Americanist Culture History

Fundamentals of Time, Space, and F

Un

Americanist Culture History

Fundamentals of Time, Space, and Form

Edited by

R. Lee Lyman
Michael J. O'Brien
University of Missouri–Columbia
Columbia, Missouri

and

Robert C. Dunnell
University of Washington
Seattle, Washington

PLENUM PRESS • NEW YORK AND LONDON

Library of Congress Cataloging-in-Publication Data

Americanist culture history : fundamentals of time, space, and form /
   edited by R. Lee Lyman, Michael J. O'Brien, and Robert C. Dunnell.
      p.   cm.
   Includes bibliographical references and index.
   ISBN 0-306-45539-0 (hardbound). -- ISBN 0-306-45540-4 (pbk.)
   I. Lyman, R. Lee. II. O'Brien, Michael J. (Michael John), 1950-
   III. Dunnell, Robert C., 1942-   .
   E77.9.A45 1997
   930.1--dc21   97-22167
                                                                CIP

ISBN 0-306-45539-0 (Hardbound)
ISBN 0-306-45540-4 (Paperback)

© 1997 Plenum Press, New York
A Division of Plenum Publishing Corporation
233 Spring Street, New York, N. Y. 10013

http://www.plenum.com

Printed in the United States of America

Preface

Albert C. Spaulding wrote in 1960 that "archaeology can be defined minimally as the study of the interrelationship of form, temporal locus, and spatial locus exhibited by artifacts. In other words, archaeologists are always concerned with these interrelationships, whatever broader interests they may have, and these interrelationships are the special business of archaeology" (Spaulding [1960b:439]; references follow the Introduction). Gordon Willey (1953:361) said more or less the same thing, but he put it more simply: "The objectives of archeology . . . are approached by the study and manipulation of three basic factors: form, space, and time." The simplicity of this statement is beguiling. Unfortunately, there is no black box into which a piece of pottery or a projectile point can be dropped to learn such things as when it was made, why it was made in one location over another, or why it took on the form it exhibits. Many of the means Americanist archaeologists use to address questions of where, when, and why were formulated early in the twentieth century. These analytical tenets, or principles, were formalized and axiomatized in later years, and, by the middle decades of the twentieth century, they constituted the first formal paradigm for Americanist archaeology—a paradigm commonly termed *culture history*. That paradigm fell from favor in the 1960s, yet many of its central tenets remain in newer paradigms and continue to be fundamental within the discipline.

With Spaulding's and Willey's conceptions as our guide, we have compiled what we view as the benchmark papers in which the fundamental tenets of Americanist archaeology were developed. These papers variously introduce and/or synthesize critical concepts and procedures for understanding the archaeological record in terms of time, space, and form. We have been prompted to compile and reprint these papers because it is our strong impression that most archaeologists today appear to have forgotten or tend to overlook many of the central tenets of the discipline—tenets that underpin virtually everything we do. Moreover, contemporary knowledge of our discipline's past often seems derived from secondary sources, many of which often impart orientations and characteristics the original authors would not recognize. Finally, ignorance of the discipline's past can result in "unnecessary originality," as noted by Bohannan and Glazer (1988:xv), while detailed knowledge of it can "give one a great many good ideas, for the past never says things quite the way the present needs them said" (Bohannan and Glazer 1988:xv).

All the items reprinted here were written by anthropologists and archaeologists working and/or trained in the United States, and all were originally published in the twentieth century. Our coverage ends just after the birth of "processual" archaeology in the 1960s (see Binford [1972] and Leone [1972] for collections of relevant articles). This "processual," or "new," archaeology is seen by some as representing a major break with previous archaeological epistemology (Willey and Sabloff 1993:214–231), while others see it as a continuation and elaboration of much of what came before (Trigger 1989:294–303). The issue is not resolved, but clearly something happened in the 1960s and early 1970s. Whatever that something might have been, we have taken that time period to define the upper limit of our coverage. As a result, the items reprinted here represent much of the thinking of a group of archaeologists characterized by processual archaeologists as "culture historians."

To enhance the volume both as a reference and as a research tool, we have retained the original format and pagination of all but one of the 39 papers included. The single exception (Ford and Griffin 1938) was originally produced as a mimeographed typescript that was not acceptable for reproduction. Many papers are reprinted in full, including illustrations and references. In other cases we have chosen to reprint only portions of monographs or books—those portions which present statements of method or logic essential to an understanding of the subject.

References for the reprinted articles are given as they were in the original—as footnotes or as a reference list following each article. In cases where we reprint only a portion of a document, references for that portion only appear at the end of the reprinted portion. In several cases, the lists contain our corrections and updates of references. For example, we have indicated when and where a paper originally cited as "in press" was published in order to enhance the value of the references. This should ease the task of a citations analysis if one should choose to perform such a task. We also have attempted to keep the number of reprinted pages as low as possible, without sacrificing content. Thus, cover pages, title pages, and other relatively superfluous material are not reprinted. We reprint the papers in mostly chronological order so that one might track the intellectual development of the culture-history paradigm. Exceptions comprise two cases in which we judged the content of the reprinted items to be a more significant ordering criterion than the date of publication.

The elements of time, space, and form have, in various guises, assumed center stage in Americanist archaeology from at least the beginning of the twentieth century. That stage has been crowded with actors—some with meaty roles, others with only bit parts. Here, we assume some familiarity on the part of the reader with the basic elements of the story. Elsewhere, we present a detailed essay written from a critical viewpoint that seeks not only to document the history of the culture history paradigm but also to demonstrate why that paradigm flourished for a time and why it ultimately was discarded (Lyman et al. 1997).

Acknowledgments

Many societies, publishers, and individuals granted us permission to reprint the materials published here. In particular, for their courtesy, the following were most helpful:

American Anthropological Association (and Terry Clifford), for permission to reprint:

Ford, James A. 1954. Comment on A. C. Spaulding's "Statistical Techniques for the Discovery of Artifact Types." *American Antiquity* 19:390–391.

Holmes, W[illiam] H. 1914. Areas of American Culture Characterization Tentatively Outlined as an Aid in the Study of Antiquities. *American Anthropologist* 16:413–446.

Kidder, M[adeleine] A. and A[lfred] V. Kidder. 1917. Notes on the Pottery of Pecos. *American Anthropologist* 19:325–360.

Nelson, N[els] C. 1916. Chronology of the Tano Ruins, New Mexico. *American Anthropologist* 18:159–180.

Phillips, Philip and Gordon R. Willey. 1953. Method and Theory in American Archeology: An Operational Basis for Culture-Historical Integration. *American Anthropologist* 55:615–633.

Rouse, Irving [B.] 1955. On the Correlation of Phases of Culture. *American Anthropologist* 57:713–722.

Steward, Julian H. 1929. Diffusion and Independent Invention: A Critique of Logic. *American Anthropologist* 31:491–495.

Wright, John H., J. D. McGuire, F[rederick] W. Hodge, W[arren] K. Moorehead, and C[harles] Peabody. 1909. Report of the Committee on Archeological Nomenclature. *American Anthropologist* 11:114–119.

American Museum of Natural History (and Valerie Wheat), for permission to reprint:

Spier, Leslie. 1917. An Outline for a Chronology of Zuñi Ruins. *American Museum of Natural History, Anthropological Papers* 18(3):207–331.

Ford, James Alfred. 1949. Cultural Dating of Prehistoric Sites in Virú Valley, Peru. *American Museum of Natural History Anthropological Papers* 43(1):29–89.

Ford, James A. 1952. Measurements of Some Prehistoric Design Developments in the Southeastern States. *American Museum of Natural History, Anthropological Papers* 43(3):313–384.

Louisiana Geological Survey (and William E. Marsalis), for permission to reprint:

Ford, James A. 1936. *Analysis of Village Site Collections from Louisiana and Mississippi.* Department of Conservation, Louisiana State Geological Survey, Anthropological Study 2.

Museum of Northern Arizona (and Kathryn S. Sibley), for permission to reprint:

Colton, Harold Sellers and Lyndon Lane Hargrave. 1937. *Handbook of Northern Arizona Pottery Wares.* Museum of Northern Arizona Bulletin 11. Flagstaff.

National Academy of Sciences, for permission to reprint:

Kidder, A[lfred] V. 1917. A Design-Sequence from New Mexico. *National Academy of Sciences, Proceedings* 3:369–370.

Kroeber, A[lfred] L. 1916. Zuñi Culture Sequences. *National Academy of Sciences, Proceedings* 2:42–45.

Peabody Museum of Archaeology and Ethnology, Harvard University (and Donna M. Dickerson), for permission to reprint:

Brew, John Otis. 1946. *The Archaeology of Alkali Ridge, Southeastern Utah.* Papers of the Peabody Museum of Archaeology and Ethnology 21. Harvard University.

Phillips, Philip, James A. Ford, and James B. Griffin. 1951. *Archaeological Survey in the Lower Mississippi Valley, 1940–1947.* Papers of the Peabody Museum of Archaeology and Ethnology No. 25. Harvard University.

Society for American Archaeology (and Janet Walker), for permission to reprint:

Brainerd, George W. 1951. The Place of Chronological Ordering in Archaeological Analysis. *American Antiquity* 16:301–313.

Dunnell, Robert C. 1971. Sabloff and Smith's "The Importance of Both Analytic and Taxonomic Classification in the Type–Variety System." *American Antiquity* 36:115–118.

Ford, J[ames] A. 1938. A Chronological Method Applicable to the Southeast. *American Antiquity* 3:260–264.

Ford, J[ames] A. 1954. The Type Concept Revisited. *American Anthropologist* 56:42–53.

Gladwin, Harold S. 1936. Editorials: Methodology in the Southwest. *American Antiquity* 1:256–259.

Krieger, Alex D. 1944. The Typological Concept. *American Antiquity* 9:271–288.

Kroeber, A[lfred] L. 1940. Statistical Classification. *American Antiquity* 6:29–44.

McKern, W[illiam] C. 1939. The Midwestern Taxonomic Method as an Aid to Archaeological Culture Study. *American Antiquity* 4:301–313.

Rouse, Irving [B.] 1960. The Classification of Artifacts in Archaeology. *American Antiquity* 25:313–323.

Rowe, John Howland. 1961. Stratigraphy and Seriation. *American Antiquity* 26:324–330.

Sabloff, Jeremy A., and Robert E. Smith. 1969. The Importance of Both Analytic and Taxonomic Classification in the Type–Variety System. *American Antiquity* 34:278–285.

Spaulding, Albert C. 1954. Reply to Ford. *American Antiquity* 19:391–393.

Thompson, Raymond H. (editor). 1956. An Archaeological Approach to the Study of Cultural Stability. In *Seminars in Archaeology:1955,* pp. 31–57. Society for American Archaeology, Memoirs 11.

Wheat, Joe Ben, James C. Gifford, and William W. Wasley. 1958. Ceramic Variety, Type Cluster, and Ceramic System in Southwestern Pottery Analysis. *American Antiquity* 24:34–47.

Southeastern Archaeological Conference (and Ken Sassaman), for permission to reprint:

Ford, James A. and James B. Griffin. 1938. Report of the Conference on Southeastern Pottery Typology. Mimeographed.

Southwestern Journal of Anthropology (and Lawrence G. Straus), for permission to reprint:

Deetz, James and Edwin Dethlefsen. 1965. The Doppler Effect and Archaeology: A Consideration of the Spatial Aspects of Seriation. *Southwestern Journal of Anthropology* 21:196–206.

University of California Press, Berkeley, for permission to reprint:

Uhle, Max. 1907. The Emeryville Shellmound. *University of California Publications in American Archaeology and Ethnology* 7(1):1–107.

University of Chicago Press, Chicago (and Perry Cartwright), for permission to reprint:

Kroeber, A[lfred] L. 1931. The Culture-Area and Age-Area Concepts of Clark Wissler. In *Methods in Social Science,* edited by Stuart A. Rice, pp. 248–265. University of Chicago Press, Chicago.

University of Pennsylvania Press, Philadelphia (and Katherine Varker), for permission to reprint:

Kluckhohn, Clyde. 1960. The Use of Typology in Anthropological Theory. In *Selected Papers of the Fifth International Congress of Anthropological and Ethnological Sciences,* edited by Anthony F. C. Wallace, pp. 134–140. University of Pennsylvania Press, Philadelphia.

Yale University Press (and Donna Anstey), for permission to reprint:

Rouse, Irving [B.] 1939. *Prehistory in Haiti, A Study in Method.* Yale University Publications in Anthropology No. 21.

James Deetz, for permission to reprint:

The Doppler Effect and Archaeology: A Consideration of the Spatial Aspects of Seriation. *Southwestern Journal of Anthropology* 21:196–206.

James B. Griffin, for permission to reprint his papers of 1938 and 1951:

Ford, James A. and James B. Griffin. 1938. Report of the Conference on Southeastern Pottery Typology. Mimeographed.
Phillips, Philip, James A. Ford, and James B. Griffin. 1951. *Archaeological Survey in the Lower Mississippi Valley, 1940–1947.* Papers of the Peabody Museum of Archaeology and Ethnology No. 25. Harvard University.

Irving B. Rouse, for permission to reprint his papers of 1939, 1955, and 1960:

Rouse, Irving [B.] 1939. *Prehistory in Haiti, A Study in Method.* Yale University Publications in Anthropology No. 21.
Rouse, Irving [B.] 1955. On the Correlation of Phases of Culture. *American Anthropologist* 57:713–722.
Rouse, Irving [B.] 1960. The Classification of Artifacts in Archaeology. *American Antiquity* 25:313–323.

John Howland Rowe, for permission to reprint:

Stratigraphy and Seriation. *American Antiquity* 26:324–330.

Jeremy A. Sabloff, for permission to reprint:

The Importance of Both Analytic and Taxonomic Classification in the Type–Variety System. *American Antiquity* 34:278–285.

Joe Ben Wheat, for permission to reprint:

Ceramic Variety, Type Cluster, and Ceramic System in Southwestern Pottery Analysis. *American Antiquity* 24:34–47.

Gordon R. Willey, for permission to reprint:

Method and Theory in American Archeology: An Operational Basis for Culture-Historical Integration. *American Anthropologist* 55:615–633.

We also must thank Elliot Werner of Plenum Press for his interest in this project. We appreciate the help of Mary Curioli of Plenum and Yvonne Ball and Rita Walther, both of the University of Missouri Printing Services, all of whom were instrumental in working through the various technical problems of layout and design. Dan Glover tracked down references and helped manufacture the originals from which the reprinted pages were produced.

Contents

Introduction

Given the ever-increasing number of new developments in archaeological methods and techniques, and the many recent gains in our knowledge of humankind's prehistory, one might well wonder why it is necessary to reproduce a set of our discipline's older writings. It is our contention that the items reproduced here represent the development of some key tenets of one of the major paradigms of Americanist archaeology,[1] a paradigm generally known as *culture history* (Binford 1965; 1968; Caldwell 1959; Dunnell 1978; Flannery 1967; see Kidder [1932:2] for an early use of this term). Upon a minimum of reflection, most Americanist archaeologists would, we believe, agree that much of what we think we know about human prehistory is founded on or has some significant ties to the culture history paradigm. At the very least, none could successfully dispute the fact that most textbooks—whether they concern *how* to do archaeology (e.g., Sharer and Ashmore 1993; Thomas 1989) or the results of *doing* archaeological research (e.g., Fagan 1991; Jennings 1989)—have at their core organizational and interpretive elements that were developed by culture histo-

rians during the first half of the twentieth century. These elements revolve around three dimensions of the archaeological record (Spaulding 1960b; Willey 1953): the *form* of artifacts and how various forms are distributed across *space* and through *time*. The job culture historians chose was first to document and then to explain the variation inherent in those three dimensions in historical terms.

It was the culture history paradigm that so incensed many archaeologists of the 1960s (e.g., Binford 1962; Fritz and Plog 1970; Martin 1971) that they argued for the development of a new paradigm. Yet, the fundamental principles of the culture history paradigm were so ingrained in Americanist thought that archaeologists, whether they realized it or not, carried many of them over to the new paradigm (Meltzer 1979). Those principles remain so ingrained in our thinking today that we often fail to acknowledge them or to realize that we use them day in and day out as we go about our research and teaching. Many modern presentations of these principles are variously superficial or derived from secondary or tertiary sources and thus seldom do justice to the original thought, often garbling them to such a degree that they would be unrecognizable to their originators. Thus it is critical to read the original discussions to ensure a firm, accurate, and complete understanding of what

---

[1]We use the term *Americanist* archaeology (as opposed to *American* archaeology) to emphasize archaeology undertaken by American-trained archaeologists, regardless of where in the world their research area is located.

the original authors meant and, equally important, to place those discussions within their proper historical context. It is for these reasons that we reprint what we take to be the benchmark articles of the culture history paradigm.

We also believe there is another reason to bring these items to the attention of the discipline. Americanist archaeology's desire to be "scientific" did not, as some suggest, originate with the processual archaeology of the 1960s and 1970s. Early twentieth-century Americanists also expressed a similar desire (see Dunnell [1992] for a review). How they attempted to fulfill that desire is an interesting part of our discipline's history. More important, because attempts to fulfill that desire still influence Americanist archaeology almost a century later, it is reasonable to ask whether earlier culture historians attained their desire, and, if not, how and why they failed. In producing an answer to these queries, perhaps we will learn why Americanist processual archaeology of the second half of the twentieth century has failed to produce its desired product. We address these questions in detail in a volume that might be construed as a companion to this one (Lyman et al. 1997). Here, we provide the briefest outline of an answer.

Beginnings: Time as a Continuum

Most histories of Americanist archaeology (e.g., Browman and Givens 1996; Rohn 1973:191; Strong 1952; Willey 1968:40; Willey and Sabloff 1993) indicate that a "stratigraphic revolution" during the second decade of the twentieth century was the catalyst that prompted the emergence and development of what came to be known as the culture history paradigm. Prior to that time, anthropologists and archaeologists lamented the fact that a chronology was unavailable, yet all recognized, as did Laufer (1913:577), "Chronology is at the root of the matter, being the nerve electrifying the dead body of history," or as Tozzer (1926:283) put it a few years later, "archaeological data

have an inert quality, a certain spinelessness when unaccompanied by a more or less definite chronological background." But the fact is that many archaeologists prior to 1910 were excavating in a manner that is readily considered stratigraphic (Lyman et al. 1997); Dixon (1913:550) and Sterns (1915), for example, observed stratigraphically and thus temporally distinct artifact assemblages. The problem was that these assemblages appeared to display no *significant* formal differences among them, and thus Dixon, Sterns, and their contemporaries seldom asked chronological questions.

Prior to about 1915, most Americanists were searching for differences in sets of culture traits of the sort that would suggest major qualitative differences in cultures. These cultures could then be construed as occupying different temporal positions in such a manner as to align with a progressive evolutionary model of cultural development like that of Lewis Henry Morgan (1877). The cultural differences would be like those then being reported in Europe; anything of less magnitude was dismissed as insignificant *but not invalid or improbable* (Kroeber 1909). For culture history to emerge as a viable and *scientific* line of inquiry—one with empirically testable implications—Americanist archaeologists had to change how they were measuring culture change; they had to change the focus of their chronological questions. The view of cultural development would change abruptly between 1914 and 1916 when archaeologists modified their observation from the *presence/absence* of cultural traits to the *frequencies* of trait variants.

Clark Wissler (1915), then curator of anthropology at the American Museum of Natural History, sent Nels C. Nelson (1913, 1914, 1915, 1916[†])[2] to the Rio Grande Valley of New Mexico in 1912 specifically to find chronological evidence of Puebloan cultural development. Alfred V. Kidder, prompted by his dissertation research (e.g., Kidder 1915), began in 1915 to address similar questions of chronology at Pecos Pueblo,

[2]Articles reprinted in this volume are denoted by [†].

just northeast of the Galisteo Basin where Nelson was working (Kidder 1916, 1917[†]). Alfred L. Kroeber (1916a[†], 1916b) visited Zuñi Pueblo west of Nelson and Kidder in 1915 to do ethnographic field work for the American Museum and while there did some innovative archaeological research. Leslie Spier (1917a[†], 1917b)—also at Wissler's direction—continued Kroeber's archaeological work near Zuñi the next year.

Nelson (1916) not only collected samples of pottery sherds from distinct arbitrarily defined vertical proveniences—what he is remembered for—but he also examined how the *absolute frequencies of pottery types* varied across those distinct vertical proveniences, a novel approach that has gone largely unremarked and certainly has not been analyzed in detail by historians of the discipline. That Nelson carried out this analysis because of his close association with Wissler and Spier seems indisputable (Lyman et al. 1997). The latter two were interested in the frequency distribution of artifacts across vertical space because of their belief that such a distribution provided insight into the mode of assemblage deposition; Nelson's assemblage provided proof that culturally deposited sets of material would display a frequency distribution distinct from that displayed by naturally deposited sets of artifacts (Spier 1916; Wissler 1916).

Kroeber (1916a, 1916b), independent of any European influence (Lyman et al. 1997), invented the technique known as frequency seriation and concluded that the temporal implications of the arrangement of his surface-collected assemblages having different frequencies of pottery types could only be *confirmed* by excavation (Lyman et al. 1997). Kidder (1917) mimicked the European technique of Evans (1850) and Petrie (1899) and employed a *developmental,* or what might be better termed *phyletic* (Lyman et al. 1997), seriation technique to arrange his pottery in a temporal sequence. But he, too, sought to confirm that the arrangement was chronological via stratigraphic excavation. Kidder and Kidder (1917[†]) mimicked Nelson's technique—later referred to variously as

ceramic or *percentage stratigraphy*—but used natural rather than arbitrary vertical units and relative rather than absolute frequencies of pottery types. Spier, too, seriated surface-collected assemblages based on the relative frequencies of pottery types, excavated in arbitrary metric levels, and used percentage stratigraphy to test the chronological significance of his and Kroeber's seriations. And Spier (1917a, 1918, 1919), in remarkable anticipation of a major interpretive direction followed by later culture historians, tracked the movement of *peoples* across the landscape by studying the distribution of pottery types (e.g., Ford 1936a; Phillips et al. 1951; Schmidt 1928).

The technique used by Nelson, Kidder, Kroeber, Spier, and others to help build a chronology came to be known as the *direct historical approach* (Steward 1942). To anchor a relative chronology of pottery types, one began with the most recent, or historically known, end of the chronological continuum and then simply worked backward in time. This approach gained popularity across North America, and was used with great success by Strong (1935, 1940), Wedel (1938, 1940), and others (Willey and Sabloff 1993:124–127). The development of dendrochronological methods in the Southwest helped to make relative chronologies developed there absolute (Douglass 1921; Wissler 1921) and eventually led to the creation of pottery types that denoted smaller and smaller chunks of the temporal continuum.

By studying changes in the frequencies of artifact *types,* or variants of a culture trait, time could be measured as a continuous variable. This was an entirely new way to view the passage of time in the archaeological record. It was, however, not wholly new in anthropology. Kroeber (1909:5) had characterized perceived fluctuations in frequencies of trait variants as "passing changes of fashion" when he denounced Uhle's (1907[†]) discussion of culture change, and Wissler (1916:195–196) described them as "stylistic pulsations" when referring to Nelson's (1916) analysis. It was Nelson (1916:167), though, who formalized this notion for archaeologists when he wrote that "normal frequency curves [of pottery styles indicate types] came slowly into vogue, attained a maximum and began a gradual decline." This axiom—the *popularity principle*—was nothing more than a commonsense explanation for perceived phenomena, but it came to serve as a central tenet of the culture history paradigm.

In our view, then, the stratigraphic revolution was not so much a "stratigraphic" revolution as it was a revolution in how time could be measured using artifacts. Stratigraphy played an important role, to be sure, but it was, at least initially, a *confirmational* role rather than a role of *creation* or *discovery*. Thus, inferences regarding the passage of time could be *tested* and either empirically confirmed or shown to be wrong. This pulled Americanist archaeology out of its antiquarian phase and into one dependent on superposition and classification, the latter being the vehicle by which artifacts were sorted so as to measure time. Classification had had an inauspicious beginning (e.g., Wright et al. 1909[†]), with most typologies being built merely to enhance communication among prehistorians. The fact that areas with large pottery samples should be the places where chronological questions were first asked and answered with some success is not so surprising when it is realized that pottery—unlike the more ubiquitous stone tools—can be decorated in a virtually infinite number of ways. Such a plastic medium—once its diversity within the archaeological record began to be known in some detail—provided the ruler of units for measuring time.

Time as a Discontinuous Dimension

Stratigraphy, or more correctly, the law of *superposition,* was the ultimate arbiter in questions of chronology. With the confirmation of Kidder's, Nelson's, and Kroeber's pottery sequences in hand, Wissler (1917b) proclaimed that a "new archaeology" had emerged, and while he played a major role in its birth, he also had a major influence on its ontogeny. Simultaneous with the birth of culture history as a valid research endeavor, Wissler (1917a:275) remarked that the "uninterrupted occupation of an area would not result in good examples of stratification, but would give us deposits in which culture changes could be detected *only* in the qualities and *frequencies of the most typical artifacts*; for example, Nelson's pottery series from New Mexico" (emphasis added). But Wissler (1919:vii), like virtually everyone else at the time, perceived strata and superposition as requisite "to verify the chronological relations the [seriations of Kroeber and Spier] suggested." Thus, while some archaeologists—mostly those affiliated with the American Museum—examined the relative frequencies of artifact types in order to measure time and to discuss culture development (Nelson 1920; Schmidt 1928; Spier 1918, 1919; Vaillant 1930, 1931), most other archaeologists working after about 1920 did not. Rather, the majority simply looked for superposed materials and then labeled the aggregates of materials "cultures" or the like (Gamio 1924; Harrington 1924; Hawkes and Linton 1917; Loud and Harrington 1929; Roberts 1929).

This was precisely the conception Boas (1913[†]) had when he directed Gamio (1913) to excavate stratigraphically in the Valley of Mexico. Stratigraphic excavation was no longer used in a confirmational role; it now took the role of a technique for *discovering* chronologies, but not just chronologies of pottery types—most culture historians were after chronologies of *cultures.* The shift in the *role*—not the perception—of vertically superposed units ultimately led to various conceptions of mixed and reversed stratigraphy when what were thought to be the diagnostic remains of distinct cultures were found within the same vertical excavation unit (e.g., Hawley 1934, 1937; see also discussion in Vaillant 1930, 1931) or when a suspected pottery sequence was found to be out of order (e.g., Judd 1954).

Wissler's (1917a) impression that the presence of strata—that is, empirically discrete and distinct depositional units—denoted a discontinuous occupation by multiple successive cultures seems to have been generally accepted within the discipline. Fowke (1922:37) noted several years after Wissler's observation that "the intermittent character of occupancy is . . . shown by the distinct segregation of numerous successive layers of kitchen refuse." The impression that strata/vertical units could be used to denote discrete "occupations" reinforced otherwise nebulous notions of a sequence of "cultures"—phenomena that were clearly visible in the ethnographic and spatial records and therefore conceived as somehow real. Such luminaries as Kidder (e.g., 1936:xx–xxi) discussed what he termed "ceramic periods" while simultaneously noting that the particular pottery types denoting these periods were nothing more than "useful cross-sections of a constantly changing cultural trait [that had undergone] a slow, usually subtle, but never-ceasing metamorphosis." As Nelson (1932:105) made clear, the history of a culture was conceived as a flowing stream, and the flow could be monitored by observing "a few cross-sections of the flow taken at strategic points." Those cross sections were discrete occupations thought to be manifest within distinct depositional units usually termed strata. And herein resided the problem.

A fine example of this problem—a problem built into the culture history paradigm from the time when superposition became creational rather than confirmational, and which contributed to the paradigm's downfall—is found in Willey and Woodbury's (1942) efforts to construct a chronology of pottery types for the northwest coast of Florida. They wrote:

Any pottery type is based on a number of stylistic features found in combination, but changes occur over time, and transitions are often so gradual as to prevent sharp distinctions. However, the periods into which the pottery types have been grouped are each based on one or more "key" or "marker" types, which have been found to be sufficiently restricted in range and distinctive in appearance to allow their occurrence to be quite precisely determined. It is also hoped that the "periods" will prove to represent distinct cultures when the bare skeleton of ceramic chronology has been given flesh and body in the form of a full and "functional" culture description. (Willey and Woodbury 1942:236)

The role of "marker" types is largely that of an index fossil—to denote a particular time period within a particular area. More important, this quotation exemplifies the conflation of a conceptual model of gradual, continuous cultural change—a flowing stream—with the ethnologically informed perception of cultures as discrete units. Index fossils, or marker types, could be used to measure the passage of time, and their correlation with an ethnographic unit such as a "culture" was surely possible. Even though such a correlation was not testable, it did serve as an ad hoc, common-sense warrant for breaking up the cultural continuum into what were otherwise clearly arbitrary chunks. These chunks began to be referred to as *cultures*. Synthesis of an area's prehistory focused on precisely this kind of unit (e.g., Ford 1936a; Kidder 1924, 1927). Thus archaeologists viewed types not only as analytical units allowing the measurement of time but also as accurate reflections of distinct ethnographic units. Unclear at the time was that these units were products of two diametrically opposed ontologies (Lyman et al. 1997). Failure to appreciate this fact created an immediate problem for Americanist archaeologists and eventually led to the abandonment of culture history as a paradigm.

The Source of the Problem

To identify the source of the problem we must consider how artifacts were conceived by most culture historians. In short, artifacts were products made by humans, and as a result they must have been made to some intentional plan. Thus, we have culture historians such as James A. Ford (1935, 1936a[†], 1936b) and Irving B. Rouse (1939[†]) suggesting that artifacts probably reflected *ideas* in the heads of the artifact makers, although Ford and Rouse did not pursue this possibility in any rigorous analytical fashion. The result was a certain confusion over whether the *types* that archaeologists spent so much time discussing and arguing about were analytical—etic—units or were somehow real—emic—units. Such confusion is quite apparent in Alex Krieger's (1944[†]) seminal paper on typology. Krieger's major contribution was to argue that a good type must pass the historical significance test; that is, it must have a continuous distribution in time and space. Such temporal–spatial contiguity denoted the flow of ideas—a commonsense warrant for the distribution, but a warrant that was fully in line with how culture history was viewed by Americanist archaeologists trained as anthropologists. Such a distribution reflected the movement of ideas across time and space (e.g., Steward 1929[†]).

Cultures were clearly evident in the ethnological record; the traits of which they consisted displayed unique and continuous distributions (Holmes 1914[†]) that could be accounted for with such notions as the culture-area concept and the age-area concept (Kroeber 1931b[†]). Phenomena in the archaeological record must also be accounted for in similar terms—Americanist archaeologists were, after all, trained as anthropologists—and Wissler (1919) and Nelson (1919) showed that the culture-area and age-area notions were, as ethnological concepts, fully applicable to and confirmed by the archaeological record. Cultures could be discovered in the archaeological record, and such units could be explained using ethnological concepts and theories. The critical issues were (1) how artifacts were to be sorted and studied so that such explanatory tools could be called upon (Colton and Hargrave 1937[†]; Ford and Griffin 1938[†]; Gladwin and Gladwin 1930) and (2) how cultures as larger-scale units were to be recognized and/or constructed (Ford 1938[†]).

Artifact types were, then, dual-purpose units. They were constructed so as to measure time, and their utility as such could be tested using the historical-significance test. If collections were seriated or the frequencies of types plotted against vertical provenience, did they display normal frequency distributions? If yes, then they must reflect the waxing and waning of a culture-trait variant's popularity through—and thus serve as a measure of—time. If types in two different time and/or space positions were formally or typologically similar, then they must represent contiguity of the ideas that underlay them as well, such as if two cultural streams of flowing ideas had intersected. In other words, such similar types represented some sort of common ancestry or *homologous* similarity. Kroeber (1931a) had noted the importance to paleontologists of the distinction between homologous and analogous similarity, the latter denoting functional convergence rather than common ancestry. Archaeologists, however, tended to ignore this critically important distinction, a fact later lamented by Kroeber (1943) and still later by Rouse (1955). This failure, too, set the culture history paradigm on a course toward downfall.

The failure to make the distinction resided in the lack of a theory of culture development or evolution applicable to archaeological materials. While some early attempts to derive such evolutionary histories from the archaeological record went unremarked (e.g., Kidder 1917; Kidder and Kidder 1917), it was probably because the use of evolutionary wording such as "one type had descended from another" was largely metaphorical. When the wording became more rigid and literal and less metaphorical, however, such as it did under the guidance of Harold S. Colton (1939; Colton and Hargrave 1937), a biologist by professional training, and Harold S. Gladwin (e.g., Gladwin and Gladwin 1934), the reaction was swift and sure (e.g., Reiter 1938; Steward 1941). Favorable views existed (e.g.,

Ford 1940), but they were few and far between. The fact that one of the proponents quickly abandoned many of the connotations of such wording (Gladwin 1936[†]) signified the beginning of the end for biologically based evolutionary wording.

J. O. Brew (1946[†]) drove the final nail in the coffin when he (1) indicated that inanimate objects do not interbreed; (2) restricted his definition of evolution to the transmission of genes; and (3) noted that although a culture might be referred to metaphorically as a species, cultures were able to interbreed via mechanisms such as diffusion, trade, migration, and the like. Species, however, do not interbreed. Brew thus emphasized that more and different kinds of classifications were necessary to fulfill different analytical purposes, but he, along with others who rejected any notion that biological evolution might serve as a template from which to build a model of cultural evolution, failed to offer an alternative source of a model. The result was continued reliance on the notion of culture change involving the flow of streams of ideas, although the stream now was clearly a braided one, given explicit recognition that distinct cultures cross-pollinated one another.

William C. McKern's (1934, 1937, 1939[†]) popularization of the Midwestern Taxonomic Method seemed to offer a way out of the dead end perceived to exist with a model founded on biological evolution. The central tenets of this method were that formal similarity denoted relatedness, but similarity—which could be denoted at several levels—was to be determined without reference to temporal or spatial contiguity of the compared units. Relatedness—homologous similarity—would be revealed with the addition of the time and space dimensions. Again, complaints were immediate; time and space could hardly be ignored at the start if *historical* relatedness was the ultimate goal, and similarity could not be measured without some form of quantitative measure (Kroeber 1940[†]). While the Midwestern Taxonomic Method saw some use in the 1940s, its perceived flaws would result in less

than discipline-wide adoption. It would, however, be resurrected in modified form in the early 1950s.

Continuing Struggles

The conflation of analytical units of various scales constructed to measure time with the belief that the units somehow reflected ideas and/or cultures came to something of a head in the late 1940s, probably in part as a result of Walter W. Taylor's (1948) unsympathetic reminder that archaeologists were, after all, first and foremost anthropologists. Such reminders had occasionally appeared in the literature (e.g., Bennett 1943; Kluckhohn 1939; Steward and Setzler 1938), but none were quite so forceful as Taylor's. Some individuals, such as Ford (1949[†]), saw types primarily as analytical tools for building chronologies, but they also acknowledged that types could be used for other purposes as well, particularly writing culture histories complete with reference to ethnological processes such as diffusion, migration, and the like. Frequency seriation clearly demanded analytical units, the empirical or physical members of which allowed one to plot distributions. How the assemblages of analytical units were to be *reliably*—that is, replicably—arranged was suggested by reference to statistics (Brainerd 1951[†]; Robinson 1951). The *validity* of the arrangement for measuring time was still assessed by using superposed collections (Rowe 1961[†]).

The Lower Mississippi Valley Survey of the 1940s brought together three of the major figures in the culture history paradigm—Philip Phillips, James B. Griffin, and Ford (Phillips et al. 1951[†])—and the monograph they produced as a result of the project is more than worth the effort to read from cover to cover. Between those covers is a dialogue among the three men that not only reveals the workings of the culture history paradigm but indicates why that paradigm would early in the next decade fall from disciplinary favor. Phillips and Griffin firmly believed in the reality of the cultures they discussed; Ford saw those cultures as arbitrary chunks of the flowing stream of the cultural continuum. Phillips and Griffin used superposed collections to argue that culture change involved periods of stasis punctuated by abrupt changes; in other words, time was discontinuous. They held so fiercely to this position that they forced Ford (1952[†]) to publish some of the results of his percentage stratigraphy and frequency seriation data—measurements of time as a continuum as opposed to a series of chunks—elsewhere. This lack of agreement among the three underscores the atheoretical nature of the culture history paradigm. While some might disagree with this assessment, it is clear in the literature that the only so-called theory of the day was derived from anthropology. This is well demonstrated in two arenas, one of which was the Ford–Spaulding debate and the other the resurrection of a modified Midwestern Taxonomic Method.

The Ford–Spaulding debate actually centered around two issues. First, Spaulding (1953a) characterized Ford's (1952) seriations as unscientific—the arrangements were nonreplicable manipulations that resulted in "bloody amputations"; Spaulding recommended use of a technique such as that proposed by Brainerd (1951) and Robinson (1951). Ford (1954b) responded that Spaulding (1) simply did not know how cultures worked or changed—in this sense, Spaulding held a decidedly distinct view of culture that was not even remotely similar to Ford's braided stream—and (2) the correct arrangement was self-evident and did not require a statistical technique to verify it. Spaulding (1954a) replied by reiterating that Ford's technique was hardly scientific because (1) it was unreplicable and (2) it was not at all clear what was being seriated. The latter point involved the second issue in the debate, the reality of artifact types. Spaulding (1953b[†]) suggested a concise and explicit statistical technique for discovering types that, because they were discoverable, by implication must have some reality in the minds of the prehistoric artisans who made

them. Ford (1954a[†]), of course, responded; Spaulding (1954b[†]) replied in kind; and Ford (1954c[†]) produced a final statement on building typologies. Unfortunately, this last statement of Ford's is rife with the conflation of types as real versus analytical constructs. Spaulding's clear, concise method won the day, though most archaeologists continued to produce typologies more like Ford's—types that were useful for measuring time—than like Spaulding's.

The other indication of the atheoretical nature of Americanist archaeology during the early and middle decades of the twentieth century resides in the resurrection of a modified form of the Midwestern Taxonomic Method. Phillips and Willey (1953[†]) were concerned not only with erecting a logical method for writing culture histories but also with making culture history more anthropological. It was, after all, Phillips (1955:246–247) who two short years later coined the oft-quoted phrase, "New World archaeology is anthropology or it is nothing." Willey and Phillips (1955) not only provided a Morgan-like model of cultural evolution, but they repeated the oft-quoted phrase and the model in their later book (Willey and Phillips 1958). The model was founded in anthropology (e.g., Stocking 1987; see also papers in Rambo and Gillogly 1991) and paralleled much of the discussion then being played out in anthropology, where the efforts of Leslie White (e.g., 1945, 1949) and Julian Steward (e.g., 1955) to resurrect progressive evolutionism are implicated.

How such a model was to be applied to the archaeological record by culture historians was spelled out by Phillips and Willey (1953; see also Willey and Phillips 1958). While expressing the opinion that "archeo-sociological correlations may eventually be possible," and suggesting that "the archaeologist is on firmer footing . . . with the conception of an archeological culture as an *arbitrarily defined unit or segment of the total continuum*" (Phillips and Willey 1953:617; emphasis added), they went ahead and made correlations between archaeological and sociocultural phenomena. *Components* were more or less equivalent to *occupations* or communities, and *phases* were "time–space–culture units" equivalent to a *society*. The definitive attributes of components and phases were *derived* from archaeological materials, not imposed on them, and thus those definitive criteria could be modified in the light of new evidence. Components were vertically bounded units—the boundaries provided either by strata or metric excavation levels—that represented a phase or society at a particular site. When combined with the extracted nature of their definitive criteria, it is not surprising that Phillips and Willey (1953:622) believed their phases were "remarkably stable" in some cases—that they were real cultural units in the sense of an ethnographer's cultures.

Phillips and Willey (1953) explicitly denied the possibility of any sort of biological-like phylogenetic relation between and among their cultural units. Instead, they fell back on the axiom, formalized by Willey (1953:363–364), that "typological similarity [denotes] cultural relatedness [which in turn] carries with it implications of a common or similar history" for culture units such as phases. They argued that *horizons*—archaeological manifestations with extensive distributions in space but limited in temporal distribution—and *traditions*—manifestations with extensive distributions in time but limited in spatial distribution—were the integrative units of choice that would provide the warp and weft to culture history. Horizons, on the one hand, suggested diffusion across space; traditions, on the other hand, indicated either cultural stability and persistence or diffusion through time. Why artifact styles or whatever should diffuse across space or through time was not addressed. And there were other problems as well. While agreeing with the profession in general and Phillips and Willey in particular that components were vertically bounded manifestations of what *might be* construed as cultures, Rouse (1955[†]) was quick to point out that (1) formal similarity did not necessarily denote historical relatedness, (2) similarity of the time–space position of two or more phases did not necessarily denote historical relatedness, and (3) the first two kinds of similarity must be demonstrated, along with controlling for analogous similarity, in order to argue that historical relatedness—literally, homologous similarity or phylogenetic history—was evident among multiple culture units. Willey and Phillips (1958) simply missed this critical point, as did most culture historians.

In 1955 the Society for American Archaeology arranged a series of seminars at which leading Americanist archaeologists were asked to address several key issues, one of which involved the study of culture traditions (Thompson 1956[†]). Yet again, just as Phillips and Willey (1953) had a few years earlier, the seminar participants found that in some cases the culture units they identified within a tradition were remarkably stable over spans of time of various duration. No one questioned why this might be so; rather, they appear to have *expected* such a result. That such a result was to be expected no doubt grew in part from their *perception* of cultural phenomena as discontinuous in the ethnographic record and in part from their *conception* that culture change varied in rate. Such notions served as a warrant for the units they discussed. By allowing that change might be more punctuated than continuous and gradual, the culture units then being discussed were no longer arbitrary chunks of a continuum. Rather, they were real. No one noticed that the components from which the cultures (variously termed phases, tradition segments, or the like) were erected were either (1) accidents of deposition if extracted from distinct strata or (2) accidents of excavation if collected from arbitrary levels. Had someone noticed, the whole scheme would have collapsed as nonanthropological and atheoretical.

Final Efforts at Classification

A final effort to refine classification systems within the confines of the culture history paradigm took the form of designating *varieties* of types. A variety was meant to have a more restricted distribution in time and/or space than the type of which it was a part (Wheat et al. 1958[†]). Thus, it could serve as a measure of those two dimensions at finer scales. Interestingly, the seminal discussion of what came to be known as the type–variety system contained no mention of Spaulding's earlier efforts to discover types that were somehow real or of the emic sort. Other efforts at formalizing classification procedures that appeared at this time made several important points. Rouse (1960[†]) reiterated his earlier (Rouse 1939) discussion that types are analytical constructs—as inches and grams are—that should have a particular purpose. Others had made this point (e.g., Brew 1946; Steward 1954), but only Rouse consistently pointed out the difference between a conceptual unit—for example, Clovis points or Baytown Plain pottery—and an empirical unit—a particular Clovis point, such as one from Blackwater Draw.

Rouse's (1960) concerns were echoed by Kluckhohn (1960[†]), but apparently they fell on mostly unsympathetic ears. Spaulding (e.g., 1960a) continued his arguments that types were to be discovered and extracted from real specimens rather than imposed upon collections as analytical tools. Sabloff and Smith (1969[†]) furthered the notion of the type–variety system, but rather than focus on the original purpose for which the system was built, they, like others (e.g., Gifford 1960; Phillips 1958; Smith et al. 1960), sought some sociocultural or anthropological meaning for types and varieties. The problems with such an approach were outlined by Dunnell (1971[†]). Simply put, varieties, like types, were originally construed as analytical tools for measuring time and space. They *might* have sociocultural meaning, but such interpretations were not testable in any nontautological manner. The failure to make clear how such units were constructed and what their definitive criteria were—literally, necessary and sufficient conditions for membership—exacerbated the conflation of units and interpretations of them. Attempts to

explore the implications of the popularity principle (Deetz and Dethlefsen 1965[†]) were cast in the experimental archaeology that became commonplace in the 1960s.

An Expanded Culture History

In the Introduction to their classic *Method and Theory in American Archaeology,* Willey and Phillips (1958:5) indicate that "Culture-historical integration is . . . comparable to ethnography with the time dimension added." They go on to lament that "[s]o little work has been done in American archaeology on the explanatory level that it is difficult to find a name for it" but conclude by applying the term "processual interpretation" (in quotes) to denote "any explanatory principle that might be invoked. . . . processual interpretation is the study of the nature of what is vaguely referred to as the culture-historical process. Practically speaking, it implies an attempt to discover regularities in the relationships given by the methods of historical integration" (Willey and Phillips 1958:5–6). The integrative methods involved constructing sequences of phases, identifying horizons and traditions, and using the axiom that typological similarity denoted historical relatedness. Thus the archaeological units used had sociocultural connotations and denoted sociocultural processes. Such units were necessary because they were "intelligible in *both* the cultural and social aspects of the [human] behavior that is our subject matter" (Willey and Phillips 1958:49).

In short, sometime in the late 1940s the culture history paradigm began to shift away from its earlier focus on establishing sequences of artifact types to explaining those sequences in anthropological terms (e.g., Meggers 1955). This prompted one practitioner to proclaim that there was emerging in the 1950s a "New American archaeology" that was "tending to be more concerned with culture process and less concerned with the descriptive content of prehistoric cultures" (Caldwell 1959:304). The processes were the typical anthropological ones of diffusion, migration, and the like. The focus on homologous similarity to tell time was the obvious one to use when attempting to detect such processes in the archaeological record, but a regular failure to analytically distinguish homologous and analogous similarity, as noted by Rouse (1955), could lead to problems. Beginning in 1962, in a series of papers, Lewis R. Binford (e.g., 1962, 1965, 1967, 1968) outlined a research program designed to realign the focus of Americanist archaeology from homologous to analogous similarity. Culture was construed as humankind's extrasomatic—nonbiological—means of adaptation, and cultures were systems of interacting parts. The polemic and rhetoric that followed are legendary.

The products that emerged in the 1960s and early 1970s were somehow refreshing. Willey, Phillips, Ford, Rouse, and others had wanted to get at the "Indian behind the artifact" (Braidwood 1959:79), but their focus on homologous similarity denied them access. Analogous similarity seemed to be the key to unlock that particular door. But the anthropological theory that underpinned culture history also underpinned the "new archeology" of the 1960s and forced archaeologists who subscribed to it into some rather untenable positions. The lack of a uniquely archaeological theory of culture development, which was the unattained desire of the culture historians, plus a failure to deal with homologous similarity, denied the new generation access to testable explanations of culture history.

bined with anthropological training, produced a view of culture change that involved the transformation of one kind of culture through a series of abrupt steps. A desire to legitimize archaeology by making it anthropological reinforced these efforts and blinded archaeologists to the unique qualities of the archaeological record, which in effect is an unprecedented and unreplicated record of cultural evolution. How that dynamic evolutionary history is to be read demands a uniquely archaeological theory. No amount of ethnographic data or ethnological research will provide such a theory because these lines of inquiry are far too limited in their temporal coverage. The culture history paradigm serves as a lesson in the fallacy of such an approach to the archaeological record.

But the culture history paradigm also serves as a lesson from which we might learn what, exactly, is necessary to create a uniquely archaeological theory of culture development. At a minimum, we need analytical units that allow us to measure time; we need to distinguish analogous and homologous similarity among typologically "related" artifacts; and we need to develop a theory that provides testable implications for explanations of perceived change. It seems to us that the papers reproduced here can inform us of much of what Americanist archaeology should seek to avoid and much of what it should seek to exploit if the discipline desires to provide the truly unique explanations of culture history that it is capable of producing.

Summary

Americanist archaeology as culture history began with the invention of a way to measure time by using artifacts. The popularity principle grew from the common-sense notion that frequencies of artifact types reflected the waxing and waning of the popularity of *styles*. Superposed collections of such things confirmed that they indeed monitored the passage of time. The resulting focus on stratigraphic excavation, com-

References

BENNETT, JOHN W.
1943   Recent Developments in the Functional Interpretation of Archaeological Data. *American Antiquity* 9:208–219.
BINFORD, LEWIS R.
1962   Archaeology as Anthropology. *American Antiquity* 28:217–225.
1965   Archaeological Systematics and the Study of Culture Process. *American Antiquity* 31:203–210.

1967 Smudge Pits and Hide Smoking: The Use of Analogy in Archaeological Reasoning. *American Antiquity* 32:1–12.

1968 Archeological Perspectives. In *New Perspectives in Archeology,* edited by Sally R. Binford and Lewis R. Binford, pp. 5–32. Aldine, New York.

1972 Editor. *An Archaeological Perspective.* Academic Press, New York.

BOAS, FRANZ
1913 Archaeological Investigations in the Valley of Mexico by the International School, 1911–12. *Eighteenth International Congress of Americanists, Proceedings,* pp. 176–179.

BOHANNAN, PAUL, AND MARK GLAZER (editors)
1988 *High Points in Anthropology,* 2nd edition. McGraw-Hill, New York.

BRAIDWOOD, ROBERT J.
1959 Archeology and the Evolutionary Theory. In *Evolution and Anthropology: A Centennial Appraisal,* edited by Betty J. Meggers, pp. 76–89. Anthropological Society of Washington, Washington, D.C.

BRAINERD, GEORGE W.
1951 The Place of Chronological Ordering in Archaeological Analysis. *American Antiquity* 16:301-313.

BREW, JOHN OTIS
1946 *The Archaeology of Alkali Ridge, Southeastern Utah.* Papers of the Peabody Museum of Archaeology and Ethnology 21. Harvard University.

BROWMAN, DAVID L., AND DOUGLAS R. GIVENS
1996 Stratigraphic Excavation: The First "New Archaeology." *American Anthropologist* 98:80–95.

CALDWELL, JOSEPH R.
1959 The New American Archaeology. *Science* 129:303–307.

COLTON, HAROLD SELLERS
1939 *Prehistoric Culture Units and Their Relationships in Northern Arizona.* Museum of Northern Arizona, Bulletin 17. Flagstaff.

COLTON, HAROLD SELLERS, AND LYNDON L. HARGRAVE
1937 *Handbook of Northern Arizona Pottery Wares.* Museum of Northern Arizona, Bulletin 11. Flagstaff.

DEETZ, JAMES, AND EDWIN DETHLEFSEN
1965 The Doppler Effect and Archaeology: A Consideration of the Spatial Aspects of Seriation. *Southwestern Journal of Anthropology* 21:196–206.

DIXON, ROLAND B.
1913 Some Aspects of North American Archeology. *American Anthropologist* 15:549-566.

DOUGLASS, A. E.
1921 Dating Our Prehistoric Ruins. *Natural History* 21:27–30.

DUNNELL, ROBERT C.
1971 Sabloff and Smith's "The Importance of Both Analytic and Taxonomic Classification in the Type–Variety System." *American Antiquity* 36:115–118.

1978 Style and Function: A Fundamental Dichotomy. *American Antiquity* 43:192–202.

1992 Is a Scientific Archaeology Possible? In *Metaarchaeology,* edited by Lester Embree, pp. 75–97. Kluwer, Amsterdam.

EVANS, JOHN
1850 On the Date of British Coins. *The Numismatic Chronicle and Journal of the Numismatic Society* 12(4):127–137.

FAGAN, BRIAN M.
1991 *Ancient North America: The Archaeology of a Continent.* Thames and Hudson, New York.

FLANNERY, KENT V.
1967 Culture History v. Cultural Process: A Debate in American Archaeology. *Scientific American* 217(2):119–122.

FORD, JAMES A.
1935 An Introduction to Louisiana Archeology. *Louisiana Conservation Review* 4(5):8–11.

1936a *Analysis of Village Site Collections from Louisiana and Mississippi.* Department of Conservation, Louisiana State Geological Survey, Anthropological Study 2.

1936b Archaeological Methods Applicable to Louisiana. *Louisiana Academy of Sciences, Proceedings* 3:102–105.

1938 A Chronological Method Applicable to the Southeast. *American Antiquity* 3:260–264.

1940 Review of "Handbook of Northern Arizona Pottery Wares" by H. S. Colton and L. L. Hargrave. *American Antiquity* 5:263–266.

1949 Cultural Dating of Prehistoric Sites in Virú Valley, Peru. *American Museum of Natural History, Anthropological Papers* 43(1):29–89.

1952 Measurements of Some Prehistoric Design Developments in the Southeastern States. *American Museum of Natural History, Anthropological Papers* 43(3):313–384.

1954a Comment on A. C. Spaulding's "Statistical Techniques for the Discovery of Artifact Types." *American Antiquity* 19:390–391.

1954b Spaulding's Review of Ford. *American Anthropologist* 56:109–112.

1954c The Type Concept Revisited. *American Anthropologist* 56:42–53.

FORD, JAMES A., AND JAMES B. GRIFFIN
1938 Report of the Conference on Southeastern Pottery Typology. Mimeographed.

[reprinted in *Newsletter of the Southeastern Archaeological Conference* 7(1):10–22]

FOWKE, GERARD
1922   *Archeological Investigations.* Bureau of American Ethnology, Bulletin 76.

FRITZ, JOHN M., AND FRED T. PLOG
1970   The Nature of Archaeological Explanation. *American Antiquity* 35:405–412.

GAMIO, MANUEL
1913   Arqueologia de Atzcapotzalco, D.F., Mexico. *Eighteenth International Congress of Americanists, Proceedings,* pp. 180–187.
1924   The Sequence of Cultures in Mexico. *American Anthropologist* 26:307–322.

GIFFORD, JAMES C.
1960   The Type–Variety Method of Ceramic Classification as an Indicator of Cultural Phenomena. *American Antiquity* 25:341–347.

GLADWIN, HAROLD S.
1936   Editorials: Methodology in the Southwest. *American Antiquity* 1:256–259.

GLADWIN, WINIFRED, AND HAROLD S. GLADWIN
1930   *A Method for the Designation of Southwestern Pottery Types.* Medallion Papers No. 7. Globe, Arizona.
1934   *A Method for the Designation of Cultures and Their Variations.* Medallion Papers No. 15. Globe, Arizona.*

HARRINGTON, MARK R.
1924   The Ozark Bluff-Dwellers. *American Anthropologist* 26:1–21.

HAWKES, E. W., AND RALPH LINTON
1917   A Pre-Lenape Culture in New Jersey. *American Anthropologist* 19:487–494.

HAWLEY, FLORENCE M.
1934   *The Significance of the Dated Prehistory of Chetro Ketl.* University of New Mexico Bulletin, Monograph Series 1(1).
1937   Reversed Stratigraphy. *American Antiquity* 2:297–299.

HOLMES, WILLIAM HENRY
1914   Areas of American Culture Characterization Tentatively Outlined as an Aid in the Study of Antiquities. *American Anthropologist* 16:413–446.

JENNINGS, JESSE D.
1989   *Prehistory of North America,* 3rd edition. Mayfield, Mountain View, California.

JUDD, NEIL M.
1954   *The Material Culture of Pueblo Bonito.* Smithsonian Miscellaneous Collections 124.

KIDDER, ALFRED V.
1915   Pottery of the Pajarito Plateau and Some Adjacent Regions in New Mexico. *American Anthropological Association, Memoirs* 2(6):407–462.

1916   Archeological Explorations at Pecos, New Mexico. *National Academy of Sciences, Proceedings* 2:119–123.
1917   A Design-Sequence from New Mexico. *National Academy of Sciences, Proceedings* 3:369–370.
1924   *An Introduction to the Study of Southwestern Archaeology, with a Preliminary Account of the Excavations at Pecos.* Papers of the Southwestern Expedition, Phillips Academy, No. 1. New Haven, Connecticut: Yale University Press.
1927   Southwestern Archaeological Conference. *Science* 66:489–491.
1932   *The Artifacts of Pecos.* Papers of the Southwestern Expedition, Phillips Academy, No. 6. Yale University Press, New Haven, Connecticut.
1936   Introduction. In *The Pottery of Pecos* Vol. II, by Alfred Vincent Kidder and Anna O. Shepard, pp. xvii–xxxi. Papers of the Southwestern Expedition, Phillips Academy, No. 7. Yale University Press, New Haven, Connecticut.

KIDDER, MADELEINE A., AND ALFRED V. KIDDER
1917   Notes on the Pottery of Pecos. *American Anthropologist* 19:325–360.

KLUCKHOHN, CLYDE
1939   The Place of Theory in Anthropological Studies. *Philosophy of Science* 6:328–344.
1960   The Use of Typology in Anthropological Theory. In *Selected Papers of the Fifth International Congress of Anthropological and Ethnological Sciences*, edited by Anthony F. C. Wallace, pp. 134–140. University of Pennsylvania Press, Philadelphia.

KRIEGER, ALEX D.
1944   The Typological Concept. *American Antiquity* 9:271–288.

KROEBER, ALFRED L.
1909   The Archaeology of California. In *Putnam Anniversary Volume*, edited by Franz Boas, pp. 1–42. Stechert, New York.
1916a   Zuñi Culture Sequences. *National Academy of Sciences, Proceedings* 2:42–45.
1916b   Zuñi Potsherds. *American Museum of Natural History, Anthropological Papers* 18(1): 1–37.
1931a   Historical Reconstruction of Culture Growths and Organic Evolution. *American Anthropologist* 33:149–156.
1931b   The Culture-Area and Age-Area Concepts of Clark Wissler. In *Methods in Social Science,* edited by Stuart A. Rice, pp. 248–265. University of Chicago Press, Chicago.
1940   Statistical Classification. *American Antiquity* 6:29–44.

1943 Structure, Function and Pattern in Biology and Anthropology. *Scientific Monthly* 56:105–113.

LAUFER, BERTHOLD
1913 The Relation of Archeology to Ethnology: Remarks. *American Anthropologist* 15:573–577.

LEONE, MARK P. (editor)
1972 *Contemporary Archaeology.* Southern Illinois University Press, Carbondale.

LOUD, LLEWELLYN L., AND MARK R. HARRINGTON
1929 *Lovelock Cave.* University of California Publications in American Archaeology and Ethnology 25(1):1–183.

LYMAN, R. LEE, MICHAEL J. O'BRIEN, AND ROBERT C. DUNNELL
1997 *The Rise and Fall of Culture History.* Plenum, New York.

MARTIN, PAUL S.
1971 The Revolution in Archaeology. *American Antiquity* 36:1–8.

McKERN, WILLIAM C.
1934 *Certain Culture Classification Problems in Middle Western Archaeology.* National Research Council, Committee on State Archaeological Surveys. Washington, D.C.
1937 Certain Culture Classification Problems in Middle Western Archaeology. In *The Indianapolis Archaeological Conference,* pp. 70–82. National Research Council, Committee on State Archaeological Surveys, Circular 17. Washington, D.C.
1939 The Midwestern Taxonomic Method as an Aid to Archaeological Culture Study. *American Antiquity* 4:301–313.

MEGGERS, BETTY J.
1955 The Coming of Age of American Archaeology. In *New Interpretations of Aboriginal American Culture History,* edited by Betty J. Meggers and Clifford Evans, pp. 116–129. Anthropological Society of Washington, Washington, D.C.

MELTZER, DAVID J.
1979 Paradigms and the Nature of Change in American Archaeology. *American Antiquity* 44:644–657.

MORGAN, LEWIS HENRY
1877 *Ancient Society.* Holt, New York.

NELSON, NELS C.
1913 Ruins of Prehistoric New Mexico. *American Museum Journal* 13:62–81.
1914 Pueblo Ruins of the Galisteo Basin, New Mexico. *American Museum of Natural History, Anthropological Papers* 15(1):1–124.
1915 Ancient Cities of New Mexico. *American Museum Journal* 15:389–394.
1916 Chronology of the Tano Ruins, New Mexico. *American Anthropologist* 18:159–180.

1919 The Archaeology of the Southwest: A Preliminary Report. *National Academy of Sciences, Proceedings* 5:114–120.
1920 Notes on Pueblo Bonito. *American Museum of Natural History, Anthropological Papers* 27:381–390.
1932 The Origin and Development of Material Culture. *Sigma Xi Quarterly* 20:102–123.

PETRIE, WILLIAM MATTHEW FLINDERS
1899 Sequences in Prehistoric Remains. *Journal of the Royal Anthropological Institute of Great Britain and Ireland* 29:295–301.

PHILLIPS, PHILIP
1955 American Archaeology and General Anthropological Theory. *Southwestern Journal of Anthropology* 11:246–250.
1958 Application of the Wheat–Gifford–Wasley Taxonomy to Eastern Ceramics. *American Antiquity* 24:117–125.

PHILLIPS, PHILIP, JAMES A. FORD, AND JAMES B. GRIFFIN
1951 *Archaeological Survey in the Lower Mississippi Valley, 1940-1947.* Papers of the Peabody Museum of Archaeology and Ethnology No. 25. Harvard University.

PHILLIPS, PHILIP, AND GORDON R. WILLEY
1953 Method and Theory in American Archaeology: An Operational Basis for Culture-Historical Integration. *American Anthropologist* 55:615–633.

RAMBO, A. TERRY, AND KATHLEEN GILLOGLY (editors)
1991 *Profiles in Cultural Evolution.* Anthropological Papers of the University of Michigan Museum of Anthropology No. 85. Ann Arbor.

REITER, PAUL
1938 Review of "Handbook of Northern Arizona Pottery Wares" by Harold S. Colton and Lyndon L. Hargrave. *American Anthropologist* 40:489–491.

ROBERTS, FRANK H. H., JR.
1929 *Shabik'eshchee Village: A Late Basket Maker Site in the Chaco Canyon, New Mexico.* Bureau of American Ethnology, Bulletin 92.

ROBINSON, W. S.
1951 A Method for Chronologically Ordering Archaeological Deposits. *American Antiquity* 16:293–301.

ROHN, ARTHUR H.
1973 The Southwest and Intermontane West. In *The Development of North American Archaeology,* edited by James E. Fitting, pp. 185–211. Anchor Press, Garden City, New York.

ROUSE, IRVING B.
1939 *Prehistory in Haiti, A Study in Method.* Yale University Publications in Anthropology No. 21.
1955 On the Correlation of Phases of Culture. *American Anthropologist* 57:713–722.

1960 The Classification of Artifacts in Archaeology. *American Antiquity* 25:313–323.

ROWE, JOHN HOWLAND
1961 Stratigraphy and Seriation. *American Antiquity* 26:324–330.

SABLOFF, JEREMY A., AND ROBERT E. SMITH
1969 The Importance of Both Analytic and Taxonomic Classification in the Type-Variety System. *American Antiquity* 34:278–285.

SCHMIDT, ERICH F.
1928 Time-Relations of Prehistoric Pottery Types in Southern Arizona. *American Museum of Natural History, Anthropological Papers* 30(5):247–302.

SHARER, ROBERT J., AND WENDY ASHMORE
1993 *Archaeology: Discovering Our Past,* 2nd edition. Mayfield, Mountain View, California.

SMITH, ROBERT E., GORDON R. WILLEY, AND JAMES C. GIFFORD
1960 The Type-Variety Concept as a Basis for the Analysis of Maya Pottery. *American Antiquity* 25:330–341.

SPAULDING, ALBERT C.
1953a Review of "Measurements of Some Prehistoric Design Developments in the Southeastern States" by J. A. Ford. *American Anthropologist* 55:588–591.
1953b Statistical Techniques for the Discovery of Artifact Types. *American Antiquity* 18:305–313.
1954a Reply (to Ford). *American Anthropologist* 56:112–114.
1954b Reply to Ford. *American Antiquity* 19:391–393.
1960a Statistical Description and Comparison of Artifact Assemblages. In *The Application of Quantitative Methods in Archaeology,* edited by Robert F. Heizer and Sherburne F. Cook, pp. 60–83. Viking Fund Publications in Anthropology 28.
1960b The Dimensions of Archaeology. In *Essays in the Science of Culture in Honor of Leslie A. White,* edited by Gertrude E. Dole and Robert L. Carneiro, pp. 437–456. Crowell, New York.

SPIER, LESLIE
1916 New Data on the Trenton Argillite Culture. *American Anthropologist* 18:181–189.
1917a An Outline for a Chronology of Zuñi Ruins. *American Museum of Natural History, Anthropological Papers* 18(3):207–331.
1917b Zuñi Chronology. *National Academy of Sciences, Proceedings* 3:280–283.
1918 Notes on Some Little Colorado Ruins. *American Museum of Natural History, Anthropological Papers* 18(4):333–362.
1919 Ruins in the White Mountains, Arizona. *American Museum of Natural History, Anthropological Papers* 18(5):363–388.

STERNS, FRED H.
1915 A Stratification of Cultures in Nebraska. *American Anthropologist* 17:121–127.

STEWARD, JULIAN H.
1929 Diffusion and Independent Invention: A Critique of Logic. *American Anthropologist* 31:491–495.
1941 Review of "Prehistoric Culture Units and Their Relationships in Northern Arizona" by Harold S. Colton. *American Antiquity* 6:366–367.
1942 The Direct Historical Approach to Archaeology. *American Antiquity* 7:337–343.
1954 Types of Types. *American Anthropologist* 56:54–57.
1955 *Theory of Cultural Change: The Methodology of Multilinear Evolution.* University of Illinois Press, Urbana.

STEWARD, JULIAN H., AND FRANK M. SETZLER
1938 Function and Configuration in Archaeology. *American Antiquity* 4:4–10.

STOCKING, GEORGE W., JR.
1987 *Victorian Anthropology.* Free Press, New York.

STRONG, WILLIAM DUNCAN
1935 *An Introduction to Nebraska Archaeology.* Smithsonian Miscellaneous Collections 93(10).
1940 From History to Prehistory in the Northern Great Plains. In *Essays in Historical Anthropology of North America,* pp. 353–394. Smithsonian Miscellaneous Collections 100.
1952 The Value of Archeology in the Training of Professional Anthropologists. *American Anthropologist* 54:318–321.

TAYLOR, WALTER W.
1948 *A Study of Archeology.* American Anthropological Association, Memoir 69.

THOMAS, DAVID HURST
1989 *Archaeology,* 2nd edition. Holt, Rinehart and Winston, Fort Worth, Texas.

THOMPSON, RAYMOND H. (editor)
1956 An Archaeological Approach to the Study of Cultural Stability. In *Seminars in Archaeology:1955,* pp. 31–57. Memoirs of the Society for American Archaeology 11.

TOZZER, ARTHUR M.
1926 Chronological Aspects of American Archaeology. *Massachusetts Historical Society, Proceedings* 59:283–292.

TRIGGER, BRUCE G.
1989 *A History of Archaeological Thought.* Cambridge University Press, Cambridge.

UHLE, (FRIEDRICH) MAX
1907 The Emeryville Shellmound. *University of California Publications in American Archaeology and Ethnology* 7:1–107.

VAILLANT, GEORGE C.

1930 Excavations at Zacatenco. *American Museum of Natural History, Anthropological Papers* 32(1):1–198.

1931 Excavations at Ticoman. *American Museum of Natural History, Anthropological Papers* 32(2):199–432.

WEDEL, WALDO R.

1938 *The Direct-Historical Approach in Pawnee Archaeology.* Smithsonian Miscellaneous Collections 97(7).

1940 Culture Sequence in the Central Great Plains. In *Essays in Historical Anthropology of North America,* pp. 291–352. Smithsonian Miscellaneous Collections 100.

WHEAT, JOE BEN, JAMES C. GIFFORD AND WILLIAM W. WASLEY

1958 Ceramic Variety, Type Cluster, and Ceramic System in Southwestern Pottery Analysis. *American Antiquity* 24:34–47.

WHITE, LESLIE A.

1945 History, Evolutionism, and Functionalism: Three Types of Interpretation of Culture. *Southwestern Journal of Anthropology* 1:221–247.

1949 *The Science of Culture.* Grove Press, New York.

WILLEY, GORDON R.

1953 Archaeological Theories and Interpretation: New World. In *Anthropology Today,* edited by Alfred L. Kroeber, pp. 361–385. University of Chicago Press, Chicago.

1968 One Hundred Years of American Archaeology. In *One Hundred Years of Anthropology,* edited by J. O. Brew, pp. 26–53. Harvard University Press, Cambridge.

WILLEY, GORDON R., AND PHILIP PHILLIPS

1955 Method and Theory in American Archaeology, II: Historical-Developmental Interpretation. *American Anthropologist* 57:723–819.

1958 *Method and Theory in American Archaeology.* University of Chicago Press, Chicago.

WILLEY, GORDON R., AND JEREMY A. SABLOFF

1993 *A History of American Archaeology,* 3rd edition. Freeman, New York.

WILLEY, GORDON R., AND R. B. WOODBURY

1942 A Chronological Outline for the Northwest Florida Coast. *American Antiquity* 7:232–254.

WISSLER, CLARK

1915 Explorations in the Southwest by the American Museum. *American Museum Journal* 15:395–298.

1916 The Application of Statistical Methods to the Data on the Trenton Argillite Culture. *American Anthropologist* 18:190–197.

1917a *The American Indian.* McMurtrie, New York.

1917b The New Archaeology. *American Museum Journal* 17:100–101.

1919 General Introduction. *American Museum of Natural History, Anthropological Papers* 18:iii–ix.

1921 Dating Our Prehistoric Ruins. *Natural History* 21:13–26.

WRIGHT, JOHN H., J. D. McGUIRE, F. W. HODGE, W. K. MOOREHEAD, AND C. PEABODY

1909 Report of the Committee on Archeological Nomenclature. *American Anthropologist* 11:114–119.

From THE EMERYVILLE SHELLMOUND

Max Uhle

AGE OF THE MOUND.

The shellmounds of the environs of San Francisco Bay are almost the only witnesses of a practically unknown period in the

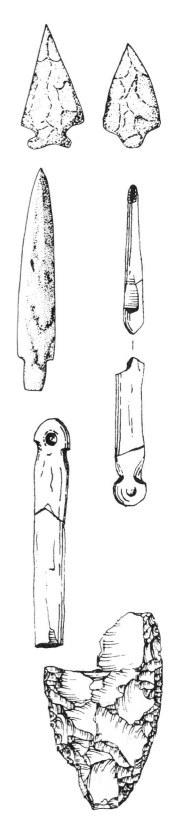

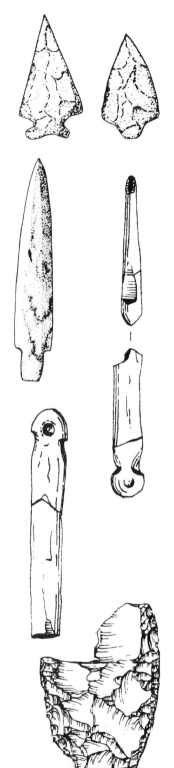

early history of this region.[54] They appear to us at first investigation unintelligible, both as regards the beginning and the end
of the period during which they served as human abodes. For a
solution of the problem before us the most diverse kinds of investigations must be carried on, before the principal facts of this
history can be clearly brought out.

Shellmounds can be found along almost all parts of the inhabited coast. In California as well as in other parts of the world
they originate by the accumulation of remnants of food, especially the shells of the mollusca which are used as articles of diet.
In the midst of the remnants of food cast aside by him, man clung
to his place of abode, raising it more and more above the general
level of the ground through the gradual accumulation of these
materials. Hence these localities represent, in certain stages of
human development, true but nevertheless low types of human
dwelling places. The manner of procuring the essentials of life
by collecting shells in itself indicates a low form of human existence. In all parts of the world, even today, people may be seen
on the shore at low water gathering for food the shells uncovered
by the retreating tide; and although under the changed conditions of life they raise no shellmounds, these people always belong
to the lower classes of society, and lead in this manner a primitive
as well as a simple life. Peoples depending for food upon collecting shells are usually not agriculturists, but fishermen, and
perhaps hunters as a secondary occupation. Their implements
are of the rudest kind, made of bone, stone, wood, and the like.
Industries of a more highly developed kind, *e.g.,* the dressing
of ore and working it up into various implements, remained unknown to them, except in perhaps a few instances.

Thus it seems natural to connect the origin of shellmounds in
general with the work of prehistoric generations, *i.e.,* man of the
stone age. The only condition necessary for their origin is, that
the people who raised them lived somewhat close together and
therefore possessed a certain social organization. For only in
many centuries or even in tens of centuries could even large
groups of men pile up such enormous quantities of kitchen debris

[54] Powers, *l. c.,* p. 375.

into hills which come to form prominent features of the land-scape. Though little is definitely known, the beginnings of human social organization evidently reached back into **Quaternary** time, just as is the case with the beginnings of human ornamentation. There is therefore no good reason why the origin of the shellmounds could not date back to Quaternary time. In this connection mention must be made of the fact that, according to Cook,[55] stone implements of argillite, which would consequently be attributed to the palaeolithic man, were found in a shellmound of New Jersey. The well known shellmounds of Denmark, the so-called "Kjoekkenmoeddings" (*i.e.*, "Kitchen debris"), which first attracted the attention of scientists to the remnants left by prehistoric men, are not so old.[56] Nevertheless, it has been possible to prove by them that Denmark had at the time of their origin a flora considerably different from that of the present, and that the Auerhahn, too, lived there, which does not exist in Denmark to-day. J. Wyman, a very careful explorer of the shellmounds of New England, does not consider the Atlantic shellmounds of this continent as old as those of Denmark.[57] He seems to have taken this view because he met with no authentic proofs of a greater age. These were difficult to obtain. Yet he calls attention to the finding of traces of the auk, the wild turkey, and the elk in those shellmounds, *i.e.*, animals which no longer exist in the region of shellmounds investigated by him. According to him, their disappearance took place in historic times.

In determining the age of the Emeryville mound we note first the fact that no traces of typical Quaternary animals were found in it. It is interesting to find that this mound resembles those just mentioned in regard to the finding of traces of the beaver, an animal no longer met with in this region. It was found in one of the lower strata of the mound. How far it reaches upward cannot as yet be decided, since the large number of bones taken from the upper beds have not all been examined. Since the time that remains of this animal were deposited in the lower strata of

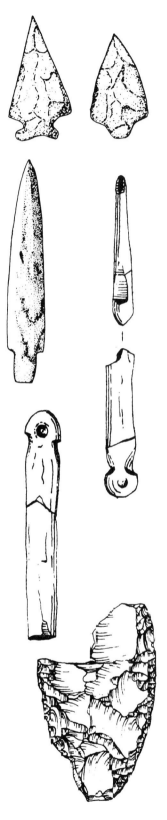

---

[55] Quoted by Abbott, *l. c.*

[56] Cf. J. Ranke, Der Mensch, II, p. 536. These shellmounds are placed in the earlier stone age of the current geologic periods.

[57] *l. c.*, p. 571.

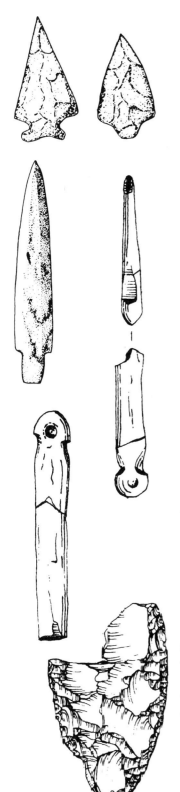

the mound, the beaver has retreated from this region, in fact from the whole of California, in a northerly direction, possibly up to Washington. When it left this region is not known. We cannot. however, be certain that this retreat may not have commenced in recent times.

Another fact of importance in fixing the age of this mound is found in the apparent change of level of the strata upon which the original layers of the mound were placed. As nearly as can be determined, the original fundament upon which the mound stands has sunk at least three feet. The base of the mound, formerly probably one foot above the usual high water level[58] of the bay, lies at present two feet below. If the mound with its environs had not since grown above the level of the original floor, it would be inundated completely for several hours twice a day. The length of time required for such a subsidence we can of course not determine with any exactness, as no measure of subsidence is available. In all probability it is to be taken as an indication of considerable antiquity.

Further facts upon which an approximation of the age of the mound may be based are of a purely anthropological nature. Usually the early period in which man made use solely of flaked stone tools is contrasted with the later age when polished as well as chipped stone implements were used. In the very lowest stratum of the hill, almost down at the base, there were found stone implements of the well known palaeolithic turtle-back form. A pestle fragment which came from the lower stratum of the mound, though having a completely disintegrated exterior, seems to have originally been artificially rounded. A mortar fragment found low down may have originated from an implement which was formed. as is often the case, out of a common boulder. But before it broke from this object the mortar was deeply worn out, just as others that have come down to our times. Also, the deep concavity of its rims speaks for long continued wear. The next stratum (two to four feet above the base of the mound) yielded the fragment of a pestle of irregular, not rounded cross-section. Here a common oblong pebble may have been used as a pestle.

---

[58] On an average once in every 14 days the high tide reaches a higher mark, which, however, is not considered here.

Besides these, the two lower strata furnished only an oval, flattened pebble, probably used as a hammer, the only one of its kind in the whole mound.

These four stone implements represent the only specimens of the two lowest strata of the mound which are not chipped. A little above these the excellently polished tool 1–8925 (pl. 10. fig. 9) was found (in stratum VIII). This is the only one of such workmanship before the IVth stratum upwards. Therefore it is by no means impossible that rubbed or polished stone implements. excepting mortars and pestles, were unknown at the time of the origin of the lower strata, and that their use was rather limited in the succeeding strata. But the presence of mortar fragments and pestles in the lowest strata points toward a higher development of the human type than is usually expected of men who use flaked tools only.

It will have become evident from the foregoing remarks that the general zoological, geological, and anthropological facts which are available for fixing the age of the mound offer only indefinite evidence; uncertain even for an approximate dating of the time of the mound's beginning. They do not preclude the possibility of an age numbering many centuries; neither do they prove it. Under such circumstances it seems proper to take into account some more general considerations which appear in a study of the shellmounds of the bay as a whole.

We shall probably not make too great a mistake if we estimate the number of the larger shellmounds around the Bay of San Francisco to be over 100. So many and such enormous shellmounds can not possibly have been constructed by human hands unintentionally in any small number of centuries. Furthermore, they form a link of a larger chain of similar mounds which stretch northerly along the coast and inland from Southern California to beyond Vancouver and possibly still farther; *i.e.*, a distance of 18 degrees of latitude. The extension of such a similar manner of life over so great an area speaks of itself for the work of a great number of centuries. Even the complete development of this peculiar mode of existence. as represented in these mounds. must have taken centuries. And this is the more probably true since in those earlier stages of cultural evolution advances in the

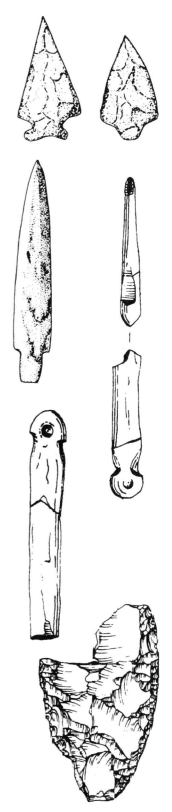

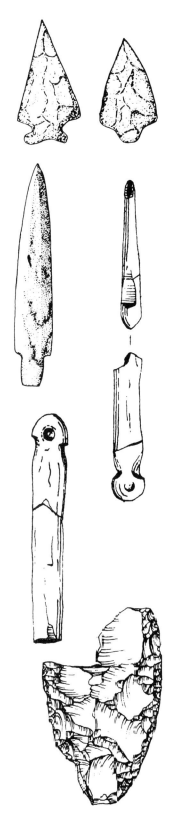

manner of living were infinitely more difficult than they were later. Under these circumstances it is only possible to assume that the origin of the shellmounds in this region represents a historical development of more than a thousand, possibly many thousand years.[59] If this holds good generally for the origin of shellmounds among which the one at Emeryville is, judged by its height, the character of its contents in the lower strata, and the observed geological facts, by no means the youngest, we have still to consider on the other hand the limits of the time up to which these mounds may have been inhabited.

For a long time it has been customary to consider the last as well as the first occupation of the shellmounds as belonging to the remote past. The fact that in California no shellmound is known which is now inhabited or has been inhabited in historic time would speak for this assumption. However, many instances point to habitation of the mounds in the most recent times, not only in a few places, but in different parts of the whole inhabited world. And this cannot surprise us; for we can see primitive man reach into the most recent, nay, even the present time, in various parts of the globe. Thus, as is well known, the first discoverers described the Indians of the Gulf of Mexico as men "living in houses of mats erected upon hills of oysters."[60] R. Schomburgh attributes a large number of mounds made of snail shells, observed by him near the mouth of the Orinoco river, to the Warrow Indians, who are still living in that neighborhood. In the desolate coast lands of the at present dry mouths of the Ica river in Peru there are two enormous shellmounds which the writer has visited. Even now there remain large parts of the wooden huts which were left behind on these shellmounds by the last shell-eaters. Painted pot-fragments, patches of woven fibres, and all

---

[59] In a similar manner, Abbott, *l. c.*, p. 449, closes a long general exposition of the reasons which speak either for or against a relatively great age of the shellmounds on the Atlantic coast, with the estimate of an age of at least 1,000 years. His deductions are based upon geological reasons (the sinking of the coast) and the dissimilarities of the cultural remains found in the mounds. Peculiarly enough, D. G. Brinton, reasoning from the analogy of the cultural character of the shellmounds with that of the Indian tribes which the explorers met in this country, thinks he has found an argument against a comparatively high age of the shellmounds. W. H. Dall considers the lower strata of his well-explored Aleutian shellmounds to have an age of about 1,000 years. (Contributions, *l. c.*, p. 53.)

[60] Abbott, *l. c.*, p. 44.

kinds of bones lie scattered about. It would be an easy matter to show that the last inhabitants of the hill exhibited the later cultural conditions which prevailed during the time of the Incas in the valleys of Pisco and Ica, about 1460 A.D.

Returning to California, there can be no doubt that the hill-like camp places of the Indians in the interior of the country represented a local variation of the shellmounds along the shore. The form and structure of these camping places resemble the shellmounds of the coast. The material differs in part, since the inhabitants of the inland had fewer shells at their disposal. These camping places were inhabited by the Indians quite recently, or are even now inhabited.[61] The time when the shellmounds of the Bay shore were vacated by their owners was therefore probably not very long ago. With this view coincides the fact that in the upper strata of the shellmound burial is represented by cremation; a form of burial observed up to the most recent times among the Indians of California. The white immigrants settled first on the seacoast, and it is therefore natural that the aborigines retreated earlier from their shellmounds than their brethren in the interior did from their camp places.

Thus, while the history of the shellmounds of this region probably reaches back more than a thousand years into the past, it must have extended almost to the threshold of modern times. The fact that their roots reached far back into the prehistoric period of California does not prevent our seeing the tops developing almost to the present day.

CULTURAL STAGES REPRESENTED.

If we attribute to the shellmound an age representing many centuries, cultural differences should be indicated in the successive strata. For it is impossible that the cultural state of one and

---

[61] The old Indian camping place at Knight's Landing (on the Fair Ranch), at the mouth of a tributary of the Sacramento river, was inhabited, according to authentic information (T. Coleman), as late as 1849 by 150-200 "Digger" Indians. They departed in 1865. The shells, of which only a small number have been found, are of *Mytilus*. A similar mound in Colusa county, 20 miles to the northwest, is still populated by Indians. The Wintun Indians are still accustomed to obtain shells for food by diving into the river. This caused Powers (*l. c.*, p. 233) to surmise that a race somewhat like theirs might have erected these shellmounds.

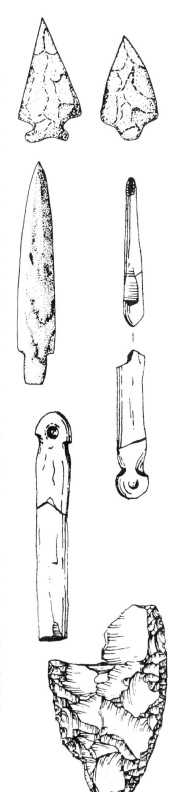

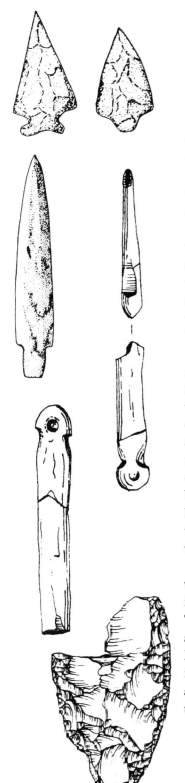

the same place should have remained stationary for many centuries and, even judging by the mass alone, the mound could not have reached such a height in less than a considerable number of centuries. In attempting to discover possible cultural differences we unfortunately meet with several difficulties. The action of the climate has destroyed in all the strata the objects which consisted of perishable materials. Only the more resistant things remained. But the perishable materials are frequently those in which the decorative sense of man expresses itself most easily, and in which cultural differences are most distinctly shown. A further unfortunate circumstance arises from the general trend to simplicity and primitiveness of the tools of the inhabitants of all shellmounds. So that the visible cultural differences which would generally appear with a people of changing forms of life are imperfectly expressed. Finally, many objects give only partial evidence as regards form and use, for they were often mutilated previous to their deposition in the strata.

In examining the implements of successive layers of the mound we find that awls and certain knife-like tools found in nearly all known shellmounds are met with in all of the strata, while ornaments consisting of *Haliotis* shells and other simple objects of decoration made of shells, corresponding in general appearance to those which are still in use among the Indians, are met with in the graves of the VIth to the VIIIth strata. In the deepest strata, however, there have not been found any bone beads, ornaments of *Haliotis* shells, or saw-like tools such as are known above the VIIIth stratum. Thus there is some support for the suggestion that cultural differences are expressed in the history of the mound.

One of the most striking differences indicating a change in the character of the people whose cultural stages are represented in the successive strata is found in the different forms of burial. The use of cremation appears for the first time in the 4th stratum and extends to the upper, completely undisturbed stratum (II). In the IVth stratum out of 11 bone awls only 4 are calcined, while in the IInd stratum 44 in 61. In the latter the great amount of ash intermingled with calcined human bones becomes very noticeable. Powers relates in his great work on the California tribes

that most of them practiced cremation, and concerning the Ka-
rok, Yurok, and Wintun he relates that they bury their dead,
while the Yokuts under certain circumstances make use of both
customs.   The inhabitants of the upper strata of the mound may
undoubtedly be assumed to have followed the customs of the majority of modern Californian tribes in the disposal of their dead.
Contrasting with this custom is burial in the ground.   In this
connection interesting evidence is furnished by the strata of this
mound: here at least cremation was preceded by interment.   In
strata IV to VIII of this mound we find this custom prevailing,
and we are forced to assume it to have been practiced by the
population living on the mound during the time from the deposition of the lower part of stratum VIII to that of the middle of
stratum V.   In their manner of burial the knees were drawn up,
resting upon the side, resembling on the whole the mode of burial
in the shellmounds of Santa Barbara county in California, and
in those found in Oregon.   Instead of suggesting that the mode
of burial is a recent one, the findings in the lower strata of the
mound at Emeryville might hint that possibly the shellmounds
of Southern California and Oregon are older than is at present
believed.   The Yokuts likewise bury their dead with drawn-up
knees, but whether lying on one side is not mentioned.   Also of
the Wintun detailed information as regards their mode of burial
is missing.   But even if a majority of tribes should still practice
the form which prevailed in the middle strata of the mound, this
would not change the fact that the whole mode of burial at this
place designates an earlier ethnical stage.   The manner in which
the inhabitants of the lower strata of the mound—say from the
bottom portions of the VIIIth stratum to the bottom of the Xth—
buried their dead is not known, because no graves or other evidences of burial appear in them.   It is not impossible that their
mode of burial differed again from the two kinds of burial found
in the strata lying above.

Another striking difference between the upper and lower layers is found in the characteristic implements of the strata.   This
difference is best represented by a comparative table.   In order
to understand this better, we give the relative volume of earth
moved for each stratum.   In the table the volume of the VIIth

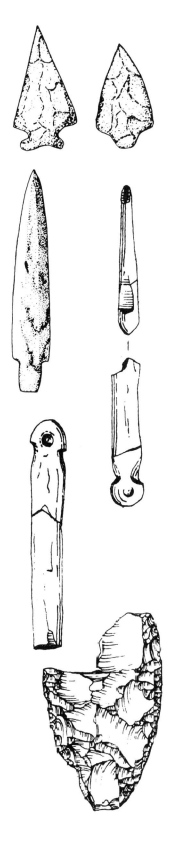

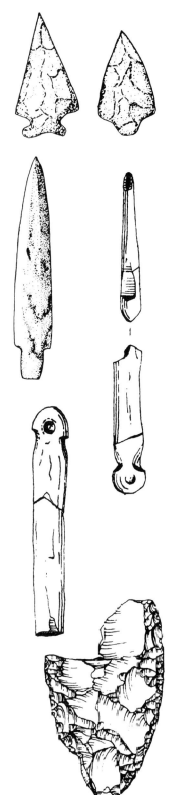

stratum (about 100 cubic feet) has been taken as the unit. Bracketed figures in the different columns denote the number of objects which might have been expected as the proportional content of one of the middle strata. In the last two columns the contents of the IXth stratum have for practical purposes been used as a basis.

Layers	Relative Contents	Rubbed* stone implements	Obsidians	Flaked stone implements excepting obsidian	Knife-like implements	Rough awl-like implements
I	5.5	2[5]	2[2]	—	[6]	—[8]
II	10.6	24[10]	11[5]	6[10]	[13]	—[16]
III	7.3	3[7]	4[4]	4[7]	[9]	—[11]
IV	4.2	4	2	4	[5]	—[6]
V	3.4	4[4]	1[1]	5(2)	[4]	—[5]
VI	1.5	—[1]	—[1]	3	[1]	—[2]
VII	1	—[1]	2[1]	6	[1]	—[1]
VII*	2.2	—[2]	—[-]	9	1[2]	[11]
VIII	7.4	1[7]	1[4]	24	1[9]	—[3]
IX	3.3	—[3]	1[2]	62	4[4]	5[5]
X	1.8	—[2]	—[1]	17	—[2]	4[3]

(Flaked stone column: VII–X bracketed with (28); Knife-like column: VII–IX bracketed with 5)*

Parentheses in the 4th column denote the number of chipped stones which may actually be assumed as tools.

It is evident that the character of the objects in the upper strata is entirely different from that of the implements which are found in the lower beds. Well polished stone implements and obsidians diminish the nearer we come to the bottom. The sporadic occurrence of a well polished stone implement in the 8th stratum of the first column has an entirely abnormal aspect, in view of the otherwise complete absence of such objects from the VIth stratum downward. The abnormal increase of objects of the 1st and 2nd kinds in the IInd stratum is doubtless due to the custom of throwing their possessions into the fire during the cremation of the dead. Still, the IInd stratum yielded a sufficient number of fragments of similar objects which were evidently lost in other ways. So few are furnished by the contents of the lower strata that their limited use is apparently indicated. In fact, even the Vth stratum shares this poverty, for its four polished implements are only represented by fragments of metate-like stones and a tablet of slate, polished on one side. In the lower strata flaked stones (of local materials), bone splinters of an awl-

---

* Except mortars and pestles.

like shape, and knife-like tools of bone predominate. Among the flaked stones, real implements are very numerous; they are missing in the upper strata. Their technique is primitive. On one side they are flat and are worked on the other side only. This working, too, is crude, and the finishing primitive. The turtle-back form is present. Different kinds of scraper-like tools of primitive form, and of drill-like sharpened stone fragments, must have been more common implements in the hands of the inhabitants of this stage than among the dwellers on the upper strata, where these tools are lacking.

A well formed implement of flaked stone, worked on both sides, was found low down in stratum VIII (a spear-like blade, pl. 10, fig. 14). Strata IX and X offer nothing similar. The leaf-like blade from stratum VIII (pl. 6, fig. 20), where a crude workmanship is paired with an attempt at more regular sharpening of the edges, does not favor the view that the inhabitants of the mound had been well versed from the beginning in the production of chipped implements.

Very remarkable is the occurrence together of crude splinters of bone, which show from long use their real value as tools, and the neat, almost elegant, knife-like implements. Among the latter we find the only ornamental fragment of a tool of bone obtained during the whole course of the excavation. The people who used the splinters of bone for their tools were not so primitive but that they possessed elegant objects of bone, and not so far advanced but that they were often satisfied with such primitive implements as common bone splinters. But both classes of these typical tools are markedly different from what the upper strata of the mound offer in the line of implements. Hence the people of the lower strata must have represented a somewhat different mental type or a different degree of mental training.

It seems advisable, from what we know, to separate the older inhabitants who had settled here and raised the foundations of the mound up to the middle part of the VIIIth stratum, from the later population of the grave period. They may have been neolithic, they may have been connected with the following generation by some common traits, although there is little evidence for this; but the two people certainly differed in cultural characteristics.

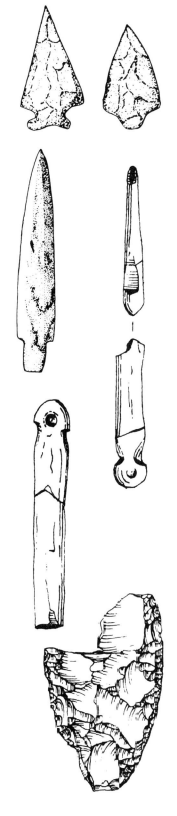

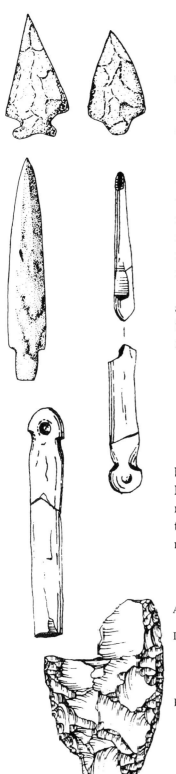

The race that commenced building in the middle of the 8th stratum was apparently less different from the population of the upper strata than from its predecessors. But differences can here, also, be discovered. The chipped tools of local materials still continue for some time (about to VIIa), and obsidian seems to have come to them as a rather rare material. Only a few bone implements from grave 8 are extant in this group of strata. Contrasted with the usage of the people of the upper strata is also the use of bone arrow blades, which the last inhabitants of the mound apparently did not possess. They had not yet departed from an extended employment of bone as a working material; a fact usually more characteristic of a primitive people than of one further advanced.

One observation should still be made in this connection. It is a striking fact that in the fifth stratum and its immediate proximity a number of objects appear, the likeness of which was not found elsewhere in the whole mound. They are:

(1) Fragments of metate-like stones, stratum V.
     A long, dull, chisel-like tool of horn, from stratum V.
     A tablet of slate polished on one side, stratum V.

(2) Pieces of antlers, truncated for use as tools, stratum V, and a knife-like implement, stratum V.

It seems possible that such sporadic types of tools were left by a people that only temporarily inhabited the mound. Since, however, up to the present time parallel investigations have furnished but little material, such an hypothesis cannot be tested as to its exactness; nor is it possible to state from what region they might have come.

REFERENCES CITED

ABBOTT, CHARLES C.
    1881   *Primitive Industry.* G.A. Bates, Salem.
DALL, WILLIAM H.
    1877   On Succession in the Shell-Heaps of the Aleutian Islands. *Contributions to North American Ethnology* 1:41–91. (U.S. Geographic and Geological Survey of the Rocky Mountain Region; edited by J. W. Powell)
POWERS, STEPHEN
    1877   Tribes of California. *Contributions to North American Ethnology* 3. (U.S. Geographic and Geological Survey of the Rocky Mountain Region; edited by J. W. Powell)

REPORT OF THE COMMITTEE ON ARCHEOLOGICAL NOMENCLATURE

The following report has been prepared by Prof. John H. Wright, Mr J. D. McGuire, Mr F. W. Hodge, Mr W. K. Moorehead, and Dr C. Peabody, chairman. The recent illness and death of Professor Wright deprived the Committee of his advice and suggestion during the final drafting ; with this exception the report is unanimous.

To the President and Members of the American Anthropological Association :

The Committee on Nomenclature of specimens has the honor of submitting the following report. It covers only certain divisions of objects in clay and of objects in stone ; the departments referred to seem to the Committee to be peculiarly suited to a rigid examination resulting in definition, classification, and meaning.

In all, the object of the Committee has been to reduce everything to its lowest terms, to use English words, if possible, and words that shall be perfectly clear in denotation to scholars at home and abroad, and to adhere as closely as may be to classifications already made standard.

As has been well said, the difficulty in classification and nomenclature comes from our lack of complete and detailed knowledge.

The classifications here offered and the definitions here proposed in some detail are based so far as is possible on form alone. It is of course taken as an axiom that a classification based on form assumes no theory of the development, interrelation, or conventionalization of forms or types in any manner whatsoever ; it has been the particular aim of the Committee to avoid or to get rid of those classes and names that are based on uses assumed but not universally proved for certain specimens.

Should the attempt meet with the favor of the members of the Association, it should be possible at a future date to apply the same principles to a detailed examination of other stone specimens and to specimens in shell, basketry, and textiles, so far as has not been already done.

ARTICLES IN CLAY

Simple vessels in clay may be presumed to cover all forms except eccentric or conventionalized (i. e., animal-shaped) forms on the one hand, and discs and pipes on the other.

It is suggested by the Committee that members of the American Anthropological Association having occasion to describe clay vessels, may classify them : first, as to material, as consisting of clay, sand, shell, and their combinations, and as possessing certain general ground-color ;

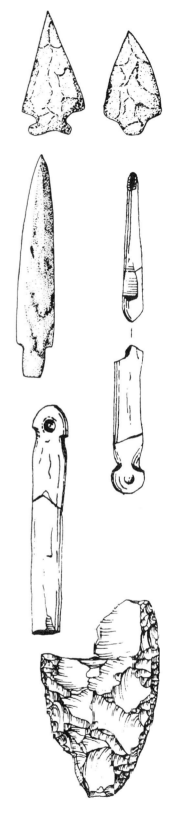

Report of the Committee on Archeological Nomenclature   29

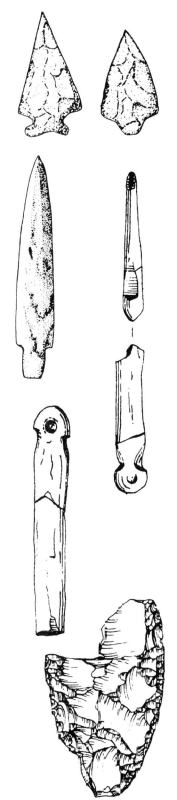

second, as to manufacture, as sun-dried or fired, as coiled or modeled — with the variations and steps of each process ; third, as to form ; fourth, as to decoration, as plain, stamped, incised, or painted. With regard to form, the Committee begs to offer the following definitions and suggestions in classifications.

[*Note.*—In all cases measurements are considered as referring to an upward direction.]

A simple vessel must consist of a body, and may have a rim, neck, foot, handle, or any combination.

1. *Body :* A formation capable of holding within itself a liquid or a solid substance.

2. *Rim :* (*A*) A part of the vessel forming the termination of the body. (*B*) A part of the vessel recognizable by a change in the thickness of the material in the terminal sections.

3. *Neck :* A part of the vessel recognizable by a more or less sudden decrease in the rate of increase or decrease of the diameter.

4. *Foot :* An attachment to the vessel which serves as support to the body when upright.

5. *Handle :* A part of the vessel consisting of some outside attachment, not serving as support.

Body : It is suggested that in comparing the forms or cross-sections of vessels particular attention be paid to the proportion of the diameter to the height, to the rate of change of this proportion, to the place of change of direction in this proportion, and to refer to the following definitions of the two dimensions :

Height : the distance from the base to a horizontal plane passing through the most distant part of the rim.

Diameter : the distance from any one point on the sides to any opposite point on the sides, measured on a plane at right angles to the height.

Base : the point of contact or a plane of contact of the body with a horizontal surface.

Types. *Body :* These are so varied, depending on relative height and diameter of the cross-section, that an analysis is too cumbersome to be of service to general reference.

Neck : 1. Expanding.
2. Cylindrical.
3. Contracting.
4. Combinations.

Lip : A part of the neck or body recognizable by a suddenly increasing diameter of neck or body, that continues increasing to the rim.

Foot : 1. Continuous.
  (*A*) Expanding.
  (*B*) Cylindrical.
  (*C*) Contracting.
  (*D*) Combinations.
 Feet : 2. Not continuous.
  Differentiated by
  (*A*) Number.
  (*B*) Angle with the horizontal.
   (*a*) Expanding upward.
   (*b*) Perpendicular.
   (*c*) Contracting upward.
Handles. Types.
 Differentiated by
  1. Number.
  2. Position on the vessel.
   (*A*) Body.
   (*B*) Neck.
   (*C*) Foot.
   (*D*) Combinations.
  3. Form.
   (*A*) Continuous with body or neck.
   (*B*) Not continuous with body or neck.
    (*a*) With constant direction.
    (*b*) With varying direction.
    (*c*) With reëntry upon vessel.
   (*A′*) Round.
   (*B′*) Flat.
   (*C′*) Coiled.

ARTICLES IN STONE

CHIPPED STONE

I. *Knives and Projectile Points.*
  Larger = 5 cm. (2 inches) or more in length.
  Smaller = less than 5 cm. (2 inches) in length.
 Types.
  1. Without stem.
   (*A*) Without secondary chipping (= flakes).
   (*B*) With secondary chipping.
    (*a*) Pointed.

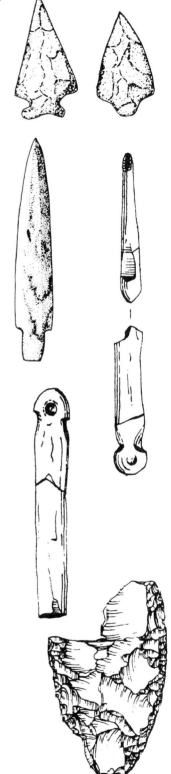

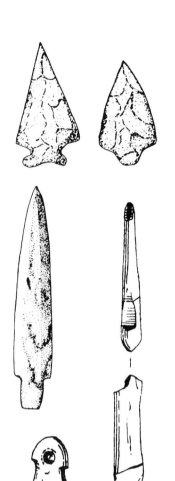

(*a'*) At one end.
  Base concave.
  Base straight.
  Base convex.
  Sides convex.
  One side convex, one side straight.
  (*b'*) At both ends.
  (*b*) Ends convex.
  (*c*) More or less circular.
2. With stem.
  (*A*) Stem expanding from base — with or without barbing.
    (*a*) Base concave.
    (*b*) Base straight.
    (*c*) Base convex.
  (*B*) Stem with sides parallel — with or without barbing.
    (*a*) Base concave.
    (*b*) Base straight.
    (*c*) Base convex.
  (*C*) Stem contracting from base — with or without barbing.
    (*a*) Base concave.
    (*b*) Base straight.
    (*c*) Base convex.

Note 1. — The proportion of the length of the base to its breadth should be observed.

Note 2. — The notches in barbed specimens may be vertical, horizontal, or with varying diameter.

Note 3. — The angles formed by the faces (i. e., " bevel ") should be observed.

II. *Scrapers.*
  Types.
    1. With one or more scraping edges.
    2. Without or with notch (including circular).
III. *Perforators.*
  Types differentiated by
    1. Cross-section.
      (*A*) Round.
      (*B*) Quadrangular or irregular.
    2. Stem.
      (*A*) Without stem.
      (*B*) With stem.

John H. Wright et al.

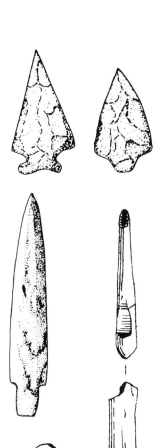

(*a*) Stem expanding gradually.

(*b*) Stem expanding suddenly.

IV. *Hammerstones.*

   Types.

    1. Spheroidal.

    2. Discoidal.   { (*a*) "Pitted."

                     { (*b*) Not "pitted."

    3. Elongated.   { (*a*) Grooved.

                     { (*b*) Not grooved.

Note 1. — Practical or ornamental serration may be applied to many forms.

Note 2. — Combinations of the types may appear in one specimen and any type may be infinitely varied by individual caprice.

GROUND STONE

I. *Problematical forms.*

    1. Laminæ (i. e., flat "spuds," "gorgets," and pendants).

  Types.

    (*A*) Spade-shaped.

    (*B*) Ovate.

        (*a*) Sides concave (not common).

        (*b*) Sides straight.

        (*c*) Sides convex.

    (*C*) Leaf-shaped.

    (*D*) Spear-shaped.

    (*E*) Rectangular.

        (*a*) Sides concave.

        (*b*) Sides straight.

        (*c*) Sides convex.

    (*F*) Shield-shaped.

    (*G*) Pendants.

        (*a*) Celt-shaped.

        (*b*) Rectangular.

        (*c*) Oval or circular.

  2. Resemblances to known forms.

    (*A*) Animal-shaped stones.

    (*B*) Boat-shaped stones.

    (*C*) Bar-shaped stones.

        (*a*) Longer, resembling true "bars."

        (*b*) Shorter, "ridged" or "expanded gorgets."

    (*D*) Spool-shaped stones.

    (*E*) Pick-shaped stones.

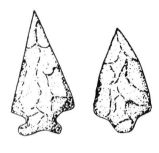

    (*F*) Plummet-shaped stones.
    (*G*) Geometrical forms.
        (*a*) Spheres.
        (*b*) Hemispheres.
        (*c*) Crescents.
        (*d*) Cones.
3. Perforated stones with wings.
    (*A*) Wings with constant rate of change of width.
        (*a*) Wings expanding from perforation.
        (*b*) Wings with sides parallel.
        (*c*) Wings contracting from perforation.
    (*B*) Wings with varying rate of change of width.
II. Tubes and tube-shaped stones.
III. Beads.
IV. Pitted stones other than hammerstones.

The Committee finally takes pleasure in thanking the following members for assistance rendered :

Prof. N. H. Winchell, University of Minnesota, Minneapolis; Prof. Henry Montgomery, University of Toronto; Prof. William N. Bates, University of Pennsylvania, Philadelphia: Dr H. Kinner, St Louis: Dr George Grant MacCurdy, Yale University; Mr M. Raymond Harrington, New York; Mrs Zelia Nuttall, Coyoacán, D.F., Mexico; Mr C. C. Willoughby, Harvard University; Dr Walter Hough, National Museum; Dr Nicolas León, Mexico; Mr F. S. Dellenbaugh, New York; Prof. F. W. Putnam, Harvard University; Dr John M. Wulfing, St Louis; Mr Harlan I. Smith, American Museum of Natural History, New York; Rev. J. D. Marmor, New York; Mr Christopher Wren, Plymouth, Penn.; Dr A. W. Butler, Indianapolis; Dr H. W. Shimer, Boston; Prof. W. H. Holmes, Washington; Mr Richard Herrmann, Dubuque, Iowa; Dr H. F. ten Kate, Tokyo; Dr J. B. Ambrosetti, Buenos Aires.

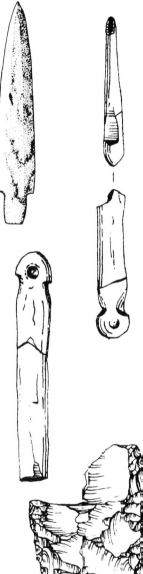

ARCHÆOLOGICAL INVESTIGATIONS IN THE VALLEY OF MEXICO BY THE INTERNATIONAL SCHOOL, 1911–12.

By Dr. Franz Boas, New York.

DURING the season of 1911–12, when I had charge of the International School of American Ethnology and Archæology in Mexico City, we gave much attention to the question of the sequence of ancient cultures in the valley. Some years ago Mr. William Niven had called attention to the wealth of material to be found in the brickyards of Atzcapotzalco, and Professor Seler proved by investigation that comparatively few objects belonging to the Aztec culture were found there, while the majority were of the type of Teotihuacan. He had also noticed a number of very curious types which were found in gravels at Atzcapotzalco and had evidently been rolled in river beds.

To ascertain the relative age of these archæological deposits, I entrusted an excavation in one of the brickyards to Sr. M. Gamio, a Fellow of the School. I also made a somewhat extended reconnaissance in the Sierra de Guadalupe to see whether the Teotihuacan type would be found there, either in surface layers or at a greater depth. I wish to express here my thanks to M. Jorge Engerrand for giving us most valuable aid in the geological interpretation of the strata investigated.

The part of the valley of Mexico in which our researches were made lies between the Sierra de Sta. Cruz and that of Guadalupe. The bottom of the valley rises gradually northward from the Lake of Texcoco. At San Miguel Amantla, where our excavations were made, the valley is probably not more than 3 or 4 metres above the present level of the lake. The surface is irregular, partly from the effects of erosion, partly owing to the removal of considerable masses of soil which have been used for centuries for the manufacture of adobes. The surface consists of vegetable mould and decomposed volcanic tufa deposited in the form of dust. In many places, one or more layers of tepetate are found at a depth of about 1 metre. This is a calcareous deposit due to the oozing out and redepositing of calcareous matter. The tepetate had been used for buildings in some places, and appears in such combination with layers of pebbles as to make an artificial origin at least plausible. Mounds of varying size are found above the tepetate all over the valley, and often rise over a paved floor, which is almost always accompanied by layers of tepetate.

At San Miguel Amantla, the deeper layers were examined. In the first excavation Sr. Gamio found loose decomposed tufa under the tepetate, and at a depth of about two metres and a half he came to the foundation of a house. The remains of an excavation and of a large hearth indicated that at this level the site had been inhabited.   Deeper down followed more decomposed tufa but much more solidly packed, and fine and coarse sands were found in between.   The whole structure of the deposit indicates that it must be considered as a subaërial deposit from which the finest particles were washed out by water during wet seasons, leaving the volcanic sand, which shows, in some places, stratification due to small watercourses.   At a depth of 7 metres the volcanic tufa ceases almost suddenly and is followed by very coarse gravel alternating with sand, clearly the remains of a stream which crossed the valley.   The gravel is about 2 metres thick.   It also ends suddenly, resting on a very hard black clay which contains impressions of plants and is evidently an old swamp.   This clay is filled with much decomposed tufa.   Under it is found a whitish sand, a lake deposit.   The present water table, at the end of the dry season, is in the hard swamp clay.   A number of control diggings showed that the swamp had a considerable extension, and that the gravel bed represents a river 100 metres in width.   At the sides of the river a sandy soil is found in place of the gravel, probably indicating that more of the fine material was washed away there than in the higher levels.   This old river-bed seems to lie under a former level of the Lake of Texcoco, which would indicate considerable climatic changes in the valley of Mexico since the deposition of the swamp clay.

In the region of San Miguel Amantla and Tacuba, Aztec remains are confined to the mounds and to surface layers.   As soon as the undisturbed decomposed tufa is reached, specimens typical of the culture of Teotihuacan are found.   The remains of houses belong to this type, which persists to the depth where the river gravel is reached.   The remains are plentiful everywhere, but most so on and under the level of the house-foundations.

Still deeper in the gravel, rolled pieces of pottery were found.   So far as their character can be determined, these do not belong to the Teotihuacan culture, but are of an entirely distinct technique.   Remains of this kind have been found wherever the gravel of this river course has been examined.   In the swamp and underlying sand no artifacts have been found.   It is, therefore, clear that the decomposed tufa represents a long period of occupancy by people who had the cultural type of Teotihuacan, while the Aztec period was very much shorter.   If it should turn out that the geographical and climatic conditions have changed considerably since the disappearance of the river course we must assume a very long time for the Teotihuacan period.

The most difficult question involved in this investigation is the identification of the cultural type of the river gravel period.   The pebbles in the gravels come from the Santa Cruz mountains, and although the bits of rolled pottery might have had the same origin, it seemed to me that many were not sufficiently rounded to have undergone transportation over long distances in a rapid river filled with pebbles, and for this reason a search in the valley seemed necessary.   In this we were favoured by luck, and Sr. Gamio found objects of this type in his fifth excavation quite plentifully and in undisturbed position.   His finds consist of small figures

N

and fragments of pottery with painted surfaces. Here he made the important observation that in the lower sands these older types occurred with the types of Teotihuacan and that the latter seemed to disappear in the lowest layers of the sand. It would seem, therefore, that there has been a gradual transition from the oldest culture to that of Teotihuacan. We had reached this conclusion before, from the types of small pottery heads, some of which showed distinct technical affiliations with the oldest culture. In the Museum at Teotihuacan a number of figurines of the same type are shown and recently objects of the same class were found at the lowest levels of the subterranean structures. These finds were made by Sr. Rodriguez, Inspector-General of Monuments, and are important because they show that in Teotihuacan also the same primitive culture occurs.

My own inquiries in the Sierra de Guadalupe enabled us to give a better identification of this culture. In the autumn of 1911, when searching with Dr. von Hoerschelmann for some point in the Sierra de Guadalupe where the Teotihuacan type might occur, our attention was called to a pile of potsherds on the slope of the hill of Zacatenco, and the similarity of the types to those of the Cerro de la Estrella, as well as the difference between these types and the valley types was at once apparent. In the course of the following months I succeeded in locating two other places with the same type in the Sierra de Guadalupe, and further objects of the same character, although not in such quantity, were secured from the Peñon de los Baños and Los Reyes. I was able to bring together a considerable collection of specimens and these are identical in type with the oldest culture of San Miguel Amantla. The whole impression of these remains is that they are closely akin to those of the State of Colima and of parts of Michoacan, so that we may conclude that a technical culture fairly uniform in its fundamental forms extended in early times from the Pacific Ocean to the Valley of Mexico, and northward to the state of Zacatecas.

The principal characteristics of the type of pottery found in the sites mentioned are : great thickness, frequent occurrence of moulded rims ; designs punched in with a dull point ; others painted in red, often with scratched outlines which the colour does not follow evenly ; a white slip with scratched designs ; the occurrence of grecques somewhat similar to those of the Pueblos of New Mexico ; feet of very large size, and handles in form of hands. Small heads are very numerous ; they were never made in moulds, but the various ornaments were built up of bits of clay, and the eyes generally consist of a clay pellet with two impressions made with the point of a stick. The legs of female figures show enormous dimensions of the thighs, while those of male figures are thin. Almost all the figures are naked, but provided with neck, ear, and hair ornaments. They were painted red and perhaps white. It may be remarked here that on the eastern slope of the Guadalupe mountains a site was found, which was covered with the remains of the Teotihuacan type.

Across the Valley, on the Cerro de la Estrella, remains of the oldest type were found, while at the foot of this mountain, at Culhuacan, enormous quantities of Aztec pottery occur. Nevertheless, in the ditches that cross this district, numerous specimens with engraved line designs are found. Since the bulk of the pottery found here has a character quite distinct from other Aztec pottery, it seemed desirable to investigate the succession of types. The characteristic yellow ware of the Valley of Mexico may be divided into three groups ; one, of very fine pottery of light colour with regular delicate line-and-dot designs ; a second, a little coarser, and perhaps a little darker, with broader line-and-curve designs ; and a third type much coarser, and darker in colour, with complex designs which bear evidence of having been executed very rapidly and carelessly. A number of small excavations which were made by Miss Ramirez Castañeda show that at Culhuacan the first-named type is the most recent. Where the soil has not been disturbed it occurs only in superficial layers. Deeper down, the third type only is found until the water table is reached, and it occurs in very great profusion. It seems likely that the older type of Culhuacan pottery had its prototype in earlier forms, since the rapidity of execution of the designs cannot be understood unless we assume that the potters were familiar with certain definite patterns and executed them with the same rapidity and individuality as we do handwriting.

Pottery with incised designs was found only in the deeper layers, although not very plentifully. A few specimens of identical type occur in the oldest Guadalupe sites, but there is not enough material available to associate these remains definitely with any cultural period. At the level of the water table the yellow pottery of the Valley of Mexico disappears and, farther down, the amount of pottery found is rather small ; all the objects of this level that can be identified have the type of Teotihuacan. I consider a more thorough search in these deeper layers very promising, because the muck has preserved objects of wood which may throw much light upon the ancient civilization. The fact that objects of pottery are found here as much as 3 metres under the water table does not necessarily indicate great antiquity, for it may well be that the so-called " floating gardens " existed in this area for a long time. A constant sinking of the soil and oozing out at the bottom occurs in these gardens and would gradually carry the old surface layers to considerable depths.

The principal results of the archæological work may thus be summarized by saying that we have obtained the proof of a very old culture widely spread in Mexico and antedating the culture of Teotihuacan. Whether the remains found in the hills indicate a late persistence of this culture cannot be stated definitely. Later on there followed a long period in which the culture of Teotihuacan prevailed. Apparently there was a gradual transition from the first to the second period. No such transition was noted between the culture of Teotihuacan and the Aztec culture : the latter seems to have lasted, comparatively speaking, a very short time. What preceded the oldest culture is not known, for in the place investigated, no earlier remains have been found. It is quite possible that in regions located on higher ground outside the limits of the ancient lake and swamp, the conditions for further research may be more favourable.

N 2

From

AREAS OF AMERICAN CULTURE CHARACTERIZATION TENTATIVELY OUTLINED AS AN AID-IN THE STUDY OF THE ANTIQUITIES[1]

By W. H. HOLMES

CONTENTS

INTRODUCTION

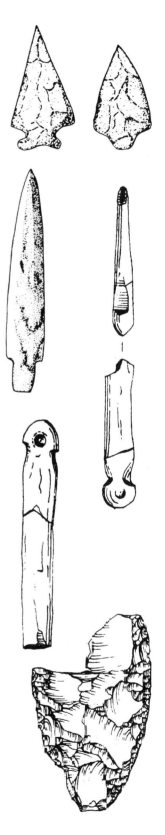

A S an initial step in the description and interpretation of the antiquities of the continent, the archeologist observes the tribes of today, their cultural characteristics and environments, and acquaints himself with what is known of them historically. He finds that their achievements are greatly diversified and that certain forms and states of culture characterize particular geographical areas and realizes that environment has had a large share in determining the course of the culture evolution. He examines the antiquities and finds that analogous geographical distinctions characterize the material culture of the past and reaches the conclusion that the relations of environment to man and culture

---

[1] The present paper is extracted from a work now in course of preparation which is intended to bring together in comprehensive form the antiquities of the continent; it is thus not complete in itself. The several areas are tentatively outlined to facilitate descriptive and comparative studies of the numerous classes of artifacts; and the brief sketches here presented are intended to familiarize the reader and student with the field as a whole and with the relative culture status of its more important subdivisions.

413

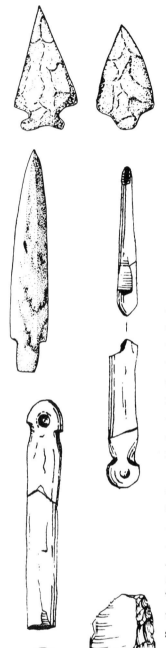

must play an important part in the prosecution of his researches and in the analysis of aboriginal history.

In the practical work of museum classification and arrangement—a work which has served in part to give form to this writing—archeological materials are necessarily grouped primarily by continents and other natural divisions, and secondarily by political divisions, such as states and territories. Separation by the larger natural divisions is always necessary, but separation by ethnic areas, or areas of culture characterization, as they are sometimes called, is most advantageous. These areas may be large or small according to the understanding or the needs of the student. By their means he approximates the real or natural grouping of the material traces of human achievement and studies to advantage culture and culture relationships and the causes of the resemblances and differences everywhere met with. The geographical limitations of culture units are, as a matter of course, not usually well defined. Cultures are bound to overlap and blend along the borders and more especially along lines of ready communication. But notwithstanding this, certain characteristics of achievement or groups of culture traits within each area will be found to separate it from its neighbors and afford effective means of comparison with other culture groups. In the present work, keeping in view the archeological rather than the ethnological evidence, it is convenient to recognize eleven areas north of Mexico (pl. xxxII), namely: (1) The North Atlantic area; (2) The Georgia-Florida area; (3) The Middle and Lower Mississippi Valley Region; (4) The Upper Mississippi and Lakes Region; (5) The Plains and Rocky Mountains; (6) The Arid Region; (7) The California Area; (8) The Columbia-Fraser Area; (9) The Northwest Coast Area; (10) The Arctic Coastal Area; (11) The Great Northern-Central Area. To these may be added (12) The Hawaiian Islands; and (13) The West Indies. These areas are here made as few and simple as possible to avoid too great complexity in conducting comparative studies of the several classes of antiquities.

The Middle and South American areas, also outlined on the broadest possible plan, are as follows: (1) Northern Mexico; (2)

Middle Mexico; (3) Southern Mexico; (4) The Maya Provinces; (5) The Central American or Isthmian Region; (6) The North Andean-Pacific Area; (7) The Middle Andean Pacific or Incan Area; (8) The South Andean-Pacific or Chilean Area; (9) The Amazon Delta Area; (10) Primitive South America, Northern Division; (11) Primitive South America, Southern Division. Detailed study of the antiquities and history of these vast regions might profit even in the initial stages of research work by further subdivision of the areas, but in the present restricted state of our knowledge this would not prove greatly advantageous, as it would prolong the summary review here contemplated without an equivalent in useful results.

These areas in all cases are based on the clearly manifested phases of their culture content. In some areas evidence has been reported of early cultures radically distinct from the type adopted as characteristic of the areas, and ancestral forms grading into the later and into the historic forms are thought to have been recognized. In these particular branches of the research, however, haste must be made slowly as the utmost acumen of the student is called for in making areal and chronological discriminations. It is anticipated, however, since the period of occupancy of the continent must have been of long duration, that not only early but more elementary cultures may in good time be identified.

Within the region north of Mexico the culture of the most advanced communities rises high in the scale of barbarian achievement—a status characterized by an artificial basis of subsistence, sedentary life, successful agriculture, and extensive town building, yet still far below the culture level of glyphic writing reached by the more advanced tribes of Middle America. Pictographic records carved on stone, engraved or painted on bark, and painted on surfaces of many kinds, were almost entirely pictorial or graphic, slight advance having been made in the use of purely conventional characters, save as separate symbols or as ornamental designs. The lowest stage ranges well down in savagery where art in stone in its rudimentary forms had barely obtained a sure foothold, as with the Seri and other Lower Californians.

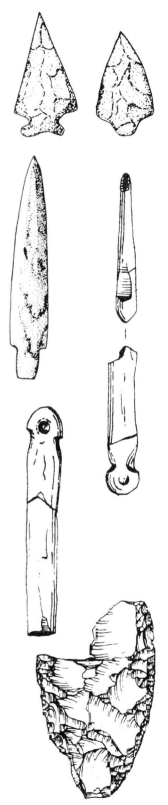

From *Areas of American Culture Characterization*

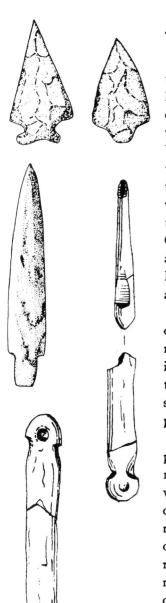

In Middle and especially in South America the culture contrasts are even greater, and nations standing upon the very threshhold of civilization, with arts, industries, and institutions highly developed, are in close juxtaposition with utterly savage tribes to which even clothing and stable dwellings are practically unknown. With the exception of a limited group at the mouth of the Amazon, the more advanced cultures were confined to the west coast and the Andean plateaus, where forests are rare and deserts common, while the primitive status was and is yet found in places throughout the vast forest regions of the eastern slope of the Andes and the Orinoco-Amazon region, in the broad pampas of Brazil, Paraguay, and Argentina, and on the entire Atlantic coastal border from Panama to Tierra del Fuego, excepting always the limited areas about the delta of the Amazon.

These differences in culture status appear to be due to a complex of causes not readily analyzed. Whatsoever the nature of the molding agencies, they have acted to diversify, differentiate, and individualize cultures in a most pronounced manner throughout the two Americas, and the results, as suggested by a study of the several areas, are among the most striking and scientifically important features of our aboriginal ethnology.

The following sketches do not assume to approximate complete presentation of the cultural remains of the several areas; they are merely intended to cultivate familiarity with the vast field as a whole and to lay out its great features tentatively as an aid in describing and comparing the antiquities and the cultures they represent. It is by no means assumed that the culture phenomena of any considerable area are uniform throughout. There may be much diversity, possibly great complexity of conditions. There may be a number of somewhat independent centers of development of nearly equal importance, or a single center may have spread its influence over a wide area. The mapping of the cultures will, in the end, take forms that cannot now be foreseen. When all available relics of antiquity have been considered and their history and distribution recorded, discussion of the culture complex may be taken up to advantage, and, enforced by the somatic evidence and illumined by the researches of ethnology, may round out the history of man in America with gratifying fullness.

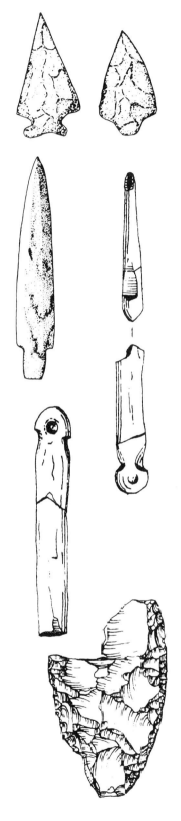

CULTURAL CHARACTERIZATION AREAS OF NORTH AMERICA AS SUGGESTED BY A COMPARATIVE STUDY
OF THE ANTIQUITIES

CHRONOLOGY OF THE TANO RUINS, NEW MEXICO [1]

By N. C. NELSON

In the course of archeological investigations pursued in New Mexico under the auspices of the American Museum during the past four years some chronological data have come to light which it seems proper to bring to the attention of students without further delay. The data consist mainly of observations on the stratigraphic relationship of several widely distributed types of pottery. Other facts of importance, such as architectural variation, exist, but these are less convincing and besides seldom immediately useful in determining the relative age of a ruin. This preliminary treatment is therefore deliberately confined to a presentation of the stratigraphy, together with a brief outline of the distinguishable ceramic features and the application of the results thus obtained to the ruins in the limited area under investigation.

GENERAL CONSIDERATIONS

As is well known, there are in the Southwest several more or less localized types of prehistoric pottery, such as ornamentally indented coiled ware, several distinct varieties of painted wares, and likewise, a somewhat varied group of glazed ware. Dr. J. W. Fewkes has only recently made us acquainted with another hitherto

[1] This article is a preliminary report of one phase of the systematic archeological exploration and excavation in the Rio Grande valley undertaken in 1912 by the Department of Anthropology of the American Museum of Natural History.

11   159

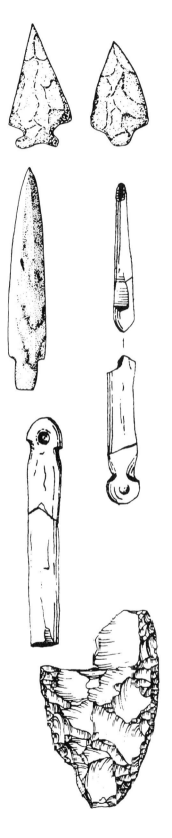

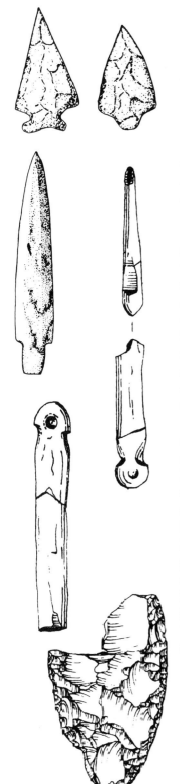

little-known ceramic type[1] of a unique character which was most intensively developed in the Mimbres valley but which occurs also in the adjacent Rio Grande country and probably beyond, towards the Pecos river. This fine, relatively ancient ware is of the painted order and seems to mark the southeastern limits of Pueblo culture in the United States.

To the north of the Mimbres center, extending up the Rio Grande drainage basin almost to the Colorado boundary, is another ceramic area characterized primarily by glazed pottery. The eastern limit of this area is somewhat uncertain, but it appears not to extend beyond the longitude of the lower Pecos and Red rivers, while in the west it remains within the Rio Grande basin except for a slender arm extended by way of Laguna and Acoma to the Zuñi valley where it again expands, taking in the country drained by several tributaries of the Little Colorado, close to the Arizona-New Mexico boundary. Leaving out of account probable sporadic occurrences in the Hopi country to the northwest, at Ysleta del Sur to the south, and also at reported minor sites along the Canadian river and elsewhere on the eastern plain, glazed pottery is distributed over an area approximating 20,000 square miles in extent, a stretch of territory which may be said to constitute the northeastern border section of Pueblo culture.

The greater portion of the country in question seems unfit for almost any sort of aboriginal existence, being either mountainous or desert-like plateau, lacking water. But the flood-plain of the Rio Grande and some of its tributaries, likewise the lower levels of the high relief with its springs and small patches of tillable soil offered inducements to a sedentary agricultural people. There is hardly a suitable spot that does not show some trace of former Indian life. To be sure, many of the settlements were small and perhaps temporary. But, disregarding those sites, there are on record for the region about three hundred ruins, some of them very large. Judging from results obtained in the Tano district alone, it is safe to say that a thorough-going examination of the entire

---

[1] "Archeology of the Lower Mimbres Valley, N. M." (*Smithsonian Miscellaneous Collections*, Vol. 63, No. 10, Washington, 1914.)

glazed pottery area would reveal probably twice the listed number of abandoned pueblos. The situation thus developed, area and environment being taken into consideration, becomes analogous to that observed in parts of California and in the Mound Builder area. That is, the implied population mounts to figures out of proportion on the one hand, to the productivity of the country and on the other, to the historically known facts. We may, therefore, reasonably suspect a lengthy occupation by either a shifting or a changing population; in other words, that the ruins in question are not of the same age.

Hitherto no archeological work of consequence has been done within the limits of the glazed pottery area, except in the northwestern part of it, *i. e.*, in the Pajarito plateau district, where Dr. E. L. Hewett and his associates of the Archaeological Institute of America have been engaged for some years. However, the conditions here do not seem thus far to have yielded precise chronological information. At the same time it is only fair to state that it has been more or less apparent to every student since Bandelier made his first observations that the Rio Grande Pueblos underwent certain cultural transformations in prehistoric times.[1] In the region under investigation by the American Museum, a district which lies southeast of the Pajarito plateau and somewhat central in the glazed pottery area, this fact was evident from the beginning. Thus, traces of "small-house" ruins marked by sherds of painted pottery of the black-on-white variety, as well as by coiled ware, were found in several places during the reconnaissance and it was easy to see that these sites antedated the large Tano ruins, say of the Galisteo basin, which were characterized chiefly by glazed pottery. At the end of the first season's work one of these glazed types of pottery had been eliminated as of historic date, having been found constantly associated with bones of the horse and other domestic animals and in fact only in particular sections of such

---

[1] Since the above was written Dr. A. V. Kidder has published his paper entitled: "Pottery of the Pajarito Plateau and of Some Adjacent Regions in New Mexico." *Mem. Am. Anthrop. Assoc.*, Vol. II, Pt. 6, 1915, in which he characterizes four styles of pottery and tentatively places the same in chronological order.

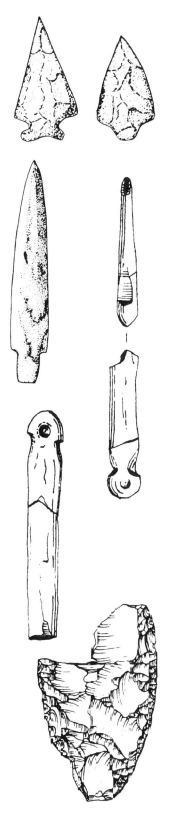

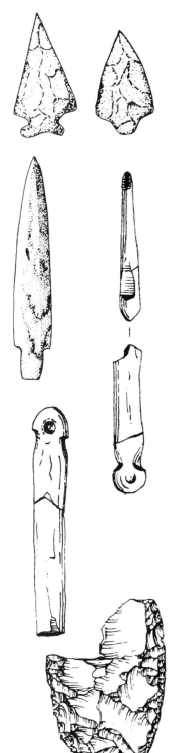

pueblos as San Cristobal, San Lazaro, San Marcos, Galisteo, and San Pedro Viejo, all but the last of which were known as Mission centers down to about 1680. But there were still apparently at least two distinguishable types—with several variants—of glazed pottery, the relative ages of which could only be surmised because both occurred in association with the strictly historic ware, though not with the same frequency. As no actual excavation was undertaken during 1913, nothing further was accomplished until 1914, when the importance of the subject had fairly impressed itself. By the opening of the season it was reasonably certain, both from internal evidence and from various general considerations, what was the chronological order of the four apparent pottery types, but tangible proof was still wanting.

This desideratum, as it happened, was obtained at the first site excavated, viz., San Pedro Viejo or Paako, a pueblo ruin lying on the southwestern edge of the Tano territory, near the head of the valley separating the San Pedro and Sandia mountains. Later, these findings were verified and supplemented by data obtained from a refuse deposit at Pueblo San Cristobal on the east-central border of the Tano country, *i. e.*, at the west base of the Trans-Pecos highlands, about seven miles south of Lamy. Again in 1915, verifications were made at the abandoned pueblos known as San Marcos, Cieneguilla, and Arroyo Hondo or Kuakaa, these last sites being all well toward the northern and northeastern limits of the Tano range and not far from Santa Fé. The result of these observations is the identification and chronological order of four, or practically five, successive styles of pottery corresponding to as many periods or stages in the history of the people occupying the late Tano and adjacent Pueblo territory. What follows is intended merely as a brief outline of the facts in the case.

STATISTICAL DATA

The data required to establish a chronology were of course to be looked for only in those places that bore evidence of long settlement. Actually superposed successions of ruins or large stratified refuse deposits are not as common, however, as might be expected, and where they do occur, there is often no appreciable differentiation in the remains. Nevertheless, at San Pedro Viejo two superpositions were discovered, one showing contact of the historic type of glazed pottery with another earlier type of glazed ware, and the other showing contact of the older of the two preceding glazed types with the black-on-white painted ware. These were, however, merely clean-cut superpositions showing nothing but time relations. Towards the end of the 1915 season another case of contact similar to the last of the two mentioned above was found at Pueblo Kuakaa. But, as before, these sections, being incomplete in that they showed no trace of the fourth type of glazed ware, could not be taken at face value. That is to say, while the positions of the two extreme members of the pottery type series were fixed, the chronological order of the two middle members was not proved, though strongly suggested. However, at Pueblo San Marcos and also at Pueblo Cieneguilla, both in the ruins proper and in the refuse heaps, the ancient type of glazed ware twice noticed in contact with the black-on-white ware was found actually mixed with it, the one gradually replacing the other. This latter was the evidence wanted, because it accounted for the otherwise unknown time interval that separated the merely superposed occurrences of types and from the point of view of the merely physical relationship of contiguity, connected them. The remaining fourth type of pottery could now take only one position in the series, namely, that of third, counting from the bottom. But all these various superpositional and transitional sections are incomplete and fragmentary, each showing merely the time relations of two successive pottery types at some place or other in the total series of four or five types. Hitherto no complete section has been found, and probably does not exist unless possibly it be at Pueblo Pecos. This site, according to Bandelier, shows evidence of settlement in the days of black-on-white pottery and, as is well known, was inhabited down to about 1838.[1] The Tano section that comes nearest to filling the require-

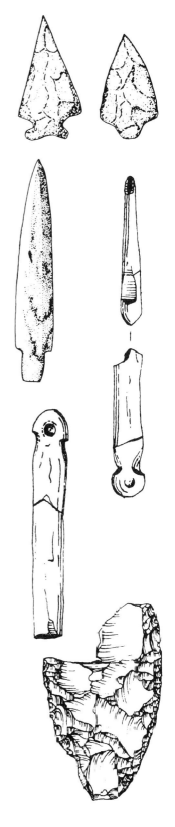

---

[1] Since the above was written Dr. A. V. Kidder of the Andover-Pecos Expedition began work at Pecos and, if I understand the situation correctly, he has found a complete chronological section which tallies quite closely with observations in the Tano district.

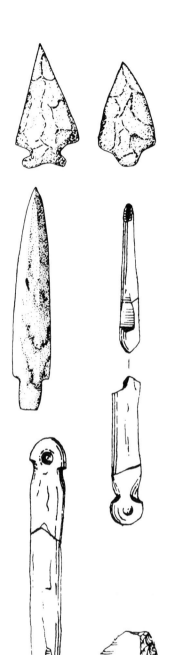

ments was found at Pueblo San Cristobal. Here are to be seen the dwindling remains of a large refuse heap, still measuring about ten feet in depth on the vertical exposure in the bank of the creek

FIG. 20.—The San Cristobal refuse section, 9 ft. 8 in. thick, yielding three successive types of pottery. Note skull protruding from original surface soil.

which has undercut and carried away the missing part (see fig. 20).[1]
Human burials were visible at different levels of this débris when
first seen in 1912, and in order to obtain some skeletal material a
five-foot bench was excavated from one side of the artificial deposit
to the other, along the edge of the creek. At that time it was noticed in a general way that different types of pottery fragments
prevailed at different levels but no effort was made, until too late,
to keep them separate. This happened partly because I was not
continually present during excavation, having decided beforehand
that chronological data were to be obtained in the ruins only and
not in burial mounds where grave diggers in overturning the débris
again and again had surely destroyed the planes of stratification.
But as all data from the ruins remained inconclusive after practically
three seasons' work I returned to San Cristobal in 1914 to make a
test. A visibly stratified section of the refuse exposure showing no
evidence of disturbance was selected and a block of this measuring
3 by 6 feet on the horizontal and nearly 10 feet deep was excavated.
I performed this work with my own hands, devoting fully three
days to the task. The potsherds from each separate foot of débris
were kept apart and the finally classified numerical results appear
in the following table.

This test is not perhaps all that could be desired; but inasmuch
as its results in their general bearings agree absolutely with the
partial data obtained before and since at other sites, no effort has
been made to strengthen the inevitable conclusions. Had a greater
volume of débris been handled, the figures of the table might possibly have lined up a little better and possibly not, because a larger
block of débris would doubtless have included areas disturbed by
burials, etc. Even with the conditions as given, viz., a visibly
stratified and undisturbed block of deposit, accidents are entirely
probable and no stress should be laid on individual figures, which at
best are more or less arbitrary. The table as a whole is, however,
both consistent and intelligible.

---

[1] For a larger general view of the refuse deposit, its relation to the topography and
adjacent ruins, see also Pl. I. of my descriptive report entitled "Pueblo Ruins of the
Galisteo Basin." (*Anthropological Papers, American Museum of Natural History*, vol.
XV, pt. 1, 1914.)

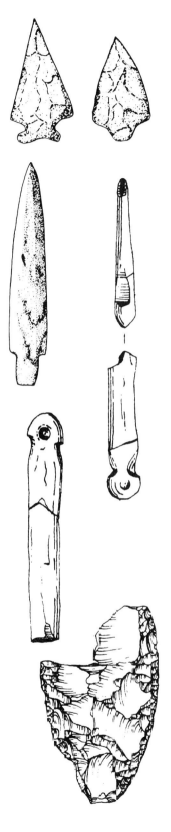

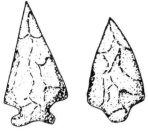

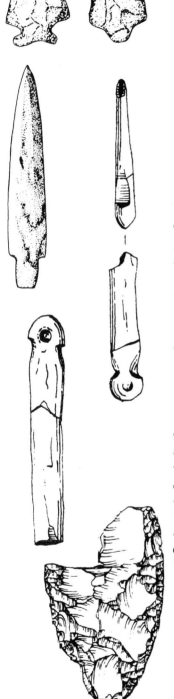

Thickness of Section	Corrugated Ware	Biscuit Ware	Type I. Two, and Three Color Painted Ware	Type II. Two Color Glazed Ware			Type III, Three Color Glazed Ware
			Black-on-White Painted Ware	Red Ware, Black or Brown Glaze	Yellow Ware, Black or Brown Glaze	Gray Ware, Black or Brown Glaze	Gray, Yellow, Pink and Reddish Wares, Combination Glaze-and-Paint Design
	(1)	(2)	(3)	(4)	(5)	(6)	(7)
1st. ft.	57	10	2	24	23	34	5
2d "	116	17	2	64	90	76	6
3d "	27	2	10	68	18	48	3
4th "	28	4	6	52	20	21	
5th "	60	15	2	128	55	85	
6th "	75	21	8	192	53	52	1 ?
7th "	53	10	40	91	20	15	
8th "	56	2	118	45	1	5	
9th "	93	1 ?	107	3			
10th "	84	1 ?	69				
= 8 in.	(126)		(103)				

Examining the table as it stands, we see at once that column 1 has no chronological significance, corrugated cooking pottery of essentially the same style having been in use throughout the time period represented by the ten-foot accumulation of débris. Column 2, likewise, is relatively useless for chronological purposes because the so-called "biscuit ware" indicated by it runs a rather unsteady course from beginning to end. The rest of the table is as satisfactory as could well be expected, whether we study the columns as individual or as related units. Column 3, representing black-on-white painted ware—called Type I—has its maximum expansion at the bottom and becomes negligible about halfway towards the top. The few fragments found in the upper four feet indicate probably heirloom vessels held over from early days or else specimens dug out of the ruins and not at all that this type of ware continued to be manufactured.[1] Whatever historical significance attaches to the fact that the ware was as its maximum development when the refuse began to accumulate we must leave for later consideration. The 4th, 5th, and 6th columns, representing contemporary variants of early glazed ware—called Type II—show

---

[1] The figures 69 and (103) in the 10th foot of Column 3 may need explanation. This 10th foot of débris in actuality measured only 8 inches in thickness and contained 69 potsherds. Had the débris measured a full 12 inches it should have contained about 103 potsherds. This will also explain the lower figures in Column I.

very nearly normal frequency curves.   That is, the style of pottery indicated came slowly into vogue, attained a maximum and began a gradual decline.   At the point where the maximum is reached the preceding style will be noticed to have come to practical extinction. Column 7, standing for a ware combining painted and glazed ornamentation—called Type III—barely gets a showing; but it appears to make the proper start for another normal frequency curve, such as would be expected.   This curve might doubtless have been completed by excavation in other refuse heaps of later date than the one here tried.   As no such supplementary test was made the succeeding style of glazed pottery called Type IV, and referred to already as of historic date, cannot appear at all in this statistical way.   Its position in the chronological type series is, however, fixed by an abundance of sound evidence.   Finally, there may be mentioned, as Type V, a painted style of ware which is clearly the forerunner of modern Pueblo pottery, though it takes its start prior to 1680.   This particular ware does not seem to occur at San Cristobal or in any but the westernmost of the supposed Tano ruins and is therefore perhaps of Keresan origin.   With these few remarks we may leave the statistical aspect of the table to speak for itself and turn our attention to its pottery classification.

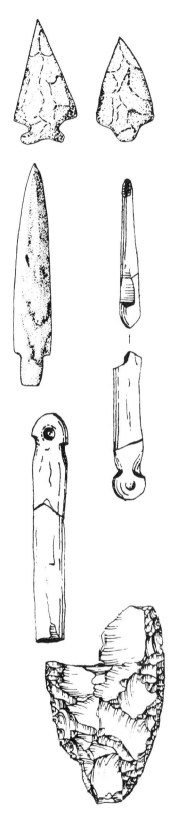

ZUÑI CULTURE SEQUENCES

By A. L. Kroeber

MUSEUM OF THE AFFILIATED COLLEGES, SAN FRANCISCO

Received by the Academy, December 8, 1915

The vicinity of the famous Indian pueblo of Zuñi in New Mexico has long been known to be rich in ruins. Many of these have been reported and described, some surveyed, and material from various sites has found its way into collections. A large body of specimens was secured through excavations by the Hemenway expedition, but this material and its data remain unpublished.

The region furnishes an unusual opportunity for an attack on the chronology, or at least the sequences of culture, in the prehistory of the

Southwest: first, because the restricted area excludes differences due to varying environments, and thus renders any observable distinctions directly interpretable in terms of time: second, because of numerous links between the historic and prehistoric periods. Several of the ruins were inhabited in Spanish times. They still bear native names that tally with those mentioned in sixteenth and seventeenth century records and some contain ruins of abandoned Catholic churches.

The tempting opportunity thus offered must of course be followed with the spade for ultimate results. I was in Zuñi during the summer of 1915. Pressure of ethnological work forbade digging; but some three thousand potsherds were gathered from the surface of about fifteen once inhabited sites within a few miles' radius of the pueblo. These were supplemented by a thousand fragments from the streets and roofs of Zuñi itself.

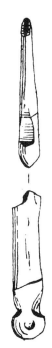

It was obvious that the pottery was of two well marked types, and that the surface of any one ruin yielded only such ware as plainly belonged to one or the other of the two classes. One set of sites is littered with sherds of which at least half are dull black or dark gray. The other half are as frequently red as white. Three-colored pieces—black and red on a white ground—are found. Corrugated ware is uncommon and about evenly distributed between dark and light.

On the second set of sites, black and red ware are both rare, white or whitish pieces constituting more than nine-tenths of the total. Three-color pottery has not been found. Corrugated sherds are common, but almost always of the light variety.

The first group of sites includes those which are mentioned as inhabited villages in the seventeenth century. Their sherds occur in nearly the same proportion as in modern Zuñi. These ruins therefore fall in part into the historic period. The second group of sites is wholly prehistoric. Their ware resembles that familiar as Cliff Dwellers' pottery. The two wares have been designated as type A, the later, and type B, the earlier.

The conditions of the ruins accords with this arrangement in time. Type A ruins normally include standing walls, and loose rock abounds. All type B sites are low or flat, without walls or rock, and show only pebbles in the surface soil. It seems more likely that this condition is due to the decay of age, or to the carrying away of the broken rock to serve as material in the nearby constructions of later ages, than to any habit of the period B people to build in clay instead of masonry. The latter possibility can be seriously entertained only if excavation reveals no building stone whatever in type B ruins.

Chips of obsidian are usually observable on period A sites, but have not been found on those of period B.

The proportions of different wares can be summarized thus:

	Eight Sites of Period A.	Nine Sites of Period B.
Wholly black	53	5
White or black on white	25	92
Containing any red	22	3
	100	100

Differences between sites of the same period can also be observed. These indicate minor periods of time. Expressed in percentages of the total number of sherds secured at each spot, the frequency of several wares is:

Period	Site	Corru-gated	Three Color	Black on Red	Any Red	Black
Present	Zuñi	0[1]	12	1		
Late A	Towwayallanna	1	8	3		
	Kolliwa	—	7	2		
	Shunntekya	2	7	2		
	Wimmayawa	2	4	1	22	53
	Mattsakya	3	4	3		
	Kyakkima	4	3	2		
Early A	Pinnawa	10	1	8		
	Site W	24	—	1		
Late B	Hattsinawa	27	—	5	10	19
	Kyakkima West	12[2]	—	4	8	—[2]
Middle B	Shoptluwwayala	40	—	2	3	7
	Hawwikku B	49	—	6	12	9
	Te'allatashshhanna	66	—	—	—	5
Early B	Site X	71	—	—	3	1
	Tetlnatluwwayala	72	—	—	2	—
Uncertain	He'itli'annanna	—	—	—	—	3
	Site Y	—	—	—	—	—

[1] Present, but less than half of 1 %.
[2] Only 25 pieces altogether are available from this site.

The material as yet at hand is too slight, and too superficial in provenience, to make this classification into sub-periods more than tentative for any particular site. The statistics however do allow of three conclusions. First, the two principal periods are almost certainly subdivisible into shorter epochs. Second, these subdivisions shade into one another. Third, there is no gap or marked break between periods A and B. So far as Zuñi valley is concerned, the prehistory of Southwestern native civilization has therefore been in the main a continuous development from the earliest known time to the present.

A. V. Kidder's recent 'Pottery of the Pajarito Plateau,' in volume 2 of the *Memoirs of the American Anthropological Association*, presents analogous results, obtained by a method differing in some details, for another

region of New Mexico; and at San Cristobal in still another part of the state, N. C. Nelson has excavated a stratified deposit showing four successive layers of different type. It is quite likely that some of the types at these three sites will prove to be similar, or even identical, as soon as the material can be compared. In this event a chronological frame work would be established that may prove capable of extension to accommodate a considerable part of the prehistoric data from the Southwest, and to fix distinctive and otherwise undatable local variations of ancient culture. The impression that there were at least two principal periods in the Southwest, the earlier represented by what are currently called Cliff Dweller forms, has of course long been prevalent, but the supporting evidence has been random. The three present sequential determinations promise not only definitely to establish but to elaborate the older general conviction.

The findings here discussed will be published in the Anthropological Papers of the American Museum of Natural History.

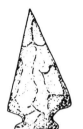

POTSHERD SAMPLES.

It cannot be doubted that the pottery art in the Southwest has run a long and varied course. It is an art with a wealth of details and to the extent to which nice discriminations in technique can be made, equally fine discriminations can be made in its fluctuating phases. It would be fatuous to emphasize here the importance of pottery for establishing a chronology of Southwestern ruins. But if we know the history of the pottery art, though only in its barest outlines, we know at once the time-relations between the ruins. Simply to state the sequence of their occupation is to tell in lowest terms of the migrations of their erstwhile occupants. Migration records are but little more than suggestive indications of former inter-tribal relations, and for just this reason seem to be the urgent need in preparing a background for ethnological study in the Southwest. In the present study we have confined our attention simply to this point.

Needless to say this type of study requires none of the intensive excava-tion necessary for the elaboration of the course of minor cultural events. It is amenable to methods possible to a reconnaissance survey. Inasmuch as several distinct methods had been indicated before the present study was undertaken, it seems advisable to discuss briefly their application to our problem.

Three methods were published almost simultaneously by Messrs. Kidder, Kroeber, and Nelson. They may be characterized respectively, as the hypothetical seriation of several pottery techniques, the hypothetical ranking of surface finds and the observation of concurrent variations, and stratigraphic observation of refuse heaps.

Dr. Kidder's method [1] rests on the association of four different wares with ruins of varying size and degree of obliteration, on their varying per-fection of technique and design, and on the extent of their distribution. With great plausibility, he tentatively ranked the wares on the basis of the combination of these factors. While the results of such a procedure are always suggestive, the objections to it are obvious. And further, wherever such a method is applicable, the methods which follow are equally applicable and certainly more productive of valid results.

Dr. Kroeber's method is outlined in the earlier pages of this volume [2]

[1] Kidder, (a).
[2] Part I.

on the basis of his experience with collections of sherds taken from the surface of ruins in the vicinity of Zuñi. Dr. Kroeber found that two general types of pottery could be distinguished. Further that sherds from any particular ruin belonged to one class only. He was thus able to distinguish two groups of ruins corresponding to the two types. Their relation in time was clearly indicated when it was noted that one group included sites occupied according to historical records and native tradition in the sixteenth century. A further analysis of the general types into their constituents, distinguished on the basis of color, suggested the division of the two general periods into minor sub-periods. Ranking these sub-periods, or rather the data for the individual ruins, by the proportion of one of the constituents, a partial confirmation of the validity of the sequence was suggested by concurrent variations in the associated constituents. A fundamental objection to Dr. Kroeber's method could be based on the quality of the original data, which obviously depends entirely on the ability of the investigator to collect a sample of potsherds at random and not by selection.

Mr. Nelson's method of stratigraphic observations on refuse heaps [1] needs no extensive comment. It is patent that the refuse heaps of every ruin contain the superposed remnants of the successive pottery styles used there, and that starting at ruins of known historical provenience we are able to trace back the successive phases of the art. More specifically Mr. Nelson's contribution consists in demonstrating the practicability of obtaining samples of sherds at random from the successive levels of the heap, and by determining the proportions of the constituent wares at each level indicating the course of the pottery art. This method is strikingly direct and entirely eliminates the error of selection, but it is only applicable to refuse heaps of considerable depth.

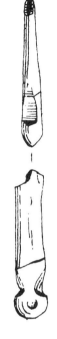

Obviously the last method is the most advantageous, but its applicability to the Zuñi ruins was strictly limited by the shallowness of the refuse heaps at most of the ruins. Stratigraphic observations were possible at only five of the one hundred ruins on the Zuñi Reservation,[2] for example. This is in itself a fact of some significance, for the necessary deduction is that the occupation of the ruins, large and small, was transitory. Fortunately, we were able to obtain good evidence connecting the pottery of Zuñi itself with Mattsakya, an historic pueblo, and Pinnawa, a prehistoric ruin, in each of which deep refuse deposits were found. For the rest Dr. Kroeber's method alone was applicable. We have therefore been forced to combine both methods in the present inquiry giving preference wherever

---

[1] Nelson.
[2] Five other ruins would probably have yielded results.

From *An Outline for a Chronology of Zuñi Ruins*

possible to the stratigraphic results. Our method of utilizing such results will be discussed after reviewing the data obtained.

It seems pertinent to inquire into the accuracy of the data obtained by the two methods. We may formulate the following questions: To what extent does a series obtained from a refuse heap represent the true sequence of types? Can we obtain a random sample of sherds by collecting from the surface of a ruin? To this end we excavated two independent sections in the refuse heaps along the eastern slope of Mattsakya, Site 48 (a ruin chosen, of course, at random). How closely these agree may be seen by inspecting the table below (p. 258). The agreement between the sections seems to be as close as may reasonably be expected, the magnitude of the deviations being relatively small and well within the range of accidental variation. This point comes out more emphatically by comparing each series with the mean series (p. 278), when it will be seen that the deviations of each series from the average have a random distribution, there being no preponderance of values on one side of the average or the other. To put the second question to the test, we compared a surface sample supposedly collected at random with a truely random sample obtained immediately below the surface. Thus, we have compared the surface sample obtained at Mattsakya by Dr. Kroeber in 1915 with the sherds from the first level obtained by the writer (p. 278). We have of necessity ignored the fact that the two samples may not be coeval, but the difference in time is probably slight.[1] The correspondence between the samples is quite close, and as in the case of the compared sections the differences are evidently accidental. In fact the differences are well within the range of variation exhibited by any two corresponding random samples in the series. A fairer test of this point would be the comparison of two samples made independently by one collector on the surface of a single ruin. We made such a test at least twice while in the field, but as the results are not at hand, we can simply state that the correspondences were similar to that above.

Pottery was obtained at most of the ruins seen. For the most part only fragments were available as no extensive excavations were made. While the absence of many complete vessels from our collection sets a definite limit on the description of the pottery wares, the preceding statements must have made it clear that this fact has but little influence on an inquiry into the sequence of the wares. Still it may be claimed that the lack of whole vessels would make an analysis of a sample of sherds into its constituent wares impossible; yet anyone who has handled material of this

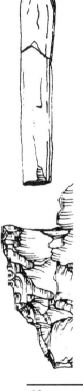

---

[1] The reader must be cautioned that such a comparison of samples obtained by different investigators does not include the differences due to personal bias since one of the samples is certainly a random collection.

sort will readily recognize that this objection is chiefly academic. It is simply a matter of experience that the variety of wares at a ruin is very limited and that sherds may be recognized without much difficulty. Indeed the fact that we have in the Zuñi region close parallels to the wares of the Tano, as determined by Nelson, rendered the segregation into classes conspicuously easy.

This brings us to a description of the chief classes into which these wares have been divided. We feel justified in abandoning Dr. Kroeber's twofold classification, for as he himself asserts, the very fact that subdivision is possible indicates that there has been "a steady continuous development on the soil." More particularly, we feel the necessity of abandoning the principle of classifying each sherd on the basis of its particular color in favor of a classification according to the several distinct wares. Surely such a classification more adequately represents the facts. However, the essential correctness of Dr. Kroeber's results cannot be doubted. The explanation for the close agreement between the results from the two methods lies simply in the small number of techniques and color combinations involved.

We have made our general classification of wares conform to those worked out by Nelson for the Tano region [1] in order to render the results directly comparable. This has been made possible, as we have already intimated, by the very close parallelism in development in the two regions. There can be very little doubt that the sequence of techniques in the Zuñi Region has been painted ware, glazed ware, combination glazed and painted ware, and finally painted ware of a distinctly modern type. On the other hand, the color combinations are somewhat simpler, for we find only three ground or body colors in use, white, red, and buff. In addition to these wares with painted decoration, we find two other types, corrugated ware and a coarse, plain, unsized, undecorated black ware. We have therefore divided the wares first on the basis of technique and secondarily on the basis of body or ground color.

In the following table we have indicated the proportions of the various wares present at each site by percentages. In the first column is the number designating the ruin in the list above, and the depths of the samples wherever stratigraphic sections were made. In the second to fifteenth columns the percentages of corrugated, black and painted wares are indicated, and in the last column the number of sherds in the sample analyzed.

---

[1] Nelson.

*   *   *   *   *

Sequences by Seriation.

Thus far the stratigraphic method has been simple and productive of unequivocal results, but beyond this point it fails us. There are no other ruins in the Zuñi region with pottery similar to that of Pinnawa, nor any which by type or proportions would appear to have immediately preceded it in point of time.[1] Nevertheless, it has long been recognized that pottery from the Zuñi region, or more generally, from the Little Colorado, presents a community of characteristics which have served to emphasize the essential unity of the wares.[2] This fact is borne in on us again by the result of the present inquiry, and indeed, one has only to observe the unity of style in the wares from Hecota'utlla and Hallonawa published by Dr. Fewkes — accidentally mixed pottery from the two ruins — or to compare them with wares figured in the present report to reach the same conclusion. Possibly we must except the pottery from "black-and-white" ruins from this general statement, for their specifically Zuñian characters are by no means marked. It is true that the red pottery painted in black which characterizes some of the earlier sites bears little more than a generic resemblance to the wares of the Hecota'utlla-Hallonawa type — those we think of as characteristic of the Zuñi region; yet, that pottery occurs with the latter wares in other ruins and occurs with them again at Pinnawa, Mattsakya, and other historic ruins.

We have then in the Zuñi region a large number of ruins, all presenting much the same general style of pottery, but with differences of technique and color scheme from ruin to ruin. It seems reasonable to believe that we are dealing with no other phenomenon than the several phases of a single pottery art. The essential need is therefore a principle for the seriation of the data, to be subjected to the method of proof by concurrent variations.

The sequence which we have already reviewed for the historic and late sites suggests such a principle. We have found among the other indicated changes that corrugated ware increases steadily in its proportions from complete absence in modern Zuñi to fourteen percent of the whole in the lowest levels of the Pinnawa ash heap. It seems possible then to utilize the fluctuations in this type for a first grouping, a preliminary seriation of the data from superficial samples. It will be recalled that Dr. Kroeber found the variations in this ware particularly suggestive.[3] It might prove

---

[1] Naturally such sites must exist elsewhere, but we will return to this point later.

[2] Thus, for example, Dr. Kidder (a, 453) is able to speak of the close affinities of old Zuñi wares with those of the Little Colorado and their less involved relations with those of the Pajarito Plateau. Similarly, Mr. Nelson was able, at the close of his reconnaissance trip of 1916, to define the somewhat restricted area of specifically Zuñian wares for the writer.

[3] This volume, page 14.

fertile then to arrange these data according to their percentages of corrugated ware in sequence from lowest to highest. But we find on referring to the data given in Table I that the samples fall into two groups. In each group corrugated ware is present in proportions varying from complete, or almost complete absence up to more than half of the whole. But any two corresponding samples from the two groups, with identical percentages of corrugated ware, have radically different wares associated with them. In one group the associated wares are black, white, red, and buff occurring in several combinations. In the other group the sole associated type is whiteware of the "black-and-white" variety. For example, of two samples with 48 percent corrugated, Ruin No. 58 has as associated wares 32 percent of redware and 20 percent of whiteware, while Ruin No. 38 yields only 52 percent of whiteware. But there can be no doubt with regard to the affinities of the two groups. The first presents wares with a style of treatment specifically Zuñian in character, bearing a marked resemblance to those in the series from the historic and late series, while we have already expressed our uncertainty as to the affiliations of the wares of the second group. It seems best for the present to consider the first group only.

The first group can be subdivided into two groups, in one of which there is no glazed decoration, the other contains glaze-decorated ware. The percentages of corrugated ware in the first subdivision average higher than those in the second. Further, the criterion of glaze would include the historic and late sites in the second subgroup. This would suggest that we are dealing here with a sequence of painted wares followed by glazed wares: a suggestion worth putting to the test by the method of concurrent variations. It will be convenient to handle each of these subgroups separately.

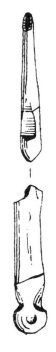

PAINTED WARE SERIES.

The first subgroup contains thirty-five samples from as many ruins. The wares are corrugated, black-on-white, black-on-red, and black and white-on-red. These samples may be arbitrarily ranked according to their percentages of corrugated ware from highest to lowest. The test of such a seriation as an historical series will lie in the observed seriation of the accompanying wares; for, when a group of three or more distinct, but mutually dependent, values are ranked according to some postulated sequence for one, and the other values are found to present serially concurrent variations, it may be concluded that the result is not fortuitous.

Ranking the samples in descending order according to their percentages of corrugated ware, we find general changes in both accompanying wares: an increase in percentage of redware and a decrease in that of whiteware.

The changes are not marked, however, as they are obscured by variations in these wares.

We have found that another seriation based on the percentages of redware yields a clearer result. That this should be so is obvious, because the percentages of redware are small as compared with those of white and corrugated ware, and by ranking redware percentages in a smooth sequence all variations will appear in relatively small magnitudes in the white and corrugated series. The seriation was suggested by the fact that redware is the predominating type in the second subgroup but does not appear at all in the group of "black-and-white" wares. It seemed reasonable to suppose, therefore, that redware had its beginnings in the subgroup with which we are dealing and rose in intensity of use therein.

On this assumption we have ranked the samples according to ascending percentage of redware (Table VI). The results are striking: there is a slight, but certain, decrease in corrugated ware and a marked decrease in whiteware. More particularly, there is rigid segregation of the values for the two wares: few values for corrugated less than 40 percent are found, while equally few values of white lie above the same point. The distribution of the wares may be indicated by curves of the type:—

for corrugated ware:—

$$y' = 49.3 - 0.26\ x$$

and for whiteware:—

$$y'' = 36.7 - 0.74\ x$$

where y' and y'' are percentages of corrugated and whiteware respectively for the deviation x from the midpoint of the redware series, 14 percent. In these equations -0.26 and -0.74 express the direction of the slope of the curves and their obliquity. Testing these curves for closeness of fit, we find that the deviations of the observed values from the theoretical values computed from these formulae are as often positive as negative; that is, that the variations appear to be accidental and that the curves represent the distributions fairly well.

Another point brought out by this seriation is of equal importance. We have included in the redware in this subgroup sherds bearing decorations in white as well as black, i. e., three-color painted ware. We find that this ware appears only in samples containing 14 percent or more of redware, that is, in the second half of the series. We pointed out above that there was every reason to assume that this subgroup of painted wares preceded that of glazed wares. Now we find that the second half of this subgroup coincides in its three-color redware with the characteristic style, three-color decoration, of the glaze subgroup. This must be considered as corroboratory of the historical reality of our assumed sequence.

TABLE VI.

<small>Painted Ware Series According to Ascending Percentage of Redware.</small>

Site	Painted Wares			Corrugated	Size of Sample
	Red		White		
	Two Color and Three Color	Three Color			
6	1–	....	55	45	131
23	2	....	64	34	117
21	2	....	74	24	167
165	2	....	56	42	146
24	2	....	50	48	230
17	3	....	62	35	109
18	5	....	45	50	153
58	6	....	29	65	105
60	7	....	48	45	118
19	8	....	36	56	184
40	8	....	38	54	79
29	9	....	29	62	56
167	10	....	48	42	101
76	10	....	37	53	44
164	10	....	28	62	161
5	12	....	43	45	118
26	13	....	43	44	61
1	13	....	35	52	59
28	14	1	33	53	110
95	15	3	25	60	116
56	16	....	28	56	29
74	16	4	23	61	68
36	18	2	17	65	200
27	18	1	38	44	133
80	18	3	39	43	104
62	19	7	27	54	164
37	20	2	30	50	247
38	20	....	35	45	134
4	22	2	25	53	335
92	22	2	35	43	93
46	24	....	41	35	298
163	25	....	39	36	38
96	30	4	20	50	136
86	32	10	20	48	117
90	39	3	23	38	112

Glazed Ware Series.

The second subgroup is characterized by the presence of decoration in glaze. In this group would be included the familiar wares of Hecota'utlla and Hallonawa figured by Fewkes. The group includes corrugated ware, painted wares of the types black-on-white, black-on-red, brown-on-buff, and black and white-on-red; glazed wares of the types black-on-white and black-on-red; and combination painted and glazed wares of the black and white-on-red type. Glazed and painted wares of all types form a homogeneous group from a stylistic viewpoint. Glazed wares may be conceived as those in which a line of glaze has been substituted in the decoration for a line of paint.

We have surface samples from only eight ruins in this subgroup. These have been ranked in the first section of Table VII in descending order of percentages of corrugated ware according to our assumption. To bring out the distribution of values more clearly these have been grouped by body color in Table VIII. The concomitant variations in the white and redwares are clear: whiteware increases slightly, while redware has a more decided increase. The distributions of these values take the form of curves of the type: —

for whiteware: —
$$y' = 23.9 - 0.24\ x$$
and for redware: —
$$y'' = 33.3 - 0.76\ x$$

where y' and y'' are percentages of white and redware respectively for the deviation x from the midpoint of the corrugated series, 42.9 percent. Here, the values -0.24 and -0.76 express the degree and direction of slope of the two curves. By the usual test for fit, we find that observed values do not differ greatly from the theoretical and are alternately positive and negative. While definite results are obtained from this seriation, it must be remembered that they are based on a small number of cases, only eight. We would therefore consider these results as indicative but not certain.

In Tables VII and VIII we have also given the data for a number of sections made with one exception in ruins east of the Zuñi Reservation. All clearly belong to this subgroup, but their sequential relations are not clear. For convenience, these tabulations have been placed in an order similar to that for the series of surface samples. This was suggested in part by progressive stylistic changes observed in them. It is hopeless to try to find a confirmation of the series for surface samples, because the samples from the sections are small and the percentages fluctuate widely. All are evidently closely related from the sequential standpoint, yet we cannot combine them since we do not know where to begin to equate values from the several series.

It will be noted that buffware enters into only one sample in the series; at Ruin No. 146 (Gigantes) where 1 percent occurs.

The point might be advanced that we have failed to link up this group with that of the historic and late ruins. That is true. However two points must be kept in mind in considering this objection: first, we have given only the data available for statistical treatment, and second, we are considering here only the arbitrarily selected area defined above as the Zuñi region. We must reserve the discussion of this point until we consider the extra-regional affinities of the wares.

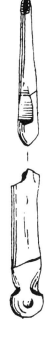

TABLE VII.

GLAZED WARE SERIES ACCORDING TO DESCENDING PERCENTAGE OF CORRUGATED WARE.

Site	Corrugated	Two Color Painted Ware			Three Color Painted Ware			Two Color Glazed Ware			Three Color Glazed and Painted Ware			Size of Sample
		White	Red	Buff	White	Red	Buff	White	Red	Buff	White	Red	Buff	
91	59	21	14			5		6	1					96
75	54	21	12			9		5	2			2		113
84	46	18	7			3		1	12			11		199
85	46	15	13			9			5			13		239
30	37	22	13			6			7			11		207
82	36	28	29						1					149
11	35	4	16					21	12			12		128
81	30	29	22			16						3		115
121 4	70	10	5			15								20
3	63	12	13			12								59
2	52	18	11			15						4		27
1	53	14	12			20						1		76
104 13	67	17	8			8								12
12	88	12												8
11	65	8	19			8								26
10	84	5	11											19
9	61	22	11			7						6		36
8	63	16	14					2	2					49
7	50	14	9			9						5		81

TABLE VII — (*Continued*).

Site		Corrugated	Two Color Painted Ware			Three Color Painted Ware			Two Color Glazed Ware			Three Color Glazed and Painted Ware			Size of Sample
			White	Red	Buff	White	Red	Buff	White	Red	Buff	White	Red	Buff	
104	6	55	24	13			5			3					38
	5	41	16	20			14							9	86
	4	50	13	16			12			3				6	32
	3	49	19	17			10			5					41
	2	55	14	23			6							2	49
	1	60	7	20			10							3	66
140a	6	64		9			18			9					11
	5	48	9	43											21
	4	47	3	35			15								34
	3	67	9	18			3			3					33
	2	44	23	23			2			6				2	48
	1	50	16	24			8			2					62
140b	14	33	10	38			14			5				1	42
	13	49	13	26			12							3	67
	12	68	14	13			4			3				3	167
	11	30	30	24			4		6	3				7	33
	10	33	17	32			12							6	41
	9	33	17	43											12
	8	12	35	29			12			6				12	17
	7	24	29	35						12				6	17
	6	26	17	15					6	9					34
	5	29	6	29			15			12					17
	4	70	5	17			18			7				1	86

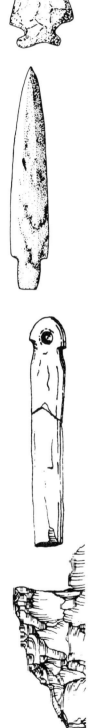

Site	149			71					101a					161a							161b			97	
Level	3	2	1	6	5	4	3	2	4	3	2	1	S	8	7	6	5	4	3	2	4	3	2	6	5
	40	51	100	12	29	38	55	81	43	51	57	150	225	36	29	36	21	28	36	61	74	50	102	13	12
	10	6				8	2	1	2	3					6		3				4				
	10	17	12	8	7	3	5	4	2	5	6		6	3		5	11				4	2	2		
							2						1	6				3	3		3		1		
	10	6	10	9	10	3	20	4	12	14	5	8	8	8	17	33	5	11	5	13	13	12	10	8	34
	20	16	24	25	21	18	13	30	23	9	9	19	16	11	4	17	23	14	25	18	22	26	16	23	50
	12	6	6	25	24	16	4	16	14	20	39	24	22	22	24	19	5	18	14	20	13	20	23	31	8
	38	49	48	33	38	52	56	45	51	51	39	43	47	50	55	25	62	43	53	46	41	40	48	38	8

TABLE VII (*Concluded*).

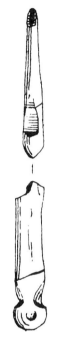

Site		Corru-gated	Two Color Painted Ware			Three Color Painted Ware			Two Color Glazed Ware			Three Color Glazed and Painted Ware			Size of Sample
			White	Red	Buff	White	Red	Buff	White	Red	Buff	White	Red	Buff	
97	4	44	21	13			19									34
	3	41	31	13			13		3					2		39
	2	46	23	8			20							3		39
146	8	42	17	25			12							4		24
	7	39	17	18			23		3							60
	6	51	12	22			9			3				3		67
	5	51	11	13			15		2	5				5		75
	4	36	17	19			16		4	6				4		84
	3	46	8	26			10			5				1		77
	2	43	12	17			19			9						103
	1	41	15	20	1		20			2				1		148
139	4	30	12	32			16			7				3		69
	3	32	11	41			7			9						44
	2	25	10	34			23			5				3		96
	Surface	27	11	30			22			8				2		95

TABLE VIII.

GLAZED WARE SERIES BY GROUND COLORS.

Site		Corrugated	White	Red	Buff	Size of Sample
	91	59	21	20	. . . .	96
	75	54	21	25	. . . .	113
	84	46	24	30	. . . .	199
	85	46	20	34	. . . .	239
	30	37	23	40	. . . .	207
	82	36	28	36	. . . .	149
	11	35	25	40	. . . .	128
	81	30	29	41	. . . .	115
121	4	70	10	20	. . . .	20
	3	63	12	25	. . . .	59
	2	52	18	30	. . . .	27
	1	53	14	33	. . . .	76
104	13	67	17	16	. . . .	12
	12	88	12	. . . .	. . . .	8
	11	65	8	27	. . . .	26
	10	84	5	11	. . . .	19
	9	61	22	17	. . . .	36
	8	63	16	21	. . . .	49
	7	59	16	25	. . . .	81
	6	55	24	21	. . . .	38
	5	41	16	43	. . . .	86
	4	50	13	37	. . . .	32
	3	49	19	32	. . . .	41
	2	55	14	31	. . . .	49
	1	60	7	33	. . . .	66
140a	6	64	. . . .	36	. . . .	11
	5	48	9	43	. . . .	21
	4	47	3	50	. . . .	34
	3	67	9	24	. . . .	33
	2	44	23	33	. . . .	48
	1	50	16	34	. . . .	62
140b	14	33	10	57	. . . .	42
	13	49	13	38	. . . .	67
	12	68	14	18	. . . .	167
	11	30	36	34	. . . .	33
	10	33	17	50	. . . .	41
	9	33	17	50	. . . .	12
	8	12	35	53	. . . .	17
	7	24	29	47	. . . .	17
	6	26	23	51	. . . .	34
	5	29	6	65	. . . .	17
	4	70	5	25	. . . .	86

TABLE VIII. — *(Continued).*

Site		Corrugated	White	Red	Buff	Size of Sample
140b	3	38	12	50	. . . .	40
	2	49	6	45	. . . .	51
	1	48	6	46	. . . .	100
149	6	33	25	42	. . . .	12
	5	38	24	38	. . . .	29
	4	52	16	32	. . . .	38
	3	56	4	40	. . . .	55
	2	45	16	39	. . . .	81
71	4	51	14	35	. . . .	43
	3	51	22	27	. . . .	51
	2	39	39	22	. . . .	57
	1	43	24	33	. . . .	150
	Surface	47	23	30	. . . .	225
161a	8	50	28	22	. . . .	36
	7	55	24	21	. . . .	29
	6	25	19	56	. . . .	36
	5	62	5	33	. . . .	21
	4	43	18	39	. . . .	28
	3	53	17	30	. . . .	36
	2	46	23	31	. . . .	61
161b	4	41	16	43	. . . .	74
	3	40	20	40	. . . .	50
	2	48	24	28	. . . .	102
97	6	38	31	31	. . . .	13
	5	5	8	84	. . . .	12
	4	44	24	32	. . . .	34
	3	41	31	28	. . . .	39
	2	46	23	31	. . . .	39
46	8	42	17	41	. . . .	24
	7	39	20	41	. . . .	60
	6	51	12	37	. . . .	67
	5	51	11	38	. . . .	75
	4	36	19	45	. . . .	84
	3	46	12	42	. . . .	77
	2	43	12	45	. . . .	103
	1	41	15	43	1	148
139	4	30	12	58	. . . .	69
	3	32	11	57	. . . .	44
	2	25	10	65	. . . .	96
	1	27	11	62	. . . .	95

From *An Outline for a Chronology of Zuñi Ruins*   73

BLACK-ON-WHITE SERIES.

The group of samples comprising corrugated and painted black-on-white wares remains to be considered. It is not certain that these form an integral part of the series we have been considering. Still it has been shown that redware comes into being in a group consisting in addition only of corrugated and painted black-on-white ware. It would therefore be reasonable to expect that some of the samples in the present group belong immediately before the painted redware series. Such samples would be those with the highest percentages of corrugated ware.

We have some stratigraphic evidence bearing on relations in this group, however. Sherds from Sites Nos. 3, 7, 14, 15, and 50 indicate an overwhelming proportion of black-on-white ware of a peculiar style associated with plain white vessels having globular bodies surmounted by straight or constricted zones sometimes bearing a few broad coils. Sherds bearing such corrugations constitute only 1 to 4 percent, but inasmuch as the bodies of the vessels were not corrugated, these values do not represent the correct proportions of the wares. We would suggest that about one-eighth of all the vessels bore coils. The characteristic feature of these ruins, as described in a preceding section, was the almost complete absence of masonry. At Shoptluwwayala (No. 40), on the edge of Zuñi village, we found remains of the regular pueblo type superposed on a "slab-house" with which the above types of pottery were associated. The relation of the two structures is indicated by the pottery data: —

	Corrugated	White	Red
Surface	54	38	8
Trench (all levels)	29	63	8

The finds in the trench are just what might be expected if the surface types were mixed at random with 2 percent corrugated and 98 percent whiteware of "slab-house" type.

The sequential relations of this type appear to be identical with stratifications found by Dr. Kidder along the San Juan River [1] and by Mr. Morris in the valley of La Plata River, San Juan County, New Mexico. [2] There can be little doubt that these are the oldest remains in the Zuñi region.

---

[1] Personal communication from Dr. Kidder, July 4, 1916. Dr. Kidder, who saw these wares before the "slab-house" structure was discovered, pronounced them closely affiliated with the sherds found by himself.

[2] Morris.

This suggested ranking the samples in this group in ascending order by percentages of corrugated ware (Table IX). We have no proof for this series, except the foregoing indications, but offer it as a tentative suggestion.

It will be noted that following the wares of "slab-house" type, the value for corrugated ware jumps to 24 percent. If as we are inclined to believe, "slab-house" corrugated really constitutes 12 percent or more, the gap is not so great.

TABLE IX.

BLACK-ON-WHITE SERIES.

Site		Corrugated	White	Size of Sample
15		1–	99	67
14	a	2	98	208
	b	2–	98	108
	c	1–	99	188
7		2	98	87
50		2–	98	107
3		4	96	83
51		24	76	87
57		30	70	62
49		33	67	32
72		40	60	35
70		42	58	12
166		48	52	39
16		50	50	10
73		50	50	6
2		62	38	28
83		67	33	29
35		75	25	48

SUMMARY.

The sequence of pottery types suggested in the preceding pages may now be summarized. It is possible that the earliest remains in the region are slab-house sites with 96 to 98 percent black-on-white painted ware with 2 to 4 percent corrugated. (These figures may be 88 and 12 percent respectively, instead). Black-on-white painted ware then decreases from 76 percent to about 30 percent, while corrugated increases correspondingly.

From *An Outline for a Chronology of Zuñi Ruins*   75

Redware now makes its appearance, increasing to 43 percent. From zero to 14 percent it consists of black painted decoration; at the latter point black and white painted decoration appears as well. At about 20 to 25 percent glaze decoration appears; the additional decorations on redware introduced being black glaze, black glaze and white paint, black glaze and white paint on a red ground with black glaze on a white ground. Meanwhile corrugated decreases from 50 to 55 per cent to 30 percent, and whiteware decreases from 45 or 50 percent to about 20 percent, then rises somewhat to 27 percent. With the rise in whiteware, black glaze appears as a decorative technique as well as black paint. Probably buffware now begins to appear. At this point a hiatus in the data interrupts the sequence.

When the sequence is resumed, corrugated decreases from 14 percent to 0 or 6 percent on the surface of historic ruins and blackware makes its ap-

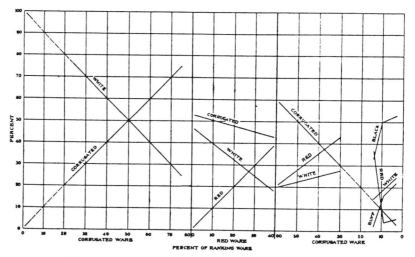

Fig. 6. Sequence of Wares, According to Ground Colors.

pearance at 33 percent increasing to about 50 percent. Redware reappears as the dominant type of painted ware, with identical decorative techniques, at 37 percent, but decreases rapidly to 4 percent, after which it remains stationary. Whiteware, including decorations in black paint, black glaze, and in addition black paint or glaze with red paint, reappears at 14 percent and increases to 23 percent. Buffware increases at the same time from 2 percent to 22 percent; decorations only in brown paint at first, then in brown and red paint, black glaze, and black glaze with red paint.

This sequence of types is shown graphically in Fig. 6. The division into groups has been retained, for, since we have no chronological unit the

percentages of the ware used in ranking each group must be used as the base for plotting. This method gives a rectilinear distribution for the ranking ware. The overlapping which appears between the several groups must be recognized as an expression of accidental variations.

Before discussing the hiatus in the suggested sequence it will be advantageous to point out the sequence of techniques corresponding to the ranking developed above. The data are given in Table X, in which the first group — the black-on-white series — is given in contracted form. The technical types are those recognized by Nelson for Tano pottery, except that biscuitware,[1] and Type IV, an historic two-color glazed ware do not seem to occur. On the other hand, a new type, a coarse plain blackware, which does not occur in the Tano ruins, is found here. We have found it necessary to separate two-color painted ware from three-color painted ware in Type I.

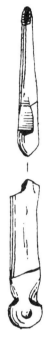

These results show no marked changes from the results obtained by ranking according to body color, yet are significant precisely on that account. Possibly corrugated ware rises from 1 percent to something less than 75 percent and then drops back to 30 percent. Correspondingly two-color painted ware decreases from 99 percent to about 50 percent and thence to about 35 percent. Three-color painted ware appears at the mid-point of the painted redware series, but never amounts to more than a few percent. Two-color glazed ware and three-color glazed and painted ware now appear together, but each as only 10 or 15 percent of the whole. Resuming the sequence after the hiatus, we find corrugated decreasing from 14 percent to 3 percent, blackware appearing at 33 percent and increasing to 50 percent, three-color glazed and painted ware decreasing slightly from about 16 to 6 percent, while the other wares remain stationary: two and three color painted wares at about 30 percent and two-color glazed ware at about 10 percent.

It seems legitimate to draw two conclusions from the foregoing: first, among the decorated wares the variations in decorative technique seem to have played a minor rôle in comparison with the variations in color combinations; and second, it is probable that glazed decoration was introduced rather suddenly into two-color and three-color decorative schemes in this region. These results are consistent with our previous findings.

---

[1] Kidder, (a), 454, says there is no biscuitware in the pottery from Hallonawa and Heshota'utlla at the Peabody Museum.

TABLE X.

Sequence of Techniques.

Corrugated Ware	Type I — Two and Three Color Painted Ware			Type II — Two Color Glazed Ware	Type III — Three Color Glazed and Painted Ware	Black Ware
	Two Color	Three Color	Two and Three Color			
1	99		99			
4	96		96			
24	76		76			
75	25		25			
45	55		55			
39	61		61			
35	65		65			
50	50		50			
65	35		35			
45	55		55			
56	44		44			
62	38		38			
55	45		45			
45	55		55			
48	52		52			
53	46	1	47			
60	37	3	40			
59	37	4	41			
53	45	2	47			
54	39	7	46			
48	50	2	52			
51	47	2	49			
35	65		65			
36	64		64			
50	46	4	50			
48	42	10	52			
38	59	3	62			
59	35	5	40	1		
54	33	9	42	2	2	
46	25		25	18	11	
46	28	3	31	10	13	
37	35	9	44	8	11	
36	57	6	63	1		
35	20		20	33	12	
30	51	16	67		3	

TABLE X.— (*Continued*).

Corrugated Ware	Type I			Type II	Type III	Black Ware
	Two and Three Color Painted Ware			Two Color Glazed Ware	Three Color Glazed and Painted Ware	
	Two Color	Three Color	Two and Three Color			
12	27	16	43	11	13	21
19	8	12	20	11	15	35
9	20	6	26	11	19	35
12	23	12	35	7	16	30
12	21	12	33	6	19	30
15	20	16	36	5	10	34
13	20	15	35	4	6	42
14	18	13	31	3	17	35
11	12	7	19	6	24	40
16	15	8	23	8	4	49
12	18	3	21	8	11	48
10	19	2	21	11	8	50
8	21	6	27	7		58
15	26	7	33	11		41
13	38		38	8	20	21
7	24	4	28	2	2	61
7	9	5	14	14	14	51
12	18	6	24	9	6	49
8	22	9	31	8	4	49
4	20	12	32	9	2	53
5	28	2	30	7	12	46
3	24	11	35	6	3	53
4	21	7	28	14	7	47
2	28	3	31	14	5	48
1	37		37	8		54
3	26	3	29	12	7	49

For comparison, Nelson's table for San Cristobal pueblo [2] is given below, the values having been reduced to percentages. The wares appear in the Tano region in the order two and three color painted wares (Type I), two color glazed wares (Type II), three color glazed and painted wares (Type III), historic two color glazed wares (Type IV), and modern painted wares (Type V), accompanied at all times by corrugated and biscuitware. The order for decorated wares (other than plastic decoration) in the Zuñi region is evidently much the same: two and three color painted wares (Type I),

[1] Average of surface samples of Sites No. 13, 45, and 48.
[2] Nelson, 166. The fluctuation in corrugated ware would appear to be as marked as that in any other type.

Thickness of Section	Corrugated Ware	Biscuit-ware	Type I	Type II	Type III
1st ft.	37	7	1	52	3
2nd "	31	4	1	62	2
3rd "	15	1	6	76	2
4th "	21	3	5	71	
5th "	17	4	1	78	
6th "	19	5	2	74	1-
7th "	23	4	18	55	
8th "	25	1	52	22	
9th "	46	1-	53	1	
10th "	55	1-	45		

two color glazed wares (Type II), three color glazed and painted wares (Type III), and modern painted wares (Type V). Biscuitware and an historic two color glazed ware (Type IV) do not appear, but a new type, blackware, appears after Type III. The principal difference would seem to be, so far as our data show, in the tendency to use painted rather than glazed wares in the Zuñi region. Glazed wares (Types II and III) appear at about the same period in this region and never attain prominence. It may ultimately be necessary to qualify the last statement, if, as we suspect, three color glazed and painted ware played a more important rôle in that section of the sequence represented by the hiatus in our data.

The sequence given by Morris for the upper San Juan Valley [1] parallels both Tano and Zuñi sequences in general outlines. It approximates the Tano more closely than the Zuñi, but the finer discriminations among the earlier wares show a close kinship to the Zuñi wares of the same period.

It is now possible to suggest definitely what the characteristics of the missing data should be. The sequence here should show a decrease in corrugated from 30 to 14 percent, and another in whiteware from 27 to 14 percent. Redware would be the dominant decorated ware, decreasing only slightly from 43 to 37 percent. Buffware would probably not amount to more than a few percent. Blackware would appear in this group and attain a proportion of 33 percent. The changes in technique which may be expected would not be great: a decrease in Type I from 35 to 20 percent, with Types II and III remaining at about 10 or 15 percent, but possibly with a rise and fall in Type III.

---

[1] Morris, 27.

MOVEMENTS OF POPULATION.

With an outline of the sequence of pottery types at hand, it is now possible to speak of the time-relations between the ruins.

In spite of the limitations on the occupation of the Zuñi region imposed by its natural resources, certain general shifts of population have taken place. While the number of localities with optimum conditions for producing food and water is strictly limited, the wide scattering of former habitations throughout the region is strong evidence for the latent possibilities of the whole. Nevertheless, the advantages of these localities are so marked that they have been the scene of repeated settlements. But the striking feature of these settlements is their transitory character. Ash heaps, as we have repeatedly stated, are a minus quantity; the fact which determined the course of this inquiry. It is certainly startling to come on ruin after ruin with long rows of rooms stretching away in straight lines or graceful curves, but with hardly a sign of ashes and broken pottery — in short, every jot of evidence pointing to a flitting occupation. The natural result has been to produce a constant movement about in the valley, a sort of milling around. It is somewhat curious to find nevertheless that the center of population has shifted from period to period.

The fact is brought out by grouping the ruins furnishing the data for the foregoing sequence. For convenience of comparison four periods are chosen corresponding to the four general groups of pottery types. The location of the ruins is shown in Figs. 7 to 10. In addition, Mr. Nelson has placed at my disposal sherds and data from ruins as far east as Acoma, south to the Rito Quemado and west to St. Johns, Arizona, some of which undoubtedly belong with the ruins in the central region.

The oldest group is shown in Fig. 7. Ruins with pottery of the "slab-house" type have been differentiated from those with black-on-white painted ware and corrugated of the ordinary type. The ruins are not localized, but are scattered through the Zuñi Valley and occur occasionally outside. Outside of the area shown, several were found along the eastern border of the great lava sheet in the Cebolla-Cebollita valleys, several west of Atarque as far as Ojo Bonito, and again at Springerville and St. Johns on the Little Colorado. Some of these, as for example, at St. Johns, are probably slab-house structures, although the reconnaissance data do not make this certain. At Sites 14 and 7 in the Ojo Caliente district there are evidences of slab-house *villages*.

In the second group ruins with less than 14 percent redware are differ-

entiated from those with 14 percent or more (Fig. 8). It will be remembered that this point marked the beginning of three-color painted ware. It also proves a significant point of division with regard to distribution. The group as a whole is scattered through the valley from the Ojo Caliente district to Inscription Rock and a number of sites appear on the plateau. But the distribution of the ruins, most of which are small, shows a different focus of occupation for the two classes. Ruins with less than 14 percent

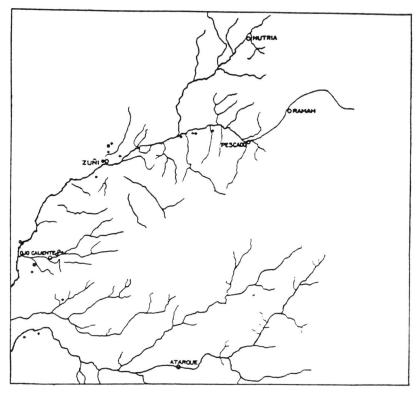

Fig. 7. Location of Ruins: Black-on-White Series. Squares, slab-house type; crosses, black-on-white type.

redware center in the Ojo Caliente district while relatively few are located up the valley. Outside of the area shown, they lie principally along the eastern side of the great lava sheet south to the Point of Malpais and several occur near Acoma. Three near Rito Quemado suggest Tularosa influence. On the other hand, ruins with more than 14 percent redware center from the Pescado district (where there are undoubtedly more than shown) through Ramah to Inscription Rock. A number are in the Zuñi district and fewer near Ojo Caliente. Similar ruins also occur in the Cebolla-Cebollita valleys north of the Point of Malpais and one further east in the

Acoma Valley.   Four lie within ten miles west of Atarque, but all except the easternmost suggest affiliations with Tularosa wares rather than with Zuñi.   The same is true for three ruins just south of Springerville.   A shift in the center of population undoubtedly occurred during this period.   The inauguration of pueblo architecture which accompanied it will be referred to later.

Ruins where glazed pottery was in use center about Pescado, Ramah, and

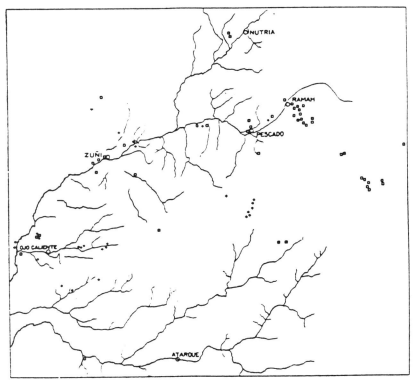

Fig. 8.   Location of Ruins: Painted Ware Series.   Crosses, two-color painted ware squares, three-color painted ware.

in the Inscription Rock section (Fig. 9).   Only three lie further down the valley.   More are situated on the Plateau to the south, but some of these (at Ojo Hallado, Ojo Pueblo, and at the Delfin Chavez ranch) strongly suggest Tularosa wares.   There are four or more east of Springerville, but again Tularosa affiliations are suggested by one.   Finally, several ruins to the east near Cebollita are of the same type.[1]

[1] Hodge in the *Annual Report of the Smithsonian Institution* for 1914 (46), refers one of these ruins tentatively to the Tangi, or Calabash, clan of Acoma.   This does not seem likely since pottery from a ruin probably identical with this one bears a marked similarity to that of the Zuñi Region.

The last group (Fig. 10) is that of the late and historic ruins. They center down the valley again, near Zuñi and Ojo Caliente, where the occupants of the region were discovered by the Spaniards of the sixteenth century. We have distinguished the post-Conquest refuge villages on the map, and it will be seen that they too cluster in the same regions. Not a single ruin of this period lies in all the country between Zuñi and Acoma, for all of which we have information. Thus, another change in the focus of occupation is indicated, a change in the opposite direction. It will be

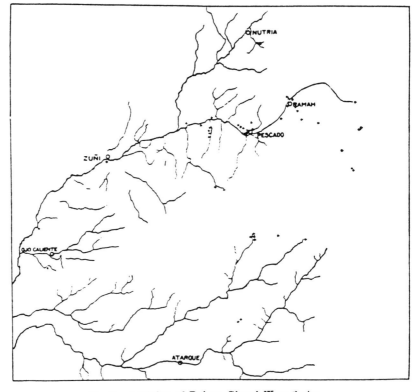

Fig. 9.   Location of Ruins: Glazed Ware Series.

remembered, however, that despite the similarity of the wares there is a hiatus in our data between the group of "glaze" sites and these late and historic ruins. No ruins with wares which would fill the hiatus in the pottery sequence lie within the bounds of this region. This gap accompanied by a shift in the center of population would inject a very strong element of doubt into the postulated relations between the late sites and "glaze" sites were not the specific points of similarity between the wares of the two groups so remarkably close.

We have at hand some suggestive data on the point. No ruins of this period lie east of Zuñi, but along the Little Colorado to the west are a number affiliated with these. Two small ruins on the west bank of the Little Colorado about three hundred and five hundred yards above the bridge at St. Johns show sherds identical with those of Pinnawa (No. 33). Three others are also of the Pinnawa type but probably slightly earlier: the first, a small pueblo ruin on a rock by the Little Colorado about four or

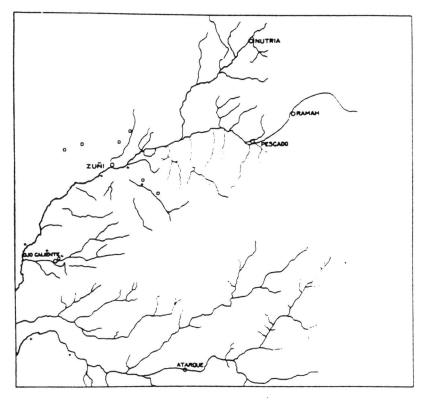

Fig. 10. Location of Ruins: Late and Historic Sites. Crosses, late and Conquest pueblos; squares, post-Conquest refuge villages.

five miles below Springerville; the second, a pueblo ruin at Ojo Bonito, ten or twelve miles due south of Ojo Caliente, and the third, a rectangular pueblo ruin about five miles southeast of Ojo Bonito on the road to Atarque.

These specific data based on sherd collections point to the west and so do all published material available. The descriptions by Fewkes and Hough of ruins and pottery in the Little Colorado Valley are fairly full and admirably illustrated. There can be no doubt that some of these ruins bear a close relation to those we have been discussing and in particular we would point out the following ruins where the essential similarity of the pottery

has been emphasized by both investigators. Beginning on the east, these are the "Stone Axe" ruins in the Petrified Forest, along the Mogollon Rim possibly those at Pinedale and Shumway on Showlow Creek should be included, "Four Mile" ruin near Taylor on Silver Creek, and along the Little Colorado, the Chevlon ruin fifteen miles east of Winslow and the Homolobi group of ruins near that town. Possibly we should include the Biddahoochee ruins north of Holbrook, but the decorative style of wares there stands somewhat apart from the others. In these ruins redware predominates, redware with decoration in black or black and white, painted or glazed or both, which is a unit with the wares from Hallonawa and Hecota'utlla figured by Fewkes in the Putnam Anniversary Volume. The essential difference between them is in the presence of a yellowware, not the "fine yellow ware" of the Hopi,[1] but the buffware of the Zuñi historic pueblos. We cannot but doubt the dictum which populates these pueblos with Hopi clans on the say-so of native informants in the face of the demonstrably close similarities between these wares and their Zuñi counterparts. It remains to be demonstrated that the Hopi wares have evolved from these. The question is still open and will never be settled by the tacit denial of historical relief and by arrogating all variations and combinations of pottery styles to the principle of clan mingling.

It is suggested then that the ruins constituting the hiatus in our sequence lie down the valley of the Little Colorado, of which the Zuñi River is a tributary. If it should ultimately prove that there was actually a movement of population eastward through this valley to the location of historic times, the fact might also demonstrate that there was no hiatus in the sequence but that we have been dealing here with the segments of two sequences which may, or may not, be of independent development. However, it must be noted that these ruins of the Little Colorado mark the western limit of the area of glaze decoration, and further, that a sequence of these ruins would be expected to begin about where the ruins of the eastern Zuñi Valley leave off. An actual continuity of occupation of the Little Colorado Valley is therefore not beyond the range of probability, but the problem merges here into that of the glaze area as a whole.

One final qualification must be placed on the sequence as a whole. It may be ultimately proven, as suggested by the marked similarities between the data for this region, the Tano country and the Upper San Juan, that there has been a parallel development over a large section of the Southwest. In that event, the several segments of our sequence may be found to be disparate parts of the general scheme and only artificially placed together here; but this point cannot be answered on internal evidence alone.

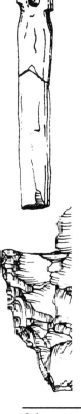

---

[1] Fewkes, (b), 59; see also 61, 64, 69, and 73 for other differences.

*　*　*　*　*

GENERAL SUMMARY.

It seems worth while briefly summarizing the preceding pages in order to emphasize the distinction between the body of data of which we are reasonably sure and the outline chronology which is in part an hypothetical structure. It does not seem fair to leave an impression of greater certainty in the results than the data seem to us to warrant. At the risk of repetition then, we will briefly indicate what we believe these data show.

Let us first turn to the methodological limits imposed by the type of remains. We have seen that the natural advantages of the region under discussion are somewhat limited. Water and arable lands are by no means uniformly distributed over its extent; rather, the combination of a copious water supply with adjacent fields is found at only a few spots. As a result the structures now in ruins seem to have had a transient occupation. With the exception of certain historic and related sites the refuse heaps at these ruins were uniformly shallow. Four of the ruins, Hawwikku, Kettcippawa, Kyakkima, and Mattsakya, were identified years ago as among the "Seven Cities of Cibola." At one, Mattsakya, a deep refuse heap was found in which the potsherds could be traced back in gradual transitions to and through another deep heap at a neighboring ruin, Pinnawa. But here was the end of direct stratigraphic information, and from this point on we were forced to fall back on the uncertain method of hypothetical seriation.

Nevertheless, the body of data available for such a seriation is, we believe, on a par with that obtained by stratigraphic methods. We have no reason to doubt that samples of potsherds collected from successive levels of the ash heaps present us with valid chronological indices. Why then cavil at the use of similar samples from the surface of the ash heaps? We have demonstrated above (p. 254) that it is possible to collect surface samples approximating in accuracy to those from refuse heaps; in fact, supposedly identical surface samples differ no more among themselves than a corresponding series of refuse heap samples. We have analyzed such potsherd samples from each of the ruins for the proportions of their constituent types. Aside from their value in our hypothetical scheme, these collected data have an absolute value in that they characterize each ruin with some precision.

A suggestion for ranking these data in seriation is contained in the short stratigraphic series: there corrugated ware is seen increasing steadily from complete absence in modern Zuñi to fourteen percent at the base of the

Pinnawa ash heap. But we cannot straightway rank all the data on the basis of corrugated percentages, although the unity of types in all the ruins suggests doing so, because we find that the values fall into two groups. In each group corrugated ware ranges from zero to about fifty percent, but in one it is accompanied only by black-on-white ware, in the other by black, red, and buff wares. The second group is further subdivided by the presence at some of the ruins of glaze-decorated potsherds as well as painted wares. Among these are the historic sites and the affiliated ruins which furnished stratigraphic information. This suggested a sequence in which corrugated ware rises from zero to about fifty percent (with only black-on-white ware present), and then drops back to zero again, while painted ware is being followed by glazed wares (the second general group). This suggested sequence was then ready to be checked by observing simultaneous variations in wares other than corrugated.

Nothing can be said as to the validity of the first half of our sequence, the "black-on-white series," beyond the fact that it seems plausible. But for the remainder of the sequence the checks employed give fairly certain results. First, concomitant variations occur in the wares accompanying corrugated. Second, the variations of individual values from the general trend of the sequence are not beyond the limits of chance. Third, a continuum of style is seen in three-color decoration which appears first at the later ruins of the "painted ware series" and continues on through the "glazed ware series." But while the general sequence is checked in its parts, it develops that a group of values belonging late in the series is missing; that is, we simply failed to cover sufficient territory in our survey to include ruins of this period. According to the available literature, such ruins probably lie further down the Little Colorado. But so long as such an hiatus remains in our data, we cannot be certain that the separated sections of our series are parts of a single historic sequence. True, the hypothetical sequence for the Zuñi country parallels that of the Rio Grande region. But if there has been a common development over a large section of the Southwest, we are still uncertain, for we may well be dealing here with parts of two separate sequences. The case for our chronological outline must rest at this point until the hiatus can be investigated. But until we then know the value of these data for this particular chronological scheme, we can at least be sure that they have an absolute value outside of it.

The suggested pottery sequence closely parallels that of the Rio Grande both in the order in which the several decorative techniques were used and in the style of decoration. It differs principally in the tendency to vary color combinations rather than decorative technique, and to use painted decoration in preference to glaze. Glaze decoration appears to have been

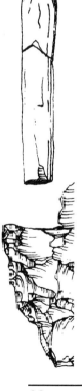

regularly substituted for certain painted decorations, but was always rather limited in use; hence we judge that glaze decoration was a borrowed trait.

So far we have used only pottery data in erecting an outline chronology in order that we might use architectural data as an independent check. When the ruins are ranked according to the pottery scheme, a parallel sequence of architectural types was found: first, probably slab-house structures (p. 228), then small houses, and finally rectangular and circular pueblos. This may be taken as a confirmation of the pottery scheme, since all students have suggested this as the probable course of development. The pueblo type appears more or less synchronously with the introduction of decoration in three colors: it probably did not develop in this region, but seems to be a borrowed trait.

Certain general shifts of the center of population have taken place. We have only a few scattered ruins belonging to the earliest period ("black-on-white series"). During the following period of the "painted ware series," the focus shifted from the lower half of the Zuñi Valley eastward to the continental divide where it remained throughout the period of the "glazed ware series." With this shift the pueblo appeared as the prevailing architectural form. The next ruins for which we have data are the historic ruins and others closely related. Again there has been a shift, for these center back in the lower Zuñi Valley. The available information suggests that had our survey been carried for some distance further down the Little Colorado Valley, of which the Zuñi is a tributary, we would have found ruins immediately antedating the historic ruins and probably intermediate between them and the ruins centering in the continental divide. This may mean that there was a general movement westward and then a return eastward to the historic location.

In short, the data assembled in the preceding pages are a reasonably certain characterization of the ruins visited. The suggested chronology may be valid in outline and even quite correct in part, but it cannot be accepted as more than indicative while an integral part of the territory remains unsurveyed. The publication of the results to date seems wholly justified as marking the completion of one important step in the establishment of Zuñi chronology, but particularly as an exposition of archaeological method.

REFERENCES CITED

FEWKES, J. WALTER
    1890   Preliminary Notes on the Origin, Working Hypothesis and Primary Researches of the Hemenway Southwestern Archaeological Expedition. *Compte-Rendu du Congrès International des Américanistes*, 7me session, pp. 151–194. Berlin.

KIDDER, A. V.
    1915   Pottery of the Pajarito Plateau and of Some Adjacent Regions in New Mexico. *American Anthropological Association, Memoir* 2(6):406–462.

HODGE, FREDERICK W.
    1921   Administrative Report. *Bureau of American Ethnology, Annual Report* 35:9–37.

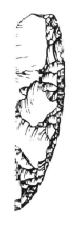

MORRIS, EARL H.
1917   The Place of Coiled Ware in Southwestern Pottery. *American Anthropologist* 19:24–29.
NELSON, NELS C.
1916   Chronology of the Tano Ruins, New Mexico. *American Anthropologist* 18:159–180.

A DESIGN-SEQUENCE FROM NEW MEXICO

By A. V. Kidder

PHILLIPS ACADEMY. ANDOVER. MASS.
Communicated by W. H. Holmes, April 2, 1917

Much has been written on the development of geometrical decoration among primitive people, and many design-sequences have been arranged; the latter, however, have almost always been based on preconceived theoretical ideas, and the material for them has usually been selected from specimens whose relative ages have not been known. Such sequences cannot, therefore, be regarded as indicating surely the tendencies of design growth, for the specimens regarded as early may in fact have been late, and the development may thus have taken place in the opposite direction to the one postulated; or, again, the specimens may all have been of one period and may represent either contemporary variants of a single design-phase, or entirely unrelated parts of other unsuspected sequences. It has accordingly been impossible in most cases to do more than guess as to whether any given change in design has been from the natural to the conventional or vice versa; whether toward simplification or toward elaboration.

The only safe method for the working out of developments in decorative art is to build up one's sequences from chronologically sequent material, and so let one's theories form themselves from the sequences. In the case of aboriginal American art this ideal has been very hard to attain because of the scarcity of stratified sites and the corresponding difficulty of obtaining relatively datable specimens.

In the Rio Grande district of New Mexico, however, students have recently been recovering stratigraphical data which establish an orderly

succession of several pottery styles; so that almost any vessel may be placed in its proper chronological relation to any other. Close studies of the decoration of these vessels should enable us to recognize and tabulate enough true design-sequences to form the basis for a correct appreciation of the art tendencies in that area. Several such sequences are already becoming apparent; the accompanying incomplete example is given as an illustration.

While the five units in the series are from vessels from various sites, stratigraphical studies by Mr. Nelson at San Cristobal and by me at Pecos allow it to be stated positively that they are arranged in their proper chronological order. A description follows.

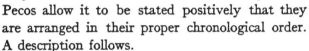

In the early black-on-white pottery a common design consists of a large triangle with two of its corners filled in with black; a pair of opposed stepped figures mounted on interlocking 'stalks' occupies the remaining rectangular space (fig. 1). In a primitive type of biscuitware which succeeds the black-on-white the same triangular element is often seen, and the two opposed stepped figures are also present but have lost their interlocking 'stalks' and hang suspended in the open space (fig. 2). In the biscuitware of a slightly later period the stepped elements drop out altogether, but the triangle holds to its original shape (fig. 3). In still later examples a progressive modification takes place in the cut-off and filled-in corners of the triangle; they become smaller and their two contiguous sides are no longer at right angles to each other (fig. 4). A final step is shown in figure 5; it is characteristic of the last type of biscuitware with which we are familiar.

This series represents, of course, only a short period in the life of this particular design; what phases it passed through in reaching the complicated form in which we first encounter it are as yet unknown; nor can we tell whether or not it had any later developments. In this short sequence we see: first, a progressive simplification due to the dropping out of elements (figs. 1, 2, 3); second, a modification in the shape of the remaining elements (figs. 4, 5). These data are, of course, too scanty for general conclusions, as they illustrate only one of many designs; they show, however, what interesting results may confidently be expected.

NOTES ON THE POTTERY OF PECOS

By M. A. and A. V. KIDDER

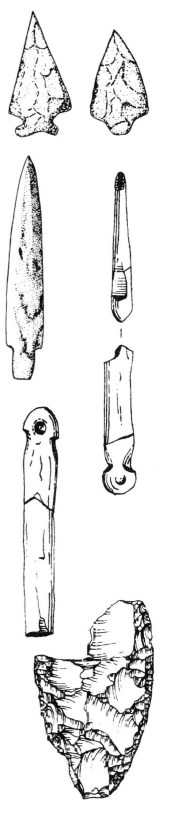

THE pueblo of Pecos in San Miguel county, New Mexico, was abandoned in 1838; after a presumably continuous occupation from an early period in prehistoric times. Its rubbish heaps, therefore, contain the accumulations of several centuries, and some of them are so stratified that by a careful study of their contents one is enabled to trace the development of the arts and industries of the community from beginning to end. Of the various objects found in these stratified heaps, pottery fragments are by far the commonest and most easily classifiable, and it is with them that the present paper is concerned.

That there have been changes in the pottery of the Rio Grande pueblos in prehistoric and historic times, has been recognized by archaeologists for a number of years, but no sure evidence as to the sequential order of the several recognizable styles was forthcoming until Mr. Nelson found at San Cristobal a stratified rubbish heap containing wares of three of the principal earlier types. Similar material from other sites enabled him to place chronologically two later types that brought the sequence unbroken down to a comparatively recent date (*ca.* 1700).[1] These investigations served, in the words of Dr. Kroeber, to convert "the archaeological problem of the Southwest from an essentially exploratory and descriptive

---

[1] N. C. Nelson, "Chronology of the Tano Ruins, New Mexico," *American Anthropologist* (N.S.), vol. 18, pp. 159–180. Here referred to as "*N.*"

23   325

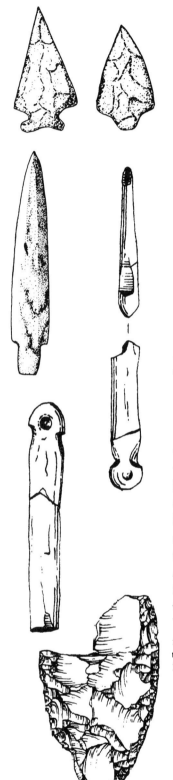

one, with interpretation based chiefly on Spanish documentary and native legendary sources, into a self-contained historic one." Mr. Nelson's discovery, and his discriminating analysis of his material constitute, therefore, one of the most important contributions that has yet been made to North American archaeology.

As Pecos was inhabited for a longer time than any other historic Southwestern site available for excavation;[1] and as its compact form, imposed by its position on a small mesa, tended to confine its rubbish heaps to a small area, an almost complete ceramic series can there be recovered in exact order. Thus we are able to cross-reference and, in some respects, to supplement the data secured by Mr. Nelson. We publish our results at this time, some years before the final report on the complete investigation can be brought out, and in their present fragmentary form, in order that they may become available for the constantly increasing number of archaeologists working in the Southwest.

The paper is in three parts: first, a classification of the wares found at Pecos, with condensed descriptions of the different types; second, the presentation and analysis of the stratigraphical evidence which has served to place them in their proper chronological order; third, a discussion of the sequence of the types.

CLASSIFICATION AND DESCRIPTION

In making this study we have used only sherds, the complete vessels found in the excavations not yet having been restored; hence we are unable to give any data on the shapes of whole pieces, or to include more than the most general notes on decoration. As it is difficult to describe in words such subtle qualities as the differences between nearly related groups of pottery, we have picked out a short series of sherds illustrating all the types. This series will be sent (on application to the Department of Archaeology, Phillips Academy, Andover, Mass.) to any one who cares to use it, either for a clearer understanding of the present paper, or for comparison with collections from other parts of the Southwest.

---

[1] Acoma is the only pueblo which has not changed its location at least once since 1540, and as to the length of its prehistoric occupation we are ignorant; it is possible, therefore, that Pecos was absolutely the longest inhabited village in Arizona or New Mexico.

The classification follows:

    I. DULL-PAINT WARE.
        1. Black-on-white.
        2. Biscuit.
            A. Rough exterior.
            B. Smooth exterior.
        3. Modern.
    II. GLAZE-PAINT WARE.
        1. Two-color.
            A. Black-on-red.
            B. Black-on-yellow.
        2. Transitional.
        3. Early three-color.
        4. Pajaritan three-color.
        5. Late three-color.
        6. Degenerate.
    III. UNDECORATED SMOOTH WARE.
        1. Polished black.
        2. Plain red.
    IV. BLACKWARE.
        1. Corrugated.
        2. Strong blind-corrugated.
        3. Medium blind-corrugated.
        4. Faint blind-corrugated.
        5. Featureless.
        6. Striated.

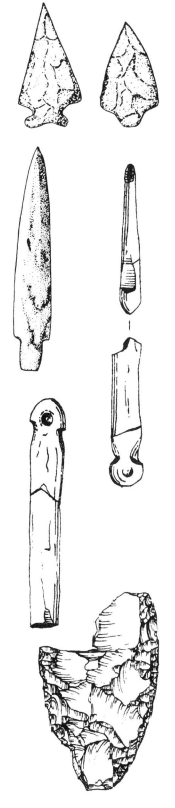

STRATIGRAPHICAL

Having classified the wares, we must turn to stratigraphy for our determination of their chronological order. Material for this study was gathered by means of test sections similar to those made by Mr. Nelson; columns of rubbish running from surface to hardpan were isolated, and from them was taken their entire pottery content, the fragments from the different levels or cuts being kept separate The Pecos tests were not divided into exactly equal cuts, as was done by Mr. Nelson, but were laid out in nearly equal divisions based on sand, ash, or other strata which indicated actual levels of deposition during the formation of the mound. This was necessitated by the fact that the Pecos deposits were for the most part laid down on sloping or irregular surfaces, and cuts made on arbitrarily chosen plane levels would have resulted in the splitting or cross-cutting of strata. This method derogates from the absolute statistical value of the material, as the cuts, not being of exactly equal thickness, are not strictly comparable statistically. The cultural results, for which these tests were taken, are, however, satisfactory; and even the statistical outcome seems fairly significant. Columns of debris have been saved intact in all parts of the heap, so that more exactly subdivided sections can be taken if desired.

Of the four tests here considered, three (whole series nos. x, xi, xii) are from the great rubbish heap on the east slope of the Pecos mesa. The earth-column of test x was 20 feet long, 5 feet wide, and 18 feet high; its eight cuts (numbered as in all the others

from top to bottom) averaged 2 feet 3 inches in thickness. Tests
XI and XII were each 25 feet long, 5 feet wide, and 12 feet high,
XI had seven cuts of about 1 foot 8 inches in thickness; XII, eight
cuts of 1 foot 6 inches. These tests were made very large in area
in order that we might get a great amount of sherds for the preliminary study, and also to neutralize as far as possible the disturbing effect of graves, from which no part of the eastern heap is entirely
free. The fourth test (XIII) was made in a midden below the northwest corner of the main pueblo; it was approximately 3 feet square,
by 4 feet high, and had seven 7-inch cuts. This section was gone
through with greater care than the other three, even the tiniest
sherds being saved.[1]

The material was handled as follows: the sherds from each cut
were classified according to ware and to vessel-forms, and the
numerical results entered under the headings given in the accompanying tables (nos. I, III, V, VII). Further, the glazed bowl-rim
sherds were subjected to closer study (for a purpose which will
be made clear below); they were classified, counted, and the results
entered in tables II, IV, VI, and VIII. Finally one set of charts was
prepared to illustrate graphically the distribution in percentages of
the principal wares (*i. e.*, all black, all glaze, all biscuit, etc.); and
another set to show in the same way the range of the types of glaze.

Looking at the four ware-charts, we see that each one of them
contains two approximately normal frequency curves: (1) for glaze;
(2) for biscuit. All show black-on-white very strong at the beginning and declining rapidly as glazed ware rises. Furthermore,
each one exhibits the start of three other curves: those for modern
painted; plain red; and polished black. The line representing
rough black runs more or less irregularly across each chart.

Blackware as a class obviously has no chronological significance.
It was evidently a somewhat variable, but nevertheless constantly
important factor in the total ceramic output of the pueblo during
its whole occupation.[2] As to the meaning of the tendency of the

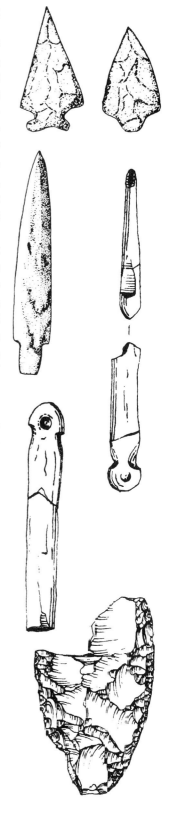

---

[1] In X, XI, and XII no fragment less than ¾-inch across was kept; pieces smaller
than this can seldom be accurately classified.

[2] We leave out of consideration the sub-types of blackware; these are without
doubt chronologically significant, but our data are not yet sufficiently full to allow us
to recognize them with certainty.

24

TABLE I

Test X

	Number of Sherds								Approximate Percentages							
Cut No............	1	2	3	4	5	6	7	8	1	2	3	4	5	6	7	8
Black olla rim[1]......	44	28	36	28	26	10	38	4	9	5	6	3	4	2	6	3
Black olla body.....	237	236	173	269	151	109	164	29	46	46	29	34	25	25	26	22
Polished black[2]......	51	19	2						10	4	X[6]					
Late plain red[2]......	87	51							17	10						
Modern painted[2]....	14	11	3						3	2	X					
Glaze bowl rim......	19	32	93	85	82	42	32	1	4	6	15	11	13	10	5	1
Glaze bowl body....	28	56	139	169	129	102	95	2	5	11	23	22	21	23	15	2
Olla-bowl[4].........	1	4	2						X	1	X					
Glaze olla rim......	2	3	7	12	10	5	6		X	1	1	1	2	1	1	
Glaze olla body.....	20	62	105	152	126	113	53		4	12	17	18	21	26	8	
Biscuit B bowl rim..		4	6	10	12	6	5			1	1	1	2	1	1	.
Biscuit B bowl body.	1	4	24	37	34	10	4	1	X	1	4	5	6	2	1	1
Biscuit A bowl rim..			2	5	9	10	16				X	1	1	2	3	
Biscuit A bowl body.	4		4	22	24	33	61		1		1	3	4	7	10	
Biscuit olla[6]........			8	9	3						1	1	X			
B.-on-W. bowl rim...	1		6	4	1	1	47	28	X		1	X	X	X	7	21
B.-on-W. bowl body.	6	1	4	4	4	6	104	60	1	X	1	X	1	1	16	46
B.-on-W. olla.......					2		9	6					X		1	4
Totals........	515	511	614	806	613	447	634	131	100	100	100	100	100	100	100	100

[1] Only ollas occur.

[2] Only ollas occur; body and rim sherds listed together.

[3] Bowls and ollas; body and rim sherds listed together.

[4] Glazed ware; body sherds of olla-bowls are not certainly distinguishable from those of undecorated bowl body sherds, hence only rims are listed.

[5] We cannot yet distinguish Biscuit A ollas from Biscuit B ollas.

[6] Present, but less than one half of one per cent.

TABLE II

Occurrence of Glazed Ware Types as Shown by Bowl-rims.　Test X.

	Number of Sherds								Percentages							
Cut No.............	1	2	3	4	5	6	7	8	1	2	3	4	5	6	7	8
Type 6.............	4	1	1						.7	.1	.2					
Type 5.............	10	15	15						1.9	2.9	2.4					
Type 4.............		6	22							1.1	3.5					
Type 3.............	2	5	44	32	5	2			.3	.9	7.1	3.9	.8	.4		
Type 2.............	1	3	8	35	57	2			.1	.5	1.3	4.3	9.5	.4		
Type 1 (yellow)....	2	2	2	10	14	28	15		.3	.3	.3	1.2	2.2	6.2	2.3	
Type 1 (red).......			1	8	6	10	17	1			.2	.9	.9	2.2	2.6	.7
Totals........	19	32	93	85	82	42	32	1	3.3	5.8	15.0	10.3	13.4	9.2	4.9	.7
Type I (both phases)	2	2	3	18	20	38	32	1	.3	.3	.5	2.1	3.1	8.4	4.9	.7

M. A. Kidder and A. V. Kidder

TABLE III
TEST XI

Cut No.	Number of Sherds							Approximate Percentages						
	1	2	3	4	5	6	7	1	2	3	4	5	6	7
Black olla rim	59	38	23	16	27	15	4	10	8	6	7	6	4	6
Black olla body	165	116	56	64	92	75	17	29	23	16	30	20	21	27
Polished black	41	15	1					7	3	×				
Late plain red	54	32	1					9	7	×				
Modern painted	21	18	1					4	3	×				
Glaze bowl rim	105	116	92	42	79	61	1	18	23	25	20	17	17	2
Glaze bowl body	68	73	76	50	115	82	2	12	15	21	23	25	23	3
Alla-bowl	7	12	12	4				1	2	4	2			
Glaze olla rim	12	19	19	2	8	9		2	4	5	1	2	3	
Glaze olla body	44	62	83	28	53	50		8	12	23	13	12	14	
Biscuit B bowl rim	1		1	5	16	4		×		×	2	3	1	
Biscuit B bowl body	1	1		3	46	9		×	×		2	10	2	
Biscuit A bowl rim				1	3	13	1				×	1	4	2
Biscuit A bowl body					8	27	3					2	8	5
Biscuit olla					6							1		
B.-on-W. bowl rim				1	2	4	7				×	×	1	11
B.-on-W. bowl body				1	6	8	23				×	1	2	37
B.-on-W. olla		1			1	1	4	×				×	×	7
Totals	579	502	365	217	462	358	62	100	100	100	100	100	100	100

TABLE IV
OCCURRENCE OF GLAZED WARE TYPES AS SHOWN BY BOWL-RIMS. TEST XI

Cut No.	Number of Sherds							Percentages						
	1	2	3	4	5	6	7	1	2	3	4	5	6	7
Type 6	16	11	1					2.7	2.1	.2				
Type 5	83	101	74	15	3			14.3	20.1	19.1	6.8	.6		
Type 4	2	3	12	17				.3	.6	3.2	7.8			
Type 3	2	1	2	8	58	5		.3	.1	.4	3.6	12.5	1.5	
Type 2			1	1	10	20				.2	.4	2.1	5.5	
Type 1 (yellow)			1		4	21				.2		.8	5.8	
Type 1 (red)	2		1	1	4	15	1	.3		.2	.4	.8	4.1	1.6
Totals	105	116	92	42	79	61	1	17.9	22.9	23.5	19.0	16.8	16.9	1.6
Type I (both phases)	2		2	1	8	36	2	.3		.4	.4	1.6	9.9	1.6

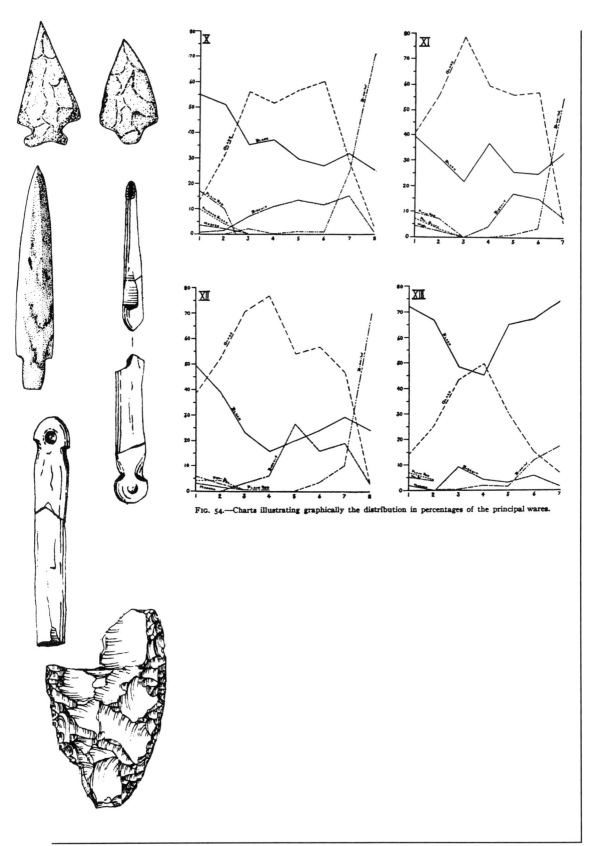

Fig. 54.—Charts illustrating graphically the distribution in percentages of the principal wares.

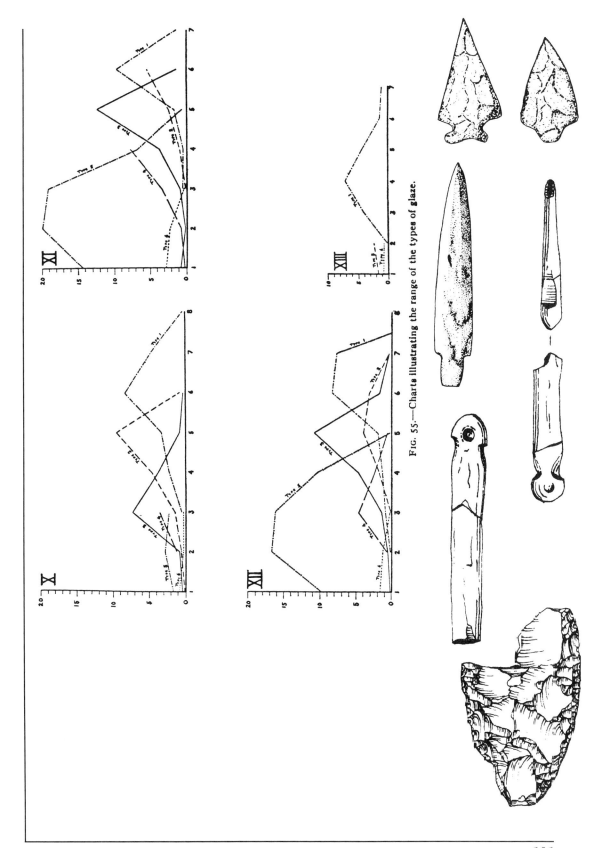

FIG. 55.—Charts illustrating the range of the types of glaze.

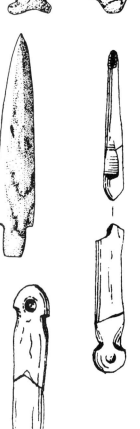

TABLE V

Test XII

Cut No.	Number of Sherds								Approximate Percentages.							
	1	2	3	4	5	6	7	8	1	2	3	4	5	6	7	8
Black olla rim......	41	132	32	6	20	31	10	6	11	11	7	4	5	5	4	7
Black olla body....	143	335	75	20	63	128	66	14	38	28	16	12	15	19	25	17
Polished black.....	14	54	3						4	4	1					
Late plain red......	20	23	4	2					6	3	1	1				
Modern painted....	11	25	4						3	2	1					
Glaze bowl rim.....	43	232	114	34	74	83	23	2	12	19	23	21	18	13	9	2
Glaze bowl body...	53	201	104	55	88	131	49	1	14	17	21	33	21	20	18	1
Olla-bowl.........	2	34	15	3					1	3	3	2				
Glaze olla rim......	2	20	20	6	10	17	4		1	2	4	4	2	3	2	
Glaze olla body....	35	131	94	29	53	141	35		10	11	20	17	13	21	13	
Biscuit *B* bowl rim .		5	2	1	16	8	1			×	×	1	4	1	×	
Biscuit *B* bowl body	1	1	9	1	65	42	4	1	×	×	2	1	16	6	2	1
Biscuit *A* bowl rim .				2	3	21	13	2				1	1	3	5	2
Biscuit *A* bowl body	1		5	3	8	36	32		×		1	2	2	6	12	
Biscuit olla........		1		1	12	3				×		1	3	×		
B.-on-W. bowl rim .		1			2	5	9	18		×			×	1	3	21
B.-on-W. bowl body		1			2	13	15	40		×			×	2	6	48
B.-on-W. olla.....							3	1							1	1
Totals........	366	1,196	481	163	416	659	264	85	100	100	100	100	100	100	100	100

TABLE VI

OCCURRENCE OF GLAZED WARE TYPES AS SHOWN BY BOWL-RIMS. TEST XII

Cut No.	Number of Sherds								Percentages							
	1	2	3	4	5	6	7	8[1]	1	2	3	4	5	6	7	.8
Type 6.............	6	16	1						1.6	1.3	.2					
Type 5.............	36	201	78	17	1				9.8	16.7	16.2	10.4	.2			
Type 4.............		8	23	4	2					.6	4.7	2.4	.4			
Type 3.............	1	6	7	8	46	7	1		.2	.5	1.4	4.8	10.9	1.7	.3	
Type 2.............			1	3	17	21	1				.2	1.8	4.0	3.1	.3	
Type 1 (yellow).....		1	2	2	6	28	7			.1	.4	1.2	1.4	4.2	2.6	
Type 1 (red)........			2		2	27	14				.4		.4	4.0	5.3	
Totals........	43	232	114	34	74	83	23		11.6	19.2	23.5	20.6	17.3	13.0	8.5	
Type I (both phases)		1	4	2	8	55	21			.1	.8	1.2	1.8	8.2	7.9	

[1] The two glazed bowl rims in cut 8 were too battered for identification.

blackware curves to dip toward the middle of the charts, and to rise toward their upper ends, we cannot attempt to judge. The total frequency of black relative to other wares seems to depend on the size of the sherds collected. Black vessels break into very many very small fragments, so that if only sherds of 3 inches square were kept, black would fall to almost nothing; whereas if the most minute bits were saved it would rise to well over 65 per cent. An example of this is seen in the plot of test XIII, a section including small fragments.

Black-on-white ware is shown in each chart to drop rapidly from a high initial percentage, its appearance in very small quantities in the middle and upper cuts (as in test X) being due, probably, to churning of the heaps during deposition, or to the dumping of old rubbish from the mesa top. In no case does black-on-white make a respectable showing after the real beginning of the rise of glaze.

Glazed ware is represented by normal frequency curves in all the charts, rising from practically nothing at the bottom, to a high percentage at or somewhat beyond the middle, and declining toward the end little less rapidly than it rose. Although no test is free from glaze in its lowest cuts, nor does any one show the entire extinction of glaze as a ceramic trait, we believe, from evidence other than stratigraphical, that there was a short period at the beginning when the art was not practised, and that no glazed ware was made during the closing years of the occupation of Pecos.

The curves for biscuitware are comparable to those for glaze; both rise together, and both tend to have similar contours. There are, however, these important differences: (1) that biscuit is always a minor or secondary ware in point of frequency; (2) that while glaze runs as far as or even beyond the upper limits of each test, biscuit has a considerably shorter life, its curves becoming negligible in every case while those for glaze are near their highest points.

The remaining three curves: those for polished black, plain red, and modern painted, have their origin at about the point of extinction for biscuit, and are on the rise in the last cut of each test. There is, however, so little overlapping of the biscuit curves

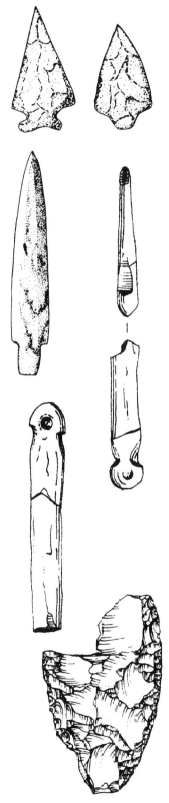

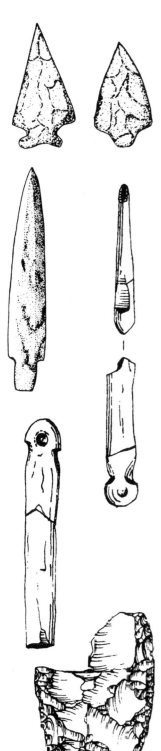

and of these three later ones that we do not believe that the wares actually overlapped in time. It seems more probable that polished black, plain red, and modern painted are all parts of a single ceramic group that replaced the glazed wares.[1] This we may call for convenience the late group.

To sum up: it appears that there were three main stages in the ceramic history of Pecos: the black-on-white, the glazed, and the late; that the black-on-white ended soon after the settlement of the mesa, and the late began only shortly before its abandonment. Within the glazed period,. then, falls most of the history of Pecos. For this reason a close study of the glazed ware is essential and is greatly facilitated by the fact that the pottery is subdivisible into six easily recognized types.

A cursory examination of the test material, when sorted and laid out cut by cut, shows that three of these glazed ware types, namely nos. 1, 3, and 5, succeed each other in the order given. The chronological positions of the three others (nos. 2, 4, and 6) are strongly indicated: (1) by their occurrence at certain levels in the tests; (2) by technological and decorative features. One would like, however, to have more tangible evidence as to the exact relations of these latter to the more obviously placeable groups (1, 3, 5) than can be had by a mere inspection of the test material. For this purpose we have plotted the distribution of all six types.[2] In the resultant diagrams each of the plotted types tends to form a normal frequency curve, indicating that each one had a natural rise, vogue, and decline. One's general impression is that they are all successive phases of the single glazed pottery trait, and that each one of them developed from its predecessor.

As to the position of Types 1, 3, and 5 there can be, as was remarked above, no doubt. Type 1 is surely the oldest, it being

[1] Here we seem to get a hint that when a style breaks up it is succeeded by two or more new styles (as black-on-white by glazed and biscuit); and that one of these eventually dominates. More research is needed.

[2] As it is impossible to classify accurately undecorated sherds from glazed vessels, and as there is often uncertainty even in the case of decorated fragments which do not show the rim-contour, we have used only rim-sherds in making the type distribution study. What is lost in bulk of material is more than made up for in certainty of identification.

the only one represented in the bottom cut of each of the tests; in test x, indeed, it is the only type in the two bottom cuts, and it stands by itself in the five lowest cuts of test XIII.   In test x it is succeeded quite definitely by Type 2, which in turn reaches its maximum and is well along in decline before the real rise of Type 3. In tests XI and XII the evidence for placing Type 2 between 1 and 3 is somewhat less decisive, and were it not for test x and for the marked transitional appearance of the ware itself, we might perhaps have been led to consider it as a contemporary variant of Type 3.

In the case of Types 4 and 5 we are confronted with rather greater difficulty.   Type 5, as is shown by the plots of tests XI and XII, is without question a later style than 3; furthermore it has from the technical and decorative points of view the appearance of being a direct outgrowth from it.   Type 4, according to the plots, lies within the limits of distribution of Type 5; in tests x and XI it comes in abruptly; nowhere do we get any direct evidence, as was the case with Type 2 in test x, for calling Type 4 transitional or even chronologically intermediate between 3 and 5.   The ware itself does not help us, as it fails to fit well into what seems to be the developmental series.   One point, however, should be noted: that the curves for Types 2 and 4 are very similar in test XI; and also very similar (though of different form from those in test XI) in test XII.   Type 2 is fairly well established as transitional, so that the resemblance between its curves and those of Type 4 may be significant.

Type 6 is shown by the plots to begin at about the time of the maximum frequency of Type 5; it is in the ascendant at the top of each test.   The glazed trait as a whole, however, being decidedly on the wane at the top of each test, we may reasonably consider Type 6 to be the last phase of the industry.

Summing up the foregoing, we see that Type 1 is the earliest; Type 2 is without much doubt transitional between it and Type 3, which latter in turn may develop directly into Type 5; the exact morphological position of Type 4 is still uncertain, but chronologically it is either between 3 and 5 or contemporaneous with early 5; Type 6 represents the last stage of glazing.

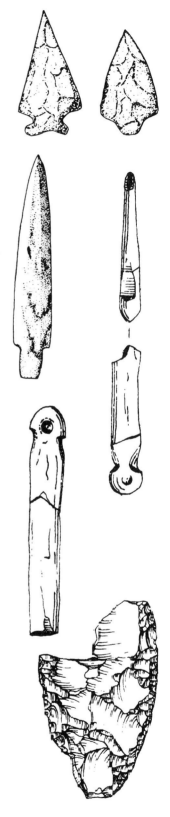

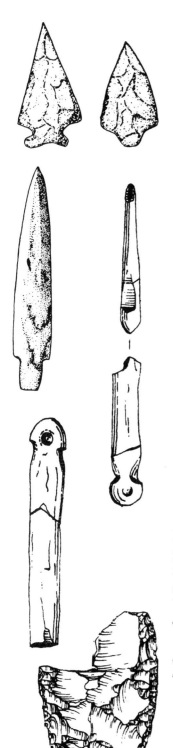

The value of glazed ware as an archaeological index for Pecos is now obvious. It was made from almost the beginning to shortly before the end, and it may be subdivided into easily recognized types which are chronologically sequent. Glazed ware can therefore be used for assigning relative dates to burials, refuse beds, rooms, kivas, etc.; and also as a criterion for assigning to their proper chronological positions other wares, types of artifacts and the like, which are found in conjunction with one or another of its phases.[1]

Having made out the succession of the three main ware classes, black-on-white, glaze, and late, and having also arranged the principal types of glazed ware in their proper order, we have built up the framework, so to speak, of the ceramic history of Pecos. The greater part of our work, however, still remains to be done; for it is more important to know how and why the observed changes took place than to have merely learned that they did so. The method to be pursued in further research is clear: we must make an intensive study of the wares themselves. For this we must have not only large amounts of material, but also as nearly as possible unmixed material, from each archaeological horizon. The purest representation of any given period is, of course, to be derived from isolated sites inhabited only during that period. For the earlier stages such sites can easily be found, as in early times the people lived in small scattered communities, which often shifted their locations.[2] The one-period site of later times is, however, much rarer, the Pueblos then having been gathered together in large and more or less permanently established towns whose rubbish heaps contain the inevitably somewhat mixed debris of several periods. Isolated heaps must therefore usually take the place of isolated sites; and, though they are difficult to find, careful search at any large ruin will be rewarded by the discovery of pure deposits.[3]

---

[1] Black-on-white, biscuit, modern, and even black, are all undoubtedly sub-divisible and will eventually also be of use for the above purposes.

[2] *Cf.* "*N*," p. 179.

[3] Most often to be found among the houses, in places where rooms have fallen temporarily into disuse, have been filled with dumped rubbish, and have then been sealed up by the construction of new floors.

For certain transitions, and for periods from which no isolated heaps can be found, we must, however, turn to the large middens, and make stratigraphical tests. To pick out only the best for the illustration of the desired horizons, we must be able to analyze these tests understandingly. To make this point clear, let us consider the ones we have before us.

Test x, according to its glaze-type chart, contains an orderly deposition of Types 1, 2, and 3. Types 4, 5, and 6, on the other hand, are very weakly represented and their curves are far from normal. We conclude, therefore, that at the end of the Type 3 period the heap was practically abandoned as a dump, and that its top cuts accumulated so slowly as to be nearly valueless for close study.[1] We should, then, concentrate on the six bottom cuts for information as to Types 1, 2, and 3. Had we been guided in this case by the total-glaze curve alone, we should have fallen into error, as we would doubtless have believed (because the total-glaze curve falls in this test most nearly to zero) that the upper cuts would give us excellent material for the concluding phases of the ware.

Tests XI and XII are quite different from X, but are similar to each other. The plotted analyses of their glaze types show that their lower parts were built up much more slowly than was the case with x (two cuts from the bottom to the apex of Type 3, as against six cuts in test x); whereas they have five cuts containing the strong curves for Types 4, 5, and 6 (as against two cuts in x with very weak curves). Interpreting this, we see that tests XI and XII came slowly at first, but finished rapidly; they are therefore best for the study of the later glazes. Test XIII is in some ways the most useful of all, though this fact would not be suspected by examining its ware-group chart alone, for there the curve for total-glaze is much like the glaze curves of the other tests. Turning to the glaze-type chart, however, it is seen that following Type 1 there is no representation whatever of Types 2, 3, and 4, Types 5 and 6 coming in abruptly at a relatively high per cent. This shows

[1] It may be considered axiomatic that the faster a heap accumulates the purer and less disturbed will be its contents.

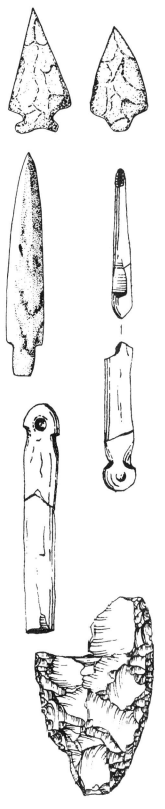

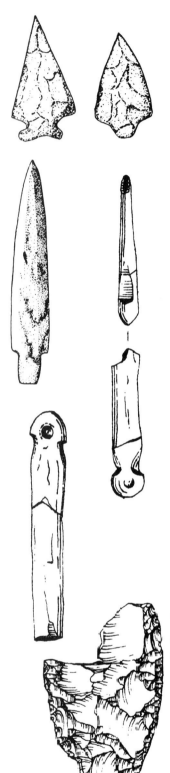

that there was no deposition whatever of refuse, from some time during the life of Type 1, until the comparatively late date when glaze as a trait was on the decline, and the late wares had already come into vogue (see curves for modern, polished black, and plain red).[1] We have, then, in test XIII a long section of pure Type 1 debris, making clear the rise and development of that type, and providing helpful knowledge as to its relation to the precedent black-on-white and the contemporaneous phases of biscuit. This test proves, for example, a thing which we had not hitherto suspected, *viz.*: that biscuit *B* came into limited use before the origin of Type 2 glaze.

We cannot, within the limits of this paper, and with the scanty material now at hand, go further into detail; but enough has been said to show the value of test analysis and the importance of plotting the results graphically.

RECAPITULATION

The earliest ware found on the Pecos mesa is the black-on-white. With it occurs blackware of the strong blind-corrugated variety and a small percentage of true corrugated, but never as far as our investigations have shown, is there any indented corrugated. Further, the dull-black-on-red and the black-on-white with basket-marked exterior, both classes noted by Mr. Nelson from Tano ruins and by the author from the lesser sites on the Pajarito and near Santa Fe,[2] are not represented at Pecos. They are to be found, however, at "Bandelier Bend," a ruin a little below Pecos on the opposite side of the arroyo, and at several other places near Glorieta. As the corrugated technic gradually fades out at Pecos from the early strata upwards, the most strongly marked specimens there occurring at the bottom, it is reasonable to suppose that the ruins which produce the best grades of the ware are earlier still. Hence we conclude that the Pecos mesa was not settled until toward the close of the black-on-white period. Whether or not glazing

---

[1] As an illustration of the purely archaeological value of test analysis it may be said that the lacuna in this particular rubbish heap throws very important light on the method of growth of the north end of the Pueblo.

[2] "N," p. 171; "K," p. 414.

had been discovered or introduced at that time is still an open question.   The great preponderance of black-on-white pottery in the early strata prove that glazing could not have attained any considerable vogue, yet the lowest cuts in all our tests show traces of glazed pottery.   On the other hand, isolated rubbish heaps of the north terrace, and a black-on-white cemetery on the west slope, contain no glazed sherds at all.   We believe, therefore, that for a short time at least, the black-on-white industry was the only one practised at Pecos.

When glazing did come in it very quickly drove out the older style.   This is clearly shown by the charts; they indicate, however, that glazing and black-on-white existed for a short time side by side. This is of course only natural, for we have no reason to think that there was an abandonment of the pueblo during the transition, or that any wholesale influx of outside clans brought the change about abruptly.[1]

Glazing was probably not of simultaneous origin in the whole country.   It was undoubtedly discovered accidentally at some one site by the mixing of a flux in the pigment, and spread outward from there, the novelty and beauty of the paint aiding rapid dissemination.   While it is of course futile to try to locate the point of origin with any exactitude, we believe that it lay to the west, probably in the Little Colorado; our reasons for this belief are as follows: The earliest form of glazing in the Rio Grande was the black-on-red.   This has been pointed out by Mr. Nelson, and is confirmed by the Pecos finds.   Now black-on-red is exceedingly rare in dull-paint pottery of the Rio Grande black-on-white period; and, if our Pecos observations are correct, it had entirely disappeared during the later phases of that period.   Hence, it seems strange that a new paint, if discovered locally, should first have been applied over a slip of a color that was seldom if ever used locally at the time.   The southern and western parts of the pueblo district seem always to have been the greatest centres for the manufacture of red wares,

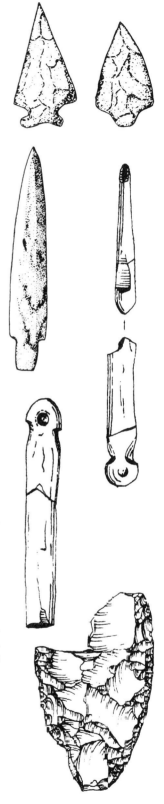

---

[1] Clan-migration should only be called upon as a last resort to explain pottery changes, for while we know that such movements were common and a very potent factor in the makeup of all the later pueblos, we have no evidence that they were capable of producing radical overturns in resident cultures.

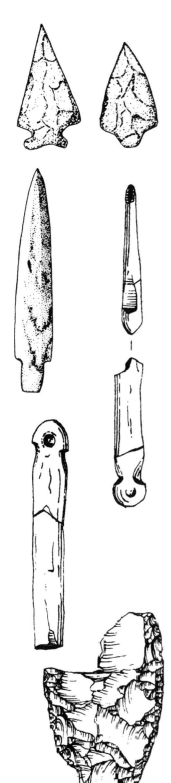

therefore the sudden appearance of a redware with a new form of paint in the east suggests western influence.

The above conclusion is entirely theoretical; to strengthen it, however, we have a few bits of archaeological evidence. In the Little Colorado drainage there occurs a redware with glaze decoration, whose bowls bear characteristic exterior designs in chalky white paint. Although Fewkes and Hough have figured a number of pieces, the chronological position of the style has never been fixed; the vessels, however, bear internal evidence of belonging to a fairly well-developed ceramic industry. We know of four fragments of such vessels from the Rio Grande: one from the Rowe ruin, an almost straight black-on-white site; two from Agua Fria "schoolhouse," which from its preponderance of black-on-red glazed ware we are justified in assigning to an early period; one from cut 7, Test x, a very early stratum, as it contains 25 per cent. of black-on-white ware. These were presumably all trade pieces and so serve to indicate with some degree of probability that glaze decoration was present and perhaps even fairly well advanced in the Little Colorado while it was still a very young art in the Rio Grande.

The locating of the origin of glaze to the west rests, of course, on possibly faulty theoretical grounds, and at best very meagre archaeological evidence. It is, however, a convenient working hypothesis which further research in the western districts and a close study of the designs will either prove or disprove. Whether or not glaze was first discovered in the west, it reached its maximum development in the east; and that development was, as far as we can see, a gradual and purely local one.

Returning to the Type 1 glazed wares, we may repeat that the black-on-red phase was at first the preponderating one. The black-on-light, however, slowly gains in importance and, as we approach Type 2, the red falls away. Type 2 is marked by a degeneration of the glaze, which becomes thicker and less adaptable to the production of fine-line designs; by a parallel deterioration of the clear yellow color of the slip; by a thickening inwards of the bowl rim (which, however, still remains square on top); and by the appearance on bowl exteriors, first of slashed marks and crosses, then of red-filled decorations. The transitional nature of Type 2, both technologically and stratigraphically, was pointed out in the preceding section. Although the ware is less uniformly specialized than those of our other groups, it appears at Pecos in large quantities, indicating that its manufacture was carried on during a considerable period of time; further, the ware is characteristic of at least one isolated site which contains nothing else.[1] For these reasons we have given it typical rank.

The other wares associated with Types 1 and 2 glaze are the black and the biscuit. Of the former little need be said; it shows a steady elimination of the visible signs of the structural coil and a progressive modification of the rim. Biscuitware presents several interesting features. Biscuit *A*, the early variety, is unslipped on bowl exteriors and bears decorations which seldom if ever conform to the highly specialized design-system of biscuit *B*; but which seem, on the basis of the sherds, to be allied rather closely to those of the black-on-white. That the ware is a development from the black-on-white would naturally suggest itself, and indeed seemingly transitional pieces are not rare. The change from biscuit *A* to biscuit *B* consists in the raising and straightening of the bowl-rim, in the specialization of the design, and in its extension with the slip to bowl exteriors. In general, biscuit *A* is associable with Type 1 glaze, *B* with 2, 3, 4, and very early 5.[2]

Returning to the development of the glazed wares, we see that in Type 3 the slip on visible surfaces is almost invariably light, but is of poor and uncertain quality; the glaze lines also are seldom sharp-edged and clear black, but are heavy, "runny," and of various shades of rusty black, brown, and greeny-brown. Because of the intractability of the paint the interior designs of bowls and the body designs of ollas are considerably simplified; the exteriors of bowls and the necks of ollas, on the other hand, bear handsome decorations (usually oblique variants of the double-ended key figure) in red with glaze outlines. Type 5 seems to be merely a further growth along the same lines, *viz.*: glaze becomes even heavier;

[1] The "Frijolito" ruin, see "*K*," p. 454.

[2] Test XIII shows biscuit *B* to have originated a little earlier than Type 2 glaze.

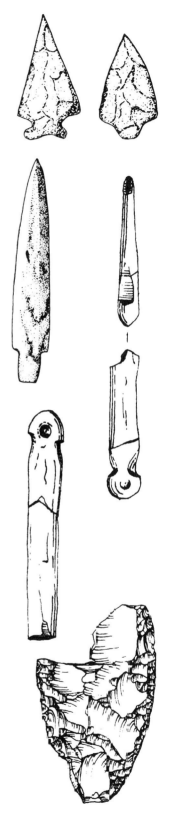

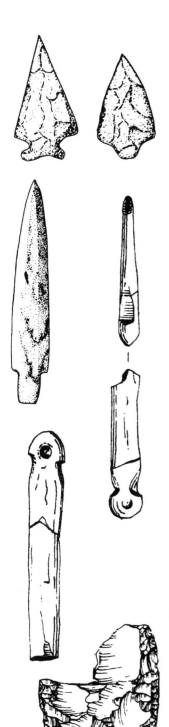

interior decoration of bowls is simplified to a mere pair of red filled lines encircling the piece just below the lip; exterior design grows more varied; and finally the rim reaches a maximum of thickness.

Found in the same strata that produce the latest forms of Type 3 and the earlier forms of Type 5, is a certain percentage of pieces scarcely, if at all, different from the pottery which in a former paper we have called "Pajaritan,"[1] and have described as Type 4 in the present one. It seems to come in abruptly, runs but a short course, and abruptly disappears, apparently with no preceding or succeeding type. Its high rather thin rims, red color, good glaze, and specialized decoration, do not fit at all well in the Pecos series. It was commonly buried with the dead, as were Types 1, 2, and 3; while Type 5 vessels were almost never so deposited. One of three conclusions might be arrived at:[2] (1) that it was really transitional between 3 and 5, but that we have not sufficient evidence or sufficient acumen to enable us to recognize it as such; (2) that it was a short-lived secondary style, arising from Type 3 and running a course parallel to early Type 5; (3) that it was made by a group of people from the Pajarito who settled at Pecos, as the Hano did at Hopi, were assigned a section of the site, made their own style of pottery, and continued their own mortuary customs; finally losing their cultural identity or moving away. Careful work in the rubbish will, without much doubt, eventually settle this interesting problem.

The wares found in conjunction with Type 5 glaze are the featureless black and, towards the end, the striated black; with its earlier phases, or roughly synchronous with the Pajaritan admixture just noted, there is a considerable amount of biscuit *B*, which seems to average yellower than the earlier biscuit *B* and to have higher rims. This ware rapidly decreases in importance and, shortly after the middle of the Type 5 glaze period, it entirely disappears.

Type 5 continued well into historic times. This is proved by the finding in Type 5 rubbish of the bones of domestic animals

[1] "*K*," p. 417.

[2] Specimens are too common to be considered trade pieces.

25

and objects of European manufacture.   At just what period in the life of Type 5 the Conquest occurred cannot yet be stated, as the bones and artifacts from the tests have not yet been studied, nor can we as yet put a date to the appearance of Type 6, the last stage of native glazed ware.

Type 6 is distinguishable from the preceding one by the diversity and eccentricity of the vessel shapes, and by the extremely "runny" nature of the glaze.   We quote Mr. Nelson's excellent description:

> Generally the iridescent glaze substance is of such striking and excellent quality as to incline one to believe that it was compounded after a Spanish formula. The fact that the artist could not control it at all seems suggestive of the same idea.   The designs attempted, though of the very simplest geometric nature, were almost invariably spoiled by the running of the glaze.   The color and general appearance is a very characteristic dark brown when thickly applied and of a greenish hue when the coating is thin.

The fact that the ware is all of historic date lends much weight to Mr. Nelson's supposition that the glaze was compounded after Spanish formulae.   If such was the case, the style must have been a very short-lived one indeed, as Spanish influence strong enough to have seriously affected the manufacture of pottery can hardly be believed to have exerted itself prior to the actual settlement of the country at the beginning of the seventeenth century, and Mr. Nelson has shown that the making of glazed pottery ceased at about the time of the revolt of 1680.[1]

Next came in the dull-paint vessels described above as "modern-painted ware."   Their whole appearance, color, pigments, and decorative elements are radically different from those of glazed pottery. The only resemblance is in the high, outcurved rim that is common both to modern and to glaze Type 6.   As to the rapidity of the rise of modern ware we cannot yet supply much data, as our tests all tend to become unreliable toward the top.   That it eventually completely superseded glazed ware is proved by the total absence of the latter from certain isolated heaps of late rubbish found at Pecos, and by Mr. Nelson's observations at Cienega no. 1 and Cieneguilla.[2]   The origin of the style is as yet a mystery.   On its

---

[1] "*N.*," p. 175.   The Pecos ruin can hardly be expected to add corroboration to this, as the site was not deserted at any time during the rebellion.

[1] "*N.*," p. 176 and table p. 179.

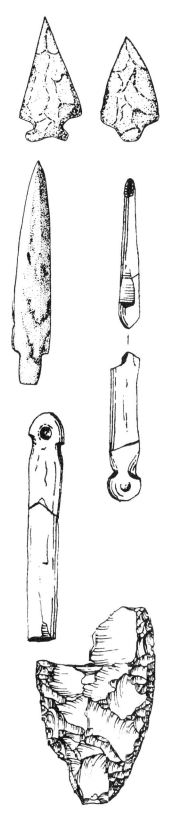

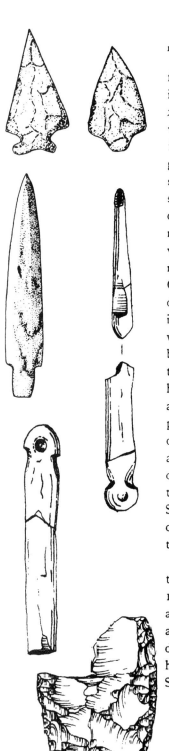

first recorded appearance it bears designs that by no stretch of the imagination may be believed to be the direct descendants of any of the glazed designs.   Technically it is most nearly allied to biscuit-ware, and some of the decorative elements may possibly be derived from biscuit prototypes.   If it is a late outgrowth of biscuit, that growth can hardly have taken place at Pecos, for our test material shows that the making of biscuit had probably ceased completely some time before the modern came into vogue.   Mr. Nelson throws out the hint that the type may have been derived from the Keresan region to the north, and this is a particularly useful suggestion in view of the fact that biscuitware was primarily a northern product, reached its maximum development in the upper reaches of the Rio Grande and the Chama, and seems to have continued in use in that district rather longer than it did in the central Rio Grande.   It is possible, therefore, that we may yet find that modern painted ware was a normal growth from an ancient prototype, probably biscuit, in some region to the north, and that the unsettled conditions of the rebellion, with their constant movements of people, may have brought about its introduction to the central Rio Grande as an already perfected style.   If this is so, we will not be forced to postulate a conscious revolt against what Mr. Nelson calls "the degenerative tendency of the seventeenth century"; or to believe, as we have sometimes done, that the modern ware was the result of an archaistic revival carried out by the Pueblos at the time of the rebellion in a desire to do away with everything savoring of Spanish influence, and to return to the dull-painted wares that observation of the sherds about their villages must have shown them were made by their prehistoric ancestors

That there were changes in the modern ware after its introduction and continuing until the time of the abandonment of Pecos in 1838, can be seen by examining the pottery fragments in and around the houses on the mesa-top.   Similar changes evidently also took place in the polished black and the plain red.   Late debris, however, in large enough quantities for satisfactory tests, has not yet been found lying conformably upon earlier strata. Such deposits surely exist at Pecos, but until they have been located and examined it is idle to attempt to carry the study of type-sequence beyond the end of glaze-making times.

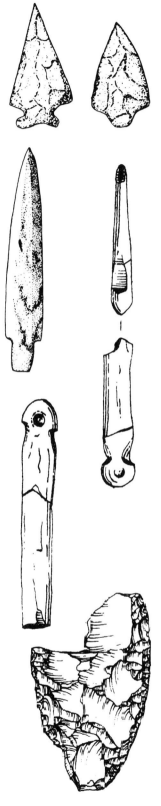

Tentative division of the culture-history of the east-central Rio Grande into chronological periods (the leading ware of each period is italicized).

I. Formative period.	Wares?	Nelson's pre-pueblo, not yet found in Pecos valley.
' II. Archaic period....	Indented corrugated, *black-on-white*, black-on-red.	Nelson's I. Not found at Pecos, but present at other nearby sites.
III. Late archaic......	Corrugated (little), strong blind-corrugated, *black-on-white*.	Nelson's I.
IV. Period of introduction of glaze.[1]..	Strong and medium blind-corrugated, *glaze 1*, biscuit *A*.	Nelson's II. Author's Agua Fria "schoolhouse."
V. Period of concentration.[2].......	Faint blind-corrugated, *glazes 2 and 3*, biscuit *B*.	Nelson's III. Author's "Frijolito."
VI. Late prehistoric. ?–1600........	Featureless black, glaze 4, *glaze 5*, biscuit *B*.	Nelson's III. Author's "Pajaritan."
VII. Early historic (1540) 1600–1680.........	Striated black, late glaze 5, *glaze 6*, modern begins (?).	Nelson's IV.
VIII. Late period 1680–1840..........	Striated black (?), plain red, polished black, *modern*.	Nelson's V.
IX. Present period 1840–1917......	Polished wares (Santa Clara), *painted wares* (San Ildefonso, Santo Domingo, Tesuque, Cochiti).	

Phillips Academy,
    Andover, Mass.

---

[1] And possibly also of the kiva.

[2] Concentration had been going on from the earliest times, but apparently became particularly strong at about this time in the Pecos valley and on the Pajarito. In the Tano country it took place somewhat later (see Nelson's chart, p. 179), perhaps because the Galisteo basin was less exposed to raids from the north and east.

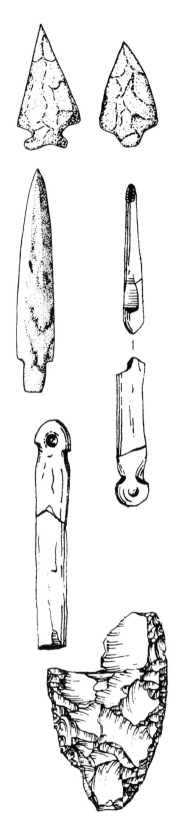

DIFFUSION AND INDEPENDENT INVENTION:
A CRITIQUE OF LOGIC[1]

BY JULIAN H. STEWARD

THERE exists a large proportion of anthropological data which admits of no clear-cut methodology but is usually handled according to inference and common sense logic. While this method may be soundly rational, the possibility of an enormous subjective element and fallacious logic is ever present and is demonstrated by the existence of the diffusion controversy. This controversy is made possible not only by the personal bias of the investigator but also by a confusion of the principles upon which the solution is based.

It is not my purpose to present a rule-of-thumb method for the settlement of the diffusion controversy but to inquire into its logical implications and discover whether these are not capable of formulation. While this will but formulate the principles implicit in most work, it will also reveal the possibility of certain confusions and inconsistencies.

Certain factors are involved in every instance where there is doubt concerning independent invention or diffusion: the spatial proximity of the localities where the culture element in question occurs, the apparent uniqueness of the element, the possibility of its derivation from a common ancestral culture, and the number of other elements shared by the localities. While all of these are usually taken into consideration through a method of common sense logic, certain of them are frequently ignored or one made to depend upon another in an illogical manner.

This may be illustrated by inverted speech[2] which occurs in North America in the Plains area, California, and the Southwest, and also occurs in Australia. Shall we account for these four occurrences by diffusion or independent invention? The solution depends upon inference from the assembled facts, but what is the

---

[1] Read at the meeting of the American Anthropological Association, Dec. 28, 1928.

[2] A custom of clowns and others of saying the reverse of what is meant.

491

logic of our reasoning? We ask: How probable is communication between these areas? How difficult an achievement is inverted speech? It is tempting immediately to postulate diffusion between the North American occurrences but independent invention for Australia. This would be solely on a basis of distribution and by this we should be prone to judge the uniqueness of the element. A consideration of California, the Southwest, and the Plains alone would lead us to regard the invention of this trait as an inherently difficult accomplishment, largely because of the comparative ease of communication between the three areas which it seems to have diffused. But the Australian data, in view of the difficulty of communication between Australia and America, lead us to regard inverted speech as not so difficult an invention after all, for it clearly has been invented a second time. What logical justification would there be for the assumption that independent invention is inherently less possible for the Plains, California, and the Southwest than for Australia because the first three happen to be geographically more accessible?

If we conclude that communication was quite possible between two or more localities possessing the same trait, we are prone to regard the trait as unique. Conversely, if we decide that the trait is not unique and may frequently appear, we are less impressed with the possibility of communication. Thus by disposing of one factor we beg the question for the other. Thus, those who regard all elements as unique and impossible of multiple invention beg the question in favor of the probability of communication everywhere and are called "extreme diffusionists." On the other hand, those who regard all elements as easily arising everywhere, the "evolutionists," beg the question against the probability of communication. Without looking to the extremist, we find that everyone is constantly called upon to make decisions in problems of this kind. Personal bias and a confusion of factors which must logically be kept distinct may affect the solution.

We are concerned here, however, not with reconciling the extremists but in defining the methodology used by unbiased investigators—if there be such—and stating its logical justification.

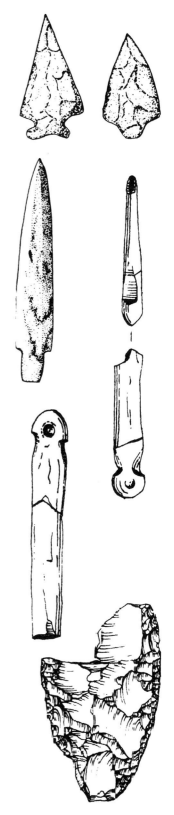

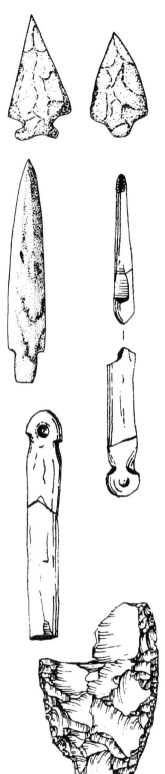

I therefore submit the following three principles as logically valid formulations of the methodology employed, implicitly or explicitly, in the solution of these problems. These principles are stated in terms of probabilities, and for this I make no apology to scientists for the most exact scientific laws are philosophically but statements of high probabilities.

When a culture element is found in two or more localities (and it is assumed that the element is identical in each case), the probability that independent invention has occurred is:

(1) Directly proportionate to the difficulty of communication between the localities.

(2) Directly proportionate to the uniqueness of the element—the "qualitative criterion."

(3) Inversely proportionate to the probability of derivation from a common ancestral culture.

(1) *The probability of independent invention is directly proportionate to the difficulty of communication between the localities.* The logical validity of this lies in the fact that as communication is difficult, the chance of its having occurred to transport the element is small. Factors determining the difficulty of communication are: geographical accessibility and means of transportation, intertribal relations, and cultural receptivity. These have been clearly discussed by Sapir in his *Time Perspective in Aboriginal Culture.*[3]

A measure of the difficulty of communication is the number of other culture elements shared by the localities. Other things equal, each culture element common to the localities strengthens the probability that communication has occurred. Therefore as a supplement to (1), we may state as

(1a): *The probability of independent invention is inversely proportionate to the number of traits shared by the two localities*—the "quantitative criterion."

That culture elements of different types diffuse with varying degrees of facility would be taken into consideration under cultural receptivity and intertribal relations.

A further supplement to (1) is:

(1b): *The probability of independent invention is inversely proportionate to the elapsed time since the appearance of the trait in either locality.*

---

[3] Canada, Department of Mines, Mem. 90 (Anthr. series, no. 13), 1916.

That is, the amount of communication between the localities is, other things equal, a function of time.

(2) *The probability of independent invention is directly proportionate to the uniqueness of the element.* The uniqueness of a culture element—that is, the probability of its being invented— is the most difficult problem to determine. This will be decided by the investigator upon his experience and knowledge of the cultural setting and circumstances under which it may have been invented. But his decision must not depend upon either of the other two principles stated here. To the probability of an element of culture arising in a particular culture, the existence of this element in other localities and the difficulty of communication between the localities are totally irrelevant.

(3) *The probability of independent invention is inversely proportionate to the probability of derivation from a common ancestral culture.* The solution of this depends partly upon the number of other culture elements which the localities have in common so that (*1a*) may also apply here as a possible supplementary principle:

(3a): *The probability of derivation from a common ancestral culture is proportionate to the number of elements shared by the localities.*

It also depends upon known factors of racial and linguistic relationship. These have also been discussed by Sapir.[4]

Where one or two of these three principles fails to yield data in terms of probabilities, our inference as to what has occurred must be drawn entirely from the known. Most commonly the unknown will be (2), the possibility of invention of the trait—its uniqueness—and we shall consequently be thrown back upon distributional inferences. Thus, to return to inverted speech, if the possibility of its arising in any culture is totally unknown, we are forced to decide its origin in any locality upon the possibility of its diffusion from another locality also having it or its derivation from a common ancestral culture. This, however, will establish probabilities merely as to whether independent invention or diffusion has occurred in this particular instance and does not

[4] Ibid.

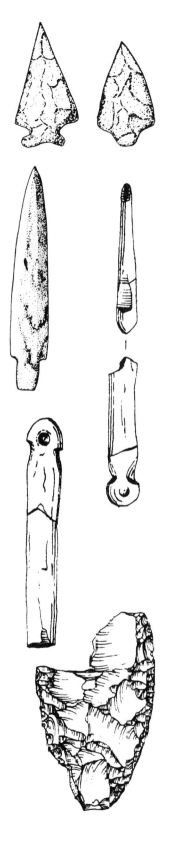

throw light on the problem as to whether or not inverted speech is a trait that is inherently difficult to invent.

The final solution of any problem of this type will rest upon a summation of the probabilities derived from each of these three principles or criteria but the principles themselves must logically be weighted separately without the least interdependence.

MUSEUM OF ANTHROPOLOGY,
UNIVERSITY OF MICHIGAN

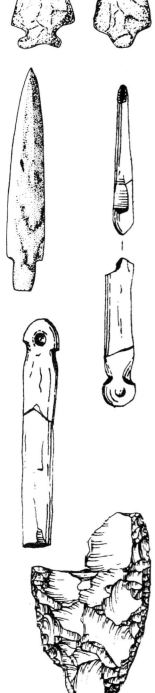

THE CULTURE-AREA AND AGE-AREA CONCEPTS OF CLARK WISSLER

By A. L. KROEBER

University of California

The concepts of the culture-area and of the age-area ("age and area") method as applicable to culture have been developed by Clark Wissler in three books: *The American Indian* (1917); *Man and Culture* (1923); *The Relation of Nature to Man* (1926).[1] The two concepts have this in common, that they deal with the space distribution of culture phenomena. They differ in that the culture area refers to culture traits as they occur aggregated in nature, whereas the age-area method is applicable to separate traits or isolable clusters of elements. They differ further in that the culture area, as such, is not concerned with time factors, whereas the age-area concept is a device for inferring time sequences from space distributions. Both ideas have long been in use in the biological sciences. An areally characterized fauna or flora, such as the Neo-tropical or Indo-Malaysian, obviously corresponds to the culture aggregation within a culture area. The term *age-area* was coined in the field of natural history, and the method of inferring areas of origin from concentration of distribution, and antiquity of dispersal from marginal survivals, has long been in use in so-called systematic biology. Perhaps because the comparable method applied to culture developed independently, the term *age area* has not gained currency in that field. Anthropologists have not been wholly happy in their terminology. They speak consistently of *culture areas*, whereas it is the content of these areas, certain culture growths or aggregations, that they are really concerned with, the areal limitation being only one aspect of such an aggregation.

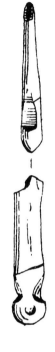

ANTICIPATION

Both concepts are not new in anthropology, although for long they were employed implicitly, or without methodological formulation. Ratzel, who spoke of marginal peoples and backward cultures as long ago as

---

[1] *The American Indian*, (1st ed., New York: McMurtrie, 1917; 2d ed., New York: Oxford University Press, 1922); *Man and Culture* (New York: Thomas Y. Crowell Co., 1923); *The Relation of Nature to Man in Aboriginal America* (New York: Oxford University Press, 1926).

248

1891,[2] was close to thinking in age-area terms. Sophus Müller's main thesis was that prehistoric Europe is to be conceived as culturally belated, marginal to, and dependent on, the higher centers of the Orient.[3] His notable five principles and three extensions not only embody the cardinal age-area idea, but state some of its chief qualifications as they are generally accepted today. Had Müller's prime interest been theoretic instead of concretely historical, he would no doubt have formulated his principles in terms of abstract methodology. In 1916 Sapir, in his "Time Perspective,"[4] discussed "the concept of culture area from an historical standpoint."

The germ of the culture-area idea is still older. It is implied in such concepts as Orient and Occident, vague though these be. The idea has had its most active development among Americanists. Among the reasons for this is the far greater length of the documentary historic record in much of the Old World. This tended to set a pattern of narrative approach which Americanists could not follow. Further, culture phenomena were on the whole more varied and their currents more complex in the Eastern than in the Western Hemisphere. This is a consequence of the fact that the Americas are smaller and were more sparsely populated (probably later) by what was essentially a single race, containing no extremely advanced civilizations. They were more isolated from the totality of the larger land masses of the Eastern Hemisphere than almost all parts of this were from one another. This comparatively uniform and undocumented mass of native New World culture almost necessitated a static, descriptive approach. The result was that Americanists grew more and more to think in terms of naturally given culture aggregates or types of the order of the Southwestern United States, Mexico, the North Pacific Coast, the Plains; whereas students of the Old World tended to pass more rapidly to direct historical interpretations of the mass of non-historic culture. It is probably no accident that the diffusionist historical explanations of both the Graebner-Foy-Schmidt school and the Rivers-Smith-Perry school, which make almost no use of culture areas as such[5] but attempt to account for most of prehistoric culture, originated

[2] *Anthropogeographie* (Stuttgart: J. Engelhorn, 1891), Vol. II.

[3] *Urgeschichte Europas* (1905). Abstract in Kroeber, *Anthropology* (New York: Harcourt, Brace & Co., 1923).

[4] "Time Perspective in Aboriginal American Culture, A Study in Method," *Canada, Geological Survey, Memoir 90* (1916) (Anthropological Series, No. 13); see esp. pp. on p. 260.—EDITOR.]

[5] [Cf. Herskovits (see n. 7): "The 'culture-area' and the 'kulturkreis' are not the same thing, and must be differentiated." Cf. also the distinction drawn by the analyst on p. 260.—EDITOR.]

in Europe; that they have had almost no following in America; and that they have not even been countered by rival theories here. In the same way, within the Americanistic field Europeans like Rivet and Uhle have advanced views as to the sequence of interrelations of North and South America that are both more ambitious and more specific than any which Americans have ventured to express. In Africa, Frobenius, a German, long ago formulated a Congo-West Coast culture[6] but it was Herskovits, an American, who first attempted to lay out the whole continent in areas.[7]

So far back as the nineties, culture areas were not only "in the air" but actually being used in American ethnology. Eskimo, North Pacific Coast, Plateau, California, Southwest, Plains or Prairies, Eastern Woodland, and Mexican areas had indeed scarcely been defined as to content or delimited on the map, but they were generally accepted as obvious empirical findings, and referred to in placing tribal cultures or culture traits. The evolutionistic display of museum materials had given way to a geographical arrangement, and in this the culture areas were implicit in the names of sections or halls. In 1900 the California Academy of Sciences exhibited a sketch map of North American Indian culture areas. In 1907 Otis Mason, in the article on "Environment" in the *Handbook of American Indians North of Mexico*,[8] listed twelve "ethnic environments" north of Mexico, which, although ecologically conceived, at the same time anticipated the culture areas that later became generally accepted. They were: Arctic, Yukon-Mackenzie, St. Lawrence–Great Lakes, Atlantic Slope, Gulf Coast, Mississippi Valley, Plains, North Pacific Coast, Columbia-Fraser, Interior Basin, California-Oregon, Pueblo Country. In 1912 Wissler used in the American Museum a map label of American archaeological areas; and in 1914 Holmes published[9] an article defining a set of fairly coincident areas.

THE CULTURE AREA

These details are adduced here to make clear that the culture-area concept is in origin a growth, a community product of nearly the whole school of American anthropologists, although largely unconscious or implicit. In 1917 appeared Wissler's *The American Indian*, which has ac-

[6] *Der Ursprung der Kultur: I, Afrika* (Berlin: Gebrüder Bornträger, 1898).

[7] "A Preliminary Consideration of the Culture Areas of Africa," *American Anthropologist*, XXVI (1924), 50–63. *The Cattle Complex in East Africa* (reprinted from the *American Anthropologist*, 1926), 137 pp.

[8] *Handbook of American Indians North of Mexico*, ed. F. W. Hodge (published by the Smithsonian Institution, *Bureau of American Ethnology Bull. 30*), Part I.

[9] "Areas of American Culture Characterization Tentatively Outlined as an Aid in the Study of the Antiquities," *American Anthropologist*, N.S., XVI (1914), 413–16.

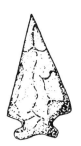

quired some repute as having originated the concept. Wissler himself never made such a claim. He says (p. 218):[10] "A perusal of the literature of our subject shows it to be customary to divide the two continents into fifteen culture areas, each conceived to be the home of a distinct type of culture." This is an overmodest statement; custom before 1917 was still too chaotic to agree on specified areas. Yet it does justice to the essential situation. What Wissler did in his *American Indian* was to name and delimit areas for the whole hemisphere; to list the principal traits characterizing each; to discuss internal subtypes and define the one most characteristic, thereby throwing the ultimate emphasis on culture *centers* instead of culture areas; to examine the relations of these culture aggregates to classifications of earlier culture, of language, and of physical type, as well as to individual culture-trait distributions and to environment. In short, the culture area was both formulated concretely and examined as to its meaning. The standardization, although by no means hard and fast, appealed as so sound that it has been generally accepted by anthropologists, modified or supplemented only in details,[11] and the theoretical findings have never been seriously attacked. At the same time it is historically significant that so important a piece of work was not issued as a contribution to theory but as part of a concrete review and an interpretation of the culture of one native race.

Wissler begins (chap. i) by setting up eight areas of characteristic food: Caribou, Bison, Salmon, Wild Seed, Eastern Maize, Intensive Agriculture, Manioc, Guanaco. These are later (chap. xiv) elaborated into fifteen culture areas, essentially though not formally through subdivision.

Food Areas	Culture Areas
Caribou	Eskimo, Mackenzie (and north part of Eastern Woodland)
Bison	Plains
Salmon	North Pacific Coast, Plateau
Wild Seed	California
Eastern Maize	Southeast, Eastern Woodland (except north non-agricultural portion)
Intensive Agriculture....	Southwest, Nahua-Mexico, Chibcha, Inca-Peru
Manioc	Amazon, Antilles
Guanaco	Guanaco

[10] Page reference is to the second edition (1922).

[11] The only other hemispheric map and list of areas, by Kroeber, *op. cit.*, p. 337, is based on Wissler and differs chiefly in attempting to follow natural boundaries instead of representing the areas diagrammatically.

In the Plains, for example, eleven named tribes, centrally situated, possess the typical culture of the area as defined by some twenty enumerated traits (bison, tepee, dog-traction, camp circle, round shield, sun dance, no pottery, no agriculture, etc.). To the east were fourteen tribes "having most of the positive traits" of the former group, plus some that these lacked (agriculture, pottery); to the west three or four tribes substituting new traits for certain of those possessed by the group in the heart of the area; and similarly on the northeast two or three tribes.

The rather "difficult" Eastern Woodland is treated as follows: There are four subdivisions: (1) Northern (Cree, Naskapi), non-agricultural, similar in material culture to the adjoining Mackenzie area; (2) Eastern Algonkian (Abnaki, Delaware), similar to the last but with feeble cultivation of maize; (3) Iroquoian (Huron, Iroquois), with most intensive cultivation of maize, and culture largely of southern origin; (4) Central Algonkian (Menomini, Fox, Winnebago). This last group is taken as typical of the whole area and defined by forty or fifty traits. The three less typical divisions are more briefly defined.

The summary of the chapter emphasizes intergradation between areas, but disposes of this as an obstacle to classification because the "condition arises from the existence of culture centers, from which culture influences seem to radiate." While a culture area on the map "is in the main an arbitrary division," it contains a culture center which coincides with the habitat of the most typical tribes. Hence the areas "serve to differentiate culture centers." Their mapped "boundaries, in fact, are merely diagrammatic." (The "centers," it must be remembered, are not points, but rather extensive nuclei.) "Social units" (tribes) are a different kind of phenomenon from "culture complexes" (aggregations of culture material).

Subsequent chapters (xv, xvii, xviii) give an analogous classification into twenty-four archaeological, an indefinite number of linguistic, and twelve somatic areas. Chapter xix correlates the classifications. Archaeological cultures are found to tend to coincide with recent cultures, except that in the regions of eastern and intensive maize culture the ancient areas or centers are more numerous, owing to a fundamental change having taken place with the introduction of agriculture (pp. 364, 374). Language and physical type show "a kind of agreement" with culture. The three are "independent groups of human phenomena, each of which tends toward the same geographical centers" (p. 366). Each "culture area tends to have distinctive characters in language and somatology. However, the reversal of this formula does not hold," owing to causes

The Culture-Area and Age-Area Concepts of Clark Wissler

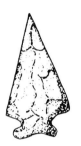

not yet perceived (p. 367). Migration has not been a normally important factor in America, else the centers would have been less stable. In general, populational "shifting was by successive small units" (p. 369); "migratory groups seem unable to resist complete cultural assimilation" (*ibid.*).

A number of environmental correlations are noted. The southeastern culture lies below an altitude of 500 feet; the Eastern Woodland, between 500 and 2,000; the Nahua, above 5,000; the eastern and western divisions of the Plains are separated by the 2,000-foot contour (pp. 368, 369). These altitudes are recognized as only rough indices of areas of climate, flora, and fauna. Wissler is not an environmentalist. Human phenomena, he says,

manifest a strong tendency to expand to the limits of the geographical area in which they arise, and no farther. Language and blood seem to spill over the edges far more readily than culture [p. 369]. . . . . [Although] the location of food areas laid down the general lines of culture grouping . . . . , yet not even all of the more material traits can be considered dependent upon the fauna and flora; for example, pottery [p. 371]. . . . . While the environment does not produce the culture, it furnishes the medium in which it grows, and . . . . when once rooted in a geographical area, culture tends to hold fast [p. 373]. . . . . The origin of a culture center seems due to ethnic factors more than to geographical ones. The location of these centers is largely a matter of historic accident, but once located and the adjustments made, the stability of the environment doubtless tends to hold each particular type of culture to its initial locality, even in the face of many changes in blood and language [p. 372].

In *Man and Culture* (1923) Wissler comes back to review the culture complex, type, area, and center (pp. 51–63), without adding anything new except a greater emphasis on zonal distribution as indicative of age. This inferring of time relations from culture-trait distributions had already been touched upon in *The American Indian* (p. 296). *Man and Culture* further presents time charts of New World culture and Old World prehistory suggested by Spinden and Nelson, and one of Old World culture by Wissler (pp. 216, 218, 220), in which cultural areas (roughly defined in geographical terms) are expressed as abscissae of a time scale. Farther on in this chapter on "The Genesis of Culture," in answer to the question as to where and how the universal culture pattern (chap. v) first arose, the "fundamental lines of cleavage at the dawn of cultures" are defined as arising in a setting of partly arboreal Tundra, warm dry Mesa, and humid tropical Jungle (pp. 227–32); and in the following pages, Euro-American (map, p. 346), Oriental, and Middle

American culture are examined as to their rooting in these three type areas. With reference to the historical functioning of culture centers, an analogy is drawn (pp. 156–57)

to volcanic activity, these different centers appearing as so many crater cones of varying diameter, all belching forth the molten lava of culture, their respective lava fields meeting and overlapping, but, as in true volcanoes, the lavas differ one from the other and from time to time, and each crater contributes something new to the growing terrain. Again craters become extinct and new ones break forth in between.

AGE AREA

The age-area concept or method of inferring at least the relative time sequences of stages of culture-trait or culture-complex developments from the more or less concentrically zonal distribution of phases of such developments is briefly approached by Wissler in *The American Indian* (pp. 296–99, with references to use of the method of Sapir, Boas, Spinden, Lowie, and Hatt) ; it is enlarged upon in *Man and Culture* (pp. 57–63, 110–57) ; and it is made the theme of a book in *The Relation of Nature to Man in Aboriginal American* (1926). In this last work, the concept is systematically developed by Wissler, analogous to its use in the biological sciences, but, as in the case of his forerunners, apparently as the result of independent empirical findings. Essentially, this concept implies that of the culture center as a locus of superior productivity. This center, normally maintaining itself for some time, tends inevitably to radiate culture content or forms to a surrounding zone, which in turn imparts the contribution to a more peripheral belt, while the center, in the interim, is likely to have advanced to subsequent phases of development which normally obliterate more or less the earlier ones. These earlier phases, however, are likely to survive, with greater or less modification, in the marginal zone which they have only recently reached. In principle, a distinction must be made between cases in which the time sequence is independently known through history, inscriptions, or cultural stratigraphy (in biology through paleontological evidence resting ultimately on stratigraphy), and is in agreement with the observed recent space distribution; and cases in which the time sequence is unknown and becomes the goal of investigation, being in that case merely deduced from the space distribution. In anthropology, at least a number of seemingly clear-cut instances of the first type were established[12] before Wissler's venture to set up the principle as a generally valid one and employ it for the finding of the time factor in

[12] As by Sophus Müller, cited above, and Nelson, reproduced in Kroeber, *op. cit.*, p. 191. [Cf. analysis 19, esp. p. 280.—EDITOR.]

cases lacking time data. A still further logical step, though apparently an inevitable one, is the inference that the present center of culmination is also the presumptive locus of origin. In short, there are three elements involved: related phases of a culture trait or complex or culture whole; the spatial or geographical distribution of these; and the time consumed in the accomplishment of the distribution of the phases. When all three elements are known and correlate approximately, there can be no reasonable doubt as to the story of what happened. When the time factor is sought instead of given, the result is no more than an inference; and since the known factors are usually either complex or variable, and difficult of exact measurement, judgments are likely to differ as to the degree of validity of the findings.

In *The Relation of Nature to Man*, Wissler reviews seven traits of material culture (chap. i: tipi, stone collars, hoop and ball games, etc.), nine of social culture (chap. iii: age societies, sun dance, vision-seeking, etc.), and four cases of segregated distributions (chap ii: monolithic ax, feather mosaics, lip plug and the nose stick, ring-neck vase). He concludes that an approach without preconceptions justifies the principle. Segregated distributions of typologically related but differentiable traits warrant the inference of independent invention in each area on the basis of an antecedent "plateau" of continuously distributed culture from which these inventions rise like peaks. Chapter iv applies the same method to somatic traits, with similar results. These have been vigorously assailed by Boas;[13] but as the involvements are biological and not cultural, neither set of arguments need be considered here.

In the fifth and final chapter, on "The Distribution Form and Its Meaning," Wissler first sets up a law of diffusion, "that anthropological traits tend to diffuse in all directions from their centers of origin" (p. 183). Several "dated distributions" (peyote cult, introduction of the horse, grass dance) are next examined and found to support "the assumption that when the distribution of a culture trait-complex takes the concentric zoned form, the zones can be safely interpreted as superpositions, and from these, time relations can be inferred" (p. 197). From this follows a generalized "New World chronology," or sequence of culture stages (p. 203). The concluding section on "The Ecological Basis" (pp. 211–22) inquires into the mechanism which has brought about a form of distribution that is universal, and finds it in ecological factors. However, only a few examples of partial correspondence between ecological and culture areas are suggested; no systematic review of data is attempted; and the conclusion

[13] *American Journal of Physical Anthropology,* IX (1926), 503–6.

is the essentially reasoned one that the American Indian in an ecological area is the end result of a sequence of factors such as climate, flora, fauna, culture.

Of the three books, *The American Indian* presents, organizes, and interprets the largest mass of concrete data; *Man and Culture* is the broadest and most philosophical; *Nature and Man,* the most concisely diagrammatic.

CRITICISMS

The Wissler points of view as to culture area and age area have apparently been used extensively in only one other general work, Kroeber's *Anthropology* (1923) (esp. chaps. vii–viii, x–xiv). There are indications of some growing readiness to apply the method in special cases, as in a recent monograph by Davidson.[14] In Europe, Wissler's works, while commended, appear to have made relatively little impression. This is the more surprising in that *The American Indian,* apart from everything else, provides a most useful outline organization of American data. The reasons apparently are: the current European preoccupation for or against diffusionist theories of single or few origins, and the habit of many students of dealing with actually or essentially historic data.

The first general criticism, of points of view rather than of Wissler's particular works, came from Wallis in 1925.[15] He argues that actual historical data do not bear out the age-area principle. In 3000 B.C. mudbrick dwellings had a wider distribution than bronze; in 100 B.C. bronze extended more widely. Also, the center of distribution or intensive development of a trait shifts within the area with the passage of time. Inference of age from distribution is impossible except at given moments, and these can be determined only from historical data. Wallis' first objection is valid largely when intrinsically unrelated elements of culture are compared, much less so for traits of the same complex. As Wissler points out (*Man and Culture,* p. 146), side-blown trumpets used within an area of end-blown trumpets are almost certainly the later development, whereas comparison with the distribution of rubber balls means very much less. Wallis' counter-examples are of the latter class. His second objection, as to shifting centers, does not seem to strike at the root of the age-area principle, which is not committed to permanent centers, although it may tend to assume them. On his third point Wallis offers no substitute

[14] *The Chronological Aspects of Certain Australian Social Institutions as Inferred from Geographical Distribution* (Ph.D. Thesis; Philadelphia: University of Pennsylvania, 1928).

[15] "Diffusion as a Criterion of Age," *American Anthropologist,* N.S., XXVII (1925), 91–99.

suggestions, and his attitude seems negativistic toward a historical attitude or the recognition of diffusion except within the field of conventional history.

Kroeber, in two papers,[16] has touched on Wissler's ring-neck-vase and arrow-release interpretations. In the first case, additional data lead him to modify certain of Wissler's special findings. In the second case, the same evidence is gone over with partly different construals. The age-area method is accepted in principle by Kroeber, but employed more cautiously. The different conclusions are due partly to a somewhat different rating of the relationship of the five forms or phases of release examined—a point on which agreement is obviously necessary before identical results are even possible; partly to a greater readiness of Wissler to assume probable continuities of distribution across geographical gaps in knowledge; and partly to his not hesitating to relate all the world-wide data in one grand scheme. Kroeber considers this last attempt as of possible but unproved validity.

Dixon's *The Building of Cultures* (1928), which aims to balance diffusion with independent origins, migration, and environmental influences, takes issue with the age-area method on general grounds (pp. 65–75, 179–85) and specifically attacks a number of Wissler's applications: the outrigger (pp. 75–104), the moccasin (pp. 124–28), the grass dance, and the peyote cult (pp. 176–79). Dixon concludes that specialization and modification of traits arise not only at the center of origin, but independently near the margin of diffusions (p. 74); that "the most striking specializations take place as a rule at the very end of the diffusion stream" (p. 140); and that trait complexes disintegrate as they pass into neighboring culture, incorporating as well as losing elements, until they may become quite unrecognizable (p. 180).

Dixon's contention that specializations occur mostly at the peripheries of diffusions seems to be based on the history of the alphabet, which is in its nature an essentially closed system, like a dogma, an established religion, or an art style, which can alter, wear down, split into varieties, disintegrate, or be absorbed, but hardly develop into something else with which it stands in "organic" or intrinsic relation. Its "specializations" are essentially distortions and of a different order from the "specialization" of a three-piece or hard-soled moccasin as against a one-piece moccasin, or of the string-pull Mediterranean release or the ring-engaging

[16] "Ancient Pottery from Trujillo," *Field Museum of Natural History, Anthrop., Memoirs*, II, No. 1 (1926), 1–43 (see pp. 20–21); "Arrow Release Distributions." *University of California Publication in American Archaeological Ethnology*, XXIII, No. 4 (1927), 283–96.

Mongolian release compared with the Primary arrow-hold which a novice with the weapon almost invariably resorts to. Dixon's specializations are, in fact, the Ogham writing with new signs and values, the essentially syllabic Indian systems, Manchu and Korean written vertically in imitation of Chinese, Ethiopic with consonant characters altered for vocalic context. The only fundamental specialization in the alphabet comparable to most of Wissler's cases would be the addition of vowel signs to the original pure consonantal Semitic system; and the historically earliest case of this, by the Greeks, occurred near the hearth of the invention soon after it, and did not spread nearly so far. On the other hand, a highly complex, accreted, presumably recent phenomenon like the sun dance, many of whose parts demonstrably have no intrinsic interrelation but only a secondarily historical and functional interrelation, is also different from elements like moccasins and arrow releases. When Wissler, therefore, subjects the sun dance to the same distribution treatment as moccasins and releases, even though he gets analogous results, the meaning of these results must be different. There is likely to be further argument at cross-purposes in these matters until the various kinds of culture phenomena are more sharply conceptualized.[17]

Dixon's criticisms of Wissler's specific interpretations are based on the grounds that the latter's classification of traits or complex forms is at times arbitrary; that carefully plotted maps show a far less regular distribution than the diagrams or schematic maps used; that data are sometimes loosely employed; and that considerations favorable to the method are weighted at the expense of contrary considerations. When accuracy of scholarship is involved, Dixon's strictures are probably true. Yet, if Wissler suggests or forces interpretations on incomplete or discordant evidence, Dixon evidently combats the age-area method in general, since he concerns himself with it only to refute it. He disinclines as consistently as Wissler inclines.

The sun dance is a case in point. Dixon reproduces Wissler's schematic

[17] Even Sapir, usually extremely exact, speaks of a culture phenomenon appearing "in its most typical or [sic] historically oldest form at the cultural centre" (op. cit., p. 26) and of "the centre of distribution" (in time or space?) of American agriculture as probably assignable to the valley of Mexico (ibid.). Again, he holds that the simple plank house of the marginal Hupa, as compared with the more elaborate one of the Kwakiutl who are central in the North Pacific Coast area, "undoubtedly represents a later period of diffusion, though not necessarily a later type of house" (p. 27). To the contrary, it seems reasonable that the simple house is the earlier in the area, but there is no evidence one way or the other whether the *arrival* of the simple house at the margin or the *development* of the elaborate one at the center is the earlier. Apparently all thinking along these lines of distribution and age is so recent that the categories involved in processes like "diffusion" or phenomena like "complexes" have not yet become sharply defined.

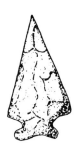

arrangement of Plains tribes (on a basis both of geography and degree of participation in this dance complex) and contrasts it with precise distribution maps, which are far less regular (pp. 168–73). Actually, the case is rather weak both ways: first, because the movements of the tribes in question render a map not very much more significant than a geometric diagram, in this particular instance; second, because both authors leave out of consideration the known historic affiliations of tribes. Both maps (pp. 171, 175) show the Arapaho and Gros Ventre as the tribes possessing most primary traits of the complex. These two tribes spoke closely related languages, associated frequently, and considered each other offshoots of one stock. Next in order come the Blackfoot, with whom the Gros Ventre were in intimate alliance during most of the nineteenth century; the Cheyenne and Wind River Shoshone, who have actually been on reservations with the Arapaho; and the Crow, who were situated between Gros Ventre and Arapaho. Then follow the Teton Dakota, also more or less intermediate geographically; the Kiowa, allies of Arapaho and Cheyenne, who although now marginal on the south were originally farther north; and the Plains Cree and the Assiniboine, for whom no cogent explanation is obvious. The other Plains tribes participate less extensively. Spier's original data on *all* traits in the complex show clearly the influence of the same historic associations. The Arapaho show 54 traits, Cheyenne 46, Blackfoot 37, Gros Ventre 36, Teton 30, Crow 29, Kiowa 28, all others below 25. Only the Wind River fall out here, as might be expected from what is known of their general culture as well as associations; evidently the selection of "primary" traits has happened to read them in. Both proof and disproof are, therefore, largely not pertinent, because the historic facts have been disregarded for a formal distributional approach, which in this case touches accidentals chiefly. What no doubt is significant is that all the highly participating tribes inhabited a continuous territory in the western Plains and were non-agricultural as well as in close relation of some sort with one another; and that the agricultural tribes to the east, and those west of the Rockies, possessed the complex in an attenuated form.

While the other instances examined by Dixon are not wholly parallel to this, they tend also to be technically correct refutations of essentially technical misapplications of the method in question.

REVIEW

If now we attempt to place and appraise the culture-area and age-area principles, it becomes clear that, first of all, they are essentially historical concepts. Wissler says expressly: "In so far, then, as anthropology deals

with culture, which is, after all, the only distinctly human phenomenon in the objective sense, it conceives of it as historical phenomena and this conception is in so far the soul of its method."[18] Whether cultural anthropology is necessarily historical may be and has been questioned; but there is no doubt that the development of the two principles by Wissler is in accord with his enunciation. At the same time, cultural data are being treated from other approaches than the historical. There is the method of examining the functional relations of the parts of one culture at a time, in the hope of finding more or less fixed relations—presumably psychological—that hold good universally or prevalently. This is the "functional" method of Radcliffe Brown and Malinowski, in a measure and less avowedly of Lowie and Goldenweiser, to a greater or less extent of Fraser and other earlier students, and by implication perhaps of Bastian. Another attack recognizes the historic aspects of culture phenomena so far as these aspects are actually demonstrated, but dissects the phenomena in order to isolate their processes as such. This is the aim of Boas and his school, which has sometimes been called, not wholly appropriately, "historical," but might be characterized as "dynamic." In the main the functional, dynamic, and actually historical methods are of course not in conflict, but they differ in objective and weighting of interest. Each is presumably equally legitimate, and its results in its own field should be equally valid. The three approaches have however not often been clearly differentiated and formulated; perhaps because no student has consistently followed one alone.

The difference between Wissler and the English diffusionist and the German *Kulturkreis* schools, which also aim to supply history for historically undocumented periods and areas, lies in the fact that these make their explanations in terms of a single or few origins, respectively, in place of an indefinite number of variable centers. The limitation of factors yields a simplified scheme, but almost inevitably involves an arbitrary or subjective choosing of the original centers. It is characteristic that discussion of the views of these two schools has revolved not so much about the validity of determination of the asserted centers as to whether the facts of culture can be made to fit the schemes of derivation from them. By comparison, Wissler is inductive. The culture areas dealt with are in their nature empirical, and the age-area method, provided it is critically used, is an inductive device.

Turning now specifically to the culture area, we may fairly say that it represents normally a synthesis useful in the organization of knowledge, tinged with a subjective element, and yet evidently resting on something

[18] *The American Indian*, pp. 387–88.

objective because empirical opinion tends to be in essential concord in specific cases. In all these points the culture area is analogous to the faunal or the floral area. In other words, it aims at determining and defining a natural area. Adjacent areas normally intergrade, and progressive dissection can therefore always analyze them out of existence. When analytic interests predominate, this dissecting away happens through the stressing of the intergradations, though even then current culture-area concepts are likely to be retained as lowly, useful tools. The core of the concept, in particular instances, is likely to be the culture center, as Wissler has recognized. This, however, is likely to be not only a "crater" of diffusing productivity, as Wissler has in the main treated it, but also a "focus" or gathering-point. The prevalence of fraying-out margins and intergradations is no warrant for merely diagrammatic representation, except in a preliminary and tentative stage of investigation. A classificatory areal study that cannot be mapped has not found its permanent basis. The same holds true of the center, whether this be conceived as a nuclear area or drawn to a point. If it is worth determining and using, it is worth delimiting. In fact, its utility value in further penetration into history is bound to depend on the accuracy with which it has been determined. Centers shift; they may be multiple for one area; or the centers for different aspects of culture within an area may be more or less distinct. All this is likely to be slurred over if there is no sharp definition. Wissler has done a broad piece of organization where chaos or indecision prevailed before, and perhaps should not be held too heavily responsible for failing to carry his pioneer work into finer detail. The danger is in stopping with his often sketchy and diagrammatic formulations, when they ought to serve as a stimulus for revision and surer knowledge.

For instance, Wissler[19] gives a diagram map of the Plains area with "the most typical tribes" underlined. This "center" however includes a full third of the tribes in the area, and the basis for its determination is only summarily stated. However, an approximation toward a more intensive center can be made from Wissler's own data.[20] The tribes possessing the greatest number of traits of the sun-dance complex are (as above): Arapaho, Cheyenne, Blackfoot, Gros Ventre, Teton, Crow, Kiowa. Of tepee foundations, the three-pole form is probably the most specialized, and is central in distribution. These same tribes use this, except the Blackfoot and the Crow. Age-grading, a specialization on men's societies and also central to the distribution of these, does not occur among Cheyenne,

[19] *Ibid.*, p. 221.

[20] *The Relation of Nature to Man in Aboriginal America*, pp. 2, 81, 85, 233; *The American Indian*, p. 383.

Teton, Crow, or Kiowa. This gives a total of participation in the most intensive forms of these three traits as follows: Arapaho, Gros Ventre, 3; Cheyenne, Blackfoot, Teton, Kiowa, Mandan, 2; other Plains tribes, 1 or 0. This result tallies well with the geographical position and historic affiliations of the tribes. Of course three traits are not enough for final judgment; but twelve or fifteen would begin to furnish a fairly representative sample of the various tribes' status. In this way there might be segregable a nucleolus as well as a nucleus, a median, a submarginal, and a truly marginal series of tribes; and significant subcenters might become apparent. The relations of these in turn to the various intensification stages of adjacent culture areas could then be examined. With enough exact data, precise findings of fairly high probability should result. Of course the point in this example is not the specific conclusion but the method of attaining greater refinement.[21]

Another point at which the Wissler scheme can probably be elaborated with advantage is in the recognition that the culture areas are not equivalent in culture-historical significance but are of different orders. Sapir long ago dwelt on this fact in his *Time Perspective*. In North America, Mexico is obviously unique in being of the first order of intensity of culture. Of second order are the Southwest, the Southeast, and the North Pacific Coast. Of these, the first two are about equally similar to Mexico and therefore presumably partly derived from it, though in different ways. The North Pacific Coast is much less dependent on Mexico, and represents either a largely independent intensification or considerable derivation from Asia. The remaining areas in North America would have to be rated as of the third or even of the fourth order. The Northeast, for instance, is obviously dependent on the Southeast. It differs less in sum total of its culture content from this than the Southeast differs from Mexico, and is more immediately derived. The eastern Plains or Prairies (Pawnee, etc.) are also clearly dependent at many points on the Southeast. It is very doubtful if their total culture is less rich than that of the tribes of the western or true Plains (Arapaho, etc.). The question therefore arises whether a "Plains culture area" as formulated by Wissler and accepted by American anthropologists has full historic validity. What has been considered the "Plains center" may be only a quaternary and late specialization developed on the tertiary culture of the Prairies, which

[21] In an earlier paper, "Material Cultures of the North American Indians," *American Anthropologist*, N.S., XVI (1914), 447–505, 472–73, Wissler actually uses the method suggested above, though with different traits as material to operate on, and comes to the conclusion that "we have good grounds for localizing the center of Plains culture between the Teton, Arapaho, Cheyenne, and Crow, with the odds in favor of the first." The point, however, has not been developed further by him.

in turn is a marginal form of the culture of the Southeastern center, which is secondary to the primary South Mexican growth. Views of this kind cannot be vindicated by evidence here, hardly even fairly developed, but the suggestions cited may suffice to indicate the point of view.[22]

In short, the culture areas codified by Wissler are unduly uniformized as to size, number of included tribes, and implied level. They remain essentially descriptive; their historical potentialities have only begun to be exploited. Wissler recognizes this, but scarcely attempts to use his culture areas for larger historical interpretations. These interpretations[23] are chiefly built up on his reviews of culture traits, complexes, and aspects;[24] the review of culture areas[25] stands apart as a promising but largely unutilized block of organized knowledge.

As regards the environmental basis, Wissler has clearly discerned the primary relation of this to the culture area as a stabilizer and a binder, and has given some apt illustrations of ecological-cultural correlation. These relations, however, in spite of some striking cases, promise on the whole to be highly complex and to yield satisfactorily only to accurate analysis. This aspect of the subject has scarcely been opened as yet.

As to the age-area principle, the analogy to recognized biological method gives support to the essential soundness and the utility of this concept, the more so as its anthropological use was empirically and independently arrived at, not borrowed from the life-sciences. Interest in this method will vary directly with the ultimate objective of study; and when historical interest is slight, distrust of the method will be pronounced. It is in its nature merely a method of inference, supplementary to the direct evidence of documentary history and archaeological superposition; but, as such, it is warranted when it is desired to push beyond the confined limits of this sort of evidence. The age-area principle may never be applied mechanically; culture is too complexly irregular, the resultant of too many factors, to be approached without care, accuracy, and discrimination.

[22] Somewhat analogously, Sapir (*op. cit.*, p. 45), suggests three "fundamental" areas in North America: Mexican, Northwest Coast, and a large "Central" area with Pueblo and Eskimo as its "most specialized developments." The Plains culture he is inclined to see either as a specialization of a more general Eastern Woodland (Northeast) or as a "culture blend" by tribes with original Woodland, Southeastern, Plateau, and probably Southwestern affiliations. In the latter case, the specific Plains features would be construable as "superimposed" or historically late, but as strong enough to have broken up and reassembled the older culture within the Plains area. As regards the fundamental areas, it is interesting that Ratzel (*op. cit.*, Vol. II, map) is not so far from Sapir's suggestion with four North American areas: Mexican, Northwest Coast, "Northeastern," and Eskimo.

[23] *The American Indian*, chap. xix–xxi.

[24] *Ibid.*, chaps. i–xiii.   [25] *Ibid.*, chap. xiv.

The relations of distributional facts assembled by Wissler do seem on the whole to substantiate his claim that migration was culturally a rather unimportant factor in pre-Columbian America. But it did occur; and his own Euro-American area shows that it may at times be of fundamental importance. This is true, similarly, with respect to all other factors that may cut across the operation of normal diffusion and the age-area principle. The danger lies in utilizing the latter too exclusively.

In general, Wissler is circumspect. He is constantly qualifying with terms like "seem" and "suggest," and issuing his findings as merely preliminary indications subject to revision. Their cumulative effect on the reader, however, is likely to be much stronger, and one-sided; and occasionally, in summarizing or in framing broader syntheses, Wissler slips and speaks as if his inferences were proved. Also, Wissler has attempted something rather unique. Two of his books, and much of the third, are historical in objective and yet emphasize process more than result. The historically minded, therefore, complain of looseness and inexactness of facts; those who are interested in processes take alarm at the historical reconstructions as too speculative. Basically, however, this means that Wissler's approach has been broad but lacking in intensiveness and reliably sharp edges. He has done enough with the age-area concept to show that it is not a mere instrument of speculation but a legitimate means of inferential reconstruction when other data fail. That it must be critically handled goes without saying. The age-area principle cannot be applied as between diverse and unrelated elements of culture. Wissler has made this clear. Much of the criticism leveled at the method rests on failure to understand this fact; which also holds in biology. No one would infer respective age of birds and snails from their distribution; but within the limits of a group such as an order, and especially within the genus, the method is constantly being used and apparently with fair reliability.

The culture-area and age-area concepts both rest on the idea of a normal, permanent tendency of culture to diffuse. This principle seems well established. It is accepted even by those who find satisfaction in pointing out cases where other factors have produced contrary results. The two concepts, however, have been brought into little relation so far. The one aims at a static description of large natural aggregations of culture; the other, at discovering sequential developments within isolable items or parts of culture. The concept of the culture center seems to hold the potentiality of co-ordinating these two approaches. It can give the culture area historic depth, and can synthesize discrete age-area findings so as to be interpretable in generalized areal as well as in temporal terms.

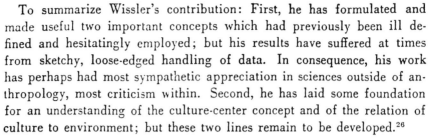

To summarize Wissler's contribution: First, he has formulated and made useful two important concepts which had previously been ill defined and hesitatingly employed; but his results have suffered at times from sketchy, loose-edged handling of data. In consequence, his work has perhaps had most sympathetic appreciation in sciences outside of anthropology, most criticism within. Second, he has laid some foundation for an understanding of the culture-center concept and of the relation of culture to environment; but these two lines remain to be developed.[26]

[26] [This analysis was first written in August, 1928, and received the analyst's final revision in June, 1929.—EDITOR.]

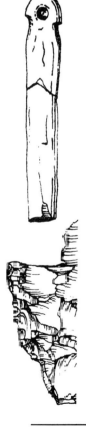

A. L. Kroeber

METHODOLOGY IN THE SOUTHWEST ... It has been said that a new physical type, *Homo americanus*, is evolving out of the various peoples who have made their home in the New World. This is, of course, a matter for the physical anthropologists to decide, but, as archaeologists, it is fitting for us to try to find the cultural characteristics which distinguish such a type. It seems to me that one of the outstanding traits of the species *americanus* is his addiction to filing systems, card catalogues, coloured labels and pins, and the great range of devices which help us to put everything in its place, and have a place for everything. There are probably no other people in the world today who have developed methods of classification to the same degree as have modern Americans, and it is perfectly natural that some of these methods should have crept from business into the sciences.

As a consequence, our fauna and flora, our libraries, and our golf clubs are all neatly tagged with a number, a name, or a label, and the innate yearning of the stamp collector, which is in all of us, can be assuaged by placing the 2 between the 1 and the 3, and our sense of the fitness of things is satisfied.

In recent years, this obsession for method has entered into archaeology, particularly into that of the Southwest, and, in some respects, I have been partly responsible. In about 1928 and 1929, three institutions were founded in the Southwest: the Laboratory of Anthropology, the Museum of Northern Arizona, and Gila Pueblo. Each one of these institutions began a type of investigation which had not theretofore been emphasized, archaeological surveys in which as many sites as possible were visited, surface indications were described, and collections made of sherds and flints, without excavation.

It became immediately apparent that it would be essential to agree on a method of naming and describing what was being found during the course of these surveys, so, at Pecos in 1929, and again at Gila Pueblo in 1930, conversations were held with various interested persons and methods were discussed. As a result, in the summer of 1930, we published *A Method for the Designation of Southwestern Pottery Types* (Medallion Papers VII; W. & H. S. Gladwin, Globe, 1930), in which we proposed a binominal system of naming various pottery types, the main idea being a generic name based on colour, such as black-on-white, and a specific name based on some geographical feature, such as Tularosa. By this means we would avoid any chronological or cultural connotation such as is implied in such terms as pre-Pueblo Black-on-white, or Caddoan Redware.

For several years this method has worked fairly well; most men in the Southwest knew what we were talking about when we mentioned a ruin containing St. Johns Polychrome or Tularosa Black-on-white. Sometimes we found that a large series of ruins, as in the Upper San Francisco Valley, contained Tularosa Black-on-white to the exclusion of St. Johns Polychrome, whereas larger ruins, farther north around the town of St. Johns, contained a smaller amount of Tularosa wares and a great deal of St. Johns Polychrome. It was a logical step for us to begin speaking of a Tularosa *Phase* and a St. Johns *Phase*.

As time went on, a number of such Phases began to form. Then dates were established from tree-rings; a chronological perspective began to form, and, as our surveys covered more and more ground, certain Phases disclosed relationships through common features of pottery designs, architecture, and so on, and the Phases grouped themselves into *Branches*. These Branches, in turn, resolved themselves into *Stems*, so that we had a fairly comprehensive archaeological tree which covered a good deal of territory, and covered the evolution of the Southwest from Basketmaker times up to the present day. Recognizing that our modern tribes are made up of several linguistic stocks, Keresan, Tanoan, and others, it was again rather a logical step for us to employ a little speculation and try to fit these modern features into our picture and see how well such things as physical types, linguistic stocks, material culture, and chronology could be combined to make an intelligible theory.

The result was the publication, in 1934, of *A Method for the Designation of Cultures and their Variations* (Medallion Papers XV; W. & H. S. Gladwin, Globe, 1934). This paper came out at about the same time as the McKern classification, and it is a very remarkable fact that the two methods are almost identical except for the terms employed. There is probably a little more emphasis on chronology in our Phase system than in the McKern method, but this is only because we have had the advantage of tree-ring dating in the Southwest. We have also indulged in a little more speculation in our Roots, possibly more than is justified, but this may be attributed to an over-developed desire on our part to have everything accounted for. Other than this, the methods agree:

McKern	*Gladwin*
Basic Culture (Fundamental determinants)	= Root (Physical Type; Language Stock)
Phase (Important cultural limitations)	= Stem (Major cultural and geographical divisions)

Harold S. Gladwin

Aspect (Characterized by more spe- = Branch (Corresponding in impor-
  cific traits)   tance to Kidder's culture areas)
Focus (Exhibiting peculiarities in cul- = Phase (covering consistent variations
  tural detail)   in culture)
Component (A specified manifesta- = Components have been listed in our
  tion)   Phases, but not named as such.
                                        This designation will be added in
                                        our next revised edition.

Up to this point there is not much to quarrel about; the method has been put to a severe test in our excavations at Snaketown and came through with flying colours. Every feature at the site has been fitted into its Phase, and our analysis of early Hohokam culture has been made infinitely easier because of the system.

But now men are beginning to ask: "How much further are you going in this business of naming things"? Speaking only for ourselves, I think we have gone almost far enough in those cultures of the Southwest which are more or less familiar to most field workers. There will undoubtedly be a few more Phases needed to fill existing gaps, and possibly one or two more Branches, but the end is now more important than the means. If the classification were carried much beyond this point, I should expect to run into a confusion of tongues.

My original suggestion in Medallion VII of using a generic and a specific name for pottery types implied a biological analogy which I now think was a mistake. The idea is being carried too far along biological or zoological lines, and men do not realize the profound differences which exist between zoological species and the things which have been made by men and women.

Zoological species do not cross and intergrade; evolution is so slow as to be hardly distinguishable. The evolution of culture, particularly in the Southwest, was stepped up to almost incredible speed, and on every side we find evidence of merging and cross-influences. The analogy is closer to the barnyard than to zoological species, and the danger is just as great in archaeology of defining new types which some individual may believe to be distinct as it would be to expect that some types of domesticated animals will breed true. We are really dealing with varieties rather than species, and, in consequence, there are bound to be a great many intermediate and transitional types.

If new types shall be created on insufficient evidence, particularly on sherds only, it will be just as if one should find the green tail-feathers of a Brown Leghorn rooster and announce "Ah! a Green Orpington!",

give it an A.O.U. number, and add one's name in brackets as the discoverer of a new species.

Besides the confusion which must inevitably result from an over-indulgence in classification ("Taxonomic Measles", according to Dr. Kidder), there is the difficulty of adequately describing types so that other persons will know what is meant. In the five series of Southwestern pottery types which we have published up to date we have confined ourselves to naming various pottery types which we have believed were distinguishable from one another. To the best of my knowledge there has been no confusion between any two of these types, but recently others have defined and described variations of these types, and actual experience has demonstrated that it is practically impossible to describe such variations in words which avoid confusion.

Several suggestions have been made which have been designed to solve this problem; presence or kind of slip, of tempering material, or of characteristic cross sections. It is probable that such criteria could be determined by petrographic analysis, and used to good advantage, but this requires a thoroughly trained technician and, as the application of petrographic methods to the analysis of pottery is a new technique, it is very difficult to obtain such training in most universities. In addition, this kind of analysis involves considerable expense in the grinding and preparation of thin cross-sections (3/100 mm.). For the average field man such analysis is out of the question, and yet Miss Anna Shepard has shown that these criteria are of little value unless they have been determined by petrographic analysis.

I do not wish to give the impression that I am trying to tell anyone else how his work should be done. At Gila Pueblo we have inaugurated certain methods; some of these have proved to be successful; after giving them a thorough trial, we have published them so that others could take advantage of them if they wished to do so. As far as we are concerned, we have reached the point where we think it is better to strengthen what has been done by more intensive study than to name new variations of pottery or phases which may tend to confuse rather than clarify our minds. This does not mean that finer distinctions will not be made as knowledge increases, nor that such distinctions would not warrant publication when they could be shown to indicate cultural or chronological relationship. It does mean that no method is as important as the result which it is designed to achieve, and that it is possible to defeat both the purpose and the method by too great elaboration of non-essential details.

HAROLD S. GLADWIN, *Vice-President*

From *ANALYSIS OF VILLAGE SITE COLLECTIONS FROM LOUISIANA AND MISSISSIPPI*

James A. Ford

THEORY AND METHODOLOGY

Chronology

At the conference on Southern Pre-history held at Birmingham, Alabama, in 1932, the point was stressed that no program of archeological field research is warranted that is not directed toward the solution of some problem. Unsolved problems are not difficult to find in the south. In fact, to become acquainted with the archeology of the area at present is to realize how little of the great mass of available data has been critically compared and arranged. For analysis and synthesis the south is practically a virgin field.

Work of various degrees of excellence has been done in all the southern states. Unfortunately the programs of the serious investigators have been limited at most to one or two seasons of excavation at sites chosen more or less at random. No sustained, clearly defined program has been attempted. This has resulted in a large conglomerated mass of data that appears to defy all attempts at analysis.

Possibly this state of affairs has caused some observers to fall into the habit of visualizing the cultures that formerly existed in the south as a flat picture—a picture without perspective or time differentiation. That this cannot be the case even a casual survey of the available literature will show. In numerous instances adjacent sites present materials and situations differing to such a degree that there can be slight probability of contemporaneity.

The writer's impression of the general outline of the history of prehistoric southern cultures will perhaps assist in comprehending the reasons for the methodology applied in this paper. The impressions are partly the results of work and general observation in southeastern arche-

4

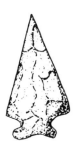

ology; partly they are derived from experience and reading in other fields where cultural histories have been more thoroughly determined.

It seems that most of the country was inhabited by a semi-sedentary population that derived at least half its subsistence from agriculture. Small village communities with outlying farmlands were the rule. Every village was more or less a self-sustained unit, but a certain amount of trade and other intercourse was carried on. Probably some of the town sites which today show large ceremonial earthworks were the religious centers of the surrounding areas. The lives of these early people were comparatively tranquil. The frequent mass movements with consequent friction, which are recorded at the dawn of written history, are probably due to the disturbing influence of the invading white man. Though the population was probably very conservative culturally, there is little doubt but that all through the relatively undisturbed prehistoric period the insidious phenomenon of cultural change was in operation. This process is at work in even the most "static" of cultures. The peoples involved were not necessarily aware of what was occurring. Slow evolutionary changes were probably usual, but marked changes occurred in certain areas through wholesale adoption of foreign styles or the actual replacement of populations either through gradual infiltration or conquest.

Territorial distinctions in cultural features were developing as the result of geographic isolation of groups. Probably some shifting of population brought widely variant cultural groups into proximity. A certain amount of merging and refocalizing might be expected along the lines of contact.

As the cultures moved on in a restless everchanging flow through time, local communities were undergoing certain geographic changes. At various times new village sites were occupied and some old ones abandoned. Possibly part of this shifting might be accounted for by depletion of the land through primitive agricultural methods or changes in natural features, that is, movements of rivers, silting up of lakes, etc. It is futile to guess at the causes. The large number of old villages found in uninhabited areas at the time of the coming of the white man indicates that there was a constant shifting. A few of these were pointed out by the Indians as sites from which their groups had recently moved.

With this sketch in mind, it is apparent that no true treatment of materials in an area can ignore temporal relationships. The results of careful research will not be a closely knit, flat picture of everything found, but must be a series of such pictures, each representing a sample taken at a definite time horizon.

This concept leads directly to what has been called the historic method of attack. A plan applicable to the southeast may be outlined as follows:

I. Develop a measure of time in terms of cultural changes.

    A. By working from the historic period back into the prehistoric.

    B. By using the most practical means available, preferably a cultural element (or elements) which:

        1. Is available in quantities sufficient for adequate comparison without extensive excavation,

        2. Is least subject to a logical form dictated by the materials of manufacture.

        3. Is least likely to be subject to possible conservative influences of religion or taboo.

II. With the cultural time scale at hand, excavate sites which will elaborate the details of the cultures at the various time levels. At the same time test, and if possible subdivide, the time scale.

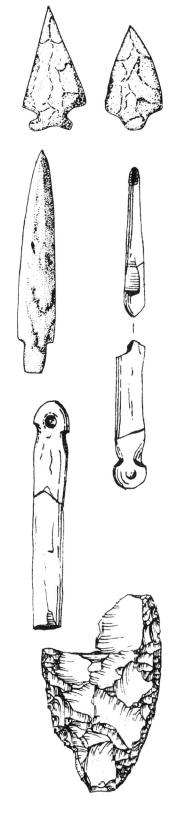

From *Analysis of Village Site Collections from Louisiana and Mississippi*

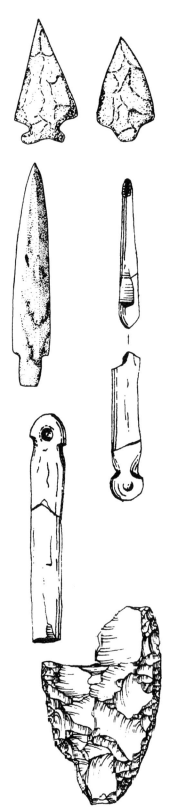

This paper is an attempt to carry out the first part of this program in portions of Louisiana and Mississippi. If this is successful and a fairly reliable time scale can be determined, the archeologist is placed in somewhat the same enviable position as the geologist who collects fossils from different strata of known comparative ages. In this way the true relationships of cultural materials may be expected to appear.

A fundamentally different approach to relationship problems is being applied by McKern, Deuel, and other investigators to the Indian remains in the northern United States. On the basis of taxonomy, they are arranging the cultural complexes into a biological-like system of general culture bases which are subdivided into patterns, aspects, foci, and most specific divisions of components. This method appears to be most valuable in clarifying the degree of relationship between the various cultural complexes. Finally it may solve, or assist in solving, temporal relations.

The nature of the McKern method demands a comprehensive number of carefully excavated sites to determine the cultural characteristics from which comparisons must be made. The southeast is lacking in a sufficient number of such sites to permit a very significant analysis of this kind. That the next step should be a program of excavation to secure this data is very doubtful. Situations and material are disturbed in excavating and cannot be duplicated. More intelligent observation may be expected if this can be done with a knowledge of the significance of the material.

Effective attack demands method. Underneath the methodology must lie a foundation of theory. Our problem has already been presented: to determine chronological relationships. The methods used in the work and the theories which led to the adoption of these methods will be discussed in the following pages.

8

In the Lower Mississippi Valley, the requirements for a cultural factor suitable for an analysis of time change appear best to be met by the fragments of domestic pottery which have been broken and unintentionally deposited on the sites of the old villages. The specific advantages are that: (1) potsherds are available in almost unlimited quantity without disturbing the sites; (2) clay, the material of which pottery is made, has a great range of possible and practical shapes and ornamentations; and (3) conservative influences retarding changes of style were probably at a minimum on these domestic utensils. Comparison is facilitated and made more profitable by the fact that southeastern ceramic art was in a rather complicated and specialized stage. No midden deposits have been found in the local area that lack decorated potsherds.

As has already been demonstrated in the archeology of the southwest, it may be expected that the ceramic art of this region will be held stylistically within fairly definite bounds of time and space, will show influence from neighboring contemporaneous areas, and will have evolved or changed with time. Concentric diffusion may also be expected. However, the relatively small area under consideration probably is not sufficient to measure this phenomenon. The writer has the impression at present that the entire eastern United States is closely involved in the diffusion of ancient pottery styles.

There are certain material limitations to potsherds as the basis of ceramic study. The sites of the old villages in the local area are generally excellent for purposes of modern agriculture, and usually have been in cultivation for a number of years. As a consequence, the vessel fragments are reduced through breakage to very small sizes. This makes difficult the significant correlations of decoration with vessel appendages and shapes, and, in a number of cases, obscures the plan of the decoration.

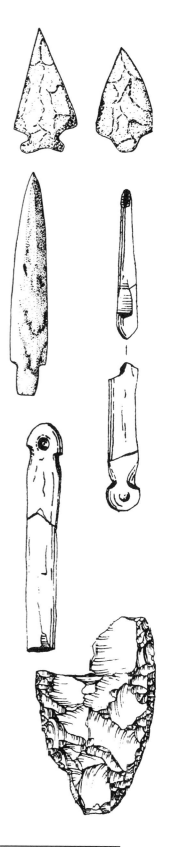

From *Analysis of Village Site Collections from Louisiana and Mississippi*

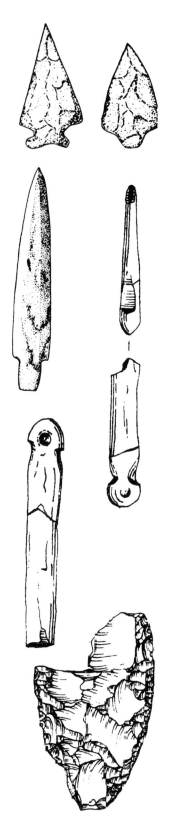

These failures of sherd collections should eventually be corrected by the supplementary evidence of entire vessels secured from burials.

In the past, burial collections have been given major emphasis by archeologists working in the Lower Mississippi Valley. The intact condition of the material is a distinct advantage, and, when the sites are properly excavated, it is often possible to determine directly the relative age of specimens at any one site. However. burial collections are subject to possibilities of selection, peculiar mortuary styles, and possible lag due to ceremonial conservatism. There is also the possibility that some of the mound building peoples did not inter their dead, or at least buried only a few. This may explain why no pottery of the exceedingly common Coles Creek types was secured in the local area by Clarence Moore or other investigators. As a matter of fact the writer does not know of a single entire vessel representative of some of the common Coles Creek types.

Several of these objections are material and are the sources of some of the errors that have been made in attempting to visualize the relationships of southeastern ceramics. No attempt is being made to minimize the usefulness of burial collections. When the degree to which they reflect the real trends of domestic ware is determined, invaluable supplementary evidence is provided. At the same time the burial ware may present a special set of cultural features which will be parallel to, and will assist in checking the relations evident from, the domestic ware.

There is another very evident possibility of limitation of the diagnostic value of surface sherd collections for determining the relative age and period of time covered by a site. This lies in the chance that the midden deposit at a site may be of such a thickness that the oldest material, laid down in the lower strata, will not appear on the surface. This would result in an incorrect impression as to the extreme age of the site. The chances that this will have happened frequently are slight. Few sites have refuse dumps of greater thickness than the depth to which plowing penetrates, and most of the sites are in cultivation. Many villages are on slightly rolling ridges. Cultivation has taken most of the surface soil off the highest part of the ridge, exposing the top of the subsoil; and, in making collections, special attention is paid to washes and gullies that have eroded into the site. There is usually a concentration of material in such places. Except in cultures which either accumulated garbage very rapidly, or which remained static for long periods of time, such a thing as completely buried strata is improbable. Although super-position may be found at definite spots at some village sites, almost certainly a shifting of the houses, or of the village sites as a whole will have occurred during the period of deposition, leaving the older stratum exposed in some places.

The possibility of a buried stratum at any one site is not a matter of great importance. In this study the desired results are not the ages of individual sites, but the relative ages of the different schools of ceramic art. It is not probable that there could be a buried stratum, representing an old time period, buried at every site at which that stratum occurs. Considering the large number of sites found in this area, there should be many villages which were abandoned during each period, and which were not reoccupied, thus leaving the pottery characteristic of each period on the surface.

After the foregoing, it is hardly necessary to mention that the theories in this study are based upon the assumption that the collecting surveys have succeeded in obtaining a sample of all of the schools of pottery art that have been used in the region. In view of the intensiveness of the surveys, especially in certain parts of the area, this assumption seems fair.

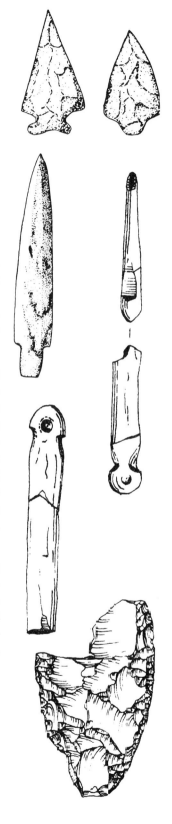

From *Analysis of Village Site Collections from Louisiana and Mississippi*

It is also evident that no conclusions can be based on the collection from an individual site. Since comprehension of the stylistic periods and areas is the object of the study, the conditions on any one site must be compared and checked by others in order to be certain of the true conditions that obtain.

Collecting methods

The methods of collecting the material were practically uniform. In all cases, unless otherwise stated, collections were not excavated, but came from the surface. Most of the old village sites are found in plowed fields. Since the middens are not ordinarily more than six to eight inches deep, the material has been thoroughly mixed by years of cultivation.

The collectors have tried to secure as much material as possible from all parts of the village dumps. Collecting conditions vary at different times of the year, and many of the collections used have been obtained by making repeated visits to a site.

Careful surface examination of a number of sites has shown no tendency for certain types or combinations of types to be segregated in different parts of the area covered by village refuse. Such segregation might be expected in some cases from shifting of individual houses, or the entire village, while styles were changing. This phenomenon is often observed in carefully excavated sites. Possibly long cultivation of most of the old villages, with the consequent dragging and washing of surface material has destroyed evidence of this nature.

Either while making the collection, or later in the laboratory, the sherds were sorted. Only those pieces were retained which promised to yield information concerning vessel decoration, shape, tempering material, or appendages. All rim sherds and all pieces that showed untypical texture or thickness were saved.

Detailed descriptions of sites, including maps where desirable, were made on mimeographed form sheets. As much information as possible has been obtained on the few sites not visited by the survey parties.

The collections presented here represent only a very small portion of all sites located and examined. Many other collections which are not considered ample for quantitative study are on file. All have been examined, and appear to substantiate the situations outlined in this paper.

Necessity for quantitative analysis

Quantitative analysis of site collections is necessary in order to evaluate correctly the relative popularity of different decoration types. Such evaluation is of paramount significance in comparing sites for the following reasons:

(1) It may be expected that two sites occupied through the same period of time, under the sway of the same school of ceramic art, will yield nearly identical decorations in about the same proportions.

(2) The assumption is usually possible that, while decorations characteristic of a school of art will form a major proportion of the material at their native sites, on contemporaneous sites of different modes to which they might have been traded or were the results of imitation, they will be in the minority.

(3) Provided the factor of population had remained nearly constant, a village inhabited through two style periods could be expected to show a majority of the material characteristic of the period in which it existed the longer. This assumption involves the very uncertain population factor; hence, it is fortunate that it is not essential in building a relative time scale.

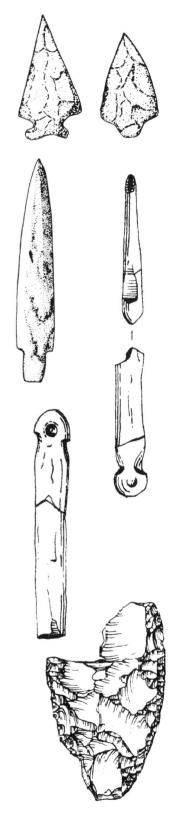

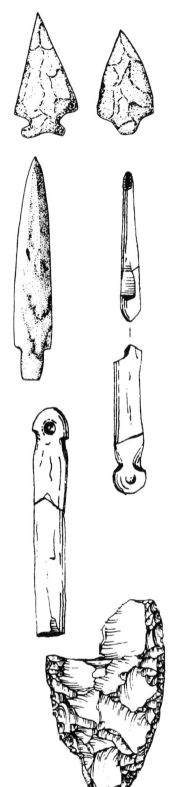

Quantitative reliability of random collections

There follow certain possibilities, inherent in the method of collecting, of quantitatively misrepresenting the prevailing modes at any one village site.

One source of error might be the possibility that the collection would contain duplicate sherds from the same vessel. This is rather improbable because a very small percentage of the total amount of the material on any site is exposed on the surface and recovered by the collector. In a few cases, when sherds from the same vessel are found among excavated material, they are readily detected due to identity of decoration, execution, paste, thickness, curvature, and color.

A more important problem is the extent to which random surface collections actually represent the different types of material present on the surface of the deposit. An attempt has been made to determine this reliability by comparing collections made at different times from thirteen sites.

The percentage of the different types in each collection was first determined. Then the average differences between type percentages in collections from the same sites were computed. This is called average variation. Where three collections were involved, the difference between the largest and smallest percentage of each type was taken as the variation of the type. If a type appeared in one collection but not in the other, the variation was considered to be from zero to the percentage to which the type was present.

The range is the greatest variation found in comparing any one type.

In the following table, repeated collections from thirteen sites are arranged in order of increasing average variation:

Site	No. Sherds			No. Types Involved	Average Variation	Range: Extreme Variation
	Coll. A	Coll. B	Coll. C			
Prichard Landing	64	118	....	32	.016	.05
Coles Creek	77	98	....	38	.021	.14
Churupa Place	97	101	89	12	.024	.06
Mazique Place	95	70	....	24	.024	.09
Harrison Bayou	99	74	....	23	.028	.12
Sidney Biggs	48	76	....	31	.030	.104
Wilkinson Place	68	84	....	18	.030	.105
Smith Creek	60	87	203	23	.034	.08
Old Rhinehart	31	111	....	15	.034	.085
Pocahontas	129	73	....	25	.036	.155
Chase Place	32	115	....	26	.041	.27
Colbert Place	61	44	....	21	.05	.23
Alphenia Landing	25	38	....	14	.073	.29

Extreme variation increases in the same order, but at a somewhat faster rate. Both of these factors are in rough inverse proportion to the number of sherds comprising the collections; the larger the collections, the smaller the variations, and vice versa.

It is very improbable that the types in several collections from a site should differ from the true conditions on the site in the same numerical direction. It seems more probable that the type percentages in different collections are both more and less than the true percentage, so that the difference between the percentages in two collections will not be greater than the difference between either collection and the true conditions.

If this is correct, the average and extreme variations shown above may be accepted as marking the probable degree to which random collections of different sizes will reflect the true conditions on a village site.

Qualitative reliability

Obviously a consideration of ceramics solely on the basis of decoration and such notable features as square bottoms, handles, lugs, and peculiar rim types is not giving a complete picture of the original ceramic complex. There are certain types of ware, which are often discovered at excavated sites, that are marked by simple though

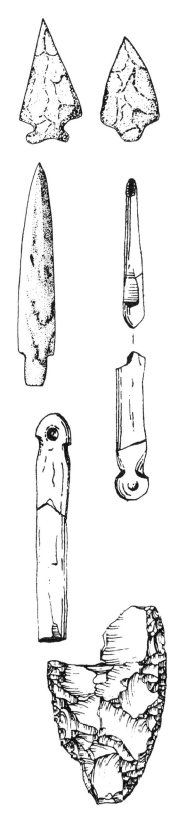

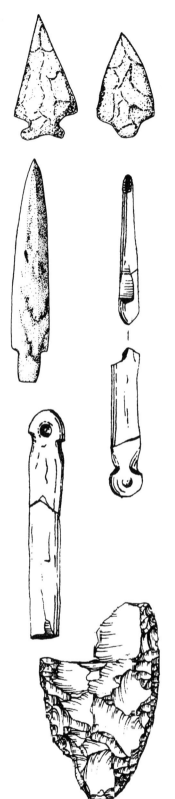

distinctive shapes and peculiarities of paste. These have certainly been overlooked in this study. This is regrettable, but is not particularly material to the real objective. A comparison must be based on specific features. The information that may be gleaned from these is intended to serve as a guide to more detailed investigation. This will give fuller information on the pottery complexes as well as on the many other cultural elements that are also neglected in this work.

Discussion of classification

In order to facilitate minute comparisons, the large mass of material composing the village site collections made necessary a uniform system of classification. Empirical classifications, such as must be used for this material, are not simple, and always must leave much to be desired in the way of objectivity.

Limitations of village site collections of potsherds as sources of information concerning vessel shape, size, and associated features have been discussed. Decoration is the most variable factor of vessel design that can be consistently determined to any degree of certainty. For this reason, it must serve as the principal basis of the classification system. Peculiarities of shape, size, and appendages must be determined wherever possible and treated in a more general manner. They appear to correlate more or less with particular decorations; hence it is possible to describe these features as the "usual accompanying characteristics".

The ordinary difficulties inherent in all attempts to categorize cultural phenomena are present in potsherd decoration classification. While specific types are apparent around which most of the material clusters, there are cases of intergradation of types and of unusual combinations of features. It is a difficult matter to try to describe as well defined types the remains of what once were living artistic styles. Fortunately the few rebels practically never succeeded in entirely divorcing themselves from their artistic background. Relationships of unconforming sherds can usually be determined by peculiarities of the decoration elements and by characteristic combinations of these elements. However useful such diagnosis may be to the worker in the field or laboratory who has developed a "feel" for the material, naturally it cannot be used as the basis for a comparative study. Fortunately widely divergent pieces are rare.

The fragmentary nature of potsherds demands an intimate knowledge of the different parts of the decorations. Two pieces from separated parts of the same decoration may appear entirely different, and it is only through thorough knowledge that they can be correctly identified. Certain types of decoration are more readily and certainly identified than others. For example, cord marking is apparent from a very small sherd, but even a large piece of a decoration with a complicated motif sometimes will not give a clue to its nature. In the work of classifying, where there is any possible doubt as to the identification of a type, the type is not allowed unless it occurs in easily recognizable form on other sherds in the same collection.

There is still another way in which errors are bound to occur in classification. In types which are formed by the combination of two or more elements, and where the isolated elements also form decoration types, there is the possibility that only one of the elements may appear on a sherd. The other element may have been present in the original decoration, but through its loss the sherd will be referred to the wrong type. For example, the combination of a number of overhanging lines drawn parallel to the vessel rim with a single row of triangular punctates just below and parallel to the lines forms a common decoration. Another type consists of the arrangement of overhanging lines without the row of punctates. It is clear that if a sherd of the first described decoration is broken so that it does not include

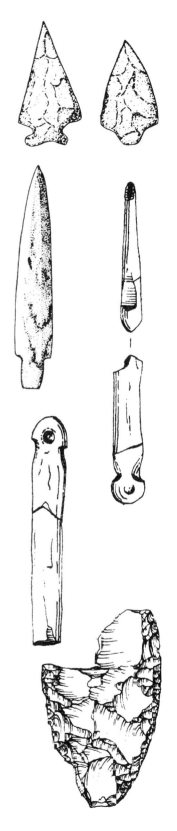

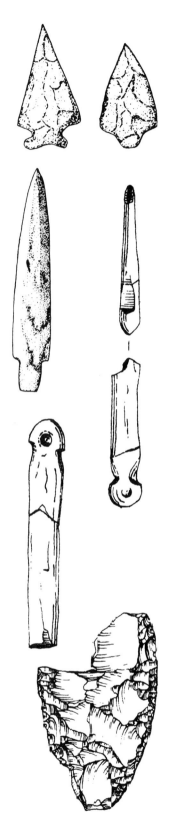

the lower part, it will be included in the second described type. This is usually not a very serious mistake, and no great errors are likely to come of it. The types that can be mistaken for others are generally very closely related, and occur in the same groups of decorations.

In each site collection, there are always a few sherds that have so small a part of some decoration that they cannot be used. Often this is nothing more than a single incised line. Such pieces have been ignored in presenting tabulations of classified material; they can add nothing. Introducing them into the tables would only result in upsetting the percentages of the serviceable material. None of the collections examined show as much as ten per cent of such pieces; the average is more like two or three per cent.

Proper orientation of a potsherd will often aid materially in determining the decoration of which it is a part. Orientation is generally possible because of the tendency of fractures to occur along coil lines. All of the pottery of the region, except an occasional very small bowl, was made by the coiling process. The flattened coils are from one to two inches wide, and the lines along which they have been joined are weak places in the vessel walls. Coil line breaks run almost parallel to the vessel rim, and can be recognized by their straightness and the concavity or convexity of the broken surface. From vessels whose coil junctures are weak, sherds break out as fairly regular rectangles.

Classification systems

A system of classification that will deal satisfactorily with such an elastic and variable thing as art is yet to be found. The writer has considered and tried several different plans.

Noteworthy among the discarded methods is a morphological, biological-like arrangement of decorations into orders, suborders, families, etc. This proved unsatisfactory because of the extreme flexibility of pottery types, as well as doubt as to their generic relationships. The frequent migration of decoration elements from what seemed to be their native types was of significance, and could not be indicated by the method. Zoological classification is not embarrassed by such anomalies as would result from the frequent crossing of different species.

An analytical system of classification was tried on collections from twenty-seven sites. It attempted to record specific decoration features, combinations of these features, execution, temper, paste, texture, thickness, hardness, vessel shape, and vessel appendages. The impracticability of this plan developed in attempts to detect significant correlations.

The system which was finally applied was very simple and uncomplicated. In effect, it was merely a list of decorations recorded on index cards and arranged under general headings to facilitate filing and reference. The index was expanded as new types were found. Unusual specimens were sketched. Later, if they conformed to newly determined types, they were classified. From time to time, as the general characteristics—temper, execution, vessel shape, etc.— became apparent, they were noted on the type cards.

This method is highly subjective; much is left to the judgment of the classifier. This was limited as much as possible by having only one classifier, by expanding the index freely to accommodate minute type variations, and by excluding all doubtful specimens from detailed classification.

The "index" method, dependent as it must be on the classifier's acquaintance with the material, was not suitable for presentation. It was only semi-systematic, was non-analytical, was meaningless unless memorized in detail, and was not capable of logical expansion.

Near completion of the work of classification, another system was developed which overcame some of these objections. Since all of the collections were not readily available for direct reclassification, and the types could easily be transferred to the improved method, this was done directly.

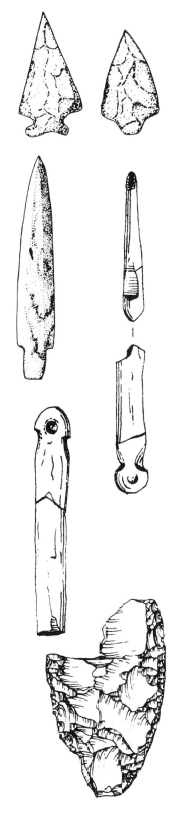

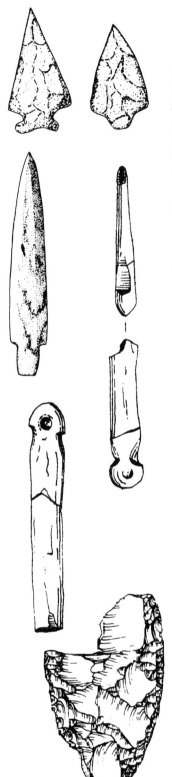

The present system is analytical in nature. Two components are considered to be present in every decoration: motifs and elements. Motif is the plan of the decoration: scroll, parallel features, herringbone, etc. Elements are the means used to express the motif, i. e., incised lines, rows of punctates, rouletting, etc. Another significant factor which deserves consideration is the specific and peculiar manner of using the elements to form the motif.

Motifs, elements, and specific applications occurring in this study are listed below.

Decoration motifs

Symbols in this list occupy the first position in the type expressions.

00 Motif uncertain.
    01 Too small a fragment to permit identification.
10 **Irregular** application.
    11 Elements arranged without order over the vessel surface.
20 **Regular** application.
    21 Elements spaced at regular intervals over surface of vessel.
30 **Features arranged in bands.**
    31 Curving bands from one to two inches wide. Bands often branch.
    32 Straight bands that turn at right angles; one to two inches wide.
    33 Straight bands dropped at right angles to the rim; one to two inches wide.
    34 Bands forming curving, unconvoluted, compressed scrolls.
40 Scroll and scroll-like arrangements.
    41 Convoluted scrolls formed by a number of lines.
    42 Guilloche, or rope-like arrangement.
    43 Curvilinear meander.
    44 Scroll figures formed by straight lines with right angle turns.
    45 Curving scroll-like lines that often branch.
50 **Chains of triangles or flags.**
    51 Chain of isosceles triangles in a row parallel to the rim. Alternate triangles are inverted and nested so that a solid band of decoration is formed.
    52 V-shaped flags in a row parallel to the rim and hung either from the rim or from a line just below and parallel to the rim.
    53 U-shaped flags arranged in a row parallel to the rim.

54   Features arranged in **zigzags**; similar to a "worm fence" made of rails.
60   Features arranged parallel to one another or in parallel rows.
    61   Arranged parallel to the vessel lip.
    62   At forty-five degree angle to the vessel lip.
    63   Perpendicular to vessel lip.
    64   Series of herringbone arrangements **parallel** to vessel lip.
    65   Series of herringbone **arrangements perpendicular** to lip.
70   Crosshatching.
    71   Features run forty-five degrees to vessel lip.
    72   Lines run forty-five **degrees** to vessel lip. A punctate is centered in each diamond formed.
    73   Lines run forty-five **degrees** to vessel lip. Alternate diamonds are filled with **features**.
80   Features applied to the vessel lip.
    81   In the flat top of square lip.
    82   On the inside of outflaring lip.
    83   In flattened, outward-slanting lip.
    84   Features applied to rounded or pointed lip.

Decoration elements

Symbols in this list occupy the second position in the type expression.

20   Incised lines.
    21   Lines incised with a pointed instrument. These were made while the paste was still soft.
    22   Lines made with a blunt instrument. As much as one-fourth inch wide. Usually rough. Made while vessel paste was soft, so that the lines are plowed with uneven and ragged edges.
    23   Wide, deep lines, semicircular in cross section. Apparently made with a cane held at an acute angle to vessel surface. Paste was firm enough to result in clean cut (not plowed) lines.
    24   Overhanging lines. Incised with a flat, pointed instrument, held at such an angle that the tops of the lines are deeply incised, while the bottoms rise flush with the surface of the vessel wall. Made when paste was firm.
    25   Incised lines made with a pointed instrument. Small punctates are spaced in lines at short intervals.
    26   Lines, either incised with a pointed instrument before firing, or scratched after firing. Sometimes even incised after the surface was polished. Small spurs are spaced at short intervals on one side of the lines. Where the decoration was made in soft paste, the spurs are short lines; where scratched, they are often tiny triangles.
    27   Scratched lines. These were made after the vessel was fired.

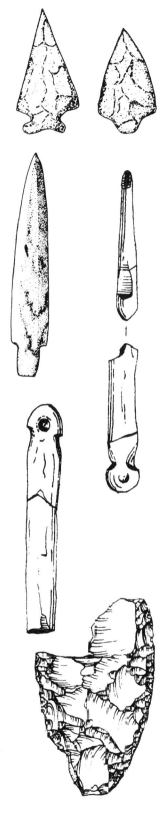

28   Fine crosshatching made with delicate lines. This is either incised or scratched.

30   Combed lines.

    31   Narrow bands of lines made with a comb-like instrument. From four to six lines are usual. Lines are fine, and were incised in firm paste before firing.

40   Brushed decoration.

    41   Brushed with a bundle of fibers while vessel surface was plastic.

    42   Brushed by fingers held side by side while paste was plastic.

50   Rim notches.

    51   Deep notches cut into lip. Rough finish.

    52   Shallow scallops cut from outside edge of lip.

    53   Large scallops cut into rim.

60   Finger tip markings.

    61   Fingernail imprints.

    62   Rough areas raised by pinching between two fingers.

    63   Modeled teats or small nodes. Made with fingers, rough.

    64   Rough ridges raised by pinching between the fingers.

70   Punctates.

    71   Punctates made with a pointed instrument. Rough.

    72   Imprints made with the end of a cane cut at right angles.

    73   Semi-conical punctates, made with the end of a cane held at an acute angle to the vessel wall.

    74   Triangular punctates, shaped as though made with the corner of a cube. These are both large and small.

80   Fabric and cord imprints.

    81   Imprints of a cord wrapped paddle.

    82   Imprints of coiled basketry.

90   Stamp impressions.

    91   Check stamp (Louisiana coast types).

    92   Curvilinear stamp (Atlantic coast types).

    93   Zigzag stamp.

100   Rouletting.

    101   Large zigzag made either by an unnotched wheel or rocker stamp.

    102   Linear rouletting made with a notched wheel. Teeth about .1 inch square.

    103   Linear rouletting. Delicate. Made with a notched wheel with pointed teeth.

    104   Rows of delicate punctates that are almost indistinguishable from the delicate rouletting described as element 103.

110   Paint.

    111   A brick red, applied as a wash, before firing.

Adaptation and arrangement of features

Where used, these symbols occupy the third position in the type expression.

1 Motif brought out in negative. Inferior elements are used to fill or stipple the background so that the motif is formed by the undecorated surface.

2 Positive motif. Elements are used to fill the area of the motif so as to differentiate it from an unmarked background.

3 Bands an inch or more wide formed by a number of lines.

4 Four to six lines used to form bands not over half an inch wide.

5 Narrow bands not over half an inch wide formed of three lines; less often of four lines. This is usually accompanied by small circles used as nucleuses, and triangles made with a three-line band that serve as fillers in the vacant parts of the decoration.

6 Elements placed closely together; generally touching.

7 Elements placed over three-eights of an inch apart.

8 Only one or two lines used.

9 Single row of the feature described by the lower numbers in type used below the main decoration.

10 Features described by the lower numbers in the type used at the ends of lines.

11 Described features alternate to form pattern.

12 Features are used in the top of a short thickened area in the lip. Viewed from above this area is triangular in shape.

13 Decoration is on the vessel interior.

14 Decoration is applied to the entire exterior of the vessel.

In the above list, it will be noted that motifs and elements are arranged in typologically related groups. Each item is given two numbers: the first designates the group to which the motif or element belongs; the second specifies the particular members of each group.

Simple vessel decorations are expressed in terms of this classification by three sets of numbers which are separated by semicolons. These represent respectively: motif, element, and combination (example: type 45;23;6). Where no peculiarities of combination need be expressed, this designation is omitted; the index then consists of only two sets of figures (example: type 11;63).

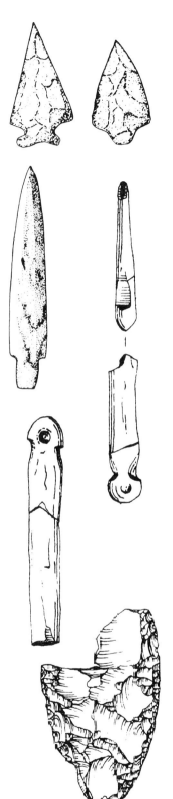

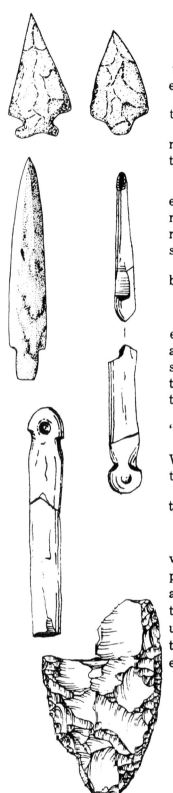

Cases of two motifs or two elements involved in the same decoration are described by placing the most essential feature over the less important (examples: type $\frac{53}{61}$;21;2 and type 61;$\frac{24}{74}$;11). Body motifs are over motifs applied to the lip. Elements which outline motifs take precedence over those used as stippling.

Where two motifs are used in the same decoration and each is expressed by a different element, the dominant motif with its element is placed over the inferior. If the manner of combination applies specifically either to the superior or inferior features, it also is placed either above or below the line (example: type $\frac{61:24;6}{81;25}$).

In some cases the old classification included two sets of elements or modes of application, either of which was allowed in the same type. To transfer these it is necessary to show that either one or the other comprises the type. This is effected by listing both feature designations and separating them by a slanting line to signify "or" (examples: type 63;$\frac{24\ 21}{71}$;10, and type 53;111;1/2). Where two elements were used to express the same motif, their designations were divided by commas (example: type 34;$\frac{26,27}{21/28}$;1).

The principal advantage of this system is the facility with which specific parts of the different types may be compared from a list of the type symbols. Thus, if it is desirable to know how often overhanging lines (element 24) or triangular punctates (element 74) appear in the list of types used in the table given as figure 1, all that is necessary is to note where the appropriate numbers are used in the element column.

Decoration complexes

As the work of classifying the village site collections progressed, it became apparent that on the basis of decorations the sites could be placed in several different categories. This tendency is clearly shown in the comparative table, figure 1. The types found at sites thus differentiated were so very dissimilar that it appeared probable that they were the results of the sway of distinct and separate schools of ceramic art styles. The term "decoration complex" will be used to refer to each of these groups of peculiar artistic styles.

Nearly all the decorated material conforms to the types of seven different complexes. Four have been associated with historic tribes and from these have received their names: Choctaw, Natchez, Caddo, and Tunica. The other three appear to be entirely prehistoric in the local area and are named for sites at which they were first recognized: Deasonville, Coles Creek, and Marksville.

The few scattered types that cannot be associated with any of these complexes are of two classes: either they are found so infrequently that their association is uncertain, or they are commonly found in more than one complex. These are listed in the comparative table as "unrelated" types (see Figure 1).

The seven complexes that have been found in the Louisiana-Mississippi area have rather well defined geographical limits along the boundaries that occur within the region studied. In dealing with semi-sedentary cultures this development of localized areas is to be expected. The few cases where isolated villages are found far outside the normal range of their particular pottery complex can be attributed to the white man's interference with the normal life of the people. Such examples are the Choctaw site found in Louisiana on the Marksville prairie (Site No. 4, Nick Place, page 48), and the Natchez Fort site, near Sicily Island (Site No. 7, page 65).

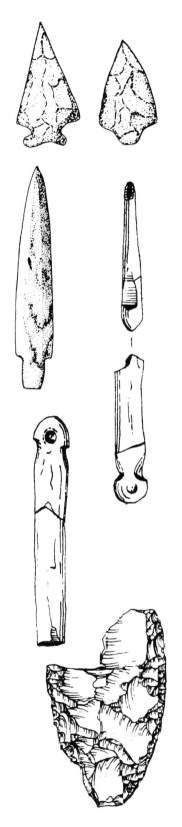

From *Analysis of Village Site Collections from Louisiana and Mississippi*

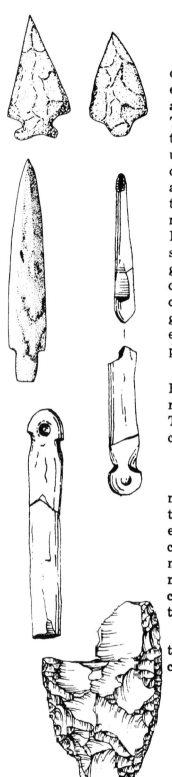

As far as historical evidence goes, the types of pottery determined for the various tribes found by the European explorers are very consistently associated with those tribes, and are confined to the areas they are known to have held. This is true in all except one case—the late Tunica site at the mouth of Red River (see page 129). In view of this usual correlation, it seems best to attach the names of the different groups to the types of ware with which they are associated. It is recognized that back of the historic period there can be no certainty that the historic Choctaw type of material was always and only made by the Choctaw tribe. However, it is as simple to keep this fact in mind as to associate a different name for the material with the historic groups of Indians. As used here, the tribal names have become archeological terms that describe certain decoration complexes. All attempts to project political or linguistic groups back into the prehistoric era are questionable; archeology can only speak with confidence in terms of a small part of the material culture.

The names of the complexes refer only to ceramic styles. It is intended that they serve for this purpose only until all recoverable evidence of the old cultures has been secured. Then appropriate names, arranged according to some accepted system, may be adopted for the cultural divisions.

Internal characteristics of decoration complexes

All the complexes in the area except the Choctaw are made up of several decoration types. In the Coles Creek, there are as many as thirty-six distinct types. Of course, every type is not found on each site where any one of the complexes dominates. This probably results from the smallness of some of the collections. That a type appears on a majority of the sites representing a complex must be accepted as evidence that it is associated with that complex of types.

The numerical proportion of the different types in their respective complexes proves to be of special significance. In each complex one or more decorations form a strikingly large proportion of the site material. These are the decorations that are more likely to be found in small site collections. From their role as the most typical features, they have received the name of "marker types". The marker types are identified in the type descriptions that follow, and on the table comparing the percentages of types at the various sites (Figure 1) they are marked by asterisks. The percentages of these types are indicated by bolder figures.

Type sites

In geological field-work a new horizon is presented by fully describing the characteristics of a type site. All subsequent finds of a comparable nature are measured by this standard.

Cultural complexes cannot very well be introduced by this method. The features are more flexible than the products of organic evolution, and variation is the rule rather than an exception. For this reason it seems best to present descriptions of several type sites for each new complex. Only in this way is it possible to demonstrate that specific features are products of real styles spread over certain areas, and are not local variations or inventions.

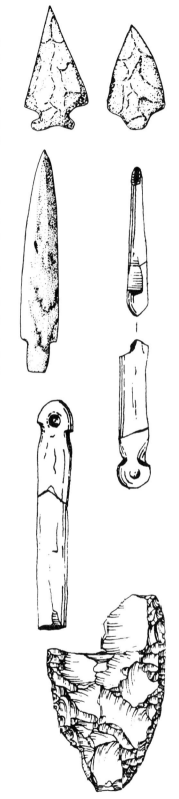

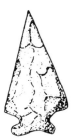

A Chronological Method Applicable
to the Southeast

Any archaeologist who considers that his science is pledged to the task of rediscovering unrecorded and lost history, rather than to the collection of "curios," is hardly in a position to deny the paramount importance of chronology. Lacking a scale which demonstrates the relative ages of the various activities of an ancient people, we are at best merely the collectors of disconnected fragments of history, and can never hope to fit these fragments together to form a complete and logical story of the past.

Before the work of Nelson and Kidder in the Southwest, the archaeology of that area was in about the same condition as that which exists today in the Southeastern states. However, the work of these pioneer scientists and the well directed researches of those who have followed them have succeeded in giving a clear picture of the course of prehistoric Southwestern cultures that in some ways is better and more complete than would have been the story of the Indians themselves, had they left written records of their history.

Although the Southeastern states seem to be as wealthy in evidences of prehistoric occupation as the Southwest, unfortunately the same conditions of thick refuse deposits are not usually present, and the same reliable methods of vertical stratigraphy cannot be applied as frequently as in the Southwest. It seems that in this area archaeologists will have to adopt existing standard methods or develop new ones to determine relative age. The largely accidental discovery of superposition in occasional village sites, and similar evidence given by later intrusions into old burial mounds, provide valuable evidence, but such cases have so far been too infrequent to give anything like a complete chronology for even one small area. If we must trust to similar accidental discoveries to complete the entire picture, we must reconcile ourselves to a long wait.

However, there is the possibility that direct and constructive work may be done on southern chronology along lines that have been somewhat neglected. It is commonly accepted, apparently with good reason, that the pottery found so abundantly at the old sites must bear the main burden of comparative dating. Considerable attention has been given this cultural feature by a number of investigators working in this region, but the major part of their material has been burial furniture found accompanying the dead in mounds or cemeteries. Usually they seem to have overlooked the apparent fact that the potsherds found in the village refuse may be expected to give a better example of the full range of the people's ceramic styles than the pieces that were chosen to accompany the dead; moreover, the refuse material is usually much more abundant. Logically it appears that the approach to chronological problems lies in the study of the changes that have occurred with time in ceramic decorations as revealed by potsherds. This is not a new idea. Kidder's chronology at Pecos was based essentially upon the same thing.

260

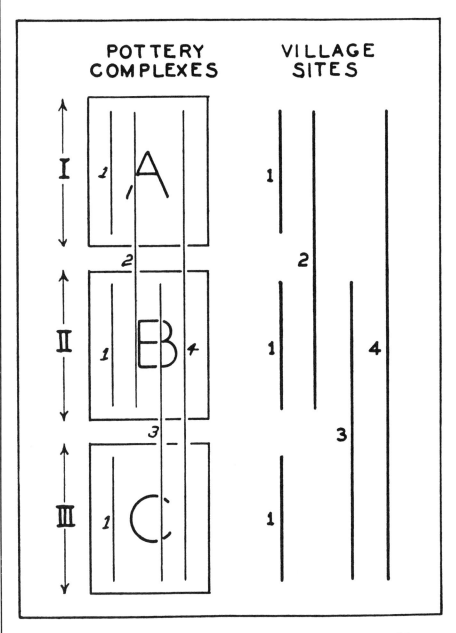

FIG. 18—Theoretical diagram of a chronological history illustrating possible actions of complexes (A, B, and C), pottery types (*1, 2, 3,* and *4*), and village sites (1, 2, 3, and 4).

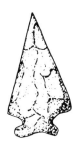

(cleaning)

In order to fully apply the methods of analysis outlined in the following pages, it is necessary that a collecting survey be made and representative samples of refuse material be secured from as many sites as possible in some area of comprehensive size—say one hundred miles square. The survey must be thorough enough for the investigator to be reasonably certain that he has secured at least a sample of every variety of material found in the area. The village sites of the Southeast are now very often cultivated fields, and the field-worker engaged in this type of survey will find little use for his spade.

The next step is that of classifying the material. The classification should be detailed. Repeated occurrence of a certain decoration at separate sites will determine for the investigator whether or not the decoration represents a real and significant type or is merely a local variation. It will probably develop that not only one but several distinct decorations will be found associated at a number of different sites. These associated decorations will be a group of styles that occur together, and form what has been termed a "decoration complex." A decoration complex covering a restricted area such as that under consideration probably represents a distinct time horizon. The stylistic time horizons that have existed in the area may now be logically separated.

However, there are numerous possibilities of becoming confused in this attempt. A review of conditions present in chronological histories that have been thoroughly developed will probably explain some of the peculiar conditions that are found. A generalized representation of a chronology is given in Figure 18. In this diagram the time periods I, II, and III are represented by the stylistic groups (or complexes) A, B, and C. These are shown by blocks placed one above another as they occurred in time. Within these blocks are lines representing the actions of definite style types. Such types as those marked *1* serve to differentiate the complexes. However, some types, such as those marked *2* and *3*, may have extended through two of the time periods but not the other. Others (*4*) may have extended through the entire time scale.

The length of tenure of a village site may act in a similar manner. This is indicated in the diagram by heavy black lines. Some sites, such as those marked 1, may have been inhabited only during the time when one complex of styles was in vogue. Others (2 and 3) may yield samples of two of the time periods but not of the third. Still others (4) may have existed all through the time scale.

Application of these phenomena of cultural chronology will not only serve to explain some of the conditions that are met with in attempting to determine complexes; they will also assist in arranging the complexes in their temporal relations. A linkage may be provided both by the overlapping of specific decoration types and varying lengths of tenure of village sites. Additional evidence may lie in the evolution of decoration types from one complex to another. This is not necessarily true. The area chosen for investigation may be distant from the region in which the actual evolution took place, and one complex may be replaced by another with no indication as to how the later types came into existence.

Another kind of overlapping may be present if, in the region adjoining that in which there were two subsequent complexes, an entirely different one existed through the time when one of the complexes was being replaced by the other. Trade material from this overlapping complex may then be expected on sites representing both of the subsequent complexes.

Of course the possibilities of readoption of abandoned decoration styles and reoccupation of old village sites would complicate this ideal scheme, but neither of these phenomena may be expected as a usual occurrence.

Preponderance of evidence must be accepted in determining types, in separating them into complexes, and in discovering relationships. Therefore, the reliability of these processes is in direct proportion to the size and number of site collections

Collections should be made from as many historic and protohistoric villages as can be located. The material from these sites will show which complex was the most recent and will determine which end of the chain of complexes constructed by overlapping is the latest. Without this tie-up it would be as logical for one end of the chronology to be recent as for the other. In some cases it may be more expedient to begin by determining the historic complex. Working back from this, the other complexes can be arranged in their true order.

A sequence of stylistic periods determined in this manner cannot be accepted as more than tentative. There are many possibilities of error in this method. Most of the work of classifying and comparing is highly subjective, and the worker is called upon to make many close decisions where he may be influenced by his preconceived ideas and desires. Then too there is the possibility that some unforeseen complication may be present to upset the apple cart.

However, such a tentative chronology is far better than no beginning at all. It is now possible deliberately to select sites at which superposition of materials may be expected. Stratigraphic study of these sites will provide a reliable check on the relative ages of the parts of the time scale that are involved.

After the chronology is established, the archaeologist will find himself in a position that, for the Southeast at least, will be novel. No longer must he excavate sites because they "look good." Instead, by paying attention to surface material, it will be possible to develop all the recoverable features of the various time levels in the area. New finds will appear in their true relation to one another instead of being a source of wonder and vague hypotheses.

However, it cannot be accepted that these ceramic complexes will represent different cultures or culture phases. It is entirely possible that two cultures may have used the same pottery, or at different times a culture may have changed its pottery types. What the method attempts to do is to use ceramic decoration, probably the most flexible of the remaining cultural features, as "type fossils" to distinguish the passage of time.

I do not insist that the foregoing is the only, or even the best method by which Southeastern chronology can be determined, but it is impossible to see,

A Chronological Method Applicable to the Southeast

without chronology, how we can ever hope to rediscover the cultural history of the Indians of the Southeast.

Bibliography

FORD, J. A. Analysis of Indian Village Site collections from Louisiana and Mississippi, Anthro. Study No. 2, La, Geol. Survey, Dept. Conservation, New Orleans, La.

KIDDER, M. A. and A. V., Notes on the Pottery of Pecos, Amer. Anthro., N. S., Vol. 19, No. 3, July–Sept., 1917, pp. 325–360.

KROEBER, A. L., On the Principle of Order in Civilization as Exemplified by Changes of Fashion, Amer. Anthro., N. S., Vol. 21, No. 3, July–Sept., 1919, pp. 235–263.

NELSON, N. C., Chronology of the Tano Ruins, New Mexico, Amer. Anthro., N. S., Vol. 18, pp. 159–180, 1916.

SPIER, LESLIE, Stratigraphic Technique in the Reconstruction of Prehistoric Sequences in Southwestern America, Methods in Social Science, Steward Rice, editor, University of Chicago Press, 1931.

J. A. FORD
School of Geology
Louisiana State University
Baton Rouge, Louisiana

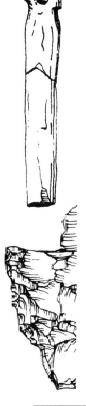

REPORT OF THE CONFERENCE ON SOUTHEASTERN

POTTERY TYPOLOGY[1]

Held at

The Ceramic Repository for the Eastern United States,

Museum of Anthropology, University of Michigan

Ann Arbor, Michigan

May 16–17, 1938

---

[2] The Conference on Southeastern Ceramic Typology was an informal meeting of archeologists directly concerned with the problems of analyzing the pottery recovered in the course of archeological investigation of aboriginal sites in the Southeastern United States.

The purpose of the meeting was to attempt to establish in the Southeast a unified system of pottery analysis. Methodologies that have been successfully applied in other areas were reviewed. Viewpoints and procedures listed in the following pages were selected as being most applicable to the Southeastern area.

Additional copies of this report may be secured from J. A. Ford, School of Geology, Louisiana

---

[1] No authorship is indicated on the original of this paper; however, James A. Ford and James B. Griffin wrote it (Williams 1960). The original unpaginated manuscript was issued in mimeographed form as *The Proceedings of The First Southeastern Archaeological Conference*. It was reprinted in 1960 in the *Southeastern Archaeological Conference Newsletter* 7(1):10-22 (Williams 1960). Page numbers are assigned here on the basis of the original manuscript and are indicated in [brackets] on the left margin. Much of the original format is retained, including several inconsistent heading forms and underlined rather than italicized text. As well, several typographical errors in the original mimeographed report have been retained; their locations are noted by * in the right margin of the line containing the error. Spacing errors within and between words have been omitted, and several modifications in the spacing of lines and paragraphs have been made in the interest of saving space. Footnotes have been added to clarify several points. The list of participants in the conference, which appears at the end of the original manuscript, has been omitted.

State University, University, Louisiana.

PURPOSES OF POTTERY STUDY

1.   For the purposes of discovering culture history, pottery must be viewed primarily as a reflector of cultural influence. Its immediate value to the field and laboratory archeologist lies in its use as a tool for demonstrating temporal and areal differences and similarities. Interpretations of technological processes are of value in making comparisons of the similarities of the material. However, at this time, when there is still so much disagreement among the specialists in that field, the more subtle technological distinctions cannot be depended upon to provide a basis for classification. It is possible to make useful divisions in material which was manufactured by processes that are not yet completely understood.

2.   The inadequacy of the procedure of dividing pottery into "types" merely for purposes of describing the material is recognized. This is merely a means of presenting raw data. Types should be classes of material which promise to be useful as tools of interpreting culture history.

                              IDENTIFICATION OF TYPES

3.   There is no predetermined system for arriving at useful type divisions. Types must be selected after careful study of the material and of the problems which they are designed to solve. A type is nothing more than a tool, and is set up for a definite purpose in the unfolding of culture history. If divisions in an established type will serve that purpose more accurately, they should be made; otherwise there is little purpose in crowding the literature with types.

[4] 4.   A type must be defined as the combination of all the discoverable vessel features: paste, temper, method of manufacture, firing, hardness, thickness, size, shape, surface finish, decoration, and appendages. The range of all of these features, which is to be considered representative of the type, must be described. By this criteria two sets of material which are similar in nearly all features, but which are divided by peculiar forms of one feature (shell contrasted with grit tempering, for example) may be separated into two types if there promises to

be some historical justification for the procedure. Otherwise they should be described as variants of one type.

5.   A type should be so clearly definable that an example can be recognized entirely apart from its associated materials. Recognition must be possible by others who will use the material, as well as by the individual proposing the type.

SYSTEMIZATION OF TYPE RECOGNITION

6.   As it is possible for certain features of pottery, such as shape or decoration, to be distributed apart from the specific features with which they may formerly have been associated, it is necessary to select a set of mutually exclusive features to serve as a primary framework for the classifications. This is to prevent the possibility of defining one type mainly on the basis of a paste feature, and still another on the basis of decoration. This procedure would eventually lead to a condition in which almost every vessel would be of two or more "types."

[5] 7. As in practice the classification will usually be applied to sherds, it was decided to utilize the features of surface finish and decoration as the bases for the primary divisions of the material. There is also the possibility of difficulty if one type is selected on the basis of a rim decoration and another has its reference to body decoration. Crossing of types would again occur as the results of a defect of the system. It was decided that body finish and decoration should define the type.

LIST OF CONSTANTS

8.   The term constant is applied to each of the list of apparent techniques selected by the conference as the primary divisions of Southeastern surface finishes and decorations. The constants selected, with some modifying adjectives, are as follows:

Constant	Modifiers	Definition
1. Plain - - - - - - - - - - - - - - - - -		No marked alteration of vessel surface.
	smoothed - - - - -	Hand smoothed, no reflective surfaces.

	polished - - - - - -	Marks of polishing tool show - some reflective surfaces.

2.   Filmed - - - - - - - - - - - - - - - - - Material added to surface of vessel after initial scraping of surface.

                  red - - - - - - - - Red slip or wash applied all over vessel exterior.

                  red and white - - - - Red and white pigment applied in separate areas to contrast with one another.

                  zoned red - - - - - Red pigment applied on uncolored vessel surface in areas.

3.   Incised - - - - - - - - - - - - - - - - Lines drawn in paste while plastic.

                  narrow - - - - - - Made with pointed tool.

                  bold - - - - - - - Lines both wide and deep.

                  broad - - - - - - - Wide lines.

                  punctate - - - - - Punctates spaced in incised lines.

[6] 4.   Engraved - - - - - - - - - - - - - - - Lines made by a pointed tool after paste had hardened. This may have been done either before or after firing.

5.   Roughened - - - - - - - - - - - - - - - Surface scarified or made irregular in a number of ways. Some of the techniques that will be included in this constant are not fully understood.

                  brush - - - - - - - Surface apparently stroked while plastic with a bundle of fibres.

                  stipple - - - - - - Shallow indentations apparently made by patting the plastic surface with a brush.

6. Combed - - - - - - - - - - - - - - - Lines similar to incised lines but made with an instrument having several teeth so that width between lines is mechanically constant. (Choctaw is only known example).

7. Stamped - - - - - - - - - - - - - - Impressions made in vessel surface with tool having designs carved on it.

    simple - - - - - - Impressions apparently made with a paddle having parallel grooves cut in it. In some cases these impressions may have been made with a throng-wrapped paddle.

    complicated - - - - Die in which were carved complex designs used to make impressions on vessel surface.

    check - - - - - - Die in which incisions were arranged in crosshatched fashion. Result of use of stamp is a "waffle" surface.

    dentate or linear - - Single or double row of square impressions evidently made with a narrow stamp.

8. Punctated - - - - - - - - - - - - - Indentations made one at a time with the point of a tool

    finger - - - - - - Indentations apparently made with the tip of the finger, or finger nail.

    triangle - - - - - - Punctates triangular shaped, as though made with the corner of a cube.

    reed - - - - - - Punctated circles made with a hollow cylinder, apparently a piece of cane, reed, or bone.

zoned - - - - - - Punctations arranged in areas which contrast with unpunctated areas of the vessel surface.

[7] 9. Pinched - - - - - - - - - - - - - - - - Tips of two fingers used to raise small areas of the vessel surface by pinching.

ridge - - - - - - - Raised areas form ridges.

10. Applique - - - - - - - - - - - - - - - - Clay added to vessel surface to form raised areas.

effigy - - - - - - - Applied clay indicates parts of some zoomorphic form (frog bowls, etc.)

ridge - - - - - - - Applied strips of clay form ridges.

node - - - - - - - Applied clay forms small protuberances.

11. Cord marked - - - - - - - - - - - - - - (Pragmatically cord marking might be considered as a stamped. However its distinctiveness, wide areal range, and usual name warrant the use of this separate constant.) Vessel surface roughened by application of a cord wrapped paddle. Twist of cords usually discernible.

12. Fabric marked - - - - - - - - - - - - - Surface marked by application of fabric to plastic clay. This constant will include the so-called "coild basket" (plain plaited) imprints. Also applied to fabric impressions found on salt pans.

-----

9. It is recognized that there is no assurance that each of these constants includes techniques

which can be considered as genetically related. They do attempt to describe all that can be determined regarding the technique of decoration. However, in some cases the techniques are in dispute and there is no certainty that this arbitrary placement is correct.

_____

[8]   TYPE NOMENCLATURE

10.   In order to facilitate reference to a pottery type, each type will be given a name, which will normally consist of three parts.

11.   The Geographical Name

The first part of the name will be taken from a geographical locality. It may be the name of a site at which the type is well represented, or the name of an area in which a number of sites bearing the type are found. If possible, the names of sites from which the type has already been described in the literature should be selected. It is advantageous that the name be both distinctive and associated with the material in the minds of the workers in the area. Numerically common types should not be given the same geographical name. In practice, the type will usually be referred to by its geographical name only. Confusion will result if more than one common type can be designated this way. Illustrations of some good geographical names are: Lamar, Lenoir, Marksville, Moundsville, Tallapoosa, Tuscaloosa, etc.

12.   The Descriptive Name

The second part of the name will sometimes consist of a descriptive adjective which modifies the constant. In certain cases the "modifier" is practically demanded by peculiarities of the constant. Some of these modifiers were determined by the Conference and are contained in the foregoing list of constants (paragraph 8). Examples are: check (stamped), complicated (stamped), red and white (filmed). In other cases the modifier may be a term which serves to suggest the [9] peculiarities of the constant. Examples: bold, fine, narrow, etc. However, it should be stressed that to be useful, a name must be as short as possible. Unless the middle term is particularly helpful in calling the type to mind and fits naturally into the type name, it should be omitted.

13.   The Constant Name

        The last part of the name will consist of one of the listed constants given in paragraph 8. The material should be examined carefully to determine to which of these categories it appears to belong. If it does not belong to any of them, a new constant may be proposed.

Examples of Type Names

14.   Examples of some names which are already in use and which promise to become standard are:

Georgia - Lamar Complicated Stamped, Swift Creek Complicated Stamped, Vining Simple Stamped, Deptford Linear Stamped.

Louisiana - Marksville Zoned Stamped, Coles Creek Incised, Fatherland Incised, Deasonville Red and White Filmed.

Which Types Should be Named?

15.   Only the materials which appear to have been manufactured at a site should receive type names based upon materials from the site. Extensive aboriginal trade in pottery seems to have occurred. Trade material had best remain unnamed until it can be examined in a region where it seems to have been manufactured and consequently is more abundant.

----

[10]   Plain Body Sherds from Decorated Vessels.

16.   Most Southeastern site collections will include a number of plain sherds which come from the lower parts of vessels that were decorated about the shoulder. These sherds should not be set up as types but should be described, with some indication as to the pottery types with which they may have been associated.

        In cases where there is little doubt as to the derivation of the plain pieces, they may be listed under the type name but should be distinguished from the sherds showing more fully the requisite type features.

DISTRIBUTION OF TYPE SAMPLES

17. The Conference decided that in order to permit consistent use of Southeastern Ceramic types it was necessary to provide each of the institutions working in the area with sets of specimens representing the recognized types. Each set should illustrate the range of material to be included in the type. Accompanying the specimens should be outline drawings of the vessel shapes.

For the present these collections are to be distributed to the following:

Mr. William G. Haag
Museum of Anthropology and Archeology
University of Kentucky
Lexington, Kentucky

Mr. David DeJarnette
Alabama Museum of Natural History
University of Alabama
University, Alabama

Mr. T. M. N. Lewis
Department of Archeology
University of Tennessee
Knoxville, Tennessee

[11]   Dr. James B. Griffin
Ceramic Repository for the Eastern United States
Museums Building
Ann Arbor, Michigan

Mr. Joffre Coe
Archeological Society of North Carolina
University of North Carolina
Chapel Hill, North Carolina

Dr. A. R. Kelly
Ocmulgee National Monument
Macon, Georgia

Mr. J. A. Ford
School of Geology
Louisiana State University
University, Louisiana

Board of Review for Proposed Types

18. The Conference recognized the need for a Board of Review to control and unify the processes of type selection, naming, and description. The board selected to serve until the time of the next meeting is composed of James B. Griffin, Gordon Willey, and J. A. Ford (addresses in paragraph 26).

Handbook of Recognized Type Descriptions

19. Descriptions of recognized types are to be issued in the form of a loose-leaf handbook. This form is adopted to permit additions and replacements from time to time as necessary. For the present the handbook will consist of mimeographed sheets, to be issued by J. A. Ford.

Procedure for Proposing a Type

20.   The procedure for proposing a new type will be as follows: the investigator proposing the type will send a representative collection

[12] of sherds specimen to all the corresponding institutions (paragraph 17). With the type   *
specimens will be a tentative description (paragraph 24).

All comments on the proposed type should be sent both to the investigator proposing the type and to the Board of Review. If the type appears to be a valid and necessary one, the Board of Review will approve it, and the type description will be issued as pages of the handbook. To avoid confusion type names should not be used in publications without this recognition.

DEFINITION OF SOME DESCTIPTIVE TERMS   *

21.   In order to make possible a more uniform description of pottery, the Conference recognized the desirability of a defined nomenclature. This problem required too much discussion to be fully considered at this time. It was only because of the immediate demands of type description that the following terms were discussed and agreed upon.

The following parts of vessels were not to be considered as accurately definable and measurable sections of the vessels, but rather as areas of the exterior surface. As these areas are formed by peculiarities of vessel shape, and there is a wide variation of shapes, all the defined areas are not present on every vessel.

Lip area - The area marking the termination of the vessel wall. More specifically, the lip lies between the outside and inside surfaces of the vessel. It is thus possible to speak of a squared lip, a rounded lip, a pointed lip, notched lip, etc.

[13] Rim area - The area on the outside of the vessel wall below the lip which may be set off from the vessel wall by decoration or other special treatment. (thickened rim, smoothed rim, decorated rim, wide rim area, etc.)

Neck area - The neck area is found only on vessels which show a marked constriction between body and rim. In general, it is an area of constriction below the rim.

Shoulder area - Shoulder area appears only on certain forms. It is marked by inward curving walls. The area is considered to lie between the point of maximum diameter and the area of constriction that marks the neck.

Body - The body is the portion of the vessel which gives it form. This means that necks and rims are not considered to form part of the body.

Base or basal area - The base is the area upon which a vessel normally rests. In the case of vessles with legs the base is the area of the body to which the supports are attached.

Appendages - Appendages are additions to the vessel which may have either functional or decorative utility. This term will refer to handles, lugs, feet, effigy heads, spouts, etc.

Strap handle - A handle which is attached to the vessel wall at two points and which in cross section is definitely flattened and strap like.

Loop handle - A handle which is attached to the vessel wall at two points and which in cross section is rounded and rod like.

Complex of types - A complex is considered to be all the types that were in use at any one village at the same period of time. The association of the different types found on any village site must be [14] proven - it cannot be assumed that every village site presents only one complex of types. Many sites show two or more recognizable complexes.[2]

22.   Measurements

Gross measurements - In presenting measurements of vessels and of their parts, the members of the Conference have agreed to use the Metric System.

Hardness measurements - Hardness is to be measured on the exterior surface of the vessel wall by means of the Mohs scale of graded minerals. The procedure is described in March: Standards of Pottery Descriptions pp. 17-22.[3]

Color - Surface coloring, paste interior coloring, and color penetration are to be described by the terms already in use. (White, grey, brown, buff, fawn, black, red, yellow, etc.)

---

[2]The concept of "complex" is discussed in Ford (1935, 1936, 1938).

[3]The full reference is given below.

23. <u>Shapes</u>

Present descriptive terms will continue to be used for shapes. Mr. Charles Wilder, who has already done some work on the classification and nomenclature of Mississippi Valley pottery shapes, has consented to prepare a simplified classification and nomenclature of shapes to be presented for consideration at the next meeting. Members of the conference are requested to send to Wilder outline drawings of all vessel forms found in their areas (address in paragraph 26).

----

[15] 24.   OUTLINE FOR DESCRIPTION OF TYPES

Illustrations of specimens of type should be placed here. Both body and rim sherds should be shown. Photographs or outline drawings may be used to show the range of shapes.

SUGGESTED TYPE NAME - - -

PASTE:

<u>Method</u> <u>of</u> <u>manufacture</u> - coiled, moulded, etc.

<u>Tempering</u> - material, size, proportion.

<u>Texture</u> - consolidated, laminated, fine, coarse, etc.

<u>Hardness</u> - use geological scale on exterior surface.

<u>Color</u> - surface mottling, penetration of, paste core.

SURFACE FINISH:

<u>Modifications</u> - smoothing, paddling, brushing, scraping.

<u>Filming</u> - slip, wash, smudging. (In cases where there is any doubt as to whether the surface treatment should be classed as either finish or decoration, the terms may be combined into Surface Finish and Decoration. Discussion of both may be included under this heading.)

DECORATION:

<u>Technique</u> - the method by which the decoration was executed; engraving, incising, punctating, etc.

<u>Design</u> - describe the plan of decoration, scroll, negative meanders, etc.

<u>Distribution</u> - portion of vessel surface occupied by the decoration.

FORM:

> Rim - treatment of rim area, i.e., thickened rim (tell how thickened) out-curving rim, cambered rim, etc.

> Lip - features of, or modifications of, i.e. squared lip, pointed lip, notched lip, etc.

> Body - general form of vessels.

> Base - shape of, peculiar treatments of, additions to.

[16] Thickness - of the different parts of the vessel wall.

> Appendages - handles, lugs, legs, etc.

USUAL RANGE OF TYPE: Geographical position of sites at which type is found in sufficient abundance to be considered native.

CHRONOLOGICAL POSITION OF TYPE IN RANGE: Time position in relation to other types and complexes. Be certain to state reliability of evidence supporting this conclusion.

BIBLIOGRAPHY OF TYPE: References to publications where material representative of type has been illustrated and described.

––––––––––––––––––––––––––––––

It will be noted that in general this outline follows the form given in Guthe's introductory section to Standards of Pottery Description, by Benjamin March (Occasional Contributions from the Museum of Anthropology of the University of Michigan, No. 3.) Any details which are not considered in the foregoing will conform to the suggestions set forth in this volume.

25.   WORDING OF DESCRIPTIONS

Make the descriptions of material as concise as practical. Complete sentences are not always necessary. First give in detail the usual conditions of each feature; then the range of variation allowed for the type.

––––––––––––––––––––––––––––––

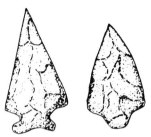

From *HANDBOOK OF NORTHERN ARIZONA POTTERY WARES*

Harold Sellers Colton and Lyndon Lane Hargrave

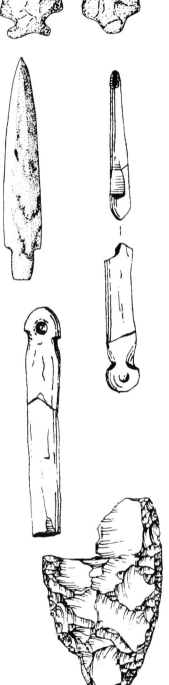

INTRODUCTION

In the present status of Southwestern Archaeology, Ceramics is the one cultural factor that can be studied at almost every site—even at sites that have not been excavated. Therefore, ceramics has an importance all out of proportion to its position in the complex of cultural traits. This being so, it is of immediate necessity to organize the study of Southwestern Ceramics so that the trends and influences can be recognized and studied and the details of Southwestern History can be compiled.

In any branch of science it is necessary first to analyze the material on which the science is based, to separate it into as many pigeon holes as possible. Bateson (1913, p. 249) once stated, "they will serve Science best by giving names freely and by describing every thing to which their successors may possibly want to refer, and generally by subdividing their material into as many species as they can induce any responsible journal to publish." But analysis is but one side of the picture. After analysis comes synthesis. By this we mean that the data collected should be assembled into a story, as complete as possible. In this paper we are considering Southwestern Ceramics in that light. We are attempting to analyze the pottery types that are found on the plateau of Arizona, north of the Mogollon Rim and south of the Utah border, and using these types as a basis, to build up a history of the region.

Pottery types will be described and named but the describing and naming of pottery types is not an end in itself but is the basis on which synthesis must be built. *Synthesis is only as accurate as the analyses which preceded it.* Many students think that Southwestern Archaeology is a finished study because works of synthesis have been published, but the analysis that preceded this synthesis is, in many cases, insufficient for the conclusions drawn.

The outline of such an analysis and the immediate fruits thereof may be indicated as follows: First, the identification of materials used, which, in a broad, although practical, manner determines certain groups of ceramic factors to be characteristic of certain regions (this is a stable character); second, recognition and knowledge of certain techniques of manufacture which make it possible to trace genetic relationships in time and space (another stable character since it is inherited); and third, characters acquired through personal contact as revealed in vessel form, style of design, and in other methods of ornamentation which reflect such factors as trade relations, and vogue. Through a proper correlation of this knowledge with knowledge from other sources, it then should be possible to determine pottery indigenous to a locality (based upon a study of materials used); to recognize the advent into a locality of new peoples (through changes in techniques that are inherited); or to trace the trend of the times as they swept across the country from one people to another (through a study of styles of design). Factors of these three kinds, over a long period of time, would combine to produce a variety of pottery types in a given region. Since we are trying to combine the stories of all of these types into one history, we cannot overlook the opportunity offered through recognition of each change in pottery. Because pottery is so durable and yet is so sensitive to change much is retained and preserved for all time in the firing of the vessel.

Most cultural factors, other than architecture and ceramics, give us relatively little material for study. At present, changes in cultural traits in the short time of pueblo evolution and geographic distribution in bone, stone and textiles have been determined in their broadest outlines only. This does not mean that textiles cannot tell as complete a story as does pottery, but it does mean that studies of textiles, to reach the same point as that of pottery, must be eminently costly. As an example, the Museum of Northern Arizona, in order to procure textiles from a dated site known to contain textiles, spent about $3,000.00 at Wupatki Pueblo and procured only a few fragments. In four years of study of 101 Pueblo II pithouses, the Museum found arrowpoints on pithouse floors in but two cases. The very sparseness of this material makes it difficult to build up a chronology based on textiles or stone points as has been done with pottery.

Textiles seem as sensitive to stylistic changes as does pottery but in very few cases have textiles been correlated with tree ring dates; moreover, much of the material is stored in eastern museums and must be studied in that area. We hope that some of the eastern institutions will turn their students to those important problems, for the material is available and crying for study.

Implements of bone and stone have been investigated but they are so insensible to individualistic expression that they have contributed very little to pueblo history. Architecture, being more sensitive than bone, has therefore contributed much but still is less sensitive to change than is pottery.

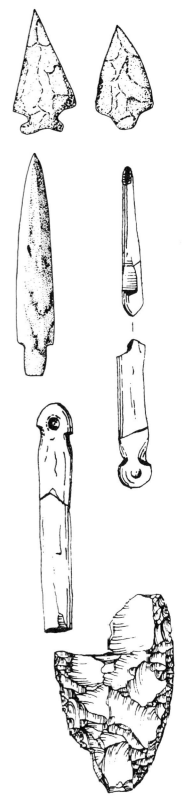

From *Handbook of Northern Arizona Pottery Wares*

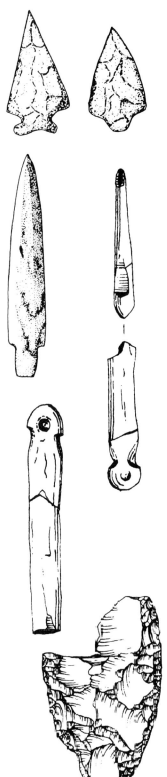

Having realized the value of pottery in recognizing time and cultural change, it is feasible to use pottery as a stage indicator. In assigning pottery types to designated chronological stages we use herein the terminology proposed at the First Pecos Conference in 1927 (Kidder, 1927) for the Basket Maker—Pueblo Culture; for the Hohokam, we use the terminology proposed at the Globe Conference in 1931 as modified by Gladwin (1934, p. 3). These stage designations are now firmly established in literature so until some radical change is made in the determination of cultural stages we believe this terminology should be continued in use.

Recognition of stages of cultural development came through the use of stratigraphy by Southwestern archaeologists. These stages were later dated by dendro-chronologists led by Dr. A. E. Douglass (Colton, 1935).

The approximate dates of the stages represented in northern Arizona differ from those in New Mexico. There seems to be about 100 years of cultural lag before 1200 A.D. Previous to that date, Arizona stages date later in time than do the same cultural levels in northern New Mexico. We cannot use dates from northern New Mexico in outlining Arizona history. Arizona has its own chronology, in part, as follows:

BASKET MAKER–PUEBLO STAGES IN NORTHERN ARIZONA

Pueblo V Stage; 1600–1900 A.D.; European influence
Pueblo IV Stage; 1300–1600 A.D.; Great pueblos
Pueblo III Stage; 1100–1300 A.D.; Pueblo evolution
Pueblo II Stage; 900–1100 A.D.; Emergence from pithouse to pueblo
Pueblo I Stage; 750–900 A.D.; Ceramic expansion; house type nearly static
Basket Maker III Stage; 500–750 A.D.; Introduction of pottery
Basket Maker II Stage; ?–500 A.D.; Pre-pottery

HOHOKAM STAGES IN SOUTHERN ARIZONA*

Modern	1700–1900 A.D.
Recent	1500–1700 A.D.
Classic	1200–1500 A.D.
Sedentary	900–1200 A.D.
Colonial	? – 900 A.D.
Pioneer	?

* Gladwin, 1934, fig. 10.

Harold Sellers Colton and Lyndon Lane Hargrave

CHAPTER I

TYPES, SERIES, AND WARES

THIS work is the result of an attempt to organize the study of Southwestern Ceramics as it appears in a small area, i.e., Northern Arizona. Until the pottery types of this area are arranged and classified it is impossible to interpret the information gathered in excavations. Because we do not know what to look for and what to record, information important in unravelling the history of the Southwest frequently is lost.

Few people outside of the active workers in Southwestern Archaeology realize the great variety of pottery that the prehistoric inhabitants of the Southwest manufactured nor do they realize how vitally pottery is contributing to an understanding of the history of the region. Not only do pottery types vary in time but they also vary from place to place at a given time. When two investigators have worked in a region, in many cases they have given different names to the same pottery type; in other cases when studies have been made in neighboring regions, investigators have failed to compare the pottery types from the two regions. In Arizona a sufficient number of pottery types have been described and named to make a system of classification possible (Hargrave, 1932). It may seem that any system is premature because so many types have been inadequately described and others have been described but not named, but the mere publication of the described types will focus attention on the weak spots and so will lead to their rapid obliteration.

Of the pottery types described from the Southwest, some are quite alike and some differ by many characters. When we have to deal with a large number of diverse objects it is necessary to arrange them in groups so that we may better grasp their characteristics. This is the reason for a system of classification.

Hargrave (1932) proposed a classification of pottery types based on fundamental structure of the material, such as paste, temper, and surface treatment. His classification is ideally perfect in that the material falls into definite pigeon holes. But because it does not always bring together in groups pottery types obviously related genetically, i.e., having a common derivation, it does not satisfy certain requirements of a logical

1

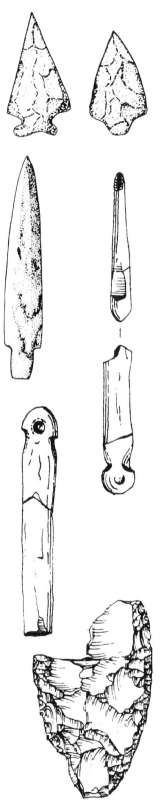

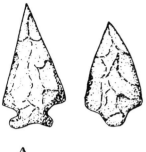

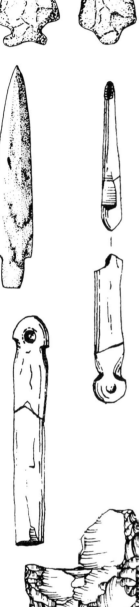

classification system. For this reason a more realistic definition of *ware* becomes necessary. In practical use it has been found unnecessary to refer to Hargrave's "genus" and "order," but the subdivisions, whatever they may be called, are useful in building a key that may be used for aid in identification. In a classification of pottery the *ware* is the important group.

Stevenson (1883, p. 319) was the first worker in the Southwest to use the word *ware* as a basis of classification. He was followed by Holmes (1886) who spoke of *Whiteware, Redware,* etc., and Fewkes (1904) who spoke of *Coarse Gray Ware, Black-and-white Ware, Yellow Ware, Brown Ware,* etc. Thus there is plenty of respectable precedent for the use of the word *ware* as a group term in ceramic classification.

Before we can define a ware we must define the word "type," because the definition of a ware is dependent upon the types within the ware. *A pottery type is a group of pottery vessels which are alike in every important characteristic except* (possibly) *form.* In general these characteristics are as follows:

1. Surface color—white, buff, yellow, red, and gray.
2. Method of handling the clay—thinned by scraping ("coiled") or by pressure ("paddle-and-anvil").
3. Texture of the core—varying from almost no visible temper to coarse temper.
4. Chemical composition of the temper if the difference is obviously caused by a difference in technique. For example: sand gathered from a stream bed might show differences in mineral content from one place to another and so is not of much significance in determining a type; but the addition of ground sherds or crushed rock to a paste is a difference in technique and is important.
5. Chemical composition of the paint—such as carbon, iron-carbon, manganese, or lead.
6. Styles of design in decorated pottery.

The definition of a ware may then be stated thus: *A Ware is a group of pottery types which has a majority of* (the above) *characteristics in common but that differ in others.*

While studying certain types in the preparation of this Handbook, it became obvious that wares could and should be subdivided on the basis of genetic series of types that were observed in several wares. These types were readily recognized as belonging to a certain ware but consistently occurred within a given subdivision of the ware area. Since genetic relationships within the ware clearly are revealed and since also a change in ecological factors is seen to have resulted in the development of new pottery types in minor geographic areas, recognition of these facts is indicated through the use of the term "series."

For many years series have unconsciously been spoken of in this manner when speaking of "Zuni glazes" or "Hopi Yellow." The unconscious recognition of the existence of series was indicated, although this fact has never been analyzed or systematized for general usage to the extent of definitely grouping specific types together according to a uniform system. Nothing new, therefore, is being proposed in the present method of classification.

In selecting a series name, the geographic portion of the name adopted was usually that of a late or culminating type in the series.

A Series, therefore, *is a group of pottery types within a single ware in which each type bears a genetic relation to each other, including all those types and only those types that occur:*

(a) *in the direct line of chronological genetic development from an original primitive or ancestral type to a late type: and*

(b) *as collateral developments or variations from any type in that line of development, but which are not themselves followed in chronological genetic sequence by derived types other than types derived through the main line of development from the type of which the collateral type is a development or variation*, as illustrated below. Fig. 1.

The earliest known type in a series is called the *ancestral type* of that series; several series may (and usually do) have a common ancestral type. Any type, however, may be spoken of as *ancestral* to all other types chronologically subsequent to it in the same series.

A type is called a *derived type* with reference to other types preceding it chronologically in the same series.

Two or more types in the same series which are derived immediately from the same ancestral type are said to be *collateral*.

Two or more types which are derived from a common *ancestral type*, no matter how remote, and two or more series which are derived from the same ancestral type, no matter how remote, are said to be *related* through that type.

The geographical occurrence of a series usually (although not necessarily) is limited to a definable subdivision of the ware area. An example may be graphed as follows:

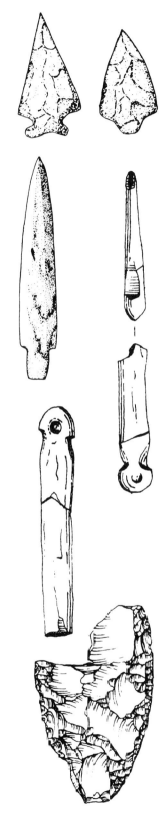

From *Handbook of Northern Arizona Pottery Wares*

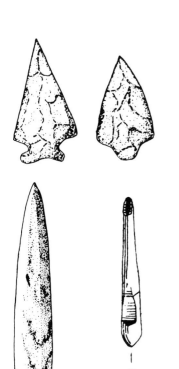

STAGES	SERIES P	M	J	F	T
Pueblo V	p	m	j	f	t
Pueblo IV	o	l		e	s
Pueblo III	q	k	i	d	r
	n				
Pueblo II			h	c	
Pueblo I			g	b	
Basket Maker III				a	

Fig. 1.
Example of Series within a ware.

Series F is composed of Types a, b, c, d, e, f.

In figure 1, type A is ancestral to all other types; type C is ancestral to types d, e, f, r, s, and t; type C is collateral to types d and r, derivative from type b, and ancestral to types f and t; all types are related to each other through type a; types i, j, k, l, and m, are related to each other through type h; types q and n are both ancestral to type o, but collateral to each other, and derivative from types h, g, and a.

The important thing in a classification is to have material, obviously related, placed in the same pigeon hole. So we must try to place pottery types obviously related in the same ware. It is impossible to make rules that will pigeon-hole the material automatically because in humanly manufactured articles so many variable influences have governed their manufacture and have affected their finished condition. Only personal judgment can care for some cases. A classification to be of value must aid our minds in grasping relationships. It cannot, however, be mathematically absolute.

Satisfactory and useful classification is impossible, however, without an orderly system of nomenclature wherewith to discuss the material classified. An object without an individual and significant name might be said not to exist in the mind of an observer. In general, most persons perhaps would admit this fact, but with some southwestern workers there is still a belief that names should not be given to various kinds of pottery, at least before the history of a type is known. But certain field and laboratory workers who have worked seriously and intensively in the field of ceramics, long ago recognized the need and value of names for various kinds of pottery in order that they might better understand each other. The action of the

Harold Sellers Colton and Lyndon Lane Hargrave

1927 Pecos Conference (Kidder, 1927) in making a rule for naming pottery types is a general recognition of this need, which admittedly is most vital to those students active in purely technical investigation. The question may be asked: "Why are such purely technical studies necessary?" The answer is: "To understand and to command the full value of a thing or a condition, each factor that has influenced or that is responsible for a thing or a condition must be isolated and studied separately so that the whole may be understood and properly interpreted." Complete analysis followed by synthesis is the only means known by which to accomplish this result.

Let us consider the technical study of ceramics. The principal object in studying ceramics is to learn as much about pottery as it is possible to learn, so that the accumulated data may be correlated with data contributed from other sources. Specifically the technical study of pottery already has contributed much. As early as 1928, Hargrave had worked out the sequence of pottery types so that the relative ages of many ruins were known. With this knowledge Dr. A. E. Douglass was directed to desired sites which gave timbers or charcoal.

As definite evolutionary characters were recognized at definite horizons in different regions—which incidentally destroyed the old theory that color and design were characteristic of clans—divisions of pottery types became necessary; such broad terms as "black-on-white" or "black-on-red" pottery no longer would fulfill the needs of the student. Regional, or geographic, names became necessary.

With the recognition of types, series, and wares we are thus able to understand better the intricate archaeological history of local districts. We are able to recognize migrations and to evaluate the part played by the acculturation of certain arts of the people. Moreover, this analysis, as applied herein to pottery, must precede synthesis in reconstructing this history of the prehistoric inhabitants of the Southwest.

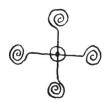

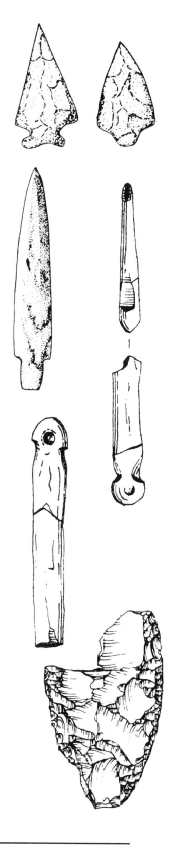

From *Handbook of Northern Arizona Pottery Wares*

CHAPTER III

METHODS OF STUDYING POTSHERDS

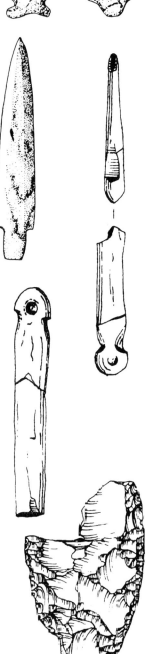

IN THE past few years many new methods have been used in the study of Southwestern Ceramics and in the use of these methods new fields of research have been opened. Although the use of these methods has not progressed far enough so that definite conclusions can be drawn in every case, yet, as a result of the application of these methods, certain trends of culture can now be observed so that bits of history that have been obscure now are reasonably clear. Methods of surface surveying have been developed by Mera, Gladwin, and Colton; Hawley has used simple chemical tests in determining paint pigments occurring on pottery; Shepard has studied the temper of pottery by petrographic methods; Fowler* has studied potsherds by means of the spectroscope; Shepard and Chapman have studied the firing temperature of modern Pueblo potters; Shepard, Fowler,* and Colton have studied the effect of oxidizing and reducing atmospheres upon various wares and clays; and Woodward has proposed a nomenclature for describing vessel forms. The importance of these new methods in the study of southwestern Ceramics cannot be too greatly stressed. A beginning has been made which will lead in time to definite conclusions.

A new method that has proven of practical value deals with the analysis of vessel rims. This method is herewith presented in print for the first time. Most readers have experienced difficulty in clearly understanding descriptive terms generally used when writers have referred to rim forms. That there is a great variety of rim forms is well known to students of Southwestern Archaeology, and, though attempts to describe these rims have been frequent, verbal or written descriptions have fallen short of accuracy and clarity. In some instances drawings have been made; these are better than word pictures. But neither of these means is adequate. Not only should the shape of the form be shown, as in a drawing, but there must be some way which, when referred to verbally, will bring to mind a picture of the rim form. A name will do that but before a name can be conveniently used there must be an adequate "description." Because of the instability of descriptive terms in certain branches

* Manuscript in files of Museum of Northern Arizona.

9

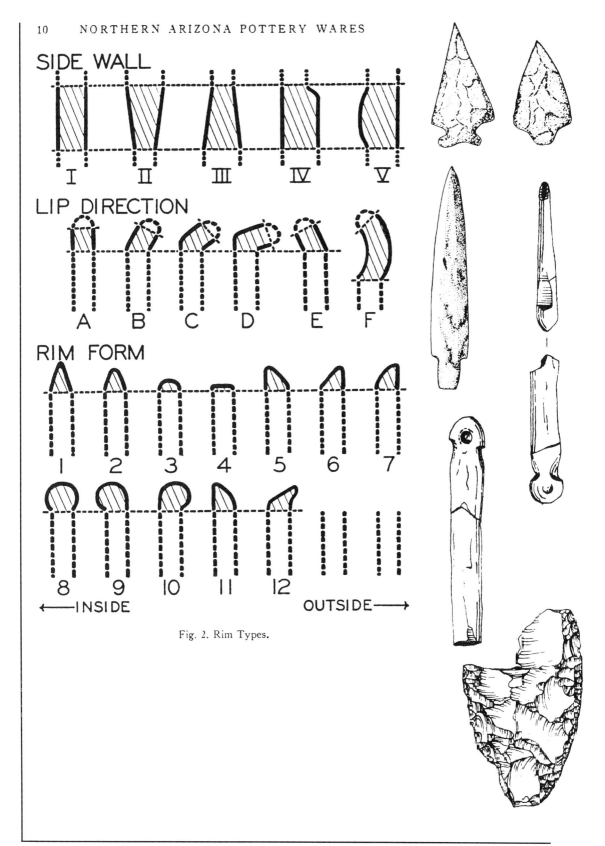

SIDE WALL

I   II   III   IV   V

LIP DIRECTION

A   B   C   D   E   F

RIM FORM

1   2   3   4   5   6   7

8   9   10   11   12

←—INSIDE   OUTSIDE—→

Fig. 2. Rim Types.

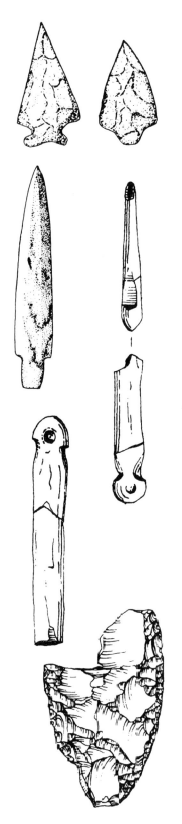

of Southwestern Archaeology the Museum has devised a mechanical method of analyzing a rim form, a symbol being used in lieu of descriptive terms. An advantage of this method is that all rim forms can be analyzed, thus segregated from other forms, and, further, all examples of a given form can be properly placed as to form. By using symbols, in conjunction with a model chart, any form can be referred to in print and by always using the master chart, consistency in form determination is maintained. Familiarity with the rim forms designated by various symbols makes it possible to use these symbols in lieu of a name. Although technically these symbols, when spoken, are names, they are not meant to be interpreted as such.

To use the chart (Fig. 2) view a sherd in vertical cross-section and compare the shape of the vertical cross-section with that section of the chart indicated by the Roman numerals (i.e., vessel walls); next, determine the lip direction, indicated by capital letters; and, finally, compare the rim form, indicated by Arabic numerals. The symbol for the rim analyses would be the combination of the three divisional symbols, say "IA3."

This method is flexible and can be used on any forms of pottery vessels by adding to the chart any forms not previously recorded.

In the study of potsherds there are several preparatory steps. The material having been gathered, the study is begun by a dry examination for which the sherds are prepared by brushing off all loose earth, etc., so that sherds decorated with fugitive paint can be recognized. All sherds then should be washed and those sherds that are coated with lime should be placed in a crock containing a weak solution of hydrochloric acid until the lime has been removed. Sherds should be washed again to remove the acid. Concentrated acid may stain gray or white sherds.

After cleaning, major separations are made of the material, as black-on-white, black-on-red, corrugated, etc. The detailed study is started by breaking off a small piece of each sherd in a group. The core is examined (preferably with a 10 X hand lens) for kinds, quantity, and mixture of temper. Temper will be recognized as grains of sand, as angular fragments of crushed rock or sherds, or may not be detected at all if the temper is very fine and of the same color as the core. Temper frequently is difficult to identify as to material, particularly when the temper is crushed rock. For instance, sands may be composed of particles or crystals of several minerals in which case a broad descriptive term must be used. The crushing of material for temper is a technique of manufacture. Although it is known that in some regions, at least, potsherds were crushed and used as temper (Haury, 1931, Pl. 10) still it is difficult definitely to identify temper as "sherd." Light-colored angular fragments is the designation used for sherd temper, and, in fact, for any temper having the appearance of ground-up potsherds.

Since the size of temper is an important criteria in recognizing types, some standard is necessary in describing size. Therefore, in the Handbook we will use a series of standards based on common pottery types. Examples of these are on file in the Museum of Northern Arizona. Very coarse temper—Jeddito plain, over .8 mm. Coarse temper—Tusayan corrugated, about .5 mm. Medium temper—Tusayan polychrome, about .2 mm. Fine temper—Deadmans Black-on-red, about .1 mm. Very fine—Jeddito Black-on-yellow, less than .1 mm and invisible to naked eye. (Hargrave and Smith, 1936.)

Other characters are noted at this time, as color of the core, presence of carbon streak, fracture, and general appearance of the core in cross-section. Color aids in determining the method of firing. *If the core has shades of color other than gray, white, or black, the specimen was fired in an oxidizing atmosphere.* The methods used in firing vessels slipped with iron-free clay can best be determined by the color of the core; in whole vessels this color may be seen in spots where the slip has worn away. Sherds of Zuni White Ware illustrate this case (p. 128).

Carbon streaks probably are a result of incomplete oxidation of organic matter within the paste. These streaks most frequently are seen in sherds fired in a reducing atmosphere, possibly because the lack of oxygen prevents the burning out of the carbon.* Moreover, core color of sherds fired in a reducing atmosphere often may be a gray on one or both surfaces, darkening, sometimes to black, as the center of the core is approached. Sherds fired in a reducing atmosphere have a greater strength, normally, than sherds fired in an oxidizing atmosphere and seem to have been fired at a higher temperature.

Methods of firing are most frequently determined by surface color, *the color of the exterior surface in nearly all instances being the criterion.*

Fracture, or the manner in which a sherd breaks under force, is determined by a combination of factors: materials, relative amounts of the mixed materials; and the degree of firing. Sherds containing large amounts of coarse temper, when fired in an

---

* Colton has mixed organic carbon with clay and fired it in oxidizing and reducing atmospheres.

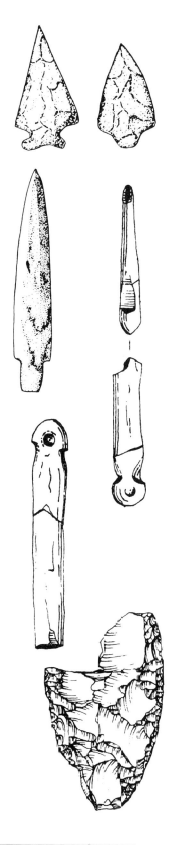

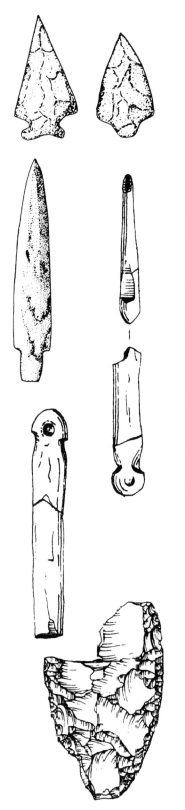

oxidizing atmosphere, will crumble when broken; those containing small amounts of fine, or sometimes even a coarse temper, when fired in a reducing atmosphere, will have a clean break, sometimes flaking or shattering. The appearance of the cross-section is dependent primarily upon the size and quantity of temper plus firing temperature. This appearance is recorded as "shattering" or "crumbling."

Subdivision of the color groups may be conveniently made at this time by separating sherds with painted decoration from those without a painted decoration. Both groups should be subdivided further on the basis of surface finish, i.e., unpolished, polished, impacted, or slipped. Among sherds with painted decoration usually will be found more than one style of design. The smaller divisions should be types but in some cases type identification cannot be determined definitely until a comparison has been made with known material or until it has been checked with a good description.

If the Handbook is used for reference, comparison by use of the key should simplify ware and type identification, if the ware or type is listed. Should specimens not key to one of the wares, regroup the unidentified specimens on the basis of materials used and techniques of manufacture employed. This grouping is to determine WARE characters.

When dealing with undescribed material, separate into types and describe each following the order used herein.

The study of Southwestern Ceramics is a promising field of research and the above methods all are far from perfect. Much technical information is needed to round out descriptions of pottery types and wares; ranges must be determined and mapped; and, finally, a synopsis of each type giving all known characters and correlations should be made.

Harold Sellers Colton and Lyndon Lane Hargrave

CHAPTER VI

DATING POTTERY TYPES

THERE are three methods of dating pottery types, namely: relative dating by seriation as a result of archaeological surveys, seriation resulting from stratigraphy, and dating through direct correlation with dated wood specimens. To make seriation clear let us take a concrete example. In an archaeological survey let us suppose that we discover on certain sites both Flagstaff Black-on-white and Deadmans Black-on-white, and on other sites both Kana-a Black-on-white and Deadmans Black-on-white. Since Deadmans Black-on-white is common to both sites we can make a series. Kana-a Black-on-white, Deadmans Black-on-white and Flagstaff Black-on-white, but without data from another source we cannot state which type lies at the older end of the series. By cutting a trench through a trash heap, suppose we discover the same series but in addition we can now determine the oldest member of the series which, in simple cases will be on the bottom of the section. In this example, the oldest is Kana-a Black-on-white and the latest Flagstaff Black-on-white. By means of Dendrochronology or the dating of wood specimens by studying the annual rings, we can now actually date each member of the series in terms of our own era. Although this may occasionally be done with accuracy the method is cast about with difficulties.

To date pottery types by the tree ring method it is necessary to excavate a large number of small sites which were occupied but a short time. Besides these sites must be in a region where Yellow Pine, Douglas Fir or Piñon wood was used in the construction of the houses because these species, at the present time, are the only ones that furnish reliable rings for dating.

Large sites usually furnish poor material for dating pottery (1) because during a long occupation of a site the pottery fragments from many time periods may be recovered and (2) because beams from one portion of a site were sometimes robbed to roof new rooms. Besides we find that as the end of a long period of occupation approaches, while the pueblo was diminishing in population, no new trees were cut and the robbing of old rooms was the general practice. This occurs at the Hopi pueblos at the present time.

In reviewing situations under which ceramic specimens occur in correlation with datable timbers we find that there are occa-

23

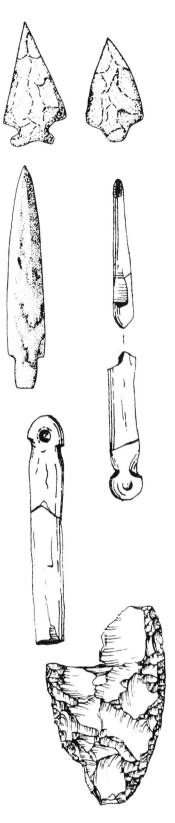

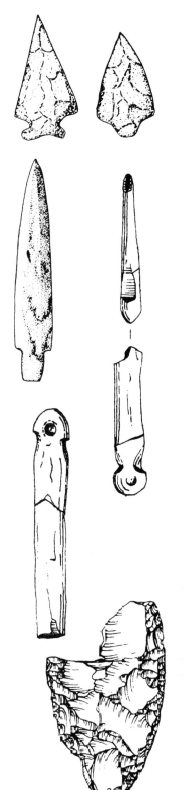

sions when the student would assign specific dates, or to make positive correlations of dates with sherds, where no such correlation is certain, because sherds occur in many situations and each situation should be carefully studied. Sherds from an excavation, for instance, consist of (1) surface sherds, (2) sherds within the earth fill of a room which may have come from the clay of the roof or from within the walls, (3) sherds resting upon the floor, (4) sherds that obviously belong to vessels crushed by falling walls or the roof, (5) sherds associated with charcoal in the fire pit and (6) sherds mixed with charcoal in trash or ash heaps

When a pit house or kiva is abandoned the roof collapses as well as a portion of the side walls, sherds on the surface of the ground, sherds that may have been imbedded in the clay of the roof as well as sherds in the fill behind the walls are found in the fill of the room. There is, therefore, no positive correlation between those sherds and the dates derived from the timbers. They may be much earlier. In a surface pueblo the fill in the rooms will contain sherds, (1) these may have been originally placed in the mortar found between the stones, (2) may have been supplied by sherds imbedded in the clay of the roof or (3) from trash deposited in the room after the room was abandoned. These sherds might cover a considerable time interval and may not be correlated with the timber found in the room. No positive correlation between sherds from within the earth fill of a room can be made with beams from this fill or with pottery specimens from within the structure proper. i.e., the dates from the two situations *cannot* be the same.

Sherds found upon or almost resting upon the floor are often considered contemporary with the structure. It must be mentioned that small miscellaneous sherds are not habitually seen knocking about floors of occupied pueblos. We cannot assume that this was true in prehistoric times. If datable timbers are recovered dates *cannot* be assigned to miscellaneous sherds found upon or near the floor since these sherds most probably came from the collapsed roof or wall, unless modifying conditions were encountered in the excavation. They must then be considered with the same doubt as "surface sherds." Moreover, it is not only possible but is probable that the dates from timbers may be of one stage while all sherds, surface and otherwise, may belong to an earlier stage. This condition was observed when a Pueblo II structure (based upon dated timbers) was built immediately upon an old Pueblo I site (based upon surface sherds). Not one single sherd of a type occurring later than Pueblo I was found in the room which was devoid of all artifacts suitable for time determination. Therefore, the structure was built, occupied, and abandoned, without leaving either whole or parts of vessels that would indicate the period of occupation.

Another case comes to mind, where every sherd found, indicated Pueblo I but a single pottery object, definitely Pueblo II, was found on the floor. Its position *directly upon the floor*, its size, and depth beneath the ground surface (about 7 feet), minimized all chances of the object having reached this position accidentally. Pueblo I sherds were found on the surface. Thus this site was Pueblo II in point of time, as the preceding example must also have been. It is to be recalled that in neither case was there found one sherd definitely referable to Pueblo II alone, yet in one site the occupation stage was determined by tree-ring dates, and in the other by ceramics. The time of abandonment of these two sites is thus stated as Pueblo II.

Sherds that belong to vessels crushed by falling walls or roofs or whole vessels in situ or in the floor, constitute a more definite criterion for accurately correlating pottery with dated house timbers. But even there, the elapsed period of time between the construction of the room and its abandonment would make an error of some years.

A more accurate determination of the *date of abandonment* might be made by studying charcoal and sherds from firepits, but branches which were used for fire wood are poor material for dating. The rings are unreliable, the record short and the outside rings are usually lost.

Hawley (1934) has used the sixth method—the dating of charcoal from fuel used in cooking, associated with sherds in a trash heap. It is assumed that when a firepit is cleaned out and the charcoal is carried to the heap, potsherds from recently broken vessels will become associated with it. Hence there will be a direct correlation. The method is sound but open to the same difficulties as is charcoal from firepits.

Even with the difficulties that have been outlined which are mostly concerned with a long or multiple occupation of a site, if many small sites of short occupation are studied, it is possible to date pottery types with reasonable accuracy. Although it is not possible to give a date more accurate than within twenty-five years, this is accurate enough for most purposes.

In Northern Arizona, the Museum has excavated more than one hundred small sites of short occupation from which a number of pottery types have been dated. These types bear what we like

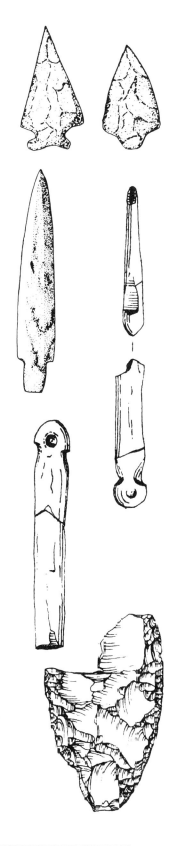

From *Handbook of Northern Arizona Pottery Wares*

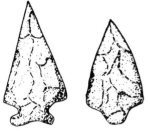

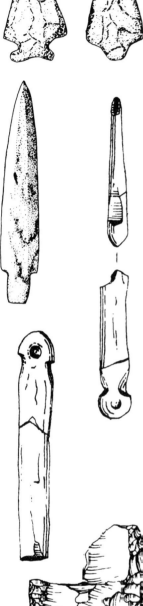

to call "index styles of design." When these types are associated with other types in a great number of small sites, these other types become dated also.

The approximate dating of pottery types has been one of the greatest advances in Southwestern Archaeology in the last ten years. By the recognition of index styles of design it has been possible to date with reasonable accuracy nearly every prehistoric site in Northern Arizona on which pottery fragments are found. For purposes of Archaeological synthesis, the importance of these results cannot be overstressed.

*   *   *   *   *

REFERENCES CITED

BATESON, WILLIAM
    1913   *Problems of Genetics.* Yale University Press, New Haven.
COLTON, HAROLD S.
    1935   Stages in Northern Arizona Prehistory. *Museum Notes* 8(1):1–7. Museum of Northern Arizona, Flagstaff.
FEWKES, J. W.
    1904   Two Summers' Work in Pueblo Ruins. *Bureau of American Ethnology, Annual Report* 22(1):3–195.
GLADWIN, WINIFRED AND HAROLD S. GLADWIN
    1934   *A Method for Designation of Cultures and Their Variations.* Medallion Papers No. 15. Globe, Arizona.
HARGRAVE, LYNDON L.
    1932   *Guide to Forty Pottery Types from the Hopi Country and the San Francisco Mountains, Arizona.* Museum of Northern Arizona Bulletin 1. Flagstaff.
HARGRAVE, LYNDON L. AND WATSON SMITH
    1936   A Method for Determining the Texture of Pottery. *American Antiquity* 2:32–36.
HAURY, EMIL W.
    1931   Recently Dated Pueblo Ruins in Arizona: Showlow and Pinedale Ruins. *Smithsonian Miscellaneous Collections* 82(11):1–79.
HAWLEY, FLORENCE M.
    1934   *The Significance of the Dated Prehistory of Chetro Ketl, Chaco Canyon, New Mexico.* University of New Mexico, Bulletin 246, Monograph Series 1(1).
HOLMES, WILLIAM H.
    1886   Pottery of the Ancient Pueblos. *Bureau of [American] Ethnology, Annual Report* 4:257–360.
KIDDER, ALFRED V.
    1927   Southwestern Archaeological Conference. *Science* 66:489–491.
STEVENSON, J.
    1883   Illustrated Catalog of the Collections Obtained from the Indians of New Mexico and Arizona in 1879. *Bureau of [American] Ethnology, Annual Report* 2.

From *PREHISTORY IN HAITI, A STUDY IN METHOD*

Irving Rouse

CONCEPTUAL TECHNIQUE

INTRODUCTION

BEFORE the main task of this paper, report of the second study made of the Ft. Liberté artifacts, is begun, it will be necessary to present the new methodological technique which was used in the study. As stated in the preface, this technique was experimental. It is hoped that the present paper will demonstrate that it is feasible to use the technique more widely in archeology.

New techniques which can be introduced into archeological methodology might be of several different kinds. Field techniques of excavation and survey are constantly being refined, for example in the work done by the University of Chicago in the Mississippi valley.[1] New methods for laboratory analysis of specimens are devised from time to time, for example by Shepard in her work on Southwestern pottery.[2] New conceptual approaches to the problem of historical reconstruction from the specimens are sometimes suggested. McKern's recently established system for the classification of cultures in the Mississippi valley is an example of this latter kind of contribution to methodology.[3] Ford's suggestion for outlining chronological history in the Southeast is another example.[4]

It is solely in this latter aspect of archeological method that the present study pretends to offer anything new. A number of existing concepts, including those of Ford, have been correlated. The attempt has been made to fuse these concepts with several new ones into a consistent, balanced conceptual scheme, useful for reconstructing certain aspects of culture history. This scheme has been employed to make a second study of the Ft. Liberté collections.

The attempt is made in Appendix 1 to explain how the new conceptual scheme might be used to supplement a number of existing archeological concepts. It is only necessary to say at this point that the scheme, as employed in the present study, is intended to be auxiliary to McKern's classificatory scheme which was used in the first study of the Ft. Liberté specimens.[5] Like the McKern scheme, it has been systematized as much as possible, with the hope of making procedures more precise and less confusing.

NATURE OF THE CONCEPTUAL SCHEME

The new conceptual scheme was divided in two parts, a series of concepts and a number of postulates. It will be necessary to describe the differences between the two before presenting the scheme itself.

[1] Cole and Deuel (1936).
[2] Shepard (1936).
[3] McKern (1934 ms.).
[4] Ford, J. A. (1938).
[5] Rainey and Rouse (1938 ms.).

9

A concept, as the term is used in this paper, is any idea about an archeological specimen (or a group of specimens) which serves as a methodological device for studying the specimens. The idea of "sharpness," as it is used to describe one of the attributes of a specimen like a stone ax, is a concept in this sense. So also is a more abstract idea like "diffusion," when it is employed to express a part of the history of certain specimens.

The postulates to be presented in the present paper are theoretical assumptions, which underlie the concepts. A definition of "culture," if it explains in theoretical terms what sort of data archeologists study, is an example.

Concepts are tools, which one can use to reconstruct prehistory. As such, they have two main functions. In the first place, they are the means whereby one formulates the descriptive data used in the reconstructions. Except for illustrations, one has to describe specimens in terms of concepts, such as the "temper" and "coiling" of pottery. If these concepts did not exist, it would be impossible to describe pottery at all, at least in words.[6]

Secondly, concepts must be employed to indicate the historical relationships between specimens. By use of the concept of diffusion, for example, one is able to postulate a historical connection between a number of sites which have the same type of pottery, providing that the sites are distributed over a contiguous area. Likewise, the concept of culture, when used in its narrow sense to refer to the artifacts deposited in a site by people who are related in culture, permits one to assume that all groups of specimens of the same kind had the same historical origin and can be considered a single historical unit.[7]

Unlike such concepts, the postulates to be presented below have no direct bearing upon the procedure of historical reconstruction. Instead, they are intended to provide a theoretical background for the study. They should clarify and systematize the meanings of the concepts, for one thing. Also, they are expected to relate the concepts to basic anthropological theory and to that of the social sciences in general.[8]

THE CONCEPTS[9]

The conceptual scheme used in this study contains three sets of working concepts. Since these are methodological devices, they will have to be described in reference to the procedure of this study. One set of concepts was introduced into each of the three main

[6] This function of concepts has been pointed out by a number of writers, including Blumer (1931) and Gumplowicz (1892, pp. 22-23). The reader is referred to these writers for a more adequate statement of the descriptive function of concepts (and of the effect they have upon conclusions) than it has been possible to give here.

[7] This role of concepts is well illustrated in Sapir (1916).

[8] One possible way in which the concepts and postulates might be used to contribute to general theory is investigated in Appendix 2, at the close of this paper.

[9] The following paragraphs concentrate upon concepts (i.e. ideas); not upon the terms which are used to characterize the concepts. As Pareto has expressed it, "Words . . . are of no importance to us; they are merely labels for keeping track of things. So we say, 'Such and such a thing we are going to call A'; or, 'We suggest calling it A'. We do not say—an entirely different matter—'Such and such a thing is A.' The first proposition is a definition, and we are free to word it as we choose. The second is a theorem, and requires demonstration. . . .

parts of the procedure, viz., the formation of culture traits, the tracing of the distributions of these traits, and the reconstruction of the history of the traits from the distributions.[10] The set introduced into each of these parts will be described in turn.

TYPES AND MODES

A set of two concepts was used to form culture traits. These were called "type" and "mode" respectively.[11]

In current anthropological literature, the term "type" seems to have been applied to at least two different concepts, a group of artifacts or an abstract kind of artifact which symbolizes the group.[12] Some writers have defined "type" in the former sense,[13] others in the latter.[14] The term was used in the former sense in the previous Ft. Liberté paper. In the present one, however, it is employed in the latter. It refers to the attributes which artifacts of a given kind have in common, not to the artifacts themselves.

Types of this abstract kind have been formulated in the following manner. First, the Ft. Liberté artifacts were classified into groups.[15] Then, a selection was made of the most characteristic attributes which appeared on the artifacts in each group. These attributes were listed, and treated as a type, or pattern of artifact characteristics.

The present paper deals with these types, or patterns of attributes which appear characteristic of classified groups of artifacts. In addition, it deals directly with the attributes themselves. It treats each attribute separately as a culture trait, equivalent to each of the types.

The term "mode" is applied to each of these attributes, in order to distinguish it from a type. Each mode consists of a single design which appears on the Ft. Liberté artifacts, or a technique like stone carving which was used in the manufacture of the artifacts, or else some specification like hardness which a number of the artifacts have in common.

Modes like these have been formulated in a manner quite different from that used to

---

[We] would gladly have replaced word-labels with letters of the alphabet, such as a, b, c [to avoid their being mistaken for parts of theorems]. . . ." (Pareto, 1935, vol. 1, p. 64).

Terms in use below, such as "mode," are treated merely as labels (or symbols) for the concepts to which they are applied. It would have been possible to substitute any other intelligible symbols in their places.

As it was, the attempt was made to apply to each concept the term whose common usages most resembled that of the concept. In this way, it was hoped that the misunderstandings which sometimes arise over choice of terminology could be avoided.

[10] These three parts of the procedure are described in the next section.

[11] The term "mode" was suggested to me by Dr. Cornelius Osgood.

[12] Other differences in the use of the term are described in Rouse (1939 ms.).

[13] E.g., Gorodozov (1933, p. 98), Colton and Hargrave (1937, p. 22).

[14] E.g., Linton (1936, p. 23, 36–9). The types discussed there are physical rather than artifact types, but the principle is the same.

[15] As described in Rainey and Rouse (1939 ms.), the classification was based upon the original appearances of the artifacts, not upon their present fragmentary conditions.

form types. The Ft. Liberté artifacts have been treated individually rather than in terms of classificatory groups. Each artifact was analyzed into single attributes of the three kinds just mentioned. The attributes which seemed from a historical standpoint to be most significant were abstracted from the artifacts and treated as modes.

This procedure might be termed "analytical," in order to emphasize the fact that it splits up the artifacts into their individual parts instead of classifying them. One could likewise term the procedure used to form the types "classificatory," because it deals with the artifacts as a whole and in groups.[16]

Modes, then, are single attributes which have been analyzed from the Ft. Liberté artifacts. Types are patterns of attributes which have been obtained by classifying the artifacts. Not all the attributes listed as modes occur also in the patterns of attributes which are called types, however, for two reasons. In the first place, the modes include attributes which have been analyzed from the artifacts, like techniques of manufacture, as well as designs and material specifications which characterize the specimens as objects. The types, however, include only the latter, for they have been formed by classifying the artifacts on the basis of their appearances as objects.[17]

In the second place, the modes include all the attributes of the artifacts which seem to be historically significant. The types, on the other hand, list merely the attributes which are definitive of each classified group of artifacts.

To summarize, both types and modes are used as culture traits in this study. They form the subject matter for historical reconstruction. Each type has been formulated by classifying the Ft. Liberté artifacts into groups, and listing the attributes which appear to be definitive of the artifacts in a single group. Each mode, on the other hand, has been formed by analyzing the Ft. Liberté artifacts into their individual attributes, and selecting the attributes which seem to be historically most significant. Each type, therefore, consists of a list (representing a pattern) of the attributes which characterize the type group (or kind of artifact). Each mode, however, is a single attribute which seems to be worthy of historical study. Each type is a list of the designs and specifications which appear on the surfaces of the artifacts. Individual modes include not only these designs and specifications, but also techniques of manufacture.

Time Scale

A single important concept has been used in this study to trace the distributions of the types and modes, viz., "time scale." This concept can best be described in terms of the functions which it served in the tracing of distributions. There were two of these, one for each of the procedures used to trace distributions. They will be discussed in turn.

The concept of "time scale" was needed, first of all, for the procedure of tracing geo-

[16] Using the biological analogy suggested by Holmes (1897, p. 147), one might also term the procedure used to form modes "morphology." Then, the procedure of forming types would become "taxonomy."

[17] This point is discussed further on pp. 25–26 below.

graphical distributions. Spier's ethnological work was used as a model for this procedure.[18] Spier had traced the distribution of culture traits from tribe to tribe. In the same way, the attempt has been made in the present study to trace the types and modes from site to site.

Spier traced his distributions without regard for the ages of the tribes, since the latter were approximately contemporaneous. In the present study, on the other hand, it has been necessary to determine which sites were contemporaneous before tracing distributions in Spier's manner.

In Spier's case, one might say, traits were traced from tribe to tribe as they existed there during one short period of time, namely the period of first European contact. In the present study, to be comparable, types and modes have been traced from site to site during a series of successive time periods.

In Spier's case, the time of his period, i.e., of European contact, was known relative to our own calendrical system. In the present study, however, it has been impossible to correlate the periods within which the distributions of the types and modes were traced with any existing calendrical system.

Instead, the periods themselves have been treated as a calendrical system comparable to our own. The entire sequence of periods which forms the system has been termed a "time scale."[19] Like our calendrical system, this time scale has been made a measure of a continuous span of time, each period on the scale being a unit within the total span. As a result, each period is comparable to a unit like "year" or "century" in our own calendrical system.

The second use made of the concept of time scale was to help trace the distributions of the types and modes in time, as opposed to the spacial distributions just described. Olson's study of Chumash prehistory was the model for this procedure.[20] Olson set up a series of time periods and traced the distributions of his artifact types from the beginning to the end of each period. In the present study, the same procedure has been followed. The distributions of the types and modes have been traced from the beginning to the end of each period on the time scale.

In Olson's case, the time distributions were determined separately for the two parts of the region he studied. Apparently, the assumption was that each of these parts was culturally homogeneous. In the present study, on the contrary, time distributions have been traced within the Ft. Liberté region as a whole, because it seems evident that the region was culturally homogeneous (see p. 31 below).

[18] Spier (1928, sections entitled "Comparative Notes"). Works like Nordenskiold (1919) are also similar. The procedure used in these works consists simply of tracing the distributions of culture traits from place to place. It differs, therefore, from attempts to determine the ages of the traits by tracing distributions, as Davidson (1928), Strong (1927), and others have done.

[19] The term used for this concept was obtained from Ford, J. A. (1936, p. 6).

[20] Olson (1930, fig. 3, p. 21). Similar procedures are also used by Sayles (in Gladwin, et al., 1937, p. 118), Kroeber (1923, p. 178), and Hrdlička (1930, p. 8), among others. Ford, J. A. (1938) outlines the procedure in theory.

To summarize, the distributions of the types and modes have been traced in both space and time during the course of the present study. In space, the types and modes have been traced from site to site within each time period. In time, they have been traced from the beginning to the end of each period within the Ft. Liberté region as a whole. In both cases, it was necessary to use a time scale, or sequence of periods similar to the sequence of centuries in our own calendric system, for measuring distributions.

PROCESSES

The set of concepts used in this study for reconstructing history from the distributions of the types and modes may be termed "processes." They conceptualize the distributions, so as to make them represent historical events.[21] Each process indicates the history of an individual culture trait along the paths of its distribution.[22]

The process usually employed by anthropologists to make historical the distributions of culture traits in space is that of "diffusion."[23] Accordingly, "diffusion" was used in the present study in order to indicate the spread of types and modes from site to site within each period.

There exists no corresponding process to make historical the distributions of culture traits in time. For this purpose, a concept had to be invented. It was termed "persistence."[24] It expresses the perdurance of types and modes in time, in the same way that "diffusion" expresses their spread in space.

Three additional processes were used to conceptualize the limits of the distributions as opposed to the distributions themselves. The first is "origination."[25] It refers to the process by means of which a type or mode comes into existence. The second is "extinction." It refers to the process by means of which a type or mode dies out, without being replaced by another. The third process is "replacement." As the name implies, it expresses replacement of one type or mode by another, rather than simple extinction of the first type or mode.[26]

In addition, "increase and decrease in the popularity" of types and modes are studied in the present paper. These terms refer to an increase in the frequency of a type or mode as it persists in time, or to a decrease in frequency.

[21] This conception of process was obtained (at least in part) from Dr. Leslie Spier.

[22] As described in Appendix 1, the processes can also be used to express the histories of trait complexes. They are not so used in the present study, however.

[23] Cf. Sapir (1916, pp. 25-27).

[24] The term "persistence" has been used in an incidental manner by several writers, including Sayles (in Gladwin et al., 1937, p. 118). To my knowledge, it has never been presented as a formal process before this, however.

[25] This term is also used by Goldenweiser (1937, p. 465).

[26] The concept of "replacement" should not be likened to the concept of "evolution." The latter implies development of artifact types, somewhat like the growth of plants. Replacement, however, expresses merely a change in types or modes. Each type or mode is assumed, by definition, to be an immutable pattern. Hence, it cannot grow or evolve like a plant. It merely comes into existence, persists, and dies out. It is analogous to a culture trait which diffuses, not to an artifact type which evolves.

The complete set of processes, then, is the following. A type or mode may have come into existence at a site by origination on the spot, or by diffusion from a neighboring tribe. It will then persist for a certain length of time, at first (perhaps) increasing in popularity, later decreasing in popularity. Finally, the type or mode will die out, either by becoming extinct or by replacement by another type or mode.

THE POSTULATES

Since the postulates are supposedly assumptions which constitute the theoretical basis for the conceptual scheme, they may be expressed in the form of propositions, in the following manner. It is assumed that:

1. Culture does not consist of artifacts. The latter are merely the results of culturally conditioned behavior performed by the artisan.
2. Types and modes express the culture which conditions the artisan's behavior. Types are stylistic patterns, to which the artisan tries to make his completed artifacts conform. Modes are community-wide standards which influence the behavior of the artisan as he makes the artifacts.
3. Artifacts are concrete objects. Types and modes, on the contrary, are conceptual patterns set up by the archeologist to represent ideas possibly held by the artisan.
4. Artifacts have little historical significance. Types and modes, however, are well suited for historical study.
5. For historical study, the persistence of types and modes in time is as important as their diffusion in space.

Each of these postulates will be discussed in turn. The treatment will be dogmatic, for none of the postulates is susceptible to proof.

1. *Culture does not consist of artifacts.*[27] It must be understood at the outset that the first postulate refers to a theoretical definition of the term "culture," not to any practical concept which might be designated by the term. From a practical standpoint, the term "culture" usually does apply to artifacts. In ethnology, for example, the term commonly denotes "any socially inherited element in the life of man, material or spiritual."[28] In archeology, too, culture is often used to denote a group of artifacts which have a similar historical origin.[29]

Nothing in the following discussion is intended to negate technical definitions of culture like these. In order to do so, the discussion would have to treat "culture" as a concept, equivalent to the three described above, and it does not. The term is used solely to denote a theoretical difference in the kinds of cultural data, not the data themselves.

It might have been preferable to use some other term than "culture" in this theoretical sense, in order to indicate that the latter is not intended to be comparable to technical

[27] Postulates 1, 2, and 3 were inspired (at least in part) by opinions on culture held by the late Dr. Edward Sapir.

[28] Sapir (1923, p. 402).

[29] E.g., Childe (1929, p. viii).

usages of the term. Unfortunately, there is considerable literature discussing culture in a theoretical sense.[30] In conformity with this literature, one has to treat the term "culture" theoretically, even though such a treatment may give the appearance of conflict with practical usages.

From a theoretical standpoint, it seems an error to regard artifacts as culture. In so doing, one overlooks the fact that the significance of artifacts varies with the cultural setting in which they are placed. The Ft. Liberté artifacts may be taken as an example. The Indians undoubtedly regarded these artifacts as tools. On the other hand, the present day inhabitants of Haiti, who possess a very different culture, consider the artifacts to be merely stones. Laymen in our own culture give the specimens a third significance, by regarding them as curios.

In the opinion of the writer, any person who is interested in studying aboriginal culture in the Ft. Liberté region must treat the artifacts from the standpoint of the aborigines.[31] In other words, he must give the artifacts the first of the three significances just described. If he were to use the second or third significance, the artifact would become a part of some other culture than that of the aborigines.

This being so, culture cannot be inherent in the artifacts. It must be something in the relationship between the artifacts and the aborigines who made and used them. It is a pattern of significance which the artifacts have, not the artifacts themselves.

Tylor's classic definition of culture speaks of the "habits and capabilities acquired by man as a member of society."[32] If his definition were accepted, culture could not be inherent in artifacts. It would have reference to man's behavior towards artifacts rather than to artifacts themselves.[33]

In gross terms, Tylor's definition of culture has been accepted as a basis for the present paper. In this paper, it is assumed that culture is connected with the behavior which people perform in dealing with artifacts, rather than with the artifacts themselves.

The behavior which people perform in reference to artifacts is of at least two different kinds, that concerned with the manufacture of the artifacts and that associated with their use. Depending upon which kind is discussed, the artifacts can be considered either as the end point of a process of manufacture, i.e., as the result of certain culturally conditioned behavior, or as objects used in certain situations, i.e., as the means for culturally conditioned behavior. In this discussion, they will be considered in the former sense rather than the latter, since it is impossible for an archeologist to obtain reliable data on the latter.[34]

---

[30] See, for example, the compilation of theoretical definitions of "culture" which is given in Blumenthal (1936).

[31] Cf. Boas (1911, p. 63), where ethnology is defined as "the science of dealing with the mental phenomena of the life of the peoples of the world."

[32] Tylor (1899, Vol. 1, p. 245).

[33] It has to be noted, however, that the nature of the artifacts is largely determined by the nature of the procedure used by the artisan in making them. In this sense, the artifacts are cultural, or at least culturally conditioned.

[34] The latter attitude, of considering the artifacts only as a means for culturally conditioned behavior, is the

For purposes of this study, then, the artifacts have to be the results of the behavior of the artisans in making them. This relationship may be expressed as follows:

Artisan's Procedure (or Behavior)

Artifacts

Parts of the artisan's procedure are probably peculiar to himself. These parts cannot be considered cultural.[35] Other parts, however, undoubtedly conform to the behavior of the rest of the artisans in the community. These conforming elements, apparently, are the ones which give cultural significance to the procedure, and to the artifacts which result from the procedure.[36]

In most cases where the artisan conforms to what other artisans do, he probably does so without awareness of what he is doing. Nevertheless, figuratively at least, he may be considered to conform to certain community standards of behavior, to which other people working as artisans in the community also conform.[37] It is these standards (or patterns) of behavior which are considered cultural in this paper, not the artisan's procedure or the artifacts themselves.

These standards may be called "elements of culture." They are related to the artifacts in the following way:

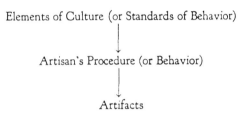

Elements of Culture (or Standards of Behavior)

Artisan's Procedure (or Behavior)

Artifacts

To speak in physical terms, elements of culture are analogous to forces which react upon the individual artisan, causing him to behave in a certain way, i.e., to make artifacts of certain kinds. They are not the only forces which react upon the artisan and affect his

one taken by Malinowski (1931, p. 636). The former attitude, of considering them as the results of behavior, I have heard suggested (among others) by Spier (in class).

[35] Cf. Tozzer's criticism of Vaillant for considering all "minute differentiations in technique and style" to signify "a change of fashion and therefore of time" rather than "personal and chance variations." (Tozzer, 1937, p. 340.)

[36] As stated above, the artifacts also derive cultural significance from their uses, which are not being discussed here.

[37] Cf. O'Neale's statement (1932, p. 161–3): "Basketry as practiced by a Yurok-Karok weaver is thoroughly molded by a compact body of established traditions. . . . It would seem, then, that as long as there is a Yurok-Karok basketry in the Klamath region it will be made according to traditional convention, which has established choices of materials, selection and arrangement of elements, and the placement of these as design motives."

procedure, however. Chance, peculiar elements of his personality, differences in his innate ability, and environment all may have affected the artisan and moulded his procedure. In fact, the procedure itself may be considered to have been an equilibrium, into which all these factors were able for a moment to enter. The artifact is the result, somwhat of a fixation, of the equilibrium. These relationships may be diagrammed as follows:

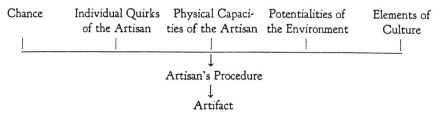

Culture, then, is merely a single one of a group of factors which influence the artisan's procedure in making an artifact. The artifact is, in a sense, a result of the interplay of all the factors. Culture may be the most important of the interplaying factors. Nevertheless, it would not seem justifiable to consider the artifacts themselves to be equivalent to culture.

2. *Types and modes express the culture which conditions the artisan's behavior.* The types formulated in the previous Ft. Liberté paper and the modes set up in the present one are assumed to be elements of culture. Both, it is hoped, are standards of behavior which influenced the artisan as he made the artifacts.

Each type is a pattern of artifact characteristics which constantly recurs on a given kind of artifact. Supposedly, it is the result of conformity by the artisans to a cultural standard which indicated the proper kind of appearance for a completed artifact to have. For practical purposes, it may be considered to be the cultural standard itself.

Each type, then, is a standard of artifact appearance towards which the artisan was working in making a given kind of artifact. It is analogous to a style, to which the artisan tried to make his completed artifact conform. Like a style, it outlines limits within which the appearance of an artifact can vary. It prescribes the alternative features which an artisan can apply to an artifact and still have it remain in style. In effect, therefore, it is a visual image of the ways in which such an artifact may look when completed.[38]

Each mode, on the other hand, is an abstraction of a recurring feature from the specimen. Supposedly, this recurring feature has resulted from conformity by the Ft. Liberté artisan to a certain cultural standard which prescribed how to proceed in making the feature. For practical purposes, the feature can be considered to be the pattern itself.

Each mode, then, is a cultural pattern, or standard of behavior, which influenced the artisan's procedure as he made his artifact. It is a community-wide technique design, or other specification to which the artisans conformed.

[38] The fact that the Ft. Liberté types list alternative features, which may appear on the completed artifacts, is discussed more fully in Rouse (1939 ms.).

Modes representing techniques might be considered analogous to habits, which the artisans learned to perform by imitation of other artisans in the community.[39] Modes consisting of designs, on the other hand, might be conceived as visual patterns, which guided the artisan as he made the artifacts. Similarily, modes which specify certain material qualities in artifacts would be ideas, to which the artisan conformed in making the artifacts.[40]

To speak in physical terms again, types and modes are cultural factors, which reacted upon the artisans as they made the Ft. Liberté artifacts. As such, they bear the equilibrium type of relationship to the non-cultural factors that was diagrammed above, namely:

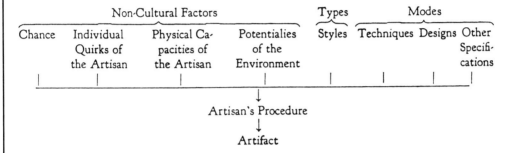

The types and modes, then, express the cultural significance possessed by the Ft. Liberté artifacts. In effect, they separate the cultural factors which produced the artifacts from the non-cultural factors which are inherent in the artifacts.[41]

3. *Artifacts are concrete objects; types and modes are conceptual patterns.* As a basis for this postulate, there is the fact that both the types and the modes formulated during the course of the Ft. Liberté research are artificial concepts, set up by the writer. They are not objects, like the artifacts, which were possessed by the Ft. Liberté aborigines.

If the aborigines had been trained to think in cultural terms, they might possibly have conceptualized the artifacts in terms of community standards of behavior, as the writer has done. It is not within the power of the writer, however, to determine whether or not they did so. He can only assume that the types and modes are products of his own mind, whereas the artifacts were objects made by the aborigines.

[39] Cf. Wissler's discussion of culturally (i.e., historically) determined habits and of their differences from motor factors (Wissler, 1914, pp. 494–501).

[40] Cf. Ford's formulation of specifications to which the artisan supposedly has to make his artifacts conform (Ford, C. S. 1937).

[41] If one limited the use of the term "culture" to the types and modes, as is done in this discussion, then it would be impossible to speak of environment or race having a direct effect upon culture, even though these factors might directly influence the manufacture of an artifact. It would likewise be impossible for one culture trait directly to affect another, as some functionalists seem to imply. All these factors would affect each other only indirectly, in that they compete and reach an equilibrium in specific situations.

Because the types and modes are artificial concepts, they are assumed in the present study to be the same whatever the artifact upon which they occur. The artifacts, however, are never identical. Each is a concrete object rather than an idea. It differs somewhat from all other objects.

Each artifact is a product of the interaction of a number of abstract factors which have moulded the artisan's procedure, including a type, several modes, the environment, the personality of the artisan, and chance. In the case of each artifact, these factors may be said to reach an equilibrium. The equilibrium will be slightly different in each case, and consequently every artifact will differ more or less from all other artifacts.

Being intellectual concepts, the types and modes overlap and intermingle somewhat. They are not independent, mutually exclusive entities like the artifacts. Each type, for example, refers to an entire artifact, whereas the modes refer to its parts. One type and a large number of modes can occur on a single artifact.

One can conceive of a group of artifacts as a number of objects laid side by side. One cannot conceive of a type and its associated modes in this fashion, however. Many of the individual modes would tend to integrate into higher patterns. Unit techniques of manufacture, for example, would tend to be linked by the fact that they form necessary parts of one or more alternative procedures of manufacture.

Unit design concepts would fuse into ideas of the arrangement of the units as complete designs.[42] Different techniques and design concepts would be linked by an abstraction of something which they all have in common, for example that all of them are intended to portray animals and are not merely geometrical.[43] One might imagine the result to be a more or less irregular pyramid, with the modes for unit techniques and designs employed by the artisan at the bottom and the type for the completed artifact at the top.[44]

4. *Artifacts have little historical significance; types and modes have much.* Artifacts are inert objects which exist only where they are kept. Types and modes, however, are assumed to be intellectual ideas, like styles, fashions, and conventions in our own culture. They do not have the limitations of objective existence.

Unlike an artifact, a type or mode can exist simultaneously in a number of different places. Consequently one can trace its distribution over a wide area where it formerly existed at one time. One cannot trace the distribution of an artifact in this manner, however. One can only show that the artifact existed in a single place at a given time.

[42] Cf. Lowie's statement (1922, p. 279) that "for purposes of characterization the combination of the geometrical elements into units of higher order and the method of arrangement of these units within the decorative area are of considerably greater significance than the use of such geometrical abstractions as rectangles and triangles."

[43] Cf. Boas' discussion of the symbolism of art designs. Boas (1927, pp. 88–143).

[44] This conception may appear inconsistent with the procedure followed in the present study, where the history of each mode is traced independently (see pp. 30–33). How can one study each mode separately, if they are linked together like this?

The attempt is made in Appendix 2 to solve this inconsistency.

While it is fashionable, a type or mode is current among a number of different people in many different communities. Each artifact in each community, however, exists only once.

A fashionable type or mode diffuses rapidly from place to place over a wide area. An artifact, however, can only be transported from one place to another.[45]

Artifacts are relatively short-lived phenomena. The life of each artifact lasts only so long as its possessor has use for it. Types and modes, on the contrary, tend to persist over long periods of time, since they are current among large numbers of people and are consequently difficult to replace. Accordingly, one can trace the history of each type and each mode over a long period of time as well as over a large geographical area. To do the same with an artifact, however, would be impossible, since one would have to deal with a minute space in time and with data which are not ordinarily available to the archeologist.

Considered from the standpoints of both space and time, then, artifacts are not in themselves profitable material for historical study. Being objects, they have limited distributions and only momentary existences. On the other hand, types and modes, which spread like ideas and are traditionally inherited, can be studied over wide areas and during long periods of time. Consequently, their histories are much more significant than those of the artifacts.

But types and modes are abstractions from the artifacts. In effect, therefore, they make the artifacts historically more significant. In the two Ft. Liberté papers, it has been assumed that they abstract the historical significance from the artifacts.

An analogy may make this point clearer. The chemist sees fit to describe changes in the substances he studies in terms of abstract formulæ which indicate changes in chemical substances. A similar assumption underlies this study. It is considered necessary to describe the history of artifacts in terms of the history of the abstract factors which have produced them. As formulated during the discussion of the first postulate, these factors include the environment, chance, the individual peculiarities of the artisan, the types, and the modes.

Of the factors mentioned, only the types and modes would seem to be potential subject matter for historical study. They are supposedly traditionally transmitted from place to place, or traditionally inherited from generation to generation, and hence their history can be traced over large areas and during long periods of time. The other factors cannot be studied historically, at least by means of existing archeological methods. They are either momentary, or else relatively constant, and they are not traditionally inherited.

As a result, the history of the artifacts has to be presented in terms of the history of the types and modes. Just as the chemist assumes that changes in the substance he studies are

---

[45] If this argument is valid, archeologists like Lovén (1935) who compare artifacts (or types defined as groups of objects) with the apparent intention of searching for diffusions, fail to utilize the full possibilities of their data. Comparison of artifacts themselves will indicate only whether artifacts have been traded or carried from one region to another, not whether there has been spread of styles or techniques of manufacture from one region to another. To accomplish the latter, one has to treat the artifacts as examples of types and modes, and compare the types and modes rather than the artifacts.

the result of the changes expressed in his formulæ, so in this study it is assumed that historical changes in the artifacts are the result of historical changes in the types and modes.[46]

5. *The persistence of types and modes in time is as important as their diffusion in space.* The best way to explain this postulate is to diagram the relationship between diffusion and persistence. In order to develop such a diagram, it will be necessary to consider the theoretical basis for the distributive procedure used to study the types and modes in the present paper.

It will be remembered that the time scale used for tracing distributions is similar to our own calendric system. It consisted of a series of periods, each of which is comparable to a unit like "century" on our own calendar.

To make the time scale completely resemble our calendrical system, one thing should be added to it. There ought to be a series of points in time, comparable to our concepts of "100 A.D.," "200 A.D.," "300 A.D.," etc. These points would mark off the beginning and end of each period, just as the dates given mark off the beginning and end of each century of our calendric system.

For the sake of simplicity, points like these have not been expressed on the time scale used in the present study. It has been considered sufficient to use the beginning and end of each period as the time points. Even so, one can say in theory that types and modes have been traced from point to point in time just as they have been traced from site to site in space.

Considered in this sense, each point on the time scale (i.e. the limits of each period) is similar to the geographical position of each site in space. In fact, one might term the sites, as mapped, a scale in space, similar to the time scale. Just as a theoretically complete time scale would consist of the periods, and of the points marking off the limits of the periods, so this theoretical space scale would consist of a series of areas, and of the sites which occur within those areas.

By using this formulation, it is possible to re-phrase the two distributive procedures described above (pp. 12-13) with greater accuracy. From a theoretical standpoint, what has been done in this study is to trace the distributions of the types and modes, first from point to point in time within each unit area of space, and, secondly, from site to site in space within each unit period of time.

These relationships may be diagrammed as follows:

[46] Throughout the above discussion, reference has been made only to culture history. It should be noted that the history of the people possessing the culture can also be inferred from the types and modes, probably more readily than it can be inferred from the artifacts themselves.

It should also be noted that the above discussion refers only to attempts at what might be called dynamic reconstruction of historical events, rather than to static historical descriptions. From the standpoint of the latter, descriptions of actual typical artifacts made during a given period of time are just as historical as the sort of reconstruction which is made in the present paper.

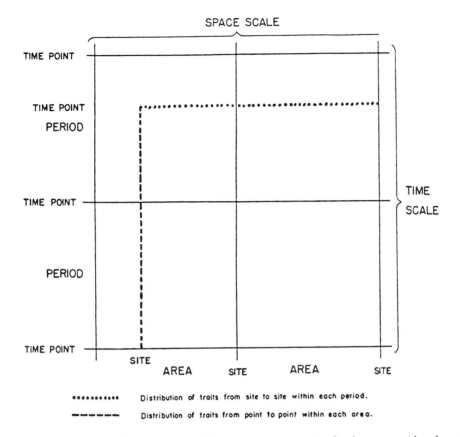

SPACE SCALE

Distribution of traits from site to site within each period.

— — — — — Distribution of traits from point to point within each area.

On this diagram, each area marks off a homogeneous unit of culture, considered geo-graphically, and each period likewise marks off a homogeneous unit of culture, considered chronologically. The two units are made similar in size, in order to avoid distorting the distributions in favor either of time or of space.

The distribution of the modes from point to point on the diagram is the basis for the concept of persistence. The distribution of the modes from site to site, on the other hand, indicates diffusion.

From the standpoint of the diagram, it will be seen, persistence is the logical counter-part to diffusion. One who traces the distribution of a type or mode only in space, thereby studying diffusion but ignoring persistence, reconstructs only part of the culture history. Likewise, one who traces the distribution of the type or mode only in time, thereby study-ing persistence but ignoring diffusion, produces a fragmentary reconstruction. A person must study both the diffusion and the persistence of culture traits if he desires to make a balanced historical reconstruction.

* * * * *

REFERENCES CITED

BLUMENTHAL, ALBERT
    1936   The Nature of Culture. *American Sociological Review* 1:875–904.
BLUMER, HERBERT
    1931   Science without Concepts. *American Journal of Sociology* 36:515–533.

reau of American Ethnology, Annual Report 15:13–152.
BOAS, FRANZ
    1911   *Handbook of American Indian Languages.* Bureau of American Ethnology, Bulletin 40.

1927   *Primitive Art*. Oslo.
CHILDE, VERE GORDON
    1929   *The Danube in Prehistory*. Oxford University Press, Oxford.
COLE, FAY-COOPER AND THORNE DEUEL
    1937   *Rediscovering Illinois: Archaeological Explorations in and around Fulton County*. University of Chicago Press, Chicago.
COLTON, HAROLD S. AND LYNDON L. HARGRAVE
    1937   *Handbook of Northern Arizona Pottery Wares*. Museum of Northern Arizona, Bulletin 11. Flagstaff.
DAVIDSON, DANIEL S.
    1928   *The Chronological Aspects of Certain Australian Social Institutions as Inferred from Geographical Distributions*. Philadelphia.
FORD, CLELLAN S.
    1937   A Sample Comparative Analysis of Material Culture. In *Studies in the Science of Society,* edited by G. P. Murdock, pp. 225–246. Yale University Press, New Haven.
FORD, JAMES A.
    1936   *Analysis of Indian Village Site Collections from Louisiana and Mississippi.* Louisiana State Geological Survey, Department of Conservation, Anthropological Study 2.
    1938   A Chronological Method Applicable to the Southeast. *American Antiquity* 3:260–264.
GOLDENWEISER, ALEXANDER
    1937   *Anthropology: An Introduction to Primitive Culture*. Appleton-Century-Crofts, New York.
GORODOZOV, V. A.
    1933   The Typological Method in Archeology. *American Anthropologist* 35:95–102.
GUMPLOWICZ, LUDWIG
    1892   *Die Sociologische Staatsidee.* Innsbruck.
HOLMES, WILLIAM H.
    1897   Stone Implements of the Potomac-Chesapeake Tidewater Province. *Bu-*
HRDLICKA, ALES
    1930   *Skeletal Remains of Early Man.* Smithsonian Institution Miscellaneous Collections 83.

KROEBER, ALFRED L.
    1923   *Anthropology*. Harcourt Brace, New York.
LINTON, RALPH
    1936   *The Study of Man*. Appleton-Century, New York.
LOVÉN, SVEN
    1935   *Origins of the Tainan Culture, West Indies*. English edition, revised. Göteborg.
LOWIE, ROBERT H.
    1922   Crow Indian Art. *American Museum of Natural History, Anthropological Papers* 21(4).
MALINOWSKI, BRONISLAW
    1931   Culture. *Encyclopedia of the Social Sciences* 4:620–645.
MCKERN, WILLIAM C.
    1934   *Certain Cultural Classification Problems in Middle Western Archaeology.* National Research Council Circular Series, Washington, D.C.
NÖRDENSKIÖLD, ERLAND
    1919   *An Ethno-Geographical Analysis of the Material Culture of Two Indian Tribes in the Gran Chaco.* Comparative Ethnological Studies 1. Göteborg.
OLSON, RONALD L.
    1930   Chumash Prehistory. *University of California, Publications in American Archaeology and Ethnology* 28(1):1–21.
O'NEALE, LILA M.
    1932   Yurok-Karok Basket Weavers. *University of California, Publications in American Archaeology and Ethnology* 32(1):1–184.
PARETO, VILFREDO
    1935   *The Mind and Society.* Dover Publications, New York.
RAINEY, FROELICH G. AND IRVING ROUSE
    1938   Archaeology of the Ft. Liberté Region, Haiti. unpublished manuscript on file, Peabody Museum, Yale University. (published as: Rainey, Froelich G. 1941. *Excavations in the Ft. Liberté Region, Haiti,* Yale University Publications in Anthropology No. 23, and Rouse, Irving. 1941. *Culture of the Ft. Liberté Region, Haiti,*

Yale University Publications in Anthropology No. 24.)

ROUSE, IRVING

1939 New Evidence Concerning the Origins of West Indian Pottery-Making.
(1940) *American Anthropologist* 42:49–80.

SAPIR, EDWARD

1916 *Time Perspective in Aboriginal American Culture: A Study in Method.* Canada, Department of Mines, Geological Survey, Memoir 90, Anthropological Series 13. Ottawa.

1923 Culture, Genuine and Spurious.
(1924) *American Journal of Sociology* 29:401–429.

SAYLES, EDWIN B.

1937 Stone: Implements and Bowls. In *Excavations at Snaketown—Material Culture*, by Harold S. Gladwin, Emil W. Haury, Edwin B. Sayles, and Nora Gladwin, pp. 101–120. Medallion Papers No. 25. Globe, Arizona.

SHEPARD, ANNA O.

1936 The Technology of Pecos Pottery. In *The Pottery of Pecos, Vol. II*, by A.

V. Kidder and A. O. Shepard, pp. 389–587. Papers of the Southwestern Expedition, Phillips Academy, No. 7. Yale University Press, New Haven, Connecticut.

SPIER, LESLIE

1928 Havasupai Ethnography. *American Museum of Natural History, Anthropological Papers* 29(3):81–408.

STRONG, WILLIAM DUNCAN

1927 An Analysis of Southwestern Society. *American Anthropologist* 29:1–61.

TOZZER, ALFRED M.

1937 Review of Vaillant's Work in the Valley of Mexico. *American Anthropologist* 39:338–340.

TYLOR, EDWARD BURNETT

1899 *Anthropology: An Introduction to the Study of Man and Civilization.* Appleton, New York.

WISSLER, CLARK

1914 Material Culture of the North American Indians. *American Anthropologist* 16:447–505.

THE MIDWESTERN TAXONOMIC METHOD AS AN
AID TO ARCHAEOLOGICAL CULTURE STUDY[246]

W. C. McKern[247]

IN DELAYED response to a certain demand for a published state-ment covering the archaeological taxonomic method introduced in the northern Mississippi Valley area a few years ago and now tenta-tively employed in this, the northern Plains, and the Northeastern areas, it seems advisable to briefly set forth in this journal the essential framework for this method, and to include a revision of previously outlined but unpublished discussions relating thereto, in addition to a brief definition of certain problems involved in its application.

Although the present writer's name has been repeatedly associated with this method, it should be made clear that no single individual can be accurately held responsible for the final product. The relatively undeveloped original plan was revised by a self-appointed committee consisting of interested anthropologists representing the universities of Michigan, Chicago, and Illinois, and the Milwaukee Public Museum.[248] A description of the taxonomic method tentatively endorsed by this group was prepared in mimeographed form and distributed[249] for critical inspection to archaeological research students throughout the country. As the result of the constructively critical response to this action, certain details relating to terminology were altered. The general re-action to this revision was one of tentative acceptance, and it was considered the proper procedure to submit the method to trial by use.

At the Indianapolis Conference[250] a change in the terminology for the classificatory divisions was adopted, creating a new division (base) at the generalized end of the frame (as was originally proposed but discarded), and substituting the term "pattern" for "basic-culture." The method as presented here follows the Indianapolis revision.

[246] A revision of the paper: *Certain Culture Classification Problems in Middle Western Archaeology*, presented at the annual meeting of the American Anthropological Associa-tion, Central Section, at Indianapolis, 1934.

[247] Curator of Anthropology, Milwaukee Public Museum, Milwaukee, Wisconsin.

[248] S. A. Barrett, Fay-Cooper Cole, Thorne Deuel, James B. Griffin, Carl E. Guthe, A. R. Kelly, and W. C. McKern, meeting at the University of Chicago, December 10, 1932.

[249] Through the facilities of the National Research Council, Committee on State Archaeological Surveys.

[250] Under the auspices of the National Research Council, Committee on State Archaeological Surveys, December 6–8, 1935.

301

THE NEED FOR CLASSIFICATION

Any adequate discussion of this or any other method relating to archaeological culture classification must logically follow some consideration of the need for culture classification in archaeology. It may be advanced that we already possess an adequate taxonomic method. I have received such questions as this: why refer to the cultural manifestation of the pre-literate Iowa as the upper Mississippi, or by any name other than Iowa? In instances we may have sufficient data to verify identification with some known historic group, such as the Iowa. However, in most instances, we can not immediately bridge the barrier between pre-literate and historic or protohistoric cultural groups, and in many instances we can not reasonably hope ever to be able to do so. Yet we perceive that there are archaeologically collected data that warrant cultural segregation. The only taxonomic basis for dealing with all cultural manifestations, regardless of occasional direct historical tie-ups, is that of culture type as illustrated by trait-indicative materials and features encountered at former habitation sites. If at any time it becomes possible to name the historic ethnic group for which the pre-literate group is the progenitor, no confusion should result from the statement that, for example, Upper Mississippi Oneota is Chiwere Sioux; no more so than from the statement that *Elephas primigenius* is the mammoth.

Aside from the inadequacy of the direct-historical method to supply the archaeologist in every instance, and immediately, with means for attachment to the ethnological classification, the latter, even if applicable, would not ideally answer the needs of the archaeologist. One ethnological classification divides the aborigines into linguistic stocks, which are subdivided first into more specific linguistic groups and, finally, into socio-political groups. The criteria for classification are social, primarily linguistic. The major portion of the data available to the archaeologist relates to material culture, and in no instance includes linguistic data. Consequently, this ethnological classification does not satisfy archaeological requirements.

It may be said that we have the ethnologically conceived culture areas to supply a basis for archaeological classification. However, these so-called culture areas involve two factors which the archaeologist must disregard in devising his culture classification if he is to avoid hopeless confusion; these are the spatial and temporal factors. First, the culture area attempts to define, or at least limit, geographic distribution. Unfortunately, cultural divisions of American aborigines did

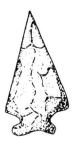

not always succeed in confining themselves within a continuous area, or in keeping culturally pure an area of any important size. Second, the archaeologist considers the American Indians from the standpoint of all time, and, certainly, there can be no cultural areas devised to account for an unlimited temporal factor.

In brief, the archaeologist requires a classification based upon the cultural factor alone; temporal and distributional treatments will follow as accumulating data shall warrant. Moreover, the archaeological classification necessarily must be based upon criteria available to the archaeologist.

Any statement that the archaeologist has no need for a culture taxonomic method is in conflict with facts which all students of the subject must have encountered. One has only to consult the pre-classification reports on research in almost any American province (outside the Southwest, where a special classification has been developed), noting the indefinite use of the word "culture" to denote anything from the manifestation of a general pattern influential over an area a thousand or more miles in extent, to the highly specialized manifestation of a culture apparent at a cluster of closely localized sites, and noting the confusion of unstandardized cultural terminology, to appreciate the need for simplifying the complexity of cultural data and concepts through the establishment of systematic order. In men's affairs, chaos does not reduce itself to order without a plan. The accomplishments of science stand as a monument to planned orderliness.

Unlike the student of ethnology, the American archaeologist has not been appreciably influenced by the initial complexity of his subject to specialize in some certain aspect of that subject; more inclined to embrace in his studies all apparent aspects of his subject within the area available to him for investigation. As his problems lead towards comparative studies over wider area, his conceptions of cultural manifestations take on broader interpretations. Starting with cultural differentiation, he begins to observe evidence of cultural affinities, not only as regards specific complexes but involving distinctive types of complexes. He lacks a specific terminology that is standard with his fellow students, by means of which he can clearly express his maturing concepts. He stretches old meanings to apply to his needs, and finds himself justly criticised, primarily by students limited to ethnological experience, for his extraordinarily indefinite, inaccurate use of the term "culture," which, for want of a more specific term, is made to serve a multitude of specific purposes for which it never was intended.

The point of all this is that the student of archaeology in the greater Mississippi Valley is greatly in need of a standardized culture scheme such as can be realized only through the medium of a taxonomic method.

There are a few who have hesitated to cooperate fully in this classificatory experiment on the grounds of not being satisfied that the time for classification has yet arrived. They perceive that we lack adequate information to warrant wholesale classification. With due respect for the caution exhibited in this attitude, I can not but feel that this caution is based upon a false conception of the very nature and purpose of classification, and a misunderstanding of the intentions of those endorsing the taxonomic method in question.

Classification is nothing more than the process of recognizing classes, each class identified by a complex of characteristics. For many years, we have all been active in this business of identifying cultural classes, no matter by what name one may call it, but we have not performed with marked efficiency because we have lacked the necessary equipment. In the *Encyclopedia Britannica*, Dr. Abraham Wolf says: "Classification is one method, probably the simplest method, of discovering order in the world. . . . In the history of every science classification is the very first method to be employed." We have tried to get along without it over long. It is classification that makes it possible for one student to describe phenomena in terms readily comprehensible to another student versed in the taxonomic method. It reduces a multiplicity of facts to simplicity and order, and supplies a standardized terminology without which students encounter difficulty in conversing intelligently on a common subject.

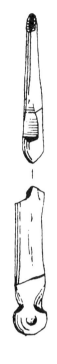

The adoption and use of a taxonomic method most certainly does not imply the immediate classification of all manifestations with apparent cultural significance. It is only in those instances in which sufficient data are available, quantitatively and qualitatively, to create a problem of cultural differentiation that classification can serve to any advantage. In some provinces little in the way of detailed classification can logically be attempted at this time; in other provinces much can be accomplished towards detailed classification; and in all provinces a taxonomic method should be adopted before any serious attempts are made at classification. Naturally, this method should be standard for the largest area possible. Following an agreement as to method, the actual classification should be a necessarily slow, deliberate procedure, constantly experimental, subject to such major and minor corrections as newly accumu-

The Midwestern Taxonomic Method

lating data may dictate, subject to a maximum of constructive criticism and resulting improvement. Such is the history of any scientific classification. It is the method of classification to be employed, not any specific classification, that offers an immediate, initial problem for which a solution is now being attempted.

PRELIMINARY TERMINOLOGY

Before describing the taxonomic system, certain details of involved procedure and related terminology should be explained and defined.

The word *determinant* is employed to denote any culture trait when and as used as a marker for any specific culture division. The term is in no sense synonymous with "trait."

In comparing any two culture manifestations, it may develop that certain traits are shared in common by the two manifestations. Such traits, to follow Ritchie,[351] may be designated as *linked* traits. Traits found to occur in one manifestation and not in that with which it is compared, peculiar to the one manifestation in this comparison, are termed *diagnostic* traits.[352] It follows, by definition, that in any comparison of two manifestations only diagnostic traits can serve as determinants for either manifestation, since only traits peculiar to each of the compared culture varieties can be used to differentiate between them. It therefore follows that traits which are diagnostic and thus useful as determinants in one comparison may be linked traits in another comparison and, consequently, useless as determinants. Therefore, there can be no truly valuable fixed list of determinants for any given culture class, serving as such in all possible comparisons; the determinants for a hypothetical Culture A as compared with Culture B may be considerably different from the determinants for the same Culture A as compared with Culture C. The term "determinant" can only be employed as applied in a stated comparison.

In brief, all the traits characteristic for a given culture manifestation comprise the culture complex for that manifestation. However, in any comparison of this manifestation with another, made for purposes of classification, certain traits may be demonstrated as present in both complexes, and these linked traits, serving to show cultural similarity between the two culture variants, can not be employed as determinants in this comparison. Certain other traits, respectively peculiar to each

---

[351] Ritchie, Wm. A., *Culture Influence from Ohio in New York Archaeology.* This series, Vol. 2, No. 3, p. 187, January, 1937.

[352] *Ibid.*

of the compared complexes and so serving to differentiate between them, are diagnostic traits and useful for culture determinants in this comparison. Other comparisons may produce an entirely new alignment of determinants.

USE OF TRAITS

One of the most difficult problems facing the classifier is that of identifying the determinants for a cultural division, particularly those more specific divisions in which cultural details are important criteria for differentiation. This difficulty is partly due to the difference in complexity between such an object as a simple bone awl and another such as a pottery vessel. Culture criteria available to the archaeologist are demonstrated by culture-indicative materials, for the most part artifacts. A simple type of artifact may serve as one element in a trait complex for one cultural division, and therefore may serve in some comparison as a determinant for that division. This may be the case with a simple type of bone awl. However, when a comparatively complex type of pottery is characteristic for one of the more specific cultural divisions, the question arises as to whether it should be considered as a trait or as comprising a number of trait elements. It certainly is more culturally indicative than a pointed fragment of bone. Single detailed pottery elements, such as shell temper, loop handles, or cord-imprinted decoration, would seem to be at least as important culture markers as a simple implement with a single differentiating trait. Thus, apparently, we may have a considerable variety of trait elements exhibited by pottery alone. Probably other subjects of cultural import in instances will each supply many, rather than a single trait; for instance, mound structure, burial methods, and house types. It may even seem advisable to recognize in the simplest of artifacts such distinct detailed traits as regard shape, material, and technique of fabrication.

The problem, then, narrows down to the selecting, from the traits comprising a complex subject, of those trait details which have sufficient cultural significance to qualify them as culture determinants. This really implies a separate classification of the essential trait elements for any given complex cultural subject. For example, pottery should be classified under such essential heads as paste, temper, texture, hardness, surface, color, shape, and decoration. Determinants in pottery for a cultural division in a specific comparison could then be selected to cover these standard pottery trait elements. In the same way, the essential detailed traits for burial method, and other complex

subjects could be standardized through special classifications, with the result that the determinants for one cultural division would cover the same ground as, and carry similar weight to those for another division with which it is compared. Simpler subjects would offer fewer but equally important trait details, or elements.

Our problem has also to deal with different types of culture, as different from each other as a broad basic type and a local specific type. The former is identified for the most part by traits that are in the nature of fundamental cultural trends. These fundamentals are quite different in character from the detailed material trait elements that are so important in determining highly specialized divisions. Thus, the character of a trait employed as a culture determinant will depend upon the type of cultural division for which it serves as a determinant. The presence of horticulture might serve as a differentiating trait for some sedentary division as distinct from a nomadic, hunting division, but it could not serve to distinguish between two subdivisions of a horticultural class. In the opposite extreme, a peculiar motif in pottery decoration might serve as one determinant of a local specific division, but not as a determinant for the less specialized division under which it is classified, since it is peculiar to the local class.

One general axiom must guide the student in attacking this problem. Traits or trait elements employed as determinants must be characteristic for that division which they serve to identify. That being the case, determinants for a *base* (see following taxonomic system), or even a *pattern*, will be for the most part general in character and relatively few in number. For the more specialized divisions, progressing from lesser to greater specialization, the determinants will be an enriched edition of the determinants for the immediately preceding, more general division, as altered to include greater detail, plus a considerable number of trait elements peculiarly characteristic of the more specialized division. For example, the *focus* determinants would be the *aspect* determinants made richer in detail and augmented by additional traits peculiar to the focus and exhibiting the greatest cultural detail apparent for the entire pattern.

TAXONOMIC SYSTEM

The method here under consideration is basically a simple one employing for its purposes complexes of cultural factors only. Five arbitrary divisions are made differentiating between specialized local types of culture manifestation and more general and broadly influential types.

Focus. Starting at the site, as any investigator must, materials and associated data are collected which have cultural significance. Expressed in terms of culture traits, these data provide a trait complex for the site. If the complex of trait units so determined, or any important complex of trait units included therein, is found to recur in characteristic purity and practical completeness at other sites, to an extent suggestive of cultural identity, this recurring complex establishes the first of our class types, the *focus*. A focus may be briefly defined as that class of culture exhibiting characteristic peculiarities in the finest analysis of cultural detail, and may in instances correspond closely to the local tribe in ethnology. It is dangerous, however, to define it as such.

The manifestation of any given focus at a specific site is termed a *component* of that focus. This is in no sense an additional type of culture manifestation, one of the five class types; rather, it is the focus as represented at a site, and serves to distinguish between a site, which may bear evidence of several cultural occupations, each foreign to the other, and a single specified manifestation at a site. In many instances several components, each at cultural variance with the other, may be found to occur at a single site.

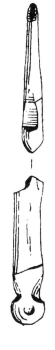

Aspect. A comparison of established foci may supply evidence that certain foci are, on the one hand, very like each other, especially when certain of the more specific trait units are eliminated from consideration, and on the other hand, as a group, show marked dissimilarity to other compared foci. When this similarity of compared foci involves a preponderating majority of the traits and trait elements, the dissimilarity apparent for the greater part in considering the more detailed elements, these foci may be classified under the same *aspect*, the second class type. All foci in a given aspect share the somewhat less specific aspect trait units, but possess additional peculiarities in fine cultural detail. Thus, the type of decorative pattern on pottery might serve as an aspect determinant, shared by all the foci in that aspect, whereas the actual patterns employed might serve to differentiate one of these foci from another.

Phase. Similarly, like aspects may determine a *phase*, the third class type. As the classifier approaches the more generalized classes, cultural detail becomes less important to his purposes, and the traits that are shared by all aspects within the phase to make up the phase complex take on a more general character. For example, whereas actual decorative patterns on pottery may serve as focus determinants, and

The Midwestern Taxonomic Method   225

less specific types of pattern decoration as aspect determinants, the trait of mechanical technique for ceramic ornamentation, shared by all its aspects, might be the most detailed trait of pottery decoration applicable to the phase. Or, the phase may be characterized by a general burial procedure, general pottery attributes, and general house-type features; whereas one aspect within the phase is differentiated from the other aspects as the result of a consideration of burials, pottery, and houses in somewhat greater detail. In addition to this qualitative factor, a near majority of traits shared in common by compared aspects determine the phase, and these traits comprise the phase complex. As previously demonstrated, it should be remembered that there is a difference between the phase complex, or any other class complex, and the complex of determinants for the phase as specifically compared with another phase.

Pattern. Several phases may be shown to share a small complex of broadly general traits, in contrast to other compared phases in which these traits do not occur. Such a complex of traits determines that the phases identified thereby bear the relation to each other of belonging to the same *pattern*, the fourth class in the taxonomic frame. The traits used as determinants for the pattern will be such as deal with the cultural reflection of the primary adjustments of peoples to environment, as modified by tradition.

For example, the Mississippi Pattern, as compared with the Woodland Pattern, offers such determinants as (tentative list): characteristic extended inhumation; a pottery ware medium to fine in texture, prevailingly shell-tempered, characterized by incised, trailed or modeled decoration, offering relative variety in shape; basically triangular chipped-stone projectile points; secondary flaking superimportant over primary, to reduce thin flakes to a desired shape and size; ungrooved axes; relative superimportance of bone, antler, and shell as materials for a considerable variety of artifacts; sedentary territorial adjustment.

The Woodland Pattern, as compared with the Mississippi Pattern, offers such determinants as (tentative list): characteristic flexed inhumation and/or secondary interments; a pottery ware characteristically grit-tempered, granular in structure, with intaglio surface ornamentation effected on the soft unfired paste by means of cords and/or other indenting tools, prevailingly sub-conoidal in shape with simple shape variety; stemmed or notched chipped-stone projectile points and cutting implements; primary chipping superimportant over secondary,

W. C. McKern

to reduce thick flakes to a desired size and shape; grooved axes; semi-sedentary territorial adjustment.

Base. In addition to the diagnostic traits respectively employed as determinants for these two patterns, there are also certain broadly general linked traits shared by both; such as pottery, sedentary tendency, and, possibly, horticulture. On a basis of these similarities, if these patterns are compared, for example, with nomadic hunting patterns, the Mississippi and Woodland patterns may be classified together within the same *base*, the most general of the taxonomic divisions. The base is characterized by a few fundamentals, such as relate in the most general way to the food quest (horticulture, hunting, seed gathering), community order (camps, permanent villages), or possession of classes of products of outstanding cultural import (pottery, basketry). Hypothetical examples of the base might include such descriptively named divisions as: Horticultural-Pottery Base; Nomadic-Hunting Base; Sedentary-Fishing Base; Seed-Gathering-Basketry Base.

To summarize briefly, the taxonomic frame consists of five major divisions: focus, aspect, phase, pattern, and base, progressing from localized detailed to large general classes. The manifestation of a focus at any site is called a component of that focus. The method is comparable to a filing cabinet equipped with labeled drawers to facilitate the orderly arrangement of culture-indicative data.

RELATED PROBLEMS

Archaeological data at best offer a very incomplete cultural picture of the people under investigation, and great care should be taken to base classification upon as representative a mass of data as possible. The exploration of a burial site has been demonstrated in many instances to produce information more characteristic of the burial customs of an ethnic group than of the complete culture. Similarly, data collected at a village site with no burials is deficient in that information on burial methods is lacking.

The error in classifying cultural divisions on a basis of site or component units, regardless of the limitations in character of such manifestations, i.e., whether burial, village, or other varieties of sites, may be corrected by a consideration of *communities* rather than components. This method of approach has been advanced by Cole and Deuel.[353]

---

[353] Cole, Fay-Cooper, and Deuel, Thorne, *Rediscovering Illinois.* University of Chicago Publications in Anthropology, pp. 34, 278, University of Chicago Press, 1937.

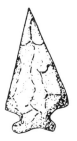

who define the community as " . . . the complete cultural manifestation of a local group or as much of it as is determined by archaeological exploration." Any classification based, for example, on data collected exclusively at burial sites is subject to greater error, and is therefore less useful than if the determinants represent a community as manifested at both habitation and burial sites.

Experience seems to demonstrate that absolute mathematical percentages in trait similarity can not be successfully employed to establish the class relationship between two compared manifestations. This is largely due to the fact that a completed list of culture-indicative data for any culture group can never be made available, and that such lists as are available will be more inclusive for one community than for another with which it is compared. Moreover, the different character of the culture elements employed for determining separate classes, i.e., the generalized traits of a pattern as contrasted to the detailed trait units of a focus, serves to complicate any mathematical treatment of the problem; it is difficult to add apples and bushels of apples.

However, the quantitative similarity in culture indicators is decidedly serviceable in determining the classificatory place of a manifestation. After trait units for a community have been formulated as the result of field and laboratory research, and this trait list is compared with similarly prepared lists for other manifestations, it may be found that, culturally, the community complex is more similar to certain of the compared manifestations than to others. If the similarity should amount to a practical identity of these detailed trait elements, a focus would be indicated. If the similarity should amount to an important majority of the trait elements, at least aspect relationship would be indicated. Similarly, a comparison on a basis of more generalized traits in all probability would serve to identify pattern, possibly phase relationships.

It is not to be expected that a complete classification for any given work province can be made immediately. Classification will grow slowly under the most favorable conditions, and, in instances, will be delayed indefinitely. In all instances, the taxonomic method should be regarded as a tool to be used only when needed.

The growth of a classification will not invariably be in logical sequence, from focus to base. After a focus has been determined, the classifier may fail for a time to find evidence of near cultural relationship and, lacking criteria indicating the proper aspect, or even phase, may assign the focus to a pattern before data indicative of the inter-

vening classes are made available; providing, of course, that the pattern complex has previously been defined.

The relative grouping of cultural divisions by any such taxonomic method does not necessarily imply evolutionary relationship. A common historical origin may be suggested, but the implication should be considered as an indicator, guiding further research, rather than as proof in itself. Cultural evolution can not be established by such a classification since time criteria, so essential to any study of directional growth, have no place in its determination; the method makes use of culture criteria only. A chronology independently constructed from available time criteria may later be determined as a parallel development and correlated with a culture classification to establish or refute evolutionary sequence.

Cultural distribution can only be portrayed on a basis of time, since distribution is not a fixed quantity for all time. Thus, any map devised to show the known distribution for a given culture division, such as the Upper Mississippi Phase, is a map of culture only; for any given time, it might offer a materially altered appearance.

In applying any taxonomic method, there is always the danger that an unleashed enthusiasm may induce the classifier to attempt to make the facts fit the method. The lure of being methodical at all costs is a constant threat to the wholly profitable use of any method. It is well to bear constantly in mind the rule that the classification is, and forever must be, subservient to the facts. It is convenience and orderliness in handling archaeological data that is required of the classification, not a flawless, natural regimentation of the facts required by the classification.

This method of classification is arbitrary, like all other scientific taxonomic methods. Under the blending influences of diffusion, and the divergent tendencies involving cultural growth by invention, there can be no hard and fast natural division lines. This absence of sharp lines of demarcation between classes applies rather equally to the subject matter of all natural sciences, and can not be advanced as a valid argument against classification. Our method is not nearly so arbitrary as the division of a continent into culture areas, which disregards an inelastic temporal factor and a confusingly mixed and unstable distributional factor. The maximum degree of arbitrariness in our method is attained in the division of cultural manifestations into five, rather than some other number of culture types. The five divisions were finally agreed upon by the authors of this method as satisfying all apparent

The Midwestern Taxonomic Method   229

needs for major subdivision. With the means provided for ultimate subclassification into specific groups under these culture-type heads, if and when needed, the major requirements of remotely separate fields seem to be satisfied, as reported by specialists in those fields.

Although the space available here has not permitted for the taxonomic method adequate illustrations by example, it is hoped that the basic idea has been stated clearly, and that some of the most essential problems relating thereto have been defined. Admittedly, the value of such a method, and the ways for making it function to best advantage as discussed herein, are controversial subjects. However, in consideration of experience obtained as the result of a rather widespread trial of the method, during the last six years, it appears to have contributed materially towards introducing order into the previously existing chaotic status of general culture concepts throughout the greater Mississippi Valley.

STATISTICAL CLASSIFICATION[1]

A. L. Kroeber

I PRESENT herewith four-cell coefficients calculated from data given in two recent midwestern archaeological reports by Webb and Griffin.[2] The purpose is not controversial, since in a simple situation involving a small number of culturally related sites a competent archaeologist saturated in his material can draw all important classificatory inferences and it would be vain to hope that any statistical device would add anything fundamental. What calculations can do in such a case is this: (1) Check errors and oversights of "intuitive" or inspectional interpretation. This of course holds both ways: if there is serious disagreement, a computatory error may be at fault. (2) Present results with added clarity and incisiveness, especially after numerical coefficients have been translated into diagrams. (3) Indicate minor revisions of classification. (4) Sometimes suggest the factor at work if a classification comes out conflicting or dubious at certain points.

Like any other inductive comparison, a statistical one, *per se*, of course yields only a classification. How this is to be read in terms of cause or sequence is a subsequent and non-statistical matter.

The usual statistical approach to culture material is through traits or elements, on which archaeologists, ethnologists, and linguists have come to depend more and more as the evidential basis of comparisons. In fact, of the three groups, archaeologists are perhaps the most familiar with the trait concept. A trait can be determined as occurring or not occurring—present or absent—in any given cultural manifestation. If it seems to be ambiguous, it can usually be broken down into two or more traits, which can then be successfully described as present or absent.

In anthropometry as the name implies, it is customary to measure on a scale. The present-absent or four-cell method of statistics has therefore been little used and is generally not even taught in anthropometry: measures of mean, variability, and correlation take its place. In all fields of culture, however, experience has shown scale measurement to be difficult. Either the scale is really subjective and only pseudo-quanti-

---

[1] Typewriting, computations, and diagram by a University of California W.P.A. project, No. 665-08-3-30, Unit A-15.

[2] Webb, W. S., *An Archaeological Survey of the Norris Basin in Eastern Tennessee.* Bureau of American Ethnology, Bulletin 118, 1938.—Griffin, J. B., *An Analysis of the Fort Ancient Culture, Notes from the Ceramic Repository . . . of the University of Michigan,* No. 1, 1935.

29

tative; or if quantitative, it seems to miss what we feel to be the significance of culture phenomena. Hence, the falling back on manipulations of presence and absence counts.

When any two cultural manifestations are compared, their trait presences and absences are of four orders or kinds: a, present in both; b, present in one, absent in the other; c, the reverse; d, absent in both. In ordinary language, a and d are agreements, positive and negative respectively; b and c are disagreements. These are the four "cells" into which the inventory of traits occurring in two culture manifestations are distributed.

The four cell-values are then treated by one of several formulae to yield a coefficient. This coefficient for cultures 1 and 2 is then compared with the corresponding coefficient for cultures 1 and 3, 2 and 3, and so on. From this comparison of coefficients there results a classification of the relative degree of likeness of the cultures dealt with, so far as they are known through evidential data. Each coefficient, of course, is a generalized expression of likeness, which takes on meaning from the relation to other such generalized expressions of likeness.

Some of the formulae are derived by mathematicians interested in statistical theory and enjoy professional repute. Others are common-sense proportions. Experience to date indicates that ordinarily there is not very much to choose between the several formulae as regards their effective representation of the "truth" of the situation.[3] I shall therefore use several different formulae by way of exemplification, without discussing their respective merits.

There is only one more theoretical point to be mentioned. Should common absences be dealt with? Almost everyone at first makes this objection. Why are two nothingnesses significant? Do they not introduce something artificial and unreal? The simplest answer is that given by Driver. If culture 1 has a trait and culture 2 lacks it, everyone will concede that the fact is significant. Therewith, however, we have admitted one zero. Since we all deal with such oneway zeros without qualm, why boggle at double zeros? Of course they must be pertinent to the field of investigation. That is, they must occur somewhere in the area or complex dealt with; otherwise they are gratuitous and may lead to mis-

---

[3] As my colleague and collaborator, H. E. Driver, has shown, all formulae give more or less misrepresentative results when one or two of the four values a, b, c, d differ very greatly from the others, that is, when their distribution is markedly skew. According to the nature of the particular skewness encountered, each coefficient can be specially misrepresentative, speaking broadly.

leading results. If we are comparing sites x, y, and z and none of them has pottery, there is no sense bringing pottery into the trait count. If, however, site z has pottery, the 0–0 relation of sites x and y on this point evidently is significant, precisely because x and z, and y and z, show a 0–1 relation.

Conversely, universal positives are omitted from counts. If all sites dealt with possess pottery, three uniform 1–1 relations add nothing when we are investigating degrees of differentiation and likeness. If the three potteries are identical in all their features, we might in fact add twenty 1–1 relations for twenty pottery traits, swell the values in the a cells, and thereby tend to distort all coefficients more or less.

In practice, common negatives sometimes present a problem, because we do not always know whether a trait was really lacking in a culture or has simply failed to be found in the excavations or collections made. In ethnology and linguistics such risks also occur, but are often more easily dealt with because they are evident, or the situation can be remedied. If the question is whether a given language has or has not a subjunctive, and the author of a grammar on it discusses modes in detail but does not mention a subjunctive, it is reasonably probable that this feature is lacking. But if his grammar is sketchy and he fails to consider modes altogether, it would be rash to infer either presence or absence of a subjunctive. Similarly, in ethnology we can to a certain degree estimate the probability of absences by fulness of context. When ethnologists, through localization of interest, cite almost no trait absences—which by their nature express a comparative point of view—even though they describe in great detail features that are present, it is always possible to retrieve the negative information, and sometimes rather rapidly, by special new inquiries. Our Element Survey in California, for instance, represents to a large extent, though not wholly, just such an endeavor.

With extinct cultures, however, there are corresponding limitations: there may be nothing left of a site, or to repeat an excavation would be prohibitively costly; and on account of perishability, whole classes of objects are ordinarily lost. If one site is favored by exceptional conditions favoring preservation, and has yielded a series of wooden objects, textiles, and the like, it is better to omit these from any quantitative comparison rather than to construe them as jointly absent from the manifestations at the other sites to which the first is being compared. This of course is only common-sense. A similar caution would be exercised as between a cemetery of the evidently wealthy and one of the

poor; though luxury and art objects might become important at a later stage of investigation, in comparisons made between a whole series of related sites and another such series. On the whole, a safe rule seems to be to compare only sites or cultures whose trait inventories are not too disproportionate. If one site has yielded only a tenth as many traits as another, it is evidently an inadequate sample; if it yields half as many, the sample may be reasonably adequate for comparison; just as in anthropometry we would not build heavily on the difference shown by the means of ten individuals measured in one population and a hundred in another, though if there were fifty and a hundred we should feel that the result had fair reliability. After all, it is desirable to avoid pedantic perfectionism: all study of men must rest on sampling. In archaeology, it is perhaps generally wise to make primary comparisons between the more adequate samples, and then tentatively attach inadequate ones— minor sites, the results of incomplete excavation, and the like—to the classification built up on the fuller samples: more on this matter in the concrete analyses that follow.

TENNESSEE

On pages 367–368, Webb gives a table of traits occurring at ten Norris Basin village sites showing post-mold patterns. This table lists seventy-five traits,[4] of which twenty-four relate to house structure. Webb finds that his sites Nos. **2, 4, 5, 6, 8, 9, 17** are of one type, which he calls "small-log," and **10, 11, 19** of another, the "large log." Webb follows his table with a list of forty-five lines, such as: "Sites Nos. **2** and **4** have a total of 46 traits—17 in common, or 37 percent."[5] The values in a list of this sort are hard to conceptualize; and on page 370 he gives a tabular arrangement of percentages which shows that the thirteen highest of the forty-five comparisons (values of 41% or more) are all either between small-log and small-log or between large-log and large-log sites, whereas the fifteen lowest (22% or less) are all between small-log and large-log sites. While this presentation is not particularly incisive, it is convincing enough.

Webb's percentages express the values of the formula $a/(a+b+c)$, with a, b, c the same as in the four-cell table. Thus, for sites **2** and **4**,

---

[4] Actually only seventy three show variation: two are universal positives (rectangular post-mold patterns, clay floors) and should not have been counted. I noted them as universal only after the computations had been made; but they are too few to affect the coefficient relations materially.

[5] Two of these, **4–6** and **5–17**, seem to have been erroneously counted, either by Webb or by me.

a = 17, b = 22, c = 7, a+b+c = 46. For sites **2** and **5,** the values are 32, 7, 13 = 52.

Adding d, the number of traits jointly lacking at the pair of sites being considered, though occurring somewhere in the group of ten sites, we have, for **2** and **4**: a = 17, b = 22, c = 7, d = 29 (= 75 − 46). As a matter of record, I first list the values a, b, c, d for the forty-five combinations of sites.

2-4: 17, 22, 7, 29	4-17: 18, 6, 22, 29	8-9: 18, 3, 23, 31
2-5: 32, 7, 13, 23	4-19: 10, 14, 25, 26	8-10: 8, 13, 36, 18
2-6: 14, 25, 5, 31	5-6: 13, 32, 6, 24	8-11: 7, 14, ?4, 13
2-8: 17, 22, 4, 32	5-8: 19, 26, 2, 28	8-17: 12, 9, 28, 26
2-9: 30, 9, 11, 25	5-9: 32, 13, 9, 21	8-19: 8, 13, 27, 27
2-10: 15, 24, 29, 7	5-10: 24, 21, 20, 10	9-10: 16, 25, 28, 6
2-11: 12, 27, 19, 17	5-11: 19, 26, 12, 18	9-11: 9, 32, 22, 12
2-17: 24, 15, 16, 20	5-17: 29, 16, 11, 19	9-17: 25, 16, 15, 19
2-19: 12, 27, 23, 13	5-19: 19, 26, 16, 14	9-19: 14, 27, 21, 13
4-5: 23, 1, 22, 29	6-8: 11, 8, 10, 46	10-11: 27, 17, 4, 27
4-6: 9, 15, 10, 41	6-9: 18, 1, 23, 33	10-17: 24, 20, 16, 15
4-8: 11, 13, 10, 41	6-10: 8, 11, 36, 20	10-19: 33, 11, 2, 29
4-9: 22, 2, 19, 32	6-11: 5, 14, 26, 30	11-17: 17, 14, 23, 21
4-10: 12, 12, 32, 19	6-17: 11, 8, 29, 27	11-19: 22, 9, 13, 31
4-11: 10, 14, 21, 30	6-19: 6, 13, 29, 27	17-19: 19, 21, 16, 19

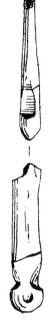

I will now apply to these counts two formulas of the several available. The first is R_{hk}, which has theoretical standing.

$$R_{hk} = \frac{ad - bc}{\sqrt{(a+b)(a+c)(b+d)(c+d)}}$$

The values obtained lie between 1.0 and −1.0.

The forty-five coefficients are best presented not in the accidental order in which the ten sites were numbered, but according to a plan which places together the sites whose intersite coefficients are highest, that is, which are most similar. The best arrangement can be found by inspection or a trial or two. This arrangement throws the higher values along a diagonal from upper left to lower right corner of the crossway table. The lowest values will then tend to cluster in the two other corners.

TABLE 1: R_{hk} VALUES

	5	2	9	4	8	6	17	11	10	19
5	1.0	.47	.41	.50	.39	.10	.27	.02	−.13	−.11
2	.47	1.0	.47	.26	.36	.25	.17	−.22	−.43	−.33
9	.41	.47	1.0	.51	.39	.46	.17	−.43	−.44	−.28
4	.50	.26	.51	1.0	.27	.19	.30	.01	−.12	−.07
8	.39	.36	.39	.27	1.0	.39	.05	−.10	−.26	−.11
6	.10	.25	.46	.19	.39	1.0	.05	−.18	−.20	−.18
17	.27	.17	.17	.30	.05	.05	1.0	.25	.03	.18
11	.02	−.22	−.43	.01	−.10	−.18	.25	1.0	.49	.41
10	−.13	−.43	−.44	−.12	−.26	−.20	.03	.49	1.0	.68
19	−.11	−.33	−.28	−.07	−.11	−.18	.18	.41	.68	1.0
Traits present	60	39	41	24	21	19	40	31	44	35

The second formula is a common-sense or simple proportion one: $Z = (a-b-c+d)/(a+b+c+d)$; or $(a+d)-(b+c)$ divided by N; verbally, shared traits less diverse traits, the difference being divided by the total number of traits dealt with. The limits of the values obtained again are 1.0 and -1.0. The arrangement of coefficients is as before.

TABLE 2: Z VALUES

	5	2	9	4	8	6	17	11	10	19
5	1.0	.47	.41	.39	.25	−.01	.28	−.01	−.09	−.12
2	.47	1.0	.47	.23	.31	.20	.17	−.23	−.41	−.33
9	.41	.47	1.0	.44	.31	.36	.17	−.44	−.41	−.28
4	.39	.23	.44	1.0	.39	.33	.25	.06	−.17	−.04
8	.25	.31	.31	.39	1.0	.52	.01	−.01	−.30	−.07
6	−.01	.20	.36	.33	.52	1.0	.01	−.07	−.25	−.12
17	.28	.17	.17	.25	.01	.01	1.0	.01	.04	.01
11	−.01	−.23	−.44	.06	−.01	−.07	.01	1.0	.44	.41
10	−.09	−.41	−.41	−.17	−.30	−.25	.04	.44	1.0	.65
19	−.12	−.33	−.28	−.04	−.07	−.12	.01	.41	.05	1.0

It is evident that while the particular values differ in the two tables, the *relative* values of the forty-five coefficients come out much alike.

Graphically, the results can be presented effectively by symbols each covering a certain range of coefficients. Figure 5 will be self-explanatory

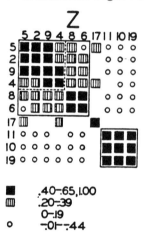

FIG. 5. Graphic presentation of Z values.

with its key. It groups the Z values of table 2, and thus puts no strain on the memory as the eye passes from one part of the table to another.

Now on comparison of either table or the diagram with Webb's classification, it is evident that they largely corroborate each other. Sites **11, 10,** and **19,** Webb's large-log sites, form a clearly marked-off class. They show rather high positive coefficients with one another,

prevailingly negative coefficients with the remaining small-log type sites. "High" does not refer to any absolute value, such as .40, but high in relation to the majority of coefficients in the table. If a group of extremely similar sites were examined, .40 might be a low coefficient. If the sites were very diverse, the table might not contain a single .40, and any positive coefficient would be a high one. For this reason there can be no rule about the range of values to be denoted by one symbol in the graphic representation. One is free to choose as many or as few symbols as one likes, and to assign to each any value-range that will best bring out the salient lines of the grouping.

It will however be noted that one site, No. **17**, does not fall clearly into the small-log group. By both formulas it has no negative coefficients and no first-order positive ones. By R_{hk}, for instance, its coefficients with the six small-log sites range from .30 to .05, with the three large-log ones from .25 to .03. This is not very decisive as to affiliation. Here then I differ from Webb: site **17** is intermediate between his two types, with only slight leaning one way.

Next, it is observable that the six remaining small-log sites segregate into two sub-classes. Sites **5, 2, 9, 4** form a compact group, with high coefficients *inter se*, only one falling below .39 by Z. Sites **8** and **6**, however, average lower coefficients with these four; one of them, according to Z, even is negative.

However, these two aberrant small-log sites are also those which yielded the smallest number of traits present: twenty-one and nineteen, respectively. Their *d* is consequently the highest of any: 46. It seems reasonable to infer that their partial deviation from "standard" small-log type is due to this paucity of material, and that if the two sites had been richer, their inventory would have proved to be typically small-log.

Following up this point of paucity of material recovered, we find that the next most meager site is No. **4**, with twenty-four positive traits, and that it is this site which shows the lowest coefficients within the **5-2-9-4** cluster. The next meager site is **11**, with thirty-one positive traits. This is in the large-log group, but yields lower coefficients with its fellow members **10** and **19** than these have toward each other; also, its coefficients with the small-log group are less consistently negative.

We can infer therefore that, *in this case*, trait inventories of about thirty traits begin to be slightly inadequate as samples of the culture which they represent, and when they fall to around twenty they are definitely unsatisfactory. They still suffice to indicate *probable* adhesion to a class, but not with the degree of conviction of a site which has

yielded thirty-five or more positive traits. These values of course are not absolute, but are empirically derived for this case alone.

Returning now to our "intermediate" site, **17,** we find that this has a full complement of forty traits. Consequently the indecisiveness of its coefficients can be construed as presumably due to a real ambiguity of its cultural position.

While we have in this way obtained a classification mainly corroborative of Webb's, the figures cannot tell us which of the two culture types is earlier. This must be determined from other evidence—stratigraphy, greater similarity of one type to a known historic culture, or the like. Webb has made an attempt to secure such evidence. On pages 371–374 he compares two of his large-log sites, **10** and **19,** with four sites or groups of sites attributed to the Cherokee and explored respectively by Harrington, Thomas, Heye (Nacoochee), and Lewis, using a presence and absence table of sixty-two traits.[6] He finds the results "unsatisfactory," and the connection with the historic Cherokee "not definitely established."

Of Webb's sixty-two traits, thirteen are universal positives. On omission of these, there remain forty-nine. I have calculated from these as before, but leave out site **10** because the positive inventory is considerably smaller than that of all the others. I omit also the Lewis group of which Webb says that it "possibly may represent Cherokee" culture.

The four-cell values are:

     H-N: 31, 11, 4, 3   N-T: 23, 12, 8, 6
     H-T: 27, 15, 4, 3   N-19: 20, 15, 8, 6
     H-19: 21, 21, 7, 0   T-19: 20, 11, 8, 10

From these we derive the Z values:

	H	N	T	19
Harrington	X	.39	.24	−.14
Nacoochee	.39	X	.18	.06
Thomas	.24	.18	X	.22
Webb 19	−.14	.06	.22	X

These figures show at once that site **19** is more different from the known Cherokee sites than these differ from one another. Accordingly, Webb's hesitation to construe his large-log sites as Cherokee is justified.[7]

---

[6] Webb says, page 372, that this list includes traits occurring at two or more of the six sites; all traits occurring on only one site having been eliminated "as having no value in this comparison." The last phrase may be doubted. He is not trying to prove similarity but to establish degree of similarity, and on this degree, unlikenesses, even if unique, certainly have a bearing.

[7] They might, of course, be prehistoric Cherokee, from a time when Cherokee culture had not yet attained its historic form.

The one exception is the Thomas sites. Their coefficient with site **19** is about equal to those which they have with Harrington and Nacoochee. A reason for this irregularity is however apparent. Thomas failed almost wholly to report on pottery traits, as was customary in his day. Webb therefore visited his sites in 1934 and made a collection of sherds. The 18 ceramic traits of the "Thomas" list are therefore really Webb-secured traits, like those of the site **19** list. These eighteen traits are distributed thus: 10, 3, 0, 5; yielding a Z of .67! It is this Webb ingredient of Thomas which has produced the exceptional high **19**-Thomas coefficient. The non-ceramic Z of **19**-Thomas is only $-.03$, which does not differ seriously in import from the **19**-Harrington non-ceramic Z of $-.29$ and **19**-Nacoochee of .10. In short, the apparent exception of the Thomas sites is dissolved, and Webb is confirmed in his conclusion that his large-log sites in Norris Basin cannot yet be positively equated with known Cherokee culture.

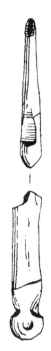

This case illustrates two points of method.

First, archaeologists do not yet collect or describe quite uniformly. There appears to be a personal equation sufficient to affect the inventory of a trait list.[8] The moral is that no calculations or comparisons are better than the excavations and typology underlying them are accurate and reliable.

Second, the case may serve to reassure those who fear that once statistics are embarked on, there is no stopping even if they lead to nonsense. Intelligence is of course needed whether one does or does not use statistics, and equally so. Statistical method is a tool, not a mechanical substitute for thought. In the present instance it has served as a means of analyzing out discrepancies in the primary data.

FORT ANCIENT

Griffin's analysis of Fort Ancient aspect sites—four in Ohio, one in Kentucky—is summarized in a folded-in sheet of convenient diagrams. He lists forty-nine non-pottery traits which occur at all five sites. These traits I omit. There remain seventy-four non-pottery traits which occur at from one to four sites. Griffin's pottery traits are not listed as simply present or absent, but as abundant, medium, rare, absent. I have preferred not to complicate matters by introducing these data measured on a four-step scale among those described on a two-end scale. It would

---

[8] It is of course possible that the Thomas sites are really similar to the Webb sites in pottery, to Harrington and Nacoochee in the remainder of the culture; but it would be hazardous to assume this without intensive reëxamination of all the material recovered.

have been possible to count abundant, medium, and rare occurrence as simply "present;" but little would have been gained by this, as thirty-three of the thirty-six traits would have come out as universally present at all five sites. I have therefore simply discarded the three remaining pottery traits.

The distribution of seventy-four non-ceramic traits is:

Gartner-Baum: 30, 6, 18, 20
G-Fox Farm: 16, 20, 20, 18
G-Feurt: 21, 15, 23, 15
G-Madisonville: 14, 22, 33, 5
B-FF: 27, 21, 9, 17
B-Fe: 29, 19, 15, 11
B-M: 25, 23, 22, 4
FF-Fe: 27, 9, 17, 21
FF-M: 25, 11, 22, 16
Fe-M: 28, 14, 19, 13

I use this time two new formulae: Q_2 and W. $Q_2 = (ad - bc)/(ad + bc)$. It is one of those devised by a mathematician, and is the quickest of these to compute. It is useless when one of the four values is 0, and gives exaggerated coefficients when one of the values approaches 0. $W = (a+d)/N$; in other words, agreements divided by the total number of traits. It differs from all the others in that its range is from 1.0 only to 0, instead of to -1.0. As a tie with the previous calculations, the Z coefficients are also added, although the two bear a constant re-

Q_2

	G	B	FF	Fe	M
G	X	.69	$-.16$	$-.05$	$-.82$
B	.69	X	.42	.06	$-.67$
FF	$-.16$	.42	X	.58	.25
Fe	$-.05$	.06	.58	X	.16
M	$-.82$	$-.67$	.25	.16	X

W

	G	B	FF	Fe	M
G	X	.68	.46	.49	.26
B	.68	X	.59	.54	.39
FF	.46	.59	X	.65	.55
Fe	.49	.54	.65	X	.55
M	.26	.39	.55	.55	X

	G	B	Z FF	Fe	M
G	X	.35	−.08	−.03	−.49
B	.35	X	.19	.09	−.22
FF	−.08	.19	X	.30	.11
Fe	−.03	.09	.30	X	.11
M	−.49	−.22	.11	.11	X
Differential traits present	36	48	36	42	47

lation, the W values being spread only half as far from 1.0 as the Z values, so that the rank order of coefficients is identical by the two formulae.

The tables are so simple that it is not necessary to convert them into graphs; but to guide the eye I have introduced lines which box together the higher coefficients.

While the absolute coefficient values differ from table to table according to the formula used, it appears that the relative size or ranking of the coefficients, which is what is of significance, is the same by formula Q_2 and formulas W and Z.

Now it is at once evident that the Gartner and Baum sites form a related pair, and the Fox Farm and Feurt another. As between these two pairs, similarity of Baum and Fox Farm is closest. Madisonville is the most apart of the five sites. It has no high coefficients and the two lowest of all. Such relationship as it has is with the Fox Farm-Feurt pair. The total set of relationships thus is linear, not crossing or ramifying. It can be adequately represented by this simple diagram, in which closeness of relationship is expressed by spatial nearness of the site symbols.

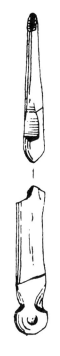

G   B   FF   Fe   M

Griffin interprets the situation similarly on the whole, but with differences in detail. He unites Gartner and Baum into one focus or subclass, Fox Farm and Madisonville into another. Feurt, he finds in discussing pottery (p. 3), "seems to be intermediate between these two groups and to constitute, at least temporarily, a division by itself." I unite Feurt definitely with Fox Farm and set Madisonville most apart.

It remains to inquire into the reasons for this subsidiary difference in classification. One appears to be that Griffin bases his conclusions on

a series of thirty-five diagrams, most of them dealing with classes of traits such as Stone Implements or Burial Content. Even ignoring most of these, and confining ourselves to his diagrams on Total Traits, we have five graphic representations to be compared mentally. Another reason is that Griffin has included and I have excluded pottery. A third is that the older investigators, as in Tennessee, apparently slighted pottery as compared with modern practice, and that Griffin, like Webb, perhaps tried to correct for this inequality in the data.

GENERALITIES

In both cases we have come to the same result: General agreement, but specific minor differences, according as the same material is classified by a method of mixed statistics and inspection and a straight statistical procedure. Which yields the more reliable result? I do not wish to answer dogmatically. While my method seems simple, consistent and rigorous, I do not know at all either the Tennessee or the Fort Ancient material at first hand, and this is a factor not to be ignored. My collaborator, Driver, takes the view that proper statistical analysis is a self-sufficient technique and that if its results have to be validated by checking against results obtained by inspection or "intuition," it might as well not be applied. I am not ready to go quite so far. For one thing, while I understand what a formula like W or Z means, I do not, like most anthropologists, understand how R_{hk} is derived in mathe-material theory, and how justly applicable it is, or when it is properly applicable, to a body of concrete data. For this reason I want to see how it works: what kind of a result it gives in specific cases, as compared with results by the intelligible W or Z, or results by the old-fashioned inspectional method which we all use. And I am submitting this essay so that archaeologists at large may also judge between the methods, as to which seems the more valid when there are differences in result, and, above all, why.

I do think I have shown that the coefficients can be sensitive, as when the Webb-collected pottery from Thomas sites comes out more similar to Webb sites than does the non-pottery Thomas material. However, there is such a thing as over-sensitiveness when we are looking for general results. And while we have found indication of a factor of collectors' personal equation, we have thereby also thrown some prima facie slur on all comparative interpretation of material assembled by more than one collector. That this doubt applies also to inspectional interpretations does not increase the reliability of statistical results.

A. L. Kroeber

What we have gained is cognizance of a potential disturbing factor against which we must be on guard.

Somewhat similar is the matter of the quantity of material necessary to ensure reasonable certainty of conclusions. Anyone would assume that in a comparison involving a total of a hundred traits, with the majority of sites averaging around fifty, a site from which only ten traits were recorded—whether because it was small, or partially excavated, or imperfectly reported—could presumably not be classified other than tentatively. But would it become validly usable when its inventory reached twenty, or thirty, or forty traits? It would be difficult to give an answer on the basis of inspection. In the case of Norris Basin we did find a seeming answer. Again, the statistical approach has proved to be an analytic tool. This is in general its primary value.

Sites are not the only archaeological phenomena which can be classified statistically. It is equally feasible to correlate elements. The data are then simply counted the other way: for element 1, sites I and II may show $++$ and therefore tally one in the a cell; I and III $+ -$ and therefore b; I and IV another a; II and III, b; II and IV, a; III and IV, c; etc. The same count is made for element 2, then element 3, and so on. The result is a series of coefficients which show the degree to which the elements tend to adhere among themselves, to use Tylor's happy old phrase; in more modern language, how they segregate out into culture-complexes or culture-strata.

I have not computed the trait-complexes for either the Webb or the Griffin data because the number of cases—that is, sites—is so small (only ten and five respectively) that the coefficients would not be very significant. Besides, the complexes or strata are easily enough determined by inspection of the authors' tables and diagrams. Had the number of sites treated in either work approximated fifty, inspection findings would have been more difficult to make, and inter-trait correlations would probably have justified themselves in spite of the labor, especially as with many more sites the list of traits would almost certainly also have grown.

In such a larger situation, tabulated coefficients may be of more service. The culture complexes or strata at the fifty sites would automatically shake down, and with the best trial and error arrangement would clearly show their segregations and blends. This is difficult to do from direct inspection of many varying presences and absences distributed in many columns. The tendency is to think in terms of traits already known to be significant as culture markers. For instance, there

has been much discussion lately of the Hopewellian. One may therefore have Hopewellian criteria in mind, and proceed to classify sites into a minority that are Hopewellian and a majority non-Hopewellian. But the latter might really be an aggregate of several cultures, say three phases or aspects of Mississippian, plus transitions between them. These aspects would crystallize out in the coefficient table, and the transitions would also be indicated as such. An exceptionally acute inspection, it is true, might well reveal these several aspects and transitions, but rather as a "hunch," which one would want to demonstrate, in order to convince others, by some form of objective evidence. The coefficient table, to be sure, is not the only such objective demonstration; but it is probably the most comprehensive and compact.

A third procedure is to intercorrelate site classes with trait complexes after both have been determined. This shows how far any given site belongs wholly to one culture, or is hybrid, or belongs primarily to one but with influence from another; and conversely, the relative strength of say the Hopewell complex in all the sites compared.

By this time, however, one has done a good deal of computing, and spent even more time counting and recounting; and many situations do not warrant the labor. There is also a substitute device available. This has been employed before, somewhat occasionally and haphazardly, it is true, but my associate, Driver, has called my attention to it as a rapid and expressive equivalent for the site-trait correlation. It carries the further recommendation, to many, of avoiding all coefficients. In principle this device is merely a grouping of related sites in adjacent columns, irrespective of their geography or order of exploration, plus a grouping of correlated or adhering traits on adjacent lines, irrespective of whether they are of stone, bone, pottery, or part of structures or burials. This arrangement clusters out classes of trait-groups characteristic of site-groups, along a diagonal of the table; only this time the clusters consist of plus symbols, and elsewhere of minus symbols, for the traits themselves, in place of numerical coefficients. I illustrate by a rearrangement of the "structural traits" part of Webb's table, limiting myself to this to save space.

It appears that the small-log sites possess nine structural traits peculiar to themselves as against two peculiar to large-log sites; that seven traits are shared by small-log and large-log; further, that all nine of the site-17 traits occur in small-log sites, only five of them also in large-log ones. On the contrary, in burial traits, not rearranged here, site 17 goes with large-log. In a complete table, this vacillation of 17

STRUCTURAL TRAITS, FROM WEBB, REARRANGED TO SEGREGATE

	5	2	9	4	8	6	17	11	10	19
Cardinal orientation	x		x	x						
Corners closed by stakes	x	x	x	x	x	x				
Horizontal log molds outside trench	x	x	x		x					
Burned town house, primary floor	x	x	x			x				
Cane impressions, town house floor			x		x	x				
Vertical cleavage plane over post molds		x	x							
Horizontal log molds inside trench		x			x					
Woven mats on roof		x				x				
Bark slabs on roof	x	x								
Small log dwellings	x	x	x	x			x			
Small log town house	x	x	x		x	x	x			
Wall posts in trenches	x	x	x	x	x		x			
Door in corner	x		x	x			x			
Cane and grass as thatch	x	x	x	x	x	x	x		x	
Earth-covered town houses	x	x	x		x	x	x	x	x	
Dwelling-house patterns under mound	x		x	x		x	x		x	
Successive superposition of town houses	x	x	x		x		x		x	x
Dwelling patterns, not earth-covered	x	x					x	x	x	
Corners not closed by stakes	x						x	x	x	x
Dwellings of large logs	x							x	x	
Town house of large logs								x	x	
Horiz. large log molds, town house floor								x	x	

would be brought out, just through burial traits and others being set *in their affiliation place* among structural traits.

In any event, I think it is evident how much culture segregation and affiliation can be brought out by this device of tabular arrangement, without any coefficients; though if the number of sites is considerable, their prior objective grouping by inter-site coefficients will probably remain desirable.

Finally, the question naturally emerges, to what extent and over what range the coefficient method promises to be applicable. Is there any prospect, for instance, that it could ultimately be employed to classify all the prehistoric cultures of the eastern United States both geographically and into their patterns, phases, and aspects? I believe it is too early to say yes or no. If the task were undertaken mechanically and wholesale, the labor would be prohibitive. A thousand sites, for instance, yield nearly half a million interrelations. Also, between most of them, the number of d's—common absences—would be so great as to make the four-cell values heavily skew. On the other hand, done step by step, the task would be much reduced. For instance, a group of Fort Ancient sites determined by their coefficients as a true group ("aspect") on comparison with other Ohio sites, could then be merged or pooled

and their traits reduced to a unitary Fort Ancient list. And so on.

A year ago at the University of Chicago, stimulated by the local archaeological activity and the Milwaukee meeting, I went so far as to begin compiling a trait list for the eastern United States. This was based on specific archaeological reports from New York, Ohio, Illinois, Iowa, and Nebraska, and quickly ran to several hundred items, many of which McKern was good enough to revise. This list was left at Chicago and no doubt is available to anyone interested. On further consideration I am less sure that this is the way to commence. It may be better to compile and compute local trait lists, expanding these until their range covers an area about as large as a state, then tie together such areas. Trial alone can tell. I am certain that in any larger comparison dealing with materials collected and described by a number of archaeologists, the first requisite will be a clearly defined typology. "Plummet," "discoidal," "cord-marked" may each be a true and constant element or they may prove to have been used in different senses and to break down, each into several traits. Determination between these alternatives can only be made by Eastern archaeologists genuinely familiar with more than local material. The first requisite seems to be a sound comparative typology. Once we have this, the rest will follow, whether with the help of statistical devices or otherwise. The main help that statistics promises is in arriving at an objective basis, instead of an essentially agreed basis, for the grouping of sites into foci, these into aspects, and so on down to bases, or whatever other categories may be demanded by the phenomena.

University of California
Berkeley, California
September, 1939

ADDENDUM

A year's further experience since this article was written reenforces the cautions expressed on pages 31, 35, and 41. The difficulty is that under the four-cell method a trait lacking at a site is counted as lacking from the culture, whereas actually it may have been present but happened not to be left at the site, or not to be found. We experience the same difficulty with ethnological trait lists compiled from the literature: that an author does not mention a trait does not necessarily mean that it was absent. (On the contrary, in a planned presence-absence field inquiry, a mere third or fourth of a trait list, being a random sample as far as it goes, will compare reliably with a full list.) Archaeological sites with markedly meager inventories must therefore be used very cautiously: some of their apparent c's and d's may have been actual a's and b's. The error is not excludable, but may sometimes be reduced by using Webb's formula $a/(a+b+c)$. In fact his 45 percentages yield a diagram comparable with mine. It differs somewhat, and is not quite so definite; but its classification may be as true, or more so. The moral is that reserve is necessary where trait inventories vary by more than about a third in size.

THE TYPOLOGICAL CONCEPT[1]

ALEX D. KRIEGER

THIS paper is an attempt to clarify the meaning of the terms "type" and "variation" when applied to archaeological materials. Although they are used constantly in speech and literature in almost every conceivable context, it must be admitted that archaeology has no generally accepted, impersonal methods of establishing the scope and application of these terms. Kluckhohn[2] has recently written:

> Our techniques of observing and recording are admittedly still susceptible of improvement, but they seem much further advanced than our development of symbols (verbal and otherwise) by which we could communicate to each other (without loss or inflation of content) the signs and symptoms we observe. In archaeology, for example, methods of classifying pottery wares on the basis of highly technical and rather precisely defined operations have been elaborated. But I am aware of but a single paper (by a Russian!) where there has been even a tentative and fumbling consideration of the implications of the typological method. Such archaeologists as Vaillant, Strong, Setzler, Gladwin, and Paul Martin are (but only very recently) evidencing searchings of their theoretical consciences, and this is a happy omen. Meanwhile typologies are proliferated without apparent concern as to what the concepts involved are likely to mean when reduced to concrete human behaviors . . . .[3]

If analytical methods fail to interpret archaeological material in terms of "concrete human behaviors," the historical reconstructions based upon them must be in greater or less degree fictitious. Traditionally, masses of specimens are grouped in one way or another to facilitate their description or to demonstrate "culture complexes" and "cultural change" through space and time. Since these groupings, regardless of

---

[1] Prepared in connection with researches in Texas archaeology, as part of a program in Research in Anthropology generously supported by the University of Texas. The analysis of material gathered over a period of twenty-five years by the University, and, more recently, by WPA-University of Texas projects, demands the settling of basic methodologies. I am much indebted to Professor J. Gilbert McAllister, Chairman of the Anthropology Department, T. N. Campbell, J. Charles Kelley, Walter Taylor, and Perry Newell for liberal discussion and unstinted criticism. I wish to emphasize particularly that Kelley has long been familiar with the main principles given here, has experimented for some time with graphic devices for expressing the results, and has been very instrumental in shaping my own convictions on the subject.

[2] Kluckhohn, 1939. The paper to which he refers is Gorodzov, 1933. The latter's arguments center about the thought that "this theory demands the subdivision of all material simple objects into categories, groups, genera, and types." To form the first three groupings the types must first be determined, and he cites the many difficulties to be faced. The general insistence throughout is on the careful use of historical methods, but the paper lacks specific statements on how to do this.

[3] This was probably written before the appearance of Rouse's valuable study of type in terms of behavior. (Rouse, 1939, esp. pp. 9–35).

271

their determining characters, are commonly termed "types," and as such form the medium for nearly all discussion of cultural relationships, it is of the utmost importance that archaeologists reach some agreements on organizational methodology.

THE PURPOSE OF A TYPE

It may be said that, ideally, an archaeological type should represent a unit of cultural practice equivalent to the "culture trait" of ethnography. Although the same difficulties in delimiting such a unit are met in ethnography as in archaeology,[4] it is apparent that both concepts may serve the same purpose, namely, that of identifying distinct patterns of behavior or technology which can be acquired by one human being from another, and thus serve as tools for the retracing of cultural developments and interactions.

In all study of behavior it is essential to distinguish between the traditional or ideal pattern and the actual enactments which result from individual variability in skill, interest, or effectiveness. Variations which never acquire social recognition or meaning beyond their originators are, however, of little historical significance. It is therefore the task of the analyst, working with the variable products of primitive manufacturing techniques, to recover, if possible, the mental patterns which lay behind these manifold works, the changes in pattern which occurred from time to time, and the source of such changes.

Thus the purpose of a type in archaeology must be to provide an organizational tool which will enable the investigator to group specimens into bodies which have *demonstrable historical meaning in terms of behavior patterns*. Any group which may be labeled a "type" must embrace material which can be shown to consist of individual variations in the execution of a definite constructional idea; likewise, the dividing lines between a series of types must be based upon demonstrable historical factors, not, as is often the case, upon the inclinations of the analyst or the niceties of descriptive orderliness.

Before entering upon the possible techniques for accomplishing these ends, we may examine briefly some of the concepts of type most commonly met in the literature. There appear to be four principal attitudes toward the organization and description of material.

1. Full description, wherein specimens are described individually in detail, in the hope that nothing of consequence will be overlooked.

---

[4] Wissler, 1923, p. 50, defines a trait as a "unit of observation," as, for example, a fire-making instrument; "Such is, for practical purposes at least, a unit of the tribal culture and is spoken of as a trait." In practice, a *particular style* of instrument would constitute a more tangible trait than Wissler's definition calls for.

Alex D. Krieger

2. Visually determined "typologies," wherein grouping is primarily to reduce repetitive description, the divisional criteria being chosen at random or based upon impressions received through personal experience.

3. Classification systems which aim toward the standardization of description and comparison over wide areas. These generally take the form of outline headings and subheadings, expressed by symbols, which provide a series of pigeonholes into which specimens are sorted and then tabulated.

4. The true typological method wherein types are taken to be specific groupings of structural features which have proved historical significance. Determinative criteria are not of constant value, but are discovered as the material is analyzed, in the manner to be discussed below.

Of methods (1) and (2) there is not a great deal to say except that the first leaves the digestion and meaning of the material to the reader to discover for himself, while the second may or may not be reliable for comparative purposes, depending upon how much explanation accompanies the presentation. In the case of isolated or new material which is little understood, the full-descriptive method may be the only possible one, but where quantity of comparative material permits reduction into better defined groups, one of the other three methods may be used. Of these, the use of "classification systems" has enjoyed wide popularity among archaeologists, and considering the vast amount of time and thought put into the perfection of such schemes, we may examine their basic tenets critically.

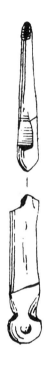

CLASSIFICATION SYSTEMS

Although the purpose of schemes presented in the literature must generally be taken for granted, a few authors have troubled to explain their position. Nelson,[5] for example, has written as follows:

... The naturalists since Linnaeus call their system of grouping *The Natural Classification*. In zoology this seems to mean nothing more or less than grouping so as to express blood relationship. In archaeology it would mean grouping by primary, secondary, and tertiary characters or traits in such a way that when the task is done the whole can be assembled in the shape of a sort of genealogical tree, in which those forms showing only the basic or primary traits would appear near the bottom or stem, while those forms showing various secondary modifications and specializations would appear near the top or on the branches, some distance away from the stem. The obvious advantage of such a system is that it hangs together and therefore, once it is grasped, will be easily remembered, while any other *artificial classification* is not, in all probability, going to be easy to remember and therefore cannot be successfully used unless we carry a printed copy of the scheme about with us.

As to how such a system of classification is to be devised, or whether we are fully ready to devise it, and to use it, I am not at all sure. Several attempts are already on

---

[5] Nelson, N. D.

record and these, so far as I have examined them, all have their particular excellences and defects. Broadly considered, they are more or less satisfactory as far as they go; but they are not complete and, worse than that, they tend to end up in confusion because the makers have generally failed to distinguish primary and secondary classificatory characters. That is, of course, merely another way of saying that there is no one basic idea or underlying trait running through and thus connecting up the whole scheme, but, instead, several unlike traits have been given equal value. All this is natural enough in first empirical attempts in a new untried field, and our recognition of previous shortcomings should at least help us to avoid some of the useless modes of procedure. The various earlier attempts also suggest that a really adequate system of classification may not be a one-man job, or at any rate that it may have to come by slow growth. The chief thing required at present, obviously, is to find the right start. Towards this proper beginning, as well as the future completion of a classificatory scheme, we can all make our contributions, or at least supply suggestion.

Nelson has stated well the exploratory nature of the problem, although his suggestion that classification systems may eventually lead to formation of a "sort of genealogical tree" on the basis of primary and secondary characters is open to serious question. The supposition that such characters exist in archaeological material reflects a common attitude towards classification problems which may have no basis in fact.

Deuel[6] has expressed a different point of view:

> The need for a convenient grouping of chipped stone and spearpoints is indicated by the occasional publication of tentative classifications. For the comparison of specimens from different regions or tribes, for the preparation of state surveys, or for the investigation of the distribution of types, a simple, easily defined classification is highly desirable.
>
> Such a classification should answer the following requirements: (1) simple major divisions of easily distinguished forms, (2) each capable of further separation into a small number of sub-types, and (3) these last susceptible of continued subdivision where necessary to embrace readily the majority of divergent shapes. A type and its sub-types should depend on a small number of related criteria, and be easily differentiated from other types and sub-types without necessity for frequent references to a complicated key.

Deuel, like Nelson, stresses *convenience* and the facilitation of memorizing the structure of a system, so that once it appears workable it can be applied anywhere without reference to the original key.

In one of the early attempts to formulate an artifact classification, Thomas Wilson[7] offered a brief statement of purpose:

> These engravings are intended to serve as a classification of these implements by which their names, and possibly their functions, may be known, and by which archaeologists throughout the country, and perhaps the world, may be better enabled to understand and describe them. When we consider that it is beyond the power of mere words to describe a form, and that a figure, cut, or representation of it must be or must have been made at some other time in order to communicate knowledge of a form to any person

[6] Deuel, N. D. On July 11, 1939, in response to a plea from the Anthropology Department, University of Texas, for information on the subject, Mr. Deuel kindly forwarded this manuscript together with copies of several others on projectile-point classification.   [7] Wilson, 1899.

who has not previously seen it, the author trusts that he will be justified in the classification and the engravings by which it is sought to be represented.

Wilson's classification formed the basis for several subsequent schemes which have been widely used, especially in the far western states.[8]

In certain circumstances, systems have been devised for the reduction of masses of material into a digestible form to facilitate reference.[9] Still others have been presented for the consideration, and presumably for the use, of other archaeologists, without statement of purpose.[10] There are also examples of classifications which appear to be mixtures of grouping by form and distributional knowledge, yet we look in vain for explanations as to how the "types" were determined.[11]

Some of the early classifications attempted to employ historical knowledge based upon European archaeological horizons. "Primary" traits corresponded to the narrow range of simple artifact forms characteristic of the Lower and Middle Palaeolithic periods, while "secondary" groupings were determined by the more specialized and diversified forms appearing in subsequent periods.[12] The assumption in these cases was that the specialized forms were genetic descendents of earlier generalized ones, the supposed evolution having taken place within the same region.

Most of these classifications consist of balanced outline divisions, each symbolized by a combination of letters and numbers which provide the key to the outstanding features of shape, proportions, workmanship, etc. For the sake of symmetry and ease in memorization the headings and subheadings are usually carried out into a complete system of pigeonholes, whether or not specimens are found to represent all of them. The number of headings to be carried varies with each author's inclinations and the complexity of the general material. The classification of axes, for example, is simple in comparison with that of projectile points. The ultimate purpose of such systems is either stated or presumed to be one or more of the following: (1) to standardize comparison of specimens over wide areas, (2) to save time in sorting, tabulating, and describing masses of material, (3) to provide convenient reference forms and terms to expedite field recording, surveys, and cataloging. *Whatever the reason and method behind such schemes, their authors automatically refer to each grouping as a "type."* This bespeaks an assumption that all

[8] For example: Gifford and Schenck, 1926; Strong, 1935, esp. pp. 88–89. The so-called "Strong system" was in use, but in an incomplete form, in the earlier work of Gifford and Schenck.

[9] For example: Kidder, 1932; Lillard, Heizer, and Fenenga, 1939; Gifford, 1940.

[10] Rau, 1876; Renaud, 1931; Renaud, 1934; Finkelstein, 1937.

[11] For example: Fowke, 1896, pp. 47–178; Cole and Deuel, 1937, esp. Chapt. IV.

[12] Wilson, 1899, pp. 888–889, cites several such cases.

that is needed for the delimitation of archaeological types is the perfection of successive subdivisions from the "most important" to the "least important" characters. Without entering into details, these premises may be variously criticized.

1. In arranging and balancing an outline of divisional criteria, it becomes necessary to give preference to some criteria over others; that is, to choose those that are "basic" for the main divisions. This choice may be guided by several considerations: by the frequency with which certain simple geometric figures such as the triangle, oval, and rectangle appear in a series; by real or supposed historical changes in form; or by arbitrary "logic." Now, the search for morphologically "basic" characters on which to build a classification is fallacious because the frequency with which certain shapes occur constantly shifts in different runs of material. Therefore, while form is a consistently valuable criterion when interpreted in conjunction with other characters, its use as an *aid* in defining types should not be confused with its use as a *base* for classificatory headings. On the other hand, the use of historical periods in the formation of a typological system is largely a matter of putting the cart before the horse, for the reconstruction of historical change should depend upon the correct ordering of known types and traits. Furthermore, the proof of genetic relationship in a series extending through successive historical periods is one of the major objectives of research and cannot be assumed to be a working tool in the analysis.[13]

2. Specimens which in actuality form a closely related group of variations may be forced, by the demands of a classification arrangement, into positions far removed from one another in the tabulations. If the divisional criteria are strictly followed—and they usually are for the sake of "scientific accuracy"—it is constantly necessary to make hairsplitting decisions on individual specimens, finally assigning them to one group or another on the basis of a final desperate summary of their minute differences, or, which is worse, by forcing artificial lines through them for lack of really decisive breaks. Persistent and complex overlapping in features of construction *may* be the very proof that the series should not be broken down in answer to outline subheadings. Again, a breakdown which works well in one collection may be hopelessly arti-

---

[13] When the archaeology of restricted regions is known well enough and there are ample typological data from distinct but connected cultural horizons, it is sometimes possible to state with assurance that certain types of material have developed out of others. The papers of Gila Pueblo, for example, contain numerous developmental charts dealing with pottery and projectile styles. However, unless accompanied by ample proof of descent, such charts may be largely imaginary.

Alex D. Krieger

ficial in another. The inflexibility of outline systems precludes their adaptability to such conditions.

3. Conversely, specimens falling into the same pigeonhole because they answer a given set of selected criteria may, through other differecens, actually belong to two or more completely distinct cultural types.

4. It is next to impossible to express variation in an outline system except by increasing or decreasing the number of subheadings—the number of criteria, that is—that are considered pertinent to the problem of discovering relationships. The broader the application of a system, as, for example, a projectile-point classification proposed for continental standardization, the more features of construction must be arbitrarily dropped for fear of overburdening the system with symbols. Such reduction leads back to the endless and unanswerable speculation on what features are of basic importance in comparative studies.

5. The arrangement of outline pigeonholes under a selection of main headings is apt to carry the implication that the subdivisions under one main head are more closely related with one another in the genetic sense than they are with the subdivisions of any other heads. This may be true in certain circumstances, as when coiled basketry techniques form one major grouping, twined another, plaited another, etc., while in the field of chipped stonework any presumptions as to genetic relationship for a starting point would only lead to complete and needless confusion.

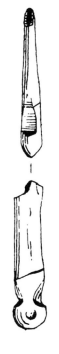

In summary, the objections to classificatory "systems" which are being created from time to time for the standardization of analysis may be expressed somewhat as follows: considering the vast amount of time and thought put into them, is there any reason to believe that their groupings will help to discover the true historical meaning of the myriad works of man? If not, what sort of method will serve this end? We will now consider what may be called "the typological method," though I am not aware that it has been so termed or described before, as a definite approach to analysis.

THE TYPOLOGICAL METHOD

The general tenets of this method may be seen in the formation of Southwestern and Southeastern pottery types. Thus each recognized type is defined by a specific and cohesive combination of features of paste, temper, texture, hardness, finish, vessel shape, technique and arrangement of decoration, use of appendages, etc., and furthermore includes what is believed to be individual variation within the technical pattern; the type as a whole is also understood to occupy a definable historical position, that is, its distribution is delimited in space, time,

The Typological Concept　　　　253

and association with other cultural material.[14] It must be thoroughly grasped that this approach represents an *attitude* toward the archaeological analysis which is almost diametrically opposed to that of the classification method. The differences between them center about the manner of choosing and applying determinative criteria to specimen grouping; where the classification method is rigid and unadaptable to varying conditions, the typological method is flexible and can be adjusted to the material and problems at hand. The theoretical scope of this concept may be summarized under these points:

1. Each type should approximate as closely as possible that combination of mechanical and aesthetic executions which formed a definite structural pattern in the minds of a number of workers, who attained this pattern with varying degrees of success and interpretation.

2. Each type, with its probable variations, must hold its form with essential consistency wherever found. *Absolute* consistency is neither possible nor necessary for the analysis. With geographical spread of a type, slight alterations in the structural pattern inevitably occur.

3. Distinguishing criteria for type determination are not of constant value; what may serve to differentiate types in one circumstance may prove to be variation in another. The number of criteria needed for proof of clean distinctions may also vary with circumstances.

4. No matter how small the difference between specimen groups, these differences are of type importance if their distributions in space, time, and cultural association are distinct.

5. There are no criteria of basic or universally primary importance in forming a typology. Each *specific combination* of features—i.e., the manner in which they combine—is of greater determinative value than any single feature.

6. The differences between types must not be so obscure that others will encounter excessive difficulty in recognizing them.

7. The typological framework for any given class of material must be flexible enough to allow for additions, subdivisions, recombinations, rewordings, and the like, in the groups where needed, without disturbing others.

8. A type, when satisfactorily blocked out, must be named (not numbered or lettered) and described. Names may be derived from sites,

[14] Several handbooks serve to illustrate the framework of pottery-type description, such as: Gladwin and Gladwin, 1930a, 1930b, 1931, 1933; Hargrave, 1937; Hawley, 1936; Gladwin, Haury, Sayles, and Gladwin, 1937. The last-mentioned work departs from the others in that type description is considerably shortened but supplemented with copious drawings of vessel shapes and decorations, thereby greatly adding to its usefulness for comparative work. For the Southeast, see the mimeographed reports of the Southeastern Archaeological Conference, esp. Vol. I, 1939; Ford and Willey, 1940.

towns, persons, geographical features, etc., but to avoid confusion and unwarranted assumptions they must *not* be taken from ethnic, linguistic, or other cultural labels. Some names derive from the sites in which they were first discovered in situ. The type is thenceforth known by the same name wherever found, but only so long as its identity with the original find can be ascertained.

Descriptive forms for pottery types have been devised in the Southwest and Southeast (see note 14), but as yet do not exist for other classes of material. In the next section, one will be suggested for projectile points. It is desirable that other such forms be created for all major classes of archaeological specimens, as well as for house and burial types. Basketry techniques, knives, scrapers, axes, bone implements, various ornaments, pipes, ceremonial objects, etc., all lend themselves to the typological method of organization and description.

Procedure by the Typological Method

The first problem facing the analyst is the sorting of specimens into major groups which *look as though they had been made with the same or similar structural pattern in mind*. This step is somewhat subjective, for there will be different opinions on what amount of variation can be

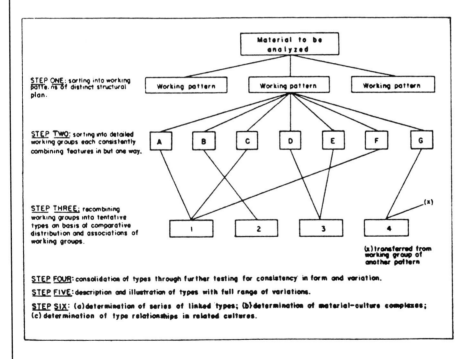

FIG. 25.—Diagram of procedure in the typological method.

allowed for. The main point is to sort the material into groups which contrast strongly. The collection need not be completely sorted, questionable or odd specimens being set aside for the present. This initial sorting into trial patterns is largely experimental, and differences of opinion over what constitutes a pattern will be more or less eliminated during succeeding steps. The greater the number of specimens available, the stronger and clearer will be the main contrasts.

It cannot be said too strongly that, during the primary division into working patterns, one must expect similarities and differences to manifest themselves in almost any character in almost any degree. There is no set order of examination and it matters little what the habits of different analysts may be in this respect. Thus in projectile-point sorting, the various features of stem expansion or contraction, shoulder width, base shape, blade shape, proportions, method of chipping, etc. must all be considered, but without insistence on any particular order. Likewise, such categories as pottery and basketry should be free from preconceived ideas of the relative importance of any particular characters of shape or treatment.

The second step is the breakdown of the working patterns according to differences which are seen to be consistent within some, but not all, of the specimens in each pattern. For example, a series of pottery bottles, while they belong to a structural pattern readily distinguished from other vessels in both form and function, may reveal details of neck shape and length, body curvature, base construction, paste, finish, etc., which are consistent through a number of specimens from one or more sites. This sorting will result in a large number of very uniform groups, each of which reveals but one specific combination of features.[15]

The third step is a process of recombining the groups obtained in the second step, through the study of their comparative distributions. It cannot be assumed that there are any *a priori* grounds for recombining these groups without a careful plotting of their distributions. This plotting must consider the three dimensions of geographical (i.e., site-to-site), temporal, and associational occurrence of the detailed groups. *Only* in this way can it be determined that certain characters are variations of single underlying plans, while others which do not fall together consistently are not variations but culturally distinct ideas. Those details which do consistently combine through site after site, in the same temporal horizon and in the same culture complex, may thus be safely regrouped into *tentative types. These differ from all other so-called types in*

---

[15] It may be argued that the step of division into "working patterns" is unnecessary because these patterns are subsequently broken down and then rebuilt. They do appear to be an aid in visualizing and organizing the material in its initial stages, especially if great quantities of specimens must be examined in limited space.

that the cohesiveness of their elements has been proved through the use of archaeological data rather than simply supposed through a variety of assumptions.

The fourth step consists of testing the "tentative types" of the third step with whatever further information is available. New collections may provide a valuable testing ground, so that it becomes possible to check the persistency with which the elements of each proposed type fall together again and again, *in the same essential pattern with the same variations.* It often comes as a pleasant surprise to see what one has regarded as a definite type turn up in some other area or collection with exactly the same features. Exact duplication is not, however, necessary for type identity, for differences in natural materials available may directly affect the workmanship and final appearance of objects made with quite the same plan in mind.

In the fifth step, after they appear to be satisfactorily composed and tested, the types must be named and described. As I do not know of any descriptive form for materials other than ceramic, the following is offered merely for illustration. Similar forms can easily be devised for any material category. Names may consist of a site or locative term plus some identifying words which stress the least variable feature within the type. There is nothing particularly significant in the order of itemization, for distinguishing features may appear anywhere in the description. A sample form which may be used for projectile points is given below.

SAMPLE TYPE DESCRIPTION FOR PROJECTILE POINTS
TYPE: YARBROUGH STEMMED
Illustrated: plate _____, figure _____

Greatest width: across shoulders.
Stem: edges usually concave in uniform curve from shoulder to somewhat flaring stem tip, but grades into straight edge without flare; edges are commonly ground or rubbed smooth.
Base: usually concave with sharp stem tips, but grades into straight line.
Shoulders: slight and formed only by outward curve of stem edges meeting blade corners.
Blade: edges essentially straight but may be irregular with crude chipping; usually, if not always, beveled with two parallel pitches on opposite faces; bevel narrow and difficult to see if chipping crude.
Cross-section: stem elliptical; blade more or less rhomboid with convex faces.
Material: poor grade of flint or "chert," dull reddish or grey.
Chipping: percussion, with pressure retouching along beveled blade edges.

Dimension ranges:	(334 specimens)
A. Widths: Base:	14–18 mm.
Stem neck (narrowest part above base):	12–15 mm.
Shoulders:	17–22 mm.
B. Lengths: Stem (base to constriction below shoulders):	14–19 mm.
Blade (remainder of specimen):	21–39 mm.
Total:	38–55 mm.
C. Thickness:	5– 8 mm.

Distribution: see map 3. All in situ specimens from Fred Yarbrough site, Van Zandt County; surface specimens from Wood County. Insufficient data for placement in definite focus but apparently earlier than Sanders Focus.

Such a form would naturally have to be fully supplemented with line drawings and photographs so as to make the variations clear.

Those specimens which were set aside as uncertain or aberrant in the initial step may now be re-examined. Many of them may be typed as the result of a better understanding of the various type compositions; the remainder may be illustrated individually and labeled "miscellaneous" or "unclassified."

The sixth step consists of the employment of typological knowledge in the reconstruction of cultural relationships. If enough data are available, the plotting of type distributions in space, time, and association may reveal consistency in the way that certain types tend to fall together in site after site. Such persistently associated types, within the same material category such as pottery, basketry, projectiles, etc., are now termed "series" in some quarters. In early Mogollon the pottery complex centers around the "Alma series": Alma Plain, Alma Punched, Alma Scored, Alma Neck Banded. In an early Southeastern period, Alexander Incised, Alexander Pinched, and Alexander Dentate Stamped form an "Alexander series." With ample evidence that such linked types, together with some others bearing different names, occur repeatedly in close association, it eventually becomes possible to shorten the identification of material as belonging to a "series" representing a single culture during a restricted time period. Thus it may be said that a certain run of pottery belongs entirely to the Texarkana Focus series, and so on.

An aggregate of types in different categories of material culture may be termed a "complex" if all types belong to a definite, delimited cultural configuration. The complex may be named after the key site or locality in the same way that a focus or phase is named.

Again, it is sometimes demonstrable that several well established types, each of which is normally identifiable with a distinct culture complex, are in fact related to one another because continuities of one kind or another show that the cultures are related. This circumstance involves the problem of genetic affinity in the products of human activity. The postulation of such affinity is based upon the principle that objects of a generally similar appearance found in related cultures are the products of changing tastes or values wrought upon some original ancestral form. Arguments for genetic affinity and evolution in artifact types must, however, be regarded with great caution. Rouse[16] has discussed this point and employed the term "replacement" as an alternative culture process to evolution:

---

[16] Rouse, 1939, p. 14.

The concept of "replacement" should not be likened to the concept of "evolution." The latter implies development of artifact types, somewhat like the growth of plants. Replacement, however, expresses merely a change in types or modes. Each type is assumed, by definition, to be an immutable pattern. Hence, it cannot grow or evolve like a plant. It merely comes into existence, persists, and dies out. It is analogous to a culture trait which diffuses, not to an artifact which evolves.

Rouse has further discussed the various aspects of historical reconstruction based upon established types:[17]

The set of concepts used in this study for reconstructing history from the distributions of the types and modes may be termed "processes." They conceptualize the distributions, so as to make them represent historical events. Each process indicates the history of an individual culture trait along the paths of its distribution . . . the processes can also be used to express the histories of trait complexes . . . .

The complete set of processes, then, is the following. A type or mode may have come into existence at a site by *origination* on the spot, or by *diffusion* from a neighboring tribe. It will then *persist* for a certain length of time, at first (perhaps) *increasing in popularity*, later *decreasing in popularity*. Finally, the type or mode will die out, either by becoming extinct or by *replacement* by another type or mode.

In other words, the proof of evolution in cultural products by means of exhaustive historical study is one thing, its assumption on the basis of visual impressions of similarity quite another. Thus basic relationships between specimens cannot be *assumed* to exist in any form, however close their superficial resemblances may be.

The Status of a Subtype

In general usage, the concept of "subtype" is that it provides a subdivision primarily useful in clarifying a description. For example, a pottery type may include several vessel shapes and design motifs, or different pastes and colors. To make such a composition easier to describe and illustrate, recourse may be taken to "subtypes."

As envisaged herein in connection with "the typological method," the subtype is a purely temporary placement of a specimen group which cannot definitely be termed a variation of one type or a type in itself. The implication is that when sufficient evidence is gathered, the group will either become a type or will be incorporated as a variation in another known type. If all specimens could be satisfactorily typed there would thus be no subtypes.

The description and illustration of complex types with much variation may then be itemized and explained to the extent that their content is clear. This may be done through forms devised for the purpose or through simple itemization lists of "modes" such as used by Rouse[18] for Haitian material.

---

[17] Rouse, 1939, pp. 14–15. Italics mine. See also the discussion in Ford, 1938.
[18] Rouse, 1939, pp. 42–56.

Application of the Typological Method

The significance of the above discussions is already quite clear to many archaeologists, and we are particularly indebted to certain pioneers in Southwestern pottery research for having put the principles into practice. What is now most needed is a general application of the same analytical concept to all archaeological remains, and a general dissatisfaction with anything that falls short of it. There are, of course, many instances of new or isolated material which cannot be accurately typed for lack of distributional knowledge, and in such cases one must describe the material as fully as possible.[19]

There is considerable danger in the presentation of so-called types drawn up without comprehension of their implied meaning, for the "facts" of relationship and sequence deduced from them may be quite unreliable. Often a loose usage of the term is fairly obvious, "type" being applied to any kind of difference between specimens, or even between individual parts of specimens. Illustrations accompanying such works may show nothing more than a scattering of objects, perhaps only the complete or "best" specimens, or those that particularly interest the author. This difficulty probably is largely due to failure to handle the problem of variability, i.e., what kinds and how much of it are to be included in each type range. The typological method is directed specifically at this problem, with the conclusion that variations can only be determined through careful distributional comparison of all executional elements. There appears to be no possibility of devising "standard" classificatory systems, for procedure must be adjusted to the material and problems in given areas, with a maximum of flexibility.

It is also essential that when a typological analysis is made, there be some adjustment in its perspective. Too-general inclusions will tend to obscure differences which may well have real historical significance, while, conversely, too-fine divisions may raise individual or minor local variations to an unwarranted importance. In the long run, it appears likely that the typological method will act toward reducing our great masses of objects into fewer and more cohesive groupings than we now face, with varying degrees of objective treatment, on every hand.

The establishment of sound typologies also effects a very great saving in publication space by the use of simple name-references to those types already described. In Southwestern and Southeastern pottery reports, for example, the general recognition of many types has eliminated repetitive description on a very appreciable scale.

---

[19] See Griffin, 1942, for a good example of discussion, description, and tentative identification of the kind necessitated by conditions.

Alex D. Krieger

The concept of the typological method has already been extended somewhat beyond the ceramic field through such terms as "Folsom Point," "Gypsum Point," "Lake Mohave Point," and the like. However, there has as yet been little attempt to formulate the complete inclusiveness of these terms, and until this is done, strict comparisons are difficult and precarious. There is a great need for more study of the variations which are to be included in these "types," although this is considerably hampered by their relative rarity and wide dispersion.

It appears to the writer that pending definition and common recognition of historically reliable types, the word "type" should be avoided as much as possible. It is perfectly easy and feasible to speak of "form," "shape," "style," or "these specimens," "this group," etc. in discussing any sort of artifact or part thereof. Suspected identity with recognized types can be discussed without confusing the issue with loose applications. Eventually "type" could be restricted to one definite meaning.

Greenman[20] has described a system which reflects dissatisfaction with the traditional approach to classification, and at the same time reveals the germ of a typology based on cultural association. Because of this conflict, his application of the term "type" is inconsistent. If he had not felt a certain obligation to begin with a typical symbolic outline, and then convert it according to experience with distributions, this ambiguity would have been avoided. The paper does, however, indicate that such dissatisfaction has been felt by some authorities for a considerable time.

Black and Weer[21] have suggested three concepts or stages in the classification of artifacts. They term these "geometric, morphological, and cultural forms." If I understand their argument, geometric forms are those which can be described by simple geometric terms; these artifacts may consist of a single shape or a combination of two or more simple shapes. The morphological and culture forms would consist of elaborations upon the simple "basic" forms which have special meanings in various culture settings.

Byers and Johnson[22] have also made an important step toward more realistic treatment of material. They demonstrate an unusual sense of obligation to the reader by explaining their position and method in considerable detail. Like Greenman's, their system of analysis arises from dissatisfaction with traditional classifications and incorporates distributional knowledge in the formation of types. Their Figure 9 is an example of such types, for there is no particular order in the sequence

[20] Greenman, 1929.
[21] Black and Weer, 1936.
[22] Byers and Johnson, 1940, esp. pp. 32–40.

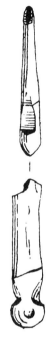

of forms shown; in other words, they felt no compulsion to present the forms in any "logical" order, for each has a meaning of its own independently of the others. Their approach, adapted from Black and Weer,[23] retains such classificatory ideas as a search for characters of "basic importance"; in this case workmanship is used and the classes are "crude," "finished," and "exceptional." The term "type," say Byers and Johnson, "is intended to represent the perfect example, exhibiting all the characteristics which differentiate it from other types. It is the mean, falling between the extreme variations." While this interpretation of type may be questioned, their discussion is interesting and valuable.

In a short paper, Adams[24] has discussed the relative diagnostic value of certain types in different circumstances. This value is far from constant, for a given type may be "diagnostic" of a certain culture complex in one area, but too elusive or too general in another.

Probably the most important single paper yet to appear on typological methodology and its implications in terms of history and behavior is that of Rouse.[25] It includes careful definitions of terms such as "concept," "postulate," etc. incidental to the discussion of "type" and "mode," the basic tools for analysis. If anything, the work is overinvolved and rather wearyingly repetitive in its insistence on certain premises. In the present paper, my use of "feature" and "character" in regard to specimen and group description, although undefined, appear to be equivalent to Rouse's "attribute" and "mode."

CONCLUSIONS

Analysis of archaeological material has not been fully effective because of such assumptions as:

1. Arrangement for descriptive orderliness and symmetry is equivalent to analysis for the discovery of cultural relationships.

2. Any grouping in a classificatory outline is automatically a "type."

3. There are basic characters underlying the products of human workmanship which, if they can be discovered, will provide the means for more uniform and standardized classifications.

It is recommended that:

1. Outline systems of classification be abandoned for purposes of research in cultural relationships. (This does not preclude their usefulness for abbreviated cataloging description, note-taking, filing, etc.)

2. The typological concept exemplified by pottery research be pro-

---

[23] Black and Weer, 1936.
[24] Adams, 1940.
[25] See notes 3, 16, 18.

jected into other material categories; type descriptions likewise to be organized toward full range of variability and illustrated for maximum comparability.

3. All instances of the use of "type" in archaeology be viewed with reserve unless accompanied by full explanation of their method of determination.

BIBLIOGRAPHY

ADAMS, ROBERT MCCORMICK
    1940. "Diagnostic Flint Points." AMERICAN ANTIQUITY, Vol. 6, pp. 72–75.
BLACK, GLENN A., AND PAUL WEER
    1936. "A Proposed Terminology for Shape Classification of Artifacts." AMERICAN ANTIQUITY, Vol. 1, pp. 280–294.
BYERS, DOUGLAS S., AND FREDERICK JOHNSON
    1940. *Two Sites on Martha's Vineyard.* Papers of the Robert S. Peabody Foundation for Archaeology, Vol. 1, No. 1.
COLE, FAY-COOPER, AND THORNE DEUEL
    1937. *Rediscovering Illinois.* University of Chicago Press.
DEUEL, THORNE
    N.D. "A Proposed Classification of Stone Projectile Points." Ms. dated 1927. Copy in Anthropology files, University of Texas.
FINKELSTEIN, J. J.
    1937. "A Suggested Projectile-Point Classification." AMERICAN ANTIQUITY, Vol. 2, pp. 197–203.
FORD, JAMES A.
    1938. "A Chronological Method Applicable to the Southeast." AMERICAN ANTIQUITY, Vol. 3, pp. 260–264.
FORD, JAMES A., AND GORDON F. WILLEY
    1940. *Crooks Site, A Marksville Period Burial Mound in La Salle Parish, Louisiana.* Dept. of Conservation, Louisiana Geological Survey, Anthropological Study 3. New Orleans.
FOWKE, GERARD
    1896. *Stone Art.* Bureau of American Ethnology, Thirteenth Annual Report.
GIFFORD, E. W.
    1940. *Californian Bone Artifacts.* Anthropological Records, Vol. 3, No. 2. University of California Press.
GIFFORD, E. W., AND W. E. SCHENCK
    1926. *The Archaeology of the Southern San Joaquin Valley, California.* University of California Publications in American Archaeology and Ethnology, Vol. 23, pp. 1–122.
GLADWIN, W., AND H. S. GLADWIN
    1930a. *Some Southwestern Pottery Types. Series I.* Medallion Papers. Globe, Arizona.
    1930b. *A Method for the Designation of Southwestern Pottery Types.* Medallion Papers. Globe, Arizona.
    1931. *Some Southwestern Pottery Types. Series II.* Medallion Papers. Globe, Arizona.
    1933. *Some Southwestern Pottery Types. Series III.* Medallion Papers. Globe, Arizona.

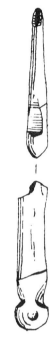

GLADWIN, H. S., E. W. HAURY, E. B. SAYLES, AND N. GLADWIN
     1937. *Excavations at Snaketown, Vol. 1, Material Culture.* Medallion Papers, No. 24. Globe, Arizona.

GORODZOV, V. A.
     1933. "The Typological Method in Archaeology." *American Anthropologist,* Vol. 35, pp. 95–103.

GREENMAN, E. F.
     1929. "A Form for Collection Inventories." Bulletin of the National Research Council, No. 74, pp. 82–88.

GRIFFIN, JAMES B.
     1942. "Adena Pottery." AMERICAN ANTIQUITY, Vol. 7, pp. 344–358.

HARGRAVE, L. L.
     1937. *Guide to Forty Pottery Types from the Hopi Country and the San Francisco Mountains, Arizona.* Museum of Northern Arizona, Bulletin 11. Flagstaff.

HAWLEY, FLORENCE M.
     1936. *Field Manual of Prehistoric Southwestern Pottery Types.* The University of New Mexico Bulletin, Anthropological Series, Vol. 1, No. 4.

KIDDER, A. V.
     1932. *The Artifacts of Pecos.* Yale University Press. New Haven.

KLUCKHOHN, CLYDE
     1939. "The Place of Theory in Anthropological Studies." *Philosophy of Science,* Vol. 6, No. 3, pp. 328–344.

LILLARD, J. B., R. F. HEIZER AND F. FENENGA
     1939. *An Introduction to the Archaeology of Central California.* Sacramento Junior College, Dept. of Anthropology, Bulletin 2. Sacramento, California.

NELSON, N. C.
     N.D. "Classification of Projectile Points." Ms. sent to Carl E. Guthe for Committee on State Archaeological Surveys, dated June 11, 1929. Copy in Anthropology files, University of Texas.

RAU, CHARLES
     1876. *The Archaeological Collection of the United States National Museum, in Charge of the Smithsonian Institution, Washington, D. C.* Smithsonian Contributions to Knowledge, Vol. 22.

RENAUD, E. B.
     1931. "Typology and Description of Projectile Points." Ms.
     1934. *The First Thousand Yuma-Folsom Artifacts.* University of Denver, Dept. of Anthropology. Mimeographed.

ROUSE, IRVING
     1939. *Prehistory in Haiti, A Study in Method.* Yale University Publications in Anthropology, No. 21.

STRONG, W. D.
     1935. *An Introduction to Nebraska Archeology.* Smithsonian Miscellaneous Collections, Vol. 93, No. 10.

WILSON, THOMAS
     1899. "Arrowpoints, Spearheads, and Knives of Prehistoric Times." United States National Museum, *Annual Report for 1897,* Pt. 1, pp. 811–988.

WISSLER, CLARK
     1923. *Man and Culture.* New York.

The University of Texas
Anthropology Department
April, 1942

John Otis Brew

THE USE AND ABUSE OF TAXONOMY [1]

Scepticism is a powerful aid to scientific thought. One must be bold enough to cast doubt both upon the theories of others and upon one's own, and even upon the foundations of one's own science and its method. — TALLGREN

DEVELOPMENTS during the last 10 years make it apparent that the time has come for a general consideration of cultural classification and taxonomic determination, or systematics, as applied to archaeology. In a few recent articles, particularly by Kidder, Roberts, and Kluckhohn, critical discussion of our current Southwestern systematics has appeared. With the exception of the last named, this, however, has been very limited, largely because included in short papers or in introductions to monographs. A few writers have referred to difficulties in the application of systematic methods but have tacitly or expressly passed them off as unworthy of discussion longer than a few sentences or paragraphs. With this I do not agree. The present condition of archaeological research in the Southwestern field leads me to believe that a thorough and careful examination into the mechanical processes of classification, and into the logical assumptions behind it, is not only desirable but necessary.

When the reader has finished this section, I hope that I shall not be considered presumptuous in stating that a perusal of much of the recent archaeological literature of the Southwest leads me to believe that many archaeologists do not fully understand the meaning, applications, and technique of systematic analysis. I hasten to add that I do not claim a complete grasp of it myself, but I firmly believe that it does not and can not do some of the things archaeologists seems to expect of it.

This is a statement which probably needs defense at the outset. That defense is simple and I believe forceful enough to justify the rather lengthy consideration which follows. It is, merely, that in biology, from which most of our systems are borrowed or adapted, the problems of taxonomic method are by no means settled, and much of current biological literature is occupied with attempts to solve those problems and to determine just what such techniques will and will not do in that branch of science.

Professionally, we are dealers in conceptual schemes, and we must keep before us at all times the realization that we are dealing with them. When a student says "Pueblo II," or "Mogollon," or "Vahki Phase," and fits cultural traits into them, he talks in terms of arbitrary concepts, and not of "objective realities."

These concepts we must have. We can not get away from them because they are inherent in our processes of thought. They are the terms in which we think. In other words — and here I address myself to those among us who express distrust or disapproval of what they call "theory" as opposed to "fact" — we can not get away from theory. We all use "theory," whether we admit it or not, *in all we do, in all our thinking.* Consequently, if we are not to waste our own time and that of others, we must analyze and attempt to understand it.

It is unfortunately the case, recently ably demonstrated,[2] that while archaeologists are becoming more and more proficient in the gathering and presentation of "facts" they, for the most part, do not seem to have much understanding of the concepts which of necessity

---

[1] Taxonomy — "Classification, esp. in relation to its general laws or principles; that department of science, or of a particular science or subject, which consists in or relates to classification": definition in *A New English Dictionary on Historical Principles* (The Oxford English Dictionary), Sir James A. H. Murray, ed., Oxford, 1919. Some confusion has arisen in archaeological discussions from the practice, common east of the Rockies, of restricting the term "taxonomy" exclusively to phylogenetic or pseudo-phylogenetic classifications. It is herein applied in its basic meaning to all classifications. By those who use the restricted definition the title of this chapter should be read as "The Use and Abuse of Classification."

[2] Kluckhohn, 1939b.

44

must be built up with those facts to give them significance.

This is not an attack on taxonomic methods as such. It is not an attack upon classificatory analysis of specimens or of culture complexes. It is a fervent plea for a better understanding of these methods and for scientific use of them.

The objections which I shall raise to parts of our current procedure are of such a nature that, when clearly presented, they are usually admitted by most workers in the field. I contend, however, that the publications show that many archaeologists who in oral discussions admit the validity of these objections and recognize the limitations of their techniques do not carry those realizations into their actual work when they are deep in the analysis of their material.

In this connection I shall quote from a recent article on theory in anthropology,[3] which in America includes archaeology. "In any case the alternative is not, I think, between theory and no theory or a minimum of theory, but between adequate and inadequate theories, and, even more important, between theories, the postulates and propositions of which are conscious and which hence lend themselves to systematic criticism, and theories, the premises of which have not been examined even by their formulators. For I am afraid that many of our anthropologists who are most distrustful of 'theory' are like Molière's character who spoke prose without knowing it, for a complex theoretical viewpoint is usually implicit in some of the most apparently innocent 'statements of fact.' "

What I suggest, then, is a critical examination of our own thinking, including those archaeological concepts which at any given time we consider as "basic" or "established." Another quotation from the author cited above is appropriate here. "While in certain aspects of scientific investigation it is absolutely necessary we should take certain things for granted, it is equally necessary that at other times we should consider our subject, coming as close as we can to taking nothing for granted." [4] The first part of this sentence is of supreme importance to our work. In building up a "theory," an "argument," an "historical reconstruction," we must make assumptions, must take certain

things for granted. But we must also realize that we are doing so. We must know what we are assuming. And furthermore, it is our professional obligation to state those assumptions so that our readers may understand them, too. Otherwise we may mislead the reader. We shall be open to misconception, and, through this misconception, our work may be submitted to criticisms which would be unjustified were our assumptions clearly stated.

The quotation continues: "We must be eternally on guard against the insidious crystallization of dogma (unrealized as such) at the expense of that freshness of outlook which is surely a prerequisite to real scientific discovery." To maintain such a guard is extremely difficult, particularly for those of us who are also teachers. As teachers we must present our subject to untrained minds and in such a way that the enthusiasm of the beginner is not stifled and in such a way that he does not give up in disgust with the observation, "These archaeologists apparently do not know anything."

This is certainly not easy. During my first year in college, in a course designed to blast preconceived opinions and provide an introduction to science and scientific procedure, I was told to take nothing for granted. Yet a large part of my subsequent instruction, as an undergraduate, was nothing more than a piling up of dogma. That most of this dogma was arbitrary in nature was very rarely so much as intimated. In a large measure this report is an attempt to alleviate that situation in a way which may prove useful.

The primary problem has already been stated. There are certain very definite things which a student can accomplish by means of taxonomic studies and there are other things which can not be done by such means. It is the latter group which is perhaps of most importance to us in 1945, for the failure to realize the limitations has created a large number of totally unnecessary problems in Southwestern archaeology which will take years to straighten out, thus occupying the energies of students who might otherwise have been more gainfully employed. I refer here, among other things, to the waste of time, energy, and space in publications spent in disputes as to the placing of a

[3] Kluckhohn, 1939b, p. 330.

[4] Kluckhohn, 1939b, p. 342.

given trait in "Pueblo I" or "Pueblo II," the "identification" of a potsherd as belonging to one type or another, and, perhaps most important of all, the attempts to place cultural material, that is to say, specimens, in a single taxonomic system which will describe them completely and solve the problems of relationship in *one* operation. In order to show these limitations, it will be necessary to examine the very foundations of classificatory analysis.

The main points which this examination will attempt to establish are easily stated and had best be mentioned briefly here at the outset of the dissertation. Perhaps the basic one is the most readily admitted and the most thoroughly ignored of all; namely, that classificatory systems are merely tools, tools of analysis, manufactured and employed by students, just as shovels, trowels, and whisk brooms are tools of excavation. Upon this concept a number of others depend:

1) The system is "made" by the student, the diagnostic criteria are defined by him, and objects or cultures are placed in a particular class or type according to his designation: therefore:

2) Cultures are not "discovered," "types" are not "found." The student does not "recognize" a type, he *makes* it and *puts* the object in it. Objects do not "belong" or "fall into" types, they are *placed* in types by the student. Developing from this it can be stated that:

3) No typological system is actually inherent in the material. Systematic classifications are simplifications of and generalizations of the natural situation. The classes are entities and realities only in the minds of students, they have no other existence. Consequently:

4) There is no such thing as *the type* to which an object "belongs." The full implication of this is that:

5) There is no naturally or divinely created classificatory system in which the objects all have a place, so to speak, ex officio. This is of particular importance when considering attempts to design, let us say, a single taxonomic system into which all pottery may be placed, irrespective of the particular characters such as form, design, surface treatment, or paste composition being studied. Attempts to set up and use such a system introduce a series of insuperable difficulties which can best be stated by an example: given 100 potsherds for analy-

sis from a stratigraphic level in a site. These may be grouped according to determinations of paste composition and placed thereby in 4 classes of 40, 30, 20, and 10 individuals, respectively. Then let us jumble them together again and classify them by certain criteria of surface finish, again for shape, again for design or any other series of characteristics. Do they "fall into" the same groups? Those who have handled such specimens can answer this immediately. Usually they do not! This brings our first positive conclusion as to the proper use of classification, namely:

6) A group of objects to be studied must be classified in a number of different ways depending upon the information the student wishes to obtain, and generally the classes will not coincide. The negative corollary to this is:

7) A student whose purpose is to find out all he can about his material restricts his findings to but a small amount of the possibilities when he uses only one classification.

Thus at the end of the first avenue of the subject explored we come to the conclusion that we advocate not less but *more* classification of a given series of objects, specifically more than one classification. The classifications, however, are personal to the student and his problem and are conditioned by the nature of the information he seeks to extract from his series.

The second avenue of thought to be followed throughout this discussion is perhaps not so clear-cut and straight. It has to do with a serious misconception, again denied as such, but continually used in practice. This is that relationships exist between cultural objects and between culture complexes which are either the same as or similar to the genetic relationships between living organisms. That this concept exists in the minds of many archaeologists is again apparent in their publications. It can be demonstrated, I believe, that it is fostered by the way in which systematics has been applied or, more specifically, by the misuse of systematics arising from a regrettable disregard of the fact that we are dealing with inanimate objects. This arises naturally because, as already stated:

8) Our systematics has been borrowed and adapted from biology. In this connection it will subsequently be shown that:

From *The Archaeology of Alkali Ridge, Southeastern Utah*   *267*

9) The authors of most of the outstanding classificatory systems in the Southwest were at one time biologists or received their early scientific training in a biological discipline. This will not be presented as a criticism of their attempts to apply their training to the new subject but, rather, as evidence providing a logical explanation of a source of this particular difficulty. Because of this:

10) Cultural material has been thought of and discussed in terms of kinds of relationships impossible in the nature of the material; and because of this:

11) There has been a tendency to ignore or subordinate certain relationships and phenomena which do exist. As J. H. Steward says in a recent review of Colton's adaptation of the Gila Pueblo Phase System: "It is apparent from the cultural relationships shown in this scheme that strict adherence to a method drawn from biology inevitably fails to take into account the distinctively cultural and unbiological fact of blends . . . between essentially unlike types. . . . The inherent inability of this method to take cognizance of cultural blends is not surmounted in its application to archaeological data; it is ignored. . . . Those of us who have ventured to question taxonomic methods in archaeology are suspected of having disorderly minds. Obviously, our objection is not to order but to the supposition that classification is synonymous with order. We do not see the advantage of simplification, even for the general student and layman, when the method employed inevitably distorts true cultural relationships. If the purpose is to represent the development, interaction, and blending of diverse cultural streams, surely one can find a method that does not require the wholly unsuitable categories of biology."[5] It will also be shown that:

12) Serious doubt now exists that actual genetic relationships in biology are always properly presented in the taxonomic systems of that science. Consequently, it is absurd to expect that similar systems will show such relationships between objects which do not receive their characteristics through the transfer of genes; in other words, where actually such relationships do not exist.

Throughout the discussion the arbitrary nature of classificatory schemes will be emphasized and, I hope, established beyond doubt. The uses to which they may profitably be put will be presented along with considerations of their limitations. General problems of taxonomic nomenclature will be explored along with the difficulties encountered in establishing diagnostic criteria to distinguish groups and phases. And the dangers will be pointed out, in the so-called ideal or comprehensive schemes, of overemphasizing single criteria or selected groups of criteria which, although of value in studying those particular characters, can not fail to give a warped picture of the whole.

In support of the various points to be made examples will be given and opinions will be quoted. The examples will, insofar as possible, be taken from archaeology; the opinions must perforce be quoted largely from the literature of biology because archaeologists, for the most part, have not turned their critical faculties in this direction.

I have mentioned before the necessity of examining the logical foundations of our work. Such examination should go on *all the time*, if we wish to be useful and to have our works withstand the increasingly critical judgments being brought to bear upon them, just as we continually examine the edge of a knife blade, the point of a drawing pen, or the effective member of any tool which we use. Because of developments in experimental physics and experimental biology, certain men engaged in these sciences have recently devoted themselves to epistemological studies, particularly to the manner in which scientists obtain their knowledge of the external world. A biologist, J. S. L. Gilmour, has recently published a paper which clearly shows the trend of these studies.[6] I shall present the pertinent statements he makes about the nature of classificatory schemes, paraphrasing them to apply to our particular archaeological problems.

Citing H. Dingle,[7] Gilmour believes there is a primary duality in our processes of obtaining knowledge. This consists of (1) a series of sense-impressions received through experience; (2) the mental processes which give order and

[5] Steward, 1941a.

[6] Gilmour, 1940, pp. 461–74.   [7] Dingle, 1938, p. 148.

coherence to these sense-impressions. To quote directly from Gilmour: "This account of the thought-process gives an entirely different picture of the acquisition of knowledge from that usually accepted by working scientists. In both there is a duality. The commonly accepted picture is that of mind, on the one hand, and the objects of the external world, on the other, the business of science being to bring to the knowledge of mind an ever greater number of these objects. Mind in this picture plays no active part in *creating* the objects of the external world, but merely records what already exists. In Dingle's picture, however, the duality is not one between a passive, receptive mind and a pre-existing external world, but between an active, subjective, reasoning agent, and the countless sense-data of experience out of which reason builds that logically coherent pattern which we call the external world. The 'objects' of this 'external world,' therefore, consist of two distinct elements, one derived from sense-experience, the other supplied by the activity of the reasoning agent."

For example, a pot consists partly of a number of experienced sense-data such as color, shape, paste composition, and other qualities and partly of the concept *pot* which the mind of man has constructed to group these data together.

According to this, the process of classification is outlined by Gilmour as follows. The investigator experiences a large number of sense-data which he groups in classes, each defined in terms of certain specific data. Thus a class called bowls may be made for sense-data exhibiting a certain range of shape. Any series of data can be grouped in a number of different ways, depending on the purpose of the investigation. Thus the range of data placed under the class "pottery vessel" can be subdivided into colors, surface treatments, shapes, uses, and so on. The important thing here is that the making of these groups is an activity of reason and can and should be manipulated at will to serve the purposes of the student.

Concluding this argument Gilmour says: "Classification, then, has always a pragmatic element as well as an empirical and a rational

one. Broadly speaking, the purpose of all classification is to enable the classifier to make inductive generalizations concerning the sense-data he is classifying."

This starts us fairly upon a consideration of the purposes of classification. It also casts grave doubts upon the possibility of obtaining that ideal of archaeological systematists, the "objective" classification of pottery or the "objective" classification of cultures.

The desire for "objectivity" in classification arises, I think, from the belief that the manufactured groups are realistic entities and the lack of realization that they are completely artificial. Thus the desire is essentially a paradox. Implicit in it is a faith, based upon the species concept of biology, in the existence of a "true" or "correct" classification for all objects, cultures, etc., which completely ignores the fact that they are all part of a continuous stream of cultural events.

It will be well here to examine the species concept in the context in which it was developed. Doubts as to the validity of species as real entities are not new, but difficulties encountered by many experimental biologists and physiologists in applying the concept, particularly to the smaller organisms, have recently brought them to the fore. Early expressions of the arbitrary nature of species are to be found in Darwin's writings. He regarded the term as one arbitrarily given,[8] and the furthest he ever went in his use of the concept was to regard species as "tolerably well-defined objects."

Later-day biologists have varied from complete denial of the concept to complete acceptance of it as representative of objective reality. E. Rabaud[9] denies its usefulness and declares that the individual is of greater consequence than species. At the opposite extreme Bateson[10] believes that "specificity" is a universal attribute of organized life. Most zoölogists and botanists now hold beliefs somewhere between these two. G. C. Robson in his book on the species problem says, ". . . while many of the groups called 'species' by the systematist are readily distinguishable one from another, there is no universal criterion by which species as opposed to other systematic

[8] Darwin, 1859, p. 66.   [9] Rabaud, 1920, pp. 291–93.   [10] Bateson, 1913, p. 12.

---

units may be recognized." [11] He believes the concept useful, though, for ". . . while there is no essential and absolute 'specificity' which can be attributed to certain assemblages of individuals, but not to others, the groups which the systematist treats as species have a tolerable degree of homogeneity. The systematic status of such groups is generally recognized as a *purely conventional matter*."

One of the common definitions of species, still held by many zoölogists, is that a species is made up of individuals capable of fertile union.[12] This definition has been repeatedly shown to be impractical [13] and, because of the difficulties of obtaining an acceptable precise definition, biologists are gradually adopting a generalized one very similar to that by which the more cautious archaeologists define their taxonomic categories; namely that a species, as a useful classificatory tool, is a group of individuals resembling each other more than they resemble the individuals of other groups.

The implications of this are important. The resemblances upon which the groupings are made must be observed by the classifier. The relative weight assigned to different characteristics of the individual vary and the particular interests of students vary as well. This view of the species problem does not arise from the study of such distinctive groups as the kangaroo and giraffe but from small organisms such as insects of which approximately 10,000 new species are currently being described every year; [14] a situation somewhat comparable to that developing in the ceramic systematics of the Southwest.

Thus, from a survey of biological literature, it seems that the various taxonomic categories of that science, even the fundamental one of species, are arbitrary. The diagnostic characteristics of each group are selected by the student, the groups are arbitrarily defined by the student, and the student puts the individual in the group.

Similar conclusions have been reached by certain archaeologists in the Southwest and in other fields. Kidder in the introduction to the second volume of "The Pottery of Pecos" says,

"The division of the Glaze ware of Pecos into six chronologically sequent types is a very convenient and, superficially, satisfactory arrangement. For some time I was very proud of it, so much so, in fact, that I came to think and to write about the types as if they were definite and describable entities. They are, of course, nothing of the sort, being merely useful cross-sections of a constantly changing cultural trait. Most types, in reality, grew one from the other by stages well-nigh imperceptible. My grouping therefore amounts to a selection of six recognizable nodes of individuality; and a forcing into association with the most strongly marked or 'peak' material of many actually older and younger transitional specimens." [15]

Irving Rouse in his study of the prehistory of Haiti [16] defines "types" as artificial concepts and devotes a large part of his paper to definition of his conceptual scheme and discussion of its utility and significance.

Likewise, Colton, though frankly adopting a scheme based upon biological taxonomy, says: "It must be stressed, however, that this is not a 'natural' classification but is purely artificial. The very nature of the material presupposes this." [17]

It seems, therefore, that we can conclude that the classes in these systems are artificial; that they are part of our own devices for interpreting our observations; and that it is incorrect to believe that objects or cultures "fall into" a given place in a system or that we are able to "discover" an artifact type or a culture phase.

If this can be admitted, and I believe it must be, then we can view such systems in a different light. The most important result of this conclusion is that, if the systems do not exist in objective reality, that is to say, naturally, we are under no historical or scientific compulsion to "discover" or "record" them. Thus the question becomes one of method, and we can concern ourselves entirely with evaluation of the usefulness of the various systems; a study of what they do for us, how they do it, whether a given system "does more harm than good," that is, whether it introduces more problems

[11] Robson, 1928.
[12] Diver, 1940, p. 303.
[13] Zuckerman, 1933a, 1933b.

[14] Smart, 1940, pp. 475–91.
[15] Kidder, 1936.   [16] Rouse, 1939.
[17] Hargrave, 1932, foreword.

than it solves, etc. In this regard, probably the most important part of the taxonomic technique is the way in which the various classes are defined, the criteria or diagnostics which are set up. These will be discussed at the end of the section when the specific application of this study to Southwestern archaeology will be made.

Before going on to a consideration of the genetic implications of current archaeological taxonomy, there is one more point which seems to merit further discussion. The fifth item in the list at the beginning of this section states that there is no ideal system of classification in which all objects or groups of objects have a place because of their natural characteristics. This is a very important consideration, for in recent years much time and energy has been spent in attempting to "find" or devise such schemes and in forcing objects into them. The attempts cover a great range of material, from fragments of artifacts, that is, potsherds, to large assemblages of traits called by various names such as "cultures," "periods," "phases," "aspects," etc.

Again I must emphasize that I do not criticize the manufacture of such schemes and their use in archaeological analysis and description. However, must we not condemn the practice of considering them as realities and above all of setting up one of many possible systems as the "true" classification of certain objects or of cultures?

This question, too, has been raised in biology; namely, is there a "final ideal classification towards which taxonomists are consciously or unconsciously striving"?[18] In answer to this Gilmour writes: "A natural classification is that grouping which endeavors to utilize *all* the attributes of the individuals under consideration, and is hence useful for a very wide range of purposes. . . . In so far as it is theoretically possible to envisage a classification on these lines, which does in fact embody all the attributes of the individuals being classified, it can be said that one final and ideal classification

of living things is a goal to be aimed at. In practice, however, this aim would never be attained, owing both to the limitations of our knowledge and to the differences of opinion between taxonomists." I wish particularly to draw attention to the final statement. If this is true of biologists, who, after all, have in their hands the complete organism, how much more surely must it be true of archaeologists who deal, for the most part, only with fragments of objects or cultures. Even when the experimental biologist attempts to recreate natural situations of interaction between organisms he often feels that the behavior of his individuals is conditioned by the specializing factors of his laboratory set-up. With such exceptions as experimentation with pottery firing[19] and with the reproduction of stone implements,[20] even these controls are denied anthropologists. Our discipline is for the most part nonexperimental.

With regard to "final-ideal-complete-classifications" we must step for a few moments into what might well be considered the realm of absurdity. I do not think it is, for the 2 questions I am about to pose are asked time and again in oral discussions and are really of great importance. They are: 1) If we attain a classification in which "*all* the attributes of the individuals under consideration" are utilized, shall we not end up, provided our information be complete, with a situation wherein each individual constitutes a class by itself? and 2) If we arrive at a complete classification of all living things, of all pottery "types," of all "cultures" in the world, then what have we, and what do we do with it?

The first question is a hard one to answer. I believe we shall err if we agree to dismiss it as absurd, because so many systematists in different fields have published statements which seem to mean just that, or else they mean nothing. The logical conclusion of their published aims can result only in a reduction to the individual object in the case of artifacts and to the individual person in the case of "cultures."[21] Obviously there is something wrong

---

[18] Gilmour, 1940, p. 461.
[19] Shepard, 1936, 1939; Colton, 1939b.
[20] Pond, no date, ca. 1930; Ellis, 1940.
[21] The appropriateness of the question is attested by the following quotation from a recent botanical report. "In reading the original descriptions of Crataegus

species one is impressed by the similarity of many of them in all but a few unimportant details. Some of the descriptions were so accurate that it would be difficult to find any tree or specimen except the type (specimen) that would fit them in every detail." Palmer, 1943, p. 374.

here and we need better definition. The usual answer to this criticism is in terms of "significant criteria." In studying the differences between individuals which differences are significant and which differences insignificant in terms of taxonomy? No general answer seems possible. Here again is a manifestation of the arbitrary nature of these systems. We must agree which differences are significant, and the significance will again vary with the student and with the nature of his immediate problem. Bateson in his "Problems of Genetics" [22] says: "They will serve Science best by giving names freely and by describing everything to which their successors may possibly want to refer, and generally by subdividing their material into as many species as they can induce any responsible journal to publish." This is an excellent and horrible example of the kind of thinking which brings discredit upon all scientific work and workers. If we follow Bateson we must describe our material according to the needs and interests of posterity, which we can not possibly know, and in the final analysis the arbiters of the number of our groups, of the size of our classifications, are our publishers! What folly!

The only answer I can reach for the first question is a tentative one and not an answer, really, at all, but a negation of the whole proposition. At present, it seems to me that the "ideal-complete-classification" is an impractical concept because of the impossibility of arriving at standardized criteria which can meet the needs of actual study of the material with a view to solving particular problems. As has been said above and will be said many times below, the diagnostics of classificatory groups are too closely associated with the immediate problem in hand to permit a general classification which can be generally applied to a heterogeneous mass of problems. Lothrop in a recent critique of taxonomy says: ". . . archaeological remains are human products, censored by destructive contact with the soil, and they therefore vary widely in quality and quantity. Furthermore archaeologists are individuals differing in character, training, ability and special interests. How then can there be

any one . . . method which outranks all others?" [23]

This verges upon the second question: if such an "ideal-complete-classification" can be worked out, what shall we have and how shall we use it? Some of my doubts as to its usefulness are already expressed. First let us consider what it is. By this ideal system we would have all of the pottery of the world, or the cultures of the world, arranged according to a single descriptive classification according to criteria arbitrarily agreed upon. This would be a nice orderly thing and to some workers, apparently, a sufficient end in itself. But what would it show? From it would appear certain real or fortuitous relationships, and I fear in most cases it would be impossible to tell which, based upon *the agreed criteria*. To establish other relationships and to check those suggested by the system itself it would still be necessary to reanalyze and reclassify the material according to other criteria. This would of necessity result in regrouping and in the production of various more limited classifications which would not conform to the basic one.

The famous McKern System (the Midwestern Taxonomic System) of culture classification in use in the eastern United States [24] is, insofar as I am able to understand it, one of these "ideal-complete-classifications." There are those who claim that it has produced considerable order in the eastern field. On the other hand, it has also produced a tremendous amount of dispute, even acrimonious dispute, and confusion.

The most important single objection which has been raised against the McKern System is that its usefulness is greatly restricted or nullified by the ignoring of a time factor. Ford, with regard to his own system of classifying lower Mississippi cultures,[25] says: ". . . it is impossible to see, without chronology, how we can ever hope to rediscover the cultural history of the Indians of the Southeast."

Rouse, who used the McKern System in his earlier work in the West Indies and then devised one of his own to supplement it, says: [26] ". . . it will be seen, persistence is the logical counterpart to diffusion. One who traces the

[22] Bateson, 1913, p. 249.
[23] Lothrop, 1941.
[24] McKern, 1939; see also pp. 18–21, *Bulletin, the*

Archaeological Society of Delaware, vol. 3, no. 3, 1940.
[25] Ford, 1938.
[26] Rouse, 1939.

distribution of a type or mode only in space, thereby studying diffusion but ignoring persistence, reconstructs only part of the culture history." And vice versa, "A person must study both the diffusion and the persistence of culture traits if he desires to make a balanced historical reconstruction." He does not consider the McKern System to be useless but merely insufficient for his purposes. He says: "The McKern technique made it possible to formulate static units of culture . . . and to point out the descriptive relationships between these units. The present technique (Rouse's system), on the other hand, has been used to reconstruct the history of certain individual traits of each cultural unit, and thereby to indicate how the traits changed from unit to unit. The dynamic nature of the present technique seems to have been a good contrast to the static character of the McKern classification."

The same point is brought out by Colton [27] in his "Prehistoric Culture Units and Their Relationships in Northern Arizona." He presents therein a system for classifying Southwestern cultures which is a combination of the Gladwin System [28] and the McKern System. Colton writes: "Although the various subdivisions of the Gladwin and McKern Systems seem superficially to be parallel, they really represent different dimensions of the same principle. The McKern System includes a horizontal or area dimension and omits time, while Gladwin includes area and a vertical or 'time' dimension as well. The two systems, therefore, are not parallel but one may supplement the other. . . . Since archaeology is history and history involves the idea of chronology, the most satisfactory system of classifying phases or foci is one that also involves time."

I cite these objections not as specific criticisms of the McKern System but as objections to the concept of an "ideal-complete-classification" for which I have taken the McKern System as an example. I realize that I have come far from exhausting the subject, but I merely wish to emphasize at this point that such systems do not serve the purpose for which they seem to be designed but must be modified or supplemented to meet any particular problem. And when the modification is, itself, set up as an "ideal-complete-system" it, too, suffers from similar or other difficulties. For example, the current merger of the Gladwin and McKern Systems by Colton [29] introduces the Gladwin "family-tree" concept which had been carefully and consciously avoided by McKern.

All of the above, I believe, serves to illustrate my point, which is that the McKern Classification, designed as a world-wide "single-ideal-complete" cultural classification is impractical and useless as such. To be used at all, it must be adapted to specific problems by each worker (other examples of adaptation of the McKern System can be found in the archaeological literature of the eastern United States), and these adaptations when made, constitute merely one of the classifications the particular student uses in the study of his material.

Consequently, I feel that we must express grave doubt that the "ideal-complete-classification," though perhaps superficially attractive, serves a useful end. If, however, it is used, as the McKern System is actually beginning to be used by the most advanced students,[30] not as a "single-ideal-complete" classification but as merely one of a number of tools for the orderly presentation of a mass of data, then, indeed, it may be of value.

Since the question of the "family-tree" concept has arisen in connection with the Colton-Gladwin System above, it may perhaps be advisable now to get on with the second group of basic assumptions before attempting to analyze further the present systems.

The second major misconception I wish to discuss is that relationships exist between cultural objects and between culture complexes which are either the same as or similar to the genetic relationships between living organisms. Because of that belief, it has been thought, by some, that these relationships will "fall into" or can be described by taxonomic systems modeled after those of biological systematics.

In questioning the validity of this assumption I shall show:

[27] Colton, 1939a, p. 8.
[28] Gladwin, 1930.   [29] Colton, 1939a.
[30] Ford, Phillips, Rouse, Griffin, Krieger, J. Charles Kelley, etc.

1) That grave doubt has been cast *by biologists* upon the assumption that current biological taxonomic systems describe phylogenetic relationships.

2) That similar doubt has been raised by students in specialized fields closely allied to biology, such as palaeontology, conchology, and oölogy.

3) That it is impossible for such systems to show phylogenetic relationships between inanimate objects since (a) they apparently do not show them between living objects, and (b) because phylogenetic relationships do not exist between inanimate objects.

The statement that biological systematics does not actually record and describe evolutionary relationships will occasion more surprise to many archaeologists than it will to biologists. Among the latter it has long been a question for discussion. The more critical among them even go so far as to doubt whether the real significance of the term "phylogenetic relationship" is yet fully understood,[31] and this is something to be kept in mind while we are considering the firmness of the ground upon which our archaeological systematics is based.

The purpose of this section, however, is not to argue the theory of evolution nor to discuss biological relationships. I shall merely present statements of current workers in biology which will be sufficient for my point and refer to their publications for the benefit of those readers who wish to go deeper into the matter.

In so far as this question affects biological taxonomy, it arises through the transfer by the student of the inheritance mechanisms of the individual to the taxonomic groups. In essence, it is a concept of group rather than of lineage phylogeny. According to Gilmour[32] this arose from a false analogy between taxonomic groups and individuals and was based upon the objective existence which both were supposed to possess. From this analogy came the belief that there is a relationship between groups analogous to the genealogical relationship between individuals. Gilmour concludes his argument with the statement, "It is only when taxonomic groups are seen to be collections of individuals classed together because

of the possession of certain attributes in common that the falseness of the . . . analogy becomes clear."

This does not imply that members of a group are not physically related, since in most cases biological groups are composed of closely related lineages. The point made by Gilmour is that this is not always so and that it is not implicit in the system. Therefore he believes that phylogeny does not form the basis for the "single, ideal natural classification" but that it is actually one of the many "classifications constructed for the purpose of special investigations."

This position, as intimated above, is not new. In 1877, T. H. Huxley wrote,[33] "The things classified are arranged according to the totality of their morphological resemblances, and the features which are taken as the marks of groups are those which have been ascertained by observation to be the indications of many likenesses or unlikenesses." He definitely denied any attempt, on his own part, to base classification on phylogeny.

I shall cite only one other statement on the side of general biology. Those who wish to explore it further will find numerous bibliographic references in the papers already cited. Discussing the problem of the "origins of species" Lancelot Hogben says,[34] "We name assemblages as such for two reasons. One is discontinuity of pattern among living creatures. The other is that it is necessary to have a convenient card index of distinguishable types. The procedure we adopt in making it has little to do with *experimental inquiry* into the nature of hereditable variations; and there is no necessary reason for expecting a close connexion between categories of resemblance based on the architecture of the germ-cells and categories of resemblance appropriate to the practice of taxonomy."

Later in his paper[35] Hogben gives an example which is not only amusing but foreshadows some of the factors we must consider when taxonomy is applied to archaeology. "Several local 'species' of the dog family, like races of mankind, are interfertile products of geographical specialization. In so far as extrinsic

[31] Gilmour, 1940, p. 461.
[32] Gilmour, 1940, p. 471 *et seq.*

[33] Huxley, 1877, p. 23.
[34] Hogben, 1940, p. 269.
[35] Hogben, 1940, p. 283.

barriers separate them into distinct assemblages, they may be given taxonomic rank as species, and they remain so as long as the extrinsic barriers are there. So the taxonomic distinction is relative to a certain level of transport industry. In so far as this is so, the origin of dog species is less a problem of biology than a problem of economic history. The sterility of discussing the polyphyletic origin of man is analogous, and also illustrates how difficult it is to think clearly about matters which involve social preferences." At this point I merely wish to point out the possibly even greater role played by preference in the selection of a design to be painted on a pot. And it has a looser rein, for the preference in the latter case must needs apply to only one of the parties to the transaction.

Before going on I believe it will be useful to quote a few recent definitions of "species" published by biologists, as follows:

"A community or number of related communities, whose distinctive morphological characters are in the opinion of a competent systematist sufficiently definite to entitle it, or them, to a specific name." [36]

"A practical and convenient unit by which fossils are distinguished." [37]

"A species is a group of individuals which, in the sum total of their attributes, resemble each other to a degree usually accepted as specific, the exact degree being ultimately determined by the more or less arbitrary judgement of taxonomists." [38]

All of these point one way, all of them exclude phylogeny, and all of them definitely state that the determining factor is the opinion of the classifier.

Many more citations could be made to the same end, but I believe these are sufficient to establish our right to question the assumption that biological taxonomic systems represent phylogenetic relationships.

There is one other biological concept, widely used by anthropologists and archaeologists which we *must discard*, even if we persist, as I hope we shall not, in using a system based on biology. This is the simple "family-tree" con-

cept by which the development of a graduated series of classificatory groups is represented by a diagram in the form of a tree, with parent stem, major forks, major and minor branches, etc.[39] The more critical biologists believe a diagram which is an interlocking network to be a better indicator of genetic relationships,[40] and perhaps a 3-dimensional diagram of this kind is an even closer approximation than a 2-dimensional one.

So much, for the present, for general biology. There are a number of very interesting scientific disciplines which are part way between pure biology and archaeology, in terms of the problem we are discussing. These are sciences which deal with certain characteristics of organisms without dealing directly with the organism in its entirety. I shall mention 3 of these in the natural sciences and 1 striking development in a field closly bound up with anthropology and history. First, palaeontology, where the scientist has only the fossil bones of the organism; second, conchology, where the student deals with the shell of the organism; third, oölogy, where the investigator studies the eggs of birds, especially their shape and color, in other words the visual, external characteristics of the temporary housing of the organism in its embryological stage; and fourth, a specialized study which has been made of medieval human armor.

In all of these cases I shall point out that, although classifications have been made and presented as representing evolutionary development, they do not necessarily describe or even parallel the phylogeny of the actual organisms.

Taxonomic troubles are not new in palaeontology. In 1927 F. A. Bather [41] presented doubts that phylogeny is a sound basis for palaeontological classification. In 1931 C. E. B. Bremekamp [42] denied that it is useful at all for this purpose. W. J. Arkell and J. A. Moy-Thomas have recently published a detailed consideration of the problem [43] from which I shall quote at some length because much of the difficulty they experienced is present in archaeological systematics. With regard to traditional procedure in palaeontology they say,

[36] Regan, 1926.
[37] Arkell and Moy-Thomas, 1940, p. 395.
[38] Gilmour, 1940, pp. 468–69.
[39] An example of the distortion of the cultural

situation presented in such charts is given on pp. 41–42.
[40] Calman, 1940, p. 457.
[41] Bather, 1927, p. lxii.   [42] Bremekamp, 1931.
[43] Arkell and Moy-Thomas, 1940, pp. 395–410.

"The method of classification now used by the majority of palaeontologists is the phylogenetic one, in which fossils are arranged as nearly as possible in accordance with the supposed course of their evolution. Thus classification has come to aim, not only at providing an easy means of recognizing fossils, but also at giving a summary of existing knowledge of phylogeny. It is because these dual objects frequently tend to produce conflicting results that the problems of taxonomy have arisen." This conflicting duality will be understood by those who have attempted to use the recently developed ceramic taxonomy of Southwestern archaeology. The latter aims not only at providing an easy means for recognizing pottery and for placing the specimens in time and space, but also at providing an outline for the development of cultures and the movement of peoples.

The next statement I shall quote from Arkell and Moy-Thomas is equally applicable to archaeological systematics. The palaeontologist is "torn between two irreconcilable endeavors; for as a phylogenist he strives to reveal closer and closer relationships, while as a systematist he must point out differences and divide up his material into units bearing distinct names." Here we have a statement of the basis of the conflict between the so-called "lumpers" and the "splitters" in archaeology which will be treated more fully later.

The crux of the palaeontologist's difficulty is expressed in the next quotation. "It is part of the paleontologist's business to unravel phylogeny by the study of fossils; but he can only arrive at an approximation to the truth, for he has only a fraction of the material to work on, the hard parts which alone have been preserved by fossilization." Even if we disregard for the moment the fact that objects of material culture are not sexually reproductive, I believe that the reader will agree that this objection applies equally well to systematic schemes built upon a study of potsherds.

Because of this situation, these 2 palaeontologists feel free to state that: "At the best of times his (the palaeontologist's) results are hypothetical and more or less subjective, and it may be questioned whether such results form a suitable foundation on which to build a classification and a nomenclature."

If this is true in the case of fossil bones it is even more obviously the case with the shells of mollusks. That the morphology of these shells, arranged in a taxonomic classification, does not parallel the morphological classifications of the organisms which inhabit them has been sufficiently demonstrated.[44] An interesting analogy might be drawn here between the development of house type and the evolution of human beings.

In oölogy I believe the disparity between the classificatory system and the genetic history of the organism is even more apparent. The differences in eggshells are even more minute and the range is smaller than in the shells of mollusks, while the differences in the organisms, in this case birds, are more gross and the range is greater. In any case, the same arguments apply and I think we must conclude that classifications of form and color of birds' eggs do not "reveal" genetic relationships between groups of birds.

The fourth case is of a different nature but is inserted here to help in the transition from "natural" to "cultural" objects. Bashford Dean was an ichthyologist whose interest led him to specialize in armored fishes. From that the step to human armor was made, and it is natural that Dean carried with him into his cultural study the taxonomic system he had learned in his biological work. The result is a series of amazingly detailed "family-trees" of armor which are published in the catalogue of the Metropolitan Museum in New York,[45] and which are used by T. H. Morgan to illustrate certain points in his critique of the theory of evolution.[46] The epistemological fallacy here is quite apparent. The only defense there can be for a classification of armor based upon phylogenetic theory is that the individual objects were made and used by man. Yet the connection between the object and its user is even less close than that between the shell and the mollusk or between the egg and the developed bird. And since this correlation does not exist, then armor has no phylogeny and a

[44] Arkell and Moy-Thomas, 1940, pp. 397–410.
[45] Dean, 1916, pp. 115 and 137.

[46] Morgan, 1916, pp. 4–5.

"family-tree" classification is not only meaningless but actually misleading.

This brings us close to one of the most dangerous examples of complaisance I have encountered among archaeologists. I refer to the use of biological concepts and terms with the knowledge that they do not apply. This means one of 2 things: either the concepts and definitions must be greatly modified for archaeological usage or else they are in fact either meaningless or false. Such usage is perhaps worse than in the case of the workers who really believe that biological rules of taxonomy are absolute and that they do apply to cultural matters. For it means that the user is either lazy or indefinite in his pursuit of knowledge.

In this connection I would, had I sufficient faith in the probability, express the hope that I should never again hear or see the term "evolution" applied to an artifact or to a "culture." I hasten to state that I realize that many humanists and historians who use this term do not imply by it genetic relationships. Of them I ask, in that case, of what use is the term? And I further charge them with this responsibility: that, even though they do not intend such implication, the general association of the term with the genetic history of living organisms leads their hearers and readers to make such implications themselves, to the detriment of progress in the understanding of cultural development.

I also wish to state that I realize that the phylogenetic implication has been added to the word "evolution" by the biologists and that the first meanings given in most dictionaries are of such general nature as to permit the term to be applied to cultural development. My interests, however, are in the ideas which the use of the term brings forward in our minds. In other words, I believe the recent modification of meaning introduced by biologists to be so widely accepted that, if we wish to free ourselves entirely from genetic concepts false to the processes we are studying, it will be necessary to abandon the application of the term to inanimate objects.

In support of this plea I shall quote again from the biologists who are responsible for the present specialized meaning of the word. T. H.

Morgan, in his critique of the theory of evolution, says: [47] "There is an obvious and striking similarity between the evolution of man's inventions and the evolution of the shells of molluscs and of the bones of mammals, yet in neither case does a knowledge of the order in which these things arose *explain them*." I have added the italics. This is a most important point, and I wish to emphasize here that one of the leading proponents of the biological theory of evolution does not believe that it, or a taxonomic system based upon it, can be usefully adapted to the study of fossil bones, shells, or the cultural products of human beings.

In criticizing general usage of the term "evolution," Morgan writes: [48] "We use the word evolution in many ways — to include many different kinds of changes. There is hardly any other scientific term that is used so carelessly — to imply so much, to mean so little.

"We speak of the evolution of the stars, of the evolution of the horse, of the evolution of the steam engine, as though they were all part of the same process. What have they in common? Only this, that each concerns itself with the *history* of something. . . . Clearly no more (in common) than that from a simple beginning through a series of changes something more complex, or at least different, has come to being. To lump all these kinds of changes into one and call them evolution is only to assert that you believe in consecutive series of events (which is history) causally connected (which is science)." Morgan concludes that our aims as scientists should be to find out actually what kind of causes produced the stars in the heavens and the steam engine in the mind and works of man. To confound these causes with the genetic mechanisms which have produced the modern horse does not assist that aim.

It has now been shown that many competent biologists do not believe that the taxonomic system is a proper tool for describing genetic relationships in living organisms. It has also been shown that the use of taxonomic systems for this purpose in the fields of palaeontology, conchology, and oölogy has been questioned by some of those who, nevertheless, believe it is a useful tool in descriptive biology.

[47] Morgan, 1916, p. 4.

[48] Morgan, 1925.

If there is, as there certainly seems to be, a reasonable doubt of the usefulness of phylogenetic classification for fossils, how much greater must the doubt be of the usefulness of a pseudo-phylogenetic classification of artifacts and cultures.

The defense has been offered that such systems are useful, because artifacts and cultures are made by man and closely associated with man, who as an animal is subject to the processes of phylogeny. This can be most effectively exposed as false in 2 ways. 1) The arguments presented above in the case of conchology, etc., apply even more patently to cultural objects. In other words, although the objects were made by man, there is no necessary or causal connection between the form of the object and the shape and color of the man. 2) It may also be effectively pointed out in this connection that although the objects were made by men, the classifications were not made by the same men. And, although the archaeological "cultures" are simplified expressions of life led by men, those expressions were not made by the men who lived the "cultures." A number of ideas (probably most of them) in such classifications were not present in the minds of the makers of the objects and the possessors of the "cultures." This is admirably stated by Rouse [49] in the following quotation: "If the aborigines had been trained to think in cultural terms, they might possibly have conceptualized the artifacts in terms of community standards of behavior, as the writer has done. It is not within the power of the writer, however, to determine whether or not they did so. He can only assume that the types and modes are products of his own mind, whereas the artifacts were objects made by the aborigines."

Consequently, since the relationships are expressed in terms of these classifications produced in the minds of students, they can not be assumed to be identical with the phylogeny of mankind through association. To speak of "polished pottery people," "Folsom people" or even — I almost hesitate to write it — "Bell Beaker people" on the basis of the presence in archaeological sites of a single distinctive artifact type is an epistemological solecism which

can and has warped our studies. Tallgren [50] considers this one of the major weaknesses in archaeological procedure. He describes it as ". . . the tendency to see . . . a uniform population or ethnic group behind cultural phenomena, that is behind the forms of material culture; we have also been too apt to see, in cultural connections and particularly in cultural transmissions, the movements and migrations of *peoples* instead rather of the products of different social classes and of commerce." A good example of this tendency can be found in the American field. Because of the great amount of red ochre found with caches of certain distinctive artifacts in Maine, the complex constructed on the basis of these artifacts was called the "Red Paint Culture." [51] In usage, many archaeologists as far west as the Mississippi Valley speculate upon the presence of the "Red Paint people" whenever red ochre appears in a site or a burial. Yet red ochre was generally used by most North American Indians. This, again, is not a criticism of the application of the term to the arbitrary complex, though a better one certainly could have been devised, but it is a criticism of the use of the term in a large measure out of context and in such a way as to suggest migrations and associations of physical type not justified by the evidence.

Before proceeding further with discussion of the use of this concept by archaeologists, it may be profitable to examine briefly the history of the application of biological classificatory schemes to Southwestern archaeology.

With the development of stratigraphic technique in the second decade of the twentieth century, the accumulating mass of data from excavations and surveys, still for the most part disjointed, presented a complicated picture which defied the ordinary descriptive approach current until then. The preliminary Kidder-Guernsey and Morris classifications were designed to bring order into this mass and eventually resulted in the Pecos System as described above. A definitely evolutionary concept provided the skeleton for the system, but it lacked sufficient precision to satisfy men familiar with more exacting disciplines. In an attempt to supply this precision a binomial taxonomic sys-

[49] Rouse, 1939.

[50] Tallgren, 1937.   [51] Rowe, 1940.

John Otis Brew

tem for the classification of pottery was invented and, based primarily upon it, there developed a "family-tree" concept of culture classification designed to describe all Southwestern prehistory.[52]

Colton [53] outlines the development of this system in Hargrave's original presentation of the taxonomic studies of the Museum of Northern Arizona. "The present situation of pottery nomenclature and classification resembles biology before the days of Linnaeus. In this paper the general rules of biological nomenclature have been followed and a biological classification adopted. . . . At a conference at Gila Pueblo, April 1930, several Southwestern Workers tentatively agreed to adopt a biological method in the classification of Southwestern pottery types."

Present at this conference were Mera, Colton, Hargrave, Renaud, and Gladwin.[54] From this system of pottery classification came Gladwin's phase system, even more strictly biological, if possible, in that it emphasized the evolutionary nature of the scheme in graphical representations of "lineage," "family-trees" of culture.[55]

The biological background is further emphasized by Hargrave in his taxonomic outline which included the following groups: Kingdom, Phylum, Class, Order, Ware, Genus, Type, or Subtype. The genetic basis was confirmed by the introduction of hybrid genera and types.[56] The continued use of the term "hybrid" in connection with artifacts by many Southwestern taxonomists seems to me to be one of the best reasons for a thorough examination of our concepts of cultural processes.

That these ideas are still current, despite disavowals, can be shown by a quotation from the latest taxonomic manual of Southwestern pottery.[57] "A Series, therefore, is a group of pottery types within a single ware in which each type bears a *genetic relation* to each other, including all those types and only those types that occur . . . in the *direct line* of *chronological genetic development* from an original primitive or *ancestral* type to a late

type." The italics are mine; in the original the entire passage is in italics.

An accompanying statement that pottery objects are inanimate does not remove the definite phylogenetic implications of the above quotation. I believe it is impossible to think in those terms without implying race history concepts of physical causal relationships.

That I am not waving a "red herring" in emphasizing this point is perhaps best shown by the following quotation. In an article entitled "The Family Tree of Chaco Canyon Masonry," F. M. Hawley says: "Southwestern Pueblo pottery of the prehistoric periods has been studied, named with dozens of geographic appellations, and traced back from period to period with *genealogic* thoroughness. 'And La Plata Black-on-White *begat* Red Mesa Black-on-White, and Red Mesa Black-on-White *begat* Escavada Black-on-White, and Escavada Black-on-White *begat* Gallup Black-on-White.' But the *family tree* of prehistoric Southwestern walls has not been cultivated with the ardor of the potsherd horticulturalist; the relation of roots to branches has been largely conjectural." [58] This was apparently written in all seriousness. The italics are mine.

Most of the men closely associated with this development had received a major part if not all of their scientific training in the biological sciences. Colton was a well-known biological systematist at the University of Pennsylvania; Hargrave, his assistant, was a competent ornithologist; and Mera holds a medical degree. Their energetic application of their own specialized knowledge to archaeology is extremely commendable and follows the best archaeological tradition of adapting whatever may prove useful in the techniques developed in other fields of learning. In this category are geochronology, dendrochronology, pollen analysis, soil analysis, etc. In the case of artifacts and cultures, however, there is an important difference, and it seems to me that this difference *must* be considered; namely, although applied to archaeological problems, glacial geology still deals with geological phenomena,

[*] Gladwin, 1934.

[*] Hargrave, 1932, p. 7.

[*] Gladwin, 1930.

[*] Gladwin, 1934. An example of one of the dangers

in such systems is given on pp. 41–42, herein.

[*] Hargrave, 1932.

[*] Colton and Hargrave, 1937, p. 3.

[*] Hawley, 1938.

dendrochronology still deals with the growth mechanism of trees, pollen analysis still deals with plant remains, etc. That is, the materials which these techniques analyze are still the materials they were designed to handle before they were adapted to archaeological ends. The question we must ask is simply: Is this the case with biological classifications applied to artifacts and culture complexes? The answer, it seems to me, is a negative. The systematics of biology was designed to classify living organisms. Even though we disregard the doubts presented above of the value of the technique in biology itself, we still are faced with the fact that, with the exception of skeletal material, the objects and concepts of archaeology are not living organisms or parts of living organisms. Consequently, their development is not properly represented by a classificatory technique based upon the genetic relationships of living organisms.[59]

In the foregoing pages I have attempted to show, principally, 2 things: (1) that all classification is arbitrary, that the classes are made by students for their own use; and (2) that the biological implications inherent in certain archaeological systems of taxonomy are dangerous in that they may introduce concepts at variance with the anthropological and historical processes with which we are dealing.

The question before us now is, what can we do? How should we proceed in the analysis of our data? I repeat that we must have conceptual schemes. We can do nothing without them, because we can not think without them. We need them to help make accessible and comprehensible a mass of otherwise disorganized material. The statement, often made at present by those who are dissatisfied with taxonomy, that we must abandon classificatory methods and substitute a "purely historical" scheme based upon tree-ring chronology means not what it at first appears to mean but only that one conceptual scheme is suggested in place of another. The "historical" method of classifying cultures by centuries or by dynasties is just as much an arbitrary scheme as is

the McKern System of archaeological taxonomy.

The way in which we handle our material must, first of all, be related to certain basic concepts of the nature of this material. Duncan Strong, in his essay on anthropological theory and archaeological fact conceives anthropology as "midway between" the biological and social sciences,[60] in that it deals with 2 "definitely historical" processes: (1) biological evolution and (2) cultural development. The former has to do with the animal nature of man and is physical anthropology. The latter has to do with the products of the minds, hands, and nerves of men and includes archaeology.

Here, then, is a basic scheme, which seems as good as any to serve as a point of departure for archaeological research. It assumes that we deal with a succession of human deeds and relationships. In archaeology we study the material manifestations of these deeds and relationships and attempt to reconstruct the latter. If we can then go beyond the historical task and interpret our material so that it can make contributions to the specialized divisions of modern life, so much the better for our justification before the world at large.

This reconstruction can not, it seems to me, be done solely on the basis of schemes for the classification of artifacts, or of groups of artifacts placed together in "periods," "complexes," "phases," etc.

With regard to this, Tallgren [61] in his paper on the method of prehistoric archaeology says: "Brilliant systematization, regarded as exact, has not led and does not lead to an elucidation of the organic structure of the whole life of the period studied, to an understanding of social systems, of economic and social history, to the history of religious ideas. In short, forms and types, that is, products, have been regarded as more real and alive than the society which created them and whose needs determined these manifestations."

However, it should be noted here that systematization when not regarded as exact is not only useful but also necessary in the handling

---

[*] Archaeologists of the Old World, notably Childe and Tallgren, also warn against the noncritical application of the systems of other disciplines to our problems. In "The Irish Stone Age," H. L. Movius writes, "But with the exception of the primary rule of stratig-

raphy, the laws of the natural sciences are far too rigid to provide an adequate interpretation of human culture. . . ." Movius, 1942, p. xxii.

[60] Strong, 1936.

[61] Tallgren, 1937.

of our multitudinous evidence. When the various systematizations are regarded simply as bits of evidence themselves, though of a different kind from the actual objects, and when they too are submitted to analysis, they then serve as profitable tools. In much current work I seem to see the misconception that systematic arrangement, that is, classification, is in itself analysis.

At present for the final summing up at the end of a study I see no alternative to the so-called "narrative approach" which, currently, is sometimes decried. The kind of simplification and systematization introduced by the usual classificatory schemes brings about a distortion which must be corrected by proper interpretation, and proper interpretation of such things demands narrative, not charts and diagrams, which are simplifications themselves. Improper interpretation and lack of understanding of these simplifications has definitely hampered advancement of our studies in many instances.

As an example of this distortion I shall cite the reasoning used by Gladwin in dating the "Vahki Phase" of the Hohokam culture at 300 B.C. I hasten to assert that I do not say that the objects classified as Vahki are not that old. I am perfectly willing to admit that I think it unlikely, but that is beside the point; our interest here is the argument by which Gladwin attempts to establish the date.

During the study of the material excavated at Snaketown a scheme of phases was set up based upon typological variations in pottery, house form, and other artifacts. The later phases in this sequence were cross-dated by means of intrusive potsherds with certain periods in the Pecos Classification of Pueblo cultures. The uncertainty in the minds of students over the number of years which should be assigned to the Pueblo periods is well known. However, for the sake of convenience it has become customary for many workers to consider a "period" roughly and loosely to represent 200 years. Gladwin, then, accepts this time unit for a Pueblo period, asserts that Hohokam phases are equivalent to Pueblo periods, and concludes as follows: "By using these methods at Snaketown, we have been

able to define seven phases, the last of which ended about 1100 A.D. Since each of the two latest phases lasted two hundred years, we may assume that the occupation of Snaketown, from first to last, was fourteen hundred years, which would place the beginning of the Vahki Phase at 300 B.C." [62] As pointed out on page viii, the Vahki date was revised by Gladwin shortly after the first part of this paragraph was originally written in 1941.[63] My statement is left as written because, although the new date for the Vahki Phase, 600–650 A.D., is considered by many to be a more reasonable date for that phase, Gladwin has arrived at it by exactly the same method. He has merely changed the time value of a phase from 200 years to 50 years.

As with all his theories, Gladwin quite properly states it as an assumption and allows that it may be questioned. At the same time he submits that the assumption is not arbitrary, a proposition with which I can not agree. What he has done is to correlate one set of arbitrary phases, defined by himself, in the Gila Basin, with another set of arbitrary phases, defined by the Pecos Conference and called Periods, on the Colorado Plateau. He then assumes that his phases represent a constant rate of culture change, that, if the last two represent the span of 200 years, all other phases existed over the same length of time. Yet there is more variation in house type assigned to the Pueblo I period alone than in the whole range of the Snaketown phases. The differences in diagnostic pottery types are also relatively smaller between most of the Snaketown phases than they are between Pueblo periods. Most workers in the Pueblo area would consider many of his phases. to be merely minor variations within periods, which is just another way of saying that another student might, quite legitimately, make different phase divisions, with correspondingly different results in dating by this method. It might also be pointed out here that a much different result as to date would be obtained if the original Hohokam "periods" (Pioneer, Colonial, Sedentary, Classic, etc.) should be used in the correlation instead of the later Hohokam phases.

Gladwin's assumption that his "phases" can

* Gladwin, 1937, p. 9 et seq.

* Gladwin, 1942.

be considered all to be equivalent to 200 years in the time-scale, in the argument given above, can even be questioned on the basis of his own published work. In Gladwin, 1934, he adapts the Pueblo cultures to his phase system, assigning phases throughout the Pueblo area. In the charts published in that paper he presents 62 phases in columns adjacent to the listing of Pueblo periods. However, only 16 of those 62 are equated with Pueblo periods and therefore equivalent to 200 years, in terms of his Hohokam argument. But there are 9 instances where 2 phases are equivalent to 1 period, that is, following the same reasoning, 18 phases are only *100 years* long. Similarly, 18 more come at the rate of 3 to a period, or *67 years* per phase; 8 more are at the rate of 4 to a period, or *50 years* per phase; and 2 phases are listed as equivalent to 2 Pueblo periods each, or *400 years* per phase. Thus only 25.8% of these phases are equal to Gladwin's 200 years to a phase, according to his own system of reckoning. An even smaller number, only 12.9%, equal 50 years, which is the new time value of a phase assigned in Gladwin, 1942, the Snaketown revision. And this, indeed, is what we should expect. Except for one special case, phases, by reason of what they are and how they are made, are not and can not be equivalent in time-span. The exception is in classifications like the one we often use for our modern European cultures, dividing them by centuries, with chronology as the sole determinant of period or phase. Some students are now trying to use the period names of the Pecos Classification this way, in conjunction with tree-ring dates. We can have no quarrel with this, if the dates are well established and if the original period diagnostics of the Pecos Classification are completely abandoned.[64]

I have taken my example from Gladwin's work, above, merely because of the present importance of the Snaketown dating. We have all had similar trouble and have made similar mistakes. I believe that a better understanding of the nature of classificatory systems will save us from this kind of fallacy in reasoning. We have here an illustration of one of the things which such schemes do to us, against which we must ever be on guard. The *force of the scheme* itself produces a new type of archaeological conservatism, the conservatism of false reality which, after all, is nothing but dogma dressed up in modern terminology. These schemes often lead us into what A. N. Whitehead calls the fallacy of misplaced concreteness.

The above discussion brings us to the most important taxonomic question in Southwestern archaeology. We have already decided that major conceptual schemes are not only necessary but unavoidable, and that minor classificatory schemes are also useful if properly used and understood. The greatest difficulties with them in practice have to do with the criteria or diagnostics by which the various divisions are set up.

Outstanding here is the vexing question of where to place a trait, a group of traits, a site, or part of a site. As has already been shown, the things, unfortunately, do not "fall into" categories by themselves, but must be put in them. The taxonomic rules by which the placing can be done are far from clear.

Three questions posed by Kluckhohn [65] will serve to introduce these problems. He asks:

1) "Is it absolute presence or absence of the criteria which count or merely predominance — or does the answer to this question vary in the case of various traits?

2) "Must the culture or 'culture period' check with all or with how large a majority of the diagnostics?

3) "Are certain of the criteria indispensable and others not?"

To point the question he cites a hypothetical problem. Suppose there are 8 criteria generally accepted for Pueblo I and we agree that 6 of them must check before the period designation may be applied. Then "will we still call a site Pueblo I if 6 of the 8 criteria are found indubitably associated with a masonry type or a pottery complex which has been accepted as diagnostic of Pueblo II?" The answer to this, in

---

[64] However, in this case, since Pecos period diagnostics loom so large in our thinking, and since tree-ring dates are now for the most part expressed in terms of our calendar, it might be better to apply the "century" system in the Southwest, where successfully applied it will only serve as a convenient time-scale. Classifications based on other cultural factors will still be necessary. [65] Kluckhohn, Reiter, et al., 1939.

John Otis Brew

terms of contemporary usage, is usually no. This problem presents the question of the weighting of criteria and, as all Southwestern classification systems are used at present, despite statements of cultural inclusiveness, pottery type, primarily, and house type, secondarily, are the most significant factors. The only important exceptions to this are 2: (1) the few workers who continue to use the extremely unsatisfactory criterion of physical type [66] as the most important diagnostic and (2) those who attempt to use tree-ring chronology alone.

This situation is recognized by Kluckhohn who discusses it with particular insight into the problems of systematics.[67] His statements are worth quoting at considerable length, as he has gone further into the problem than any other writer in the Southwestern field. With regard to the weighting of criteria he says:

"Observation of the actual operations of archaeologists suggests that in many cases the classification of a site is actually made on the basis of pottery complex or architectural style (including masonry type) alone. If this fact is explicitly stated, this procedure may well be the most convenient and quite unobjectionable. If, however, there is assertion or implication that the classification has been made on the basis of total culture complex, some confusion results." Here again we are faced with the difference between statement and practice, so characteristic of archaeological systematics.

Kluckhohn goes on to say:

"For what occurs is that the other culture elements found associated with the critical pottery complex or architectural style are simply dragged in after the crucial step has been taken. If we are really operating with pottery or masonry-architectural complexes (or a combination of these two) only, it would be in the interests of clear thinking if this circumstance were brought into the open, either through terminology or explicit statement. It seems possible that classificatory operations frankly based solely upon these apparently somewhat more sensitive and more consistent criteria would be most useful. The associated culture elements (not used in cultural classification)

could then be studied apart from the prejudice of a question-begging nomenclature. . . .

"It would, then, be necessary to make clear how great a proportion of traits otherwise regarded as diagnostic of, let us say, Pueblo II could be admitted *seriatim* in a Pueblo I site. It would likewise be imperative to state if any criteria are to be weighted as of greater importance and which differentiae are to be applied first. Because, as in physical anthropology, two investigators can use the same diagnostic traits in making a classification and yet get different results, depending on the order in which they are applied (with resultant eliminations). It follows, also, that the relative significance to be attached to positive and negative evidence would have to be specified."

Such analysis of our current practice is certainly necessary at present. Kidder and Guernsey worked much with sandal types, Haury and F. H. Douglas have made detailed studies of textiles, Bartlett has written a paper on metate types, R. B. Woodbury is studying stone and bone implements, respectively, but very little indeed is known about the chronological and geographical distributions of artifact types in the Southwest aside from pottery and, to a much smaller extent, architecture. Surely it is better procedure to recognize this and to govern ourselves accordingly than to cover our systems with a camouflage of completeness, admittedly a desirable ideal, but one which is far from attained. The very admission not only eliminates current misconceptions but emphasizes the urgent necessity of intensive study of the lesser-known divisions of material culture.

There is another factor here which may help us to a better understanding of our difficulties with criteria. In order to give a heterogeneous mass of data orderly classification, it is necessary arbitrarily to set up definitions of groups and to determine certain characteristics which will be considered as diagnostics for these groups. But after this is done it seems always to be the case that a number of objects can not be satisfactorily placed. And the more material and the more knowledge the investigator gathers, the greater this difficulty seems to become.

---

[66] See pp. 67-73.

[67] Kluckhohn, 1939b.

The difficulty applies to detailed classifications of artifacts and to the broader concepts of culture classification as well. In the former case the so-called "intermediate types" cause the trouble. And the glib answer, "Make a new type," does not solve the problem, because, as in the case of Jeddito Black-on-orange and Jeddito Black-on-yellow pottery in the Hopi country, when a large number of specimens is obtained, a complete series marked by almost imperceptible gradations appears between the 2 types.

In the latter case, that of the broader concepts of culture classification, the difficulty is that when a large number of sites have been excavated, it is found that the criteria do not change simultaneously, like the change of billing for a vaudeville show, but tend to change individually and to present a varied picture of lag and overlap in individual traits. In my own experience I have never seen a Southwestern site which did not present, in a single "occupation-level," criteria of at least 2 major cultural periods. The only unnatural thing about the hypothetical problem presented by Kluckhohn above was the small number of overlapping criteria.

It is this situation, shown admirably by trait charts in Rouse's first report [68] and present in the reports of all major Southwestern digs, which impels Kidder to look upon all arbitrary classifications as temporary and to say: ". . . our investigation has now reached a point at which formal classifications, such as the Pecos nomenclature, are not only of lessening value, but are often . . . positively misleading." [69]

In biology, taxonomy has also encountered this difficulty. Robson,[70] discussing the species problem, says: "The only conclusion at which we can arrive is that there is no criterion by which we can define and delimit separate units of the status required by the species-concept. There may be a general sense in which the four criteria we have discussed are simultaneously applicable. But the degree to which in any one instance differentiation is manifested in respect of these is so variable that it defies organization in the sense required by the concept. It is not only impossible to find a standardized

type of group by applying any single criterion; but also the various main criteria do not give the same results, the same indications of affinity."

On the cultural side consider a wealthy modern Hopi trader in his house which has windows purchased in Holbrook, Arizona, but a roof similar to that of a prehistoric dwelling. Imagine him seated on a stone loom weight, facing a coal range of the vintage of 1890, smoking a "tailor-made" cigarette, wearing triangular turquoise earrings, and listening to a dance orchestra from Havana, Cuba, on the short wave band of a new radio, while his son drives up in a 10-year-old Ford and his wife grinds corn in a primitive mealing bin, using, for sentiment's sake, a mano which she has picked up at the old Sikyatki ruin. This is an extreme case, but such cases can be demonstrated any day in the year. In some degree or other, it is situations like this we are called upon as archaeologists to handle. But, at the outset of any given problem we do not have in hand the information which enables us to evaluate the archaeological case as we can the modern case just cited. So, we make our schemes, and, if we are wise, as our knowledge of that particular set of problems advances, *we change our schemes*.

The overlaps are not necessarily, as some would have us believe, unimportant and of only a few years duration. Some of them last for centuries. The "intermediate types" are *not* unimportant, to be eliminated, as is often done, by disregarding them. We are dealing with a constant stream of cultural development, not evolutionary in the genetic sense, but still a continuum of human activity.

It is quite apparent, now, that we are facing a much larger question than the one so frequently asked, "Should the Pecos Classification be abandoned?" My answer to that question perhaps points the way to the general suggestions as to procedure with which this section will be concluded. I do not believe that the Pecos Classification should be abandoned. I do, however, believe that we should abandon the practice of treating it as the only classification applicable or useful to the phenomena we group under the term Pueblo or Anasazi cul-

* Rouse, 1939.   * Kidder, 1936, p. xviii, footnote 2.

[70] Robson, 1928.

ture. My contention is that it is very useful in certain stages of our studies. In many parts of the region and in many aspects of our investigations its definitions and terminology provide an extremely handy mechanism. On the other hand, in certain districts and in certain divisions of the development of material culture our accumulated knowledge now renders that sort of classification unnecessary. In his consideration of the situation in Chaco Canyon, Kluckhohn says: [71]

"But we must remember, as Whitehead has so often reminded us, that a classification is, at best, 'a half-way house.' A classification is useful so long as the facts fall without violence into it. So soon, however, as their greater bulk, greater complexity, or greater subtleties of discrimination make the classification a Procrustean bed into which the maimed and helpless facts are forced, the classification should be abandoned or radically modified." This process is going on all the time, in actuality. The Museum of Northern Arizona, the University of New Mexico, the University of Arizona, the Laboratory of Anthropology at Santa Fe, and the Field Museum all use the Pecos Classification in conjunction with concepts borrowed from Gladwin's system and concepts of cultural development by centuries based upon tree-ring chronology. Yet many of the workers in the field express dissatisfaction with the lack of precision involved in such procedure and continue to feel that they should adopt a single system and "stick to it." My contention is that to adapt and change classifications and to make new ones as needs arise is correct procedure provided it is implemented with a better understanding of the nature of systematics, a more critical examination of new systems for dangerous distortions (like the "family-tree" concept in the Gladwin System), and accompanied in the published reports by *a statement of the various assumptions used.* To adopt a single system and to stick to it would be fatal to scientific progress.

In certain minds approval of such technique will be denied because it is not precise. Admittedly, it is not. And for that very reason it is practical and scientific. We are not able to treat precisely the material with which we

are dealing. Whether or not we shall in part ever be able to do so in future can not be decided now. The fact is that the processes which govern the deeds and beliefs of any group of people at any particular time are conditioned by a large number of variables, many of which we do not understand and many of which we as archaeologists are not able to deduce from our fragmentary evidence. A flexible, nonprecise technique is more useful and more "scientific" for the kind of evidence we have of the kind of phenomena with which we deal than is the pseudo-precision which, at this time, is the only alternative.

We must make our choice between these 2 alternatives. Shall we maintain a fluid technique which can be changed as our needs change and as our knowledge develops or shall we fix our technique into a pseudo-precise system which by its very dogmatism will bar all progress beyond its level? Fortunately, we probably can not do the latter, even should we wish it. The vigorous spirit of inquiry in the mind of man certainly will not be satisfied with it for long. But why waste our time trying it on?

Thus we come to what may be a positive rule of procedure. All classificatory schemes, it seems, are arbitrary and designed to fill an immediate need. If research prospers, there comes a time, and this is what Kidder says in the quotation above, when the information gathered goes beyond the simplifications of the given systems. *The systems then become obsolete,* to use them longer is awkward and definitely warps the results. We should then pass on to new systems which will absorb all the known "facts" and systematize the new and more "advanced" unassimilated data.

Our systematics, then, must be flexible, too, as are the materials with which we deal. In all of this we must remember, as Tallgren points out,[72] that it is the *use* and not the *form* of artifacts which is important to us. Variations in form, treated systematically, can aid us greatly in prosecuting our research, but when we can fit the object into its economic or social environment, into the system of production of which it is an instrument or the ceremonial system of which it is a part, we should readily

---

[71] Kluckhohn, Reiter, *et al.,* 1939.

[72] Tallgren, 1937, p. 158.

dispense with the purely morphological classification.

That is going a long way, probably further than most of us will ever get in our lifetimes, but all our work should tend toward such an end. Similarly with "cultures"; when we can show, as I think we can in this report, the gradual development of houses, kivas, pottery, and a few other objects by numerous small changes over a period of 600 or more years, it will not advance our cause to present them in only 4 periods, which we must do if we discuss them only in the terms of the Pecos Classification.

What, then, should our procedure be? It is easy to offer destructive criticism and fashionable to leave it at that. And I am not one of those who feel that we are not entitled to indulge in destructive criticism unless we also offer constructive suggestions. But in this case I shall offer suggestions which I hope will prove to be constructive. I do this because I believe the subject of our analytical method to be of supreme importance to us and because I believe I can see some ways in which our methods can be improved and in which some current difficulties can be avoided. On the other hand, most of the suggestions I am about to make are so simple that I distrust them somewhat myself. I present them for consideration, if they seem worthy of that, and above all with the hope that this discussion will induce some further examination into the basic assumptions and analytical methods of our subject.

With regard to taxonomy, then, I believe we can say this. As archaeologists we must classify our material in all ways that will produce for us useful information. I repeat, we need more rather than fewer classifications, different classifications, always new classifications, to meet new needs. We must not be satisfied with a single classification of a group of artifacts or of a cultural development, for that way lies dogma and defeat. We are, or should be, in search of all of the evidence our material holds. Even in simple things no single analysis will bring out all that evidence.

We must continually analyze not only our material but also our methods, we must continually check our concepts for distorting factors, and we must always remember to advise the reader thoroughly of the concepts we are using.

We need have no fear of changing established systems or of designing new ones, for it is only by such means that we can progress. At the same time we must not present our new system or systems as a standard to be used and adopted by everyone and forevermore. We must recognize that any given system in its entirety will probably be applicable only to the given set of problems it was designed to meet. The main value of a published description of a given system is that it may then be *adapted* by another student to his problems, not that he should force his material into it.

Above all, we must remember that we are dealing with a cultural continuum which is *continually changing*. Even the products of the automotive assembly line are not identical, and this is probably the greatest material standardization yet achieved by mankind. We must ever be on guard against that peculiar paradox of anthropology which permits men to "trace" a "complex" of, let us say, physical type, pottery type, and religion over 10,000 miles of terrain and down through 10,000 years of history while in the same breath, or in the next lecture, the same men vigorously defend the theory of continuous change.

Before concluding this chapter, in which I have so greatly emphasized the subject of taxonomy, it will be well to dig even deeper than we have dug already and to consider the ultimate objectives of archaeology. For the devices discussed above certainly do not constitute the end of our studies. They are merely a part of the tool kit we must use in achieving that end, whatever it may be.

Although to add to our store of accumulated knowledge may be in itself satisfactory to many, I believe that our objective should be much more than the systematic amassing of information and the conjectural reconstruction of past events. Beyond that, as I see it, the aim of archaeology is to relate our newly gathered information scientifically to the immediate problems of human life and society, through an analysis of the problems and achievements of other peoples, toward a better relationship with our physical and social environments. We must broaden our cultural horizon by showing to ourselves the accomplishments of these others in the various fields of human endeavor, both material and artistic.

There are those who will object to the inclusion of the aesthetic aspects of prehistoric cultures along with the material on the grounds that, while the latter is objective, the former is purely subjective and can not be brought to life from the past. It will be said that I am injecting the personal equation, something no good scientist should ever do. It may even be said with vehemence, as though I could keep the personal factor out if I wished to do so. In this chapter I have deplored dogmatic statement but I shall now offer one for my critics to work on. *Those who say these things will be wrong.* As I have pointed out time and again in the preceding pages, the personal element is necessarily implicit even in the most mathematical systematics. To present our results so that they will be useful to men at large we must, at times, leave our systematics with

our test tubes in the laboratory. If we fail to do so, every once in a while, we shall fall short of our aim.

Such presentation, which I believe to be necessary, involves the "narrative approach" and subjective picturization. This must be done with any body of archaeological data, if those data are to be of use to anyone besides archaeologists. Our obligation to society, our aim which I defined 2 paragraphs above, has been stated much more simply by a friend of mine, a lawyer — "A reasonable degree of humanizing is the only justification for archaeological research, carefully stopping short, of course, of fanciful romance." That statement contains a challenge we must meet. We are on the defensive. Our research is costly and its products must be useful. To make them so we must vastly improve our systematics and then go beyond them. We must present much more than our systematics to society.

REFERENCES CITED

ARKELL, W. J. AND J. A. MOY-THOMAS
1940   Palaeontology and the Taxonomic Problem. In *The New Systematics*, edited by Julian S. Huxley, pp. 395–410. Clarendon Press, Oxford. (Oxford University Press).

BATESON, WILLIAM
1913   *Problems of Genetics.* Yale University Press, New Haven.

BATHER, F. A.
1927   Biological Classification: Past and Future. *Geological Society Quarterly Journal* 83(2):lxii–civ.

BREMEKAMP, C. E. B.
1931   *The Principles of Taxonomy and the Theory of Evolution.* South African Biological Society Pamphlet No. 4.

CALMAN, W. T.
1940   A Museum Zoölogist's View of Taxonomy. In *The New Systematics*, edited by Julian S. Huxley, pp. 455–459. Clarendon Press, Oxford. (Oxford University Press).

COLTON, HAROLD S.
1939a   *Prehistoric Culture Units and Their Relationships in Northern Arizona.* Museum of Northern Arizona, Bulletin 17. Flagstaff.
1939b   The Reducing Atmosphere and Oxidizing Atmosphere in Prehistoric Southwestern Ceramics. *American Antiquity* 4:224–231.

COLTON, HAROLD S. AND LYNDON L. HARGRAVE
1937   *Handbook of Northern Arizona Pottery Wares.* Museum of Northern Arizona, Bulletin 11. Flagstaff.

DARWIN, CHARLES
1859   *Origin of Species,* 6th edition. London.

DEAN, BASHFORD
1916   *Notes on Arms and Armor.* Metropolitan Museum, New York.

DINGLE, H.
1938   The Rational and Empirical Elements in Physics. *Philosophy* 13:148–165.

DIVER, C.
1940   The Problem of Closely Related Species Living in the Same Area. In *The New Systematics*, edited by Julian S. Huxley, pp. 303–328. Clarendon Press, Oxford. (Oxford University Press).

ELLIS, H. H(OLMES)
1940   *Flint-Working Techniques of the American Indians: An Experimental Study.* The Ohio State Archaeological and Historical Society, Columbus.

FORD, JAMES A.
1938   A Chronological Method Applicable to the Southeast. *American Antiquity* 3:260–264.

GILMOUR, J. S. L.
1940   Taxonomy and Philosophy. In *The New Systematics*, edited by Julian S. Huxley, pp. 461–474. Clarendon Press, Oxford. (Oxford University Press)

GLADWIN, HAROLD S.
1937   *Excavations at Snaketown, II, Comparisons and Theories.* Medallion Papers No. 26. Globe, Arizona.
1942   *Excavations at Snaketown, III, Revisions.* Medallion Papers No. 30. Globe, Arizona.

GLADWIN, WINIFRED AND HAROLD S. GLADWIN
1930   *A Method for the Designation of Southwestern Pottery Types.* Medallion Papers No. 7. Globe, Arizona.
1934   *A Method for the Designation of Cultures and Their Variations.* Medallion Papers No. 15. Globe, Arizona.

HARGRAVE, LYNDON L.
1932   *Guide to Forty Pottery Types from the Hopi Country and the San Francisco Mountains, Arizona.* Museum of Northern Arizona, Bulletin 1. Flagstaff.

HAWLEY, FLORENCE M.
1938   The Family Tree of Chaco Canyon Masonry. *American Antiquity* 3:247–255.

HOGBEN, LANCEOLOT
1940   Problems of the Origins of Species. In *The New Systematics*, edited by Julian S. Huxley, pp. 269–286. Clarendon Press, Oxford. (Oxford University Press).

HUXLEY, T. H.
1877   *A Manual of the Anatomy of Invertebrated Animals.* London.

KIDDER, ALFRED VINCENT AND ANNA O. SHEPARD
1936   *The Pottery of Pecos, Vol II.* Papers of the Southwestern Expedition, Phillips Academy, No. 7. Yale University Press, New Haven, Connecticut.

KLUCKHOHN, CLYDE
1939b   The Place of Theory in Anthropological Studies. *Philosophy of Science* 6:328–344.

KLUCKHOHN, CLYDE AND PAUL REITER (editors)
1939   *Preliminary Report on the 1937 Excavations, BC 50–51, Chaco Canyon, New Mexico.* University of New Mexico Bulletin 345, Anthropological Series 3(2).

LOTHROP, S. K.
1941   Review of Rouse, 1939. *American Antiquity* 6:364–365.

MCKERN, WILLIAM C.
1939   The Midwestern Taxonomic Method as an Aid to Archaeological Study. *American Antiquity* 4:301–313.

MORGAN, T. H.
1916   *A Critique of the Theory of Evolution.* Princeton.
1925   *Evolution and Genetics.* Princeton.

MOVIUS, HALLAM L., JR.
1942   *The Irish Stone Age; Its Chronology, Development, and Relationships.* Cambridge.

PALMER, ERNEST J.
1943   The Species Concept in Crataegus. *Chronica Botanica* 8:373–375.

POND, ALONZO W.
no date, Primitive Methods of Working Stone. ca. 1930 Based on Experiments of Halvor L. Skavlem. *Logan Museum Bulletin* 2(1).

RABAUD, E.
1920   *Éléments de Biologie Générale.* Paris.

REGAN, C. T.
1926   *Organic Evolution.* British Association Report for 1925, Southampton.

ROBSON, G. C.
1928   *The Species Problem.* London.

ROUSE, IRVING B.
1939   *Prehistory of Haiti, A Study in Method.* Yale University Publications in Anthropology No. 21.

ROWE, JOHN HOWLAND
1940   *Excavations in the Waterside Shell Heap, Frenchman's Bay, Maine.* Excavators' Club Papers 1(3).

SHEPARD, ANNA O.
1936   The Technology of Pecos Pottery. In *The Pottery of Pecos, Vol. II,* by A. V. Kidder and A. O. Shepard, pp. 389–587. Papers of the Southwestern Expedition. Phillips Academy, No. 7. Yale University Press, New Haven, Connecticut.
1939   Technology of La Plata Pottery. In *Archaeological Studies in the La Plata District, Southwestern Colorado and Northwestern New Mexico,* by E. H. Morris, pp. 249–287. Carnegie Institution of Washington, Publication 519.

SMART, JOHN
1940   Entomological Systematics Examined as a Practical Problem. In *The New Systematics,* edited by Julian S. Huxley, pp. 475–492. Clarendon Press, Oxford. (Oxford University Press).

STEWARD, JULIAN H.
    1941a   Review of Colton, 1939a. *American Antiquity* 6:366–367.
STRONG, WILLIAM D.
    1936   Anthropological Theory and Archaeological Fact. In *Essays in Anthropology Presented to A. L. Kroeber,* edited by R. H. Lowie, pp. 359–368. University of California Press, Berkeley.
TALLGREN, A. M.
    1937   The Method of Prehistoric Archaeology. *Antiquity* 11:152–161.

ZUCKERMAN, S.
    1933a   Sinanthropus and Other Fossil Men: The Relations to Each Other and Modern Types. *Eugenics Review* 24(4):273–284.
    1933b   *Functional Affinities of Man, Monkeys, and Apes: A Study of the Bearings of Physiology and Behaviour on the Taxonomy and Phylogeny of Lemurs, Monkeys, Apes, and Man.* Harcourt, Brace and Company, New York.

ber of examples of this situation were found in Virú, particularly in occupations of the Puerto Moorin and Tomaval periods. In none of these was the deposit thick enough to make vertical distinction possible. Fortunately here the later population did not occupy the houses erected in the Puerto Moorin period, but tore them down to their foundation stones and built structures of their own design, using the stones collected in the earlier period. At six of these reoccupied sites, collections made from the rubble fill of the stone walls of the later houses were almost entirely of Puerto Moorin pottery types, while in and around the same house the two periods were about equally represented. In a few instances we have not been able to establish the association between structures and one of several ceramic complexes. These are listed in the tabulation of sites.[1]

A third problem is the desirable size of a collection necessary to obtain a fair sample of the material available on the surface of the site. This is a matter discussed by Spier[2] in his study of Zuñi surface collections, and briefly by the writer in regard to collections from the Lower Mississippi Valley.[3] It seems well to offer a little additional data from the Virú Valley.

Figure 3 presents, in graphic form, a comparison between repeated collections made at different times at five sites. Type percentages of the two collections compared from each site are represented by the contrasting clear and black bars, and each pair has been marked with a small bracket. For this purpose the types involved are not significant, so their names have been omitted.

The examples compared here are inadequate to permit any definite conclusions as to the desirable minimum size of a collection. The collections from Site V-17 show the greatest variation, as is to be expected, because of the inclusion of a collection of only 51 sherds. Another thing that seems to be indicated is that when a type appears in a strength of over 5 per cent the chances are excellent that it will be represented in a collection of over 100 sherds. Out of 17 occurrences in which type percentages exceed five, the same type was found in the companion collection except in two cases.

*　*　*　*　*

RELIABILITY OF SURFACE COLLECTIONS

Several questions must be considered in regard to the reliability of surface collections when used for the cultural dating of buildings. The first and perhaps the most serious of these is whether the material exposed on the surface represents the cultural refuse of the people who built the structure. Their refuse might be deeply buried beneath later cultural material and the sand which is constantly in motion along the desert coast. This may have happened in the dating of a few of the structures in Virú, but if so, their number is very small. This possibility was guarded against by two methods of procedure. At all sites showing any promise of depth of refuse, test holes were dug, for one purpose of the survey was to discover places with an appreciable midden depth, so that the investigators making stratigraphic excavations might put down cuts. The second check was to examine the surface of all parts of the site. Generally it would not be expected that an older stratum would be covered for its full extent; at some point it would probably show on the surface, in ravines or beyond the edge of the later deposit.

A corollary of this problem is the procedure in the determination of the dating of structures when material from separated time periods is mixed on the surrounding surface. A num-

---

[1] See Sites V-24, V-26, V-28, V-29, V-33 for examples.
[2] Spier, 1917, 254.
[3] Ford, 1936, 13–14.

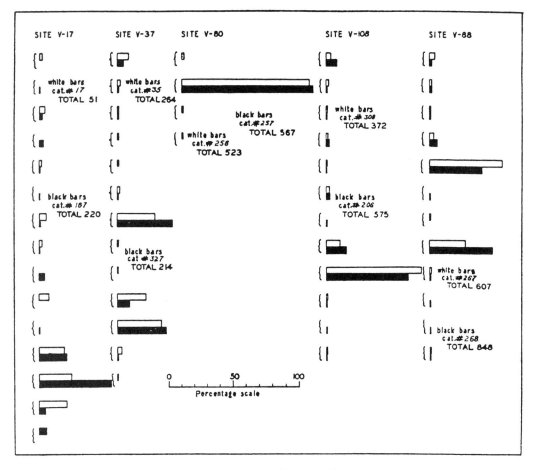

Fig. 3. Graph comparing surface collections made at
different times from the same sites.

Both these are in the small collection of 51 sherds from Site V-17.

This graph also appears to indicate that fairly substantial variation from the theoretical actual percentage conditions on the site is to be expected in types that approach 50 per cent popularity, even in collections of 300 to 500 sherds. Variation between the substantial (over 10 per cent) type pairs shown in this graph ranges from 3 to 20 per cent. In one type pair from Site V-17 the difference is 31 per cent, doubtless due to the inclusion of the small collection of 51 sherds.

This range between type pairs from substantial collections is really only half as bad as it appears. The probabilities are that the percentages of the type in each collection vary on either side of the actual proportion of that type on the site. Thus we may say that the range of variation from the actual percentage of a type on a site to be expected in a collection of over about 200 sherds is probably not more than 10 per cent.

As a result of experience in analyzing classification results, rather than from any basis demonstrated here, I have come to regard a random collection of over 100 sherds as fairly dependable, and anything over 50 sherds as usable for rough dating.

There is still another qualification which must always be made when dealing with fragmentary pottery from refuse deposits. The quantities of different kinds of pottery fragments recovered are never an accurate reflection of the number of vessels of these varieties that had been in use. Difference in size of vessels is an obvious factor. Big pots make more sherds than little ones. Thin vessels can be expected to break into smaller pieces than thick ones. This, however, need cause no concern over the use of quantitative studies for chronological purposes. Vessel size and thickness changed with time, as did other cultural features, and were subject to as strict stylistic control. A percentage increase of a type due to the vessels' becoming larger or thinner is as good a measure of time change as it is when it reflects greater popularity of that type. The primary aim of a chronological analysis of ceramics is to provide a time and space scale by means of which other and more important cultural elements may be ordered, thus making possible a reconstruction of culture history. To provide a "true" qualitative and quantitative history of ceramics is of lesser importance, if not impossible of accomplishment with the type of data that can be obtained from refuse deposits, and the fact that such uncontrolled variables as those just described are hidden in the pottery counts is not of much concern.

CLASSIFICATION

THEORY

MANY STUDENTS of ancient cultures seem to regard the classification of cultural remains as a somewhat esoteric business in which the classifier, aided by some inherent insight, examines an assembled mass of prehistoric handiwork and separates the type groupings which the ancient artisans have put there. He decides which features are important and which may safely be ignored. If the classifier is competent, the groupings are believed to approximate the true ones; if not, the classification is incorrect and useless.

This attitude is highly questionable. It derives directly from the notion that there is a basic order in these phenomena, and the scientist's duty is to search for and discover this order. This was the viewpoint of the "natural sciences" in the nineteenth century. It fails to recognize that the apparent order has been imposed on the material either by chance circumstances or, more commonly, by the classifier himself. In actuality the same group of archaeological material may be classified in an almost unlimited number of ways, each equally valid from an empirical point of view. A single inevitable and natural order apart from a posed problem is not there to be found, and each classificatory arrangement of material must be tested by the question of how well it serves the end purpose that the classifier has in view.

The primary purpose of classifications of archaeological material until about 1920 was description of the material. In the second decade of this century, the pioneer work of Kroeber,[1] Spier,[2] and Kidder[3] has introduced the concept of the classification system as an instrument for measuring culture history in time and space. This is the major goal of classification in most present-day archaeological studies.[4]

The reasons for this change in point of view, and the resultant procedures, are not obscure. They have resulted from a gradual, perhaps not always conscious, acceptance by archaeologists of the concept that culture is most usefully viewed in what Kroeber[5] has defined as a "superorganic" realm of phenomena. According to this concept, culture may be briefly defined as a stream of ideas,[6] that passes from individual to individual by means of symbolic action, verbal instruction, or imitation. The present-day archaeologist is primarily concerned with the histories of what can be recovered or reconstructed of these streams of ideas. Stone tools, pottery, and other artifacts are not collected and examined for their esthetic qualities, or to discover and concentrate upon their uniqueness. They are useful as recorders of cultural influence. It follows then that archaeological materials are classified primarily to measure culture and trace its change through time and over area.

There is nothing difficult about the application of a classification system after it has been set up. Illiterate workmen can often be trained to be excellent classifiers. All that is necessary is to learn the bounds of the variation that has been allowed the type groups and to maintain a strict consistency in handling the materials. The setting up of a system and the constant adjustment that is necessary as the result of increasing knowledge of a cultural history are more involved. These demand a grasp of the theories of cultural change and a clear conception of the end results expected from the use of the classification.

This is the point to introduce a discussion of the theoretical assumptions that apply specifically to the problem of setting up a time scale in the small area of Virú Valley. These are the probabilities in accord with which work was carried forward until analysis of the material should demonstrate otherwise:

A. At any one time in the past the features of the culture in this restricted area were essentially the same all over the valley. Some locali-

[1] Kroeber, 1916.

[2] Spier, 1917.

[3] Kidder, 1931.

[4] Brew, 1946, 44 ff. Rouse, 1939, uses his classifications in this manner without making an explicit statement to this effect.

[5] Kroeber, 1917.

[6] Webster's definition of "idea" does not quite serve here, yet the writer does not wish to use an obscure word or coin a new one. For the purposes of this paper, it is understood that individuals do not "create" ideas. The concept of "free will" seems to have no place in science. Individuals receive ideas from other humans, sometimes combine them, less frequently discover them in the natural world about them, and almost always pass them along to others.

38

ties may have lagged slightly in the process of cultural change, and at different times people with a foreign culture may have held portions of the valley. Or, less likely, extraneous cultural influences may have found acceptance in some parts of the valley but not in others. If true, these conditions must be demonstrated. The probabilities are against areal cultural differentiation having occurred often or having lasted for any length of time in such a small valley. Probably then the areal dimensions of the problem can be factored out.

B. It may be assumed that with the passage of time marked changes of style occurred in all elements of culture. The ideas of the ancient people as to the proper ways in which things should be done and made were quite different when they are observed at 500- or 1000-year intervals. The difference may appear relatively small if the culture is protected from outside influence either by its simplicity and consequent inability to absorb new ideas or by geographic isolation. Or it may be observably great, as in the recent history of our present culture. In any span of cultural history some change will have occurred, but sometimes the problem is to find tools delicate enough to measure it.

C. Normally cultural change will have taken place gradually, so gradually that the people making the artifacts and following the customs were probably under the impression that they were doing everything exactly as their fathers and grandfathers did. Any rapid change in these relatively simple cultures will have been forced by external pressure.

In the less complex cultures, where handmade articles are produced, each object made is different. No two women can make identical pieces of pottery, and no craftsman can duplicate his own handiwork exactly. While at any given period the cultural styles stayed in more or less narrow limits, the accumulation of variations resulted in slow shifting of the norms. Emulation of the variations affected by outstanding individuals and the acceptance of new ideas from adjacent cultures may have speeded up this process at times. It is to be expected that the foreign ideas which are readily accepted will not be entirely new and strange. They are more likely to be variations originally derived from the same source as the custom which they are replacing. Entirely new ideas will

almost certainly be strongly modified in the course of merging with the local culture.

D. In a strictly literal sense, there is never anything new in a cultural history. Each cultural entity has one or, more often, numerous parents, to which it will show a rather strong family resemblance in most characteristics. Change in culture occurs by only two processes: first, combination of ideas already available in the cultural environment; and, second, discovery and adaptation to cultural purposes of new phases of the natural environment. Cultural change is always a gradual process in which the new is founded on the old. It is this fact that gives cultural history its strongest resemblance to biological history. However, the relationship ties in a cultural history weave back and forth between the different cultural categories in a bewildering fashion entirely foreign to the history of living organisms, and only the strongest and most easily detected can be traced with any assurance. These evidences of relationships are to be expected, but in dealing with the materials that will be used to form a hitherto unknown cultural chronology, they must be set aside and carefully ignored. Assumptions as to relationship are impossible until the chronological factor is completely under control.

E. The foregoing discussion is not intended to convey the impression that there was homogeneity in the cultural material of any category at any one time. All the pottery vessels did not vary about a single stylistic norm. On the contrary, it is to be expected that several norms will have existed side by side which were kept somewhat separated by the manufacturer's ideas as to either the function or the derivation of the classes. Chicha jars, cooking vessels, and water containers each may have characteristic features. Introduced ideas may be used but kept separate from the local ideas in a conscious fashion. This is directly comparable with modern dress styles. At one moment there now exist, side by side: types of house dress, sport dress, street dress, and evening dress. This is a functional separation. Introduced ideas accepted as a complex are such things as modified Chinese costume used for a house dress. All these varieties, separated in the minds of the present-day users by function or origin, undergo time change.

We cannot always guess at the ideas carried

in the minds of the prehistoric culture bearers that caused this separation. Indeed, it is not necessary that such an attempt be made. For present purposes it serves to be aware of the phenomenon and to take it into account in the work of classification, for these divisions will be more or less reflected in the classification system.

F. It is of fundamental importance that distinctions be drawn between the histories of a culture, a people, and a region. Regions, such as Virú Valley, are fixed in space, but both populations and cultural ideas were free to move. Evidently they did. The remarks above as to the characteristics of cultural development apply to *culture*. Neither people nor area is involved. This study will not be a history of people, nor entirely a history of culture. It is a study of the cultural history of a restricted geographical area. If attention were to be focused on cultural history, it is evident that we would have to examine many parts of South and Central America to complete all details of the story. History of *people* is something we are not prepared to touch upon. To be strictly literal in the present viewpoint, it lies completely in the field of physical anthropology.

What Is a Pottery Type?

Different parts of the foregoing discussion have been previously considered a number of times by various writers. The point of view is summarized here because it must be kept in mind if the nature of the ceramic analysis presented is to be clearly understood. The ceramic chronology of Virú is the story of the change of pottery styles with the passage of time. Most of the change was slow and gradual. This change can be visualized as fluid in nature; sharp breaks, due to the factors cited above, were rare in the continuity. No two pottery vessels made during that long history were exactly alike, and every sherd has some feature that makes it unique. Yet all this material that represents any one time level is clearly imprinted with the prevalent cultural ideas or styles. Just as today, there seemed to the individuals involved to be proper, and apparently inevitable, ways of attaining their objectives. Ancient potters conformed to prevailing ideas exactly as we do in everyday experience. The several different styles of pottery that may have been in use at any one time are due to the difference in function of the vessels or origin of stylistic ideas.

The pottery that the classifier groups into a type is nothing more than material that exhibits a high degree of similarity in the features that reflect the influence of the ideas prevailing in the ancient cultures. Each type established will be found to grade insensibly into other materials that were made coevally or particularly those that preceded or followed. This will lead to "drifting" of the type concept in the mind of the classifier unless it is guarded against by strict definition of the type limits. It must be clearly understood that the type does not exist in the material. "Type" is an artificial concept created by the classifier, and it is here created for one purpose: to serve as a measure of time and space. However, we have here assumed the spatial factor to be negligible, owing to the restricted area to which this study has been applied. Types must be described to be defined, and that the description of all the types of a chronology adds up to a complete description of the material is merely a welcome by-product.

As a type is primarily a time-space measuring tool, it is clear that its validity depends solely on how well it serves for its end purpose. Recombining of types that have proved useless with others that are highly similar and thus are inferred to be culturally related and the splitting of one type into two are both quite valid if this procedure can be justified by the results obtained.

The separation of pottery into types is limited by the ability of the classifier to differentiate readily and consistently between the groups. It is desirable to have the groups as restricted as possible in order that they may be more sensitive measures of cultural change. This is a practical matter that must be settled by usage. If the material has a different position areally or chronologically, and classifiers well acquainted with it can consistently separate the groups, then a division is justified.

The Popularity Characteristics of Types through Time

Pottery types are to be viewed as artificial units set up by the archaeologist in what actually was a continuous stream of ideas, expressed in durable form, that were changing with the passage of time. In consequence, when the relative popularity of a type is measured through time the resultant graph will resemble a normal distribution curve. The type will appear to have been made at first in very small quantities. As time passes it reaches its period of maximum popularity, more or less great. Then it declines in popularity and finally vanishes. (See Fig. 4 for examples.) This apparent life cycle of a type is misleading, for it is really created by the act of classification. For example, the change of features from the type Guañape Red Plain to typical examples of Huacapongo Polished Plain and on into Castillo Plain and Valle Plain are seen to be quite gradual if the material is laid out on a table in the same sequence that it came out of the ground. The fact that a few sherds of Huacapongo Polished Plain are illustrated as from the lower levels of Site V-272, Cut B (Fig. 4), means that at the time represented by these lower levels that proportion of the pottery had passed from the bounds of the ceramic features set by the classifier for Guañape Red Plain to the group of features called Huacapongo. By the time represented by the upper levels of this excavation, nearly all the pottery had crossed this line set up by the classifier, and only a small percentage is left in the type Guañape Red Plain. Many of the sherds from this site were so near the border between these two types that one classifier might put them in one type and another in the other without being in essential disagreement at all.

To illustrate the nature of this process further, it should be pointed out that in the stream of cultural ideas represented by this series of pottery types, one type concept might have been established on the basis of this border material that now appears to be between Guañape and Huacapongo, and another on the present border material between Huacapongo and Castillo Plain. If that had been done, then the material that is now considered typical Huacapongo would be on the border between the two new types. Such a procedure would be fully as valid as the course followed.

SETTING UP THE VIRÚ VALLEY CLASSIFICATION

Field-work was continued for several weeks and collections were gathered from about 50 sites before any attempt was made to set up a classification. I was considerably surprised to note how little of the beautiful pottery that fills museum collections from the North Coast of Peru was found on the occupation sites. In the looted cemeteries, of which Virú has its full share, fragments of pottery representing the well-known styles of Gallinazo, Mochica, and Tiahuanaco of the North Coast variety were abundant. These styles were rare in the rubbish collections and, when found, were often explained by the presence of a looted cemetery near-by. Obviously the already known ceramic chronology promised to be of little assistance in the dating of dwelling site refuse.

Most of the pottery collected was undecorated and rather crude, as compared with a collection of rubbish heap material from the southwestern United States. The sophisticated ancient Peruvian potters spent little skill on their domestic ceramics, or, more likely, separate classes of potters made the two wares. For the first few weeks, the prospect of success in developing a time scale any more sensitive than that already provided by the grave pottery seemed very small. The dating of structures appeared hopeless.

However, as more material accumulated and I became better acquainted with the refuse pottery, consistent dissimilarities became apparent. Suggestions of time difference in the plain wares also began to accumulate from the deep strata excavations which Strong and Evans were making at the Castillo of Tomaval. A classification was begun by pouring out on a large table the sherds from half a dozen sites which seemed to show the full range of ceramic differences encountered in the valley up to that time. Then the pottery fragments were divided into a number of groups, each characterized by observable distinctions in paste, composition, surface finish, hardness, thickness, firing, or decoration when present. Consistent differences in any of these categories of features were accepted as a basis for a separate grouping. Thus a group of sandy, oxidized-fired, hard, unpolished ware which ranged from 6 to 12 millimeters thick was segregated from similar ware from 12 to 40 millimeters thick. This division resulted in the types named Castillo Plain and Valle Plain.

Each of these arbitrary groups was given a type name and was defined, both mentally and in notes, with very rigid boundaries which the classifier expected to observe as consistently as possible. The types thus set up were guesses. In each one the classifier was guessing that the observable differences would be significant temporally or areally, or would be the coeval results of different function or of distinct cultural influences. These types were not final; all were held on probation until analysis should prove whether or not they would be useful in determining cultural history. Analysis by the seriation method was begun as soon as enough collections had been classified, and this tentative work resulted in the re-combination of several types which were highly similar and proved to have identical cultural histories. It also resulted in the splitting of some of the types. If a slight difference was detected in certain sherds that fell in the range set for a type and there was any reason to suspect that this difference indicated any change in time, two types were made. Later, as the classified results of the stratigraphic work of Strong and Evans and Collier became available, their evidence served as a more detailed basis for the evaluation of the type divisions. This balancing of typology against a growing knowledge of the chronology continued right up to the end of the work of classification. Each time a type was split, all the sherds of that type which had already been classified had to be re-checked and the records corrected accordingly.

Brief descriptions of the pottery types set up for Virú are given in Appendix I. Full descriptions will be published by Strong and Evans and Collier, and duplication here appears unnecessary.

*   *   *   *   *

* * * * *

Time Gap Filled by Seriation of Surface Collections

After all the useful strata cut graphs had been fitted, there still remained a gap in the chronology. This was in the Puerto Moorin period, a time during which there seems to have been no accumulations of very deep refuse deposits in the valley; at least the survey found none. At this period the people were living in scattered, single-room houses which probably were not occupied for a very long time. Eighteen surface collections from as many sites were arranged from top to bottom, according to an increasing percentage of the type Guañape Red Plain, a dying type of the earlier Guañape period. Then the later of these sites were rearranged according to their increasing percentage of Castillo Plain, the predominating type of the succeeding Gallinazo period. The results are shown in the summary graph, Fig. 4.

Critique of the Summary Graph, Time Range of Types

The graph (Fig. 4) that resulted from the fitting of the strata excavation results and seriation is presented as the story of the popularity of the pottery types described in the Virú Valley. In viewing this graph, one should keep two things in mind. First, the ceramics represented here were classified over a period of five months by four different people: Collier, Strong, Evans, and myself. Despite efforts to be consistent, some variation doubtless occurred. Evans, who made most of the plainware classifications for his unit, may have drawn the line between the types Valle Plain and Castillo Plain so as to include more sherds in the former type than did the others. I am certain that my concept of each type at the beginning of the work was not identical with that held towards the end. This factor of human variation is inevitable and must be kept in mind.

A second source of variation may be due to differences between the communities of the prehistoric peoples of Virú. While, for general purposes, we have assumed a high degree of similarity of the culture in all parts of the valley at any one moment in the past, this cannot be carried so far as to insist that there was necessarily an exact degree of uniformity in the popularity of pottery styles. Some of the common styles may have reached a slightly higher degree of popularity in comparison with the other styles of the moment in one part of the valley than in another. The strata excavations were made in various parts of the valley, and some of the percentage variation shown may be due to this factor. Still another uncontrollable factor is the sampling error.

The variation between type percentages, however, is not great, and the major trends shown by the excavations are in almost perfect agreement. That Valle Plain came in later than Castillo Plain and reached a lower peak of popularity is shown by all the cuts that cover the early part of the Gallinazo period. The fit of the stratigraphic cuts is much better than was hoped for when I began putting them together.

Still another factor seems to have introduced a certain amount of distortion in the summary graph. That is the tendency for older pottery types which were originally deposited in the lower strata of a midden accumulation to occur in decreasing percentages right up into the top levels. This slow fading away of popularity is, of course, the way in which a type is expected to die. However, it seems that the types did actually disappear sooner than is apparent from the evidence supplied by deep strata cuts. The reason for this appears obvious. While the midden was in the process of accumulation and people were living on and around it, the ground was constantly being dug into and overturned to a shallow depth. In the course of this constant stirring of the soil, potsherds that were originally deposited in the lower levels were brought higher and higher in the midden.

That this weighting of a type history towards its later phase does occur is demonstrated by comparing these slightly mixed sites with middens that began their life history after the type actually had disappeared. Site V-51, Cut 1, shows that the type Huacapongo Polished Plain continued in very small percentages almost to the end of the Gallinazo period. Site V-162, Cut 1, which begins its history after the first half of this period had elapsed, contained very little of this type only in the lowest levels. The absence of the type Castillo Plain in the short-lived late Site V-108, Cut A, is in contrast to the other sites which cover the same time but were settled at an earlier date, Site V-171, for

example. The comparison of surface collections from sites which were occupied for very short periods and produce samples free from this kind of mixture also shows that this tendency existed in deep midden deposits.

RELATIVE TIME REPRESENTED BY VERTICAL SPACING IN MASTER GRAPH

The amount of midden accumulation suggests that the earlier Guañape and Gallinazo periods were several times longer than the later Huancaco, Tomaval, and following periods. The brevity of the late periods is indicated by the *average* of several cuts: if such an excavation as Site V-167, Cut A, with its total depth of 3.5 meters had been taken as a guide, the Tomaval period would have been represented as about two-thirds as long as the Gallinazo period. However, deposits like Site V-171, Cut A, and Site V-60, Cut A, suggest that this is not true.

It will be noted that time periods become shorter from the bottom to the top of the graph. The suggested acceleration in cultural change from early to late periods probably did occur, for there was a factor in operation throughout the history of the valley which would tend to mask such evidence for relative speed of change as is used here. That factor is the trend towards urbanization which will be discussed by Gordon Willey in his paper. Populations were much more concentrated in the later periods, and relatively greater depths of refuse should have been accumulated in a given length of time. This is another of the uncontrollable factors that enter into our time estimates.

It has been mentioned above that probably not enough vertical space, representing time, has been allowed for the Puerto Moorin period. This is suggested by the fact that as the chart is now arranged the type Huacapongo Polished Plain appears to change much faster than either the preceding popular type Guañape Red Plain or the succeeding one, Castillo Plain. In fact, the present arrangement gives Huacapongo about the same rate of change as Tomaval Plain, the most recent popular type which existed at a time when considerable cultural acceleration probably had developed.

It is also very likely that too much vertical space has been given to the upper two-thirds of the Estero period (Time B-C on the time scale). Above the horizontal position of the tops of the two compressed strata-pit graphs, Site V-305,

Cut A, and Site V-108, Cut A, the graphic spacing of the upper levels of Site V-171, Cuts A and C, should have been placed closer together. They should have been drawn to conform to the average spacing illustrated by such excavations as Site V-51, Cut 1, and Site V-71, Cut 1.

SMOOTHING THE CHRONOLOGY

After the graph representing the valley chronology had been completed, the curves indicated for the percentage popularity of each type were drawn. This smoothing was done by eye, and an effort was made to strike an average between the variation shown by the several collections covering the same sections of the chronology. The smoothing lines are dotted and are identical in both the strata chart derived from the strata excavations (**Fig. 4**) and the graph illustrating the fitting of surface collections (**Fig. 5**).

DATING SCALE

The smoothed strata graph was inspected to determine the number of divisions that might be made in it to date the surface collections. It was not to be expected that surface collections when graphed would fit perfectly at one and only one point along the smoothed graph. Even if some did, this fitting would still be suspect. Too many variations were involved to make possible such accuracy in dating. Short spans of time to which each collection might be referred would allow for the error factors hidden in the graphs.

The appearance of Inca Painted pottery, the beginning of the decline of Tomaval Plain, and the end of the types Corral Incised and Niño Stamped provided one such point. Accordingly a line was drawn across the graph. Other points were chosen as shown and lines drawn. Space was left at the top for a Colonial period on which very little data were recovered, but this period is known to exist both from historic records and collections in the Chiclín Museum. This is the arbitrary scale to which the dating of surface collections will be referred. The divisions are lettered "A" to "N" on the right-hand side of the four graphs (**Figs. 4, 5, 6, 7**).

*   *   *   *   *

REFERENCES CITED

BREW, JOHN O.
    1946   *The Archaeology of Alkali Ridge, South-*
             eastern Utah. Peabody Museum of
             Archaeology and Ethnology, *Papers* 21.
             Harvard University.

FORD, JAMES A.
    1936   *Analysis of Village Site Collections from*
             Louisiana and Mississippi. Louisiana State
             Geological Survey, Department of Con-
             servation, Anthropological Study 2.

KIDDER, ALFRED V.
    1931   *The Pottery of Pecos, Vol. I: The Dull-Paint*
             Wares. Papers of the Southwestern Expe-
             dition, Phillips Academy, No. 5. Yale Uni-
             versity Press, New Haven, Connecticut.

KROEBER, ALFRED L.
    1916   Zuñi Potsherds. *American Museum of*
             Natural History, Anthropological Papers
             18(1):1–38.

ROUSE, IRVING
    1939   *Prehistory in Haiti, A Study in Method.*
             Yale University Publications in Anthro-
             pology No. 21.

SPIER, LESLIE
    1917   An Outline for a Chronology of Zuñi
             Ruins. *American Museum of Natural His-*
             tory, Anthropological Papers 18(3):207–
             331.

THE PLACE OF CHRONOLOGICAL ORDERING IN ARCHAEOLOGICAL ANALYSIS*

George W. Brainerd

THE article which precedes this one describes a statistical technique for the chronological placement of archaeological artifact collections. The purposes of this paper are first to describe the *rationale* of archaeological analysis under which the data and problem as presented to Robinson were formulated, and upon which the validity of his solution therefore depends, and second to describe analytic and interpretive work which I have based upon his results.

The introductory section of this paper is a defense of archaeological artifact typology as a primary tool of analysis, and of mathematical and graphic working techniques in the chronologic placing of material. To the archaeologists who approve of and constantly use these techniques I apologize for my verbosity but plead that in many reports the method of sequencing is given briefly and sometimes nearly apologetically. To those ethnologists who find in trait lists at best a superficial method of culture study I plead a special purpose for typology in archaeological analysis.

TYPOLOGY IN ARCHAEOLOGICAL ANALYSIS

During the last few years there has been a growing and proper demand that archaeologists extract from their artifacts more reconstructions of past cultures, more data that will add historical perspective to ethnology. Steward and Setzler (1938) present an example of a well-reasoned plea for broader archaeological interpretation. In sympathy with this demand there

---

* See footnote on p. 293.

has been a laudable tendency among archaeologists to provide more complete and carefully considered culture reconstructions. These reconstructions have usually taken the form of amplified descriptions of archaeological phases or "horizons." The current forms of archaeological typology have been under sharp criticism during the last few years. From these two critical trends has emerged in some minds the conclusion that archaeologists should forego the barren escapism of typology and proceed directly to the goal of culture reconstruction or, a less radical cure, that whatever typology is used should of itself provide a functional description of the culture. To my mind these proposals reflect a misunderstanding of the fundamental purpose of archaeological typology.

The tracing of culture change through time by careful documentation is as major a responsibility of the archaeologist as is culture horizon description; he is a culture historian as well as an ethnographer. Although his competence in the former field has by many been taken for granted, actual performance has often not been exemplary. Human migrations have certainly too often been invoked to explain culture change. Such major errors as the misunderstanding of the Basketmaker-Pueblo transition (Brew, 1946, pp. 32-85) and of the interrelationship of the central and northern Maya groups (Brainerd, 1948) have come from failures in historical reconstruction. Some errors of this type might have been avoided if more attention had been given to careful chronologic sequencing, to working through time as a continuous variable rather than by the limitation of description to successive chronologic cross sections. Other errors have been perpetuated unduly through the uncritical acceptance as fact of theoretical interpretations of culture sequence based on thinly distributed data.

The archaeologist has a unique chance to determine empirically how preliterate cultures came to be as they were. His use of technical procedures in reaching an ever more finely drawn chronological scale needs no apology; these are prerequisite to his determination of culture change through time, a subject in which he should be able to work with unique authority.

The materials which come to the hand of the archaeologist have invariably been made by man during an interval of time, and only after these have been sequenced can he write culture history, or even know when he has arrived safely at the way station of horizon description. Few archaeologists would question the advisability of formulating horizon descriptions, both because of the insight these give into cultural configurations and the opportunity they afford for direct comparison with the richer horizon descriptions available from the ethnographers. But the techniques of close chronological placement, if not systematically explored and improved, can prejudice all future work toward culture reconstruction from archaeological remains.

The prime working tool of the archaeologist in the formulation of his time-space framework is typology. The effects of the time factor can be isolated by stratigraphic or seriational analysis of types. This procedure is a specialized archaeological technique best applied in the first stages of the work.[1] The impatience of many ethnologists with detailed archaeological typology is easily understandable. In studying a human group the ethnographer can follow the direct procedure of describing the organization, conventions, and techniques of a society, appending descriptions of the material results of its arts and crafts. The archaeologist, attempting to apply inductive methods toward reconstructing cultures from their material remains, produces a monograph the bulk of which provides frustrating reading to the ethnologist. He finds the material culture descriptions unduly detailed, organized in an incomprehensible manner, and including data extraneous to even his most exacting needs and interests. Failing to realize the purpose of archaeological typology, he is apt to suspect the archaeologist of an interest in objects rather than in their makers.

There is adequate reason for nonfunctionally oriented artifact typology, even that of the most detailed sort, if it is objectively formulated and serves the purpose of construction of the

---

[1] Although these dicta will seem self-evident to most archaeologists, they are far from universally accepted. The Midwestern Taxonomic system defers chronology for later consideration, while Taylor (1948, p. 147) defers comparative and taxonomic studies until the "culture types" existing in the archaeological material have been "separated inferentially on the basis of cultural cohesiveness." Although I do not completely understand his statement, this sequence of procedure would seem to favor the making of culture reconstructions before the establishment of the time-space framework.

George W. Brainerd

necessary time-space framework. If a chronologic sequence can be constructed by procedures unconnected with cultural interpretation, and if the process provides its own proofs of validity, it gains authority thereby. The cause and effect relationships subsequently reconstructed will then be supported by independent chronologic anchorage and are sure to be unaffected by circular reasoning on the part of the investigator.

Such an objective technique is completely feasible, as may be demonstrated by analogous techniques developed in geological sequencing and in chromosome mapping. Archaeological types may properly be formulated, as indeed they usually are (Krieger, 1944, pp. 277-9; Rouse, 1939, pp. 25-6), by noting which objectively describable artifact traits occur often in combination in single artifacts. The frequencies in artifact collections of types thus formulated can serve as the working material from which chronological sequences may be built. Furthermore such objectively determined types may reasonably be assumed to represent cultural standards (Rouse, 1939, pp. 18-23) which may be later utilized as parts of the culture description.

The value of an initial typology should not be judged by what it directly tells of the culture to be investigated but by the sensitivity and reliability of the time-space framework which it can be made to yield. Time moves by imperceptible increments through the archaeological sequence. The more finely drawn and objectively determined the chronology, the more delicate and authoritative can be the insight which it provides into the interpretation of changes undergone through time.

THE PROBLEM OF CHRONOLOGICAL ORDERING

The problem of objective and closely controlled determination of chronological sequences from frequencies of types in collections or samples is the subject of the experimental work here described. I have long felt that this type of determination can most logically be done by mathematical procedures using the largest possible number of types or trait assemblages. It is my contention that the reasoning so often advanced against necessarily simplified mathematical formulations of complexly interrelated cultural factors does not apply here

to the extent of invalidating a chronological sequence. I believe this claim is borne out by the independent checking of sequences established by Robinson's ordering techniques described in his accompanying article.

It should perhaps be pointed out here that statistical treatments of chronological ordering are not subject to certain logical complexities, inconsistencies, and uncertainties of judgment inherent in the mathematical formulation of measures of similarity between regional cultures. Variations undergone by a culture through time, although likely as complex in their causation as the regional variations found in contemporary cultures, can be arranged in a linear order which is not varied by differences of emphasis or judgment. American culture of 1900 A.D. may be related to that of 1950 A.D. by use of a linear time scale which is in itself not subject to the questions of viewpoint and interpretation which enter so profoundly into an assessment of the relationship of, for example, modern English and American cultures. Variations in judgment as to the relative importance of kinds of cultural differences can alter profoundly estimates of similarity between contemporaneous cultures, but should not alter sequential orderings of artifact material along a time axis. Although the *sensitivity* of time differentiation in an archaeological sequence is directly dependent upon the judgment of the typologist, its *ordering*, if objectively arrived at, should not be affected thereby.

If the above scheme of thought be acceptable we may start our problem with a described and tabulated mass of archaeological material which has been segregated into the divisions which will be used as our criteria in the formation of a time-space framework.

The nature of these divisions does not bear directly upon the scheme of analysis proposed here; although those employed in this problem are of the commonly used hierarchic sort whose smallest division is often called a type[2] the subdivisions used may equally well crosscut hierarchic classifications.[3] A single important

---

[2] Such types are not so restricted in definition as Krieger's; they will, for example, not meet Krieger's qualification (1944, p. 285) of having demonstrated chronologic or regional significance, since such proof is one of the by-products of our procedure.

[3] Cf. Rouse's (1939, pp. 11-12) *modes*, and Brew's (1946, p. 46) plea for "more" classifications.

qualification must be met by the sorting criteria used. Each must be of such complexity in number and organization of attributes that the presence of an artifact belonging to it suggests that its maker lived in the same cultural milieu as that of makers of all other artifacts classified into the same sorting group; thus all artifacts classified under one group must have been made at approximately the same time and place. This hypothesis is tested for each group by the subsequent analysis, and is empirically proved for various groups if the analysis is successful. These sorting groups will henceforth in this paper be called *types*.

Types are normally encountered in artifact *collections*. A collection is defined as a group of artifacts which were found together, and therefore are suspected of having been made at approximately the same time and place. The *types* associated in collections are listed quantitatively, and the frequency of occurrence of the various types defined in a collection of any size may thus be computed.

The analytic technique whereby collections of artifacts may be placed in a time-space framework is based on the concept that each type originates at a given time at a given place, is made in gradually increasing numbers as time goes on, then decreases in popularity until it becomes forgotten, never to recur in an identical form.[4]

If, in a mass of cultural material from a single region, a series of artifact types follows the course outlined above, each originating more or less independently of another, the corollary may be drawn that if a series of collections comes from a culture changing through time, their placement on the time axis is a function of their similarity; collections with closest similarity in qualitative or quantitative listing of types lie next to each other in the time sequence. This corollary allows a "seriation" or ordering of collections to be formed which, if time be the only factor involved, must truly represent the temporal placing of

the collections,[5] although determination of the direction early to late must be obtained by other means.[6] Stratigraphic excavations have abundantly confirmed this general disposition of artifact types through time in archaeological deposits.[7]

ROBINSON'S ORDERING TECHNIQUE

Brainerd posed to Robinson the problem of obtaining a mathematical measure of similarity among collections which would depend upon the comparative frequencies of a considerable number of types common to the collections. Since the variation among the collections to be analyzed was suspected to be principally chronological, an objective method for the seriation or ordering of the collections on the basis of these measures of similarity was desired.[8]

---

[4] Cf. Rouse (1939, pp. 14-15). New types do not normally originate at identical times save by chance. If a series of collections shows mass displacement of types at a single time, cultural displacement by conquest or other means seems indicated. This corollary has been much overworked in the past (as in the Basketmaker-Pueblo I transition) by reconstructing from too widely spaced series of collections.

[5] Spier (1917) first published a mathematical formulation of a chronological sequence using the above-described principle. The sequence arrived at by Spier seems to have been previously formulated by inspection by Kroeber (1916). Formulation of sequences by the principle of placing collections or artifact styles or types in order of closest similarity has been done, using a wide variety of techniques, by many workers, among whom Kidder (1915), Kroeber (1930), Olson (1930), Ford (1938), Rouse (1939), Beals, Brainerd and Smith (1945) and Ford and Willey (1949), may be cited as examples. Several have qualified their orderings as provisional, awaiting establishment or disproof by stratigraphy.

[6] Spier knew historically which end of his sequence was late. Stratigraphic placement of two or more points will also give direction. A technique for this determination from the data of the seriation itself forms part of the present study.

[7] Nelson (1916) first demonstrated such a stratigraphic sequence to Americanists. Kidder (1936) was able to check his seriational results (1915) by later stratigraphic excavation.

[8] Robinson's statistical techniques show certain obvious similaries to those used in ethnological studies. He was unfamiliar with these at the time of his work. (See Driver and Kroeber, 1932; also see Kluckhohn, 1939, for a bibliography and evaluation of such studies.) Kroeber, perceiving the similarity in ordering of data between ethnological trait lists and the trait lists employed in archaeological studies using the Midwestern Taxonomic system, applied the ethnological statistical method to a series of archaeological sites, getting results similar to those made by previously used inspectional

Brainerd's immediate need for this sort of a method was to aid in the formulation of a more closely defined chronology for the Maya ceramics of the Puuc region in Yucatan. The numerous collections made by the Carnegie Institution in Puuc ruins had failed to yield evidence of ceramic change when analyzed by Brainerd's inspectional techniques, although considerable variation of types through the collections from single sites was evident. An accurate objective serial placement of these collections in chronologic order was desirable to allow the study of the development of the associated architecture and other facets of the culture as well as of the ceramic development. Detailed results of the statistical analysis will be presented in Brainerd's subsequent monographs. This article is confined to method and theory.

Robinson, a sociological statistician, showed an immediate enthusiasm in the problem, tempered only by considerable distrust of the sort of data furnished him. His delighted comment that the results are more definitive than any he has obtained in several years may perhaps be taken to demonstrate the ease of chronologic analysis as compared to that of the interaction of factors in contemporaneous society.

As may be seen from Dr. Robinson's article, which precedes this one, the linear orderings which he formed are based upon the relative degrees of similarity among a group of collections from an archaeological site. The types or criteria used by Robinson in computing the measures of agreement were chosen by Brainerd from his field tabulations. The sum of these criteria normally constituted a high percentage of each collection but never the total collection.

The criteria of constant combination of attributes in the defining of types and of complexity of attributes in gauging their cultural validity had been adhered to in the making of the field tabulations. From types meeting these require-

ments were selected those suspected of showing significant variations in frequency among the samples. The criteria chosen belonged to various grades in a hierarchic classification; some were wares, some vessel forms, some rim shapes, since the classification had originally been made in that form. The base used for frequency computation was the sum of the criteria chosen, not the collection total.

It should be emphasized that the collections worked on by Robinson were not chosen as likely prospects but were, on the contrary, those which had failed to yield chronological sequences to Brainerd's inspectional techniques. Robinson's results are thus free of any bias from hypotheses previously formed by Brainerd on other than statistical grounds. This is not a mathematical expression of a previously hypothesized ordering[9] but a *de novo* objectively determined sequence.

To determine whether or not chronology was the causative factor in the formation of his collection orderings Robinson repeated his technique on the Mani collections which showed stratigraphic ordering, and has demonstrated that the distribution of individual types in the orderings obtained by his technique are those previously known as correct (Fig. 91). That his results checked accurately shows that his method will order collections correctly at least in certain cases when chronologic differences are present, but does not conclusively rule out the possibility of factors other than chronology causing a sequence in all instances. Certain irregularities of type frequencies in the Maya ceramic collections suggest quite definitely that factors other than chronology and sampling errors must be hypothesized to account for variation in single sites. In an effort to provide theoretical bases for the more accurate isolation and analysis of chronologic variation and thus to permit analysis of the remaining non-chronologic variation, the following series of tests was run:

The classification categories of the sites were graphed in Robinson's seriated order of collections. These graphs show the characteristic lenticular shapes previously established as characteristic in chronologic sequence. Included in these graphs are various categories

---

methods (Kroeber, 1940). Similarities between this and Robinson's work are doubtless due to the fact that both techniques were formulated to demonstrate relationships based on mathematical measures of similarity. No former work on this basis has been oriented toward chronology; clumping, not seriation of collections in matrices, was attained by previous studies. Also, qualitative rather than quantitative trait distributions have generally been used by previous workers to compute measures of similarity.

[9] Cf. discussion by Griffin (1943, p. 334) on the procedure of workers under the Midwest Taxonomic System.

not included in Robinson's computations. Figure 92 shows an abbreviated series of graphs of the Kabah pottery according to Robinson's ordering.

That these characteristic nodal curves are followed by several wares, types and shapes concurrently suggests that the causative factor must have been linear in nature, and that it is correctly represented by the linear ordering furnished by Robinson. Although it might be possible that varying frequencies of a single well-represented type, coupled with the inevitable and complementary frequency changes in all others, might yield an ordering by Robinson's technique, these graphs show concurrent changes in groups when computed on separate percentage bases, and thus their variations are not simply complementary to each other. An additional check on the possibility of the ordering being due to variation in a single type was made by Robinson. Measures of agreement were recomputed for a site after eliminating the type showing the largest percentage variations in the series. The ordering was not changed thereby.

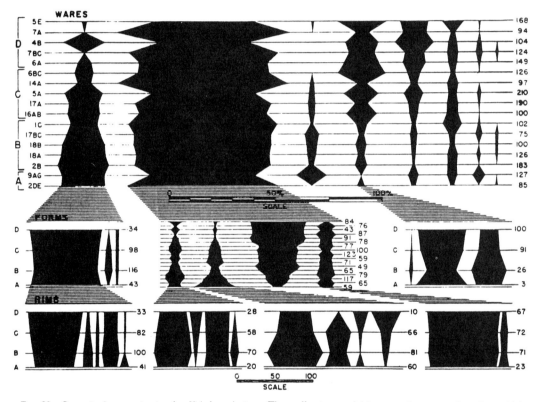

FIG. 92. Ceramic frequencies in the Kabah ordering. The collections, which came from trenches dug within the site of Kabah, are in the order determined by Robinson's mathematical technique; late collections are toward the top, early toward the bottom. The upper percentage scale applies only to the upper graph, the lower scale was used to plot the two lower rows of graphs. Numbers of fragments in the groups considered are given to the right of each graph and should be used to judge the validity of frequencies in their groups. The upper graph shows frequencies of rim sherds of the 8 major wares found. Unslipped ware, first column, decreases through time. Thin Slateware and Thin Redware, columns 4 and 5 respectively, increase through time. The second row of graphs shows frequencies of vessel forms of certain of the wares, each computed with its ware total as 100 percent. When ware totals have been too small to provide statistically useful samples the collections have been grouped as shown into four sequent clusters, A, B, C and D. Note in the center graph, which shows Medium Slateware divided into jars, basins, basal break bowls, and hemispheroid bowls, that the jars and basins decrease in frequency through time, while the basal break bowls increase. The lowest row of graphs shows the frequencies of the commoner rim shapes of certain of the vessel forms shown in the middle row of graphs.

It is believed that the above mentioned linearity of causal factor may with certain reservations be used to isolate chronologically caused variation from variations produced by other causes. Factors such as regional differences in culture and social stratification suggest themselves as the likely causes of variation alternative to chronology. The regional variations in culture studied by Driver and Kroeber by techniques quite similar to those evolved by Robinson gave matrices which, as would be expected, show clumping rather than linear ordering. Regional cultural variation can confidently be expected to show other than a linear matrix patterning since the geographic framework in which it evolved is of itself multidimensional.

The question of variation in pottery deposits due to social stratification in the site is a knottier one. In general a linear sequence running coarse to fine pottery and based on wealth or social power might be conceived to occur in sites of complex societies, complicated by such variables as industries with special uses for ceramics and in Maya sites very possibly by special ceramics used in religious ceremonies. The graph shown for Kabah (Fig. 92) may be inspected to decide whether chronology or social stratigraphy has caused our sequencing. It will be noticed that unslipped ware and Medium Slateware jars and basins decrease bottom to top while Thin Slateware, Thin Redware and Medium Slateware basal break bowls increase. This sequence in general shows coarser wares and larger vessels at bottom with finer smaller pottery at the top, suggesting a possible basis of cultural stratigraphy for the seriation. Some of the changes through the ordering are not, however, thus classifiable. It is difficult to imagine why simultaneous frequency changes should occur in so many seemingly unrelated shapes and forms unless a chronological factor were dominating the sequence. Fortunately, inspection of collections dating before and after the occupation of Kabah bears out a chronological trend through time toward finer pottery; a factor other than chronology is not needed to explain it.

ANALYSIS OF ORDERED MATRICES

From the above analysis and similar analyses done on other sites it seems safe to assume that the linear orderings shown in Robinson's matrices are the result of chronology, and that

strong deviations from a linear ordering are likely to have been caused by factors other than chronology. To aid in the judgment and interpretation of matrices I have found it advantageous to contour them in the manner of relief maps and to construct a series of matrices from geometric models to discover the significance of their "surface characteristics." Figures 95, 96, 97, 98 and 99 are matrices contoured in this manner.

If contoured, Robinson's mathematical model (Table 16) would show a central ridge of high measures of agreement with sides of constant slope diagonal to the upper right-hand and lower left-hand corners. These two slopes are mirror images of each other about the diagonal of perfect agreement. The table may be said to be analogous to results from a series of short term, unmixed collections showing a constant rate of ceramic change between each successive two. The collections may be visualized as successive points on a straight line, equidistant at one unit of measure apart. Measures of agreement between any two may then be obtained by measuring distance and subtracting it from a constant, in this case 7. For example, from point 2 to point 6 measures 4 units. By subtracting these 4 units from the 7 above we derive 3 — the figure in Robinson's table.

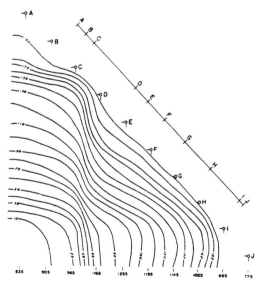

FIG. 93. Geometric model of points irregularly spaced along a straight line. Line is 200 units in length. Distances between points have all been subtracted from 200, and resultant values contoured.

Using the same geometric system we can compute and contour a matrix from a group of points irregularly spaced along a straight line 200 units in length (Fig. 93). In this and the following matrices presented, we show only the lower left half; the other half is always mirror symmetric across the diagonal axis. This matrix should be to some degree analogous to that given by collections separated

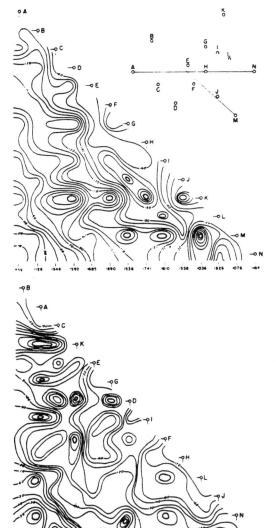

by varying degrees of chronologic (linear) change or, more properly, by relative degree of ceramic change since such change is our only measure of time lapse. Note that the contours all equally change direction along lines parallel to the axes of the matrix both horizontally and vertically between points C and D, the two most widely separated adjacent points of the sequence. Also note that the sums of the matrix columns, shown along the baseline, depart markedly from the smooth curve of those in Robinson's Table 16, the sums of close spaced points grouping closely, those of widely spaced points showing larger differences. This synthetic matrix shows markedly similar characteristics, both in contour and column sums to the Mani matrix, in Figure 99. The collections from this site, which occurred stratigraphically, show marked ceramic change among the major pottery wares at the points indicated: between 2G and 4F, between 4C and 4D and between 4A and 1A. The ceramic collections at Mani would be expected to show these sharp changes since deposits some 2.5 meters deep document over 2,000 years of ceramic change, as compared to from 150 to 400 years in the other matrices illustrated.

Another synthetic matrix was plotted using a group of points having a random pattern in a plane. Linear arrangements in two directions were tried, oriented to align with widely separated points (Fig. 94). These matrices should give some idea of the irregularity of contour to be expected if the best possible linear arrangement be made of a group of collections showing no close relationship to a linear (chronologic) pattern. All matrices from the Yucatan pottery are more regular than either of these with the exception of Uxmal thus indicating that Robinson's results are in most cases not merely artifacts of his technique as applied to nonlinear material. Graphing of the pottery types in the Uxmal collections in seriated order showed that even with this unprepossessing matrix (Fig. 96), the ceramic change of the major wares corresponds in general to those of other contemporaneous sites. The irregularity of contour seems due to "wild" values of the fine wares, a suggestion of the strong intrusion of social stratigraphy into the total variation.

Fundamental to the working methods used in this study is the assumption that each collection consists of artifacts made during a shorter time span than that covered by the whole group of collections. The formation of chronological orderings verifies this assumption but does not sort from the data the results due to variable time span of deposit of artifacts included in a single collection. The results of the latter causative factor are obviously to be suspected of bulking large when the collections come from a concentrated area or site, when deposits are shallow, when the total time period is short, and when the analysis is carried to the ultimate degree of chronologic subdivision. All these factors apply to our material.[10]

The accurate determination of these chronologic variabilities in individual collections is of course possible only in the terms of relative amount of ceramic variability in collections, since this variability is our only time indicator. In the analysis of collections for span of deposition of individual collections some separation between the causative factors may be possible: (a) the time during which the archaeological deposit was laid down in its final position before excavation, and (b) amount of admixture of earlier material through reuse of earth, and (c) that of later material introduced by animal and plant activities since deposition. The effects of factor (a) may be assumed in the main to be a mixture of artifacts more or less evenly covering a segment of the time span of the site. Factor (b) is more likely to cause a mixture of material from two markedly separated intervals of that segment of the time span preceding deposition, and factor (c) is likely to cause sporadic occurrence of small numbers of artifacts of later date in preponderantly earlier collections. Factor (c) is nearly certain to be the least active of these three in a long occupied site.

The effects of these factors on a linearly ordered matrix can be to some degree prophesied. In Robinson's synthetic model (Table 16) the measures of agreement of each collection rise steadily from a low value at each edge of the matrix to a high at each side of

the diagonal. His model is analogous to a condition where each collection represents but a point on the time scale. If, on the other hand, the deposition of a single collection covers in an even manner the whole time span of the matrix, the inverted V figure formed by profiling its measurements of agreement with the other collections in sequence will be lower at the vertex and higher at the ends than are those of the short span deposits.

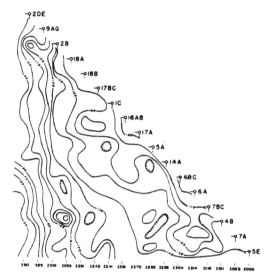

FIG. 95. Contoured matrix of the final ordering of Kabah.

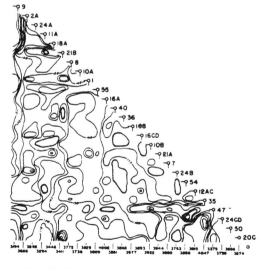

FIG. 96. Contoured matrix of the final ordering of Uxmal.

---

[10] In most analyses of sherd materials from sites this problem is met by taking only the "pure" collections, that is, those collections showing most striking differences among them, to define chronologic phases, components, or horizons. The bulk of the material is then assumed to be "mixed" or "transitional" and its characteristics are used only to augment the detail of the descriptions taken from the "pure" collections.

This diagnostic feature of long term collections has been checked empirically by inserting into sequences synthetic collections formed by combining several collections in the sequence and computing new frequencies. A synthetic long term collection when sequenced will fall into a position intermediate among that of its component collections, and will show lower measures of agreement with adjacent collections in the sequence, and higher measures

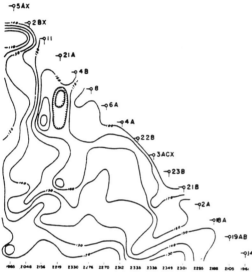

FIG. 97. Contoured matrix of the final ordering of Sayil.

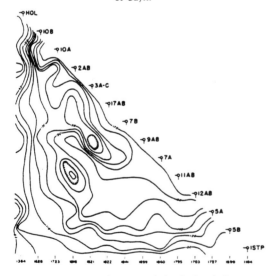

FIG. 98. Contoured matrix of the final ordering of Holactun.

with distant collections than will shorter term collections. Relative "degradation of profile" is thus a measure of the time interval covered by the materials contained in the deposit, and a mathematical measurement of relative time spans of the collections in a matrix may eventually be feasible. The column total of measures of agreement in the instances tried fitted well into the even, non-disjunctive sequence of column totals as exemplified by Table 16. Thus column total variability seems promising as a criterion in separating effects of mixed collections and variable period of depositions from those of variable spacing in ceramic change. Meanwhile much may be seen by inspection of contoured matrices.

Many profiles show multiple peaks. Multiple peaks in a degraded profile indicate the presence of materials which fit the sequence at the points indicated by the peaks. Thus a single profile may be checked for high points and the position in the matrix where such points fall will indicate the time level from which the mixed or long term deposit has received material. The actual analysis of this condition is complicated by the fact that all collections in the matrix are sure to cover varying time intervals, and each measure of agreement is a function of two collections. In analyzing which of the two component collections has caused a given peak the column and row profiles should allow a judgment. Whichever profile shows a documented upslope adjoining the peak is the one to suspect as a mixed collection. An isolated high value in a profile suggests that its complementary collection at that point has caused it. In topographic terms spurs from the central ridge or independent ridges suggest that the collections whose profiles they follow are long term. In the making of any of the above analyses the column totals of measures of agreement should first be checked to assure that irregularity of spacing along the axis of ceramic change is not the causal factor.

It should be easy for the reader to gather from the above that the interpretation of the apparently chaotic topography of Robinson's matrices has not yet reached the ordered stage of an exact technique. It may be worthwhile for Brainerd to record, however, his conviction that the fault lies in the immaturity of his working methods rather than in any permanent intractability of the data. There is considerable evidence that the results of variable deposition span and of variable spacing of collections along the axis of ceramic change (the time axis) can be objectively, and quite precisely, separated. The proper understanding of these two variables and the consequent control of the errors introduced by them into the time scale should improve the precision of time placement of collections, and concurrently allow a closer separation of variability due to time from that due to such causes as social stratification and regional variation and trade.

Early in the course of this project it was noticed that in contoured matrices from several Puuc sites there is a tendency for the matrix to slope upward toward one end of the diagonal axis rather than parallel to the axis as would be expected, and that concurrently the other end of the axis shows a very sudden rise to high value from low values at edge of matrix (Figs. 95, 96, 97, 98). Graphing of the pottery sequences covered by the collections which formed these matrices, and comparison with stratified material, showed that the four examples were uniform in that the sharply rising end of the ridge is the early end of the sequence. Reading along the profiles of the individual collections reveals that those at the early end of the sequence show the characteristics outlined above as those of short term deposits, a high peak value for adjacent collections, low values for those further

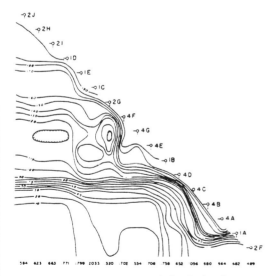

FIG. 99. Contoured matrix of the final ordering of Mani.

removed in the sequence. Collections at the late end of the sequence conversely show the degraded profiles of long term deposits. Although this tendency is not striking it was sufficient to allow recognition of time direction before its causes were known.

The cause must be progressive mixing of deposits, the factor (b) of page 309 acting with increasing strength through the depositional period of the site. This principle has been recently used by Kidder to hypothesize the priority of a phase from mixed deposits (Kidder, Jennings and Shook, 1946, p. 258). This phenomenon may be expected to show most strongly in groups of collections from a concentrated site showing continued occupation. Its value in giving time direction in sites where stratigraphy has not been obtained should be obvious.

SUMMARY OF RESULTS

The results which Brainerd believes have been gained during the work of which this is a progress report may be summarized.

First, and of major importance, Dr. Robinson has worked out a mathematically simple, objective technique for the chronological seriation of archaeological collections. This technique requires no special system of classification and recording and thus is immediately applicable to large masses of tabulated material which, if not found stratigraphically, are often difficult to place by present techniques, and it allows their more accurate assignment in a chronological scale. Such assignment greatly increases the efficiency of archaeological analysis, and there is sound reason for desiring this; archaeological deposits are not inexhaustible. I believe that undoubtedly seriations formed by this technique will allow refinements in chronology greater than those currently possible, but it should be cautioned that the number of seriated steps is no direct measure of the number of chronological substages which may reliably be defined, since spans of deposition of individual deposits are very likely to overlap considerably with those of adjacent collections. It should also be cautioned that, as has so often been said of statistical techniques, this method will not give closer results than are inherent in the data put into it; although poor typology should not give erroneous orderings, it cannot be expected to give finely graded seriations. An additional caution should be given as to the type of material suitable for this technique. Since the seriation of collections depends upon relative degrees of difference between collections, orderings cannot be obtained from collections which do not share a number of their included types. Stratigraphy is the only valid method for the sequencing of completely disparate cultural materials, and, save in deposits where progressive mixing has occurred, t is the only device for obtaining time direct on. Although stratigraphy has often been called the final proof of archaeological sequence, it seems questionable whether possible errors due to redeposition do not render stratigraphy at times less reliable than are the internal evidences of concurrent culture changes upon which seriations depend. Stratigraphic placement supported by the evidence of finely graded concurrent cultural changes through the artifacts from a series of overlying deposits is certainly a final clincher; it is unfortunate that such deposits are found so seldom!

Robinson's statistical technique for chronological ordering is a tool ready for use. Although its results will need constant testing and evaluation, its underlying *rationale* is uncomplicated enough to allow most archaeologists an adequate judgment as to the meaning of its results. Techniques for the utilization of the numerical data produced by the procedure are the present need and these must be evolved by archaeologists. Beginnings in the recognition of the relative spacing of collections along the chronological axis and of the relative spans of deposition of individual collections are described in this paper. These techniques when developed fully should allow a more precise separation of time-caused variation in archaeological collections. A promising clue to the determination of early from late end of sequences found from non-stratified collections has also been described. Adequate understanding and analysis of the variation caused by time in archaeological collections allows the close documentation of culture dynamics, and throws into sharper relief the non-chronologic variation from which the archaeologist can in turn make more finely drawn and reliable inferences as to the functional relationships shown by his material.

BIBLIOGRAPHY

BEALS, RALPH L., GEORGE W. BRAINERD AND
WATSON SMITH
    1945. "Archaeological Studies in Northeast Arizona." *University of California Publications in American Archaeology and Ethnology*, Vol. 44, No. 1. Berkeley.

BRAINERD, GEORGE W.
    1948. Review: The Ancient Maya (Sylvanus Griswold Morley). *American Antiquity*, Vol. 14, No. 2, pp. 133-6. Menasha.

BREW, JOHN OTIS
    1946. "The Archaeology of Alkali Ridge, Southeastern Utah." *Papers of the Peabody Museum of American Archaeology and Ethnology, Harvard University*, Vol. 21. Cambridge..

DRIVER, H. E. AND A. L. KROEBER
    1932. "Quantitative Expression of Cultural Relationships." *University of California Publications in American Archaeology and Ethnology*, Vol. 31, pp. 211-56. Berkeley.

FORD, JAMES A.
    1938. "A Chronological Method Applicable to the Southeast." *American Antiquity*, Vol. 3, No. 3, pp. 260-4. Menasha.

FORD, JAMES A. AND GORDON R. WILLEY
    1949. "Surface Survey of the Viru Valley, Peru." *Anthropological Papers of the American Museum of Natural History*, Vol. 43, Pt. 1. New York.

GRIFFIN, JAMES B.
    1943. *The Fort Ancient Aspect.* University of Michigan Press. Ann Arbor.

KIDDER, A. V.
    1915. "Pottery of the Pajarito Plateau and of Some Adjacent Regions in New Mexico." *Memoirs, American Anthropological Association*, Vol. 2, Pt. 6, pp. 407-62. Menasha.

KIDDER, A. V. AND ANNA O. SHEPARD
    1936. *The Pottery of Pecos.* Vol. 2. Yale University Press. New Haven.

KIDDER, A. V., JESSE D. JENNINGS AND EDWIN M. SHOOK
    1946. "Excavations at Kaminaljuyu, Guatemala." *Carnegie Institution of Washington, Publication* 561. Washington.

KLUCKHOHN, CLYDE
    1939. "On Certain Recent Applications of Association Coefficients to Ethnological Data." *American Anthropologist*, Vol. 41, No. 3, pp. 345-77. Menasha.

KRIEGER, ALEX D.

1944. "The Typological Concept." *American Antiquity*, Vol. 9, No. 3, pp. 271-88. Menasha.

KROEBER, A. L.

1916. "Zuni Potsherds." *Anthropological Papers of the American Museum of Natural History*, Vol. 18, Pt. 1. New York.

1930. "Cultural Relations Between North and South America." *Proceedings of the 23rd International Congress of Americanists*, pp. 5-22. New York.

1940. "Statistical Classification." *American Antiquity*, Vol. 6, No. 1, pp. 29-44. Menasha.

NELSON, N. C.

1916. "Chronology of the Tano Ruins, New Mexico." *American Anthropologist*, n.s., Vol. 18, No. 2, pp. 159-80. Menasha.

OLSON, RONALD L.

1930. "Chumash Prehistory." *University of California Publications in American Archaeology and Ethnology*, Vol. 28, No. 1. Berkeley.

ROUSE, IRVING

1939. "Prehistory in Haiti, A Study in Method." *Yale University Publications in Anthropology*, No. 21. New Haven.

SPIER, LESLIE

1917. "An Outline for a Chronology of Zuni Ruins." *Anthropological Papers of the American Museum of Natural History*, Vol. 18, Pt. 3. New York.

STEWARD, JULIAN AND FRANK M. SETZLER

1938. "Function and Configuration in Archaeology." *American Antiquity*, Vol. 4, No. 1, pp. 4-10. Menasha.

TAYLOR, WALTER W.

1948. "A Study of Archaeology." *Memoirs, American Anthropological Association*, No. 69. Menasha.

Department of Anthropology and Sociology
University of California
Los Angeles, California

The Place of Chronological Ordering in Archaeological Analysis   *313*

Philip Phillips, James A. Ford, and James B. Griffin

CLASSIFICATION OF THE POTTERY

TYPOLOGY

SINCE practically everything in this report depends on the mass of potsherds collected at the expense of so much bending of backs, it becomes necessary to describe with candor the methods employed in their classification. Archaeology has not reached that stage of development in which there is only one correct way to do things, and, it is hoped, never will. What follows, therefore, is in no way intended as a treatise on the proper way to classify pottery, but merely a description of what was done by us and why — especially why. To say that the choice of methods of classification is governed by the nature of the material to be classified is a truism. But it is no less governed by the predilections and general attitudes of the classifier, and particularly by the ends which the classifier has in view. The extent to which classification may be a creative activity is perhaps not sufficiently recognized. Before embarking on a description of the actual methods of classification employed in the present study, we must therefore furnish a brief statement of our position in regard to the subject of cultural typology in general and pottery typology in particular.

The Concept of Type

In the study of archaeological materials there are, among others, two basically divergent interests: (1) interest in objects as expressions of the ideas and behavior of the people who made and used them; and (2) interest in objects as fossils for the determination of time and space relations. It cannot be maintained, of course, that these two interests are mutually exclusive, but it is an important fact that one's approach to problems of classification will depend very largely on which of them is being served. The first interest we may call, following Taylor,[1] cultural, as opposed to the second which is empirical, in the sense that the classifier is interested chiefly

in what he hopes to get out of it. He is content to work with fragmentary materials such as potsherds — in fact, prefers them because of their susceptibility to statistical treatment — since he is concerned primarily with the distribution of "cultures" in time and space, and only secondarily with the cultures so revealed. The resulting apparent indifference to "culture-context" has been characterized by Taylor as little short of criminal, and there is no question that studies rigorously conducted along these lines make unconscionably dull reading. Nevertheless, the most casual glance at the history of archaeology in any part of the world where it has progressed beyond the stage of antiquarianism will show their utility. Indeed, one might go further in suggesting that at certain stages in the development of archaeological knowledge they are indispensable. Until a certain amount of order has been achieved in respect to time-space relations on a regional scale, it may be questioned whether satisfactory cultural inferences can be drawn from any archaeological materials. We are in such an early stage of development in the Lower Mississippi Valley. The classification which is to be described in the following pages, is, in consequence, the outcome of a frankly, if not fanatically, empirical attitude toward the material.

It has become practically mandatory in putting typological studies into print to declare at the outset that classification is regarded therein purely as a "tool," fashioned to suit the material in hand and the kind of information one hopes to get out of it. Unfortunately, the phenomenon of inter-changeability of ends and means is not confined to political science. Also, there is magic in names. Once let a hatful of miserable fragments of fourth-rate pottery be dignified by a "Name," and there will follow inevitably the tendency for the name to become an entity, particularly in the mind of him who gives it. Go a step further and publish a description and the type embarks on

[1] Taylor, 1948, p. 114.

an independent existence of its own. At that point the classification ceases to be a "tool," and the archaeologist becomes one. This fate we shall endeavor, probably not successfully, to avoid in the pages to follow.

The "tool" that best seems to fit the present undertaking is the system of classification formally introduced into Southeastern archaeology at the Field Conference held at Birmingham, Alabama, in 1938. It is adopted here, not because of a belief in the necessity for a single standardized pottery classification in the Southeast — a classification with a capital C — but because it was the outgrowth of work on material similar to ours by students with the same general point of view as our own. This system is essentially the binomial classification of the Southwest, without any phylogenetic implications, and with important modifications arising from differences in the pottery to be classified. So far as we are aware, the underlying concepts and assumptions of this classification system, as applied to the Southeast, have not been explicitly stated, although the methodology has been described by Krieger.[2] As interpreted by the present writers, they run somewhat as follows:

It is first of all assumed that, after the introduction of pottery-making into the Southeast, a gradual shift of all ceramic features took place.[3] Techniques of manufacture, surface finish, shape, and decoration constantly, but slowly, changed. Such changes were no doubt partly the result of new ideas from outside the area — whatever mechanisms were responsible for the introduction of pottery-making in the first place may have brought increments to the original stock of ideas from time to time — but in the main, changes are assumed to have been internal, resulting from play on the potentialities of current forms and styles. Revolutionary inventions, in the popular sense of the word, probably occurred rarely if at all. In general, therefore, pottery styles at any given time and place may be assumed to have derived from those that went before; if not in that particular spot, then in another region with which there was contact.

Each community that had reached a certain level of sophistication in pottery-making will be found to have been maintaining side by side several different vessel styles. These are normally closely related, particularly in the matter of construction, paste, and surface finish, and seem to mark vessels made for different purposes or vessel ideas derived from different sources. If any one of these particular styles is examined at a single place and a single point in time, it will be seen that, while each vessel varies in minor detail, such variations tend to cluster about a norm. This norm represents the consensus of community opinion as to the correct features for this particular kind of vessel. Variations from the norm reflect the individual potter's interpretation of the prevailing styles, and the degree of variation tolerated is also culturally controlled. With the convenient hindsight of the archaeologist, we can divide such variations into two classes: those which were not followed by the rest of the community, and those that were. The latter are, of course, significant as the means by which ceramic development was accomplished.

In areas where the distribution of population was relatively stable, as seems to have been the case in most of the Southeast for long periods, ceramic development was general and in a crude sense surprisingly uniform. There was always a tendency, however, for particularly vigorous centers to impress their ideas on less enterprising neighbors. When a cross section of a large area is viewed at a given point in time, popularity centers will be seen for certain styles. Between these centers, styles vary and trend toward those of other centers in rough proportion to the distances involved, subject of course to ethnic distributions and geographic factors.

Thus, we have in mind the concept of a continuously evolving regional pottery tradition, showing a more or less parallel development in and around a number of centers, each of which employs a number of distinct but related styles, each style in turn being in process of change both areally and temporally.

---

[2] Krieger, 1944.
[3] The word "introduction" is used here in its widest possible sense. It is not intended to imply the assumption that there was only one introduction of pottery into the Southeast, or even to rule out the possibility of independent invention. We can produce as good an evolutionary series from stone pots to Arkansas head vases as has been done anywhere else.

With this remarkably unstable material, we set out to fashion a key to the prehistory of the region. Faced with this three-dimensional flow, which seldom if ever exhibits "natural" segregation, and being obliged to reduce it to some sort of manageable form, we arbitrarily cut it into units. Such *created units of the ceramic continuum* are called *pottery types*.

The importance of this concept of type in the present study justifies a certain amount of repetition. It can be illustrated in a crude

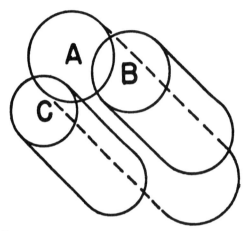

Fig. 5. Diagrammatic representation of the concept of pottery type.

diagrammatic form (fig. 5). Let the letter *A* represent a type and the circle around it, in purely abstract fashion, its limit of variability. That is to say, if an individual specimen does not fall within the range of variation represented by the circle, it does not conform to the type. We have already seen that variation and geographical range are closely related, so our circle represents, albeit crudely, the geographical range of the type as well. The circle thus describes the type two-dimensionally. To this, a third dimension, time, may be added by which our figure becomes a cylinder. The length of the cylinder represents the range of variability resulting from changes taking place in time. Several closely related and overlapping types — the most carefully defined types always overlap — can therefore be represented as above.

The length of the cylinders is shown as unequal because of the inevitable variation in

persistence of the peculiarities we have used to define the types. Actually, of course, these cylinders are a tremendous over-simplification. If it were possible to show it diagrammatically, they would be irregular in shape, expanding, contracting, branching, and coming together, so that no two horizontal cross sections would be the same. The figure is a hopelessly crude approximation to the facts, but it serves to illustrate the point of interest here, to wit, the arbitrariness of the whole typological procedure. The drawing of the circles is arbitrary and highly subjective — no two classifiers will draw precisely the same circle — the cutting-off of the cylinders is equally so. It is scarcely necessary to draw attention to the additional difficulty of determining whether a given variation is the result of spatial or temporal factors. If this is anything like a true picture of what a pottery type is, can anyone seriously ask whether it corresponds to a "natural" or cultural reality?

Whether, among the primitive communities of the Mississippi Alluvial Valley, groups or classes of pottery were recognized, and whether such entities, if we may speak of them as such, were conceptualized in terms anything like those with which we define a pottery type, are intriguing and by no means unimportant questions. We need not go into them here, however, because by reason of the very nature of the material to be classified the possibility that our and their conception of a given type might coincide is so remote as to be negligible. These are questions that can scarcely arise in the initial stages of a comprehensive pottery survey. Before leaving the subject, however, let us make it clear that, although the empirical typology here described — "working" typology as Krieger perhaps would call it — cannot be expected to show any strong relationship to cultural "reality," it does not follow that such relationship is precluded now and forever. To a certain extent, the characters we select as criteria for type definition, however dictated by expediency, not to say necessity, are bound to correspond to characters that might have served to distinguish one sort of pottery from another in the minds of the people who made and used it. We should, of course, make every possible effort to increase this correspondence. In course of time, with increased information in respect to vessel shapes and over-all patterns of design — let us not forget that we are classifying vessels, though we have for most types only sherds to do it with — our types will be redefined in ever closer approximation to cultural "realities." In short, an eventual synthesis is possible between the seemingly antithetical attitudes loosely characterized above as "empirical" and "cultural," in which the product of classification, the pottery type, will finally achieve cultural meaning. The limits of the variability of the type will then no longer be wholly arbitrary decisions of the classifier, as is now the case, but will bear some correspondence to ethnographic distributions in time and space. On this hopeful note, let us conclude this brief introduction to the problems that beset those who set out to measure and relate, by means of wretched bits of fired clay, cultural phenomena of which there are as yet no other records.

The Concepts of "Pottery Complex" and "Series"

As already remarked, in cultures of the level reached by the pottery-making Indians of the Southeast, a given site, or level in a site, will show several discrete pottery types, each of which may have a separate history. It is convenient to refer to such a group of types as a "complex." This pottery complex in a given situation is usually described in terms of percentages of the several component types and, where so described, gives a very useful measure for comparison with other cultural situations. A further step is sometimes made in which all or several of the component types of a complex are given the same site designation and the group referred to as a "series." Thus, the types Alexander Incised, Alexander Pinched, and Alexander Dentate Stamped are members, along with O'Neal Plain and Smithsonia Zoned Stamped, of the well-known "Alexander Series" in northern Alabama. However tempting from the standpoint of simplicity, we are not using the device in the present work. As Krieger has pointed out,

such linkage of types is a further step in th. typological process.[4] Furthermore, when becomes clear that related types have the sam. distribution in time and space, it may be preferable to lump them together as a single typ whereupon the concept of "series" become superfluous. Until such a time, their separate identities have to be maintained, and it is perhaps less confusing in the long run to keep th names distinct as well. It is hardly necessar to add that, in our view, neither "complex" nor "series" are classificatory terms in th sense that they represent an order, more inclusive than type, in a taxonomic system. The fact that they do tend to acquire such a meaning is an additional reason, in our view, fo. avoiding their use, except in a context tha leaves no room for ambiguity. When, therefore, in the following pages, we find it convenient to speak of a pottery complex it wil! be understood to refer only to a given archaeological situation, and the term "series" wil! be, so far as possible, avoided.[4a]

The Binomial System of Type Nomenclature

The above-described methodological freedom, however, does not by any means eliminate any of the difficulties or responsibilities of the classifier. As already pointed out, the norm of style, which we measure by means of pottery types, shifts both areally and chronologically in a manner so gradual that we are hard put to say at what point in either dimension one type leaves off and another begins. But this is not all. The separate characters of paste, surface, form, and decoration change also in time and space, and not all at the same rate. Each separate character has its own history and each history will provide a more or less sensitive register for the history of the culture as a whole. Now it would be unreasonable to hold that one character is unfailingly more important than another, or to insist that all pottery be classified on the basis of uniformly selected characters. It does, however, lessen the initial confusion to select

[4] Krieger, 1944, fig. 25.
[4a] Ford objects to this usage of the term "series" on the grounds of poor English. "1. A number of things or events standing or succeeding in order, and connected by a like relation; sequence; order; counsel; a succession of things; as, a *series* of calamities or triumphs." (Webster's New International Dictionary.)

the most sensitive — and at the same time most recognizable — characters as guides or "constants" in the process of classification. In Southeastern pottery generally, these are features of surface treatment and decoration, and thus it has come about that what may for convenience be called the Southeastern classification employs a binomial system of nomenclature in which the second term or "constant" is descriptive of surface treatment or decoration, as in Mulberry Creek *Cord-marked* or Indian Bay *Stamped*.

It may be asked why characters of shape are not regarded as equally sensitive and equally suggestive of culture change. The answer is found in our original point of departure and its paramount interest in sherds rather than vessels, and more objectively, perhaps, in the fact that except in the very latest periods the Southeastern potters had not reached an advanced stage of refinement in vessel form. Features of shape, particularly rim and lip modifications, have sometimes proved useful in sorting the present material, but it has not been found expedient to use them as constants in classification. All types set up by the Survey, therefore, are defined in the present work according to the Southeastern procedure.

By so doing, we shall have lessened but by no means removed the main typological difficulty. Type "A" let us suppose has been defined on the basis of what appears to be the "norm" at what appears to be a "center." We may as well admit that these "centers" are often only such because they first attracted our attention, or because of our ignorance of the intervening spaces. As we go away from that center in space — the same thing happens in time, but we may leave that unpleasant fact aside for the moment — the characters that we have selected as determinants for the type gradually shift, the all-too familiar phenomenon of "creep," until at some point we can stretch our original type definition no further and have to consider whether material "X" more closely resembles Type "B," already established at another center, or whether it is not sufficiently like either "A" or "B" and must be given an independent status as Type "C." These wretched hair-line decisions beset the classifier at every step. The only helpful principle the writers have been able to find is one of the sheerest empiricism — ability to sort. Rigorous application of this principle results in some rather startling distributions. For example, we were unable to distinguish certain clay-tempered, cord-marked sherds found in our area from the type Mulberry Creek Cord-marked, originally set up in the Pickwick Basin on the Tennessee River several hundred miles away. Candor compels the admission that we could not sort it from what was then called Deasonville Cord-marked in southern Mississippi and Louisiana either. If Mulberry Creek Cord-marked and Deasonville Cord-marked could be separated, as implied in the fact that they were set up as distinct types, our material obviously could not be both, so an arbitrary decision had to be made. We first encountered the pottery in the northern part of the Survey Area where it more closely approximates Mulberry Creek Cord-marked. If we had encountered it first in the south, we undoubtedly would have been struck by its resemblance to Deasonville Cord-marked. Our solution was to call it Mulberry Creek and quietly liquidate Deasonville. From this sort of dilemma there is no escape, but its effects can be minimized by more knowledge of the pottery and sharper definition of types.

It may be surmised from the above that much depends on the sort of constants by which types are defined. The "creep" of types in time or space is by no means uniform. A generalized surface treatment like cord-marking, for example, will extend farther without sortable change than a type based on a specialized scheme of decoration; a plain undecorated type may go farther than either. So far as possible, an attempt should be made to reduce these inequalities by careful choice and definition of constants. On the other hand, bearing in mind that classification is only a means to an end, the classifier will choose the sort of constants that he thinks are likely to turn out to be culturally and historically significant. Finally, let it not be overlooked in the glow of these fine thoughts that in the initial stages of classification one seizes upon *any* feature that will serve to distinguish one group of sherds from another.

Having, so to speak, walked around the pottery type as understood here, and examined some of the more obvious aspects of its anatomy, we may conclude by admitting that the practical necessities of the situation have virtually destroyed it as a concept in any *a priori* sense. We are left with — and this is as much of a definition as will be found in the present work — a named abstraction, representing a combination of selected characters, susceptible of recognition from sherds alone. An artificial, albeit useful, creation of the classifier, the pottery type has at this stage of being little, if any, correspondent cultural "reality," present or past. Exigencies of language require us to think and talk about pottery types as though they had some sort of independent existence. "This sherd *is* Baytown Plain." Upon sufficient repetition of this statement, the concept Baytown Plain takes on a massive solidity. The time comes when we are ready to fight for dear old Baytown. What we have to try to remember is that the statement really means something like this: "This sherd sufficiently resembles material which *for the time being* we have elected to call Baytown Plain." Frequent repetition of this and similar exorcisms we have found to be extremely salutary during the classificatory activities described below.

Methods of Sorting

The 1940 season's material, consisting of surface collections only, from 149 sites, mainly in the Lower Arkansas River Lowland and St. Francis River Basin, was shipped to Baton Rouge for cataloguing, and there sorted by the writers at the conclusion of the field season. This preliminary sorting was done in the time-honored way, that is, by piling the whole mass of sherds into one terrifying heap, and sorting them as many ways as possible. The experience in other Southeastern areas prompted the use of tempering differences as a primary breakdown,[5] and the result was that we ended up with 47 types loosely grouped into three temper groups: shell, clay, and sand. Fiber-tempering did not occur in the first season's collections. The "constants" selected were in the categories of surface finish

and decoration. Under the latter, technique of decoration was relied on more than design, as is necessary when sorting surface material, on account of the small size of the sherds. It should be pointed out that these 47 types were not all "new." Eight of them had been previously named and described in the Lower Mississippi Valley, and two were among the types set up in the Pickwick Basin in northern Alabama. After sorting, the material was broken up into the original site collections, counted, and tabulated. Some preliminary graphic analysis, of the sort described in a later section, was carried on by Ford, so that in going back into the field in the following spring, we had a fair idea of the probable chronological relationships of our provisional types, which was a great help, particularly in the selection of sites for stratigraphic testing.

The second and third season's material, mainly from the Yazoo Basin, was handled differently. Site collections and stratigraphic material were kept intact. By this time, we felt we had a classification and that it was therefore unnecessary to throw all the pottery together, as was done the previous year. Now, this raises a question pertinent to the discussion of typological theory just completed. There is no question that, had we sorted this Yazoo Basin material afresh, forgetting as far as possible, our existing typology, we would have come out with a classification quite different from that presented here. Not that the list of types would have differed so much, but the types themselves would have been differently defined. The norms in the Yazoo Basin are not the same as in the St. Francis Basin. Throughout all our description and discussion of types, we are constantly being reminded of the "set" that was given to our typology by the fact that it was largely determined by the first season's work. In spite of all efforts, our type definitions in many cases really apply to the St. Francis Basin pottery. We have not been able to rid our minds entirely of the notion that corresponding type material in the Yazoo Basin is deviant if not atypical. Another interesting result is that we tend to see a culture divide or "frontier" about the latitude of

---

[5] So far as we are aware, the first use of tempering differences as a primary ceramic breakdown in the

Southeast was in Griffin's study of the pottery of the Wheeler Basin in Webb, 1939.

the mouth of the Arkansas River, because it is here that the type definitions set up in the St. Francis begin to reach their limit of applicability; the types begin to lose their outlines. The fact is very neatly expressed in the increased percentages in the "unclassified" column of site tabulations south of this point. We have to be on guard against such appearances. Getting back to the point at issue, it seems now in retrospect that it would have been worth the extra effort to have piled all three season's collections together, and all subsequent material for that matter, and made a final grand sorting. However, our present purpose is to describe what we did, not what might have been done.

Sorting and analysis of the 1941 collection was interrupted by the war. When the work was resumed in 1946 the situation was as follows: The 1940 collections had been broken up. Approximately a third of the material was still in Baton Rouge. The remainder had been sorted at least once by one or more of the present writers, but it was felt that a new sorting by one of us was required not to eliminate the personal equation, which cannot be done, but to standardize the errors resulting therefrom, and accordingly all the material, to which was subsequently added the collections of 1946 and 1947, was assembled at the Peabody Museum. This was another opportunity to throw it together, but it was sorted by sites as before. In the process, a number of changes were made in the previous classification, several new types being set up to take care of the material in the southern part of the Yazoo Basin. At the same time a number of earlier types were abandoned. As each site collection was sorted, the types were segregated in small boxes and filed away by sites in cupboards where they were readily available for further study. Body sherds of the more common types were counted and put away in dead storage, and the counts entered in a dead-storage file. The material was thus in excellent shape for final analysis. This was done type by type in the following manner. All the rims and bases (in types that have bases) — or in the case of the numerically smaller types, all the sherds — were spread out on long tables in geographical order from north to south. Data sheets

listing the occurrence by site of all measurable and observable features were prepared. Direct observation, backed up by these data sheets gave an excellent idea of the nature and extent of the variations of the type in its geographical range. "Centers" for the type, and for particular features within the type, were readily apparent. The gradual shift of the type away from these centers was clearly seen again and again. In some cases, this shift became so great as to require an arbitrary decision — thus far and no farther — and the creation of a new type. While the material was in this convenient form, quantitative distribution maps were made, which proved to be very useful in further delimiting the types.

At this point, it may be well to make another confession. What Hooton used to call the "fierce typologist" does not compromise with space or time. If two things look alike, he puts them together regardless. So, in theory, do we. But it sometimes happens otherwise in practice. When confronted with one of the innumerable hair-line decisions one has to make in sorting, it may be that the mere location of the site from which the sherd comes, or its chronological position, if it comes from an excavation, is sufficient to throw it one way or another. We have not scrupled to use such adventitious aids to sorting from time to time.

With the material still spread out on the tables and the data sheets as a control, a preliminary type description was written on the spot. Now to write a close description of a type represented by collections from several hundred sites covering a range of 200 to 300 miles, to say nothing of a considerable stretch of time, is not easy. There is an irresistible tendency to orient your description around what seems to be the "central" material of the type, and to describe the variations in terms of this assumed "center." It is hardly necessary to point out again that a center may be nothing more than the place where one happened to get the most material. It is also very apt to coincide with the place where one first set up the type. Pottery descriptions have always to be read with this in mind. Ours are only exceptional in that we admit it.

The last act before putting away one type and getting out another was to select a number of specimens for the type collection, and these were also inventoried by site in a card-index file. A further distillation from these was made for the photographs in this report.

Upon completion of the analysis, there remained a considerable residue of unclassified material. This was also spread out on the tables and sorted carefully for possible new types. Actually, none were found, which was reassuring in a way, as an indication that our classification was sufficiently thorough, for the present at least. Several tentative types were set up, and these are described in this section under the heading "Provisional Types." It was felt that these would no doubt attain the status of types with more material, so they are useful in pointing to areas for further investigation.

There remained only the final unexciting task of counting and tabulating on printed site inventory sheets to which were added the counts from the dead-storage and type-collection files. Totals and percentages were then calculated, and we were finally in a position to begin to get some returns on our investment.

*   *   *   *   *

Assumptions

NOW the 346,099 sherds from 383 sites, collected by the Lower Mississippi Survey and duly classified as described in Section III, could be stored away in cabinets and forgotten for the time being. The data was safely on paper and time would heal our wounded consciences and dim our suspicions that at several points our classification was less than perfect. During the winter of 1947 Phillips turned to the problems of physiography, and the identification of historic sites; Griffin began the description of pottery types; and Ford started work on analysis, assisted and checked at every point by his somewhat fearful colleagues.

The basic assumptions which served as a foundation for the analytical procedure need to be stated in some detail. They will help to explain the procedure followed and it is hoped will prevent the reader from accepting the conclusions in an any more "positive" sense than the writers intend. We consider these assumptions as a set of probabilities which lead to conclusions that are our best guesses. Not that we intend to apologize for this admission. This we think is the real method of science. We are trying to expose our limitations and are not setting out to *prove* anything beyond all doubt.

A. In the portion of the Mississippi Valley which was surveyed and for the greater part of the span of history which is being studied, the aboriginal people were presumably agriculturists. The population was rather numerous, as will be shown later, and was collected in small villages. For these reasons it seems reasonable to think that there was comparative stability of peoples. These Indians did not wander as did the historic Indians of the Plains and, from the archaeological evidence, there seems to have been little or none of the frantic shifting of tribes that marks the post-contact history of the Eastern Indians. We are assuming then until the evidence indicates the contrary that

the people who carried the cultural traits we are studying were probably relatively stable geographically and that for the most part population changes were slow gradual ones.

B. While the prehistoric populations were comparatively stable in the larger geographic sense, this does not appear to have been true of the great majority of village sites. Some sites were inhabited throughout the time span which is being studied. Most, however, were occupied for a short time in proportion to the entire chronology. This assumption was based on archaeological experience in other parts of the Southeast and on a preliminary glance over the collections gathered in this Survey. The condition seems to be due to the limitations of the agricultural methods and equipment of the Indians. After a field had been cleared and used for crops for a few years, the grass and weeds probably moved in and took over. With the inefficient tools which the Southeastern Indians had, control of this vegetation very likely became so difficult after a few years that it was easier to ring and burn trees for a new field than it was to continue planting in the old one. In the course of a few decades, when all the desirable agricultural land in the vicinity of a village had been opened up to weeds in this fashion, the village would have to be moved to a new location.[1] This was the practice of the Southeastern tribes in the early Historic Period before they acquired plows, and such names as "Chickasaw Old Fields" and "Tuckabachee Old Fields" undoubtedly refer to such weed-grown abandoned land.

The securing of short time-span collections is essential if the method of seriating of surface collections is to be successfully applied. For this reason, careful attention was paid to the combinations of sherd material which were gathered from various parts of each village site. In the course of field work, where it was evident that one portion of a site yielded a different complex from that found on another part, two or more separate collections

[1] Linton, 1940, pp. 37-40.

219

were made. These were labeled "A," "B," etc., and were treated all through the course of analysis as though they came from different sites. A cross section of the ceramic styles in vogue at these different sites at one instant in time would have been the ideal material for seriation purposes, but that, of course, is an unattainable goal.

C. The third assumption has already been stated in the foregoing section on ceramic classification. Until the evidence suggests differently, we are assuming that in any large area cultural continuity in both time and space is to be expected as the normal state of affairs. A gradual change of feature with the passage of time and across the area, when it is viewed on any one time horizon, was our very idealized concept of the cultural history with which we are dealing. This does not mean that we did not anticipate the possibility of finding evidence of (1) the replacement of one population bearing a certain variety of culture by another population having entirely different customs; (2) the replacement of cultural features through acculturation from sources outside the region in which we are working; or (3) the specializing of cultural complexes in certain regions due to their being protected from the prevailing patterns of the area as a whole by such factors as geographical isolation, peculiarities of population distribution, linguistic barriers, or political groupings. These conditions were some of the things of which we expected to get hints from our study.

So we did not begin our analysis with any assumption that changes in ceramics, such as the shift from clay- to shell-tempering, necessarily indicate any abrupt cultural or population replacement. If the refuse deposits of the two time periods really should have a layer of clean white sand separating them after the classic model of stratigraphy, we wanted to be shown by the evidence.

D. Our fourth basic assumption has also been stated in the discussion of ceramic typology. We are assuming that each of our pottery types is a more or less sensitive instrument for measuring cultural change with the passage of time and distribution over space. We are a little complacent about this assumption and

[1a] Spier, 1917.

feel that we are on fairly certain grounds because we went to great pains to set up and adapt each type for exactly those purposes. Rearranging, merging, and splitting of type groups were guided by preliminary analysis and the resultant information about chronological relations.

However, as has been made clear in the type descriptions, all of the types are not equally well adapted for this purpose. Because of the practical difficulties of making distinctions, some of the types, especially the undecorated ones, include material that represents long spans of time and large amounts of area. In other examples we are aware that the original concepts have changed during the classifying so that the resultant categories are somewhat broader than would have been desired. Mazique Incised is an example of this latter kind of type weakness. Despite this, we feel that we are fairly aware of this factor and thus have it under reasonable control.

E. The next point to be considered is not a basic assumption but rather a logical derivative of the preceding discussions. It has to do with the relative popularity of types through time. If our pottery types are successful measuring units for a continuous stream of changing cultural ideas, it follows that when the relative popularity of these types is graphed through time, a more or less long, single-peak curve will usually result. Put in another way, a type will first appear in very small percentages, will gradually increase to its maximum popularity, and then, as it is replaced by its succeeding type, will gradually decrease and disappear.

This interesting phenomena can be illustrated by endless examples taken from any span of culture history. Consider the popularity curve of the "Charleston" dance fad in the United States. A specific political concept, a particular word, or any other carefully defined cultural type will show the same popularity curve that Spier found in the history of Zuñi pottery.[1a]

This is an interesting phenomenon but do not let us be misled. We have not discovered a natural law operating independently of our own humble efforts. This peculiar characteristic of type popularity distribution through time is something we have helped to bring about through our own conceptualization of the pottery types that manifest said behavior. How the curves come out is partly controlled by how the types are defined.

F. The sixth assumption is also a derivative of the foregoing discussions. If a complex of cultural materials representing a space-time continuum of culture history is classified in a consistent manner, the popularity curves of the various constituent types will form a pattern. Each portion of this pattern will be peculiar to a particular time and area. This concept may best be illustrated from contemporary culture. Lacking accurate data, as this sort of information is usually ignored by historians, let us manufacture some for purposes of illustration.[2] Let us say that in the State of Ohio in the year 1920, the following were the relative popularities of the indicated types of travel for distances over 5 miles:

	PER CENT
Walking	5
Riding horses	5
Horse and buggy	15
Gasoline-powered boats	5
Steamboats	5
Automobiles	20
Airplanes	2
Railways	43

Here is a ratio of popularity of transportation types which will never be exactly repeated in Ohio or anywhere else.

Now let us take a look at a supposed history of the relative popularity of transportation types in Ohio for a period extending sometime before and after 1920. This we have graphed in figure 15.[3] Not only is the pattern different for each ten-year interval, but the quantitative picture of this stretch of culture history is a unique thing. The pattern of the popularity peaks of the different transportation types have never been repeated. A simi-

lar graph for Texas would doubtless show larger popularity of horse-riding. There wouldn't have been any steamboat travel at all in Utah. Indiana would show the same type as Ohio but in differing quantities and temporal relations.

So long as we maintain our classifications strictly as they are, we may review any number of representative samples of Ohio transportation history, and the same frequency pattern will result. The only way in which the pattern might be changed would be to change the classification. This can be done in a number of different ways. Let us show a few:

1. Travel without vehicles
   Vehicles that travel on land
   Vehicles that travel on water
   Vehicles that travel in air

2. Man-powered travel
   Animal-powered travel
   Steam-powered travel
   Gasoline-powered travel
   Electric-powered travel

3. Travel 0–5 miles an hour
   Travel 5–10 miles on hour
   etc.

Note that in each case where the classification is rearranged, the quantitative-historical picture would be completely different. This is not to say that it would be any more true or false than the scheme which we have illustrated in figure 15. All of these classifications will measure time change in a cultural feature. The point of interest to the classifier is that the first scheme with the finer type divisions will do the job a little more accurately than the others. Still finer divisions which will do even better jobs will occur to the reader.

While this fanciful illustration is set up, let us go a little farther and show how the dating and seriation techniques that will be discussed later will work. Suppose that we

[2] Historical statistical data about manufacturing, trade, etc., will give this kind of information. However, it is easier to make up our illustration than to dig it out of the census

[3] Here we have used the type of diagram which will often reoccur in this study, so we might as well explain it now. The passage of time is always represented by proceeding from the bottom to the top of

the figure. Each cultural type is assigned a vertical "axis," or imaginary line, which is indicated at both top and bottom of the figure. The relative popularity of the type is shown by the length of the horizontal bars that center on the type axis. This may be measured by means of the percentage scale given in the figure. Try it for the year 1920 and see if the graph agrees with the tabulation given above.

have a sample of the transportation habits of the Ohioans for an unknown date which showed the following percentages of popularity:

	PER CENT
Walking	5
Riding horses	12
Horse and buggy	28
Paddling and rowing boats	1
Steamboats	12
Automobiles	0
Airplanes	0
Railway	40

with frequency data on the transportation customs of Ohio for a number of years. We do not know the dates of these samples and have no idea as to their chronological sequence. We can't get a complete history out of this data but we can do something. By rearranging our samples, we can find the type frequency pattern and the relative order of the samples. We will not know the calendrical dates of the samples, the relative lengths of time occupied by the various sections of the chronology, or even which end of the chronology is the most recent in time, but we can develop the quan-

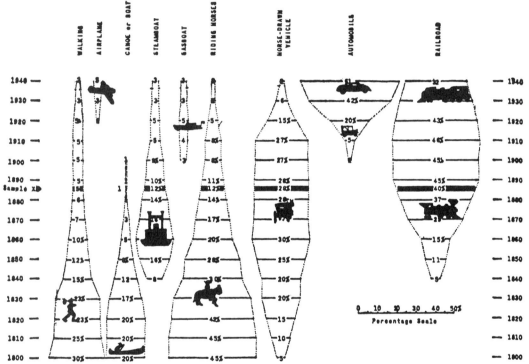

Fig. 15. Theoretical percentage frequency graph of transportation types in Ohio from A.D. 1800 to 1940.

When this information is graphed after the fashion used in figure 15, and the graph is placed on this chronology, it will be seen that the type frequencies of this sample, which we may as well call "X," will fit the chronology at only one point. As our figure shows, it dates about 1885.

Let us suppose again that we are faced with a situation in which we are merely provided

titative-historical pattern. This, in effect, is the seriation technique we have used.

This rather far-fetched bit of imaginary analysis is only worth-while if it brings out the point that systematic classification of cultural data representing a particular range of time creates in each case a characteristic quantitative pattern. We had this in mind as our sherds from the Mississippi Valley area were classified, and the analytical procedure that will be described were the steps which were taken in search of these patterns.

G. Two more assumptions which we have made may be grouped together. We have assumed that our sampling of sites in each part of our Survey Area has been sufficiently thorough. We think that we have secured a sample of the pottery which was made during each stage of the chronologies which we will present so that no large time gaps remain unrepresented.

We are also guessing that a random sample of over fifty sherds is sufficient to indicate the proportionate type frequencies existing in the refuse from which the material was collected. A total of fifty is considered to be usable, but not particularly reliable. One hundred is much better and every sherd above one hundred is all to the good.[4] It will be noted that some of our collections are quite large.

The foregoing assumptions which we made at the start of the analytical work, and which we intended to act upon until the evidence indicated that they were wrong, may be summarized as follows:

A. The distribution of prehistoric populations of the Survey Area was relatively stable.

B. The majority of the village sites were probably inhabited for a short time as compared to the entire time with which we are dealing.

C. The culture of the area in the main probably changed gradually rather than by means of mass migration from other areas.

D. If propositions A and C were true, the pottery types which we had defined would each show a single-peak popularity curve when measured through time, but the duration of such peaks, and the resulting curves, would vary from one type to another.

E. If D is true, then all the pottery-type frequency curves would be different in each part of the area on each time horizon, and a distinct pattern will appear when each part of the area is viewed through time.

F. Our sampling technique has been successful in getting samples representing continuous segments of time in all parts of the area

and also in securing enough material from the sites which we will treat to give a more or less reliable picture of the material available on the surface.

Analytical Procedure

The first step in our ceramic analysis was a simple and tedious one. On the sheets which recorded the classification of the material from each collection, the totals of these collections were run up on an adding machine, and the percentages of each type calculated by slide rule. The "Unclassified" sherds were included in these totals. This was done for all surface collections which contained more than fifty sherds, as well as for each level in the stratigraphic excavations.

Then a roll of graph paper marked with a centimeter-millimeter grid was secured. On a piece of this paper a "key" was prepared very carefully. This key indicated the position of the axis of each type from which bars showing the relative frequency of the types were to be drawn. The best spacing of the types along the key was something that had to be developed in the course of the analysis to prevent overlapping of the frequency bars. The arrangement was changed several times, and its final form is as given at the tops and bottoms of figures 17–21.

After the first key was worked out, the type frequency data for each collection was placed on a 5-centimeter-wide strip graph. This second step was also a routine mechanical matter and took some time to accomplish, particularly as this work several times pointed out defects in the positions of the types on the key. When the key was changed, all strip graphs made with the old key had to be discarded. Finally, however, all of the classification data was in this graphic form.

While this work was underway, the classification data was being analysed in another way by several student assistants[5] at the American Museum. This was a distributional study of type frequencies. For each type a sheet of tracing cloth was placed over a map showing all site locations. Then, the percentage frequency of the type at each site, say

[4] For a brief discussion of quantitative reliability of collections, see Ford, 1936, pp. 13-14.

[5] Miss Margaret Rose, Miss Eileen Boecklen, and Mr. Gary Vesalius.

Mulberry Creek Cord-marked for example, was recorded in its proper geographical position on the traced map. Now, if the above-discussed assumptions are correct, that the average village site was inhabited for a relatively short period (see assumption B, above), and that our Survey work has gathered a sample of the material from sites representing each time period in all parts of the area (F, above), then in each part of the Survey Area there should be sites which show Mulberry Creek Cord-marked near or at its popularity peak. Other sites, which cover time ranges before or after the maximum popularity of the type, will, of course, show their occurrence in smaller percentages. With all of this in mind, the completed distribution maps of Mulberry Creek Cord-marked were inspected with particular attention to maximum occurrences. It was seen that it would be possible to draw lines which would enclose maximums in descending order, after the fashion of contour lines (see figs. 6–14). If we wished to coin a new word and help our science to become more profound, we might call these "Iso-ceramic Lines" — but let's not.

These distributional studies made plain something which we knew already from classifying the material: there would be both quantitative and qualitative variation at all time periods in the different parts of the Survey Area. They also showed something else which we had suspected would be true. Regional specialization tended to increase with the passage of time so that late complexes from the northern and southern ends of our Survey were more unlike than were the early. This is a common phenomenon for cultures at this stage of development and seems to be owing to factors such as decreased population mobility due to an increased dependence on agriculture; the establishment of more stable centers, such as ceremonial mound groups and towns; and an increase in the cohesion of political groupings made possible and necessitated by the improved food supply and consequent population increase; to which was added the increased availability of cultural ideas which could be combined to form "new" varieties.

With this data in hand, it was decided that the practical way in which to treat the chron-ology of the Survey Area would be to divide it up into sub-areas based on the differences that could be observed in the material of the latest time horizons. A chronological column could then be worked out for each sub-area and comparisons between the areas could be made at the different time levels. We realized that the procedure which we were adopting was fully as arbitrary, and indeed was of the same kind of high-handed ruthlessness as were our decisions in regard to ceramic classification. We are again preparing to set up artificial boundaries, which this time are geographically defined, and draw the borderline cases back toward the selected concepts.

From the beginning, the Lower St. Francis River area in Arkansas looked like a "natural" for a "Focal Grouping." Here are a number of highly similar sites, already known in archaeological literature (Parkin, Rose Mound, etc.), that seemed to stand off by themselves. This happy condition was improved by the fact that Survey work was not extended very far up the St. Francis River above these sites, so we were ignorant of any gradual transition toward any different-appearing complex in that direction. All the arbitrary decisions which would trouble us lay to the south and east. Ignorance and a classical tradition; it couldn't be better. We immediately set up a Lower St. Francis area and accepted the sites in quadrangles 11–N and 12–N as appropriate for starting chronological analysis.

The second area also looked good. Its literary background is provided by Calvin Brown's description of the material from the Walls Site [6] near Memphis. The material from this and a number of closely related sites differed in a number of respects from the typical St. Francis area complex, as we have abundantly shown in Section IV. That this distinction proved to be partly due to difference in time does not lessen the initial lure of the situation. A *Memphis area* was definied and the sites included in quadrangles 13–O, 13–P, 14–O, and 14–P were taken as nuclear for starting the analysis.

We had a little more difficulty about the other three areas which were eventually set up. The literary background did not focus our attention so effectively, and we knew a

---

[6] Brown, 1926, pp. 288–319.

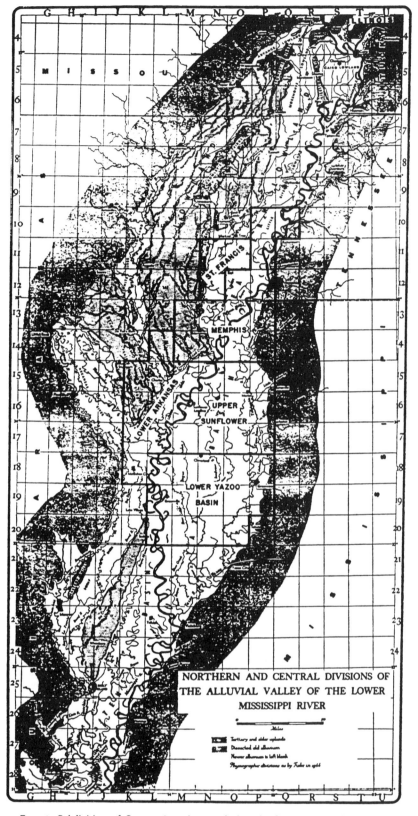

Fig. 16. Subdivision of Survey Area into analysis units for purposes of seriation.

Philip Phillips et al.

little too much about "transitional" sites and material. After several false starts the following areas and beginning quadrangles were selected (fig. 16):

St. Francis Basin 11–N, 12–N
Memphis area 13–O, 13–P, 14–O, 14–P
Sunflower area 16–N, 16–O, 17–N, 17–O
Lower Yazoo Basin area . 19–M, 19–N, 20–M, 20–N
Lower Arkansas River area . 16–K, 16–L, 17–K, 17–L

It must be emphasized again that these areas have been set up solely for purposes of seriation and are therefore not to be confused with "foci" in the Midwestern taxonomic sense, or any other sort of cultural grouping.

It will be seen that the starting quadrangles for each area are geographically separated from the starting quadrangles of the other areas. This was intentional and was for the purpose of emphasizing the differences. The borderline cases were dealt with later as will be described.

By the time the study had reached this stage, we already had at hand considerable information as to the outlines of the ceramic chronologies in the region. One source of information was the sequences which had been worked out in the adjoining regions by Webb and his associates in northern Alabama;[7] Jennings along the Natchez Trace Parkway in north-central Mississippi;[8] Ford and his co-workers around the mouth of the Red River in Louisiana. A second very essential source of information were the stratigraphic excavations made by Phillips and Griffin, described in detail in a later section of this report. These revealed portions of the ceramic histories which could be used as partial backbone for the area chronologies. Our third source of information was the preliminary seriation analyses which we had made while classifying the site collections. So we had a rather good idea as to the relative time positions and distributions of many of the ceramic types. Despite this, the analytical procedures described here were followed out in detail, so far as possible, as though we had been completely innocent of such fore-knowledge.

Five sheets of heavy paper about 48 inches long and 20 inches wide were laid out on a large table side by side. The 20-inch width

of these sheets corresponded to the length of the strip graphs which recorded the type frequencies of each collection. Each of these sheets was headed with the name of one of the seriation areas, and they were placed on the table in the geographical relation of the areas from north to south. Then all of the strip graphs that represented collections from sites included in the quadrangles that served as the nucleus, or starting point, were separated out and placed on the appropriate sheet. The strips were laid horizontally across the sheets and were held in place at the edges by paper clips. As they were arranged and rearranged, particular care was taken to see that the type axes coincided.

We were now ready to begin the search for the quantitative patterning of pottery types, which for reasons that have been discussed in the foregoing, should exist in the area chronologies. This work was started with site collections of the Lower Yazoo Basin area (see fig. 17). These were relatively easy to seriate as two stratigraphic excavations were available to serve as guides for part of the history. The deepest of these excavations, Jaketown (20–O–1) Cut A, had fourteen levels and seemed to cover the greatest range of time. Accordingly, the strip graphs representing these levels were arranged on the sheet in the order in which they had come from the ground and immediately showed the frequency patterning for the time covered by the cut. The strips representing the second strata excavation, Shell Bluff (19–O–2) Cut A, were next put in place. The graph of the top level of this cut was slid along the sheet of paper until a point was found at which all its type frequencies best fitted the corresponding frequencies of the Jaketown cut. It was clear that the second level at Shell Bluff was older than the top level, but we could not know how much older it was in relation to the picture given by the Jaketown cut. Consequently, the second-level graph was placed below the first and slid downward until the best fit was secured.

Vertical arrangement of the material in the ground gave some control over the collections from the stratigraphic pits, and we knew that the collections from the lower levels had to

[7] Webb and DeJarnette, 1942.

[8] Jennings, 1941.

be older than those from the upper. However, for the surface collections we had no such guide. All we had was our assumption that the majority of these surface collections represented relatively short spans of time (see B, above) and the logic which led us to think that a quantitative patterning must be there.

The surface-collection graphs were taken one at a time and compared to the beginning that had been made with the stratigraphic material. If they fitted somewhere along the time represented by the excavations, the graph was fastened down to the backing sheet with paper clips. If percentages of such late types as Neeley's Ferry Plain and Bell Plain were too large, and proportions of such older types as Baytown Plain, Larto Red Filmed, and Mulberry Creek Cord-marked were too small, the collection was obviously later and the graph was placed above the excavations. These surface-collection graphs were shifted about in vertical relation to one another until patterning was developed as is shown in the upper part of figure 17.

The data from the starting quadrangles of the other four seriation areas were dealt with in a similar fashion, figures 17–21. Where stratigraphic information was available, it was used as a guide. Where there was none, the surface-collection graphs were shifted about to develop the best patterning that could be secured. In this way the five chronological columns were developed side by side.

The next phase of the analysis was to assign the sites in the intervening quadrangles to one or another of the five areas which had been set up. All of the site-collection graphs for each of these remaining quadrangles were seriated and then compared to the five area graphs. For example, the chronological patterning of quadrangle 18–M looked more like the chron-

ology begun for the Lower Yazoo area than any of the other sub-areas, so the collections from this quadrangle were fed into the Yazoo graph at the points where they fitted best.

Now, the area chronological graphs were virtually complete and good patterning of types could be seen. Apparently, our assumption that most of the surface collections represented relatively short lengths of time was correct. But while the majority did, some obviously did not. In a number of collections, early and late types were associated together in a fashion that showed either that the sites had been occupied for a long time, or there had been reoccupation. In order to clear up the patterning, the strips representing these collections were taken out. The numbers of these long time-span collections as compared to the shorter-lived sites that are used in the final graph are as follows:

AREA	NUMBER OF SHORT-TIME-SPAN SURFACE COLLS. USED IN FINISHED GRAPH	NUMBER OF LONG-TIME-SPAN COLLS. TAKEN OUT TO CLARIFY GRAPH
Lower Yazoo Basin	48	1
Lower Arkansas River	19	1
Sunflower	81	9
Memphis	66	7
St. Francis	37	0
Colls. used in graphs 251		Discarded 18 *

Although eighteen surface collections with respectable sherd totals have been eliminated from the graphs because of the special requirements of this kind of analysis, this does not mean that the effort devoted to these sites has been lost. It may be expected that these are places where rather long spans of history may be examined in stratigraphic relation, if there is any depth to the deposits. So far,

---

* The full list of site collections excluded from the seriation graphs is as follows:

SHERD TOTAL

Lower Yazoo
20–O–1 (Jaketown) 4226
Lower Arkansas
16–L–3 (Stovall) 218
Sunflower
17–N–16 (Wilnot) 244
16–P–7 (Mitchell) 418
16–P–5 (Crosslyn) 127
16–P–1 (Charleston) 646

16–O–14 (Stover) 110
16–O–17 (Longstreet) 160
17–O–11 (Cassidy) 249
16–O–1 (Dunn) 94
16–P–6 (Cox) 144
Memphis
10–P–3 (Nettle Ridge) 477
10–Q–3 (Turnage) 328
14–N–6 (Helena Crossing) 80
13–P–4 (Dogwood Ridge) 354
13–P–10 (Irby) 1381
11–P–3 (Golightly Place) 241

tests have been made in one of these sites, 20–O–1 (Jaketown), the results of which are discussed in the section on Stratigraphy (VI). It was quite evident why surface collections from this site were useless for seriation purposes; the occupation covered practically the full range of ceramic history in the area.

Handling of the Data from Stratigraphic Excavations

The incorporation of the data from the stratigraphic excavations into this analysis was done in a purely arbitrary fashion. Each level was treated as though it were a separate surface collection from a distinct site, except for the fact that care was taken to keep the levels in proper vertical order. The relation of stratigraphic levels to the soil profiles revealed by the walls of the excavations, which is discussed in detail in the next section of this report, was not worked out at the time this analysis was made, but had it been available would not have received consideration in this phase of the work. The seriation of the data in these five sub-areas was an attempt to discover the chronological patterning of the pottery types in each region and to reveal the consistency with which the types followed that pattern. In this handling of the data it was expected that such anomalies as the reoccupation of sites after they had been abandoned for any considerable length of time would be revealed by comparison with the evidence given by neighboring sites as to the chronological pattern of each sub-area.

There are some discrepancies between the interpretation given to the stratigraphic data in this section, written mainly by Ford, and the section on Stratigraphy which follows, written by Phillips. These disagreements are not basic differences as to the gross outlines of the chronology; there are no differences as to this. They have to do principally with the problem of whether the evidence indicates that there was a break in the deposition between the Baytown refuse characterized by clay-tempered pottery and the shell-tempered Mississippian deposits. In most cases this involves a question as to whether late Baytown (period D–C) or the early Mississippian Phase (period C–B) is missing in the strati-

graphic sequence. With the evidence which we have at present it does not seem possible to resolve these discrepancies to everyone's satisfaction, so we will allow them to stand. However, they can be explained by the fact that Phillips' judgments have been based on detailed examination of the internal evidence supplied by each strata cut while the guesses of Ford have attempted to reconcile the evidence given by both surface and excavated collections.

Co-ordinating the Area Chronologies

We are now in possession of five quantitative graphs representing the ceramic history of the five selected areas. However, these are relative histories. There is no absolute chronological scale by which the appropriate amounts of vertical spacing, which represents time that should be given to the early, middle, or late portions of each can be measured. The best that can be done is to try to correlate them one with another. This was done in the following fashion. Six strings, spaced and running parallel, were stretched from end to end of the table on which the graphs lay. Then portions of the graphs were adjusted up or down until the same types showed comparable relative quantities under the appropriate string. Thus, the third string down from the top, which has become line C on the time scale used in the finished drawings (figs. 17–21), was made to mark the point in each graph where Baytown Plain and Neeley's Ferry Plain were about equal, Mulberry Creek Cord-marked had practically disappeared, Bell Plain was just getting a start, and Larto Red Filmed was almost gone. In each case this procedure was a compromise. If the upper portion of the Lower Arkansas graph had been slid downward until all the percentages of Bell Plain were equal to those in the Sunflower and Memphis areas along the C horizon line, then the Baytown-Neeley's Ferry relationship would have been all out of adjustment. All the type patterns were considered in this correlating process and the A to G time-scale arrangement given in the five final graphs is the end result of many compromises. So this scale is presented as a time framework for the chronologies. Time F in the Yazoo area, for example, is supposed to be the same as F in the Lower St. Francis.

The necessity for compromises of this kind was not unexpected. As a matter of fact, they are an inherent part of this kind of cultural analysis. The groups of ideas to whose products have been tagged such names as Mazique Incised did not spring up simultaneously all over the area. They moved from one part to another, and that took time. For example, the ideas of red slipping on clay-tempered vessels (Larto Red Filmed) apparently was moving from south to north through the region, while cord-marking on clay-tempered pots (Mulberry Creek Cord-marked) was moving from northeast to south. Naturally, the former is earlier to the south and the latter to the north.

The student who is particularly interested in the history of this area, or of the procedure by which this balancing was done, may check it — if he has the time and patience — by placing the five area graphs (figs. 17–21) side by side and following across the relative time position of each type. This process has been a subjective weighing of the evidence provided by each type position and of course is always open to question. As a matter of fact, there has been considerable question as to certain aspects of this arrangement which should receive attention at this point. Griffin and Phillips are of the opinion that the late materials in the Arkansas area actually date somewhat later than they are represented in the graph of that area (fig. 18). They think that the pottery type Wallace Incised probably extends up to the time when the Quapaw were discovered by the French. This opinion is somewhat reinforced by the fact that the type is practically confined to the region in which the Quapaw were described and occurred in appreciable amount in the top levels of two cuts in the Menard Site (17–K–1), and on the surface of the near-by Wallace Site (17–K–3) which there is reason to believe may have been the site of the Quapaw

village of Osotouy (Uzutiuhi), first visited by the French in 1686 (see p. 414). As additional evidence, Clarence B. Moore excavated burials in the fields near the Menard Site that were accompanied by European material. Admitting that the cemetery excavated by Moore almost certainly is of Quapaw origin, Ford has hesitated to raise the upper part of the Arkansas graph for several reasons. First, to do so would also bring the types which accompany Wallace Incised up to a later date where their proportions would not be consistent with those of the same types in the neighboring areas. Second, Moore's illustrated material does not show any examples of the types Wallace Incised. However, this does not mean that he may not have found such vessels. The third and most convincing point (to Ford) is the fact that Moore does illustrate three vessels of the type Fatherland Incised, the pottery which the Natchez tribe farther down the Mississippi were making about A.D. 1700.[10] In addition, he found "teapot vessels," another trait shared with the Natchez. Neither Fatherland Incised nor any of the late "Caddo" types with which it is normally associated appeared in the Survey collections from the Menard and near-by sites. While far from denying that this vicinity is the likely site of a historic Quapaw village from which Moore sampled the burials, it does not appear likely to Ford that the site collections and uppermost strata levels in our Arkansas area graph represent this historic occupation.[11]

Comparison of the area graphs will show that the late collections in the Memphis area have been allowed to come up to the most recent times. This was practically forced by the large percentage of Bell Plain found on the surfaces of the late sites in that area. In contrast the other areas show much smaller percentages of this type as a very late feature. It is possible, as discussed in the next section, that a part of this Bell Plain is pot-hunter refuse or is burial ware which has been ripped

---

[10] Moore, 1908a, figs. 8, 10, 19. Compare with Quimby, 1942.

[11] Griffin's reposte to this is simple. He thinks that the Yazoo and Sunflower columns also have their latest portions placed too early. More of the sites in those areas should fall after time B.

Phillips thinks that this is an instance where the

assumption of continuous distribution of a pottery type has played us false. Bell Plain, which carried the weight of identification of the late time, seems to have a discontinuous distribution in space. Therefore, according to this view, the near lack of Bell Plain in the top portions of the Lower Arkansas graph is not chronologically significant.

from graves by cultivation. However, the trends in accompanying types: decrease of Barton Incised, increase of Parkin Punctated, and the appearance of Rhodes Incised and Vernon Paul Appliqué, suggests that there is a certain consistency to this situation that makes the increase of Bell a significant marker of the passage of time in this area — whatever may be the factors involved.

It is thought that probably none of these columns extend to the beginning of reliable historic documentation about A.D. 1700. This is consistent with the fact that the French explorers of that period indicate that the population of the Mississippi flood-plain area between the mouth of the Yazoo River, where villages of Yazoo and Tunica were found, and the northern limits to which our Survey has extended was very scanty indeed. About the mouth of the Arkansas River were found the Quapaw or Arkansea, and those are the only people who can be placed with any certainty. In the upper drainage of the Yazoo were the Tiou,[12] Chakchiuma,[13] and Ibitoupa.[14] Swanton estimates that the total of this Upper Yazoo population was less than 1000 people.[15]

This is far from enough people to account for the number of sites which we have dated as occupied during the later Mississippian period, and, in fact, is markedly in contrast to the population picture given by the De Soto narratives for the year 1542 as will be shown in a later section.

Clarence B. Moore found burials accompanied by glass beads and other European material at several sites through the area we have surveyed.[16] The pottery which he illustrates from the Rhodes and Bradley Places is clearly of late Memphis area types but, as Moore's report does not associate the illustrated materials with the burials that are described, it is impossible to state definitely that the European material was found with this complex. Even if it is associated with it, it should be noted that the possibilities for the aborigines acquiring glass beads probably go back some-

what before 1700 in this area, if not back to the period of De Soto's exploration in 1542

There is some reason to expect that the ceramic complex which prevailed at least as far north as the Sunflower area in 1700 had a small percentage of incised pottery resembling in both decoration and shape the historic Natchez-type Fatherland Incised.[17] It has already been pointed out that Moore found a small proportion of this type associated with European material near the Menard Site Charles Peabody's excavations in the Oliver Site in our Sunflower area produced at least one vessel of this type.[18] Again, the association with the European material which was found in some quantity cannot be determined from the report. However, the type did not appear in any of our late collections. Clearly, further search needs to be made for rare contact sites in the Survey Area with a view to determining the exact forms of the late ceramic complexes in the different parts of the region. Until this is done, it cannot be stated with certainty exactly when these columns end.

The finished area graphs are given as figures 17, 18, 19, 20, and 21. The collections are listed by site designations, 12–N–7, etc., down the left side of each graph. Collections which were made from restricted areas in certain sites are indicated as A, B, etc. (12–N–3A). The stratigraphic cuts made in certain sites are shown by staffs on the left side of the diagrams, and each level of such excavations is indicated with depth in centimeters. Each staff is shaded to aid in relating it to the corresponding type frequency bars given in the body of the charts.

The pottery types are represented by vertical "axes" which are labeled at both top and bottom of the diagrams. Equally spaced on either side of the appropriate axes are horizontal bars the length of which represents type percentages according to the scale given in the lower right-hand corner of the graph. It will be noted that only one-half of the full length of the frequency bars for the relatively

---

[12] Swanton, 1946, p. 194.
[13] Swanton, 1946, p. 105.
[14] Swanton, 1946, p. 140.
[15] Swanton, 1946, p. 107.
[16] See Moore, 1911, pp. 406, ff., Kent Place (our

13–N–4); pp. 413, ff., Rhodes Place; and pp. 427, ff., Bradley Place.
[17] Quimby, 1942, pp. 263–64.
[18] Peabody, 1904, pl. 14, line 4.

abundant types Neeley's Ferry Plain and Mulberry Creek Cord-marked has been shown. These types are arranged at the left and right-hand sides of the graphs, respectively, and this device has enabled us to decrease the over-all width of the illustrations.

On the right-hand side of each graph are listed the collection totals. These will indicate the amount of reliance that may be placed upon the samples. The time scale, A, B, C, etc., which relate the graphs to one another in the manner which has been described above, is on the right-hand side of each. These are the smallest time divisions which we have felt justified in making in the chronologies. The more comprehensive names which we are using Tchula, Baytown, and Mississippian are also given with the time range of each period indicated.

Explanations of complicated diagrams are tedious reading and frequently serve mainly to hide the essential simplicity of the scheme. The reader who is still confused at this point may be less so after comparing the following tabulation of types at Site 19–L–6 (Refuge) with the collection as graphed at the very top of the Lower Yazoo Basin area diagram (fig. 17).

19–L–6 (Refuge)

TYPE NAME	NO. SHERDS	PERCENTAGE
Neeley's Ferry Plain	304	.463 *
Baytown Plain	31	.047
Bell Plain	263	.400
Parkin Punctated	21	.032
Leland Incised	28	.043
Unclassified	9	.014 †

* Half of percentage shown in graph.
† Not graphed.

Discussion of the Seriation Technique

Such, then, was the analytical procedure followed in developing the area graphs, and some of the reasons why it was done so. The seriation of surface collections might have carried the full weight of the evidence for developing the chronological type patterning, but as some stratigraphic excavations were available in each area it did not have to. There is a tendency among some archaeologists to affect an attitude of suspicion and doubt in regard to the seriation technique, and it has

often been asserted that the results of such "juggling" cannot be accepted unless supported by vertical stratigraphy. It seems likely that such an attitude may arise from one or both of two sources: either a misconception of the phenomena of cultural change and the part that typology plays in measuring that change, or a lack of understanding of the seriation technique. As a matter of fact, both seriation and the vertical stratigraphic technique have certain advantages and defects under different conditions and must be applied to chronological problems with a careful regard for their limitations.

The chief limitation of seriation is the fact that it must work with degrees of probability which are often quite difficult to measure or even estimate. Usually, the measure has to be the pragmatic one of the results obtained. In our area, for example, any one or all of the probabilities stated at the beginning of this section may not have been true. The population may not have been relatively stable. There might have been sudden and frequent movements of populations so that the cultural change in any one locality would have had little semblance of order. Had this been true, we might expect either that the development of a sequence by this means would have been impossible, or that cultural periods would have been developed which were clearly delimited, one from the other.

It is also possible that a majority of the villages might have been inhabited for very long periods of time. If this had been true, it would have been impossible to separate early and late pottery features by surface collecting and seriation techniques. There is, of course, a degree of this kind of error in all of the samples which we have handled, and this is probably the principal defect of the technique. None of the collections are the instant cross section of the ceramic content of the culture at each site which would be the ideal situation. The fact that each of the surface collections does represent a time span of a certain length must, in theory, result in a certain "fogging" of the quantitative history. For example, if we assume that we have done a perfect job of sampling and classifying and have placed one of our strip graphs so that its vertical position correctly represents the mean date of the site occupation, then it is plain that this graph will represent the early types which were fading or perhaps disappeared soon after the site was first occupied, too high in the chronological scale. Conversely, the late types which belong to the latter part of the occupation are also pulled back to the mean position and show as too early.

Again, the occasional reoccupation of sites after a lapse of time might be a disruptive factor. It is even possible that there might have been at some periods the general custom of utilizing older sites. This also would result in our securing a mixture of old and new cultural materials and would invalidate our assumption for continuous occupation. Had this happened in a majority of cases, the odds are very much against there having been any consistent pattern to the selection of the earlier sites which would be utilized. Only in the event that a region had been cleared of a previous population by conquest, and the conquerors had moved in and begun to utilize the settlements and fields of the people whom they replaced, could there be any probability of a consistent sequence of types. In such a case the seriation technique would reveal the cultural chronology, but interpretations as to cultural and population continuity might be led astray. It is very probable, however, that there would be "pure" deposits of the late phase of the earlier occupation, and the early phase of the later, which would illustrate the break in cultural continuity.

We can also be certain that none of the collections show type frequencies to the exact percentage that would be found if every sherd at a site had been gathered and classified. For these reasons, we would like to say again that success in this type of work demands numerous collections, and the imperfections of the technique are such that the majority of the indications must be taken as evidence. Two or three sherds of a type that seems to be quite late in a surface collection from a site that by all other indications is rather early do not worry the seriator at all. There are too many ways in which such a chance mixture could have occurred. He is more concerned by the fact that the overwhelming majority of the sherds of this type take a late position, and that

the preponderance of the material from the site fits into the early ceramic pattern. Add to all this the uncertainties of classification which we have outlined in a foregoing section, and it is easy to see why we would like to stress the fact that success in this type of work demands a number of fairly sizable collections, and that only indications given by the majority of the situations must be accepted as evidence.

The Use of Stratigraphic Data in Seriation

The analysis of stratigraphic data as such will be discussed at length in the following section. Here we are concerned principally with the use of stratigraphic along with surface collections in the seriation technique and their limitations from this point of view.

Phillips and Griffin in the 1941, 1946, and 1947 field seasons made a total of seventeen stratigraphic excavations at nine different sites. All of these gave the anticipated results and showed evidence of change in type frequencies with the passage of time. Of these, fourteen were clear-cut enough to be incorporated in the area graphs and three could not be used for reasons that are explained below. This high degree of success in the effort to obtain this type of evidence was directly due to a careful selection of sites to excavate. Before beginning, each excavator had a fairly clear notion as to at least a part of the chronological patterning which the site would reveal.

The principal defect, from the point of view of seriation, in the information provided by stratigraphic excavations is a result of what might be termed migration, particularly upward migration of material in midden deposits. This is most pronounced in middens in which refuse and soil was accumulated very slowly. Apparently, the activities of the Indians who lived on such sites, the digging of post-holes and pits, and overturning the soil in other ways, has tended to bring old pottery and other refuse to higher levels in the growing deposit. This is particularly true of the later Mississippian horizons. Analysis of stratigraphic studies in such deposits make the older type appear to have lasted much longer than really was the case. This factor is doubtless always present in the analysis of all midden deposits. Usually, however, the distortion of the graphs is so small that it falls well within the limits of the variations that have to be allowed in this kind of analysis.

The control which we have over this accidental upward weighting of midden-deposit evidence is the comparison of such unusually slow-growing cuts with the results of other excavations in the same area. A still better check is the comparison of these cuts with seriated short time-span surface collections.

The most pronounced example of upward migration which we have encountered in this study are the two strata cuts that were made at Lake Cormorant (13–P–8). These are described on pages 249–52. The site is located in the Memphis area and the excavations revealed about 120 cm. of refuse deposit, the material from which, when analyzed, proved to represent the entire ceramic chronology for the area from time G to A. All of the types found in the area are well represented, for the collections from each level were substantial. The popularity peaks of the types form a pattern which is in perfect agreement with the seriation graph of the Memphis area as a whole as can be seen by comparing the stratigraphic and seriation graphs (figs. 25 and 27 with fig. 20). However, if we were to accept the evidence offered by the Lake Cormorant Site we would have to believe that the types Withers Fabric-impressed and Baytown Plain were still being made in time B to A. All the other sites collected from the Memphis area by both the surface and stratigraphic techniques show that this was not so. We conclude then that these older types in the Lake Cormorant Site have been brought up to the surface of the midden by overturning of the soil. For this reason, it has not been possible to incorporate the Lake Cormorant data in the Memphis area graph.

The second phenomenon found in strata-cut tests is that at times they misrepresent the history of the site being studied by completely skipping or being deficient in the material that represents certain spans of time. The reason for this is not difficult to find. While a village was occupied, the midden material accumulated at any one spot only so long as it was being actively deposited at that place. In the Southwest, where intentional dumps were utilized

or in Peru where substantial buildings of stone and adobe were occupied uninterruptedly, there was little reason to change the locales of garbage disposal. However, in the eastern United States the houses were impermanent structures of wood, and from the excavation of numerous sites it is clear that considerable shifting of house locations was done in rebuilding. Thus, it may happen that one of our strata pits was put down at a spot where a house stood for the first third of the time the village lasted; was rather far from any dwellings during the second third; and was again near a house during the last third. A graph of the type frequencies will — if it is clear enough — show a definite shift in percentage frequencies at the level where deposition paused. The same thing will result if the pit chanced to pass through a house floor or a courtyard which was intentionally kept clean of débris.

The Question of Population and Cultural Continuity

One of the most interesting questions raised in the interpretation of the data which we have to present is whether there are indications of cultural and, by inference, population discontinuity between the Baytown and Mississippian periods. This has an important bearing on the matter of how and where did the Mississippian cultures develop, the major current mystery of Eastern archaeology. Did the Mississippian culture come into the Survey Area from outside, carried by a new population in such a way that there was a distinct break in the cultural sequence, or was there a period of gradual but possibly rapid cultural change at the beginning of this period when new cultural ideas (carried perhaps by some intruding people) came into the area and merged with the Baytown. We cannot pretend to settle this question, for our data are confined to ceramics. However, the ceramic histories and the villages that have been investigated give enough evidence to permit some discussion. This discussion centers about the more specific question of whether reoccupation has occurred on these sites where the shell-tempered Mississippian pottery complex is mixed with the clay-tempered Baytown ware. A glance at the five area graphs will show that there are a substantial number of such sites in each sub-area, most of them represented by surface collections and a few by stratigraphic excavations. Do all of these sites represent reoccupation?

There can be little doubt that reoccupation is represented by some of these collections. These sites where an early Baytown complex is mixed with shell-tempered pottery, such as 14–O–1 and 14–O–2 near the bottom of the Memphis area graph (fig. 20), seem to have a thin Mississippian occupation mixed with early Baytown, with material of the intervening periods missing. Some of the surface collections excluded from seriation may also be interpreted in this way. Also, there may be some examples of reoccupation where the time during which the site was unoccupied was so short that it is impossible to measure it in cultural terms. The real question is whether the *majority* of mixed sites represent reoccupation. If site reoccupation were the explanation for this mixture, it might be expected that late Mississippian material would be mixed with early Baytown pottery about as often as occupations of the early part of the Mississippian chanced to be placed over late Baytown refuse. The early Baytown sites are in just as favored geographical locations as the late, and there is little reason why these spots should have been avoided by the later invaders. In this event, little or no patterning would appear in either the attempts at seriation or in the strata excavations. However, there is also the possibility that the later people conquered the territory and settled down to use the cleared fields and villages of those whom they had displaced. The techniques applied here would not be able to clearly detect such an event. Even if this somewhat unlikely kind of population replacement had occurred, it is probable that there would be some early Mississippian villages which were established in new, unoccupied spots which would not have the late Baytown mixture, and conversely some of the conquered late Baytown villages which were not reoccupied, and thus did not show the early Mississippian mixture. There are several sites which may be interpreted in this way such as Collins (13–O–9), of the late Baytown in the Memphis area graph (fig. 20), but the number

is small. The patterning revealed by the majority of the site collections indicates to one of the present writers at least (Ford) that there was essential continuity of the ceramic complex and, by inference, of the majority of the population.

Another and parallel approach to this question of continuity lies in an examination of the possibility of certain ceramic decorations which are found on clay-tempered pottery being directly ancestral to similar decorations on the shell-tempered wares. This will be treated elsewhere, and it is sufficient to say here that this evidence does not suggest that there has been a cultural break.

Relative Dating of Village Sites

The foregoing was the analytical procedure which was directed toward the development of the five area chronological columns (figs. 17–21). Now, we call attention to the fact that in the analysis process we have also provided relative dates for the collections studied. The vertical positions in which the collection graphs have been arranged in the five chronological columns show the relative mean dating of these collections. However, it must be emphasized that this is a *mean* or *average* date. As has been mentioned above, each of these collections represents refuse which was in the process of deposition for a shorter or longer period of time — 10, 25, 50, or 100 years, we do not know. There is no external evidence which can be used to resolve this uncertainty. We are aware that what has been done is to "flatten out" the cultural evidence which accumulated during the occupation span that each collection represents and treat the collection as though it were a cross section of the cultural content at one moment in time. If our analytical operations were perfect, we might expect that the time at which the collection best fitted in the chronology would be about the mid-point of the period through which the refuse was accumulating. This is the reason for the term "Mean Date" which will be applied to the graphed time position of the collections.

Frequently, there is in the collections some evidence on which a judgment of the relative time span represented may be based. The presence of types which are chronologically earlier or later than the mean date may indicate approximately how far the time span of a site extended from its mean date. This evidence has served as a basis for the judgments of the time spans of site collections listed under the heading "Range" in table 1. The majority of collections, it will be noted, are listed as falling within one of our lettered subdivisions. These are collections which show no evidence of any long period of occupation and which seem to be about as homogeneous in content as is the usual 10-centimeter level of a stratigraphic cut in this part of the Mississippi Valley.

The above discussion has reference, it will be noted, to the dating of collections. The question as to whether a collection completely and fully dates a site is another matter. There is always the possibility that either (1) only the top and latest refuse is on the surface of the site, or (2) earlier refuse is on the surface but at some point which was not investigated. There can be little doubt that we have made this error in the dating of some sites, but we suspect that the proportion will be quite small. The principal reason for thinking so is that refuse deposits that extend below the plow zone are not common. Numerically, there are more of these deposits than has generally been supposed in the Mississippi Valley, but the proportion of deep to superficial sites is undoubtedly small. The second reason is that this possibility was kept in mind during the course of the field work, and as far as possible all sites were examined to see if areal differentiation of material could be detected. In these cases localized collections were made. Thus, while we cannot say with complete confidence that site "X" is fully dated by its surface collection, we are fairly well satisfied that the great majority of the mean dates do not suffer from serious error of this kind.

An interesting comparison can be made between the graphed positions of surface collections from certain sites and the later stratigraphic excavations in these same sites. Although Ford insists that at the time these collections were being seriated he paid not the slightest attention to site designations but concentrated on type frequencies, the reader had best judge the appropriateness of each position for himself.

On the area graphs, we make the following comparisons:

19–O–2, general surface collection with 19–O–2 strata cut (fig. 17);

17–K–1, a general surface collection with the two strata cuts made on the site, A and B (fig. 18);

17–L–1B, a localized surface collection with strata Cut A, made in same part of the site (fig. 18);

17–L–1C, a localized surface collection with strata Cut B, made in the same part of the site (fig. 18);

16–N–2,[19] a general surface collection with the two strata Cuts A and B made in old and younger parts of the site (fig. 19);

16–N–2B, a localized surface collection with strata Cut B, made in the same part of the site (fig. 19);

16–N–6,[19] a general surface collection with the three strata cuts made in this site, A, B, and C (fig. 19).

The Walls Site (13–P–1) and the Rose Site (12–N–3) are the only cases where such collections fit in the graphs at the upper end of the time span indicated by excavations in the same sites (cf. figs. 20, 21). When the fact is recalled that the sites enumerated were selected for excavation partly on the basis of their showing a depth of midden deposit, and that these depths ranging from 75 to 240 cm. are exceptional rather than the rule on sites in this region, it can be seen that the chances are rather good that we have secured samples representing the full time range of most sites. The problem of buried strata can virtually be ignored so long as we are considering the *majority* situation.

However, this slight degree of doubt which

[19] Note that the graphs of these two surface collections show mixture of both early and late types, a condition that is clearly explained by the length of time represented in the deposits as shown by the stratigraphic excavations. Their lessened value for giving a clear seriation is obvious, and possibly they should have been excluded from the graphs as were the 18 long time-span surface collections described

above. However, they are included here both to illustrate this effect and to point out the tendency of these surface collections to take a position intermediate of the time range of the site. The surface collection from site 20–O–1 (fig. 17), another long time-range site, would have illustrated the same condition, but was not included, as explained above.

must be admitted for the fullness of the site-dating shown by any particular surface collection has no bearing at all on the validity of the quantitative-chronological patterning which derives from the seriation of these collections. The probabilities are still in favor of each collection representing a continuous segment of time, whether this segment be only the latter portion of the length of time any one site has been occupied or not.

INTRODUCTION

Seriation and Stratigraphy

BEFORE embarking on a detailed cut-by-cut analysis of the stratigraphic excavations conducted by the Lower Mississippi Archaeological Survey, it will be well to clarify further the relationship, from the standpoint of method, between seriation and stratigraphy as used in the present study. In a sense we have to regard them as independent methods of analysis. This is perhaps less a result of choice than necessity, owing to the circumstances that the seriation analysis was done in New York by Ford in 1947 and the stratigraphic analysis by Phillips in Cambridge in 1948, both assisted by long-range advice and criticism from Griffin in Ann Arbor. Ford made significant use of stratigraphic data in the seriation by interpolating strata with surface collections as explained on page 228 and shown in figures 17–21. Wherever practicable, the strip graphs representing individual levels in strata cuts were laid down first as a guide to the ordering of surface collections, so it might be more correct to say in such cases that the surface data were interpolated into a stratigraphic framework. The results in our opinion fully justified this unorthodox combination of two distinct kinds of data.

However, it might be pointed out that this is not stratigraphic analysis *per se* and cannot take its place entirely. It was done, in fact more or less has to be done, without regard for what may be called the ground context, i.e., without consideration for the sometimes complex relationships of pottery-type frequencies to special conditions on the site. It is the latter "tied-down" sort of interpretation that will be described in the present section. That the results will always tally with the broader patterning produced by the seriation technique is hardly to be expected, and in fact they do not. Instances of disagreement will be noted as we come to them, and a general discussion of their over-all significance will be given in the concluding remarks at the end of the section. It may be asked why we do

not resolve — "hide" would be a better word — such disagreements by adjusting the discrepancies on the seriation charts. Such a procedure would carry the implication that stratigraphic analysis is a more "accurate" and sure method of dating than seriation, which is by no means certain. We must not lose sight of the fact that interpretation of a stratigraphic cut is accurate, assuming that it *is* accurate, for that cut only. In attempting to extend that interpretation to the site as a whole, or beyond, we have to make use of the same concepts of patterning upon which the seriation technique is based. No, we may as well admit that, in most cases of disagreement, we simply do not know which method has produced the correct interpretation and let both stand — for the present. Fortunately, the discrepancies are not serious. Given the conditions of physical separation under which the two analyses were carried out, and the not identical points of view of those who carried them out, the extent of agreement is a matter for self-congratulation.

The Chronological Framework

It cannot be too strongly emphasized that we have not yet reached the stage of having, or even requiring, a cultural typology in the Survey Area. In fact, we have not yet taken the first step toward such a typology, the determination of significant cultural units or "foci," if you prefer the term. The nomenclature used in this and all other sections of the present report is derived solely from the seriation analysis described in the preceding section. As may be readily seen by reference to any of the charts in that section, the scheme consists of six time divisions set off by the letters A to G, which are in turn grouped into three periods, Mississippi, Baytown, and Tchula. Thus we have two different ways of designating time position, by the use of letters or by the use of names. Both are subject to the ambiguity that attaches to most archaeological designations. They refer primarily to time but have cultural, or better say, since we

239

are dealing with pottery alone, typological implications. As an example of such limited typological implication, it will be recalled that C on the seriation time scale, representing the division point between the Mississippi and Baytown periods, was arbitrarily fixed at the point where Baytown and Neeley's Ferry Plain were approximately equal in percentage frequency; in other words, at the mid-point of a theoretical transition from the use of clay- to shell-tempering in the area. It would be vain to assert, therefore, that the distinction between Baytown and Mississippi is wholly chronological and in no sense typological.

Such being the case, we have to guard against confusion between our period designations and typological concepts already in use. Fortunately, the archaeology of the earlier periods, Tchula and Baytown, has not been sufficiently dealt with in this area to have become seriously involved in concepts of culture type. That of the Mississippi Period, however, has long been identified with the generic concept "Middle Mississippi," which, in our understanding, is primarily a typological concept, not without chronological implications to be sure, but fundamentally a concept of culture type. As indicated above, our studies have not reached the stage of total (archaeological) culture analysis leading to the delineation of "cultures" or culture types. Furthermore, the pottery of the Mississippi Period in our area, while included within the general definition of Middle Mississippi pottery, does not appear to exhibit its full typo-chronological range. Except as faintly foreshadowed in one or two stratigraphic components to be described presently, we have not found anything typologicaly comparable to early Middle Mississippi pottery as exemplified elsewhere in Hiwassee, Old Village, and related foci. We have, therefore, deemed it advisable to substitute for Middle Mississippi the more general term Mississippi, carrying (we hope) a minimum of cultural and typological implication. This involves us in certain terminological difficulties, which must be made as explicit as possible. Like Middle Mississippi our Mississippi Period is also di-

vided into two parts, early and late, C–B and B–A, but this is an arbitrary and strictly chronological division, as devoid of typological significance as can be, being based on differences in percentage frequencies rather than differences in constituent types. If, in the interest of clear expression, it becomes necessary to refer to the "early portion of the Mississippi Period" or simply "early Mississippi" it is not to be understood that this means that the local early Mississippi material dated between C and B is typologically correspondent to what has been referred to as early Middle Mississippi in other parts of the Southeast.[1] If this point has been made sufficiently clear, we should be able to proceed without undue misunderstanding and without raising the sort of questions with which we are not yet prepared to deal.

Definitions: Stratification and Stratigraphy

As outlined in the introductory section of this report, the original over-all Survey program contemplated three successive stages of investigation: (1) preliminary site survey and analysis of surface collections; (2) stratigraphic testing; and (3) site excavation. To date, only a slight beginning has been made on stage (2). To what follows in this section, therefore, the word "preliminary" is more than usually applicable. The results, however, justify a rather detailed presentation, not only for their bearing on the immediate problems, but from the broader point of view of archaeological method in the Southeast.

The use of stratigraphic methods in the eastern United States has not yet developed to an extent comparable with their use in other areas of American archaeology. This is mainly due to an earlier impression on the part of Eastern archaeologists that the method was not applicable, owing to the paucity of deep deposits yielding long cultural sequences. It is also partly due, perhaps, to a misconception regarding the stratigraphic method. To many archaeologists, stratigraphy necessarily involves a situation in which materials can be segregated on the basis of distinct and separable soil zones. Such is fortunately not the

[1] Ford and Willey, 1941; Griffin, 1946, fig. 6.

case. It frequently happens, as we shall show, that a homogeneous deposit, without observable soil stratification, may be made to yield a stratigraphic record of the utmost value. Obviously, such an unstratified deposit will have to be excavated by arbitrary levels, to which method the term "metrical stratigraphy" has sometimes been applied in derogation,[2] as opposed to "natural stratigraphy" obtained by peeling stratified layers. If we were to regard "natural" stratigraphy as the only valid method, the discouraging outlook referred to above would be justified. On the other hand, unstratified or weakly stratified midden deposits of sufficient depth for excavation by "metrical" analysis are not rare. An example of successful exploitation of such deposits is to be seen in the excavations of Willey and Woodbury on the Gulf Coast of Florida in 1940.[3]

There is no need for injecting this terminology into the present discussion, since our stratigraphy — so far at least — is all of the metrical variety. The distinction, however, between "stratification," the description of the actual ground situation, and "stratigraphy," as applied to the chronological interpretation of the ground situation, whether by "natural" or "metrical" methods, is a useful one and will be maintained here. Under the heading "stratification," we shall refer to soil zones as revealed by trench profiles; under "stratigraphy," the analysis of the excavated material and interpretation of the results. The one is what you find, the other is what you do with it. The separation will serve to bring out the fact that it is possible to have stratigraphy without stratification and *vice versa*. In line with this distinction, the terms "stratum," "zone," "deposit," etc., will be hereinafter used to refer to the ground stratification, the term "level" being reserved for the arbitrarily excavated unit of "metrical" stratigraphy.

Methods of Excavation

The simple methods of stratigraphic testing used by the Lower Mississippi Archaeological Survey may be described very briefly. Vil-

lage site deposits in the Alluvial Valley rarely exceed 1 to 2 meters in total depth. Ten centimeters was therefore chosen as a unit of depth, convenient for seriating, without presenting serious difficulties in excavating. The first cut (Walls A) was dug 3 meters square, but on finding that a sufficient yield of sherds could have been obtained from a smaller area, subsequent cuts were made only 2 meters square. Ideally, cuts should be dimensioned to get an adequate sherd sample per level from the smallest possible space, but we could never agree as to just what constituted an adequate sample, and therefore adhered to the convenient 2-meter square throughout. In only one instance (Rose A) was the yield per level below what we should have liked.

Field procedures were of the most elementary description. Cuts were laid out with a compass, corner stakes leveled with a carpenter's level lashed to a two-by-four and used as datum for all subsequent leveling. Plans at successive levels and profiles upon completion of cut were drawn to scale. Cuts were located by reference to a "permanent" bench mark, consisting of an iron pipe with brass cap stamped with symbols guaranteed to mystify all future visitors to the site. Cuts were designated by the site number and a capital letter A, B, C, etc., in the order made. Levels were numbered from top to bottom. Finds catalogued 16–N–6/A–9 would therefore read "Oliver Site (16–N–6), Cut A, Level 9."

Excavated material was put through ½-inch screens. It was found that one shovel hand could keep two to four men busy at the screens, but constant supervision was required to maintain accuracy of level. With such a crew, two or three working days were sufficient for the completion of a cut. As far as practicable, sherds were washed, catalogued, and sorted on the spot to avoid useless labor on unsatisfactory cuts.

In all, 17 cuts were made in 9 sites, not including several which were abandoned for one reason or another, usually lack of depth. These cuts varied from 50 to 240 cm. in depth, the average being 106 cm. or between

[2] In the Southwest. Information by J. O. Brew.

[3] Willey and Woodbury, 1942; Willey, 1949.

10 and 11 levels. Not one of the 17 failed to yield some stratigraphic information of value, several of them revealed pottery sequences covering almost the entire known span of pottery-making in the Lower Mississippi Valley. No other answer is needed for those who may still be skeptical about the practicability of stratigraphic studies in the Southeast.

Method of Analysis

The crucial operation in the interpretation of stratigraphic data is the correlation of pottery distributions with soil stratification, if the latter is present. In a homogeneous deposit without observable profiles you have to take the pottery distribution at face value so to speak, assuming that the changes or lack of changes from level to level mean just what they say. Where stratification has been recorded, however, an opportunity is given to evaluate such changes a little more realistically. It is hardly necessary to point out that the effect of local conditions and events, as revealed by the profiles, may be such as to materially affect the distribution of pottery in the ground. Thus, two distinct phases of interpretation are involved: (1) interpretation of profiles for what they may reveal of events on the site, or that particular portion of it; and (2) interpretation of pottery distributions in the light of such events. No attempt is made here to minimize the possibilities for error in such a complicated interplay of guesswork. Limitations of excavation technique guarantee that the chances of 100-per cent successful interpretation are nonexistent. One simply does the best one can with the available information.

Assuming for the moment that there is a complete record of the four profiles of a given cut, the specific mechanical difficulty is how to effect a graphic comparison of that record with the pottery picture. After considerable experimentation, we have found the most satisfactory method is to construct the pottery graph by the usual manner of seriating bar graphs for each level, in the same vertical scale as the profile drawing, and superimpose one upon the other. Unfortunately, it happens rarely that stratification is so congruent that the profile of one wall of the cut may be allowed to stand for the other three. One

way around this difficulty is to construct an ideal profile by averaging the stratification of all four walls of the cut. This method is sometimes sufficient, but has to be used with caution, because it gives a misleading effect of conformity. In most cases we have found it more satisfactory to use an alternative method involving a composite profile drawing, a sort of palimpsest of all four profiles such as may be seen in figure 23. This, of course, has the opposite effect of exaggerating incongruities, but the resulting errors of interpretation are more likely to be on the side of safety.

*   *   *   *   *

SUMMARY OF STRATIGRAPHY

The results, if such they may be called, of the small-scale excavations described above may be summarized under three headings: (1) the actual stratigraphic results; (2) the light they throw on the stratigraphic and, indirectly, on the seriation methods; (3) the Baytown-Mississippi problem.

(1) Stratigraphic Results

These were, in general, most encouraging. Out of a total of seventeen cuts, all but two gave positive stratigraphic results. In both cases the failure was due to the fact that the cuts had been put down into low mounds. In one of these (Alligator A) stratigraphy, as between mound and sub-mound, was indicated but was masked statistically by the large percentages of early types in the mound fill. The other (Massey B) was completely negative. Of the fifteen successful cuts, four gave information on relationships within the Mississippi Period (Walls A, B, Menard A, Rose A); six on relationships within the Baytown Period (Lake Cormorant A, B, Oliver B, C, Jaketown A, Shell Bluff A); all but one (Walls A) gave evidence of the relationship of the Baytown and Mississippi periods; one (Jaketown A) covered all three periods, Tchula, Baytown, and Mississippi; and two (Jaketown A and B) furnished a glimpse of a possible pre-pottery period underlying the Tchula. In relation to the time and expense involved, these excavations paid off extremely well.

Not only were they individually successful, but the story they tell is completely consistent, so far as it goes. In no case was there conflict or uncertainty so far as the position of individual types or complexes is concerned. They are always in the same — hence we can call it the right — order. The uncertainties are on a higher level of interpretation, but before considering these, it will be well to summarize the results of this study under the second heading outlined above.

(2) The Stratigraphic Method

First, let it be recalled that any remarks made here on the subject of method apply solely to "metrical" stratigraphy. Most if not all of our difficulties of interpretation might have been avoided if we had been able to "peel" stratified deposits instead of digging them in arbitrary horizontal levels. The first generalization, then, is that "metrical" stratigraphy is not good enough. On the other hand, it is, in most cases, the only practicable method. Of the seventeen cuts described here, only four (Oliver A, C, Menard A, and Rose A) were in deposits that might possibly have been peeled by means of the block. The others, among them some of the most successful cuts from the point of view of pottery stratigraphy, could only have been dug by arbitrary levels. We did not consider using the block technique, for reasons of economy, but will in the future be on the look-out for opportunities to do so. Comparison of results of the two methods applied side by side might be very revealing.

While on the subject of excavation technique, another detail we learned the hard way is that great care should be taken to eliminate material from pits and post-holes in the course of digging. We were deliberately careless in this regard on the theory that such material would not be in sufficient amount to upset the over-all statistical results. As a matter of fact, it rarely does so, but in questions having to do with continuity or discontinuity of deposits, in other words, the presence or absence of a "transitional" phase, out-of-place material

in pits and post-holes may be important if not decisive. A great deal of tedious discusison in this section might have been avoided if we had not such material to account for.

Of first importance, on the side of interpretation, is a repetition of the warning, several times repeated in the foregoing pages, that interpretations based on one cut are valid for that cut only; insofar as they are extended to apply to the site as a whole, or a larger area, they lose their force in direct ratio to such extension. We have pointed out several instances in which the interpretation of an individual cut would have been very different but for additional information derived from other cuts on the same site. This leads to the recommendation that, except under special circumstances, more than one cut should be made on a site. This seems so obvious it may be wondered why we mention it. However, it is often overlooked. In our own private disagreements, the existence of which the careful reader may detect here and there, we have often found ourselves using what we *think* happened in 4 square meters of deposit as proof of cultural events on an extensive regional scale.

(3) The Baytown-Mississippi Problem

The most difficult problem raised by these excavations is the nature of the relationship between the Baytown and Mississippi complexes in the area. This problem was repeatedly brought into sharp focus in the course of the interpretations of the several pits. It could only be dimly perceived in the course of the seriation analysis, because that method assumes that the collections used represent continuous occupation. Collections that could be seen to be from stratified or reoccupied sites were not used in the analysis. Collections containing a mixture of Baytown with Mississippi types that were used were assumed to include a transitional phase between these two periods in a continuum and were placed on the graphs in that position. There are certain mechanical factors involved in this that must not be overlooked. Depending on the number of such mixed sites, the resulting pattern in each area was one of a gradual replacement of Baytown by Mississippi types. The precise shape of the individual type frequency patterns, i.e., the degree to which they show a sharp or gradual increase or diminution, is to a certain extent influenced by the mere number of these mixed collections, since space for them has to be found on the graph. In other words, the seriation technique, without more careful controls than we were able to bring to bear, tends to draw out the patterns vertically, with the result that changes and replacements tend to look more gradual than they are in fact. The net result is to reinforce the assumption of continuity upon which the method is based. The effect of stratigraphic diagramming is just the reverse, particularly in a refuse deposit of slow accumulation. Compare the generally abrupt pattern of the first appearance of Neeley's Ferry Plain on the stratigraphs with its slow, gradual increase on the seriation charts. There is no point in discussing which is right. Such terms are meaningless until you have absolute chronology by which to scale the charts. But the difference is important in terms of interpretation and general thinking. The slowly expanding figures on the seriation charts fortify the original assumption of gradual change in a cultural continuum. The rapidly expanding figures of the stratigraphic charts lead to an impression of abrupt cultural change, an impression not a little influenced by the fact that sites were *selected* for excavation on the expectation that they would show cultural change. In short, the results of both methods, as used here, are "rigged" to a certain extent

in favor of one side or the other of this important question.

With this in mind, we may summarize the stratigraphic evidence on the Baytown-Mississippi question. Of the fifteen cuts, that showed superposition, one (Shell Bluff A) appeared to show positive evidence in favor of continuity; two more (Walls B, Menard B) favored, but weakly, the same interpretation; three (Oliver A, Alligator B, Rose A) showed definite evidences of discontinuity; and three more (Oliver B, C, Massey A) were interpreted that way with somewhat less assurance; the remaining six gave no indications on this particular issue one way or the other.

It is important to note that certain cuts that gave the clearest evidence of a discontinuity (Oliver A, Alligator B, Rose A) showed up as transitional on the seriation charts. The final conclusion is that, while the assumption of general continuity between Baytown and Mississippi periods in this area is not disproved, there is sufficient evidence on the other side to call it into question. If this is correct, it follows that more vigorous controls have to be introduced into the seriation method to eliminate the use as "transitional" of mixed collections that are actually the result of reoccupation. In the meantime, if we have succeeded in exposing some of the difficulties inherent in *both* seriation and stratigraphy, the foregoing pages will not have been written in vain.

* * * * *

SUMMARY AND CONCLUSIONS

THE results of the first phase of a continuing survey program in the northern part of the Lower Mississippi Valley have been presented in the foregoing pages under various headings written by various hands not always animated by identical points of view. The effect has been perhaps to create the impression that we have settled many questions, whereas we have all too often only settled the same questions in several different ways. This cannot fail to have left the reader, provided he has not already left the report, in considerable confusion, and it now becomes our duty to straighten him — and ourselves — out. What is required at this point is a general summary of what the three authors can agree on, or failing that, at least to bring together their conflicting interpretations so the reader may compare and judge between them. Up to now, we have attempted to keep such disagreements in the background by writing more or less consistently in the first person plural, giving an effect of praiseworthy unanimity. We have bribed each other's silence by promises of an opportunity to express dissenting opinions and prejudices in the concluding section. A change of style is therefore indicated if we are to give scope to these individual interpretations. From here on, the third person singular will frequently appear in order to make clear which author's point of view is being expressed.

The plan of this concluding section is as follows. We shall first review briefly what we have done and what we, each and severally, think of it. Following this, we shall present a summary of the archaeology of the area period by period, a sort of culture-historical reconstruction, in which we shall use any information that is available whether obtained by us or others. Finally, we shall conclude by attempting to fit our findings into the general picture of Eastern archaeology with a few observations in regard to their bearing on the over-all chronological problem.

AUTHORS' REVIEW

It may not be good form to forestall adverse criticism by offering a review of one's own work, but in the case of a report that makes no pretense of finality it is excusable. Nothing is more exasperating than being criticized for failure to succeed in something one has not tried to do. That is sure to happen to the Lower Mississippi Archaeological Survey. We have merely presented a progress report and are as dissatisfied with it as the most carping critic could possibly be. This is our opportunity for expressing that dissatisfaction, but, since there are three of us, it takes different forms and applies unequally to different sections of the work. A rather detailed review is required for which we beg, once more, the reader's indulgence.

In the long opening section, dealing with the geographical conditions of the Survey Area, a great deal of emphasis was placed on the physical differences between the various areal subdivisions and it was confidently predicted that these differences would be reflected in the archaeology. We now have to explain why this expectation has not been fulfilled, or at least why very little more was said about it. At the time when Phillips was writing this section, inspired by the enlightened environmentalism of Kroeber, Ford was carrying out the seriation analysis described in Section V, in which Mississippi River Commission quadrangles were used as convenient units of area and grouped into five subdivisions on a purely empirical basis. In other words, while Phillips was saying all those fine things about natural conditions and their effect on culture and the shape of cultural distributions, Ford was working out a grouping quite independent of natural subdivisions, in many cases crosscutting them, which nevertheless seemed to give satisfactory results, and eventually became the framework for most of our archaeological generalizations about the area. Phillips is, not unnaturally, unhappy over this and harbors a

425

suspicion that an analysis that took these natural subdivisions more into account might have produced better results. However, it may be pointed out here that the work of the Survey has so far been confined almost entirely to the St. Francis and Yazoo basins which are both comprised in one major type of area, to wit, flood plain of Mississippi-Ohio derivation (see classification, p. 20). Very little work was done in flood-plain areas of "other than Ohio-Mississippi" derivation. A few sites were located in the lower part of the Arkansas River Lowland, but the Survey was not carried into the White-Black River Lowland nor the Boeuf Basin. Thus, no opportunity is yet afforded to make cultural comparisons between these two major categories of flood plain. From general information, however, it can be fairly confidently predicted that the flood-plain areas of other than Mississippi-Ohio derivation are not going to show as dense an occupation, particularly in the Mississippi Period, as the more fertile portions of the flood plain covered by the Survey. As for the older alluvial plains and upland remnants, we have produced no new comparative information at all. Thus, it cannot be said that the moderate environmentalist point of view in Section I has been refuted. It has remained unfulfilled simply in the sense that it has not been tested.

The pottery classification described in Section III is a joint responsibility. We all had a hand in it and are all equally dissatisfied with it. This is normal. The archaeologist who thinks he has achieved a final classification of anything is a rare and probably untrustworthy individual. Most of the shortcomings of our classification have been fully exposed in the type descriptions. Our guess is that very few of our types will stand up when more and better material is available. Many of them will break down into more specialized groups, a few (we may hope) will be combined into more general groups. It is not likely that the total number of types will be reduced. The outlook for the Southeast as a whole, so long as present typological methods remain in favor, is not pleasant to contemplate. Where we are now counting types in tens, they will be counted in hundreds. However, the proof of

the typing is in the using. Our classification cannot be too bad or it would not have produced the consistent patterning of types through time that is shown in the seriation and stratigraphic analyses of Sections V and VI. It seems to have been equal to the purposes for which it was devised, which is all that should be asked of any classification.

Section IV presents a series of distributional studies of certain characteristic pottery forms and designs that have a special interest from the wider point of view of relationships with Mesoamerica and the Southwest. These have been entirely the work of Griffin and have led him to several important conclusions, to wit, that in the Mississippi Period there were more or less direct contacts between the northern part of our area and the Southwest, that these contacts may have begun fairly early, as early as Developmental Pueblo, that the exchange of traits may not have been entirely in one direction, and that the route was not through Texas. It is Griffin's belief that in the recent emphasis of Southeastern students on connections between the Southeast and Mesoamerica, these important evidences of Southwestern connections have been overlooked. His co-authors heartily endorse this opinion. There are in fact many other ceramic traits not covered by Griffin, coming under the heading of miscellaneous small pottery objects, such as disks, ladles, trowels, etc., that point the same way. But to agree that this is a neglected phase of research is not to regard it as *the* answer to a long-standing problem. Griffin's findings in this section present one more evidence of the complexity of processes that underlies any focalization of traits that we refer to as "culture." There is enough of this kind of evidence already to make an expression such as "the origin of Mississippi culture" look faintly ridiculous.

The seriation analysis described in Section V is at once the most fruitful source of results in the report and conflict among the authors. Results, because the chronological framework upon which our findings are hung derives from it; conflict, because, although we all profess belief in the general validity of the method, no two of us have the same degree of confidence in its results. Before commenting further on the nature of our disagreement, it may be well to point out wherein the seriation technique differs from other methods of analysis. The usual method of organizing archaeological data over a large area is to isolate culture groupings, "phases," [1] "foci," or whatever one chooses to call them, by combining units, usually sites or levels within sites, and to rationalize on the basis of fairly complete trait inventories the inter-relations of these groupings in terms of space and time. This is an inadequate statement of a complicated procedure but the essential features are that it is a process of combination, of "building-up" from smaller to larger units, and that a good deal of detailed information is needed even to begin it. We have not yet made an attempt to organize our findings in this way; in fact, it may be doubted whether it is possible at the present time. If we have occasionally referred to groups of sites or localities by some convenient designation outside of the seriation framework, no classificatory significance has been implied. The grouping in question is valid only for the particular matter in hand.

The seriation method, on the other hand, makes an effort to grasp the main outlines of the prehistory before the details are known, by means of graphic delineation of the behavior of one trait complex, in this case pottery, through time. Having established the over-all pattern, the stream of time represented is cut into units at points where shifts in patterning occur. Thus, in a sense, the seriation method works from the general to the particular, the reverse of the conventional method, and is therefore well suited to an initial attack on an area. The contrast must not be over-stressed, however. The results are not as different as the methods. The "periods" derived from seriation are not as different conceptually from "foci" as one might think. They have typological as well as temporal implications, since the cuts are made at points where typological shifts affect the general pattern. Ford stands on the unshakable philosophical ground that none of these concepts have any cultural "reality" anyhow, all being arbitrary con-

structs of the archaeologist. If there are differences they are differences of degree not of kind. This is consistent with his view that the predominating characteristic of culture is continuity both in space and time. To the extent that such a view is correct, any divisions spatial or temporal, however derived, must of course be wholly arbitrary.

As applied specifically to pottery, the only thing we are in a position to generalize about, Ford's idea is that it was developing in a continuum throughout its entire history in the Mississippi Valley, that whether new types evolve by modification of older ones or come in as new ideas from outside, they take their place in an uninterrupted cultural flow. The logical consequence of such a view is that, in most cases a "mixed" pottery complex represents a single brief span of time on that continuum, an "instant" for all practical purposes, when both elements of the mixture were being made and used side by side. The importance of this postulation for the seriation method can hardly be exaggerated. Ford does not deny that mixed complexes sometimes do result from reoccupation of sites. Such collections he frankly banishes from his graphs and says so (p. 233).

Griffin and Phillips, on the other hand, while not rejecting the general theory of continuity, are inclined to feel (with emphasis in order named) that there are more instances of mixture through reoccupation of sites than Ford has recognized. In particular, as pointed out in the individual sections written by them, they have tended to see indications of at least one significant break in the otherwise placid stream of pottery continuity at the point where the tempering material shifts from clay to shell, in other words between the Baytown and Mississippi periods. They feel that, by including mixed collections on the graphs, Ford has effected a spurious transition that seems to prove his continuity hypothesis, but in reality leaves the question open. Another way of putting it would be that the seriation technique, being based on the assumption of continuity, is unable to cope with a "break"

[1] In the sense in which this term is used in Mesoamerica and the Southwest.

of the nature described above, consequently, to establish whether such a break is really there or not, some other method of analysis is required. The upshot is that this compact majority of two, while perfectly willing to endorse and even use the results of the seriation analysis, do not regard the evidence it shows of such continuity as final.

Griffin would like to have it stated that he started with the opinion that there was a break between the earlier horizon and the Mississippi Period. Phillips only came to it gradually as a result of his independent analysis of stratigraphic collections in Section VI, where the reader may follow his painful lucubrations on the subject. One might have thought that stratigraphy would have settled the Baytown-Mississippi continuity question one way or the other. It did not. The only conclusion we are able to agree on is that the subjective element enters into the stratigraphic method just as surely as into the seriation method. That more stratigraphic cuts gave evidence of discontinuity than the reverse Ford attributes to a bias on the part of Phillips in favor of that solution. Phillips naturally protests his innocence, but the reader will have to decide between them. We have perhaps made too much of this issue, which, after all, involves only one point on the time scale. In general, the results of seriation and stratigraphy were in satisfactory agreement.

The experimental correlation of archaeological and geological time scales presented in Section VII is so tentative, and the various possibilities of error are so thoroughly exposed in that section, that nothing further need be said about it here. We are all agreed that the results are sufficiently promising to justify further work along these lines. We cannot predict that this is going to result in a new archaeological technique that will supersede those now in use in the area. What is more likely is that by using the channel sequence as a control in seriation and stratigraphic studies some of the present difficulties of interpretation that have been so fully confessed above will be eliminated.

More important from a long-range point of view is the possibility that correlation of archaeology and hydrography plus C^{14} dating

will result in an accurate absolute time scale for the entire Mississippi Alluvial Valley, which would be as welcome to the hydrographer as to the archaeologist.

The study of spatial and temporal distributions of sites as to type in Section VIII is another promising approach. In its present form it can be no better than the dating on which it is based. The difficulty of dating sites from surface collections whether by seriation or any other method has been repeatedly emphasized and the lack of agreement among the three authors as to the dating of individual sites freely exposed. The period date for the first appearance of new types of mounds and site plans, as set forth in Section VIII, cannot be regarded as final. Phillips and Griffin, for example, hold reservations concerning the appearance of small ceremonial centers with rectangular platform mounds as early as the middle Baytown Period (E–D). On the other hand, there can hardly be any question about the relative order of appearance of the various types of sites, and the population distributions during the several periods indicated by the maps (figs. 64 to 69) is probably in the main correct. With more and better data of the same sort, some very interesting demographic questions might be indicated.

The long Section IX dealing with the problems — but containing no solutions — of the identification of sites from documentary sources might, in its author's (Phillips) opinion, better have been published separately, if at all. It is principally due to Griffin that it has been included here. He feels that, notwithstanding the meager results, it is a valuable contribution as an object lesson for archaeologists who brashly enter the field of history. It also contains leads for further research. The search for Quapaw sites of the contact period was shown to be difficult but not quite hopeless. The Lower Mississippi Survey has not been back in the Lower Arkansas region since this study was made. In particular, further investigation of the Wallace Site (17–K–3) is indicated, but the entire area should be thoroughly searched as well. The importance of establishing the latest pottery typology in this area is sufficiently apparent in the uncertainties and disagreements that crop up whenever the late Mississippi Period falls under discussion. In some respects this most recent period, which ought to be the best known, has been the hardest to deal with chronologically. This will continue to be the case until we can fix its terminus by means of a few good contact sites.

REFERENCES CITED

BROWN, CALVIN S.
1926   Archeology of Mississippi. Mississippi Geological Survey, University, Mississippi.

FORD, JAMES A.
1936   Analysis of Village Site Collections from Louisiana and Mississippi. Louisiana State Geological Survey, Department of Conservation, Anthropological Study 2.

FORD, JAMES A. AND GORDON R. WILLEY
1941   An Interpretation of the Prehistory of the Eastern United States. American Anthropologist 43:325–363.

GRIFFIN, JAMES B.
1939   Report on the Ceramics of Wheeler Basin. In An Archaeological Survey of the Norris Basin in Eastern Tennessee, edited by William S. Webb, pp. 127–165. Bureau of American Ethnology, Bulletin 122.
1946   Culture Change and Continuity in Eastern United States. In Man in Northeastern North America, edited by F. Johnson, pp. 37–95. R. S. Peabody Foundation, Andover.

JENNINGS, JESSE D.
1941   Chickasaw and Earlier Indian Cultures of Northeast Mississippi. Journal of Mississippi History 3(3):155–226.

KRIEGER, ALEX W.
1944   The Typological Concept. American Antiquity 9:271–288.

LINTON, RALPH
1940   Crops, Soils, and Culture in America. In The Maya and Their Neighbors, edited by Hay, Clarance L., Ralph L. Linton, Samuel K. Lothrop, Harry L. Shapiro, and George C. Vaillant, pp. 32–40. D. Appleton–Century Company, Inc., New York.

MOORE, CLARENCE B.
1908a   Certain Mounds of Arkansas and of Mississippi—Part I: Mounds and Cemeteries of the Lower Arkansas River. Journal of the Academy of Natural Sciences of Philadelphia 13:480–557.
1911   Some Aboriginal Sites on Mississippi River. Journal of the Academy of Natural Sciences of Philadelphia 14:367–480.

PEABODY, CHARLES
1904   Exploration of Mounds, Coahoma County, Mississippi. Peabody Museum of Archaeology and Ethnology, Papers 3(2):23–63. Harvard University.

QUIMBY, GEORGE I., JR.
1942   The Natchezan Culture Type. American Antiquity 7(3):255–275; 311–318.

SPIER, LESLIE
1917   An Outline for a Chronology of Zuñi Ruins. American Museum of Natural History, Anthropological Papers 18(3):207–331.

SWANTON, JOHN R.
1946   The Indians of the Southeastern United States. Bureau of American Ethnology, Bulletin 137.

TAYLOR, WALTER W.
1948   A Study of Archeology. American Anthropological Association, Memoir 69.

WEBB, WILLIAM S. AND DAVID L. DEJARNETTE
1942   An Archeological Survey of Pickwick Basin in the Adjacent Portions of the States of Alabama, Mississippi, and Tennessee. Bureau of American Ethnology, Bulletin 129.

WILLEY, GORDON R.
1949   Archaeology of the Florida Gulf Coast. Smithsonian Miscellaneous Collections 113.

WILLEY, GORDON R. AND R. B. WOODBURY
1942   A Chronological Outline for the Northwest Florida Coast. American Antiquity 7:232–254.

From *MEASUREMENTS OF SOME PREHISTORIC DESIGN DEVELOPMENT*

James A. Ford

CORRELATION OF CHRONOLOGIES

Figure 2 presents a pattern of type frequencies that can best be visualized from the forms and relative vertical positions of the curves made by the dotted smoothing lines. In this attempt to correlate the Red River chronology with those in adjacent areas, I am concerned with these smoothed curves. The process of correlation is tedious and must be a total comparison of frequency peaks, duration, and internal features of types. This is most readily accomplished with chronological graphs representing neighboring areas laid side by side on a table. Then, bearing in mind the fact that we have no absolute time control over either the entire span of each chronology or of its segments, the parts of the chronologies are shifted upward or downward, until the best agreement is achieved between the patterning formed by corresponding or closely related types.[4] It has never been tried, but the process would probably be easier if the chronologies

were drawn on thin rubber sheets, so that they could be stretched and lengthened, both overall and in part, to achieve the best matching of patterns. I am not recommending that the student with similar problems should rush to the nearest hospital supply house, but the suggestion will serve to illustrate the process.

In a comparison of chronological patterning, area to area, it is not to be expected that temporally corresponding sections will resemble one another completely. The same degree of fit that is found in a comparison of stratigraphic graphs that represent the same span of time in one area cannot occur for several very good reasons.

A. The act of defining a cultural type automatically creates a geographical frequency center for that type (in a stable population, of course). This should be clear enough, but I shall provide an illustration to becloud the matter. Suppose, in a frequency study of United States architecture, we were to define

[1] Cotter, 1951.
[2] Brown, 1926, 36–40.
[3] Ford, 1936, 50–71; Quimby, 1942.

[4] This procedure has been described in a previous paper; see Phillips, Ford, and Griffin, 1951, 226–231.

James A. Ford

a type "Gambrel-roofed red-painted barn." The largest proportion of total barns of this class would undoubtedly be in the Midwest. Another type, "Gambrel-roofed barn with basement and stone foundation" has a frequency center in New England. "Unpainted gambrel-roofed barns" are most common in the South. "Red-painted gambrel-roofed barns with a hex sign" have a frequency center in Pennsylvania and are of rather limited frequency and distribution. On the other hand, we might attach little importance to the shape of the roof and classify barns on the basis of other criteria so that the groupings cross-cut the above categories: i.e., Dairy Barns, Work Animal Barns, Hay Barns, Machinery Storage Barns. The possibilities for varying the classificatory groupings are as numerous as they are for any other cultural feature. As a result of each class definition a geographical frequency center (or centers) will be made.

B. Cultural influences take time to move across geographical areas, whether the fraction of a second required by the modern telephone or the longer spans of time more usual under primitive conditions. One certainty when comparing types in different regions is that they do not represent the same instant of time. This means that it is to be expected that identical types or types that have been defined on the basis of the same stream of cultural influence will shift their relative positions in the neighboring chronologies, depending on the direction in which they were moving. If cord-marked pottery diffused from north to south in the United States, its initial appearance must be, and its peak of popularity probably will be, later in the south than in the north.

The matching of patterns is somewhat simplified, however, by the fact that for immediately adjacent areas our time measuring devices seem not to be accurate enough to gauge the majority of ceramic trait movements. Only the slower drifts can be detected with any confidence. This seems to be particularly true for a fairly stable population that shared the same basic culture, and in which specific cultural changes proceeded in an almost parallel fashion, with relatively rapid diffusion of new ideas. Apparently it is safest to assume that the frequency peaks of the majority of the comparable types in immediately adjacent areas represent the same time horizon; the more unusual

instances in which there is a marked displacement from one area to another may then be interpreted as evidence of relatively slow trait movement. Fortunately, it will sometimes be found that the pattern displacement of one influence moving north to south, for example, will be balanced by another traveling in the opposite direction.

This factor of time lag of similar types in adjacent areas makes it necessary to draw conclusions as to direction of movement of influences when the columns are being aligned. This may appear to the reader as advice to lift himself by tugging on his bootstraps, but perhaps it is not quite that bad. Once again, conclusions must be based on the major part of the evidence and the most probable interpretation. It is hoped that the diagram in Fig. 3 will assist in this discussion. It compares the patterning formed by three cultural types, A, B, and C, in three neighboring chronological columns labeled Areas 1, 2, and 3. These patterns have been aligned in what appears as the most probable time relation, but this is not by any means the only interpretation that can be made. As arranged, the diagram indicates that Type A moved from Area 1 to 3, diminishing in frequency; C went from 3 to 1 at about the same rate of speed; and B moved at a slightly faster rate in the same direction as C, decreasing as it diffused.

An alternative interpretation that would be just as good as the first, if we had to rely entirely on the internal evidence shown by this figure, might be that the pattern alignment is wrong and that all three of these types had moved from Area 1 to Area 3, with the types shifting their relative positions in the time scale in the course of the process. The reverse direction of movement also might be true. The relative time positions of the patterns would then have to be shifted upward or downward. Only if we have some supplementary evidence as to the direction of movement of these cultural influences can we choose between these possibilities. It is not necessary to have this information for all the types; just one or two are sufficient. If it is virtually certain that Type A spread from Area 1 to Area 3, then the present alignment would become very probable. If, in addition, it were possible to show that Type B was moving in the opposite direction, there would be no question.

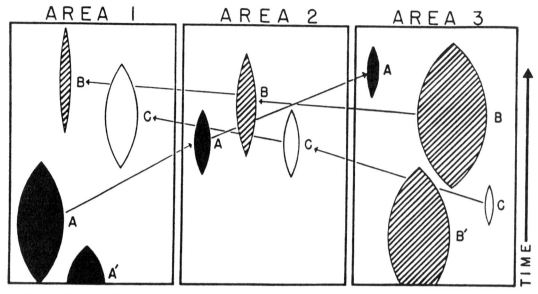

FIG. 3. Diagram illustrating quantitative change and time lag in diffusion—phenomena that must be considered in making temporal alignments of relative chronologies.

Fortunately, the direction of movement of a trait can be deduced in at least two ways. The less reliable of these is the comparison of relative frequency. It is not always true, but most of the time influences diffuse from the areas where they were most popular into the regions where they are found in lesser frequencies.[1] This is the usual situation, but it is not inevitable. Sometimes a trait becomes more popular in the course of diffusion. Type C in the simplified diagram given as Fig. 3 will serve as an illustration.

The most reliable basis for such judgment is the question of ancestry for the trait. If Type A in the illustration (Fig. 3) has older ancestral forms in Area 1, such as the type graphed as A', and no possible earlier forms are found in Areas 2 and 3, then the direction of diffusion becomes obvious.

C. As the third complicating factor in the matching of chronological patterning, it is well to recall that the device that is being used to measure cultural chronology is much less than perfect. Stratigraphic excavation and seriation of surface collections do not give an accurate record of what has transpired. Not that

they will be so inaccurate as to place cultural influences in an incorrect relationship with one another, but rather that each chronology will be "fuzzy." Each graph is a more or less out-of-focus picture of the culture history that it represents. Inadequate samples introduce some quantitative distortion, but this is fairly easy to evaluate and check. The most serious type of distortion for which allowance must be made in the Southeast is caused by the comparatively slow growth of refuse deposits. On village sites, when the accumulation was slow and thin, the overturning of the soil in the course of the normal activities of the inhabitants, digging post-holes, pits, etc., will have intermixed earlier and later artifacts so that types will appear to begin earlier and, particularly, to last longer than actually was the case. This is an element that should be taken into consideration in all stratigraphic samples, as has been discussed in another place.[2] Fortunately, this sort of distortion varies from one deposit to another according to the rapidity of accumulation for each. Where several excavations present parallel evidence, the data from the most clear-cut can be followed; this will be the situation in which the time spans of the types are

[1] As a fairly clear-cut illustration, see the discussion of Mulberry Creek Cordmarked in Phillips, Ford, and Griffin, 1951, 82–87, Fig. 7.

[2] Ford, 1949, 48; Phillips, Ford, and Griffin, 1951, 232–233.

the shortest and the greatest vertical separation is found in the pattern formed by the type frequency maximal. This distortion can be minimized by focusing attention on the patterning formed by type maximums and by placing less weight on the apparent starting and stopping points of type occurrences. For example, in Fig. 6 I am not inclined to consider as at all decisive the fact that Weeden Island Incised seems to appear in western Florida slightly later than French Fork Incised first occurs in the Red River chronology. More important is the position of the frequency peak of French Fork as slightly later than Weeden Island.

REFERENCES CITED

FORD, JAMES A.
1949   Cultural Dating of Prehistoric Sites in Virú Valley, Peru. *American Museum of Natural History, Anthropological Papers* 43(1):29–89.

PHILLIPS, PHILIP, JAMES A. FORD, AND JAMES B. GRIFFIN
1951   *Archaeological Survey in the Lower Mississippi Valley.* Peabody Museum of Archaeology and Ethnology, Papers No. 25. Harvard University.

STATISTICAL TECHNIQUES FOR THE DISCOVERY
OF ARTIFACT TYPES

ALBERT C. SPAULDING

WITHIN RECENT YEARS there appears to have been an increasing awareness on the part of archaeologists that certain statistical techniques offer economical methods of extracting information of cultural significance from archaeological data. The discussions of Kroeber (1940), Robinson (1951), and Brainerd (1951) have appeared in *American Antiquity*, and the last two even evoked a comment* (Lehmer, 1951). In addition to these papers, which are primarily devoted to exposition of method, a considerable number of special applications can be found in the literature. Archaeological research inevitably brings the researcher face to face with the problems of ordering and comparing quantities of data and of sampling error. There seems little doubt that the best approach to these problems involves a search of statistical literature for appropriate methods.

The discussion which follows is an attempt to apply certain statistical methods to the discovery and definition of artifact types and to suggest other applications to related problems. No effort has been made to explain such important statistical concepts as population, random sample, sampling error, and so on; these explanations are the proper function of textbooks, and any paraphrasing here would be presumptuous. I am indebted to Paul S. Dwyer, Consultant in the Statistical Research Laboratory of the University of Michigan, for reading and commenting on an earlier version of the manuscript.

The artifact type is here viewed as a group of artifacts exhibiting a consistent assemblage of attributes whose combined properties give a characteristic pattern. This implies that, even within a context of quite similar artifacts, classification into types is a process of discovery of combinations of attributes favored by the makers of the artifacts, not an arbitrary procedure of the classifier. Classification is further an operation which must be carried out exhaustively and independently for each cultural context if the most fruitful historical interpretations are to be made. It is the primary purpose of this paper to argue that with the aid of suitable statistical techniques the degree of consistency in attribute combinations can be discovered in any meaningful archaeological assemblage provided sufficient material is at hand, and hence that valid types can be set up on the basis of analysis of material from one component.

Wholesale acceptance of these views entails modification of a widely held concept of typology which has been clearly expressed by Krieger (Krieger, 1944; Newell and Krieger, 1949). Under this concept, the method employed to demonstrate the existence of a valid type is a site-to-site comparison to show consistency of the identifying pattern, range of variation, and historical relevance. In the absence of a method for investigation of consistency and range of variation within the site, this is indeed the only convincing technique available for validation of a proposed type. On the other hand, the presence of an adequate method for investigating consistency and range of variation within the site obviates a comparative study so far as the questions of the existence and definitive characteristics of a type are concerned. Historical relevance in this view is essentially derived from the typological analysis; a properly established type is the result of sound inferences concerning the customary behavior of the makers of the artifacts and cannot fail to have historical meaning. This is not meant to imply that corroborative evidence from the other sites would not be welcome in the case of a dubious type, i.e.,

---

* See pp. 341-53 in this issue for an application of the Robinson technique.

305

one which is on the borderline of probability owing to a deficient sample or lack of clear evidence of attribute clustering, nor is it meant to imply that the classifier is relieved of the responsibility of avoiding synonymy. Finally, it is not intended to assert that artifact types are the only useful units of attribute association for site-to-site comparison; numerous examples of good comparative work with body sherds are sufficient refutation of such an assertion, although the common practice of failing to distinguish between kinds of body sherds and types of vessels is a stumbling block in understanding the cultural meaning of a comparison. It should be pointed out that this discussion owes much to the expositions of Rouse (1939, especially pp. 9-23), Krieger (1944), Newell and Krieger (1949, pp. 71-74), and Taylor (1948, especially pp. 113-130).

The customary technique of classification consists of inspection and segregation of obtrusive combinations, or occasionally of attempting to describe all of the observed attribute combinations on an equal basis. Categories resulting from both of these methods are called "types," although they are not exactly comparable. Both methods fail to yield surely artifact types in the sense in which the term is used here. In the first case, segregation of obtrusive combinations, the cultural implications of the data are usually not exhausted, although under favorable circumstances all of the types may be discovered and described. In the second case, description of all combinations, the problem of typology is not faced at all; some of the "types" described will in all probability consist of combinations habitually avoided by the makers of the artifacts. Questions of typology arise, of course, only in a situation where a considerable variety exists within a group of generally similar artifacts — it is obvious that a stone projectile point and a pottery vessel belong in two separate artifact types. But within a group of similar artifacts the propriety of division into more than one type may be anything but obvious. It follows from the concept of the type adopted here that a pronounced association of two attributes is the minimum requirement for the demonstration of the existence of an artifact type, since two is the smallest number which can be considered an assemblage.

Application of this concept to concrete material can be illustrated by a few simple examples. Inspection of a collection of 100 vessels which represent all the pottery from a component results in the noting of the following attributes: smooth surface, cord wrapped paddle stamped surface, grit tempered paste, and shell tempered paste. The question to be answered is whether the vessels represent one or two pottery types with respect to these attributes. The data necessary to answer the question are the frequencies of vessels in each of the four possible categories into which two pairs of alternatives can be grouped, here smooth surface and grit temper, smooth surface and shell temper, cord wrapped paddle stamped surface and grit temper, and cord wrapped paddle stamped surface and shell temper. Table 7 presents these frequencies in 2 x 2 form under the assumption that the count in each category is 25 vessels.

TABLE 7. FOUR-CELL FREQUENCIES WITH NO ASSOCIATION OF ATTRIBUTES

	Grit Temper	Shell Temper	Total
Stamped Surface	25	25	50
Smooth Surface	25	25	50
Total	50	50	100

It is evident by inspection that the 100 vessels cannot be separated into two types under these circumstances. The cord wrapped paddle stamped vessels are equally divided with respect to grit temper and shell temper, the same is true of the smooth surfaced vessels, and conversely both the shell tempered and the grit tempered vessels are equally divided with respect to surface finish. A mathematical statement to the same effect can be obtained by applying the simple and useful four-cell coefficient of association described by Kroeber (1940). If the upper left cell is designated a, and the upper right cell b, the lower left cell c, and the lower right cell d, the coefficient of association for the attributes grit temper and cord wrapped paddle stamped surface would be computed as

$$\frac{(a+d)-(b+c)}{a+b+c+d} = \frac{(25+25)-(25+25)}{25+25+25+25} = \frac{0}{100} = 0.$$

The same result would follow for the other three pairs. The opposite situation would be that of Table 8. Here there are plainly two types with respect to the traits considered, a cord wrapped paddle stamped and grit tempered type and a smooth surfaced and shell

TABLE 8. FOUR-CELL FREQUENCIES WITH PERFECT
ASSOCIATION OF ATTRIBUTES

	Grit Temper	Shell Temper	Total
Stamped Surface	50	0	50
Smooth Surface	0	50	50
Total	50	50	100

tempered type. The computed coefficient of association for the attributes grit temper and cord wrapped paddle stamped surface is

$$\frac{(50 + 50) - (0 + 0)}{50 + 0 + 50 + 0} = +1.0,$$

and the same coefficient would be obtained for the shell tempered, smooth surfaced category. On the other hand, the calculation for the smooth surfaced, grit tempered category shows

$$\frac{(0 + 0) - (50 + 50)}{0 + 50 + 0 + 50} = -1.0,$$

and this is also true of the cord wrapped paddle stamped, shell tempered category.

This discussion of four-cell coefficients has been introduced chiefly to illuminate the concept of the two attribute association as the minimum requirement for the establishment of an artifact type, although the simple four-cell coefficient of association and its more sophisticated relatives are by no means to be ignored as working methods under the proper conditions. One of the serious deficiencies of the four-cell coefficient is its failure to consider the vagaries of sampling, since a conservative interpretation of the material from any archaeological component requires that it be considered no more than a sample drawn from a universe of artifacts manufactured by a society over some vaguely defined period of time. Other precautions to observe when using four-cell coefficients are discussed by Kroeber (1940).

Methods do exist which give answers expressing the combined result of the error involved in sampling and the extent to which the observed data fit the expected with respect to a hypothesis. The remainder of this paper will be devoted to illustrating the application of these methods to typological problems and some other archaeological data. All of the techniques presented are drawn from the literature of biological statistics dealing with the analysis of binomial distributions, especially the discussions of Mather (1947, Chapter XI) and Snedecor (1946, Chapters 9 and 16), and

the reader is referred to these sources for an adequate explanation of the underlying concepts. The most practical method of recording and subsequently extracting the variety and quantity of data needed for a thorough analysis of any sizable collection would appear to be one of the mechanically or electrically sorted punch card systems.

TABLE 9. FOUR-CELL FREQUENCIES WITH INDEPENDENCE
OF ATTRIBUTES

	Grit Temper	Shell Temper	Total
Stamped Surface	53	64	117
Smooth Surface	32	43	75
Total	85	107	192

Using Table 9 as an example, an analysis which fulfills the stipulated conditions can be made by means of a formula for computing a statistical entity known as chi square. The formula which is most convenient for a 2 x 2 table is

$$x^2 = \frac{n(ad - bc)^2}{(a + b)\ (c + d)\ (a + c)\ (b + d)},$$

or verbally, the number of specimens multiplied by the squared difference of the product of the diagonals divided by the product of the marginal totals. Substituting the values of Table 9 gives

$$x^2 = \frac{192\ [\ (53 \times 43) - (35 \times 64)\ ]^2}{117 \times 75 \times 35 \times 107},$$

which reduces to

$$\frac{192 \times 231 \times 231}{117 \times 75 \times 35 \times 107} = 0.128.$$

With a x^2 of 0.128 and one other argument, the number of degrees of freedom, it is possible to enter a table of x^2 and read the probability of the occurrence of so large a x^2 through the operation of sampling variation alone in a population having independent attributes in the ratios indicated by the marginal totals. The appropriate number of degrees of freedom is 1 because the computation imposes the restriction that the frequencies must add up to the marginal totals, so that as soon as a frequency is assigned to any cell those of the other three can be found by subtraction. The probability corresponding to a x^2 of 0.128 with 1 degree of freedom is between .80 and .70, which means that a x^2 this large would arise by chance alone between 70 and 80 times in 100 in a population having independent attributes.

It seems reasonable to accept the hypothesis of independence of attributes and conclude that the marginal totals present a fair picture of the potters' habits, there being very little evidence that the individual cell frequencies fall outside the range expected in a random drawing from a homogeneous population having the proportions of attributes indicated by the marginal totals. In other words, there is no discernible tendency for the attributes to cluster into types. Here, in contrast to the coefficients of association mentioned above, it has been possible to make a statement in terms of numerical probability and a definite hypothesis, which reduces the data to their most comprehensible form.

Chi square for Table 8 would be computed as

$$\frac{100\,[\,(50 \times 50) - (0 \times 0)\,]^2}{50 \times 50 \times 50 \times 50} \;=\; 100,$$

a value exceeding by a large amount the tabled value of 10.877 for a probability of .001 for 1 degree of freedom, and the probability that the marginal totals fairly represent the potters' habits is astronomically remote. The attributes are not independent; inspection of the table shows that the sample is derived from two populations, one characterized by grit tempering and a cord wrapped paddle stamped surface, the other by shell tempering and a smooth surface. This is the same conclusion as that based on the coefficient of association, but again a numerical expression of the odds against the occurrence of such a distribution in a random drawing from a population having an independent distribution of the four attributes has been provided.

It is important to note that the proportions used in testing attribute independence or lack of it were derived from the sample, and consequently the calculations have not tested the proposition that the observed proportions exactly represent those of the population from which the sample was obtained. What has been tested is the hypothesis that the two samples, those in the two rows or the two columns, were randomly drawn from a common binomial population. In the first instance (Table 9) the hypothesis was accepted, in the second (Table 8) it was rejected. Acceptance in the case of the data of Table 9 indicates that both cord wrapped paddle stamped and smooth surfaced vessels were randomly drawn from a population of vessels having grit temper and shell temper in a ratio estimated to be in the neighborhood of 85:107, or alternatively, both grit tempered and shell tempered vessels were randomly drawn from a population of vessels having cord wrapped paddle stamped and smooth surfaces in a ratio estimated to be 117:75. The estimated ratios are simply the marginal totals, and the inferences about the nature of the parent population can be completed by finding confidence limits for these estimates. This can be accomplished easily by means of a calculation or by reference to a table of confidence intervals such as that presented by Snedecor (1946, p. 4). Rejection of the hypothesis of independence in the case of Table 8 leads to the conclusion that cord wrapped paddle stamped vessels were drawn from a population of vessels estimated to be exclusively grit tempered, and smooth surfaced vessels were drawn from a probably exclusively shell tempered population. Again confidence intervals can be assigned to the estimates.

The next question to be investigated is that of a suitable technique for situations involving combinations of more than two pairs of attributes. The method to be employed is closely related to that just illustrated, but the resemblance is obscured by the streamlined computing routine used for the 2 x 2 table. There are two basic steps required: (1) calculation of an expected frequency for the combination, customarily under the hypothesis that the combination in question does not constitute a distinctive type, i.e., that the attributes making up the combination have independent distributions; and (2) comparison of the expected frequency with the observed frequency to determine whether or not the difference between the two can be reasonably attributed to sampling error. If the observed frequency exceeds the expected frequency by an amount too great to be considered the result of mere sampling error, it will be concluded that a genuine tendency for the makers of the artifacts to combine the attributes in question has been discovered — that the existence of a type has been demonstrated.

The following data will be used to explain the working method: in a collection of 297 pottery vessels, it is suspected that a combination of grit tempering, stamped surface, and a collared rim occurs often enough to provide sufficient grounds for the definition of a pottery type. A count made of the frequency of the triple combination gives 83 vessels; of the frequency of grit tempering alone, 117 vessels; of stamped surface alone, 91 vessels; and of collared rims alone, 136 vessels.

Under the hypothesis of independent distribution of attributes (no type), the frequency of the combination would be expected to be a simple function of the relative frequencies of the component attributes. Calculation of the expected number is a straightforward problem in compound probability, here

$$\frac{117}{297} \times \frac{91}{297} \times \frac{136}{297} \times \frac{297}{1} = 16.42 \text{ vessels.}$$

In practice it is necessary to compute the proportion (p) characteristic of the combination for reasons to be explained below. The computation of p here is

$$\frac{117}{297} \times \frac{91}{297} \times \frac{136}{297} = .0553.$$

The next step is to obtain the deviation (d) of the observation from the expectation by subtracting 16.42 from 83.00, which results in a deviation of 66.58.

It is necessary here to introduce some new symbols required for the final comparison of the expected frequency (E) and the observed frequency (O). The proportion of vessels not expected to exhibit the combination will be designated q, which is simply $1 - p$ or $1.000 - .0553 = .9447$ in the example. The expectation for the various possible frequencies of two alternative types (in this example grit tempered, cord wrapped paddle stamped, collared rim vessels and vessels not having this combination) can be found by expanding the binomial $(p + q)^k$, where k is the symbol for the number of individuals in the group (297 vessels); in addition, and of immediate importance in the solution of the problem, is the fact that the variance of the expanded binomial distribution is pqk (.0553 x .9447 x 297 = 15.52). The standard deviation (σ) is $\sqrt{pqk}$, which makes it possible to compute easily either the deviate in units of standard deviation as $\dfrac{d}{\sigma}$, or $\left[\dfrac{d}{\sigma}\right]^2$ as $\dfrac{d^2}{pqk}$. Both $\dfrac{d}{\sigma}$ and $\left[\dfrac{d}{\sigma}\right]^2$ can be converted into statements of probability by means of widely available tables.

In the case of d, σ, tables of areas of the normal curve or tables for t for infinite degrees of freedom may be used; $(d/\sigma)^2$ is the familiar χ^2 for 1 degree of freedom. Choice of formula is a matter of individual preference since the answers obtained are identical; tables for χ^2 are less closely computed than those for d/σ owing to their two dimensional character, but the precision of the latter does not appear to have any advantage for archaeological purposes. In both cases the tables were computed on the basis of a continuous curve rather than the binomial curve with discrete steps used here, and consequently they are not exactly applicable. A widely recommended· procedure for avoiding excessive distortion is to group categories so that the expected numbers are not too small, say 5 or less. A partial correction (the Yates correction) can be made by adjusting d, and precise methods of adjustment for small numbers can be found in statistical literature. The simple adjustments do not seem to change the results markedly, but anyone planning to use these techniques should be familiar with informed discussions of the subject.

Calculations for $(d/\sigma)^2$ for the example are

$$\frac{(66.58)^2}{15.52} = \frac{4432.90}{15.52} = 285.62.$$

Entering a table of χ^2 with this figure and 1 degree of freedom, a probability of finding a fit with hypothesis through chance at least as bad of very much less than .001 is noted. A similar calculation for d/σ indicates that the odds are actually less than 1 in 400,000,000,000 that so large a difference between observed and expected frequencies would arise through random sampling in the expanded binomial. It can be concluded that the chance of a sampling vagary as the explanation is exceedingly remote, and the large number of vessels exhibiting the combination must be attributed to the habits of the potters. The calculation does show that a pottery type exists. Further research would be necessary to investigate whether (1) on the basis of other attributes it might not be possible to identify a group of pottery types sharing the specified combination, or (2) whether there are other combinations differing by only one attribute which should be included in the type description as variants. The original conclusion — that the existence of a pottery type was demonstrated — is not modified by either case.

The evaluation of probability can perhaps be clarified by two other examples. Had the observed frequency been 24 vessels, χ^2 would have been computed as

$$\frac{(7.58)^2}{15.52} = \frac{57.46}{15.52} = 3.70,$$

which for 1 degree of freedom represents a probability of between .10 and .05, but much closer to .05. The conclusion is not at all clear. There is an appreciable chance that no real preference for the combination was exhibited by the potters, and the evaluation must be made with the aid of all the experience which the archaeologist can muster. If related sites plainly show that the combination is elsewhere a valid type, the interpretation would probably be that in this case the type was just appearing or disappearing. In the absence of other data, one could say only that there is a very good possibility that a type has been discovered. In certain types of statistical investigation a χ^2 of more than 3.841 (the .05 level of probability for 1 degree of freedom) is considered significant, or in our terms the hypothesis of independence would be rejected. It would appear unwise to carry over blindly such concepts into archaeology. Had the observed frequency of the combination been 8 vessels, d would have been 8.42 and $\chi^2 = 4.57$ with a probability between .05 and .02. The same general reasoning applies again, but here the situation is reversed because the expected frequency exceeds the observed frequency; there is a strong probability that the potters tended to avoid the combination, and the examples observed might best be considered the work of unorthodox potters.

A thorough investigation of a collection requires the calculation of d/σ or χ^2 for every possible combination of presumably important attributes. The number of combinations possible can be found by grouping the mutually exclusive attributes and multiplying together the number of attributes in each of the groups. If the groups of attributes consist of (1) smooth surface, stamped surface; (2) incised rim, plain rim; (3) incised lip, plain lip; and (4) bowl shape, jar shape; the computation is $2 \times 2 \times 2 \times 2 = 16$ possible combinations. If the groups are (1) smooth surface, stamped surface; (2) rectilinear incising on shoulder, curvilinear incising on shoulder, plain shoulder; and (3) grit tempered, shell tempered; there are $2 \times 3 \times 2 = 12$ possible combinations. These 12 combinations will be used in an example with the following data given: total number of vessels (k), 186; frequency of smooth surface, 121 vessels; of stamped surface, 65 vessels; of rectilinear pattern incised on shoulder, 47 vessels; of curvilinear pattern incised on shoulder, 28 vessels; of plain shoulder, 111 vessels; of grit tempering, 70 vessels; and of shell tempering, 116 vessels. Combination counts and computations are shown in Table 10. The computations are exactly like those described above. For example, p in the first combination is

$$\frac{121}{186} \times \frac{47}{186} \times \frac{70}{186} = .0619.$$

The expected number (E) is $186 \times .0619 = 11.51$, and so on.

TABLE 10. COMPUTATION OF $\dfrac{d^2}{pqk}$ FOR TWELVE COMBINATIONS OF ATTRIBUTES

Attribute Combination	O	E	d	d²	pqk	$\dfrac{d^2}{pqk}$
Sm. surf., rect. sh., grit t.	0	11.51	−11.51	132.02	10.78	12.25
Sm. surf., curv. sh., grit t.	2	6.84	−4.85	23.52	6.59	3.56
Sm. surf., plain sh., grit t.	14	27.17	−13.17	173.45	23.21	7.47
Sm. surf., rect. sh., shell t.	38	19.07	+18.93	358.35	17.11	20.94
Sm. surf., curv. sh., shell t.	26	11.36	+14.64	214.33	10.66	20.11
Sm. surf., plain sh., shell t.	41	45.04	−4.04	16.24	34.13	0.48
St. surf., rect. sh., grit t.	3	6.18	−3.18	10.11	5.97	1.69
St. surf., curv. sh., grit t.	0	3.68	−3.68	13.54	3.61	3.75
St. surf., plain sh., grit t.	51	14.60	+36.40	1324.96	13.45	98.51
St. surf., rect. sh., shell t.	6	10.25	−4.25	18.06	9.69	1.86
St. surf., curv. sh., shell t.	0	6.10	−6.10	37.21	5.90	6.31
St. surf., plain sh., shell t.	5	24.20	−19.20	368.26	21.04	17.50
Total	186	186.00	0.00			

Statistical Techniques for the Discovery of Artifact Types

Table 10 is to be interpreted simply as a list of χ^2 values, each of which has its corresponding probability for 1 degree of freedom. The individual χ^2 values, computed as d^2/pqk, do not have additive properties in contrast to the contingency table discussed below. Interpretation in terms of pottery types follows the principles already discussed. Three combinations have large positive deviations and large χ^2 values with probabilities well beyond the .001 level. These are stamped surface, plain shoulder, grit temper; smooth surface, curvilinear incised shoulder, shell temper; and smooth surface, rectilinear incised shoulder, shell temper. The last two combinations differ by only one attribute, and hence are to be lumped in one type. The same is true of the smooth surfaced, plain shouldered, shell tempered combination, which is important numerically but has a very small χ^2 value. Accordingly, there is definitely a smooth surfaced, shell tempered type having three kinds of shoulder treatment in a ratio estimated to be about 26:38:41. This can be confirmed by calculating a χ^2 for a 2 x 2 table testing the degree of association of smooth surface and shell temper. It will be found that they are very strongly associated, as are grit temper and a stamped surface. It can be inferred that the indifferent χ^2 value (0.48) of the shell tempered, plain shouldered, smoothed surface combination is the result of the fact that plain shoulders are shared with and are rather more characteristic of the stamped surfaced, grit tempered combination. This conclusion is at sharp variance with conventional type analysis, where the shell tempered, plain shouldered, smooth surfaced combination would almost surely be distinguished as a separate type, as would the other two smooth surfaced, shell tempered combinations. The calculations above are intended to be an objective demonstration that the fundamental pattern of the type is the smooth surfaced, shell tempered vessel. Shoulder treatment can be described only in terms of estimated ratios of a group of mutually exclusive attributes.

The stamped surfaced, plain shouldered, grit tempered vessels constitute a second definite type; χ^2 for the combination is very high (98.51) and it can be shown that stamped surface and grit temper are strongly associated. The 14 vessels having smooth surfaces, plain shoulders, and grit temper would not be as-

signed to either type; they are genuinely intermediate and would be so described. The same reasoning applies to the 5 vessels having stamped surfaces, plain shoulders, and shell tempering. The remaining few vessels share two attributes with one or the other of the types and would be assigned accordingly as somewhat aberrant examples. Combinations of this sort, characterized by negative deviations and crossing over of attributes from two types, offer interesting evidence on the degree of conventionality of the potters. In this connection the combinations with a frequency of 0 are highly informative.

A second sort of table can be computed which offers summary evidence on the total pottery making habits of the group. For this table, the individual contribution of each combination would be computed as d^2/E, which for the first combination of Table 10 is 132.02/11.51. The total of these contributions is a χ^2 value for the 12 combinations taken together, for which a probability can be found in the χ^2 table using 7 degrees of freedom. A verbal explanation of the appropriateness of 7 degrees of freedom is too cumbersome for inclusion here, and a clear graphic presentation of a 2 x 3 x 2 table is also difficult, but it can be stated that the particular restrictions imposed by the attribute totals used as basic data allow 7 of the 12 cells of the table to be filled in freely within the general limitations of the attribute totals. The remaining five can be determined by subtraction and hence do not contribute to the degrees of freedom. A χ^2 computed in this manner gives an over-all measure of the tendency of the potters to group attributes and offers cogent material for comparison with other sites having the same categories. Other sorts of comparisons between sites can be made by using the observed number for each combination from one site as the expected number for the other and calculating the resulting χ^2 or by calculating a χ^2 testing the proposition that both sets of observed values could reasonably be considered random samples from a common population. The latter process is illustrated below in the example dealing with the problem of site homogeneity (Table 12).

All of the examples have been concerned exclusively with attributes which are physical properties of the artifacts. It is well known, however, that artifacts have other kinds of attributes, notably provenience, which can be pertinent evidence for the existence of a type. Thus a site might yield two kinds of vessels which differed only in the presence or absence of a single physical attribute, say a lip flange on one. If nothing but physical properties were considered, both kinds would be included in one pottery type because a difference of one attribute is not sufficient evidence for separation. But if the flanged lip appeared only on vessels found in graves and the plain lip was confined to village debris, it would be obvious that the potters had in mind two types with different functional connotations. Provenience furnishes the second attribute required to differentiate two types. The attributes "found in graves" and "found in village refuse" can be included in a probability calculation in exactly the same way as can any physical property of an artifact.

An example, this time not fictitious, of the application of this technique to a non-typological problem will be presented. The data of Table 11 are from the Columbia University excavations at the Arzberger Site, Hughes County, South Dakota, and summarize provenience data of grooved paddle stamped body sherds and other types of surface finish. The

TABLE 11. SURFACE FINISH OF BODY SHERDS BY PROVENIENCE, ARZBERGER SITE, SOUTH DAKOTA

Excavation Unit	Surface Finish		
	Grooved Paddle Stamped	Other	Total
House I	396	1,279	1,675
House II	135	546	681
House III	172	532	704
House IV	178	657	835
Ditch	0	4	4
Unknown	22	79	101
Total	903	3,097	4,000

problem to be investigated is one of site homogeneity. If the site is homogeneous, one excavation unit should be much like another within the limits of sampling error. With respect to the data given on surface finish of body sherds, a hypothesis of independence can be set up: the proportion of grooved paddle stamped sherds will be a function of the frequency of the totals and will be independent of the locus from which the sample is drawn if the site is truly homogeneous. Chi square is computed by the $d^2 pqk$ method used above, although this is not the most common technique for a $2 \times n$ contingency table such as is given. The value

of p is $903/4,000 = .2258$, $q = .7742$, and k is successively the total number of sherds for each sample. The values are shown in Table 12 (a few rounding errors have not been adjusted). The result is good evidence that the

TABLE 12. TEST OF HOMOGENEITY OF EXCAVATION UNITS, ARZBERGER SITE, SOUTH DAKOTA

	O	E	d	d^2	pqk	$\dfrac{d^2}{pqk}$
House I	396	378.21	17.79	316.48	292.81	1.08
House II	135	153.77	18.77	352.31	119.05	2.96
House III	172	158.96	13.04	170.04	123.07	1.38
House IV	178	188.54	10.54	111.09	145.97	0.76
Other[1]	22	23.70	1.70	2.89	18.35	0.16
Total	903	903.00				$\chi^2 = 6.34$

[1] The expected frequency for "Ditch" is less than 6, and accordingly it is incorporated in a new category by adding its value to "Unknown."

hypothesis of independence is correct. Individual values are small, and the total for 4 degrees of freedom (this is a 2×5 contingency table) corresponds to a probability of between .20 and .10, which does not give any very convincing reason to suspect significant differences in the various excavation units. It can be concluded that so far as the evidence at hand is concerned, the site may reasonably be considered the product of a single occupation over a restricted period of time.

An attempt to appraise the usefulness of this approach to typological and related problems should consider the amount of labor necessary in making the computations. In view of the general availability of computing machines, this seems trivial. The writing of the exposition was far more tedious than the computing of the examples. There is a great deal of work required in making, recording, and assembling the observations needed for a thorough study, but this is not the fault of the statistical methods. It is rather an inevitable part of any detailed study. The methods of calculation used here were selected on a basis of clarity of exposition, not economy of labor; those interested in computing routine are referred to the statistical textbooks cited.

With regard to the more serious question of general usefulness, these are the methods generally recommended for handling data of this sort, although no claim is made that the particular procedures illustrated here completely exhaust the resources of statistics. The information derived from them is important in an earnest attempt to discover the cultural significance inherent in archaeological remains, and there is no other way in which such information can be obtained. There is no magic involved, however; the usefulness of the result is entirely dependent upon the wisdom with which attributes are observed and investigated and on the relevance of the context to meaningful archaeological problems. Moreover, the inference to be drawn from a statement of probability is sometimes not altogether clear, but at least the degree of uncertainty is put into objective form.

A source of uncertainty which has been mentioned is the fact that the proportions on which the hypothesis of independence is evaluated are derived from the sample and hence are themselves subject to sampling error. This difficulty is inescapable; we can work only with the samples we have, and the observed proportions are surely the best estimate of the proportions of the population, the properties of which must be inferred from the sample. Nevertheless, the cautious student will interpret his results with one eye on a table of confidence limits. To add to this uncertainty, the dimensions of which can at least be estimated on the basis of statistical theory, there is the purely archaeological problem of the nature of the relationship of the sample to the living culture which produced the artifacts. The whole problem is summarized by the often repeated warning that statistics are never a substitute for thinking. But statistical analysis does present data which are well worth thinking about.

BIBLIOGRAPHY

BRAINERD, GEORGE W.
1951. The Place of Chronological Ordering in Archaeological Anaylsis. *American Antiquity*, Vol. 16, No. 4, pp. 301-13. Salt Lake City.

KRIEGER, ALEX D.
1944. The Typological Concept. *American Antiquity*, Vol. 9, No. 4, pp. 271-88. Menasha.

KROEBER, A. L.
1940. Statistical Classification. *American Antiquity*, Vol. 6, No. 1, pp. 29-44. Menasha.

LEHMER, DONALD J.
1951. Robinson's Coefficient of Agreement — A Critique. *American Antiquity*, Vol. 17, No. 2, p. 151. Salt Lake City.

MATHER, K.
1947. *Statistical Analysis in Biology*. New York: Interscience Publishers.

NEWELL, H. PERRY, AND ALEX D. KRIEGER
1949. The George C. Davis Site, Cherokee County, Texas. *Memoirs of the Society for American Archaeology*, No. 5. Menasha.

ROBINSON, W. S.
1951. A Method for Chronologically Ordering Archaeological Deposits. *American Antiquity*, Vol. 16, No. 4, pp. 293-301. Salt Lake City.

ROUSE, IRVING
1939. Prehistory in Haiti, A Study in Method. *Yale University Publications in Anthropology*, No. 21. New Haven.

SNEDECOR, GEORGE W.
1946. *Statistical Methods Applied to Experiments in Agriculture and Biology*. Ames: Iowa State College Press.

TAYLOR, WALTER W.
1948. A Study of Archaeology. *Memoirs, American Anthropological Association*, No. 69. Menasha.

Museum of Anthropology
University of Michigan
Ann Arbor, Michigan
August, 1952

* * * * *

COMMENT ON A. C. SPAULDING,
"STATISTICAL TECHNIQUES FOR THE
DISCOVERY OF ARTIFACT TYPES" *

First let me say that I am thoroughly sympathetic to all efforts toward development of more accurate methodology. But the application of statistics and other techniques to our problems, without regard for basic culture theory, cannot be regarded as an advance in technique.

For years there have been arguments as to whether cultural types — pottery types to be specific — were pre-existing units in culture history that could be discovered by a good archaeologist and missed by an incompetent one. I have been on the negative side in these debates — which arise, it seems to me, because people are talking about two different things.

It is well known that any given culture is a classificatory device which offers its bearers patterned ways of meeting the problems of existence. Not only are

* American Antiquity, Vol. 18, No. 3, 1953.

there categories of correct ways to dress, dance, talk, and solve the mother-in-law problem, but also there are proper ways to manufacture food vessels, water containers, cooking pots, etc. This is the patterning that is found imposed on the sherds in any time level in a village dump. The degree to which cultures allow variation in patterning varies widely from one culture to another; at different times; and from one aspect of the culture to another. The flexibility of the styles in Weeden Island is in contrast to the rather rigid patterning of Caddoan or Mississippian ceramics.

Spaulding's suggestion that statistical analysis of the patterning to be found in a collection from a village site will establish pottery types useful in study of culture history is amazingly naive. It will reveal the relative degree to which the people conformed to their set of ceramic styles at one time and place, but that is all it will do. Whether this information about ceramics is worth the work, I hesitate to say. However, it should be pointed out that Spaulding is advising the use of data in which variation due to the degree of conformance to standards is welded to variation due to style change with time. Such studies could be better made after the chronology is controlled.

The search for the natural units in culture history, which still haunts the work of archaeologists, is directly analogous to the early 19th century biologist's faith in immutable species following one another in orderly procession down the misty corridors of geological time. Surely it is time we progressed beyond cataclysmic archaeology where deposits representing each period are separated by layers of clean white sand. We now have techniques by which cultural development can be studied.

Patterning is not the central problem of typology, rather it is the framework in which the problem of setting up measures of time-change and geographical space-change of each unit of the pattern have to be solved.

To try to make this clear, I will discuss an actual situation. It is well known that a ceramic association consisting of a grit-tempered ware with a range of conoidal-base shapes and cordmarked decoration forms a fairly stable unit of the patterning that is found at a number of village sites in the northeastern United States. Let us make the entirely unwarranted assumption that we can view the distribution of this association of features at the year A.D. 700. As we cross geographical space to the southward, it will be seen that change took place in the "mean" — or we might say "ideal" — about which the actual specimens cluster. In Kentucky and Tennessee, grit is replaced with sand tempering; clay tempering appears in northern Alabama, and becomes the rule in the lower Mississippi Valley. Form changes from conoidal to rounded to flat base. Similar minor changes can be seen in the application of the surface finish.

Change of these associated traits tends to be gradual as space is crossed, and there is a good reason — which need not be detailed here — why this should be so. There are no inevitable, necessary breaks which will force the classifier to cut this ceramic distribution into segments. However, diffusion does not operate unaffected by other factors. When enough information is available, it will doubtless be found that rate of change in this pattern unit across geography was speeded up by competition with other cultural forms or by natural, political, or linguistic boundaries. Also, change was probably slowed by movements of people, or routes of easy communication.

After chronology is well under control, it may be possible occasionally to associate recognizable units of ceramic pattern with tribes as Ritchie and MacNeish have recently done. However, there is no inherent reason why such divisions must coincide.

Similar change can be seen in the cordmarking tradition as it is viewed through time. For example, there is a drift from large to fine cords. Here, too, there were doubtless periods of acceleration and deceleration in change due to a variety of possible factors. However, there are no natural inevitable factors operating that will establish neat segments in this change. Replacements of populations will cause sudden breaks in the culture history of Fulton County, Illinois, but that is another matter.

To set up historically useful type units in a tradition such as is represented by cordmarked pottery, I can see no way to avoid detailed comparisons made site to site and through time. Also necessary is a wary awareness that it is the date and geographical position of the site which you chance to dig that give the association of features that look so significant. Had your site been a hundred miles to the north and a hundred years earlier, "Klankenburg Cordmarked" would have been slightly different — a category into which one could place only about half the sherds now called by that name.

James A. Ford
American Museum of Natural History
New York, N.Y.
May, 1953

REPLY TO FORD

Ford's objections to the ideas advanced in "Statistical Techniques for the Discovery of Artifact Types" appear to revolve around (1) the notion that use of such techniques somehow constitutes a denial of continuous variation of culture in time and space and (2) certain implicit definitions of such terms as "artifact type" and "historical usefulness" which in effect make their use the exclusive prerogative of the archaeologist engaged in inferring chronology by ranking sites or components of sites in order of likeness as judged by relative frequency of attribute combinations. I shall attempt to show that the first objection is a gratuitous error and that the second is no more than a semantic quagmire.

The issues involved can be clarified by describing three levels of organization of artifacts with respect to the attributes which they exhibit. I wish to point out in advance that the result of classification at each of these levels has been called an artifact type, and that the levels have an orderly logical relationship to each other. This relationship is lineal; each level represents an elaboration of that immediately preceding it by the addition of new concepts.

Level I is the primary organization of the empirical data, which are the artifacts or fragments of artifacts in an archaeological assemblage. Operating procedure at this level consists of observing and tallying the attribute combinations present. If, as is frequently the case, the researcher plans to conduct comparative investigations by means of these attribute combinations, the tallies are expressed as proportions in order to provide commensurate data. A type at this level is a group of artifacts linked by the possession of a specific attribute combination which someone chooses to call a type.

Level II is an elaboration of the data provided by the Level I classification; the combination counts of Level I are analyzed to provide the total frequencies of each attribute noted, and the relationship of these attribute frequencies to the combination counts is investigated to provide information on the amount and nature of attribute clustering present in the assemblage. A type at this level is a group of artifacts exhibiting a consistent and distinctive cluster of attributes.

Level III is in turn based on the data of Level II, but adds the attribute of function to the attribute clusters of Level II. A type at this level consists of a group of artifacts exhibiting a cluster of distinctive attributes and having a distinctive function or functions. In the case of archaeological data, the function in most situations must be inferred from the attribute clusters of Level II by means of attributes which are not physical characteristics of the artifact (provenience, for example) or by imputing function on the basis of ethnographic analogy.

In order to avoid confusion here, the classificatory entities of Level I will be called simply attribute combinations, those of Level II attribute clusters, and those of Level III functional types. The major purpose of my paper was to suggest suitable techniques for discovering the amount and nature of attribute clustering in any archaeological assemblage — in short, how to perform the characteristic operations of Level II. It was further suggested that the definite attribute clusters isolated by these techniques were artifact types, i.e., corresponded closely to a general idea of the signification of the word "type." I supposed that an especially valuable feature of types so defined was the fact that they included inferences as to the behavior of the makers of the artifacts, in contrast to the boldly empirical attribute combinations so often called types (and even dignified by a "Binomial System of Nomenclature"). The attribute clusters are "natural" units in the sense that they represent a special effort to infer the behavior patterns of the makers, not the particular needs of an archaeologist working on a particular problem.

These preliminary remarks lead up to the semantic question mentioned in the first paragraph. Ford's comments, although never rising to the level of a coherent definition of what he means by an artifact type, indicate that in his view an artifact type is something which cannot be delineated on the basis of data from a single society over a restricted period of time, thus nearly excluding the possibility that our current knowledge will allow us to describe the artifact types of our own culture in 1953. Dismissing this result as nonsensical, I move on to infer that on the positive side a Fordian artifact type is "historically useful" and that an attribute cluster is not. Unfortunately, we are not favored with an intelligible statement of what is meant by historical usefulness, but it is plain that it has something to do with site to site comparisons extending through some undefined segment of time. Ford's default leaves a clear field for my own definition of historical usefulness: I would argue that any reasonably consistent and well defined social behavior pattern is historically useful, i.e., meaningful in assessing similarities and differences between any two components. The major purpose of my paper was to explore techniques for discovering consistent and well defined behavior patterns, and if the techniques actually do what they are supposed to do they cannot fail to yield historically useful units. The crucial point is adequacy of sample, not occurrence at 2 or 20 or 200 sites.

The alleged incompatibility of attribute clusters and a situation of continuous cultural development (disregard for "basic cultural theory" in Ford's terminology) can be dealt with simply. The methods I described are supposed to be an efficient process for discovering and describing the attribute clusters in any archaeological assemblage, and are nothing more than that. No suggestion was made that any statistical operations would disclose the ultimate significance of the clusters described; significance depends on the nature of the assemblage. The clusters may be the product of contemporaneous patterning, or of a systematic shift in styles over a considerable period of time, or the result of mixture of two more or less discrete cultural traditions, or combinations of these and other factors. Judgment of significance is primarily a matter of interpreting the nature of the archaeological deposit, which, even in the case where a single tradition is involved, can range from the group of projectile points imbedded in the Naco mammoth to the meters of continuous deposit found at some southeastern sites. But the attribute clusters are an excellent device for describing the outcome of such judgment in culturally meaningful terms. Formal recognition of transitional combinations (those differing by only one attribute from each of two distinct types) is particularly helpful in the exposition of continuous cultural change. I would like to make the malicious observation that the pottery attribute combinations used in site-to-site comparison by Ford fail to disclose ultimate significance in precisely the same fashion and to the same degree as do the attribute clusters, and to query Ford as to whether or not the binomial southeastern pottery types should be abandoned forthwith on the ground that they disregard basic cultural theory.

At this point, it seems more profitable to abandon debating tactics and go to what I take to be the root of Ford's dissatisfaction with the attribute clusters (he has not challenged the validity of the techniques used to discover the clusters). This root is simply the fact that the attribute clusters are obviously not identical with the pottery types used by southeastern archaeologists and hence, in Ford's reasoning are certainly not pottery types, and moreover are probably not good for anything else. The southeastern types are attribute combinations which have been found to be useful in ranking components in order of likeness for the purpose of inferring relative chronology; usefulness here means occurring in varying proportions at several sites (Phillips, Ford, and Griffin, 1951, pp. 61-66). Although this point of view has been criticized above, the argument can be summarized by pointing out that (1) inferring relative chronology is not the sole objective of archaeology, the problem of description of assemblages in terms of patterns of human behavior being equally important; and (2) the attribute cluster with its explicit investigation of patterning has a somewhat better claim to the name "type" than does the attribute combination (the functional type has the best claim of all). By way of comment on statement (1), it might be asked whether anyone has shown that simple attribute counts would not discriminate sufficiently well between components to permit ranking; if they can discriminate, the Fordian type is both an inefficient tool for inferring chronology and an incomplete descriptive tool without any cogent reason for existence. The dispute over names mentioned in (2) is trivial, although it is certain that some confusion in classification has resulted from calling attribute combinations "types" owing to a more or less inchoate recognition that the word does imply patterning. If any semantic boundaries are to be set, clearly the functional type is entitled to the label, the attribute cluster probably is, and the attribute combination is probably out of bounds. I should add that I do not favor setting any boundaries by legislation; I am quite willing to let Ford have his types if he will let me have mine. The important thing is to be explicit about what kind of type one is talking about.

BIBLIOGRAPHY

PHILLIPS, PHILIP, JAMES A. FORD, AND JAMES B. GRIFFIN

    1951. Archaeological Survey in the Lower Mississippi Valley, 1940-1947. *Papers of the Peabody Museum of American Archaeology and Ethnology, Harvard University*, Vol. 25. Cambridge.

ALBERT C. SPAULDING
Museum of Anthropology
University of Michigan
Ann Arbor, Michigan
Nov., 1953

On the Concept of Types

An article by J. A. FORD

The Type Concept Revisited[1]

SEVERAL years ago, Kluckhohn (1939) upbraided anthropologists in general and archeologists in particular for failure to examine critically the assumptions and concepts which lie at the foundations of their methodologies. Perhaps this well justified censure has prompted the healthy introspection that has developed in the past decade and resulted in valuable papers such as those by Rouse (1939), Krieger (1944), Brew (1946), Taylor (1948), and Ehrich (1950).

As soon as students of cultural phenomena cease to be satisfied with comparisons of mere qualities of cultural traits and begin also to treat their data quantitatively, it becomes apparent that the basic conceptual tool of cultural research is that of the type. To the present it is the archeologists who have been most concerned with the formulation and use of cultural types, but this hardly redounds to the credit of this branch of the profession. Archeologists have been forced into this position by the necessity for reconstructing cultural histories from a very limited range of cultural material. Although the term has been used indiscriminately, in practice the typological concept has been thoughtfully applied almost entirely to ceramics. The principles are the same, however, for all other aspects of culture, and we may expect to see it more widely used as sufficient evidence accumulates to make it possible and necessary.

To utilize the concept of type efficiently, it is very necessary that the cultural student have a clear idea of what a type is, how it is defined, and what purposes it may serve. At present there seems to be some confusion. The debate seems to center around the question of the "reality" of cultural types; a debate which is very similar to that carried on by the biologists for a number of years in regard to the significance of the species concept. To state it clearly, the question may be put this way: "Do cultural types exist in the phenomena so that they may be discovered by a capable typologist?" This is an important question for the answer not only determines how investigators may proceed in identifying types, but it also determines how types may be employed in solving cultural problems.

Both Rouse (1939) and Krieger (1944) have given excellent discussion of the application of the concept of type but have failed to clarify this debated point. Neither am I entirely satisfied with the statement in Phillips, Ford and Griffin (1951:61–64). Recently the question has again been brought up as a result of an article by A. C. Spaulding (1953) which describes a method for discovering cultural types by statistical methods. This discussion takes for granted the assumption that types do exist in culture and may be discovered by competent methodologies. This I doubt.

42

Perhaps it will clarify the problem to say a word about the history of the type concept, for the purposes of classification of archeological material have undergone a change beginning in this country during the second and third decades of this century. Initially archeological classifications were made for the purpose of describing collections, and the smallest divisions of the items were frequently called types. These groupings were defined without reference to the temporal and spatial coordinates of culture history. Where chronological information is lacking such descriptive classifications are the only sort that can be made and are extremely useful. A good example of such a classification is S. K. Lothrop's (1926) analysis of pottery collections from Costa Rica and Nicaragua.

The classifying of ceramics into type groupings that are designed to serve as measuring devices for culture history began in the southwestern United States and is now standard practice among American archeologists. Descriptive systematization is subordinated to the necessity for emphasizing spatial and temporal change in the material. Perhaps it is unfortunate that the word "type" has been retained for this new function because to some it seems to carry a connotation of its earlier descriptive usage. Krieger (1944:272) has stated the current purpose of formulating types in the following words:

> Thus the purpose of a type in archaeology must be to provide an organizational tool which will enable the investigator to group specimens into bodies which have *demonstrable historical meaning in terms of behavior patterns.* Any group which may be labelled a "type" must embrace material which can be shown to consist of individual variations in the execution of a definite constructional idea; likewise, the dividing lines between a series of types must be based upon demonstrable historical factors, not, as is often the case, upon the inclinations of the analyst or the niceties of descriptive orderliness.

Spaulding (1953:305) seems to agree that to be useful each type must have historical significance: "Historical relevance in this view is essentially derived from the typological analysis; a properly established type is the result of sound inferences concerning the customary behavior of the makers of the artifacts and cannot fail to have historical meaning." I certainly am in agreement with both these authors that to be useful, each type must have a limited range in time and space and thus have historical significance.

The discussion that follows will retrace some of the same arguments set forth by Rouse and Krieger but will consider typology from a slightly different angle. Instead of emphasizing the problem from the point of view of archeological specimens, I shall examine the concept as it would apply to a living culture. Further, to make the task easier and to attempt to clarify basic problems which the typologist must face, this will be fictitious culture history which has not been subjected to the complicating factors that operate in all actual histories. These factors are barriers to diffusion such as uneven population distribution, natural obstacles to communication, political and linguistic boundaries, or boundaries between competing cultural items of different geographic origin. Neither will it be subjected to the forces that speed and retard

cultural change—wars, epidemics, alien cultures with high prestige, or advertising by influential innovators. Each culture bearer has been the normal minor innovator that has borne the responsibility for most of the change that has taken place in culture histories.

The fairy tale which follows is the sort of "stripped" description of phenomena which has proved very useful in more mature fields of science, such as physics. Every physical "Law" states that if certain modifying circumstances were nullified such and such would happen. In experience the modifying circumstances are always present and events never conform exactly to the "Law." This, then, is my excuse for introducing the Gamma-gamma people of the Island of Gamma, situated in the curious sea of Zeta.

A CULTURE IS A CLASSIFICATORY DEVICE

With no intention to disparage the work of fellow anthropologists, it may be said that the synchronous view of the ethnologist is the most simple way to consider cultural phenomena. When an ethnologist first arrives among the Gamma-gamma of the Island of Gamma, their culture will impress him as a confused conglomeration of absurdities. The Gamma-gamma will do strange, unreasonable things and on many occasions will appear to be lacking in common horse sense—an impression that has been shared by every tourist who has come into contact with people having a culture different from his own.

As the more-or-less impartial ethnologist becomes better acquainted and begins to acquire something of the point of view of the Gamma-gamma, social actions and cultural objects begin to fall into classes. It will be discovered that these classes are well organized to solve the problems that confront this group of human animals: procuring food, providing shelter and protection from enemies, regulating mating and other social relations, and magical techniques that affect otherwise uncontrollable forces such as diseases and the weather. There are patterned ways of dancing, of constructing a canoe, of clothing and decorating the body, etc. In addition, if the basic premises of Gamma-gamma thought are accepted, many of these cultural categories have a logical, apparently inevitable, relation to one another and these relations are cross-ties that reinforce and stabilize the entire cultural structure. Certain dances are necessary as a preliminary to catching fish; a man cannot marry until he has killed an enemy—human or shark—and has been tattooed; houses are the property of women because they build them; children belong to the mother's family for where is the child who can be certain of his father?

This compartmentalization and order are necessary and will be found in all other cultures. To add to the definitions recently listed by Kroeber and Kluckhohn (1952), it can also be said that culture is an organized system for handling human and social problems. However, different segments of a culture will vary as to the range of variability which is permitted as acceptable behavior. The Gamma-gamma group has very strict rules as to how a man may address his mother-in-law: he must face away to avoid seeing her and preface all remarks with polite formal phrases—to do otherwise would cause great

scandal and what else no one knows for it has never been tried. However, there are a number of perfectly good ways to make an adze. Virtually any hard stone will serve as a blade, four varieties of hafting are used, and there are six shapes of handles. In addition, a man takes some pride in carving the handle in an original fashion, as different from those of his fellows as possible. Still, any ethnologist acquainted with the material culture of this region can recognize a twentieth-century Gamma-gamma adze at a glance. Despite the fact that it permits and even appears to encourage variability, this cultural trait is a classificatory device similar to the mother-in-law taboo and has wider but still rigid limits. The variation follows patterns and these people haven't thought of.turning the blade around and making a hatchet of the tool.

It is this inherent order in culture of which archeologists must be aware when they begin the search for types for this is the framework within which the typology must be constructed. This is certainly the order that will be revealed by applying statistical devices to the ceramics of prehistoric dwelling sites as recently advocated by Spaulding (1953). However, this order does not provide the historically significant grouping of traits which the archeologist must have to measure culture history.

THE ETHNOLOGIST'S VIEW OF A CULTURAL TRAIT

The Gamma-gamma have each aspect of their culture well compartmentalized: pottery food-serving vessels have a limited range of shapes and decorations; water bottles have their appropriate range; and the containers in which the mild alcoholic drink is fermented have their range. However, the actual specimens that are manufactured for these various purposes are by no means identical duplicates such as would be turned out by a machine. Instead, each vessel is recognizably different from every other vessel in its class. As the ethnologist studies the pottery, and other aspects of the culture, he will observe that the variation in actual artifact tends to cluster about a mean, which he can then visualize as the central theme of the type.

The ethnologist cannot rely upon the culture bearers to define this central theme. They may or may not be aware of it, or may have rationalizations in regard to it which are at considerable variance with actual practice, as Dr. Kinsey's study of male sexual practices has demonstrated for our own culture. A statistical average must be arrived at, either by actual counting or by estimating. If desirable, the rationalizations may be considered apart for they are also cultural features and are subject to the same kind of analysis as actions.

The cultural trait, then, is an abstraction made by the ethnologist and derived from the cultural activity. It has a mean and a range of variation. This range of variation may be visualized as a scatter diagram—a three-dimensional scatter diagram similar to a swarm of bees clustering about the queen might better represent the situation, but there are limitations to the printed page and a two-dimensional diagram will have to serve. In Figure 1, I have attempted to represent the variation in houses that was observed among the Gamma-gamma on the Island of Gamma in 1940. As the diagram shows, the

majority of houses were medium-sized rectangular structures about 4 by 6 meters and 5 meters high, placed on low piers above the damp ground, and had gabled roofs, one room, and one door. Variations from this norm are observed in several directions. Houses illustrated toward the right of the diagram, mostly occupied by older people, were on high stilts, and one is in a tree. They

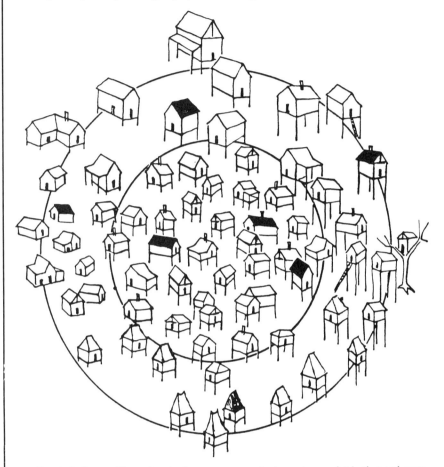

Fig. 1. A diagram illustrating the frequency mean of a type at one point in time and space. The small houses grouped in the inner circle represent the mean. Variation from this mean is illustrated in four directions—a simplification of the variation that is found about the frequency means of actual types.

tend to be smaller than the average. Toward the left side of the diagram, the houses are larger and are on very low stilts, or are built on the ground. A few have two rooms. Variation toward the top of the diagram tends toward larger size, and toward the bottom the houses are small, square, and the roofs approach the pyramidal in shape.

This description is an obvious simplification. As the diagram shows, there

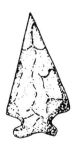

are all sorts of variations between the four poles described and, in addition, there are other variables which could also serve as poles in this diagram. For example, some buildings are roofed with the white palm fronds and on others the dark gray *kilea* grass is used. Still, these combinations have definite limits of variation. None of the houses has more than one living and sleeping room, all are constructed of bamboo and thatch, and no one has introduced bathrooms such as are observed in the local mission buildings. To the ethnological observer it is quite clear that there is a Gamma-gamma house type with a mean and range of variation as just described. In Figure 1, what may be considered the mean of the type lies within the inner circle.

THE ETHNOGRAPHIC TYPE IS FORMED BY THE OBSERVER AT A CHOSEN LEVEL OF ABSTRACTION

The dwellings of the Gamma-gamma at first glance offer a convenient segment of their culture composed of tangible elements and would seem to be ideal for the purpose of measuring. Upon closer examination, the apparent concreteness of this category can be broken down in two directions, for this aspect of the culture is part of an integrated whole and became a measurable unit merely because attention was focused upon it. First, it must be recalled that these buildings are cultural products—not the culture. These arrangements of wood, bamboo, and grass are of interest to the ethnologist solely because they illustrate the aborigine's ideas as to the proper ways to construct dwellings. The cultural concept "house" can be broken down into elements. There are a range of methods to anchor piers, to arrange plates, to lash rafters, and at least four standard methods of thatching. Each of these elements can be measured in the same way as the entire houses have been and each will be found to have a frequency mean and range of variation. "House" may quite legitimately be considered as a cultural complex rather than as a unit.[2]

On the other hand, the concepts dictating the proper ways to build a house are not isolated in the culture. For one thing, they are intimately connected with the form of the family. These people are monogamous and married children set themselves up in separate establishments. There is never need for more than one living room, nor is large size necessary. In turn, the single-room small houses tend to reinforce this pattern of family life. The house, then, might legitimately be considered as one element of the 1940 Gamma-gamma family type.

It is evident that "cultural types" are abstracted on different levels of apparent complexity by the observer.[3] One level is no more "real" than another. What the classifier must do is to select a level which will serve the purposes in view. If the objective is a comparison of religions, the student will set up religious types; if it is concerned with priestly paraphernalia, the types will be formed of cultural traits which are mere elements for the preceding purpose. The cultural scientist must be aware of this necessity and not allow chance focalization of interest to provide categories that are accepted as immutable units.

THE ETHNOGRAPHIC TYPE IS ABSTRACTED BY THE OBSERVER AT ONE POINT IN SPACE

So long as the ethnologist stays among the Gamma-gamma on the Island of Gamma, the house type described above appears to form a satisfactory unit. It seems to be a natural division of the culture. However, in the surrounding territory live people with the same general cultural tradition as the inhabitants of Gamma. After the ethnologist finishes his preliminary survey of Gamma and begins to visit their neighbors, he will discover that there is another reason why the house type which he has described for the Gamma-gamma is not a natural cultural unit.

In Figure 2 is illustrated the frequency distributions of dwellings on the islands that lie about the Isle of Gamma. This is a very simplified diagram. On each island the house in the center represents the mean as illustrated in Figure 1; the four buildings arranged about each mean represent the range of varia-

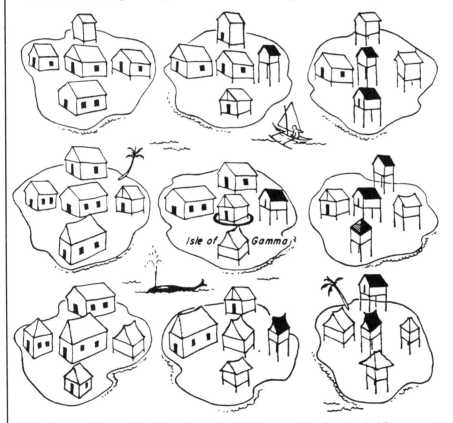

FIG. 2. Diagram illustrating trait variation in geographical space. The Island of Gamma occupies the center. The frequency of the Gamma-gamma house type is in the center of this island and the less numerous variations are grouped around it. On neighboring islands mean and range are similarly indicated.

The Type Concept Revisited

tion. It becomes apparent that the Gamma-gamma house type, illustrated in Figure 1, is not the cohesive cultural type which it appeared to be. The variants from the mean have to be assigned to house types typical of the neighboring peoples north, south, east, and west. As a matter of fact, this diagram shows that the polarity of Figure 1 was not correct. All the black-roofed houses are related to a type that centers to the eastward. Very few examples need be left to be classed in the Gamma-gamma type house.

Figure 2 illustrates the point that each locality will have a distinctive mean and a range about that mean which tends toward the means of surrounding culture. However, Figure 2 is an unsatisfactory diagram in that the geographical separation of the islands has created nodes in the pattern of distribution. If the landscape had been undivided, the geographical variation would be a more gradual function of space, similar to that shown in Figure 3. Although this latter figure is designed to demonstrate the nature of change with time, it will serve equally well for this discussion of space-change. For this purpose it will be considered that each building shown represents a local type. Variation about the mean in each locality is not shown. The building near the upper center of the figure, just above the hurrying female in a grass skirt, will represent the mean type at Gamma-gamma. The gradualness of the change in means in all directions becomes apparent.

Lest the reader suspect that this description is pure fiction, he is referred to an article by Wilhelm Milke which summarizes several illustrations that qualitative differentiation in culture is a function of distance.[4] For an illustration that the *popularity* of specific cultural categories is also a function of geographic space, see Phillips *et al.* (1951: Figs. 6–12) and Ford (1952).

Setting aside the fictional Gamma-gamma for the moment, in actual distributions of cultural items change in form is accelerated by natural, political, and linguistic barriers, or at the zones where competing cultural items of different origins meet. For several reasons these barriers cannot be depended upon to furnish limitations to the spatial aspect of the variations that may be included in a cultural type. First, there may be no such barriers operating on the selected cultural item in the region under study—it is certainly not legitimate to assume that there were before their effect can be measured by the typology. Second, the effect of such barriers is often less than might be imagined. With the exception of impassable terrain, the effect of a barrier is usually to produce a more or less broad zone in which the rate of change with geographic space is accelerated.

It follows, then, that the particular locality where an archeological collection chances to be made will be one of the factors that determines the mean and the range of variation that are demonstrated in any particular tradition in the culture that is being studied. On the same time level, the cordmarked pottery from a village site in northern Illinois is different from that on a site in southern Illinois. If the archeologist has only these two collections to study and is not conscious of the nature of the problem, separate types may be "established"[5] and considered as realities, unconscious of the favor performed

by the chance geographic separation of samples. However, if additional collections, all of the same date, are available to fill in the intervening space, then the problem usually becomes the difficult one of fixing boundaries in a continuum which Phillips has described (Phillips *et al.* 1951:66–68).

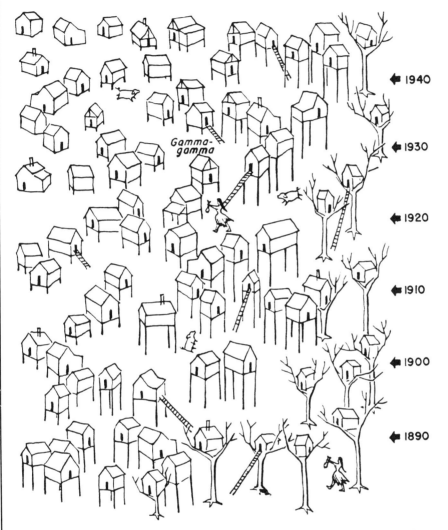

Fig. 3. This diagram will serve two purposes. First, it will represent geographical distribution of variation and for this purpose each house represents a trait mean. Location of the Gamma-gamma mean is shown and position of the houses represents geographical location. Second, this will serve as a chronological diagram. For this purpose time is the vertical ordinate of the figure and decades are indicated on the right-hand side. Variation is shown horizontally with frequency means in the center of the diagram.

THE TYPE IS ABSTRACTED BY THE OBSERVER AT A POINT IN TIME

The ethnographic view of a culture resembles a snapshot taken in the middle of a race for it is a static view of a very fluid process. Stretching back in time from each cultural element described and measured by the ethnographer there is a long history which must be traced if we wish to know why the trait assumes its particular form. For cultural traits that did not find expression in durable form, this is impossible; it can be done, however, for enough streams of thought to demonstrate the principle beyond reasonable doubt.

As illustration, again consider the mythical Gamma-gamma. In the 1940 static diagram, Figure 1, house structures are shown varying four ways from the mean of the type—already a simplification of the variation as explained above. To give a temporal picture of variation, it will be necessary to simplify still further and show only two directions of variation from the mean. This has been done in Figure 3, which now will be used for the purpose for which it was designed. From bottom to top this diagram represents the passage of time. Decades are indicated on the right-hand side. House form variation is shown horizontally and the frequency mean forms are illustrated down the center of the figure.

The phenomena of cultural drift with the passage of time is so well known to archeologists who have dealt with adequate samples of material culture representing appreciable time spans of culture history that it does not seem necessary to elaborate the illustration. Even in modern Western culture, with all of the acceleration of change that has developed, the well paid innovators who control design of automobiles, architecture, and clothing have learned that while minor innovations will sell new models, the buying public will tolerate no marked jumps in the development of stylistic patterns.

Figure 3 cannot fully illustrate the phenomena of time change among the houses of the Gamma-gamma for close inspection of these structures would show that not only did the gross outline of the structures change, but similar change was taking place in minor details such as systems for placing rafters, lashing, the methods of thatching, etc. The ethnologist's view of this cultural type in 1900 would have had the same order of mean and range as his 1940 view, but the types would have been recognizably different. A glance up and down the time scale demonstrates that there are no natural limits to temporal change in this cultural element which may be utilized as type boundaries.

In actual culture histories there are instances of major innovations which will cause one stream of cultural development to be replaced by another. An example is the addition of the gasoline motor to the buggy to make the horseless carriage. This is a different order of innovation from the numerous small changes that have occurred in the design of wheeled personnel carriers from the invention of the first cart to the rubber-tired buggy, or from Charles Duryea's automobile of 1892 to the 1953 Cadillac. Such major innovations are so rare that the archeologist cannot depend on them to provide temporal

limits for typology. They are of little use for the working out of *details* of culture history.

Abrupt change may also be caused by accidents, or profound shocks to the culture. For example, many Pacific island peoples have taken advantage of abandoned military establishments to change their dwelling types entirely. These are also relatively rare and typology based upon them would measure cultural change in great blocks, not in any detail.

To summarize the preceding discussion, there are four dimensions to the cultural type of which the archeologist must be fully aware if intelligent use is to be made of the concept. These are:

(1) The inherent organization that exists in culture at all times and places. The cultural type will, to a greater or lesser degree, be a reflection of the boundaries to one stream of ideas which the cultural bearers considered related. This requires an analysis of the consistency of association of features which may, if necessary, be tested by statistical analysis.

(2) The level of abstraction from the tightly interwoven cultural structure at which the typology is to be formulated. For archeologists this may be at the level of the artifact, or, if desirable, features of artifacts may be utilized as Rouse has done for ceramics in the West Indies.

(3) The cultural type will encompass variation due to cultural drift across geographical space. The apparent mean of the type is the function of the locality at which it is defined.

(4) The cultural type will include variation that occurred with the passage of time. The apparent mean of the type is a result of the particular point in the history of the cultural stream at which it is selected.

In most archeological research, chance has determined the form of the typological structure to a great extent. The fact that Site X was in a certain locality and represented a certain short span of culture history has determined the nature of the cultural types defined there. Permitting sampling chance to determine typology operates very well so long as the archeologist has only a spotty sampling of the culture history. Types are easily separable and they look natural. However, when the gaps are filled in so that the history may be viewed as a continuum through time and across space, the naive typologist is certain to run into serious difficulties. Overlapping of types will render the typology a meaningless conglomeration. The artificiality of the groupings must be taken into consideration and type groupings consciously selected if a workable typology is to be developed.

The type concept as discussed in this paper is the working tool of the cultural student—the device which is used to examine the most minute fragments of culture which the student can grasp. This tool is designed for the reconstruction of culture history in time and space. This is the beginning and not the end of the archeologists' responsibility. After culture history has been outlined various other methods of classification become possible and may be designed to measure different facets of the culture history. This, I think, is the place for classifications based on function as described by

Steward in the accompanying paper. For example, the functional classification which Gordon Willey (1953) applied to the prehistoric settlement patterns in Viru Valley, Peru, very neatly clarifies the history of this aspect of culture and permits comparison with the growth of communities in other parts of the world. However, the necessary prelude to this study of Willey's was the strictly morphological classification of thousands of potsherds.

JAMES A. FORD, *American Museum of Natural History*

NOTES

[1] I wish to thank Alex Krieger, Philip Phillips, Gordon Willey, Julian Steward and Irving Rouse for reading the manuscript of this paper and making a number of helpful comments. The title is a bow to the late Clarence B. Moore who frequently revisited prolific archeological sites.

[2] This is comparable to what Irving Rouse and others have done when they have utilized ceramic traits as bases for comparison. Rouse termed such elements "modes."

[3] "Apparent complexity," for all these levels are infinitely complex and it is the limitation of the observer's ability to perceive differences that set the limits. Ehrich (1950:468–81) gives an able discussion of this matter.

[4] Milke 1949. The word "Quantitative" in Milke's title refers to the numbers of items in the compared cultures which are similar to the reference culture—not to relative popularity.

REFERENCES CITED

BREW, J. OTIS
    1946 Archaeology of Alkali Ridge, southeastern Utah. Papers, Peabody Museum of American Archaeology and Ethnology, Harvard 21.

EHRICH, ROBERT W.
    1950 Some reflections on archeological interpretation. American Anthropologist 52:468–82.

FORD, JAMES A.
    1952 Measurements of some prehistoric design developments in the southeastern states. Anthropological Papers, American Museum of Natural History 44, Pt. 3.

KLUCKHOHN, CLYDE
    1939 The place of theory in anthropological studies. Philosophy of Science 6, No. 3: 328–44.

KRIEGER, ALEX D.
    1944 The typological concept. American Antiquity 9, No. 3:271–88.

KROEBER, A. L. and CLYDE KLUCKHOHN
    1952 Culture, a critical review of concepts and definitions. Papers, Peabody Museum of American Archaeology and Ethnology, Harvard 47, No. 1.

LOTHROP, S. K.
    1926 Pottery of Costa Rica and Nicaragua. Vol. I. Contributions, Museum of the American Indian, Heye Foundation, New York.

MILKE, WILHELM
    1949 The quantitative distribution of cultural similarities and their cartographic representation. American Anthropologist 51:237–52.

PHILLIPS, PHILIP, JAMES A. FORD and JAMES B. GRIFFIN
    1951 Archaeological survey in the lower Mississippi alluvial valley, 1940–1947. Papers, Peabody Museum of American Archaeology and Ethnology, Harvard 25.

ROUSE, IRVING
    1939 Prehistory in Haiti, a study in method. Yale University Publications in Anthropology, No. 21.

SPAULDING, ALBERT C.
    1953   Statistical techniques for the discovery of artifact types. American Antiquity 18: 305–13.

TAYLOR, WALTER W.
    1948   A study of archeology. American Anthropologist 50, No. 3, Pt. 2 ("American Anthropological Association Memoirs," No. 69).

WILLEY, GORDON
    1953   Prehistoric settlement patterns in the Virú Valley, Perú. Bureau of American Ethnology, Bull. 155.

METHOD AND THEORY IN AMERICAN ARCHEOLOGY: AN OPERATIONAL BASIS FOR CULTURE-HISTORICAL INTEGRATION

By PHILIP PHILLIPS and GORDON R. WILLEY

INTRODUCTION

IN REVIEWING past and current trends of American archeological think-ing, it seems possible, without violent oversimplification, to discern three general and more or less sequent points of view. The older antiquarianism of the nineteenth century gave place to the "scientific" archeology of the twentieth, and this in turn is undergoing profound modification, the end of which is not in sight. The motivations of antiquarianism were almost as numer-ous and diverse as the antiquarians and their private interests, whereas the prev-alent point of view of the "scientific" era was order and system. The archeolo-gist not only concerned himself with phenomena, but sought their meaning in patterned relationships. Such patterns were pursued through descriptive taxonomy or taxonomy combined with temporal and spatial distribution studies. For the most part the outlook was that, with sound field work, careful analysis, and classification, the archeologist discharged his duties to science and society. The over-all problem, so far as it was envisaged at all, was seen as the bit-by-bit discovery of a pre-existing order in the culture-historical uni-verse, the outlines of which would miraculously emerge when sufficient pieces were ready to be fitted together. Thank Heaven, archeology was not a "theo-retical" science but something "you could get your teeth into." As time wore on, however, and the archeologist got his teeth into mountainous accumula-tions of facts, the expected miracle failed to take place. Something was appar-ently wrong with the "jigsaw" hypothesis. It became apparent that such order as could be discerned was not altogether inherent in the data but was in large part the product of the means employed to organize the data. In short, the means, if not becoming the ends, had assumed a determinative importance in relation to them. It became, then, necessary to examine those means and the conceptual bases that underlay them. That is the stage we are in at present and in the following pages we propose to examine the main lines

615

of theory that have so far emerged in the Americas and to make certain suggestions about future possibilities.

THE NATURE OF ARCHEOLOGICAL UNIT CONCEPTS

The ultimate objective of archeology is the creation of an image of life within the limits of the residue that is available from the past. The procedural objectives toward such a goal may be dichotomized into reconstructions of space-time relationships, on the one hand, and contextual relationships on the other.[1] Operationally, neither is attainable without the other. The reconstruction of meaningful human history needs both structure and content. Cultural forms may be plotted to demonstrate geographical contiguity and contemporaneity, but when we move to establish an historical relationship between forms so placed we immediately invoke processes like diffusion, trade, or migration and in so doing shift the problem from the bare frame of space and time into the realm of context and function. Conversely, processes such as diffusion have no specific historical applicability without control of the spatial and temporal factors. Taylor (1948) is undoubtedly correct in stating that American archeologists have placed heavy emphasis upon skeletal chronicle at the expense of the recovery of context, but a review of the more recent literature indicates a drift in the opposite direction. Although there is little agreement upon what kind of problem should be pursued (and this lack of agreement is a healthy sign), there is every reason to believe that American archeology will be increasingly concerned with cultural and natural contexts and functional interpretation. Without slighting Taylor's contribution, we submit that this is an area of agreement for American archeologists: history—and prehistory—is both the space-time scale and the content and processes which it measures.

A method basic to archeology—as to all science—is taxonomy, in the general sense of typology and classification. Some recent disputes reveal the fact that fundamental differences in attitude toward the concept of type still obtain in American archeology. Opposition is between those who believe that types are "designed" and those who think of them as "discovered." According to the first view types are segments of the cultural continuum—a segmentation made or imposed by the classifier. The second maintains that types reflect—or should reflect—a cultural segmentation that is inherent in the data, that "designed" or empirical types, while admirably suited to space-time measuring, only accidentally correspond to types or models which were in the mind of the artisan who made the artifacts. Our attitude is that these opposing views are not hopelessly antagonistic. We maintain that all types possess some degree of correspondence to cultural "reality" and that increase of such correspondence must be the constant aim of typology.[2] Types which had cultural significance to the makers, if such can be "discovered," would not only have greater historical value, but would in addition be better adapted to problems of functional understanding. Their determination will involve considerably more testing than the first sort, but statistical analysis along these lines holds promise (Spaulding 1953).

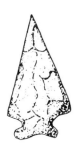

Taxonomy applies to "cultures," as well as artifacts. Inverted commas are appropriate when the archeologist speaks of "culture," for reasons of which he is only too painfully aware. He doesn't need to be reminded what a small segment of the total cultural content is represented by his pitiful pots and stones. Nevertheless he can not, and should not, dispense with the term. Those poor stones and pots are meaningful only in terms of culture. They are indeed the raw materials of his craft, but culture—or the reconstruction of culture—is the finished product. But, because that product is never finished and never can be, the word has a special interim meaning for the archeologist. Childe (1950: 2) has defined an *archeological culture* as "an assemblage of artifacts that recur repeatedly associated together in dwellings of the same kind and with burials of the same rite. The arbitrary peculiarities of implements, weapons, ornaments, houses, burial rites and ritual objects are assumed to be the concrete expressions of the common social traditions that bind together a people." If this sounds as though he were describing a discrete unit, *a* culture, we have only to recall the essential conditions of its existence. Before it in time was another "culture" separated from it by a transition which is usually difficult if not impossible to fix, after it another; beside it in geographical space, contemporary "cultures" with frontiers quite as difficult to draw. It is in effect merely a chunk torn loose from the cultural matrix. It cannot be said to have existed as an entity until the archeologist named and defined it. Putting the case in terms of current jargon, an archeological culture is an arbitrary division of the space-time-cultural continuum[3] defined by reference to its imperishable content and whatever of "common social tradition" can be inferred therefrom.

The same problem confronts us here as in the matter of artifact typology. An archeological "culture" conceived of as a sliced-out section of the space-time-cultural continuum corresponds to the observed facts of cultural continuity and cultural interrelationships; but, as with the empirical "designed" artifact types, it may or may not parallel the reality of a past social unit as this might have been conceived by the peoples who composed it. Archeosociological correlations may eventually be possible but it is our opinion that the archeologist is on a firmer footing at present with the conception of an archeological culture as an arbitrarily defined unit or segment of the total continuum.

If this view be accepted, it follows that a fundamental unvarying characteristic of all archeological concepts, whether in the domain of artifact typology or cultural taxonomy, is the fact that they are the resultant combination of three unlike basic properties: space, time, and form. It is impossible to imagine an artifact type or a cultural "unit" that is not defined with reference to specific forms and does not also have distribution in space and duration in time. However, though invariably present, these three diverse properties may and do vary enormously in proportion one to the other. Probably a large share of our classificatory difficulties and the ensuing arguments could be avoided by the recognition of that simple fact. It becomes essential,

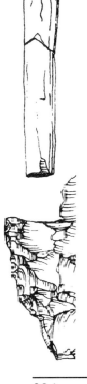

Philip Phillips and Gordon R. Willey

therefore, in the definition and use of archeological concepts of whatever nature to understand precisely what quantities of space, time. and formal content are involved in the mixture.

Thus far, we have argued that the unifying themes of spatial-temporal ordering, contextual reconstruction, and taxonomic identification afford a common ground for archeological research. In so doing we have been talking in general terms, skirting many of the questions as to how these objectives may be drawn together into a comprehensive methodology. To construct such a methodological apparatus we must strive for maximum coverage and utility and, at the same time, minimum complexity of machinery. An operational system is needed that will be sufficiently broad and flexible to incorporate past research in all fields of American archeology and to facilitate its integration on the basic levels of historical synthesis. It must, similarly, provide for current and future investigations. Its theoretical bases must be clearly stated and understood. Above all, it must serve as the foundation for further theoretical formulations in the fields of culture continuity and change as these processes are observed and plotted from the data of prehistory. Such a system should in no way inhibit the development of multiple, successive, and radically differing trial hypotheses but should be the common starting point of more searching exploration.

NOMENCLATURE

In the search for practicable units of study archeologists in the Americas have invented a large number of taxonomic concepts and designated them by an even larger number of names. The initial task, then, is to reduce a diversity of existing terminology to some degree of order and it seems both necessary and practicable to do this by means of a scheme, which is in no sense another taxonomic system for doing archeology, but merely a standard nomenclature by means of which existing systems and their working parts can be roughly equated. Fortunately, as already pointed out, all such concepts, whatever the actual intentions of their originators, have three elements in common: formal content, and space and time dimensions. For intelligibility we need to know not only what forms, but what order of space and time, are involved. Taxonomic concepts can, therefore, be roughly classified by reference to the amounts of space and time they take up. If this be granted it seems a practical approach to bring one of these two variables under control before considering it in combination with the other. The spatial factor is clearly the easier to deal with, so we may start by setting forth a series of geographical categories that we have found useful in characterizing space-time-culture formulations.

SPATIAL DIVISIONS

Locality:—The smallest unit of area ordinarily dealt with in archeology, varying in size from a single site to a district of uncertain size, generally speaking not larger than might be occupied by a single community or "local group." It is hardly necessary to add that such limits as are implied in this qualifi-

cation have the variability found in the size of local groups from one sort of society to another. In strictly archeological terms the locality is a space not large enough to preclude complete cultural homogeneity at any given time.

Region:—A considerably larger unit of area usually determined by archeo-logico-historical accident. Quite often it is simply the result of concentrated research by an individual or group. Rightly or wrongly such a region comes to be thought of as having problems of its own that set it apart from other regions. Regional terms are those most often found in the titles of archeological papers of wider scope than excavation reports. Through constant reiteration they become fixed in the literature and achieve a kind of independent existence. Regions are not altogether without reference to the facts of geography, how-ever. In stressing the accidental factor in their formulation, we must not overlook the tendency for environmental considerations to assert themselves. In portions of the New World where physical conditions of sharp diversity obtain, archeological regions are very apt to coincide with minor physiographic subdivisions. Of the various units of area defined here, the region certainly offers the most practicable field for the study of culture-environmental correlations.

In socio-political terms—and here we must tread warily—the region is roughly equivalent to the space that might be occupied by a social unit larger than the community, to which we may with extreme trepidation apply the term "tribe" or "society." This rough equation is based on what we know of American tribal distributions in historic times and must be accorded the same flexibility that we see in the size of those distributions. The same caution is re-quired in attempting to qualify the definition of region in archeological terms. Generally speaking it is a space in which at a given time a high degree of cul-tural homogeneity may be expected.

Area:—A unit very considerably larger than the region corresponding roughly to the culture area of the ethnographer. Archeological areas, like regions, have come into existence by common consent, but they also have physiographic implications of a fairly definite nature. In the formulation of areas the element of historical accident is reduced by the fact that so many more individuals and institutions are involved in their investigation. That the Southwest has maintained its identity as an area through a half-century of intensive investigation is almost certainly due to culture-environmental determinants beyond the control of the investigators.

It is hardly necessary to add that, though the area as defined here may have considerable physiographic reality, its limits are not so easy to draw on a map as those of the smaller regions. The problem is familiar in all culture area studies.

FORMAL OR CONTENT UNITS

Component.—This useful term which has achieved currency in eastern North American archeology has been defined as the manifestation of a given *focus* (here called *phase*, see below) at a specific site (McKern 1939: 308).

Strictly speaking the component is not a taxonomic unit. In theory the basic unit (McKern's *focus*, our *phase*) comprises a number of components. It is a working assumption that no culture worthy of the name will fail to manifest itself in more than one component. In practice, of course, it often happens that a phase is initially defined on the strength of one component, i.e., a site or a level within a site—but the expectation is implicit that other components will be found and the original definition modified accordingly. It will be noted presently, however, in connection with the sociological implications of the phase, that it is theoretically and actually possible for a phase to consist of only one component and in such cases the latter word, with its suggestion of incompleteness, would not apply.

Phase.—The *phase* is the basic space-time-culture concept in all that follows. It is, in our opinion, the practicable and intelligible unit of archeological study. Choice of the term accords with prevailing usage in a preponderance of New World areas, including the Southwest, sections of South America, and Middle America. Kidder (Kidder, Jennings, and Shook 1946: 9) has defined it as:

> A cultural complex possessing traits sufficiently characteristic to distinguish it for purposes of preliminary archaeological classification, from earlier and later manifestations of the cultural development of which it formed a part, and from other contemporaneous complexes.

Like him we prefer phase to the approximately equivalent "focus" commonly used in eastern North America, because of its stronger temporal implication.[4] The emphasis cannot be placed entirely on time, however. Modifying Kidder's definition, we would prefer to describe the concept in the following terms: A space-time-culture unit possessing traits sufficiently characteristic to distinguish it from all other units similarly conceived, whether of the same or other cultural traditions, geographically limited to a *locality* or *region* and chronologically limited to a relatively brief span of time. It must be acknowledged that this gives a specious impression of uniformity. It would be fine if phases could be standardized as to the amount of time and space they occupy. One thinks with nostalgia of the former neat 200-year phases of the Hohokam. Unfortunately there are so many variable conditions entering into the formulation that it is neither possible nor desirable to define its scope except within rather broad limits. A phase may be anything from a thin level in a site reflecting no more than a brief encampment, to a protracted occupation represented in a large number of sites distributed over a *region* of very elastic proportions.

It will be noted that Kidder's definition of phase lays more emphasis on cultural continuity than ours does, since it implies necessary relations to what goes before and what comes after. We have freed it from this requirement in order to provide for the many instances in which we simply do not know what goes before or comes after, or those less frequent occasions when a new phase appears as an intrusion without apparent relation to the precedent

continuity. In any case, whether as an instance of continuity or discontinuity the phase most often appears as one member of a series which will be referred to hereinafter as a *local* or *regional sequence*. These terms will be defined presently, but let us first examine some further implications of the archeological phase.

We have already alluded briefly to the impossibility of close delimitation of phase in respect to the dimensions of time and space. It may help clarify the problem to consider it in relation to various levels of cultural development. We propose to submit in the near future a developmental sequence for the New World with six general stages, Early Lithic, Archaic, Preformative, Formative, Classic and Postclassic. It is not necessary to anticipate the definitions of these stages to point out here that the space and time dimensions of phase are not going to be the same in all six stages. For example, in the Archaic, in which a semisedentary catching and gathering economy is assumed, phases can be expected to occupy wider spaces than in the sedentary Formative. There is no regular reduction from stage to stage, however; in the Classic and Postclassic stages the space dimensions may also be larger than in the Formative, but for a different reason, this time because the socio-political groups are larger. Time dimensions, on the other hand, may actually exhibit a regular diminution from stage to stage, if the common assumption is correct that the rate of cultural change accelerates with increased advancement and complexity. It does not seem necessary to elaborate on this point here or to attempt any further refinements of definition. It is enough if we have made it clear that the concept of phase has no appropriate scale independent of the cultural situation with which it happens to be involved. This is not as great a deficiency as it might appear. Looked at *internally* so to speak, the phase may have very considerable and highly variable space and time dimensions; looked at from the standpoint of the total range of New World prehistory they are very small quantities indeed, and it is from this point of view that they assume a rough sort of *relative* equivalence that enables us to use the concept of phase as an operational tool regardless of the developmental stage involved.

In considering the phase concept from another point of view, we must recall that the archeologist is constantly admonished by his cultural anthropological brethren to remember that his ridiculous stones and pots are products of social behavior, with the result that he is ever guiltily conscious of his inability, except on the very lowest levels, to relate his formulations to sociological units. The sociological equivalent of the component is the "community," as defined by Murdock (1949: 79) and others, "the maximal group of persons who normally reside together in a face-to-face association." Murdock's three types of community: band, neighborhood, and village, manifest themselves archeologically in the component, and it is even possible as a rule to tell which type is represented. So far, so good. The equivalent of phase, then, ought to be "society," and in a good many cases it probably is. The fact that in practice phases often consist of a single component need not disturb us; on the lower levels of cultural development the society like-

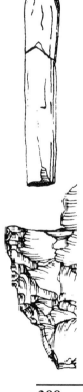

wise frequently consists of only one community. At the other end of the
developmental scale, however, society becomes a larger concept, spatially at
least, than phase. For the purpose of this discussion, however, let us think of
society in the terms most often implied in the older ethnographic studies, i.e.,
a relatively small aggregate comprising a number of closely integrated communities. How does this correspond to the concept of phase? Logically the
correspondence is perfect. The society consists of a number of communities;
the phase consists of a number of components; component equals community;
therefore phase equals society. Q.E.D. Unfortunately in practice it doesn't
work. We have no means of knowing whether the components we group
together into a phase are the same communities an ethnographer (supposing
such a person happened to be on hand when these components were living
communities) would group into a society. We cannot be sure that the individual members of these communities would recognize themselves as belonging
to the same "people." They might not even speak the same language. Ethnography offers abundant examples of different societies sharing a material culture that would be impossible to differentiate archeologically. Probably it
would be only slightly more difficult to find examples in which the culture of
individual communities within a society diverged sufficiently to cause them
to be classified archeologically in separate phases. A frontier garrison community specialized for defense might be a case in point.

More vexing perhaps are questions having to do with the relative stability
of material and social culture through time, a dimension happily ignored by
the ethnographer. Within the time span of a phase, determined by material
traits which can, under certain circumstances, be remarkably stable, it is
conceivable that sociological changes might be sufficient to enable our hypothetical ethnographer to speak of several societies. Conversely, under special
conditions even a primitive population may exhibit revolutionary changes in
material culture without losing its identity as a society. We have abundant
examples of this in recent history.

In sum, it looks as though the present chances were against the phase
having any sociological meaning whatever, but that is not to say that it cannot have. Our attitude here is the same as that already expressed in relation
to the problem of typology. As archeology develops to a point where it can
afford the luxury of Taylor's "conjunctive" or contextual approach, it will
become increasingly possible to define archeological culture in terms that
reflect sociological realities. The phase might then become in effect an "extinct
society" and the archeologist could legitimately experience the emotional
satisfaction he now purloins by the simple substitution of the word "people"
for "culture."

This is a possibility, but it is not really the point of the present discussion.
We do not maintain that any specific archeological phase corresponds to a
former society. We simply call attention to the fact that there is a certain
conceptual agreement between phase and society. Both are the intelligible
units of their respective fields of study. They have a similar *role* and a similar

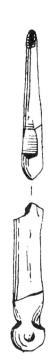

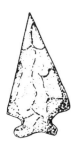

scale—subject to the important difference that in phase the temporal dimension is explicit whereas in society it is implicit—and in this crucial matter of scale both exhibit the same relativism with respect to the level of cultural stage. Our contention is, therefore, that this congruence, which can as yet be demonstrated only on the theoretical level, offers the best hope of incorporating archeology into general anthropological science. Even if this hope be illusory, it may be still maintained that the phase is the best available instrument for the integration of culture-historical data at the present stage of archeological development.

TEMPORAL SERIES

Local Sequence.—In its purest form a local sequence is a series of components found in vertical stratigraphic relationship in a single site. It may, however, also be a composite series made by combining shorter stratigraphic "runs" from several sites within a locality, or it may be derived from seriating components without benefit of stratigraphy at all. However derived, the important feature of the local sequence is that it is local. The spatial dimension, not larger than the locality, is small enough to permit the assumption that cultural differences between components reflect differences in time.

We have already referred to the fact that members of a local sequence, though technically regarded as components, are often referred to as phases on the ground that they are local manifestations of the larger units; also that it is theoretically possible for the phase to be represented by a single component only, in which case the "higher" designation is appropriate. The local sequence, therefore, may be defined as a chronological series of *components or phases* within a locality as defined above.

Regional Sequence.—A regional sequence is not the same thing as a local sequence with merely a larger spatial dimension. The difference can best be approached from the operational standpoint. In the normal course of extension of archeological information, components, phases, and local sequences multiply and questions of relationships come to the fore. Ideally, the archeologists of a region come together in harmonious session where a careful matching of local sequences produces a new sequence of larger scope. Actually this happy event occurs but rarely. What more often happens is that phases and local sequences gain in scope by a sort of osmosis. They flow outward so to speak, not seldom propelled by their inventors, uniting to themselves their weaker correlates over a widening circle. The process is necessarily accompanied by a progressive generalization of definitions until their original usefulness is impaired.

Nevertheless we will assume that local sequences remain local and that regional sequences are the result of correlating them—not combining them, be it noted; this is not a taxonomic operation, because in the process the original formulations are retailored to fit the wider spatial and (perhaps) deeper temporal requirements. The phase now appears in its widest extension and at its furthest remove from the original data, for it is our contention (to be discussed

Philip Phillips and Gordon R. Willey

further along) that the concept of phase cannot be safely extended beyond the limits of a region.

With these operational differences in mind we may define the regional sequence as a chronological series of phases within a space defined here as a region.

At this point it may be well to emphasize the artificiality of the relationship between phase and region in a regional sequence. We have said that the maximum practicable spatial dimension of a phase is comparable to that of a region, but no actual geographical coextension is implied. Such a one-to-one relationship may occur fortuitously because it oftens happens that a region comes into existence on the heels of a phase, so to speak, but there is no reason whatever to expect that earlier or later phases in the sequence will also coincide with that region.

Period and Area Chronology.—We now move onto a "higher" plane of abstraction where definitions become more difficult to frame. An area chronology may be described as a series of cultural formulations—here called periods—conceived on the scale of an *area* as defined in this study. Logically, *period* is simply phase with amplified space and time dimensions. Operationally this is not the case. Progress from region to area involves a greater leap into the abstract than from locality to region. A shift to the word *chronology* is made because sequence no longer seems applicable. The regional sequence, notwithstanding differences in operational procedure, is not radically different conceptually from the local sequence. It still maintains some contact with the primary stratigraphic data. With the area chronology, however, the spatial dimension has become so large that the interpretation of cultural similarities as evidence of contemporaneity becomes a theoretical question; the ever-present possibility of cultural "lag" comes into play. It would seem reasonable that the time dimension subsumed in the concept *period* would also be larger, that is to say the period would be of considerably longer duration than the phase. The fact is, however, that most area chronologies operate on approximately the same temporal scale as the local and regional sequences from which they took their original departure. For some mysterious reason they usually wind up with exactly the same number of subdivisions. This has a very important bearing on general archeological theory, for obviously it can only be justified on the assumption that cultural changes do take place synchronously over wide geographical spaces. Now whether this proposition is the cause or the result of area chronologies is one of those impossible chicken-egg questions, but there is no question that it has become one of the basic assumptions of American archeology. It might be termed the microcosmic theory since it sees reflected in the locality or region the pattern of culture-history of the area. To examine this theory critically would take us too far afield. It was necessary to allude to it only to show that the concepts of period and area chronology are different in kind, not merely in scale, from those already dealt with, in that they involve an assumption that it was not necessary to make in proceeding from the local to the regional level.

It may also be pointed out that area chronologies almost invariably tend to take on the characteristics of a developmental sequence, in which case it is more appropriate to refer to *stages* rather than *periods*. More often in such cases, however, the two terms are used interchangeably as though they meant exactly the same thing. Fortunately, deliverance from this kind of ambiguity will come, as it has for the later periods in the Southwest, when current techniques of absolute dating have reached a point of sufficient dependability. Then we shall be able to place a given unit within a temporal framework, on the one hand, and a developmental sequence, on the other, without confusing the two operations.

The above remarks are an evaluation unfavorable to area chronologies in general. They have undoubtedly served a useful purpose in focusing attention on larger issues, but have done equal disservice in fomenting endless controversies over fictitious problems. We submit that, when it comes to dealing with major spatial and temporal distributions on levels so far removed from the concrete data, it is preferable to employ formulations of a more fluid nature, those which carry the least implications of precision in respect to the dimensions of space and time. Such are the terms remaining to be defined. Before proceeding to do so, it may be well to pause long enough to explain again what we are doing, or rather what we are not doing. This is not a description of a taxonomic method either actual or contemplated. A regional sequence may be the result of correlating local sequences, but it is not the result of combining them. That would be taxonomy. The area chronology has even less formal relationship to the regional sequence. In sum, we are simply recognizing the fact that certain cultural and chronological formulations differ from others of larger spatial and temporal dimensions, because the operations involved are different, and we find it useful to distinguish them by the nomenclature suggested here.

INTEGRATIVE DEVICES

Horizon.—The horizon style concept, first introduced into Andean archeology by Max Uhle (1913) and formulated by Kroeber (1944), has amply proved its utility in that area. It represents an idea different in kind from those already considered here, in that the usual ingredients of space and time are mixed in very unequal proportions. A horizon style, as the name implies, occupies a great deal of space but very little time. It may be briefly described as a spatial continuum represented by the wide distribution of a recognizable art style.[5] On the assumption of "historical uniqueness of stylistic pattern" coupled with the theory that styles normally change with some rapidity, the time dimension is reduced to a point where the horizon style becomes useful in equating in time phases of culture widely separated in space. As one of the present authors (Willey 1945: 55) has already observed: "The horizon styles are the horizontal stringers by which the upright columns of specialized regional development are tied together in the time chart."

Unfortunately this excellent synchronic device has a limited application

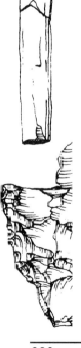

Philip Phillips and Gordon R. Willey

since it presupposes a level of esthetic sophistication that many New World cultures failed to reach. In some cases it has been possible to regard certain highly specialized and widely traded artifacts as horizon "markers," but they must be used with considerable caution on account of the possibility that such highly prized objects may be preserved for long periods as heirlooms or "antiques."

Tradition.—This is another methodological tool that seems to have originated in South American archeology, but has recently found favor in other areas of the New World. A familiar, not to say indispensable, word in any historical context, it has of late acquired a special archeological meaning, or rather a number of meanings, for it is still in an incipient stage of formulation and doesn't mean quite the same thing to all who use it. Owing to the fact that this concept is designated by a term that has always been used in archeology, it is difficult to say just when it began to be a definite methodological tool. In the Andean area it came about in connection with the very different idea of horizon style, and was first applied to pottery only. Once it became apparent that the utility of the horizon style depended upon the combination of wide space and short time dimensions, it was equally clear that some other formulation was required to express a somewhat different kind of ceramic unity in which these proportions were reversed. This gave rise to the term *pottery tradition*, certainly not a verbal innovation, but perhaps the first time the idea of tradition entered into a definite space-time formulation.

The relationship of the two concepts, horizon style and pottery tradition, is so important that one of us may be permitted to repeat himself, as follows:

> These speculations concerning the relationships of the later White-on-red styles to the earlier component styles of the White-on-red horizon lead us to wonder if there are not other widely inclusive historical units of an order different from that of the horizon style. It appears certain that the Peruvian Andes and coast were a unified culture area in that the important cultural developments were essentially local and basically inter-related for at least a thousand years. This fundamental cultural unity justifies seeing ceramic developments in terms of long-time traditions as well as coeval phenomena. The concept of a pottery tradition, as used here, includes broad descriptive categories of ceramic decoration which undoubtedly have value in expressing historical relationships when the relationships are confined to the geographical boundaries of Peruvian-Andean cultures. The pottery tradition lacks the specific quality of the localized pottery style, and it differs from the horizon style in that it is not an integration of artistic elements which has been widely diffused at a given time period. A pottery tradition comprises a line, or a number of lines, of pottery development through time within the confines of a certain technique or decorative constant. In successive time periods through which the history of ceramic development can be traced, certain styles arose within the tradition. Transmission of some of these styles during particular periods resulted in the formation of a horizon style; other styles in the continuum of the tradition remained strictly localized. The distinctions between a horizon style and a pottery tradition . . . are opposable concepts in archaeological reconstruction [Willey 1945: 53].

Shortly after this first limited injection of tradition into Peruvian studies,

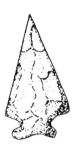

Wendell C. Bennett (1948: 1) enlarged the concept very considerably under the name "area co-tradition." This formulation, as Bennett clearly saw, is nothing more than the familiar culture area concept with the addition of time depth,[6] "the over-all unit of cultural history of an area within which the component cultures have been inter-related over a period of time." The emphasis, implied in the "co-" is on the *linkage* of "whole cultures," each with its own history and persistent traditions, and on the *area* in which this linkage takes place. Thus the co-tradition is an enlargement over the simple tradition in terms of content, since it is no longer confined to a single technological or cultural development, but becomes a broad coalescent cultural continuum. At the same time it introduces a restriction in that stable geographical boundaries are implied.

About the same time that the Peruvianists were beginning to talk about pottery traditions, John McGregor[7] introduced the term into the Southwest with somewhat different connotations. He defined tradition very broadly as "more or less deeply rooted human characteristics—persistent attitudes or ways of doing things—which are passed on from one generation to another," thus emphasizing the non-material and configurational aspects of culture. He maintained that characteristic attitudes can be inferred from material traits and that the determination of traditions (as defined by him) is not only possible but essential in making broad cultural comparisons.

This is an enlargement of the concept of tradition in another direction— it is not a co-tradition or anything like it. McGregor's traditions are actually technologically oriented; house types, pottery, ground stone, etc.; he merely advocates that they be formulated in terms of the preference and attitudes they reflect. There is nothing revolutionary about this surely, but it is a point of view that cannot be too often stated.

The first significant use of the tradition concept in eastern North America was by John M. Goggin. His definition is more like McGregor's, at least on the philosophical side:

> My concept of Florida cultural traditions is similar in theory but more inclusive in content than a ceramic tradition. A cultural tradition is a distinctive way of life, reflected in various aspects of culture; perhaps extending through some period of time and exhibiting normal internal cultural changes, but nevertheless throughout this period showing a basic consistent unity. In the whole history of a tradition certain persistent themes dominate the life of the people. These give distinctiveness to the configuration. [Goggin 1949: 17.]

Goggin recognizes ten cultural traditions in Florida, allowing to them a great deal of latitude in space and time dimensions. It seems to us that here Goggin has discovered the outstanding merit of the tradition as an archeological tool, namely its flexibility. He has treated it as a space-time-culture formulation in which the three components can be mingled in almost any proportion required by the data. In the case of the time component he has overdone it perhaps. Surely inherent in the idea of tradition is persistence through time. Actually what happens in Florida is that certain traditions make a brief

Philip Phillips and Gordon R. Willey

appearance, his "Florida Mississippian" for example. Such a configuration has a long history of development elsewhere before its brief appearance in Florida.

Goggin, rather more than others, has emphasized the importance of environmental factors in the shaping and conserving of cultural traditions. Here again he has put his finger on another virtue of the concept. It offers to the reconstructed environmentalists, in which category we are not ashamed to declare ourselves, the most effective means for giving expression to culture-environmental correlations.

We are at last in a position to essay some sort of definition. All aspects—technological, configurational, environmental—must find a place and there must be, above all, freedom from set limitations of space, time and content. A tradition, then, is a major large-scale space-time-cultural continuity, defined with reference to persistent configurations in single technologies or total (archeological) culture, occupying a relatively long interval of time and a quantitatively variable but environmentally significant space.

Climax.—There remains but to mention briefly this useful but largely neglected concept (see Kroeber 1939). It may be defined, in the terms used here, as the phase or phases of maximum cultural intensity of a cultural tradition. This is necessarily a value judgment, but only in relation to the tradition involved. So far as possible the emphasis should be placed on population density and like factors rather than exquisite developments in esthetics. The latter may conceivably take place in periods of low cultural intensity. Theoretically, there ought to be a climax development in every tradition, but it cannot always be identified archeologically. Another way to describe it would be the phase or phases when-where the tradition comes closest to realization of its full potential development within the limits imposed by history and environment.

CULTURE-HISTORICAL INTEGRATION

In the preceding sections we have outlined a terminology for reducing existing classificatory concepts to a set of common denominators. In doing so we have perhaps revealed a personal bias for or against some of these concepts and it now becomes our task to show whither these predilections are tending. What has been offered so far is in no sense a system but it will not have escaped the reader that a system lurks within.

In briefest possible terms, we submit that archeology can be historically integrated by means of a very simple apparatus consisting of the two static formal concepts *component* and *phase* and the two fluid historical concepts *tradition* and *horizon style*. The essence of this departure is, we think, recognition of the fact that taxonomy cannot be profitably carried beyond the order of phase as defined herein. The phase itself is admittedly an abstraction corresponding only roughly to *society*, but it is only one remove from the primary data and the gap between it and the ethnographic "reality" can theoretically be closed. Beyond phase we take off into the ether. "Higher" taxonomic

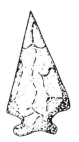

concepts—really higher, in the sense of further from the ground—are subject to variables of space and time such as to render, in the time-honored phrase, any resemblance to actual societies living or dead purely coincidental.

We are accordingly taking the obvious and straightforward course of pursuing cultural configurations of greater magnitude than phase by means of concepts that make no pretense to sociological or any other kind of reality. Tools like tradition and horizon style have come into existence precisely in response to an awareness that the main currents of culture flow through space and time without regard for social and political boundaries. It seems to us that these main currents, essential to an understanding of prehistory on an areal or continental scale, cannot be apprehended by combining with ant-like industry smaller archeological units into larger ones. It may be seen that we are at once for and against taxonomy. We believe strongly in the sound-ness of phase as a taxonomic unit. It has the importance of *species* to the biologist, or *society* to the cultural anthropologist. What happens in the higher taxonomy is that once a group or series of phases becomes an "aspect," "branch," or what you will, it seems to be taken for granted that something more significant has been created and the phases tend to drop out of sight.[3] We propose to keep them in sight. They may and should be constantly subject to modification and redefinition, always with a view to closer approximation to the theoretically possible ethnographic "reality," but they must remain to the end the basic formulations of the data.

There will be too many phases for comfort, of course. How many species are recognized in the insect world? How many societies in the ethnographic world? It has been frequently pointed out that archeology is to cultural anthropology what paleontology is to biology. It was necessary for paleon-tology to reveal the processes of organic evolution because they take time. Cultural processes are much more rapid, but they also take time and cannot therefore be fully understood without the aid of archeology. So we are con-cerned with process as well as history. This may seem far removed from the glorification of the phase, but it appears to the writers that you cannot hope to shed light on processes by means of abstractions that have no theoretically possible counterparts in cultural and social "reality." We believe that all taxonomic concepts above the rank of phase as defined herein are subject to that disqualification. On the other hand, it is not necessary to know all there is to know about all recognizable phases of New World archeology or even a major division thereof. As in all science, fortunately for its practitioners, processes are revealed by partial selected data. This disposes of the objection of too many phases. Are we trying to understand the processes of culture change or merely to simplify its manifold effects?

The apparatus that we are attempting to describe may be crudely dia-grammed as on the following page.

This diagram is intended to show that there are actually two "systems" in-volved, one formal and the other historical, or spatial-temporal. The relation-ships in the system *component-phase* are formal, even structural in a social

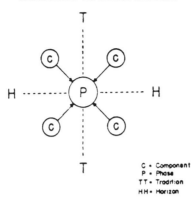

C = Component
P = Phase
TT = Tradition
HH = Horizon

sense. They are located in space and time but are not dependent on these properties for their meaning. Operationally, components are combined into phases because analysis reveals cultural uniformity amounting to practical identity. We usually know, to be sure, that they are closely associated geographically and we assume contemporaneity but neither of these considerations is necessary for the recognition of the relationship. This is because the space and time dimensions that inhere in all archeological concepts are here, on this low level of classification, reduced to negligibility. For all practical purposes the space occupied by a phase may be regarded as a point; the time, an instant. The phase, in other words, is a formal abstraction that can be manipulated independently of space and time.

Up to this point most archeologists would probably "go along" though many, depending upon the areas in which they have worked, would prefer to use other terms in place of phase. Where our point of view differs is in the conviction that phase, as defined in these pages, is the largest unit of archeological culture that can be so manipulated. When formal abstractions are expanded to embrace a wider range of forms they cease to be merely formal and become spatial and/or temporal as well. Actually, by some seemingly paradoxical process, they lose rather than gain in formal content—the familiar phenomenon of shorter trait lists for higher taxonomic divisions. Why is this? Because forms are also fluid, changing constantly through space and time, and you cannot expand an archeological concept without expanding one or both, usually both, of these dimensions. The result is that the change in forms *within* the concept are such that it can no longer be apprehended on a strictly formal basis. Space and time have become dominant in a system that is theoretically supposed to be a formal one operating independently of space and time. It should surprise no one when such a system fails to work.

These remarks apply specifically to the Gladwin (1934), Colton (1939), and Midwestern Taxonomic (McKern 1939) systems. The Gladwin and Colton schemes are phylogenetic or historico-genetic. Phylogeny involves relationships that are not only formal but also causal (i.e., based on common ancestry) and temporal. A and B are related not only formally but because

they derive from C, which is, perforce, earlier in time. The use of the organic evolutionary model is, we believe, specious (see Willey 1953: 369). The Midwest taxonomists. on the other hand, seem to be involved in a hopeless contradiction in attempting to set up a scheme so heavily committed to the same factors of phylogenic causality, and implied evolution and time, while insisting that it must operate independently of the time dimension. To be sure, it was McKern's idea that once the higher cultural units had been delineated by means of the classificatory method, they could be arranged in temporal sequence through dates obtained by some other means. Failure of this hope is becoming apparent now that Carbon 14 is furnishing evidence for the extremely long duration and overlapping of many of these units.

We now turn back to our diagram and the two "systems" it is designed to reveal. If it be granted that the component-phase system deals mainly in relationships of a formal or structural nature, it certainly will be allowed that tradition and horizon style belong to a different system in which the properties of space and time play dominant roles. The difference we are talking about here is only a difference in the proportions of the space-time-form mixture. In tradition and horizon style, form, or content is important—when is it not?—but the temporal and spatial ingredients are dominant. The real point, however, is not whether these two sets are essentially different conceptually, which is arguable, but that in actual operation they are not subject to any necessary logical or systematic relationship. Components and phases enter into traditions and horizon styles, their external relationships may be revealed and expressed by them, but they are not in any manner combined to form them. In fact, the opposite process is more nearly in accord with cultural reality; two or more traditions usually converge in any given phase. In short, the effectiveness of the method, as we see it, depends upon interplay between these two pairs of conceptual tools without systematic limitations of any kind.

To summarize briefly: insofar as this can be formulated as a program for New World archeology, we are advocating: (1) that the primary emphasis continue to be placed on the organization of components and phases (or their equivalents) in local and regional sequences under stratigraphic control; (2) that phases be studied intensively as the effective contexts of archeological culture; (3) that their internal spatial and temporal dimensions be kept within manageable limits of magnitude; and (4) that their external spatial, temporal and formal relationships be studied and expressed in terms of traditions and horizons without recourse to any taxonomic formulations of a higher order than themselves. From this, as a common platform on which it would not seem unreasonable to hope we might stand united, further studies could be carried to meet specific objectives.

PEABODY MUSEUM, HARVARD UNIVERSITY
CAMBRIDGE, MASSACHUSETTS

Philip Phillips and Gordon R. Willey

NOTES

[1] Taylor (1948) has referred to this dichotomy as "chronicle" and "historiography." See also Willey's (1953) use of the terms "historical" and "processual."

[2] Phillips, Ford, and Griffin, 1951: 63–64, discuss this problem of the "empirical" versus the "cultural" type. ". . . let us make it clear that, although the empirical typology here described—'working' typology as Krieger (1944) perhaps would call it—cannot be expected to show any strong relationship to cultural 'reality,' it does not follow that such relationship is precluded now and forever. To a certain extent, the characters we select as criteria for type definition, however dictated by expediency, not to say necessity, are bound to correspond to characters that might have served to distinguish one sort of pottery from another in the minds of the people who made and used it. We should, of course, make every possible effort to increase this correspondence. In course of time, with increased information in respect to vessel shapes and overall patterns of design—let us not forget that we are classifying vessels, though we have for most types only sherds to do it with—our types will be redefined in ever closer approximation to cultural 'realities.' In short, an eventual synthesis is possible between the seemingly antithetical attitudes loosely characterized above as 'empirical' and 'cultural,' in which the product of classification, the pottery type, will finally achieve cultural meaning. The limits of the variability of the type will then no longer be wholly arbitrary decisions of the classifier, as is now the case, but will bear some correspondence to ethnographic distributions in time and space." See also Rouse, 1939.

[3] It should be pointed out that no resemblance to the space-time continuum of the higher metaphysics is implied. It is perhaps unfortunate that archeologists in America, the present writers included, have pounced upon this high-sounding term. When the archeologist talks about space he is referring to simple two-dimensional geographical space.

[4] Also for the same reason given by Beardsley for his preference for "facies," i.e., to avoid the implication that the whole Midwestern system was to be duplicated in California. Beardsley's definition of "facies" as "groups of intimately related settlements or components" corresponds closely to our concept of phase (1948: 3).

[5] For a more detailed statement about "style" in this connection, see Willey 1951: 109–111.

[6] Kroeber's (1939) *culture whole*, for those who prefer the term, means about the same thing. Bennett (1948) indicated that the Southwest might well offer an example of the area co-tradition, a suggestion which was followed up by Martin and Rinaldo's (1951) somewhat controversial "The Southwestern Co-Tradition."

[7] McGregor 1950, paper submitted in 1946.

[8] Many students who do not accept the Midwestern taxonomic scheme as a whole nevertheless feel that up to the level of *aspect* it is a very useful tool. It will be said by them, that, in limiting our terminology to component and phase (the rough equivalent of focus) we are forgoing the use of a means of expressing relationships between phases closer than those implied in the concepts of horizon and tradition. Our reply is that if such a relationship between two or more phases can be demonstrated, and contemporaneity is indicated, they probably should be combined in a single phase anyhow. Our definition of phase is elastic enough to permit this. If, on the other hand, the formal relationship is close, but contemporaneity is *not* indicated, it would seem wiser to continue to regard them as separate and sequent phases of a common cultural tradition. In other words, the concept of phase, though approximately equivalent to focus, can be stretched to accommodate most aspects that have been established, and if it cannot, it is probably because the aspect in question is not a significant cultural "unit."

BIBLIOGRAPHY

BEARDSLEY, RICHARD K. 1948 Culture Sequences in Central California Archaeology. American Antiquity 14, no. 1: 1–28.

BENNETT, WENDELL C. 1948 The Peruvian Co-Tradition *in* A Reappraisal of Peruvian Archaeology. American Antiquity 13, no. 4, part 2. Memoir no. 4: 1–7.

CHILDE, V. GORDON 1950 Prehistoric Migrations in Europe. Instituttet For Sammenlignende Kulturforskning, Ser. A: Forelesninger XX: V, Oslo.

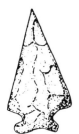

COLTON, H. S. 1939 Prehistoric Culture Units and their Relationships in Northern Arizona. Museum of Northern Arizona, Bulletin 17.

GLADWIN, W. and H. S. 1934 A Method for the Designation of Cultures and Their Varieties. Medallion Papers No. 15. Globe, Arizona.

GOGGIN, JOHN 1949 Cultural Traditions in Florida Prehistory *in* The Florida Indian and His Neighbors: 13–44. J. W. Griffin, ed. Winter Park.

KIDDER, A. V., JESSE D. JENNINGS and E. M. SHOOK 1946 Kaminaljuyu. Carnegie Institution of Washington, Publication 561.

KROEBER, A. L. 1939 Cultural and Natural Areas of Native North America. University of California Publications in American Archaeology and Ethnology 38. Berkeley.

——— 1944 Peruvian Archaeology in 1942. Viking Fund Publications in Anthropology No. 4. New York.

MARTIN, PAUL S. and JOHN B. RINALDO 1951 The Southwestern Co-Tradition. Southwestern Journal of Anthropology 7, no. 3: 215–229.

McGREGOR, JOHN C. 1950 Weighted Traits and Traditions *in* For the Dean, pp. 291–298. Erik K. Reed and Dale S. King, eds. Santa Fe, New Mexico.

McKERN, WILLIAM C. 1939 The Midwestern Taxonomic Method as an Aid to Archaeological Study. American Antiquity 4, no. 4: 301–313.

MURDOCK, GEORGE PETER 1949 Social Structure. New York.

PHILLIPS, PHILIP, JAMES A. FORD and JAMES B. GRIFFIN 1951 Archaeological Survey in the Lower Mississippi Valley 1940–1947. Peabody Museum Papers, vol. 25. Harvard University, Cambridge.

ROUSE, IRVING 1939 Prehistory in Haiti. Yale University Publications in Anthropology No. 21. New Haven.

SPAULDING, ALBERT C. 1953 Statistical Techniques for the Discovery of Artifact Types. American Antiquity 18, no. 4: 305–313.

TAYLOR, WALTER W. 1948 A Study of Archaeology. American Anthropologist 50, no. 3, pt. 2. Memoir No. 69.

UHLE, MAX 1913 Die Ruinen von Moche. Société de Américanistes de Paris. N.S. 10: 95–117.

WILLEY, GORDON R. 1945 Horizon Styles and Pottery Traditions in Peruvian Archaeology. American Antiquity 11: 49–56.

——— 1951 The Chavin Problem: a Review and Critique. Southwestern Journal of Anthropology 7, no. 2: 103–144.

——— 1953 Archaeological Theories and Interpretation: New World *in* Anthropology Today pp. 361–385. A. L. Kroeber, ed. University of Chicago Press, Chicago.

Philip Phillips and Gordon R. Willey

On the Correlation of Phases of Culture

IRVING ROUSE
Yale University

IN A recent article in this journal, Phillips and Willey (1953:628) proposed an "operational basis for culture-historical integration" which makes use of "two static formal concepts *component* and *phase* and . . . two fluid historical concepts *tradition* and *horizon style*." As Phillips and Willey point out, the first two of these concepts are not likely to arouse much disagreement. Some archeologists will prefer, in particular studies, to concentrate upon artifact types or other elements of culture, but it would seem reasonable to accept *components* and *phases* (i.e., the foci of the Midwestern Taxonomic System) as the basic units of archeological research, since these correspond, as Phillips and Willey point out, to the community and society (i.e., tribal group) in ethnology.

The establishment of relationships among the various phases or groups of components is another matter. While Phillips and Willey (1953:630–31) favor the use of *traditions* and *horizon styles* for this purpose, they concede that many archeologists will prefer other concepts. The purpose of this article is neither to advocate any of the other concepts nor to propose new ones but rather to examine and evaluate the various ways of relating phases.

COMPONENT AND PHASE

It is important at the outset to gain a clear idea of what is meant by *component* and *phase*. Phillips and Willey (1953:619) have defined a component as "the manifestation of a given focus [i.e., a phase] at a specific site." It may embrace the entire site or, if there has been more than one occupation at the site, it will correspond only to a part of it—a layer of refuse, analysis unit, or whatever other division is made. It comprises all the remains encountered within this division. Hence, it is objective and has physical reality. If one wishes, one can point to a particular set of structures, group of burials, food remains, collection of artifacts, etc., coming from a designated part of a specific site, and say that these constitute the component.

By contrast, a phase is an abstraction from the reality of the components. Phillips and Willey (1953:620) quote Kidder's definition of it as "a cultural complex possessing traits sufficiently characteristic to distinguish it . . . from earlier and later manifestations of the cultural development of which it formed a part, and from other contemporaneous complexes." In other words, it is a complex of traits which recurs from component to component and which serves to distinguish its particular components from others. It comprises "arbitrary peculiarities of implements, weapons, ornaments, houses, burial rites and ritual objects [that] are assumed to be the concrete expression of the common social traditions that bound together the people" of its components (Childe 1950:2).

713

To use an analogy, the relationship between a phase and its components is like that between a pottery type and the sherds of that type. Just as a type, in the conception of many archeologists, comprises the attributes distinctive of a class of similar potsherds, so a phase may be said to consist of those attributes which are shared by a class of similar components. And, just as a type is defined without regard to its specific position in time and space, so a phase is basically nontemporal and nonspatial. One does not need to know its chronology in order to define it although, of course, one may give its distribution in time and space after it has been defined. It is this point which distinguishes both type and phase from the corresponding ceramic and cultural periods; chronological position is not inherent in either type or phase as it is in a period.

Finally, neither a pottery type nor a phase carries within itself the implication of specific genetic connections with other types or phases. Both type and phase are conceived of as independent entities, although it may be possible subsequent to the definition of either of them to show that it was derived, wholly or in part, from some other type or phase and thus to establish its genetic relationships.

THE CORRELATION OF PHASES

The problem, then, is how to correlate a series of phases, or recurring complexes of culture traits. There are, I would suggest, three ways of doing this, which will be called respectively descriptive, distributional, and genetic. In the first of these, the phases are related entirely *per se*, i.e., in terms of their distinctive attributes. In the second and third, they are instead correlated in terms of factors external to themselves—time and space in the case of the distributional approach, and genetic connection in the case of the third approach. Each of these approaches will be considered in turn.

DESCRIPTIVE CORRELATION

The first approach seeks to answer the question: What phases most closely resemble each other? The answer is obtained by classifying the phases into one or more series of groups, as diagrammed in Figure 1. Phases are grouped together because they share the same attributes, and hence each group reflects descriptive similarities among its constituent phases. It may also reflect contemporaneity and genetic connection, but not necessarily so. For example, two phases grouped together on a descriptive basis may have been successive rather than contemporaneous, and their similarities may be due to adaptation to the same type of environment or to a correspondence in level of cultural development rather than to genetic connection. Additional research is necessary before one can give a proper interpretation of similarities among phases which have been descriptively correlated, and the interpretation will not always be the same. Each individual similarity has to be considered on its own merits.

The descriptive approach is thus on a low level of interpretation. But at the same time it has a high degree of validity. Its groupings are based directly

on the facts and are not subject to assumptions of chronological position or genetic relationship as are the groups to be discussed below.

The Midwestern Taxonomic Method is a good example of the descriptive approach (e.g., McKern 1939). In it, phases (*foci* in its terminology) are grouped on the basis of their resemblances into a hierarchy of aspects and larger units in the manner indicated in Figure 1. To be sure, some archeologists who have used this approach have made the mistake of assuming that the relationships thus established *necessarily* indicate a particular type of time-space or genetic relationship. However, the originators of the method warned specifically against this error; for example, McKern (1940: 20) pointed out the necessity for setting up a separate time chart (although he does not

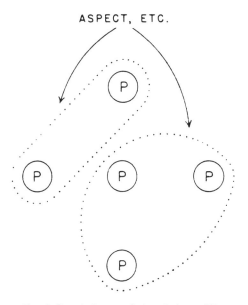

Fig. 1. Descriptive correlation of phases (P).

mention the dimension of space), and he also specified that genetic connections should be established independently. Numerous instances could be cited where this has been correctly done (e.g., Krieger 1946; Smith 1950).

The Midwestern Method has been regarded by some as a temporary expedient, designed only to meet the immediate lack of chronological information in the Middle West, with the idea that it would be replaced by the distributional approach as soon as chronology became available. It does, perhaps, have its greatest utility as a preliminary method of correlation, to be made before one has the factual basis needed to proceed with the distributional and genetic approaches. But, in addition, I would contend that either the Midwestern approach or some less systematic method of descriptive correlation—such as the kinds of statistical classification suggested by Kroeber (1940) and, in the case of ceramic attributes, by Spaulding (1953)—is a necessary pre-

requisite to proper correlation on the distributional and genetic levels. One needs to know as much as possible about the nature of one's phases before proceeding to the other levels of correlation, and the descriptive approach is a means of obtaining this knowledge, in that it brings to one's attention the principal similarities and differences between one's phases. Furthermore, descriptive correlation provides an opportunity to test the phases—to determine whether any two of them are so much alike that they should be consolidated into a single phase, for example. Any study is only as good as the units with which it deals; and hence, in so far as descriptive correlation helps one to apprehend and to validate one's phases, it should lead to improved distributional and genetic correlation.

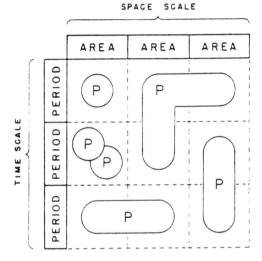

FIG. 2. Distributional correlation of phases (P).

DISTRIBUTIONAL CORRELATION

The second approach is not concerned with the nature of the phases; rather it seeks to answer the question: When and where did a given series of phases occur? The answer to this question may be obtained in several different ways but it will here be assumed, for the sake of discussion, that one does it by plotting the distribution of one's phases along space and time scales, as shown in Figure 2. Phases are placed in a certain area on the space scale and in a certain period on the time scale because the evidence indicates that they occurred there and not because of any similarities or differences among them (although the latter may be part of the evidence). The resultant arrangement cannot be considered descriptive, for the phases which are closest together temporally and spatially are sometimes quite different in content; neither can it be considered genetic, for the fact that one phase has succeeded another in an area does not necessarily mean that the former was derived from the latter. In its

pure form. therefore, the distributional approach establishes contemporaneity and contiguity, or lack thereof, and nothing else.

As is indicated in Figure 2, there may be a one-to-one relationship between a phase and its corresponding area and period; two phases may occur in a single area and period: or a single phase may extend across several areas, persist through several periods, or both. Instances of all these possibilities may be seen, for example, in the chronological charts published by Childe (1947, Tables I–III) for prehistoric Europe.

Charts like these are not easily established. Given adequate data, an archeologist should have no difficulty in locating a given phase in space, although opinion may differ as to the exact boundaries of the area in which the phase occurs. Position in time is another matter. The archeologist can occasionally obtain an absolute date (or better still, a series of them) by means of such techniques as dendrochronology or radiocarbon analysis but. lacking these, he will have to fall back upon some method of relative dating. If he is fortunate, he will be able to make use of geochronology, i.e., of a system of natural periods which, because it is independent of his phases, can be used to date them with considerable reliability (e.g., Clark 1936). More often, he has to fall back still further upon a system of culturally defined periods, based upon his phases and their content.

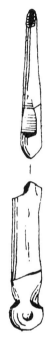

The so-called "direct historical approach" will serve to illustrate this last alternative (Steward 1942). The archeologist starts with the earliest known point of time. that of historic contact; seriates the phases of each local area back from this point; and then roughly equates the phases from area to area in terms of their order within the local sequences thus established. starting with the historic phases and giving due weight, as he works back in time, to differences in the duration of the phases which are indicated by depth of refuse, extent of cultural change, etc. This provides him with an arrangement of the phases according to their relative position in time and space, from which he may derive, for example, a threefold time scale of historic, protohistoric, and prehistoric periods, each with its corresponding phases or parts of phases, as the case may be (e.g., Strong 1935, Table 7).

The procedure of establishing a culturally defined time scale will not always be so regular as this. Often, it is a matter of fitting together various miscellaneous bits of chronological evidence, much as the pieces of a picture puzzle are put into their proper position. In such cases, all pertinent bits of evidence should be utilized since, for example, even when two sequences of phases are from distant areas, they may, by their consistency, serve to strengthen the validity of the over-all chronological picture. Some phases in the intervening areas may have to be left chronologically uncorrelated, because local sequences have not yet been established for their areas, but these phases can be included in the chronological chart in an indeterminate position (e.g.. Kidder 1948:416, 432–33).

It is important to distinguish procedures like the above, in which phases are equated solely on the basis of their absolute or relative positions within

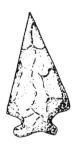

local sequences, from procedures in which the phases are chronologically correlated in terms of their presumed genetic connections. To say that a phase in one area is contemporaneous with phases in other areas because they share a given horizon style, for example, is on the genetic rather than the distributional level of interpretation, for it requires an assumption that the style has diffused from one phase to the others with little or no time lag. Too often an archeologist who has made this assumption will proceed to draw the conclusion that the style must have diffused from one phase to the others simply because all of the phases are contemporaneous, thereby involving himself in circular reasoning. It was apparently this danger which led Phillips and Willey (1953:624–25) to advise against broad-scale time-space correlations, and their point is well taken. It does not, however, preclude the use of nongenetic methods of broad-scale distributional correlation, such as have been discussed in the preceding paragraphs.

Even in its pure, nongenetic form, the distributional approach is on a more complex level of interpretation than descriptive correlation simply because it involves the factors of time and space. By the same token, it is less reliable. Nevertheless, it has tended to take the place of descriptive correlation as a means of ordering phases as soon as a relatively reliable form of chronology has became available. Some amateurs and art historians may still prefer the descriptive approach, since it is closer to the artifacts, in which they are most interested, but otherwise the distributional approach seems to provide a more satisfactory means of ordering or synthesizing the phases because it produces better historical perspective. It arranges the phases in the positions they actually occupied relative to each other in prehistory (cf. the "narrative approach" advocated by Brew 1946:66). Beyond this, distributional correlation is, in my opinion, a necessary prerequisite to proper genetic correlation, in that one cannot adequately demonstrate that two phases are genetically related without first showing that they have been in contact. This point will be discussed further below.

GENETIC CORRELATION

The genetic approach seeks to answer the question: Which phases or parts thereof are derived from other phases? This is done by arranging the phases according to their lines of development. Phillips and Willey (1953:628) seem to be suggesting this when they propose the use of the concepts of *tradition* and *horizon style*, since the former expresses the development of a series of phases through time, and the latter, a corresponding linkage through space, as diagrammed in Figure 3 (*left* and *left center*).

The term "genetic" is used here in a broader sense than by many anthropologists (e.g., Brew 1946), who limit it to the phylogenetic process, whereby one phase gives rise, wholly or in part, to two or more new phases. Phylogeny, which is also diagrammed in Figure 3 (*right center*), is here considered comparable to *tradition* and *horizon style*, since all three of them imply that one phase, or part thereof, is derived from another. There are a number of other possible forms of genetic relationship, considered in this broad sense, of which only one, the fusion of two phases to form a third, is diagrammed in Figure 3 (*right*). These various possibilities may occur singly, as is indicated in the figure, or in any kind of combination.

In order to establish a valid genetic relationship between phases, one must first demonstrate that the phases are similar and, second, that they have been in contact. In other words, one must do both descriptive and distributional correlation. Then, one may proceed to decide which phases are genetically connected and what forms the connections have taken by following out the descriptive and distributional relationships, as indicated in Figure 4.

When carrying out this procedure, it would seem advisable first to eliminate all those resemblances which do not appear to have been accompanied by contact. Next, one must decide which of the remaining resemblances are due to genetic connection rather than to some other factor such as adaptation to a

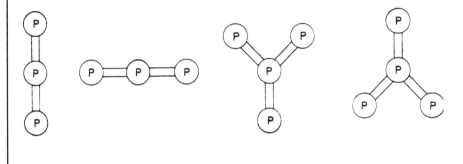

TRADITION, HORIZON, ETC.

Fig. 3. Some models for genetic correlation of phases (P).

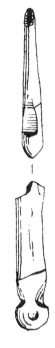

similar environment or attainment of the same level of cultural development. Only then will it be safe to choose from among the various possible forms of genetic connection, such as are diagrammed in Figure 3.

The genetic approach is on a more complex level of interpretation than either descriptive or distributional correlation and produces a more integrated picture of cultural relationships. On the other hand, it does not subsume as much of the data, since it is applicable to only one type of resemblance among phases, as illustrated above. Furthermore, it is the most difficult of the three types of correlation to carry out and the least reliable. The data are seldom adequate to indicate beyond doubt whether one phase is derived from another and, if so, in what manner—by a process of evolution, diffusion of constituent traits, phylogeny, fusion, etc. A decision among these possibilities is often a matter of opinion, as witness the current controversy whether there is a distinct Mogollon tradition, apart from the Anasazi, in the Southwest.

For these reasons, I would suggest that the genetic approach is not in itself an efficient method of ordering the phases, i.e., of making broad-scale syn-

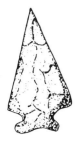

theses of cultural relationships, although it may be useful as a check upon syntheses established by other means. It would seem prudent to make one's basic synthesis by means of descriptive or distributional correlation and then to point out the genetic relationships only in the instances where sufficient data are available and they indicate that this particular type of relationship has occurred.

CONCLUSIONS

The foregoing discussion has been concerned with three approaches to the correlation of phases: descriptive, distributional, and genetic. The attempt has been made to show that these three approaches are distinct; that they require different concepts and methods; and that they are increasingly interpretative

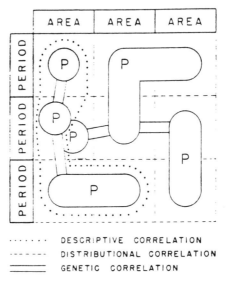

```
........  DESCRIPTIVE CORRELATION
--------  DISTRIBUTIONAL CORRELATION
========  GENETIC CORRELATION
```

FIG. 4. Use of descriptive and distributional correlation to demonstrate genetic connection among phases (P).

in the order given, but have decreasing reliability and inclusiveness. It has been further stated that the descriptive approach is a necessary prerequisite to proper distributional correlation and that both should be done before drawing any definite genetic conclusions.

It should be emphasized that the three approaches cannot properly be carried out in terms of a single classificatory system. If one were to adopt such a system, one would have to apply it to all of the phases whereas, as we have noted, both distributional and genetic correlation have to be limited to the phases for which adequate data are available. Moreover, in order to establish a single over-all system, one must assume a single form of distribution and a single type of genetic relationship whereas, as we have seen, it is advisable in each instance to consider all the possibilities, such as those diagrammed in Figures 2 and 3 (cf. the principle of multiple working hypotheses in geology in Chamberlin 1944).

The weaknesses in many historical reconstructions are, in my opinion, the result of failure to realize this point. To take an example from ethnology, one drawback of the *Kulturkreis* approach would seem to be that it does not establish valid descriptive and distributional relationships among tribes before grouping them together genetically in *Kreise* (Kluckhohn 1936:167). In archeology, the genetic classifications produced for the Southwest by Gladwin (1934) and Colton (1939) likewise suffer from a lack of independent descriptive and distributional correlation. Both Gladwin and Colton have failed to demonstrate that their phases actually are similar, contiguous, and hence genetic; and that the relationships among them actually are phylogenetic and do not, in some instances, conform to one of the other possibilities diagrammed in Figure 3 (or to some combination of these models). Their results would be more convincing if they had done so.

When Phillips and Willey (1953:628–31) propose that the correlation of phases be made only in terms of *traditions* and *horizon styles* (and thus without recourse to the other concepts previously mentioned in their article), they would seem to be making the same mistake. I cannot believe that it is wise to apply genetic concepts like these without first correlating one's phases in terms of descriptive and distributional concepts, or to work with *traditions* and *horizon styles* except on a basis of equality with all other genetic models, as in Figure 3. To do otherwise would be to adopt a priori one form of culture change without inquiring whether the data point to another.

Culture historians should, in my opinion, beware of overrefining their concepts, methods, and results. Students of history and of natural history have long since learned that there is no short cut to historical reconstruction, and it is time for culture historians also to realize this. As Brew (1946:66) has pointed out, what we need is more, not fewer, concepts and methods, and greater use of those we already have.

REFERENCES CITED

BREW, JOHN OTIS
    1946   The use and abuse of taxonomy. *In his:* Archaeology of Alkali Ridge, Southeastern Utah. Papers of the Peabody Museum of American Archaeology and Ethnology, Harvard University 21:44–66. Cambridge.

CHAMBERLIN, T. C.
    1944   The method of multiple working hypotheses. The Scientific Monthly 51:357-62. Washington, D. C.

CHILDE, V. GORDON
    1947   The dawn of European civilization. 4th ed. London, Kegan Paul, Trench, Trubner & Co., Ltd.
    1950   Prehistoric migrations in Europe. Oslo. H. Aschehoug & Co.

CLARK, J. G. D.
    1936   The mesolithic settlement of northern Europe. Cambridge, Cambridge University Press.

COLTON, H. S.
    1939   Prehistoric culture units and their relationships in northern Arizona. Museum of Northern Arizona, Bulletin 17. Flagstaff.

GLADWIN, W. and H. S.
    1934   A method for the designation of cultures and their variations. Medallion Papers 15. Globe.

KIDDER, ALFRED, II
    1948   The archeology of Venezuela. *In* Handbook of South American Indians, ed. Julian H. Steward. Bureau of American Ethnology, Bulletin 143, 4:413–38. Washington, D. C.

KLUCKHOHN, CLYDE
    1936   Some reflections on the method and theory of the *Kulturkreislehre*. American Anthropologist, n.s. 38:157–96. Menasha.

KRIEGER, ALEX D.
    1946   Culture complexes and chronology in northern Texas. The University of Texas Publication 4640. Austin.

KROEBER, ALFRED L.
    1940   Statistical classification. American Antiquity 6:29–44. Menasha.

MCKERN, WILLIAM C.
    1939   The midwestern taxonomic method as an aid to archaeological study. American Antiquity 4:301–13. Menasha.
    1940   Application of the midwestern taxonomic method. Bulletin of the Archeological Society of Delaware 3:18–21. Wilmington.

PHILLIPS, PHILIP and GORDON R. WILLEY
    1953   Method and theory in American archeology: an operational basis for culture-historical integration. American Anthropologist, n.s. 55: 615–33. Menasha.

ROUSE, IRVING
    1953   The strategy of culture history. *In* Anthropology Today: An Encyclopedic Inventory, prepared under the chairmanship of A. L. Kroeber, pp. 57–76. Chicago, University of Chicago Press.

SMITH, CARLYLE S.
    1950   The archaeology of coastal New York. Anthropological Papers of the American Museum of Natural History 43:93–200. New York.

SPAULDING, ALBERT C.
    1953   Statistical techniques for the discovery of artifact types. American Antiquity 18:305–13. Salt Lake City.

STEWARD, JULIAN H.
    1942   The direct historical approach to archeology. American Antiquity 7:337–43. Menasha.

STRONG, WILLIAM DUNCAN
    1935   An introduction to Nebraska archeology. Smithsonian Miscellaneous Collections 93, No. 10. Washington, D. C.

Raymond H. Thompson

1

Introduction

THE STUDY of cultural stability requires a knowledge of cultural development over a reasonably long span of time. The definition of this time perspective is one of the major contributions of archaeology to the study of culture. The archaeologist therefore should be in a position to make a significant contribution to the appraisal of the stability problem itself. However, the lack of a commonly accepted anthropological definition of the concept of cultural stability imposes semantic difficulties which hinder the determination of practical limits for the stability-instability problem area. Moreover, the nature of the data available to the archaeologist conditions the kind of contribution he can make.

One important aspect of cultural stability for which archaeology can provide basic data is that of the persistence and change of cultural forms through time. Our approach to the stability problem consists of a detailed analysis of this archaeologically documented aspect of it. We hoped that we might contribute significant results at a specifically archaeological theoretical level, rather than merely illustrate with archaeological examples the existing ideas about cultural change which are largely derived from ethnographic and historical data. But archaeologists cannot escape the basic limitation that the very identification of objects as artifacts is a product of the observation of existing cultures. Consequently, no claim for an absolutely independent point of view can be made. (Compare the statement by Phillips 1955, published since the seminar was held.) Under these circumstances, a specifically archaeological theory cannot be free from suppositions about the nature of culture, but it can be free from suppositions about the nature of culture change. At this level we can hope for a genuinely archaeological contribution to the body of anthropological theory.

In our effort to make such a contribution we reviewed the general character of archaeological data in order to appraise the limitations and potentialities of the basic evidence available to us and to establish a basis for defining some of the necessary conceptual tools. This examination of the kind of evidence which we can reasonably expect archaeology to produce, first reinforced the impression that the concept of tradition is one of the most important of these tools, and then led to a refinement of its current definition. We therefore undertook a study of the forms of traditions; we were especially interested in defining chronologically restricted segments of these forms which might serve as units of comparison. We developed a typology of tradition segments which seems to have promise for the formulation of causal theories about cultural persistence and change. We made a systematic analysis of the possible causal relationships between the tradition segments and various facets of man and nature, and arranged the results in the form of hypotheses to be tested by future research.

Thus, while we cannot claim to have made any startling new archaeological discoveries of a theoretical nature, we have illustrated the possibilities for an archaeological contribution to anthropological theory and have prepared the way for such a contribution by providing refinements of some of the basic conceptual tools, a sharper focus on some of the research problems, and a set of hypotheses for the investigation of these problems.

35

2

The Nature of Archaeological Data

THE BASIC UNIT of archaeological research is the artifact; the existence of the artifact implies the existence of artifact attributes. The artifact is treated here as given without further discussion; two fundamental classes (or dimensions) of attributes, the formal and the positional dimensions, can also be taken as given. A third significant dimension of artifact attributes, that of time, is not given and accordingly must be inferred. "Formal dimension" here refers to all physical properties of the artifact (shape, weight, chemical composition, etc.), "positional dimension" to physical locus, and "time dimension" to temporal locus in any sense.

Because the formal and positional dimensions are given, it is possible to describe the form and form-positional relationships of artifacts without introducing auxiliary principles and inference. Although a systematic study of the formal aspect of all artifacts has never been carried out, it seems to be generally assumed that the usual condition is one of attribute clustering rather than an endless list of all conceivable combinations of attributes. This clustering can be explained in part by inherent limitations of materials, human musculature, and the like, but even after due allowance for these is made the tendency is still evident. Similarly, any broad consideration of the positional dimension results at once in the generalization that artifacts tend strongly to occur in spatial clusters. Indeed, the tendency is so obvious that archaeologists commonly treat the site as a given, although they may be concerned about whether or not more than one component is represented.

The site provides a unit of artifact association for analysis and synthesis. It can be described with respect to the form of its constituent artifacts in much the same

fashion that an artifact can be described in terms of its attributes, and it is possible to rank various pairs of sites as more or less alike on this basis. Moreover, form classes of artifacts and a unit of artifact association provide the necessary data for quantitative description and comparison. Thus, a site can be characterized not only with respect to the artifact forms observed but also in terms of counts and proportions of these forms.

A general consideration of the formal aspect of sites leads to a judgment that, as was the case with artifacts, a clustering tendency is present. Archaeologists implicitly recognize this tendency by their habitual use of such terms as culture, culture type, and phase. Still another sort of cluster, the culture area, can be derived from an investigation of the position of the component sites of a culture type. We can accordingly list the artifact type, the site, the culture type, and the culture area as concepts derived from the formal and positional dimensions of artifacts without the aid of theories of culture change.

The classification of artifacts and sites in the time dimension is often accomplished by means of prior theories of culture change, but independent techniques for time ranking and measuring (or counting) are available and have furnished data for form-time generalizations. The independent ranking methods are borrowed from the natural sciences; they include superposition and association with successive geological and biological events. Chronological ranking furnishes a direction in time on which changes in form can be arranged. Measuring and year-counting techniques, of which the most familiar are radiocarbon dating and dendrochronology, provide information on rates of change as well. The general result of ranking and

36

estimation of absolute chronology is well known. Both artifacts and sites tend to become more complex as time progresses, and the rate-quantity methods of estimating absolute time over long periods suggest a regular acceleration in the tempo of development.

Additional inferences can be obtained by combining these generalizations. By holding the spatial dimension constant we can observe the tendency of sites to cluster into cultural types with a corresponding rarity of transitional sites. We can conclude that shifts from one culture type to another are comparatively rapid. This rapid shifting can be represented graphi-cally by plotting cultural complexity against time. The resulting curve repre-sents the continuous line of cultural de-velopment; it is characterized by a series of sharply rising escarpments connected by slightly sloping plateaus. If the concept of accelerating tempo is added, we can in-fer that the upturns of the curve are more closely spaced as time progresses. These concepts of culture change are a part of the general body of anthropological theory and historically were not derived solely from archaeological data. We wish to em-phasize, however, that they could have been so derived and in this sense constitute an independent and distinctively archae-ological theory of culture change.

* * * * *

3

The Concept of Tradition

THIS REVIEW of the theoretical background for archaeological studies of culture change sets the stage for the development of more precise formulations of the form-time and form-space relationships. The emphasis in this study is on the form-time relationship; the operational formulation for the elucidation of this relationship is the concept of tradition. A tradition is a socially transmitted form unit (or a series of systematically related form units) which persists in time.

This concept is not a new one. It has long been used in a general sense in the anthropological literature. Willey (1945: 53) first gave the concept of tradition a restricted and special meaning when he employed it as a temporal complement to the spatial concept of horizon style. More recently he and Phillips (Phillips and Willey 1953; Willey and Phillips 1955) have reviewed the further development of the concept and presented a restatement of the definition. They define a tradition as "a major large-scale space-time cultural continuity, defined with reference to persistent configurations in single technologies or total (archeological) culture, occupying a relatively long interval of time and a quantitatively variable but environmentally significant space" (Phillips and Willey 1953: 628). Our definition closely reflects Willey's original idea with its subsequent modifications, but there are differences which are worth pointing out.

In his original study of tradition Willey (1945) was concerned with formulating a concept which would help explain various observations about ceramic evidence which the spatial concept of horizon style did not accommodate. He therefore first presented the tradition concept in terms of a "pottery tradition." Through the succeeding years it has been gradually ex-

tended beyond this limited application to the full range of cultural phenomena (Willey 1953: 373). We wish to emphasize that, potentially at least, a tradition may exist for any cultural trait or combination of traits.

The temporal factor in tradition has apparently always been recognized. However, as in the case of Willey's first statements, it is not always clear whether the quality of persistence is considered an integral part of the concept itself. In their recent papers Willey and Phillips specifically state that appreciable persistence through time is inherent in all traditions. This point is fundamental to our discussions because we approach the stability-instability problem through a study of persistence. It should be noted that by the unqualified use of "persistence" in our definition we imply that the degree and extent of persistence in any tradition is a relative matter pertinent only to the problem under investigation.

In 1945 Willey placed geographic limits on the pottery tradition, probably because he was dealing with a specific problem having to do with a specific geographic range in Peru. Throughout the development of the concept, space has remained a requisite of the definition. Willey's emphasis on spatial continuity may reflect a recognition of the role of social continuity in forming traditions because archeologists often infer social continuity from the spatial dimension. However, in order to place the emphasis where it seems to belong, we specifically state in our definition that traditions are socially transmitted. By again omitting any qualifications we imply that transmittal can be in single, multiple, or cross cultural lines.

Other writers have also begun to present more precise formulations of tradition.

38

Phillips and Willey (1953) summarize this trend and comment on the statements on tradition advanced by Bennett (1948; compare Rouse 1954), McGregor (1950), and Goggin (1949). These authors have enlarged the concept in various directions. Mc.Gregor's remarks are particularly appropriate for the present study because of his emphasis on social continuity from one generation to another. The general trend seems to be toward defining the concept of tradition in terms of broad patterns of persistence. We recognize that tradition can be viewed in these broad ways and that they are appropriate for certain problems, but we prefer to keep the concept as flexible as possible in order to encompass any magnitude of cultural phenomena.

Phillips and Willey (1953: 627) also point out that "the outstanding merit of the tradition as an archeological tool" is its flexibility. Yet, while they emphasize that the concept must be free from set limitations of time, space, and content, they stipulate that the tradition must be of large scale. This size restriction seems to limit the utility of the concept because magnitude is immaterial to the concept itself, however pertinent it may be to problems involving tradition. We emphasize the logical completeness of the concept of tradition whereas Willey and Phillips (1955: 724) are more interested in its application in historical-developmental interpretation. Thus, although it is logically necessary to entertain the possibility of traditions ranging from the smallest to the largest, it is also important to recognize that the cultural and historical significance of a tradition diminishes toward either size extreme. Willey and Phillips point out the practical limits of very broad traditions, but there are probably comparable limitations in traditions of restricted size and content.

We recognize that the phase or locus (either temporal or spatial) of maximum intensity in a tradition may be formalized in terms of Kroeber's concept of climax. Indeed, we consider the articulation of the two concepts of tradition and climax to be one of the more fruitful directions in which the study of traditions may go. However, maximum intensity must be evaluated in terms of empirical data pertinent to the immediate problem rather than some inferential standard such as the "full potential development" suggested by Phillips and Willey (1953: 628). In so contingent a realm as culture such a standard is operationally meaningless because we cannot state with assurance and accuracy what *full* potential development might be.

In brief, then, we approach the problem of cultural stability-instability through a study of the persistence and change of cultural forms through time; we offer the concept of tradition as the basic tool for organizing archaeological data toward this end. A tradition is a socially transmitted cultural form which persists in time.

From *An Archaeological Approach to the Study of Cultural Stability*

4

A Method for the Study of Traditions

THE APPLICATION of the tradition concept to specific archaeological situations necessitates the consideration of certain general characteristics of traditions such as cultural context, geographical location, content, magnitude. duration, intensity, and form. The first two of these are determined by the investigator's original selection of the part of the world in which to carry out his archaeological research; they require no further discussion here.

We have emphasized in our definition of the tradition concept the need for maximum flexibility, especially in regard to content and magnitude. As anthropologists we are accustomed to think in terms of traits and increasingly larger groupings of traits such as trait complexes, patterns. and configurations. As archaeologists we often find it convenient to deal with more specific categories at the level of trait attributes: material, technique, shape, element, motif, style, function, etc.

Thus, an archaeologist may investigate a tradition of considerable magnitude such as the elaborate ritualism and symbolism of Mississippian culture, or one of smaller scope, the artistic style associated with the Southern Cult. He may focus on the hand-and-eye motif, the scalloped-edge disc as a traditional shape of one Southern Cult artifact, the cut-out technique of carving, or the tradition of using shell as a material in Southern Cult art.

Also of interest is the quantity in which the component parts of the tradition persist. However, it seems desirable to devise better methods of handling data quantitatively on the archaeological level before we attempt to study the quantitative behavior of traditions. It is in the study of the duration of a tradition that the archaeologist is perhaps most at home. In fact, archaeologists probably already have adequate techniques for answering the question of how long a tradition lasted, if not in relation to absolute time at least in terms of some relative scale.

Although a satisfactory estimate of the intensity of tradition development is often difficult to obtain archaeologically, it provides one of the most important lines of evidence for achieving a characterization of the tradition in terms of growth, maturation. climax, fulfillment, decline, disruption, and extinction. Closely related to this kind of appraisal is the interpretation which derives from the use of such essentially psychological concepts as "play" or "non-play," self-conscious or unconscious, explicit or implicit, overt or covert, closed or open. These approaches to the assessment of the broader implications of tradition development require considerable refinement before they can be used as successfully and as objectively as most students of cultural stability demand.

We devoted a large part of our seminar time to a description of the forms which traditions take. Several steps in the investigation of the problem were recognized. These consist of descriptive analysis, descriptive synthesis, and formulation of hypotheses which may be of value for directing future research.

40

DESCRIPTIVE ANALYSIS

A first step in the study of tradition consists of an analysis of those formal aspects of the archaeological data which may be treated in terms of persistence. Some of the formal categories frequently used by archaeologists are shown in Table 1. The major categories are trait attributes, traits, and culture. Subcategories of trait attributes include material, technique, shape, element, motif, style, and function. Traits can be classified or divided into classes, types, and complexes. Cultures can be con-

TABLE 1

FORMAL CATEGORIES OF ARCHAEOLOGICAL DATA IN TERMS OF PERSISTENCE IN TIME AND SPACE

WITH EXAMPLES OF TRADITIONS AND
HORIZONS FROM PERUVIAN ARCHAEOLOGY

	FORMAL CATEGORIES	PERSISTENCE IN TIME: TRADITION	PERSISTENCE IN SPACE: HORIZON
TRAIT ATTRIBUTES	MATERIAL		
	TECHNIQUE	TECHNIQUE TRADITION WHITE-ON-RED NORTH COAST PLASTIC	HORIZON TECHNIQUE WHITE-ON-RED NEGATIVE
	SHAPE		
	ELEMENT		
	MOTIF		
	STYLE		HORIZON STYLE CHAVIN TIAHUANACO
	FUNCTION		
TRAITS	CLASS	POTTERY TRADITION	
	TYPE		
	COMPLEX		
CULTURES	COMPLEX		
	PATTERN		
	CONFIGURATION		
	WHOLE	CO-TRADITION	

sidered in terms of culture complexes, patterns, and configurations, or as whole cultures. Although an attempt has been made to list under these categories the most common analytical units, the treatment cannot be considered exhaustive. The categories and units are logically related as parts of a hierarchical typology, but they are not mutually exclusive. Thus a given trait may be analyzed in terms of several if not all of the attributes listed here.

It is possible to study the persistence of forms in both time and space. Both of these dimensions are incorporated in Table 1 in order to call attention to the possibility of developing a wide variety of constructs similar to the Horizon Style already known from Peruvian archaeology. For example, Willey (1948: 15) comments that both the White-on-Red and Negative horizons in Peru are based on technical processes rather than stylistic unity. An examination of the trait attributes in the chart in relation to the space or horizon column, illustrates the possibility of a con-

cept of "Horizon Technique" which might serve better than the Horizon Style as a basis for explaining the diffusion of the White-on-Red and Negative technical ideas. Similarly, the use of this chart as an analytical guide makes possible constructs like "Technique Tradition," "Shape Tradition," or "Horizon Shape." Indeed, any of the units in the chart may be traced in time or space in terms of either the tradition or the horizon concept. Several of the traditions and horizons which have been formalized in Peruvian archaeology are arranged in the chart in order to illustrate these possibilities.

The method of any descriptive analysis is the ordering of data. The kind of ordering presented here provides both a set of units by means of which lines of continuity through time (or space) may be traced and a framework for combining these lines. It should be possible thereby to point out new relationships of the traits or trait attributes that operate within a tradition.

DESCRIPTIVE SYNTHESIS

A second step in this study is the definition of general classes of traditions. Unfortunately, the fragmentary nature of archaeological data usually makes it impossible to recognize the entire history of a tradition. Moreover, a tradition may change form. We therefore found it desirable to deal with segments of traditions. A segment represents a chronologically restricted portion of a tradition; its duration depends upon the available archaeological information or the focus of the particular problem. The classification of traditions presented here is based on the form of tradition segments rather than on the form of whole traditions.

Tradition segments exhibit different forms or patterns of persistence and change through time. In order to describe these forms, therefore, attention must be given

to change as well as to persistence. Both random (or unpatterned) change and no change (or complete stability) are theoretically possible, but for the most part change seems to be directionally patterned. Differences in this patterning may serve as the basis for a classification of tradition segments. Although the complexity of the patterning makes graphic presentation of tradition segments a gross oversimplification, Figure 1 gives some conception of the possibilities for representing ideal tendencies (compare Rouse 1955, Fig. 3). Some of the ideal tradition segments are direct, converging, diverging, elaborating, and reducing. We have found it convenient to abbreviate the names of these tradition segments, for example, "Direct Tradition" instead of the more awkward "direct-trending segment of a tradition."

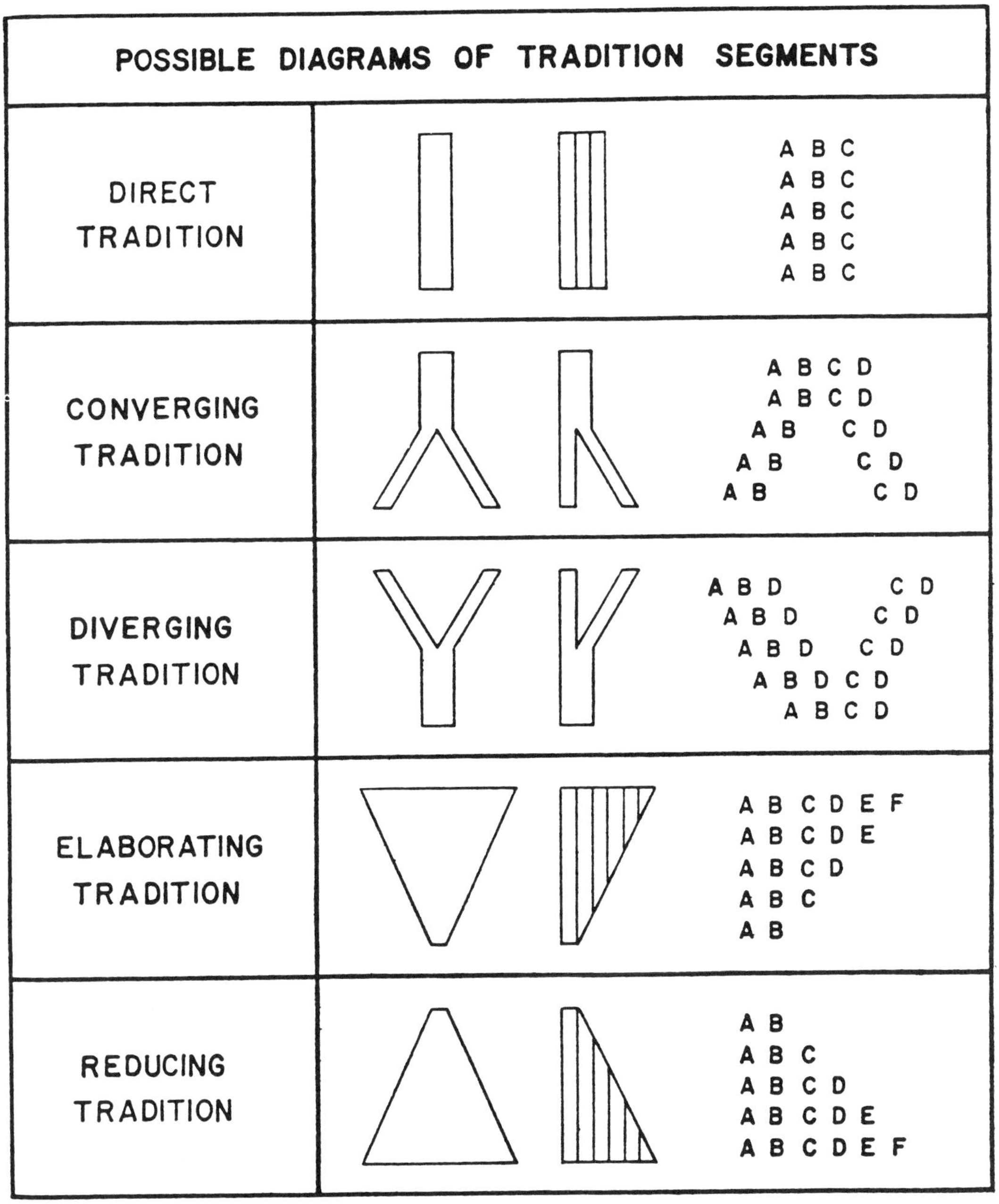

POSSIBLE DIAGRAMS OF TRADITION SEGMENTS

DIRECT TRADITION		A B C A B C A B C A B C A B C
CONVERGING TRADITION		A B C D A B C D A B C D A B C D A B C D
DIVERGING TRADITION		A B D C D A B D C D A B D C D A B D C D A B C D
ELABORATING TRADITION		A B C D E F A B C D E A B C D A B C A B
REDUCING TRADITION		A B A B C A B C D A B C D E A B C D E F

FIGURE 1

The descriptive terms may be combined in the name of a single segment, as for example, the reducing branch of a diverging tradition.

It seems unwise to offer formal definitions of these classes of tradition segments at this time. Until the method as a whole can be tested more thoroughly, the concepts should be kept flexible. Nevertheless, it is possible to set forth what seem to be their essential features.

A Direct Tradition is characterized by

an essentially unchanging continuity. Those changes which take place do not effectively shift lines of development within the tradition. An example is the preference for flat-bottom vessels in the pottery shape tradition of North Coast Peru.

A Converging Tradition describes the segment in which two or more traditions come together. Convergence may result in a merger of the traditions into a single tradition. Sometimes one of the traditions is absorbed. On the other hand, convergence may mean that the traditions impinge on one another for a time, without the submergence of either. Although contact situations between different cultures offer a ready opportunity for convergence, this process may take place between traditions within a single culture. Convergence is illustrated by the blending of the Mogollon and Anasazi cultural traditions in the Southwest.

A Diverging Tradition is in many respects the opposite of a Converging Tradition and refers to the segment in which a single tradition splits into two or more distinguishable traditions. This does not necessarily mean that the parent tradition is terminated, for it may not be appreciably affected by this process. In others, the newly formed traditions differ considerably from the original one. The development of two distinct regional variants of the Hohokam red-on-buff pottery tradition is an example of divergence.

An Elaborating Tradition is characterized by an increasing complexity resulting from the addition of traits or attributes which are integrated in a single line of development. Not only quantity and variety of traits are involved, but also their organization and embellishment. The polychrome pottery tradition in South Coast Peru is an illustration of elaboration.

A Reducing Tradition is in some ways the opposite of an Elaborating Tradition. The Reducing Tradition is characterized by an increasing simplification through loss of traits, and perhaps in terms of a less complex organization. The reduction of the Yucatecan tradition of religious architecture at Mayapan illustrates this class of tradition segments.

Disruption normally relates to the terminal phases of a tradition and describes the collapse of a tradition through the process of disorganization. Nevertheless, it is necessary to recognize the possibility of re-emergence and reconstitution of a tradition after disruption, however rare such a situation may be in reality. The revival of the decorative tradition of Sikyatki Polychrome by contemporary Hopi potters is a widely quoted example. Extinction means that the tradition has ceased to exist in a recognizable form. Stagnation might be thought of as referring to an essentially unchanging tradition which gives the appearance of lacking the capacity for further development.

In the case of a tradition whose history is well understood the segment designation may be qualified by the adjective, external or internal. External signifies that contact or diffusion has been largely responsible for the development of the tradition. Internal means that the development has taken place within the cultural unit, largely free from outside influences.

It should be pointed out that such descriptive terms as convergence and reduction could also be applied to the horizon concept. However, we did not explore these possibilities.

The descriptive synthesis offers a classification of tradition segments which permits a characterization of developments within a tradition and provides one basis for the evaluation of persistence and change. The segments may be combined in sequence to obtain a more complete picture of the history of the tradition as a whole. On the other hand, the tradition may be divided into unit segments which can be correlated more directly with causal factors and thus provide the basis for further interpretation. The ultimate test of the utility of this classification consists of the demonstration that the form segments are related meaningfully to other aspects of the cultural and noncultural world.

HYPOTHESES CONCERNING TRADITION SEGMENTS

A third step in our consideration of the tradition concept is the formulation of hypotheses about the relationship of various tradition forms to some of these cultural and noncultural factors. The suggested relationships range in character from obvious to dubious. The classes of factors to be related to tradition forms are drawn from general anthropological theory. The only innovation presented here is the systematic consideration of these classes in terms of limitations and potentialities.

Certain causal factors appear to correlate with particular classes of tradition segments. The possible correlations which we considered are presented schematically in Table 2 where they are arranged in terms of the limitations and potentialities for change within tradition. The limitations and potentialities are considered as the opposite ends of a continuum of change-producing situations. These situations are extreme cases or polar ideals which represent the theoretical expectancy in the correlation of the causal factors and the tradition segments. A perfect correlation with a single causal factor is hardly to be expected, if for no other reason than that few cultural problems can be removed from their multiple-cause matrices.

The polar ideals described in Table 2 are not offered as examples of commonly occurring cultural and archaeological situations, but rather as a means of analyzing the influence of any one causal factor by holding all others theoretically constant. Thus, the more nearly an archaeological situation approaches one of these extremes, the greater should be the tendency for a positive correlation between the tradition segment and the causal factor. Obviously, some of the ideal situations are more likely to occur than others, or at least they are more easily recognized in the archaeological record. These more frequently occurring or more readily identifiable situations are, of course, of greater immediate analytical utility than their logically satisfying but somewhat more elusive counterparts. However, these latter are included in Table 2 because they afford more than logical satisfaction. They provide a systematic approach to the identification of the less obvious elements in the multiple-cause matrices.

Table 2 is a catalog of the correlations which were discussed in the seminar. The correlations are stated as generalizations concerning the kind of tradition segment which may be expected to result from the change-producing influence of various causal factors. These factors are grouped in seven major classes: biological, inherent, environmental, demographic, societal, cultural, and contact or diffusion. The table contains the only complete check list of all the correlations or ideal situations which were formulated. However, it must not be assumed that these statements represent all possibilities for no attempt has been made to compile an exhaustive listing. While some of the theoretical or ideal situations are analyzed and stated in greater detail than others, there is no mention in the table of concrete situations or examples.

These ideal formulations are therefore offered as hypotheses which must be tested, and the formal statements are phrased in ideal or abstract rather than concrete terms in order to emphasize their hypothetical nature and their untested status. Much of our discussion of these hypotheses consisted of a kind of prelimi-

TABLE 2

CAUSAL FACTORS IN THE DEVELOPMENT OF TRADITIONS

A correlation of classes of causal factors with a continuum of change-producing situations. The focus of each correlation is on the limitation or potentiality pole of this continuum.

I. BIOLOGICAL FACTORS

Potentialities and limitations for change, which depend at least in part upon biological factors, probably affect traditions in conjunction with other causal factors. However, the nature and extent of this biological effect are largely problems for biological research and therefore not immediately germane to the present investigation.

II. INHERENT FACTORS

A. LIMITATIONS
   1. within trait attribute
      a. Limitations inherent in material or function tend to result in Direct Tradition.
   2. within tradition
      a. Limitations inherent in a tradition tend to result in Direct Tradition and possibly eventual stagnation, disruption, or extinction.

B. POTENTIALITIES
   1. within trait attribute
      a. Potentialities for "play" inherent in an attribute tend to result in Elaborating Tradition.
   2. within tradition
      a. Potentialities for variation inherent in a tradition tend to result in Elaborating Tradition.

III. ENVIRONMENTAL FACTORS

A. LIMITATIONS
   1. in constant environment
      a. Limitations in an essentially unchanging environment produce "ecologically-bound" tradition and tend to result in Direct Tradition.
   2. in changing environment
      a. A *slow* environmental change *incompatible* with the conditions basic to an "ecologically-bound" tradition tends to result in Reducing Tradition (in case of minor environmental change) or eventual extinction of the tradition (in case of major environmental change).
      b. A *slow* environmental change *compatible* with the conditions basic to an "ecologically-bound" tradition tends to result in Direct Tradition (in case of minor environmental change) or slightly Elaborating Tradition (in case of major environmental change).
      c. A *rapid* environmental change *incompatible* with the conditions basic to an "ecologically-bound" tradition tends to result in disruption or extinction of the tradition.
      d. A *rapid* environmental change *compatible* with the conditions basic to an "ecologically-bound" tradition is infrequent but tends to result in Elaborating Tradition.

B. POTENTIALITIES
   1. in constant environment
      a. Potentialities in an essentially unchanging environment produce "ecologically-free" tradition and tend to result in Direct Tradition or to permit Elaborating Tradition.
   2. in changing environment
      a. A *slow* environmental change *incompatible* with the conditions basic to an "ecologically-free" tradition may eventually produce an "ecologically-bound" tradition and tends to result in Reducing Tradition (in case of minor environmental change) or disruption and possible extinction of the tradition (in case of major environmental change).
      b. A *slow* environmental change *compatible* with the conditions basic to an "ecologically-free" tradition, while unlikely, would tend to result in Direct Tradition (in case of minor environmental change) or slightly Elaborating Tradition (in case of major environmental change).
      c. A *rapid* environmental change *incompatible* with the conditions basic to an "ecologically-free" tradition may produce an "ecologically-bound" tradition and tends to result in Reducing Tradition (in case of minor environmental change) or disruption and possible extinction of the tradition (in case of major environmental change).
      d. A *rapid* environmental change *compatible* with the conditions basic to an "ecologically-free" tradition, while unlikely, would tend to result in Direct Tradition (in case of minor environmental change) or Elaborating Tradition (in case of major environmental change).

IV. DEMOGRAPHIC FACTORS

A. LIMITATIONS

1. Limitations in small or non-increasing population tend to result in Direct Tradition.

B. POTENTIALITIES

1. Potentialities in large or increasing population tend to result in Elaborating Tradition or Diverging Tradition.

V. SOCIETAL FACTORS

A. LIMITATIONS

1. in class or occupational specialization
   a. Conservatism of specialists may inhibit change and tends to result in Direct Tradition.

B. POTENTIALITIES

1. in class or occupational specialization
   a. Interest in innovation or variation by specialists may *vastly* increase change and tends to result in Elaborating Tradition.
   b. An increase or fission in class or occupational specialization tends to result in Diverging Tradition or Elaborating Tradition.

VI. CULTURAL FACTORS

A. LIMITATIONS

1. Lack of cultural interest or closed value system tends to result in Direct Tradition.

B. POTENTIALITIES

1. Cultural interest or open value system tends to result in Elaborating Tradition, and possibly Converging Tradition or Diverging Tradition.

VII. CONTACT OR DIFFUSION FACTORS

A. LIMITATIONS

1. without migration
   a. The introduction, through *little or intermittent* diffusion, of traits or traditions *incompatible* with the receiving tradition tends not to affect the continuity of the receiving tradition.
   b. The introduction, through *little or intermittent* diffusion of traits or traditions *compatible* with the receiving tradition tends either not to affect the continuity of the receiving tradition, or to modify it toward Converging Tradition, Diverging Tradition, or slightly Elaborating Tradition.

2. with migration
   a. The introduction, through *small or intermittent* migration, of traits or traditions *incompatible* with the receiving tradition tends to result in continuity of the receiving tradition with possible coexistence of the incoming tradition. In the case of conquest there is a possibility of disruption of the receiving tradition.
   b. The introduction, through *small or intermittent* migration, of traits or traditions *compatible* with the receiving tradition tends to result in continuity of the receiving tradition or modification of it in the direction of Elaborating Tradition, or Converging Tradition (with probable absorption of the incoming tradition). In the case of conquest with convergence there is a possibility of domination by the incoming tradition.

B. POTENTIALITIES

1. without migration
   a. The introduction, through *much or frequent* diffusion, of traits or traditions *incompatible* with the receiving tradition tends to result in disruption and possible extinction of the tradition.
   b. The introduction, through *much or frequent* diffusion, of traits or traditions *compatible* with the receiving tradition tends to result in Converging Tradition, Elaborating Tradition, or Diverging Tradition.

2. with migration
   a. The introduction, through *large or frequent* migration, of traits or traditions *incompatible* with the receiving tradition tends to result in disruption of the tradition and/or possible coexistence, even disruption of the incoming tradition.
   b. The introduction, through *large or frequent* migration, of traits or traditions *compatible* with the receiving tradition tends to result in Converging Tradition, Elaborating Tradition, or Diverging Tradition.

From *An Archaeological Approach to the Study of Cultural Stability* nary test in the form of a search for concrete examples from more or less familiar and well-documented archaeological situations. Only the results of that discussion and a few of the examples are given here. While these comments are based upon a wide range of anthropological fact and theory, the examples are drawn from archaeological situations in order to emphasize that the concepts under discussion are intended to help explain the patterning of persistence in the archaeological range of the anthropological record. These summary comments are arranged, like the table, by causal factors, but the focus of interest is on the tradition segments and the modifications.

BIOLOGICAL FACTORS

Although serious problems are connected with the recognition of a class of biological factors which may affect traditions, the possibility of some kind of biologically derived causality must be acknowledged. This acknowledgment is made difficult, however, by the uncertain status of research on the relationship between biology and culture. This uncertainty is reflected in the fact that while biological factors are often acknowledged, discussion of them is usually avoided except for some token statement like the present one. The unscientific claims of racist writers have contributed materially to this overcautious treatment.

What objective acknowledgment there is seems to indicate that any possible biological causes of cultural development are considered to be remote and indirect. For example, it is often stated that the biological differences between the various fossil men found in the Old World may have some significance for the interpretation of cultural development. Slotkin (1952) discusses the methodological problems which stem from the logical necessity of recognizing this possibility. There is also a growing interest in the causal role of biological factors in the transition from or-

ganic evolution to the development of culture, an interest which is exemplified by LaBarre's recent (1954) book. (See also Kroeber's discussion of this development in the Wenner-Gren *Yearbook of Anthropology—1955*, pp. 294-5, published since the seminar was held.)

This discussion of the biological factor is purposefully brief, for we do not consider indirect biological influence in remote periods of time to be central to the problem of the seminar. Moreover, we were reluctant to undertake a study of the biological correlation without the advice of a specialist in biology. We decided that it would be more profitable to focus on those classes of causal factors which seem to have more direct and more immediate analytical value.

INHERENT FACTORS

The fact that certain classes of artifacts are inherently more susceptible to change than others has made it common practice for archaeologists to base chronological studies on those artifact classes which possess high inherent potentialities for change and variation. The analytical method presented here makes it possible to apply this familiar concept of inherent characteristics to the study of traditions. While only the potentialities for change are emphasized in chronological studies, both limitations and potentialities must be considered in tradition analysis. Moreover, these limitations and potentialities for change may be inherent either in the trait attributes which influence tradition development or in the tradition itself.

The inherent characteristics of some trait attributes impose specific limitations on tradition change which tend to produce Direct Tradition. The attributes of material and function frequently possess these inherent limitations. The *Glycymeris* shell bracelet tradition in the Southwest provides an example of the limiting influence of both of these factors. This long-lived tradition was directly patterned because of the close correlation of the circular form of the shell with the functional requisites of a bracelet (Table 2: II,A,1).

Some attributes, on the other hand, are particularly subject to minor modifications which do not significantly affect the basic form or function of the trait. These modifications need not involve deliberate or large-scale innovation; they seem rather to result from the cultural expression of the biological (or psychological) play impulse (Kroeber 1948: 29, 355-7, 387; Linton 1936: 90, 311-2). Inherent potentialities for experimentation and play-derived change tend to result in Elaborating Tradition.

Sometimes this potentiality is inherent in the material. Thus, the plasticity of clay provides an excellent opportunity for the expression of the play impulse. An example is Willey's North Peruvian Plastic Tradition which is of the elaborating type and which is based in part at least on this inherent property of clay (Table 2: II,B,1). But in general, attributes such as element and motif which are capable of almost endless recombination appear to be most subject to the play factor. At the same time it is also apparent that a single class of attributes may show great variation in this respect.

An Elaborating Tradition may often be analyzed in terms of the inherent characteristics of the attributes which contribute to the tradition. For example, the Anasazi painted pottery tradition is of the elaborating variety because of the inherent potentialities for change in the painting technique as well as in the many geometric elements and motifs used in the various regional and chronological styles.

Traditions also may have inherent limitations and potentialities for change and variation. The Maya calendrical tradition may be viewed as a closed system with inherent limitations which resulted in a Direct Tradition and which were partly responsible for its eventual stagnation and disruption (Table 2: II,A,2). The Mochica emphasis on life-scene depiction, on the other hand, constitutes a tradition with almost unlimited inherent potentialities for elaboration. Indeed, this tradition helps explain the Peruvian exploitation of the play potential in attributes like the plasticity of clay and the molding technique (Table 2: II,B,2).

ENVIRONMENTAL FACTORS

The limitations and potentialities of the natural environment constitute an important class of causal factors which must be considered in any attempt to understand the development of traditions. But, although there is extensive literature on the relationship between environment and culture, there is no consistent body of theory to serve as a guide for the analysis of the role of environmental factors in tradition formation (compare Meggers 1954). The hypotheses concerning environment which are listed in Table 2 represent a first attempt at such a guide. We present this tentative guide with some misgivings for we did not have time to examine adequately either its theoretical or practical aspects. It is offered as an approach to the problem which we consider worth more extended consideration.

Fundamental to this approach is recognition of the fact that there may be a large number of variables in any situation involving a correlation between culture and environment. Some of the more obvious of these are included in the statements in Table 2. They are arranged in pairs of opposites which can be defined in terms of the ideal tendencies in a continuum. The concept of continuum seems particularly appropriate at this tentative stage in the study of traditions because of its flexibility. Although the continuum is defined in terms of its theoretical extremes, it also includes a series of intermediate correlations which could presumably accommodate any archaeological situation. In practice, therefore, the continuum is a scale for measuring the degree to which an actual correlation approaches the ideal tendency.

Thus, the polar concepts of "ecologically bound" and "ecologically free" are offered as the extremes of a continuum of ecological dependence rather than as statements of absolute conditions. Surely no tradition is so completely bound to its ecological setting that it cannot change unless the environment changes. Although it is also difficult to conceive of a tradition which is totally divorced from the influences of the environment, traditions which involve idea systems on the order of the alphabet are probably close to being "ecologically free" in the absolute sense.

Nevertheless, the influence of the environment is one of the factors which participate in the formation of most traditions, and certain traditions, such as those based on subsistence activities, are quite intimately related to ecological conditions.

It is also important to consider whether the environmental conditions are constant or changing, for a change could cause considerable modification in a tradition, especially in the case of an "ecologically-bound" one. The problem cannot be viewed simply in terms of change or lack of change, however, because the extent of modification of the tradition will depend in part at least on the magnitude of the environmental change and the rate at which it takes place. Moreover, the development of the tradition will be directly affected by whether the environmental change is compatible or incompatible with the ecological conditions to which the tradition is already adjusted.

In Table 2 the systematic presentation of these several sets of variables has resulted in a number of rather awkward constructions. We look upon these semantic difficulties as a function of the tentative nature of these statements and not as a basic defeat in the approach as a whole. In fact, a more thorough treatment of the influence of environmental factors in terms of variables like those used in the present approach would probably eliminate such problems. We recognize that the lack of adequate techniques for identifying such variables in the archaeological record limits the exploitation of their interpretive potential, but we include them to emphasize their usefulness in tradition analysis, and to encourage continued search for more satisfactory means of isolating them archaeologically.

The uncertainties which at present surround the identification of some of these variables make it somewhat difficult to select clear-cut archaeological examples of all the ideal correlations between environmental factors and traditions which are suggested in Table 2. Moreover, in at least one case (Table 2: III,A,2,a) other causal factors sometimes so obscure the picture as to make it almost impossible to isolate the environmental one. Nevertheless, we offer some examples to show the direction of our thinking on the environmental causes in tradition formation.

The long persistence of the western Eskimo sea mammal hunting tradition illustrates the situation in which limitations in an essentially unchangng environment produce "ecologically-bound" traditions of direct form (Table 2: III,A,1). A basic artifact in this tradition is the toggle-head harpoon; it provides the archaeological evidence for this persistence. Throughout the long Aleutian sequence, for example, this harpoon remains constant except for variations in hafting.

A classic example of the result of a major environmental change which takes place gradually and which is incompatible with the conditions basic to an "ecologically-bound" tradition is the reduction of the Upper Palaeolithic traditions of art, hunting, and settlement pattern recorded in the transition from Magdalenian to Azilian (Table 2: III,A,2,a).

Limitations in the environment of northeastern North America were such that while the Postglacial increase in temperature was a change in harmony with the conditions to which the "Archaic" type of hunting tradition was adjusted, the change was so slight and took place so gradually that the hunting tradition tended to be direct in form (Table 2: III,A,2,b).

The lowering of the level of the sea which led to the extinction of whales in the Arctic Archipelago was a rapid environmental change incompatible with the conditions basic to the "ecologically-bound" traditions of the whale-hunting Thule Eskimo (Table 2: III,A,2,c). The result was the disruption and extinction of the whale-based traditions in Thule culture and ultimately the disruption of the cultural tradition itself.

The tendency of potentialities in an essentially unchanging environment to produce "ecologically-free" traditions of elaborating form is illustrated by the dry farming tradition of the Anasazi (Table 2: III, B,1). They made better use of the available water by conservation of runoff, floodwater farming on valley floors and at arroyo mouths, deep planting, and seed selection. This elaboration of the basic tradition enabled the Anasazi to achieve a relatively full utilization of their environment within the limits of dry farming.

The eruption of Sunset Crater in the Flagstaff region of northern Arizona was a rapid change of major proportions which produced conditions compatible with the agricultural base of the region and made possible a whole series of elaborating traditions (Table 2: III,B,2,d).

DEMOGRAPHIC FACTORS

It has long been recognized that both size and density of population are important for understanding processes of cultural change. These demographic factors are often invoked in attempts to explain major trends of world culture history, especially the transition from food gathering to food production and the development of urban civilizations. However, these same factors can be used in causal analysis at all levels of archaeological interpretation. Childe's (1948) reconstruc-

tion of the growth of civilization in the Old World is a familiar example of the application of standard demographic generalizations to culture-historical interpretation; our statements in Table 2 are a rephrasing of these generalizations in terms of the tradition problem. Before more precise correlations between demographic factors and tradition segments can be formulated much more detailed information on population size and distribution is needed. The growing interest in settlement patterns should provide some of the necessary data and make possible more extensive use of demographic factors in the study of tradition formation.

The influence of demographic factors is often obscured by failure to hold all other causal factors theoretically constant. The marked tendency toward traditions of direct form in the "Archaic" cultures of the Northeast is usually explained by reference to limitations in the environment. This dependence on one major causal factor masks the importance of the limitations imposed by small and static populations (Table 2: IV,A,1). On the other hand, a large and increasing population creates conditions which are favorable to tradition elaboration. At the Village of the Great Kivas the parallel development of increased size of the site and elaboration of the pottery tradition illustrates this generalization (Table 2: IV,B,1).

SOCIETAL FACTORS

Limitations and potentialities for change in a tradition are sometimes the result of conditions created by the structure of society. These conditions are particularly well defined when a society is organized into specialist groups along occupational or class lines. However, the nature of the conditions created by a given societal factor may differ widely according to the cultural setting. Some understanding of the cultural background of a tradition is therefore necessary in order to assess adequately the causal influence of a societal factor. Societal factors constitute but one end of a complex continuum of socio-cultural situations. Nevertheless, it is analytically useful to focus separately on each end of this familiar continuum in order to isolate as many as possible of the subtle causal elements in the socio-cultural whole.

In archaeological studies the social or specialist group is always an inference from the empirical data. Even when there are written sources with which to check the inferential status of the social unit, there is considerable danger of error in interpretation, resulting from circular reasoning. Reference to basic anthropological generalizations on socio-cultural situations provides the only satisfactory independent control. The correlations between societal factors and tradition segments listed in Table 2 are derived from these generalizations.

Peruvian archaeology provides examples of the opposite influences of an occupational group in different cultural settings. The relatively direct form of the Inca pottery tradition may be attributed to the presence of craft specialists in a culture interested in quantity production (Table 2: V,A,1,a), the elaboration of the Mochica pottery tradition to artisans in a culture interested in technological and artistic experimentation (Table 2: V,B,1,a). In Mesopotamian archaeology there are many examples of Elaborating Tradition resulting from increasing class and occupational specialization (Table 2: V,B,1,b).

CULTURAL FACTORS

A tradition may consist of any magnitude of cultural phenomena from trait attribute to cultural whole. Archaeologists ordinarily deal with only fragments of culture and thus with traditions of less than total cultural extent. The usual archaeological tradition is only a part of culture. But no part of culture can be completely divorced from the cultural whole, except perhaps for analytical purposes. Therefore, the direction in which a tradition develops is determined at least in part by the interests of the culture which supports the tradition. While this relationship to the total cultural setting has only been mentioned in the discussion of the societal factors, it is also important in the appraisal of the other causal factors. No analysis of the development of a tradition can be considered complete without some effort to define the value system which determines so much of the behavior of the parts of a culture.

Unfortunately, however, the definition of these abstract qualities of a culture requires information which is seldom available to the archaeologist. At any rate there are no well defined independent standards with which the archaeologist can achieve a reasonably accurate estimate of these qualities. Of course, some anthropological generalizations make possible the framing of tentative hypotheses like those in Table 2. Thus, cultures with a conservative outlook tend to emphasize Direct Tradition, while those with an interest in innovation tend to produce Elaborating Tradition.

There are only two contexts in which one can make a valid archaeological test of these and similar hypotheses. Complex civilizations preserve a record of their value systems in art form and written word, but they are of limited analytical value because they are not sufficiently representative of the usual archaeological situation. The direct historical approach is somewhat more broadly applicable. The projection of ethnohistorical data backward into archaeological horizons provides a method of inferring for both complex and simple cultures those qualities of cultural emphasis which are necessary before the cultural factors in a tradition's causal matrix can be successfully analyzed. The interpretation of Pueblo culture history is a familiar example of the application of this method. The direct form of many Pueblo traditions is correlated with the tightly integrated value system of contemporary Pueblo culture (Table 2: VI,A,1).

CONTACT OR DIFFUSION FACTORS*

The introduction of new ideas through contact with other cultures is one of the primary causes of cultural change. The identification of diffused traits has therefore been a major goal of archaeological research. Although the contact situation is extremely complex, some of the variables have been recognized and tentatively defined so that it is possible to attempt a systematic arrangement of the limitations and potentialities for tradition modification which diffused traits and traditions possess. The correlations between diffusion factors and tradition segments in Table 2 represent our effort to achieve a preliminary version of such an arrangement.

Each contact situation consists of the interaction of at least two cultural traditions: the incoming and the receiving. The hypotheses in Table 2 are stated in terms of the effect of diffusion on the receiving tradition with only an occasional comment on the incoming tradition. We have made a distinction between those introduced traits and traditions which are compatible with the receiving tradition and those which are not. But at the same time we recognize that our treatment of the concept of compatibility is greatly oversimplified. For example, we have not tried to take into account the possibility of confusing acceptability, compatibility, and need. The amount of tradition change also depends on whether the diffusion takes place by migration and whether the migration is accompanied by conquest. Moreover, the causal influence of the diffusion varies considerably according to the magnitude and frequency of the contact. The following examples illustrate the way in which some of these variables modify traditions.

The intermittent introduction of polychrome pottery to North Coast Peru did not affect the continuity of the local pottery tradition (Table 2: VII,A,1,a). The presence of bichrome styles in this tradition indicates that the failure to accept polychrome painting was caused by cultural rather than technological incompatibility.

Limited diffusion of a compatible trait resulted in tradition divergence at Point of Pines in eastern Arizona when cremation was introduced to a people who practiced inhumation (Table 2: VII,A,1,b). Cremation became popular and partly replaced inhumation, but the practice of inhumation persisted qualitatively unchanged as one part of the new Diverging Tradition.

The Oneota are an example of the Converging Traditions with subsequent elaboration created by the strong pressure of compatible Mississippian influences on the Woodland cultures of the northern Midwest (Table 2: VII,B,1,b).

A Converging Tradition was produced at Chichen Itzá during the Toltec occupation by the blending of the compatible architectural traditions of the local Yucatecan Maya and the migrating Tula-Toltec (Table 2: VII,B,2,b).

In Mesopotamia the frequent and large-scale migrations of Semites helped to create the conditions which led to tradition elaboration, convergence, and divergence. The movement of the Akkadians into the area north of Sumer and of the Amorites into Akkad are familiar examples of the causal influence of diffusion through migration (Table 2: VII,B,2,b).

---

* For a more extensive study of this and related topics, see the first seminar report in this Memoir: *An Archaeological Classification of Culture Contact Situations.*

SUMMARY

This method for the study of traditions consists of three steps: descriptive analysis, descriptive synthesis, and formulation of hypotheses concerning the causes of tradition formation. The first step is an organization of the empirical data in order to facilitate the study of their persistence. The data must be described in terms of the formal categories frequently used by archaeologists, such as trait attribute, trait, and culture. Familiar trait attributes are material, technique, shape, element, motif, style, and function. Traits are organized into types, classes, and complexes; cultures in terms of complexes, patterns, configurations, and cultural wholes.

The second step consists of a classification of the form of the tradition or segment of tradition under study. We recognize five classes of forms which tradition segments commonly take: direct, converging, diverging, elaborating, and reducing.

The third step is an analysis of the causal factors in tradition development. We discuss seven major classes of causal factors: biological, inherent, environmental, demographic, societal, cultural, and contact or diffusion. These factors are treated in somewhat different ways. Biological factors are only briefly discussed, but inherent, environmental, and contact or diffusion factors are treated in considerable detail. The comments on the demographic, societal, and cultural factors are based on more or less standard anthropological generalizations which have been rephrased in terms of the tradition problem.

Our discussion is based on an examination of the relationships between these factors and the tradition segments. The relationships are systematized in terms of limitations and potentialities for tradition change which are provided by each causal factor. The limitations and potentialities are considered as the opposite ends of a continuum of change-producing situations.

Under the ideal conditions of these polar situations there is a theoretical expectancy for certain classes of causal factors to correlate with particular forms of tradition segments. There is a fairly consistent relationship between Direct Tradition and limitations for change, and between the other forms of tradition segments and potentialities for change. Elaborating Tradition is the non-direct form which correlates with the greatest number of classes of causal factors. Diverging Tradition and Converging Tradition are most often associated with contact situations.

The formal statements of these tendencies constitute a series of hypotheses for analyzing causes in tradition development. The systematic arrangement of these hypotheses makes it possible to examine the influence of one causal factor while the other factors are held theoretically constant. Thus, each causal factor is abstracted from its multiple-cause matrix for the purpose of analysis. Then an appraisal of the relative importance of the combined factors provides a realistic and balanced view of the formation of the tradition.

Throughout our discussion we emphasize the potential utility of the method, but we are also aware of some of its difficulties and limitations. While our approach is systematic, it is not exhaustive. In fact, it can only be considered a tentative formulation. We emphasize the untested status of most of our formal statements by presenting them as hypotheses. The successful application of these hypotheses to the analysis of a tradition requires a careful definition of the problem and its focus. The utility of some of the hypotheses is seriously limited by the lack of adequate archaeological techniques for identifying and defining some of the more important variables. More serious is the fact that much of the detail that is accessible to the archaeologist is often not provided in the literature.

5

The Direction of Future Research

OUR attempt to define an archaeological approach to the study of cultural stability suggests that further research on this subject will be directed toward at least three major problem areas. These are: a systematic exploration of those aspects of traditions which we have not considered, archaeological tests of hypotheses about traditions and cultural stability, and a persistent search for techniques appropriate for such testing.

We have considered in detail only the form of traditions. One of the first tasks which future investigators will face is the examination of some of the other facets of the tradition concept. Among the more important of these are problems of quantity, duration, and intensity.

Successful quantitative analysis of traditions depends upon further advances in the application of statistical techniques to archaeological problems. But, although archaeologists already have ways of defining the duration of a tradition in some kind of time scale, many interesting problems relate still to the question of how long a tradition lasted. For example, an analysis of full histories of traditions should be made to determine whether there is a pattern in the sequences of tradition segment classes.

One of the most promising research problems in tradition study is the assessment of the degree of intensity of a tradition segment. Out of such an assessment should come a more satisfactory characterization of traditions in terms of developmental concepts like growth, maturation, climax, and decline. It would be valuable to review the possibility of correlations between these developmental stages and sequences of classes of tradition segments.

Special problems derive from the application of the tradition concept to the larger categories of our descriptive analysis. Archaeological studies of traditions on the level of cultural patterns or configurations require skillful and sophisticated interpretation. Particularly complex is the study of the tradition of a whole culture, what Kroeber has called the "slant" of a culture. In ethnological literature the slant of a culture is usually expressed in terms of the tradition concept even though the investigator may have observed but a small segment of the tradition during the few months he spent in the field. In archaeological literature the characterization of an overall cultural tradition is usually an estimate based on inferences from the empirical data and analogy with the brief tradition segments described by ethnologists. We suggest that a systematic structuring of the study of total cultural traditions somewhat along the lines which we have attempted would make possible a less intuitive approach to this broad subject.

The second major area for future work is the testing of hypotheses. We have presented our statements about cause and effect in terms of hypotheses; we suggest that they offer many rewarding topics for research. Since the validation or refutation of statements with presumed predictive value is a continual process, hypotheses like those which we have formulated will undoubtedly result from further study of the various aspects of traditions.

In addition to these hypotheses which arise from detailed study of the tradition concept there are many general statements already in the literature which relate to the stability-instability problem. Examples of these statements are in every general text in anthropology: traditions of a social or institutional nature tend to be more stable than those composed of mechanical or "practical" traits (Kroeber 1948: 522-3);

55

---

multiple function may account for many cases of long persistence (Linton 1955: 45). As the study of traditions progresses and knowledge of the behavior of traditions increases, it should be possible to attempt a systematic archaeological test of some of these anthropological generalizations about cultural stability.

The third topic for future study is the search for new techniques. Fundamental to progress in any area of archaeological research on traditions and cultural stability is marked methodological improvement in at least two directions: more precise techniques for identifying the archaeological evidence for certain kinds of cultural behavior, and quantitative techniques for more accurately determining rate of cultural change.

The direction of advance seems plain enough. Implicit and intuitive judgments of almost certain validity provide a broad knowledge of the basic principles of cultural change. In fact, it is likely that most, perhaps all, of these general principles are now known. Most future advances therefore will come from detailed exploration of the more subtle problems of cultural change by carefully explicit techniques. The crude rankings implied by such terms as rapid and slow, intensive and extensive, rare and abundant, should be augmented by more precise quantitative scales; the whole apparatus of quantitative manipulation can then be brought to bear on archaeological data.

The prospect of increasing quantification and of devising more subtle refinements of method may seem dismal in the light of the more heroic pioneering tradition of archaeology, but it is unlikely that anthropology in general and archaeology in particular can escape the fate of other sciences. Accordingly, we have attempted in this seminar a first step toward the inevitable refinement of concepts and techniques. We have tried by a conscious application of the elementary principles of scientific method to show how observations can be organized to provide the data for new insights in the problem of cultural stability.

References Cited

BENNETT, WENDELL C.

1948 The Peruvian Co-Tradition. In "A Reappraisal of Peruvian Archaeology," assembled by Wendell C. Bennett. *Memoirs of the Society for American Archaeology*, No. 4, pp. 1-7. **Menasha.**

CHILDE, GORDON

1948 *What Happened in History.* Penguin Books, Harmondsworth.

GOGGIN, JOHN

1949 Cultural Traditions in Florida Prehistory. In *The Florida Indian and His Neighbors*, edited by John W. Griffin, pp. 13-44. Rollins College, Winter Park.

KROEBER, A. L.

1948 *Anthropology.* Harcourt, Brace, New York.

1955 History of Anthropological Thought. In *Yearbook of Anthropology—1955*, edited by William L. Thomas, Jr., pp. 293-311. Wenner-Gren Foundation for Anthropological Research, New York.

LaBARRE, WESTON

1954 *The Human Animal.* University of Chicago Press.

LINTON, RALPH

1936 *The Study of Man.* Appleton-Century, New York.

1955 *The Tree of Culture.* Knopf, New York.

Mc.GREGOR, JOHN C.

1950 Weighted Traits and Traditions. In *For the Dean: Essays in Anthropology in Honor of Byron Cummings*, edited by Erik K. Reed and Dale S. King, pp. 291-8. Hohokam Museums Association, Tucson and Southwestern Monuments Association, Santa Fe.

MEGGERS, BETTY J.

1954 Environmental Limitation on the Development of Culture. *American Anthropologist*, Vol. 56, No. 5, pp. 801-24. Menasha.

PHILLIPS, PHILIP

1955 American Archaeology and General Anthropological Theory. *Southwestern Journal of Anthropology*, Vol. 11, No. 3, pp. 246-50. Albuquerque.

PHILLIPS, PHILIP AND GORDON R. WILLEY

1953 Method and Theory in American Archeology. An Operational Basis for Culture-Historical Integration. *American Anthropologist*, Vol. 55, No. 5, pp. 615-33. Menasha.

ROUSE, IRVING

1954 On the Use of the Concept of Area Co-Tradition. *American Antiquity*, Vol. 19, No. 3, pp. 221-5. Salt Lake City.

1955 On the Correlation of Phases of Culture. *American Anthropologist*, Vol. 57, No. 4, pp. 713-22. Menasha.

SLOTKIN, J. S.

1952 Some Basic Methodological Problems in Prehistory. *Southwestern Journal of Anthropology*, Vol. 8, No. 4, pp. 442-3. Albuquerque.

WILLEY, GORDON R.

1945 Horizon Styles and Pottery Traditions in Peruvian Archaeology. *American Antiquity*, Vol. 11, No. 1, pp. 49-56. Menasha.

1948 A Functional Analysis of "Horizon Styles" in Peruvian Archaeology. In "A Reappraisal of Peruvian Archaeology," assembled by Wendell C. Bennett. *Memoirs of the Society for American Archaeology*, No. 4, pp. 8-15. Menasha.

1953 Archaeological Theories and Interpretation: New World. In *Anthropology Today: An Encyclopedic Inventory*, prepared under the chairmanship of A. L. Kroeber, pp. 361-85. University of Chicago Press.

WILLEY, GORDON R. AND PHILIP PHILLIPS

1955 Method and Theory in American Archeology II: Historical-Developmental Interpretation. *American Anthropologist*, Vol. 57, No. 4, pp. 723-819. Menasha.

CERAMIC VARIETY, TYPE CLUSTER, AND CERAMIC SYSTEM
IN SOUTHWESTERN POTTERY ANALYSIS*

Joe Ben Wheat, James C. Gifford, and William W. Wasley

DURING the past 20 years, the number of named pottery types in the Southwest has increased at such a rate that it is now virtually impossible for an archaeologist to know and be familiar with more than a small percentage of them. Some of these types are totally new, but a surprisingly large number represent refinements in terminology or segregations from more inclusive categories, resulting from further study and increasingly complex technological analyses. This proliferation of named types has alarmed many archaeologists. There can, however, be no legitimate doubt that if the intricate ceramic history of the Southwest and other areas of the New World is to be understood, research analysts must be free to break down their material to as fine a point as necessary in order to localize in time and space the infinitesimal variants of pottery which constitute, with other aspects of material culture, the documents of regional prehistory. It is equally clear that some method must be found to integrate the

smallest units into meaningful groupings of a larger order. Groupings of this kind are necessary in the derivation of cultural interpretations from archaeological materials.

Based on these assumptions, the purpose of this paper is to crystalize certain taxonomic concepts into a framework to serve present needs for classification of prehistoric pottery. These concepts are here termed "type," "variety," "type cluster," and "ceramic system." The concepts themselves are not new and the term "type" is retained in the sense that has become standard in Southwestern pottery terminology. The formulations dealt with have been discussed on many previous occasions and "variety" in particular has been used in a vague manner for at least 3 decades. A formal definition of the concepts is proposed so that ideas may be more precisely expressed through the usage of these taxonomic devices. This in turn should lead to less diversity in what the different terms stand for when employed by individual workers. Whenever possible, for purposes of illustration, particular examples have been selected from the Southwest, but it is our hope that the concepts will be applicable in other areas.

In arriving at the suggested categories, the method of ordering ceramic data into type, ware, sequence, and series designations as established by Colton and subsequent workers has been used to as great an extent as possible. Basic to the study of all prehistoric ceramics is the pottery "type." This concept is well known and, as defined for the Southwest by Colton (Colton and Hargrave 1937: 2; Colton 1942: 177; 1952: 1; 1953: 51, 55), is fundamental to our proposed taxonomy. To depart from or redefine the pottery type would be to scrap all previous ceramic classification in this area. This is neither desirable nor necessary, as it is our aim to build upon the foundation established by the Museum of Northern Arizona, Gila Pueblo, and others. Several criteria are of particular importance, in that a type is recognizably distinct in terms of certain visual or tactile characteristics, and has explicit temporal and areal associations.

In scope, the most inclusive of these categories is the ware. A "ware" is a large grouping of pottery types which has little temporal or spatial

---

* This paper, from its inception, has been a cooperative endeavor to produce a taxonomic framework suited to current needs for the analysis of ceramics in the American Southwest. A draft of the present work was discussed during informal meetings and an official session of the August, 1957, Pecos Conference held at Gila Pueblo in Globe, Arizona. Many ideas were exchanged during the conference, and to those who participated we express our appreciation for their constructive and stimulating remarks. The following persons took an active part in discussions and were most helpful with suggestions: David A. Breternitz, Harold S. Colton, Alfred E. Dittert, Jr., Rex E. Gerald, Emil W. Haury, Anna O. Shepard, Stanley A. Stubbs, Nathalie F. S. Woodbury, and Richard B. Woodbury. Special thanks are due Philip Phillips, Gordon R. Willey, Stephen Williams, and Hugo G. Rodeck for reviewing the final manuscript, Watson Smith and Robert F. Burgh for encouragement and editorial advice, and Carol A. Gifford for her editorial and secretarial assistance. The authors accept responsibility for the final form in which these concepts are presented. Charts are by James C. Gifford.

Apropos of what has taken place in the field of pottery analysis since the first Pecos Conference 30 years ago and of the ideas under consideration, the following remark in a recent letter from A. V. Kidder seems particularly appropriate: "As a matter of fact, I sometimes feel like an elderly rabbit returning to his home brier patch to find that he has left ten thousand descendants. . . ."

34

implication but consists of stylistically varied types that are similar technologically and in method of manufacture (Hargrave and Colton 1935: 49-51; Colton and Hargrave 1937: 1-2; Colton 1942: 177; 1952: 2; 1953: 52, 55; 1955: 2).

A "sequence" is more restricted in scope than a ware, and carries a connotation among its constituent types of evolutionary development. A ceramic sequence is composed of pottery types similar to each other in decorative style and other manifestations, which have evolved, one from another, from early to late times (Colton 1953: 75-8). Polychrome, black-on-red, black-on-white, corrugated, or plain types can each be arranged into separate sequences. Ceramic sequences necessarily transcend wares as indicators of developmental continuity and may include types or type clusters from any number of series.

A "series" consists of technologically related pottery types which are similar in decorative technique or, in the case of corrugated and plain types, surface manipulation or technique of manufacture alone. It is of importance in distinguishing a series from a sequence that the constituent types of a series occur within a definable geographical unit without exact limitation in time, and that these types must be within a single ware (Colton and Hargrave 1937: 3; Colton 1955: 2). A series is essentially geographical with respect to the implied relationship among the types within it, in contrast to evolutionary relationships implied among the types within a sequence. It must nevertheless be pointed out that the terms series and sequence have sometimes been used interchangeably. This usage has come about because in certain instances a series may contain all the members of an entire sequence. An example is to be found in the White Mountain Series which contains the complete White Mountain Polychrome Sequence (Colton 1955: 8). Future confusion can, however, be avoided if care is taken to utilize each of these terms strictly in accord with expressed definitions and intended meanings.

The Concept of Ceramic Variety

It is clear that prevailing taxonomic custom allows many named pottery types to differ from other types only in very minor ways, as in temper or style of decoration. While it is extremely important to name these variations for purposes of analysis and study, the practice of giving them all equal status as types has often resulted in attaching too much significance to the variant. The definition of pottery type is, in many instances, not always fulfilled by this method. Moreover, since each has a separate name there is no immediate way to indicate the relationship of one type to another or to distinguish variants from types. The only mechanism presently available for the designation of ceramic entities has therefore resulted in equalizing all such entities even when it is obvious that some are very close to each other in a vast majority of characteristics, while others differ markedly. That this defect in existing terminology has been recognized is patent from the fact that the term variety, or subtype, is often loosely used to refer to minor variants of a more widely known type, and that some types have been designated in publication as varieties.

In order that each entity described may be placed in a category according to its degree of distinctiveness, some method is needed to designate entities which do not differ markedly from a described type and yet are useful if given separate recognition. The requirement is a defined designation which differentiates such entities from established types. It is suggested that the concept of the "variety" fulfills the need, and that together with type, it may be used as both a working tool and a taxonomic device in the analysis of pottery.

The criteria used in defining a pottery type are decisive in the designation of varieties and their relationship to established types. A variety differs from the type to which it is related only in one or more minor particulars. In terms of geographical distribution and time span it may be equal to that of the type, although generally it is more restricted in one or both of these elements. A variety cannot be temporally and areally distinct from the type in any radical sense; nor can it differ conspicuously from the type in the manner of design execution, surface finish, or character of paint or paste utilized, else the variety warrants designation as a type. Colton describes a ceramic variety in much the same terms but his definition attributes varieties to "the vagaries of individual potters" (1946: 315) which may or may not be the correct interpretation, and fails to point out or emphasize the usefulness of variety in classification. Borderline cases of varieties that exhibit a potential as new types must, of course, be judged and evaluated by the individual investigator in harmony with the basic definition of a pottery type and a variety. One of the reasons for stressing concepts per se is to permit the analyst of a potentially new type or variety freedom to place it within the framework without forcible insertion into any larger taxonomic category than may be deemed necessary.

A variety, then, differs from the type only in such lesser technological or esthetic features as may indicate a minor regional or temporal departure from the standard. Three aspects of variation may be enumerated: (1) one or more minor characteristics perceptibly distinguishing a variety from the type, (2) slightly differing or more restricted areal distribution, and (3) slight difference in time span from that of the type. The first factor is always foremost because it is on the basis of minor visually distinguishable characteristics that the variety is identifiable. After initial recognition, however, evidence may lead to an evaluation of the variety in terms of any one of the three factors. Therefore, as a result of the individual or collective presence of these factors, the concept of variety may be considered as manifesting itself in any of 3 possible ways and we may speak of 3 aspects of a variety: (1) technological or stylistic, (2) areal, (3) temporal. It cannot be overemphasized that in practice, varieties are first recognized by the presence of the technological or stylistic aspect, in combination with which may or may not occur either of the other 2 aspects. The nature of a particular variety may subsequently be indicated by stressing the factor or aspect which represents the most salient or significant departure from an established type. The following examples are presented to show what is meant by dominance of each of these 3 aspects of a variety.

Technological or stylistic aspect of a variety. This aspect denotes varieties which can be recognized and designated as departures from established types on the basis of a single or very few distinctive features of decoration or technology. Entities of this kind constitute technological or stylistic varieties. The smudged-interior varieties of Reserve Plain, Reserve Indented, Reserve Incised, and Tularosa Patterned Corrugated types (Rinaldo and Bluhm 1956: 155-71) are cases in point. In these the technique of smudging is the single distinguishing characteristic. Another instance is Jeddito Engraved (Colton 1956; Colton and Hargrave 1937) which is no more than a variety of Jeddito Black-on-yellow, and, as pointed out by Colton: "The recognition of this type is

based entirely upon the appearance of a new variation in decorative technique, namely, engraving." The engraved elements of design consist of lines scratched through the black paint; otherwise the pottery is Jeddito Black-on-yellow. A more restricted time range has been inferred but has not been proven stratigraphically.

Another example, in this case recognized on stylistic grounds, has been cited by Colton in distinguishing 2 types on the basis of "differences in styles of design, Sosi Black-on-white and Dogoszhi Black-on-white. They are contemporary and are usually found associated. Indeed, cases are now known in which both styles of design appear on the same vessel. Obviously they belong to the same type" (1952: 2). It is not our intent to pass judgment as to whether this is a situation actually involving 2 distinct types (a position held by some archaeologists) or if indeed a type and its variety are involved. But assuming the correctness of Colton's interpretations and those of Rinaldo and Bluhm, it would be desirable if in the future, examples of this kind were designated taxonomically by the same mechanism as is suggested in the succeeding discussion concerning a variety of Kiet Siel Polychrome as an areal aspect. The implications of situations such as indicated in the Sosi-Dogoszhi example could be solved in this manner and possibly an unnecessary type designation in this way be avoided.

From the foregoing it is plain that while a variety is differentiated from a type on the basis of minor technico-stylistic differences, it, like the type, may in addition have certain temporal and areal implications. A variety may coincide with the type in both time and area (as in a true technico-stylistic variety), or it may differ to a minor degree in one or both of these factors. An areal aspect or a temporal aspect may in consequence be attributed to a variety.

Areal aspect of a variety. The occurrence of Kiet Siel Polychrome at the ruin of Awatovi furnishes a convenient illustration of a variety that displays areal significance. Kiet Siel Polychrome as described by Colton and Hargrave (1937: 100-1); Beals, Brainerd and Smith (1945: 107-37); and Colton (1956) is found at Awatovi. In association with it occur bowls which differ from the type description by having an exterior band or panel of decoration using white or black and white paints on a red background, similar to the interior combination of colors. In the Marsh Pass-Kayenta region, exterior decoration is either absent or limited to horizontal red stripes encircling the vessel just below the rim. The paneled exterior bowl decoration executed in 2 or 3 colors is, as thus far known, peculiar to Awatovi or the Jeddito region and clearly distinguishable from Marsh Pass type sherds. Necessarily this distinction of an areal variety is confined to bowl forms.

The question arises as to whether this pottery should be accorded type status. A somewhat similar case occurred when Colton (1937: 156; 1956) accorded Kawaika-a Polychrome (called Kawaioku Polychrome by Colton) type status, distinguishing it from Sikyatki Polychrome.

In the Kiet Siel instance, although the differences are at least as great as the Kawaika-a-Sikyatki differences, it does not seem wise to establish a new type because there is no difference between the vessels found at Awatovi and Kiet Siel Polychrome, except the exterior decorative style in bowl forms. Both probably have the same temporal value; whereas a new type should not only be recognizably different from its most closely comparable type, but should also be assignable to a different time and locality.

The importance of the differences in the 2 kinds of Kiet Siel Polychrome lies in the recognition of a local or areal variety at Awatovi which is not temporally distinct from the established type. The entity is no more than a variation in style of decoration from that of the established type. This style of decoration is peculiar to a certain region of northern Arizona. Such a variation is not only distinguishable from the established type by a difference in decorative technique but by restriction of that technique to a locality within or at the margin of the larger areal range of the established type. The taxonomic status which seems best suited to this situation is expressed by the term "variety," prefaced by the site name or a geographical name selected from the immediate territory, all of which must follow the established type name; thus: "Kiet Siel Polychrome: Awatovi Variety." If such a designation had been adopted in the Kawaika-a-Sikyatki Polychrome situation previously mentioned, we would speak of "Sikyatki Polychrome: Kawaika-a Variety."

This method of identification is consonant with the rules of naming set forth by Colton and others and long accepted in the Southwest (Colton 1953: 52-5; Gladwin, W. and H. S. 1930: 1-3; Kidder 1927: 489-91; Colton and Hargrave 1937: 19-22; Hargrave and Colton 1935: 49-51). It is applicable to technological, areal, or temporal aspects of variation for the simple reason that in order to be recognized, the sherds and vessels of any variety must first be found at a site or within a given district. The name itself does not, of course, necessarily determine the "area of greatest density," for the name simply serves as a label for reference" (Colton 1953: 53). Later study may enlarge the area of its occurrence, or show its greatest frequency of occurrence to be in another locality.

It is possible that this taxonomic usage might be considered cumbersome, and when followed to its ultimate conclusion, it assumes such proportions as "Three Circle Neck Corrugated: Point of Pines Variety" (Breternitz 1957: 36). Despite such objections, this terminology seems to have overriding merit for designating what is intended, that is, an areal or temporal variation of style or technology which carries no other significant differentiation from the related type, but which constitutes a recognizable entity peculiar to a certain locality or time.

This taxonomic designation is more concise than qualification of the type name by a statement to the effect that at Awatovi a few bowls of Kiet Siel Polychrome occurred which exhibit an unusual kind of exterior decoration. Such a statement is inadequate because it fails to emphasize the distinctiveness of the variation and it is awkward for colleagues to use, especially when making comparative comments. The knowledge that certain decorative or technological ceramic features are widely distributed and others are restricted to certain localities is of great importance for the study of prehistoric ceramics in relation to the cultures which made, used, and traded them. It is therefore vital to observe and designate variations when they are discernible. The above taxonomic procedure makes it possible to do this in a systematic way.

Temporal aspect of a variety. Kiet Siel Polychrome: Awatovi Variety was described as an illustration of a geographic variant. There are also varieties which largely overlap the time range of an established type but which have a time range of their own slightly different from that of the established type. Varieties of this kind may or may not have meaning in terms of area, but in either case they have a peculiar temporal aspect which may be more important or more evident than areal or technological considerations in terms of analysis.

As an example, a variety of Reserve Black-on-white (Danson 1957: Table 19, Fig. 17 a) may be cited. This ceramic variation is described as a local development of black-on-white pottery which coincides with late Pueblo I-early Pueblo II and "with the ceramic developments of Red Mesa Black-on-white, but which differs in having a darker paste and a much heavier slip, and in showing a suggestion of the later Reserve style of decoration" (Danson 1957: 92). It is referred to by Danson as an "early variant of Reserve Black-on-white" and as "Reserve Black-on-white (early variant)" (1957: 100). On the basis of these assertions this variety may be construed as being earlier than, but probably overlapping in time, Reserve Black-on-white as described from the vicinity of Reserve, New Mexico (Martin and Rinaldo 1950: 502-19). There is a suggestion of significant areal differentiation but the temporal implications seem at the moment more demonstrable and important and it is therefore considered a temporal variety. This temporal variety of Reserve Black-on-white should not, however, be confused with Reserve Black-on-white: Black River Variety, also described by Danson (1957: 92-3). Socorro Black-on-white is another established type that may yield recognizable temporal variations (A. E. Dittert, personal communication, 1957).

Several concluding points concerning the concept of variety must be made. Circumstances of excavation may be influential in the initial or preliminary determination of a type or a variety. It is possible that due to the incompleteness of knowledge concerning a given ceramic situation the first ceramic entity excavated and described will become the type while entities recognized at a later date become varieties. To obviate the permanence of such conclusions and make it possible for new knowledge to rectify preliminary findings which may prove false, the constructs of variety and type must be kept fluid. To this end the status of a variety must be conceived as being temporary to the extent that: (1) some type descriptions may eventually be broadened to include tentative varieties, (2) within some type clusters certain varieties may eventually be dropped altogether as no longer useful, (3) some entities now described as types may be judged to be in fact varieties, or (4) some varieties may eventually be established as types in their own right.

An example of the last of these possibilities came about with the elevation of Fourmile Polychrome: Point of Pines Variety to the status of Point of Pines Polychrome. Although at first recognizably distinct and more restricted in area than Fourmile Polychrome, this pottery did not at that time appear in an archaeological context which presented more than a bare hint of temporal departure from that encompassed by the established description of Fourmile Polychrome. It was for this reason tentatively termed Fourmile Polychrome: Point of Pines Variety (Wendorf 1950: 43-59). The University of Arizona Archaeological Field School continued operations in the Point of Pines region of Arizona and subsequently demonstrated stratigraphically that this pottery was indeed associated only with the Point of Pines phase, at a time distinctly later than the occurrence of Fourmile Polychrome. In addition, greater quantities of this pottery were unearthed and its distinguishing features became more conspicuously manifest so that its distinctness rested on a configuration of major characteristics rather than minor ones (Wasley 1952; Morris 1957). Consequently, its separation from Fourmile Polychrome was justified beyond any reasonable doubt. It was therefore redesignated Point of Pines Polychrome in keeping with the basic definition of a type.

THE CONCEPT OF CERAMIC TYPE CLUSTER

The idea of the variety as outlined here has previously been utilized to a limited extent in earlier studies of Southwestern ceramics — first in Alma Plain: Forestdale Variety (Haury 1940: 72; Haury and Sayles 1947: 48-52) and in San Francisco Red: Saliz Variety (Martin and Rinaldo 1940: 80-1; Martin 1943: 240-1), in Alma Plain: Bluff Variety (Haury and Sayles 1947: 48-52), and later in Alma Plain: Point of

Pines and Black River varieties (Wheat 1954: 82-7). A uniform taxonomic treatment of recognizable varieties has, however, never been adopted even though it is generally agreed that such treatment has long since proved its usefulness for the comparative study of pottery types. Our concept of established types, each with its own constellation of varieties, is outlined here to provide a standard method for identification and designation of varieties. The definition, description, and number of varieties which are related to any given type is determined, of course, by the individual worker's appraisal of the archaeological data at hand.

If the taxonomic devices already discussed are considered useful and the implications of each are understood, it now seems desirable to crystallize and name a more inclusive concept, a unit which contains the type and its associated varieties. This will permit a grouping of individual types plus their varieties into meaningful entities which can then be considered as independent units. Units of this kind can be used in accordance with the dictates of any particular problem and larger configurations may be formed which tend to have a greater cultural significance than any more restricted unit may display by itself. The term "group" cannot be applied to this concept because Colton (1953: 65) has used it in the sense of a ceramic complex or assemblage which recognizes contemporaneity among individual types. The idea of the ceramic group is discussed more fully at a later time. The term "cluster" is, however, free of prior archaeological implication and we suggest that "type cluster" be used to refer to the constellation that is formed when one type including all of its varieties is considered as a single unit. Figure 1 illustrates several examples.

A type cluster consists of one type together with its varieties. These varieties, of which theoretically there can be any number, bear a relationship to the type such as has been detailed in the account of Kiet Siel Polychrome and Kiet Siel Polychrome: Awatovi Variety (Fig. 1). This conception of a type cluster permits free accommodation of type and variety within one unit. There is always space in a cluster for the designation of new varieties as they are recognized. A type cluster is as restricted in time and area as the temporal and areal value of the type *plus* any additional time and area encompassed by the varieties within its sphere. Furthermore, type clusters can be grouped and regrouped into categories of a higher echelon when the need arises.

The type cluster allows for a great deal of flexibility and expansion to suit the needs of any given ceramic situation. Those whose problems necessitate fine ceramic breakdowns will be able to achieve their desires within the framework of the variety, the type, and the type cluster without necessarily designating new types. Those who think about ceramics in larger, more inclusive categories may satisfy themselves by working with type clusters alone. For example, instead of particularizing Sikyatki Polychrome, Sikyatki Polychrome: Kawaika-a Variety, and Sikyatki Polychrome: Awatovi Variety, the more inclusive grouping *Sikyatki Polychrome Cluster* (Fig. 1) may be used to designate all of the 3 smaller entities (one established type plus 2 related varieties).

A ceramic type cluster takes its name from the established type. The type, as distinguished from its varieties, is determined by the fact that it has the most comprehensive descriptive, geographical, or temporal range of the cluster. The entities related to it are varieties in a technico-stylistic, areal, or temporal sense. If, on the other hand, it can be shown that all the members of a type cluster are roughly equal in typological status, as may be the case with Alma Plain and its varieties (Forestdale Variety, Bluff Variety, Point of Pines Variety, and Black River Variety), then according to Colton's rules of

naming and priority (1953: 52-5), the one first described in published form lends its name to the cluster; therefore the proper taxonomic title would be Alma Plain Cluster. It must be made clear that situations similar to that which pertains to the Alma Plain Cluster may be more frequent than has been implied (particularly with regard to relatively unstudied utility types), and indeed, in other areas may be the rule rather than the exception. The established type and its varieties within a type cluster may therefore, in certain instances, be indistinguishable in all major attributes and separable only on the basis of minor distinctions.

THE CONCEPT OF CERAMIC SYSTEM

Having formulated the type cluster as a working unit, clusters can in turn be grouped into entities having cultural significance. These larger entities derive from intercluster similarities which are relatively shallow in time depth. Basic to the concept is the fact that by an arrangement of contemporary type clusters, larger units are formed indicative of the pottery characteristic of a culture at a given period or time level in the development of that culture. The term ceramic system is proposed for this purpose.

A "ceramic system" is a grouping of type clusters which are related in design style, or surface manipulation when present, vessel form, and general technology (broadly speaking a class of

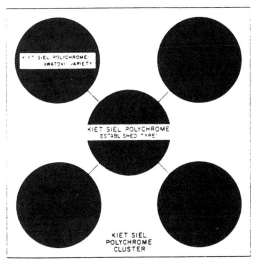
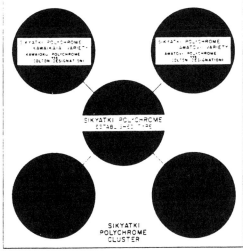

FIG. 1. The Kiet Siel Polychrome Cluster and the Sikyatki Polychrome Cluster. Solid black circles represent potential varieties of an established type, of which there may be any number.

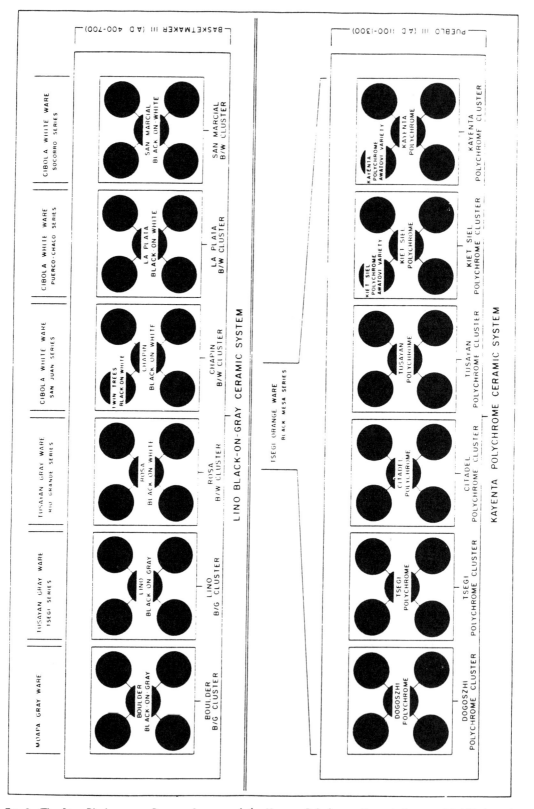

FIG. 2. The Lino Black-on-gray Ceramic System and the Kayenta Polychrome Ceramic System. Solid black circles represent potential varieties of an established type, of which there may be any number.

Joe Ben Wheat et al.

pottery), and which range over a wide area, but are roughly contemporaneous. A ceramic system usually crosscuts wares. The relationship of type clusters contained within a system rests on broad characteristics which transcend individual types or clusters. A system may, however, in its simplest form, be a single type cluster; more often and most usefully, it is composed of a number of type clusters.

Two ceramic systems are shown in Figure 2. It will be observed that in these 2 ceramic systems all units dealt with are, for purposes of illustrating the ceramic system concept, labeled type clusters on the assumption that even though there are at present no recognized varieties for a given type, there is provision for their existence and ultimate recognition. In actual practice, a ceramic system will not be made up entirely of type clusters but will be composed both of type clusters and types lacking described or recognized varieties. One such grouping of types and type clusters is the Lino Black-on-gray Ceramic System (Fig. 2), composed of type clusters from 3 different wares. It is, however, made up of all known Basketmaker III black-on-gray potteries and consequently may be defined in terms of a class of pottery made by Basketmakers during a certain period in their cultural development within their area of occupation.

If the suggested taxonomic method of designating varieties is adopted and the classification of Twin Trees Black-on-white as a variety of Chapin Black-on-white is agreed upon as shown in Figure 2, Twin Trees Black-on-white would be renamed Chapin Black-on-white: Twin Trees Variety. All of the pottery in this system sometimes, if not always, shows a fugitive red exterior. By including black-on-gray and black-on-white type clusters in the Lino Black-on-gray Ceramic System, it appears superficially as if one of the qualifications of a ceramic system (that all included pottery be of one class) is, in this example intentionally ignored. This is not the case, however, because specialists in Basketmaker III pottery recognize that the terms black-on-gray and black-on-white are almost interchangeable descriptively when applied to different types of this class. This situation has come about because the surface color of almost all Basketmaker black-on-gray pottery shades into white and black-on-white pottery into gray.

There are general attributes which are basic to every Basketmaker III black-on-gray pot; when the Basketmakers manufactured black-on-

gray pottery, they had an idea in mind as to how that pot should look. The concept of the ceramic system refers to a cultural image which the people were trying to produce in a class of ceramics during a certain interval of prehistoric time. In this way, a ceramic system takes into account cultural implications at a given period of time over a definable area. Therefore when an archaeologist picks up a Basketmaker III black-on-gray sherd, he can say that from an over-all view it is a sherd representative of the Lino Black-on-gray Ceramic System during Basketmaker III in the Anasazi area. If generally applied in the Southwest, other type clusters and types would be grouped into ceramic systems and this scheme would consolidate all pottery into some 40 or 50 ceramic systems of this kind. Thus through the recognition of these ceramic systems, it would further be possible for an archaeologist to assign to a general area and time span almost any of the plethora of specific types or varieties which only a specialist in that area might know by name. Because of certain gross characteristics, rendered explicit by inclusion within a ceramic system, a sherd or vessel could be recognized as early Pueblo III from the Kayenta or the Mesa Verde, or as Mogollon IV from the Point of Pines region, without a knowledge of its specific type name or the technical aspects of its manufacture.

During Pueblo III times ceramic specialization became more complex than in Basketmaker times. Consequently, the Pueblo III ceramic systems (black-on-white, black-on-red, polychrome, corrugated, and others, each including a number of related type clusters) became more numerous. The Kayenta Polychrome Ceramic System is shown as an example (Fig. 2). In contrast with the Lino Black-on-gray Ceramic System, the members of the Kayenta Polychrome Ceramic System belong to a single series within a single ware: Black Mesa Series, Tsegi Orange Ware (Colton 1956; 1955: 13). In this instance, although the representation of these types at Awatovi is insufficient to actually determine their type-variety status, Citadel, Tsegi, and Dogoszhi polychromes are included and shown as established types on a tentative basis for purposes of illustrating the concept. These 6 polychrome type clusters, therefore, constitute a particular entity indicative and representative of polychromes (a class of pottery) during the Pueblo III period within the Kayenta-Jeddito region of northern Arizona. Similarly, other polychrome ceramic systems during Pueblo III are expressive of other cultural affiliations and regions. For example, Jeddito, Kwaituki, Kintiel, Klageto, Heshotauthla and other polychromes might be assigned to a Pueblo III ceramic system represented in the Hopi-Little Colorado-Zuni region of Arizona-New Mexico. This hypothetical ceramic system would overlap the Kayenta Polychrome Ceramic System in the Hopi Mesas and the interrelationship is indicated in the Kayenta-Hopi Polychrome Sequence (Fig. 3) where Kiet Siel and Jeddito polychromes are shown to have developed one into the other. The ceramic systems themselves reflect cultural interchange between adjoining regions.

A ceramic system may be defined as representing a certain class of pottery (in the first example, black-on-gray; in the second, a certain class of polychrome), made or used by the people of a certain archaeological culture, in a certain area during a certain period of time. Significant criteria are the period of time and the culture or people represented, and the area or region involved. The significance of any or all of these criteria fluctuates according to the ceramic system being formulated and its over-all context. A ceramic system should be thought of in terms of a time period (Basketmaker III, Pueblo III, and so forth) rather than a phase. There may be one or several phases in a period and a period may be one or several centuries in duration. The same principle is true of the ceramic system in terms of time and one or more archaeological phases may be spanned by the length of time embraced in the duration of any particular ceramic system.

It will be noted that our definition of ceramic system is concordant with that of a pottery type, but the very important difference is that the ceramic system is far more inclusive and has a much more general cultural frame of reference. The ceramic system is usually and most usefully short in time duration (commensurate with the archaeological period it is associated with), showing little or no evolution among member type clusters, but is wide in geographical range by comparison with a ceramic sequence which shows a demonstrable evolution among member type clusters but is limited in range and long in duration. Cultural processes are implicit in the taxonomic structure here described, and all the categories, from smallest to largest, find practical employment in the taxonomic designation of manifestations and entities of culture. At

this time and for the purposes of this paper, it is suggested that only type clusters and types belonging to one class of pottery (polychrome, or black-on-white, or corrugated, or plain, and so on) be included in a single ceramic system. However, it is observed that the relationship of some polychromes to some bichromes is so close that it may ultimately prove useful to modify the definition of the term ceramic system to include such closely related types and clusters when they are contemporaneous.

In naming a ceramic system Colton's rules of taxonomic priority are followed (1953: 52-5), and the system takes the designation of the first-named type in the system. As a result, Lino (in the first ceramic system cited) and Kayenta (in the second ceramic system cited) become ceramic system names by reason of seniority in their published description. However, among the clusters of a system, no superior rank is conferred upon the one that gives its name to that system. There is no standard by which one type cluster can be rated higher or lower than another in relative importance.

Contrasts between ceramic system and other transcending terms. A brief discussion of terms which are similar but do not correspond with our concept of ceramic system may be of value. "The ceramic group is defined as an assemblage of contemporary, usually painted, pottery types recognized in a restricted area at sites occupied for a short period of time" (Colton 1953: 65). As used by Colton, black-on-white, black-on-red, and polychrome types may be included within a single group. Other analysts have also included corrugated, red, and plain types (Olson and Wasley 1956: 257-8) in arriving at ceramic groups, and in that way the terms ceramic group and ceramic complex are almost identical in use and meaning. The ceramic complex is an instrument for dating a site or the phases within a site because, in its entirety, it represents an inventory of the pottery types peculiar to a particular archaeological phase (Gifford 1957: 118-26, Figs. 31, 99, 100, 138). A ceramic system differs from a complex in that only one class of pottery is included in the former. For example, the Lino Black-on-gray Ceramic System (Fig. 2) imparts the idea of black-on-gray pottery made by Basketmaker people (culture) over a certain geographic extent (area) during the Basketmaker III period (time level). Thus the black-on-gray class of pottery is considered as an integrated whole apart from polychrome, black-on-orange, or corrugated types or clusters of the same or later periods, each of which is in its own ceramic system, according to the class of pottery it represents.

The terms "ware" and "index ware" are unsatisfactory because in scope they are too broad and in structure too loose for present purposes. "The Index Ware is defined

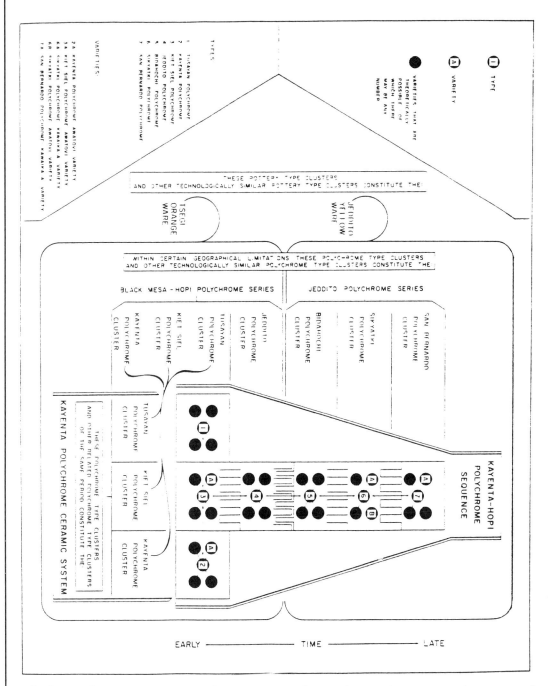

Fig. 3. A graphic summary presentation of variety, type, type cluster, series, ceramic system, ceramic sequence, and ware, used as taxonomic devices to show technological, temporal, cultural, and areal interrelationships and similarities among certain ceramic manifestations.

as a pottery ware including a number of more or less similar types used for cooking and storage and which are peculiar to a certain prehistoric tribe . . . the characters that are selected to describe a ware are usually the basic techniques of manufacture which are handed down from mother to daughter and which persist over a long period of time. Some wares we can trace over eight hundred years" (Colton 1953: 67). A ceramic system differs from a ware in that the various component parts of a system are all of one class of pottery (that is, black-on-gray) and are grouped together by reason of attributes other than the gross technological and functional attributes common to the components of a ware. A single ceramic system contains type clusters of a single class; hence polychromes are not included in a black-on-white ceramic system nor black-on-white types in a black-on-red system. A ware on the other hand may include plain, corrugated, and decorated types. Ceramic systems may be wider in cultural and geographical scope than wares, and may cut across the wares established by Colton (1955: 3-26) as is shown by the Lino Black-on-gray Ceramic System illustrated in Figure 2.

The idea of analogous types has also been promulgated (Colton 1943: 316-20): "When the same style of design is found on pottery types of the same age but belonging to different wares, those types are said to be analogous" (Colton 1953: 71). This particular concept is closely allied to that of "horizon style" as used in Middle and South America (Willey 1945: 49-56; Parsons 1957; Willey and Phillips 1958: 31-2), which is usually based almost exclusively on ceramic art styles. The analogous-type concept differs from that of the ceramic system in that the latter includes other properties besides decorative style in arriving at pottery groupings indicative of a specific period, archaeological culture, and region in prehistory. A grouping of analogous types could, nevertheless, constitute a horizon style, and it is possible that in special instances a given ceramic system may be composed entirely of analogous types. In this event, the usefulness of the unit as a whole is greatly improved by designating it as a ceramic system rather than by saying only that the types or clusters under consideration are analogous.

A "horizon marker" is any unique trait, or by definition an "item" which at a specific time horizon has spread beyond its source over a wider geographical range. "Geographically wide distribution and brief duration" (Parsons 1957: 119) are key characteristics of the horizon marker. Horizon markers are "certain highly specialized and widely traded artifacts" (Phillips and Willey 1953: 626). A horizon marker can be a method of "treating material (technique) as incising, modelling, polychrome painting, negative painting" or a special form such as "a certain vessel shape . . . a type of foot, ridges, or applied effigies, or in some cases a specific design element" (Parsons 1957: 100). The term ceramic system (representing a number of type clusters rather than any single kind of artifact, trait, or item) is not, therefore, synonymous with horizon marker. A ceramic system is larger in scope than any specific item.

Various taxonomic concepts which can be used in association with our own constructs of variety, type, type cluster, and ceramic system are most useful in throwing light on other cultural phenomena. Foremost among these are the concepts of tradition (Thompson 1956: 38-9; Rouse 1957: 123) and, as previously noted, horizon style (Willey 1945: 49-56; Willey and Phillips 1958: 29-34), which may be used in the sense of their original definitions and descriptions. A tradition has temporal continuity and may progress in time through any number of successive ceramic systems. A horizon style is comparatively short in duration and may extend on a single time level through any number of contemporary ceramic systems.

Throughout the discussion and presentation of our various concepts, many of the specific examples used are taken from among pottery found at the site of Awatovi. The Awatovi Expedition of the Peabody Museum, Harvard University, during 1935-39 excavated at the great Hopi-Spanish ruin of Awatovi on Antelope Mesa within the Hopi Indian Reservation in northern Arizona (Brew 1942). The considerable collection of ceramic material provides examples which are illustrative because of the long time span encompassed by intensive occupation of the site. A summary expression in graphic and taxonomic terms of the affiliations between certain decorated pottery types indigenous to Awatovi is presented in Figure 3. It is intended to show the technological, developmental, temporal, cultural, and areal interrelationships of the pottery involved. By means of Figure 3 it may be seen how terms such as ware, sequence, series, ceramic system, type cluster, type, and variety can actually be employed to express meanings peculiar to each of them.

Kiet Siel, Jeddito, Bidahochi, Sikyatki, and San Bernardo polychromes comprise the Kayenta-Hopi Polychrome Sequence. This is, therefore, composed of polychrome type clusters derived from the Black Mesa Series, the Hopi Series, and the Jeddito Series which in turn are extracted from the Tsegi Orange Ware and the Jeddito Yellow Ware as grouped by Colton (1955: 12-14; 1956). These type clusters develop from one another through time within the sequence and are one illustration of ceramic continuity within the region. Citadel, Tsegi, and Dogoszhi polychromes (Colton 1956) belong to a more westerly occurrence of the Kayenta-Hopi Polychrome Sequence as well as being a part of the Black Mesa-Hopi Polychrome Series. These have not been included in Figure 3 because they do not occur in quantity at Awatovi and their type-variety status has not been appraised in the light of the concepts defined here. They were nevertheless included for purposes of discussion only in the Kayenta Polychrome Ceramic System as shown in Figure 2, but Figure 3 makes due allowance for this inclusion by stating that the polychrome type clusters shown may have added to them other polychrome type clusters of the same period to complete the Kayenta Polychrome Ceramic System. Each type cluster has been given equal vertical space within Figure 3 because it is not germane to this presentation to enter into the exact relative time valuation of the individual types or type clusters.

A "series" is essentially geographical in orientation. Tusayan, Kayenta, Kiet Siel, and Jeddito polychromes are the principle constituents of the Black Mesa-Hopi Polychrome Series at Awatovi. This grouping of polychrome types, together with others included by Colton (1955: 13) from the Marsh Pass locale, is indicative of a restricted geographical unit — the entire Black Mesa or Kayenta-Jeddito region. Bidahochi, Sikyatki, and San Bernardo polychromes are the principle constituents of the Jeddito Polychrome Series at Awatovi, which is, with several other late polychromes recognized by Colton (1955: 14; 1956), indicative of a smaller district known as the Hopi Mesas or Jeddito region. As used by Colton (1953: 42; 1955: 143), sequence and series in certain instances appear synonymous, but this is, as previously pointed out, rarely the case and a sequence always connotes an evolutionary succession of related types through time, whereas a series is essentially a geographical grouping. Basically, as explicitly stated by Colton, "wares can be split into geographical series: (sub wares)" (Colton 1943: 317).

CONCLUSION

The fundamental requirement of taxonomic procedure is to make the analyst's own observations useful and available to others who now or in the future, work with the same problems and data. In any taxonomic structure designed for archaeological materials, the research worker must be allowed freedom of choice, and the structure which he uses must be flexible enough to permit the breaking of working entities into the smallest units required. These small units may then be reassembled in any desired manner at the discretion of any other archaeologist according to his estimate of a given situation, and yet still be within the framework of the established taxonomic structure. We have made every effort to leave as great a measure of flexibility as possible in the actual use of the taxonomic categories suggested here so that others may have freedom in approaching differing problems while using this framework.

It may be argued that by combining varieties and types into type clusters and type clusters into ceramic systems, the interpretation of evidence is prejudiced. If, however, bits of evidence are related on the basis of their own merits and characteristics, no prejudice is involved and the entire scheme becomes no more than a method for penetrating the unknown on the basis of objective evidence.

In our opinion, none of the foregoing suggestions does violence to existing taxonomic structures. The final test of any recommended procedure, taxonomic or otherwise, is its usefulness and workability. We therefore hope only that other investigators shall try out these concepts and taxonomic devices in the analysis of archaeological materials, both materials under active study and those already published. If they choose to arrange their observations upon this taxonomic lattice, the publication of their results together with any criticisms or suggestions for modification will be most welcome.

BEALS, R. L., G. W. BRAINERD, AND WATSON SMITH

1945 Archaeological Studies in Northeastern Arizona. *University of California Publications in American Archaeology and Ethnology*, Vol. 44, No. 1. Berkeley.

BRETERNITZ, D. A.

1956 The Archaeology of Nantack Village, Point of Pines, Arizona. M.A. thesis, Department of Anthropology, University of Arizona, Tucson.

BREW, J. O.

1942 Preface. In "The Changing Physical Environment of the Hopi Indians of Arizona," by J. T. Hack. *Papers of the Peabody Museum, Harvard University*, Vol. 35, No. 1, pp. v-x. Cambridge.

COLTON, H. S.

1942 Types and Wares. *Clearing House for Southwestern Museums, Newsletter*, No. 49. Denver.

1943 The Principle of Analogous Pottery Types. *American Anthropologist*, Vol. 45, No. 2, pp. 316-20. Menasha.

1946 The Sinagua. A Summary of the Archaeology of the Region of Flagstaff, Arizona. *Museum of Northern Arizona, Bulletin* 22. Flagstaff.

1952 Pottery Types of the Arizona Strip and Adjacent Areas in Utah and Nevada. *Museum of Northern Arizona, Ceramic Series*, No. 1. Flagstaff.

1953 Potsherds. *Museum of Northern Arizona, Bulletin* 25. Flagstaff.

1955 Check List of Southwestern Pottery Types. *Museum of Northern Arizona, Ceramic Series*, No. 2. Flagstaff.

1956 Pottery Types of the Southwest. *Museum of Northern Arizona, Ceramic Series*, No. 3c. Flagstaff.

COLTON, H. S. AND L. L. HARGRAVE

1937 Handbook of Northern Arizona Pottery Wares. *Museum of Northern Arizona, Bulletin* 11. Flagstaff.

DANSON, E. B.

1957 An Archaeological Survey of West Central New Mexico and East Central Arizona. *Papers of the Peabody Museum, Harvard University,* Vol. 44, No. 1. Cambridge.

GIFFORD, J. C.

1957 Archaeological Explorations in Caves of the Point of Pines Region. M.A. thesis, Department of Anthropology, University of Arizona, Tucson.

GLADWIN, WINIFRED AND H. S. GLADWIN

1930 A Method for the Designation of Southwestern Pottery Types. *Medallion Papers,* No. 7. Globe.

HARGRAVE, L. L. AND H. S. COLTON

1935 What do Potsherds Tell Us? *Museum of Northern Arizona, Museum Notes,* Vol. 7, No. 12. Flagstaff.

HAURY, E. W.

1940 Excavations in the Forestdale Valley, East-Central Arizona. *University of Arizona Bulletin,* Vol. 11, No. 4, *Social Science Bulletin* No. 12. Tucson.

HAURY, E. W. AND E. B. SAYLES

1947 An Early Pit House Village of the Mogollon Culture. *University of Arizona Bulletin,* Vol. 18, No. 4, *Social Science Bulletin* No. 16. Tucson.

KIDDER, A. V.

1927 Southwestern Archaeological Conference. *Science,* Vol. 66, No. 1716, pp. 489-91. New York.

MARTIN, P. S.

1943 The SU Site, Excavations at a Mogollon Village, Western New Mexico, Second Season 1941. *Field Museum of Natural History, Anthropological Series,* Vol. 32, No. 2. Chicago.

MARTIN, P. S. AND J. B. RINALDO

1940 The SU Site, Excavations at a Mogollon Village, Western New Mexico, 1939. *Field Museum of Natural History, Anthropological Series,* Vol. 32, No. 1. Chicago.

1950 Sites of the Reserve Phase, Pine Lawn Valley, Western New Mexico. *Chicago Natural History Museum Fieldiana: Anthropology,* Vol. 38, No. 3. Chicago.

MORRIS, E. A.

1957 Stratigraphic Evidence for a Cultural Continuum at the Point of Pines Ruin. M.A. thesis, Department of Anthropology, University of Arizona, Tucson.

OLSON, A. P. AND W. W. WASLEY

1956 An Archaeological Traverse Survey in West-Central New Mexico. In *Pipeline Archaeology,* edited by Fred Wendorf, Nancy Fox and O. L. Lewis, pp. 256-390. Laboratory of Anthropology and Museum of Northern Arizona, Santa Fe and Flagstaff.

PARSONS, L. A.

1957 The Nature of Horizon Markers in Middle American Archaeology. *Anthropology Tomorrow,* Vol. 5, No. 2, pp. 98-121. Anthropology Club of the University of Chicago.

PHILLIPS, PHILIP AND G. R. WILLEY

1953 Method and Theory in American Archaeology: An Operational Basis for Culture-Historical Integration. *American Anthropologist,* Vol. 55, No. 5, pp. 615-33. Menasha.

RINALDO, J. B. AND E. A. BLUHM

1956 Late Mogollon Pottery Types of the Reserve Area. *Chicago Natural History Museum, Fieldiana: Anthropology,* Vol. 36, No. 7. Chicago.

ROUSE, IRVING

1957 Culture Area and Co-tradition. *Southwestern Journal of Anthropology,* Vol. 13, No. 2., pp. 123-33. Albuquerque.

THOMPSON, R. H (EDITOR)

1956 An Archaeological Approach to the Study of Cultural Stability. In "Seminars in Archaeology: 1955," edited by Robert Wauchope, pp. 31-57. *Memoirs of the Society for American Archaeology,* No. 11. Salt Lake City.

WASLEY, W. W.

1952 The Late Pueblo Occupation at Point of Pines, East-Central Arizona. M.A. thesis, Department of Anthropology, University of Arizona, Tucson.

WENDORF, FRED

1950 A Report on the Excavation of a Small Ruin Near Point of Pines, East Central Arizona. *University of Arizona Bulletin,* Vol. 21, No. 3, *Social Science Bulletin,* No. 19. Tucson.

WHEAT, J. B.

1954 Crooked Ridge Village (Arizona W:10:15). University of Arizona Bulletin, Vol. 25, No. 3, Social Science Bulletin, No. 24. Tucson.

WILLEY, G. R.

1945 Horizon Styles and Pottery Traditions in Peruvian Archaeology. American Antiquity, Vol. 11, No. 1, pp. 49-56. Menasha.

WILLEY, G. R. AND PHILIP PHILLIPS

1958 Method and Theory in American Archaeology. University of Chicago Press.

UNIVERSITY OF COLORADO MUSEUM
Boulder, Colorado

PEABODY MUSEUM WEST OF THE PECOS
Tucson, Arizona

ARIZONA STATE MUSEUM
Tucson, Arizona
February, 1958

THE CLASSIFICATION OF ARTIFACTS IN ARCHAEOLOGY

Irving Rouse

ABSTRACT

Analytic classification consists of forming successive series of classes, referring to different features of artifacts. Each class is characterized by one or more attributes which indicate a custom to which the artisan conformed, for example, a technique of manufacture, or a concept which he expressed in the artifacts, such as a design. These customs and concepts constitute modes. They are "procedural modes" when they refer to behavior of artisans and "conceptual modes" when they consist of ideas which artisans have expressed in artifacts.

Taxonomic classification consists of formulating a single set of classes, one for each kind of artifact in the collection. Each class is characterized by two or more modes, selected from among the total number of modes obtainable by means of analytic classification. The modes diagnostic of each class constitute its type. If diagnostic modes are selected for their time-space significance, the resultant types are "historical." If the diagnostic modes are selected for what they indicate about the intrinsic nature of the artifacts, the types are "descriptive."

The situations under which it is best to use either procedural or conceptual modes or historical or descriptive types are discussed and it is concluded that all four kinds of units are essential for the complete interpretation of archaeological remains.

A NUMBER of recent papers, such as Phillips (1958), Wheat, Gifford, and Wasley (1958), and Sears (1960), have been concerned with particular methods used by archaeologists to classify artifacts. The present paper is instead an attempt to survey the range of current methods. It is intended to differentiate the various methods, to discuss their theoretical basis, and to assess their relative utility.

According to the dictionary (Nielson, Knott, and Earhart 1940: 496), the word classification refers to "the act of assigning [artifacts] to a proper class." If the class is a new one, it will have to be defined by listing the criteria used to form it and will also have to be given a name or a number. If pertinent classes had previously been established, it will be enough to determine that the new artifacts have the criteria diagnos-

tic of one of the classes, and to give them the name of that class.

Classification, like statistics, is not an end in itself but a technique by means of which to attain specified objectives, and so it must be varied with the objective. The main opportunity for variation comes in selecting the criteria which are to be considered diagnostic of one's classes. In my experience, archaeologists select these criteria to meet one of two alternate objectives: either to form modes or to establish types. If modes are the objective, the classification is called "analytic" (Whiteford 1947). If, instead, the purpose is to form types, then the classification becomes "taxonomic" (Phillips 1958). I shall discuss these two kinds of classification in turn.

ANALYTIC CLASSIFICATION

By the term "mode" is meant any standard, concept, or custom which governs the behavior of the artisans of a community, which they hand down from generation to generation, and which may spread from community to community over considerable distances (Rouse 1939). Such modes will be reflected in the artifacts as attributes which conform to a community's standards, which express its concepts, or which reveal its customary ways of manufacturing and using artifacts. Analytic classification focuses on these attributes and, through them, attempts to get at the standards, concepts, and customs themselves. In effect, it attempts to read such modes out of the artifacts.

Not all the attributes of the artifacts are indicative of modes. Some attributes will instead express personal idiosyncracies of the artisans. A unique design, which occurs only once, may be cited as an example. Other attributes fall within the realm of biology, chemistry, or physics rather than culture. The atomic structure of artifacts is an obvious example. The white color of shell artifacts is another. This whiteness does not appear until after the artifacts have been in the ground for some time, it

313

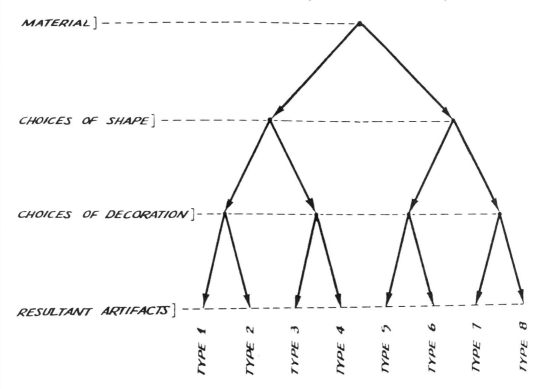

FIG. 1. Procedure of making artifacts.

is as prevalent among natural as among worked shells, and hence it must be considered a purely biological trait which has no part to play in cultural studies.

Analytic classification, then, must single out modes, which are cultural, and exclude those traits which are purely biological, chemical, or physical. One way to do this is to examine a collection in terms of the artisan's procedure, starting first with the materials he used, continuing with his techniques of manufacture, and then considering shape, decoration, and uses. At each stage in the procedure one may find that the artisan had some choice of standards or customs (Fig. 1). This makes it possible, for example, to divide a given collection into one or more series of classes on the basis of the materials used. One can then redistribute the same specimens into other series of classes on the basis of techniques, elements of shape and decoration, and uses (Fig. 2). Each class will have one or more diagnostic attributes, and those attributes will be indicative of a single mode.

For example, an archaeologist may take a collection of potsherds and divide it into two classes, one consisting of sherds with inclusions of grit and the other, of sherds with inclusions of shell. He thereby determines that the potters had two alternative customs of tempering their vessels, one with pieces of stone and the other with pieces of shell. Then, he may pick out the sherds which are from rims and regroup them into a second series of classes, each characterized by a different set of rim attributes. In this case, he will have established a series of standards to which the potters conformed in making rims. He may repeat this process of reclassification with other aspects of material, shape, decoration, and use, ending up, as I have done in the case of my Antillean collections, with as many as 80 modes of material, shape, and decoration (Rouse 1939, 1941, 1952).

It is not necessary, of course, to be so systematic and all-inclusive as this in doing analytic classification. Various authors have concentrated upon technology (Matson 1942), upon shapes (Black and Weer 1936), upon designs (Amsden 1936), or upon uses (C. S. Ford 1937). The important point is that the author be interested in establishing independent modes and not in studying the manner in which those modes are combined on the artifacts.

PROCEDURE

CATEGORIES

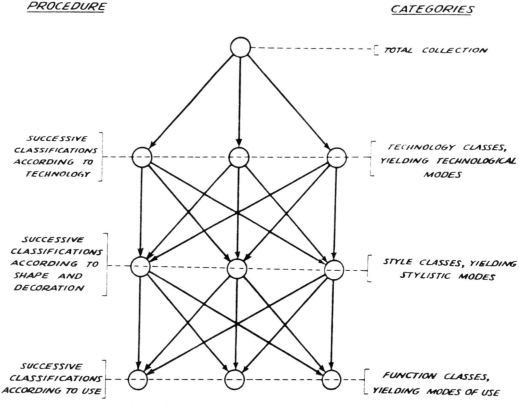

FIG. 2. Example of the analytic approach to classification.

The modes may be of two kinds: (1) concepts of material, shape, and decoration to which the artisans conformed and (2) customary procedures followed in making and using the artifacts. In the case of conceptual modes, the archaeologist need only designate one or more attributes of his artifacts to be diagnostic of each class, but in the case of procedural modes he must also infer behavior of the artisans from the diagnostic attributes. The process of inferring procedural modes has been well described and illustrated by other authors (Osgood 1942; Thompson 1958).

Once modes have been set up — whether conceptual or procedural — and their diagnostic attributes have been determined, one may identify these modes on new artifacts simply by looking to see whether the proper diagnostic attributes are present, without actually grouping and regrouping the artifacts. Many archaeologists (Waring and Holder 1945, Fig. 1) have found it helpful to make drawings of the more complex conceptual modes, such as rim profiles or designs, to assist in identification.

TAXONOMIC CLASSIFICATION

We have seen that analytic classification concentrates on the attributes of the artifacts which indicate modes. Taxonomic classification is instead concerned with those attributes which indicate types (Gladwin and Gladwin, 1930, 1931, 1933; Haury 1936; Sayles 1936). As in the case of analytic classification, the attributes indicative of types must be chosen for their cultural significance (Gifford 1960). Indeed, if the archaeologist is being completely logical, he should first do analytic clasification in order to form modes and should then classify taxonomically in terms of those modes, instead of going back again to the original attributes. In such a case, for example, he will use the technique of incision as a criterion for taxonomic classification, rather than the attribute of incised lines. In order to simplify the following discussion, I will assume that the archaeological taxonomist does work in terms of modes rather than raw attributes, in which case a type may be defined as a complex of modes which is diagnostic of a

PROCEDURE   _CATEGORIES_

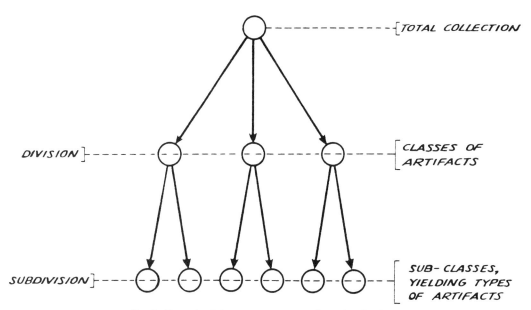

FIG. 3. Example of the taxonomic approach to classification.

certain class of artifacts and which serves to differentiate that class from all other classes.

There are several different ways of classifying a collection to form types. The most systematic one is to divide the specimens into two or more classes on the basis of one set of modes, for example, of materials; then to subdivide each class on the basis of another set of modes, such as shapes; and to continue this process until all the artifacts of the same kind have been separated into a single sub-subclass (Fig. 3). Another way is to work intuitively by simply sorting and re-sorting the artifacts until they end up in relatively homogeneous classes (Krieger 1944, Fig. 25). A third is to work statistically, for example, by noting the taxonomically significant modes of each artifact on a punch card and sorting out the cards according to the most frequent combinations of modes (Shepard 1956: 322–32). In all cases the end result is the same: a single series of classes or subclasses rather than the successive series which result from analytic classification (compare Figs. 2, 3).

In all cases, the classifier must decide how many modes he is to consider diagnostic, that is, how many are going to end up in the type. He must select more than one, since by definition a type consists of two or more modes. On the other hand, he cannot expect to use all the modes; to do so would result in too large a number of types, especially if the artisan was permitted choices of modes during the course of the manufacture of the artifacts (Fig. 1). The proportion of modes which it is practicable to use as the criteria for taxonomic classification varies with the complexity of the artifacts and with the number of alternatives open to the artisan. Simple artifacts with few alternatives, for example, no decoration, can be classified in terms of almost all their modes, whereas complex artifacts with many alternatives, such as elaborately decorated pottery, require selection of only a few modes from among many. The type "stone ball" may be cited as an example of the former extreme; here the three diagnostic modes, use of stone, grinding, and spherical shape, are practically the only ones which can be analyzed from the specimens. Pottery types illustrate the other extreme; for example, Ritchie and MacNeish (1949: 99, Fig. 36), in their study of pre-Iroquoian pottery, explicitly limited the diagnostic modes they used to rim profiles, designs, and decorative techniques, excluding all the other modes which were analyzable from the sherds.

The personality of the taxonomist may also have an effect upon the number of modes which he selects to be diagnostic. If he is a "lumper," he will group the artifacts into large and inclusive classes, each of which will contain so much variation that relatively few of its modes can be considered diagnostic. If, on the other hand, he is a "splitter," he will establish many more classes, there will be less variation within each class, and as a result the ratio of diagnostic to non-diagnostic modes will be considerably higher.

The current tendency on the part of some archaeologists to subdivide pottery types into varieties (Gifford 1960) seems designed to meet this problem. It permits one to select a relatively small number of diagnostic modes for one's types and thereby to satisfy the lumper, and at the same time to define varieties in terms of larger numbers of diagnostic modes, thus satisfying the splitter as well.

The distinction between diagnostic modes, which form part of the type or variety, and non-diagnostic modes, which do not, is frequently obscured by the practice of "describing types" (Ford and Willey 1949: 71–8). In the terminology of the present paper, such descriptions amount to a presentation of the modes analyzable from the artifacts of each class. Some of these modes will be diagnostic and, as a result, form part of the type; but others — and in many cases the majority — will not. Ritchie and Mac-Neish (1949: 100–16) provide a good example. In the case of each type, these authors specify only three "diagnostic features" and then proceed to list a much larger number of other modes of "paste," "surface finish," "decoration," and "forms." The latter modes are not part of the type, as the word is used in the present paper.

The selection of modes has a qualitative as well as a quantitative aspect. The taxonomist must decide not only how many but also what kinds of modes are to be considered diagnostic of his classes and hence constituents of his types. Our colleagues in biology solve this problem by selecting the diagnostics which best show the course of organic evolution. We archaeologists are not so consistent. In the case of pottery and sometimes also projectile points, we select those modes which best indicate differences in time and space (Ford and Willey 1949: 40). Otherwise, we tend to select modes which best express the intrinsic nature of the artifacts (Rouse 1952: 327–9). This difference is reflected in the names of our types, for example, "Glades Plain"

in the case of pottery and "semilunar knife" in the case of stonework—or "problematical form" when the nature of the artifact is not known.

This difference must be kept in mind if we are to think clearly about classification. It leads me to make a distinction between (1) historical types, whose modes have been selected, consciously or unconsciously, for their time-space significance and (2) descriptive types, composed of modes referring primarily to the nature of the artifacts.

Once types have been established — whether they are historical or descriptive — they may be used to identify new artifacts without the necessity of actually grouping the artifacts into classes. One need only determine that the new artifacts have the modes comprising a certain type and then apply the name of that type. This is easy enough to do if the types are simple. In the case of more complex types, containing a greater number of diagnostic modes, it has sometimes proved helpful to establish a key to assist in comparison. As in biology, such a key consists of a list in outline form of the modes comprising all of the types. To identify an unknown artifact, one need only trace it down through the key by means of its modes (Colton and Hargrave 1937: 36–41; Colton 1952, 1955).

Another device to assist in the identification of new material is the "type artifact(s)." Not to be confused with an artifact type, this consists of the most typical artifact(s) in a class. To identify unknown artifacts or to check identifications made by means of a key, one may compare the unknown artifacts with the type artifacts and thereby, in effect, assign them to the classes typified by those artifacts (Osgood 1942: 22–5).

MODES vs. TYPES

We have now distinguished the two principal ways in which archaeologists classify artifacts, analytic and taxonomic. Analytic classification is done by forming successive series of classes, focusing on different features of the artifacts. Each class is characterized by one or more attributes which indicate a procedure to which the artisan conformed, such as a technique of manufacture, or a concept which he expressed in the artifacts, such as an element of shape or decoration. Each custom or concept constitutes a mode.

Taxonomic classification is done by formulating a single set of classes, which differentiate the artifacts in one's collection according to type. Each taxonomic class is characterized by two or more modes, selected from among the total number of modes obtainable by means of analytic classification. The modes diagnostic of each class constitute its type.

Types, then, consist of selected modes. We have seen that the nature of the selection will vary from type to type depending upon the complexity of the artifacts, the number of alternatives which the culture offered to the artisans, the personal inclination of the taxonomist (whether he is a "lumper" or a "splitter"), and the purposes for which he plans to use the types.

To put this in another way, modes are inherent in one's collection. If two archaeologists analyze the same collection and do an equally good job of it, they should produce the same modes (Taylor 1948: 129–30). Types, on the contrary, are imposed on the collection. If two taxonomists classify the same collection and decide, for whatever reason, upon different diagnostic modes, they will produce different types (Brew 1946: 46). The mode, therefore, is a natural unit of cultural study, whereas the type is an arbitrary one.

It does not follow from this that types are any less demonstrable than modes. An archaeologist can validate types equally well by grouping them into classes and demonstrating that the artifacts of each class share the same diagnostic modes. The point is that he can then regroup the artifacts according to another set of diagnostic modes and thereby produce other types which will have equal validity.

It should not be implied, either, that a type consists merely of the sum of its constituent modes. The fact that all these modes recur from artifact to artifact gives them a reality above and beyond that of the individual modes.

We have distinguished two kinds of modes: (1) conceptual modes, consisting of ideas and standards which the artisans expressed in the artifacts and (2) procedural modes, consisting of customs followed by the artisans in making and using the artifacts. Conceptual modes are directly indicated by the attributes of the artifacts whereas procedural modes have to be inferred from the attributes. Hence, the distinction between the two is primarily a matter of relative reliability.

Two kinds of types have likewise been distinguished: (1) historical types, formed in order to establish differences of time and space, and (2) descriptive types, formed in order to express differences in the nature of the artifacts. There may be some overlapping between these two, but generally they will be distinct, because the modes comprising each will have been chosen for different reasons. Here, we have a good example of the arbitrary nature of types.

A comparison with ethnology may perhaps help to clarify these distinctions. One of the things an ethnologist does in studying material culture is to ask or observe how his informants make and use their artifacts. Such observations enable the ethnologist to distinguish various techniques of manufacture and uses of the artifacts. In the terminology of the present paper, the latter are procedural modes.

It is likewise possible for the ethnologist to ask his informants to identify the various parts of their artifacts. If the informants go on to distinguish different kinds of handles, for example, or if the ethnologist himself does so, they will be producing the units here called conceptual modes.

A third possibility is for the ethnologist to ask his informants to identify the artifacts as complete objects by saying, for example, that they are "knives" or "scrapers." If either the informant or the ethnologist goes on to define the resultant categories by listing the modes diagnostic of each, he will be producing the units which we have termed descriptive types.

Finally, the informants may refer to certain artifacts as being "old-" or "new-fashioned" and to others as being of a local or foreign style. If either the informant or the ethnologist should define these categories by listing their distinctive modes, he would be producing what are here called historical types.

In other words, the ethnologist as well as the archaeologist may do both analytic and taxonomic classification. The ethnologist, however, is able to do so with the assistance of informants, whereas the archaeologist is forced to rely entirely upon his own judgment and experience in formulating modes and types.

UTILITY OF THE METHODS

Brew (1946: 65) has observed that "we need more rather than fewer classifications, different classifications, always new classifications, to meet new needs." If Brew is correct, we ought to be able to list the needs for classification in archaeology and to state the kinds of classification which best meet each need. The remainder of the paper will be devoted to this task. It will be done in terms of the products of our two kinds of classification, conceptual and procedural modes and historical and descriptive types.

Identification of artifacts. There is probably no professional archaeologist who has not, at one time or another, had an amateur come up to him, take an artifact out of his pocket, and ask for an identification. When the amateur does this, he expects to be answered in terms of descriptive types, that is, to be told that the artifact is a "knife" or a "scraper," for example. If the artifact is a potsherd, the professional will probably answer instead in terms of historical types, calling it "Sebonac Stamped," for example. In my experience the latter answer is not so satisfying to the amateur. He does not understand it, unless he is unusually sophisticated, and tends to look upon it as an affectation of the professional. The amateur is probably right in this, insofar as he is interested purely in identification and not in the historical significance of the potsherd. It would be more appropriate for the professional to identify the sherd descriptively as "a fragment of a cooking pot" instead of terming it "Sebonac Stamped."

Interest in such descriptive identification is, of course, not limited to amateurs. The professional must do it in cataloguing his artifacts and in preparing museum exhibits, where specimens are grouped according to types. Descriptive identification is also basic to several more academic pursuits of the archaeologist, which are discussed below. It is fortunate that taxonomy has not lost prestige among archaeologists as it has in the other natural sciences, for it is a vital part of our research.

Determination of the culture of a component. Following the lead of Taylor (1948: 197), I would suggest that, when archaeologists determine the culture of a component, that is, of a culturally homogeneous site unit, they would do well to conform to ethnographic practice. As already indicated, ethnographers handle their collections in two different ways: (1) they identify the artifacts, usually in terms supplied by their informants, and (2) they discuss the manufacture and use of the artifacts (Thompson 1958: 65–146). From the standpoint of the present paper, (1) corresponds to descriptive types and (2) to the modes produced by means of analytic classification. (Ethnographers seem to emphasize procedural modes, but many of them also pay some attention to conceptual

modes.) Accordingly, I would suggest that the best way to determine and present the culture of a component is in terms of descriptive types and of procedural and conceptual modes. I doubt that historical types are necessary for this particular purpose, so long as the descriptive approach is applied to pottery and projectile points as well as to other kinds of artifacts, since the historical types will overlap the descriptive types, and anyway they are designed for a different purpose.

The descriptive types and modes will, of course, suffice only to present the material culture of the component. They must be combined with other traits and complexes inferred from the non-artifactual content of the component, for example, the settlement pattern, in order to establish the total culture of the component. The various types, modes, and other traits may simply be listed or they may be grouped into culturally meaningful categories. For example, Fairbanks (1942: 228–9) has organized them about the activities of the people inhabiting the Stallings Island component, in accordance with the concept of activity proposed by Linton (1936: 397).

Classification of components to form cultures. Many archaeologists find it advisable to group their components into cultures, known variously as foci, phases, complexes, industries, or styles. This requires a form of taxonomic classification. The common practice is to compare the components in terms of their "traits" and, as in the taxonomic classification of artifacts, to select certain traits to be "determinants" of each culture (Cole and Deuel 1937: 207–23). When one examines such determinants from the standpoint of the present paper, one finds that they consist of varying combinations of procedural and conceptual modes and of descriptive and historical types. The four appear to be used indiscriminately, without thought as to which units, if any, would be more suitable. To my knowledge, the only author who has attempted to discriminate among the various kinds of determinants is Phillips (1958: 123–4), who advocates the use of types as the primary basis for classifying components but would supplement them with modes.

Phillips does not distinguish among the various kinds of types and modes but, if the suggestions made above for the presentation of the culture of a component are correct, it would be appropriate to use descriptive types and both kinds of modes. Personally, I would hesitate to state categorically, as Phillips does, that types should be given priority over modes. I suspect that this will depend on the nature of the cultures being studied. In fact, I can conceive of cases in which modes might suffice by themselves. I do not believe that it would do merely to use single modes, but types are not the only available kinds of combinations of modes. It has been possible, for example, to establish structural relationships among modes, such as Amsden's (1936) correlation of "design vocabulary" and elements of shape. Such structural relationships have proved to be effective as determinants in other branches of anthropology, for example, in the classification of folktales (Propp 1958), and I wonder whether they might not work better in the classification of some archaeological components than typological complexes of modes, whether selected for their historical or their descriptive significance.

Alternatively, there may well be cases in which neither types nor modes are the best criteria to use in classifying components. Nonartifactual traits, such as settlement patterns and means of subsistence, may sometimes prove to be superior.

In any case, I am certain that artifact types alone cannot provide an adequate basis for the classification of components, if only because they do not cover enough of the culture of the components. For example, Brew (in Tax and others 1953: 245) has argued that there is no such thing as a Folsom culture (complex) because practically nothing is known of it but the Folsom type of projectile point. Even assuming that we have only the one type of point, the situation looks better when viewed in terms of modes and non-artifactual traits, for we know the kinds of material used; the techniques of manufacture; distinctive elements of shape; a characteristic, if assumed use; and something about the means of subsistence. All these are separate traits which Brew obscured by limiting himself to the type concept.

Dating of components and cultures. Historical types are unquestionably the most effective kind of unit to use in dating components and cultures. The fact that their constituent modes have been selected for time-space significance makes them superior to descriptive types; and the fact that they consist of multiple modes gives them greater reliability than individual modes. This is true whether the types are used

as "time markers" with which to correlate strata (components) in the manner of paleontology or are studied in terms of their relative popularity in a more purely archaeological fashion (Heizer 1958: 112–3, 114–5).

Definition of cultural periods. By the same token, historical types should be most suitable for defining local cultural periods. J. A. Ford's various chronological studies may be cited as examples: his lettered "time scale" and the correlated periods are measured against the frequency changes of pottery types (Phillips, Ford, and Griffin 1951, Figs. 17–21). If, on the other hand, one wishes to work with chronology on a regional, multi-areal basis, modes are likely to be more practicable, whether used singly or in combinations, since they tend to have a broader distribution than types (Cruxent and Rouse 1959).

Studies of cultural distribution. Following J. A. Ford's lead (1952: 319), I would suggest that modes are the best unit to use in studying cultural distributions. One may trace their persistence and their relative popularity through time (Rouse 1939, Fig. 6) or their diffusion from area to area (Wendorf 1953: 163–70). By so doing, one will not only be able to reconstruct the histories of the individual modes but also one will find that certain modes tend always to occur together and hence to form discrete historical complexes. Some of these complexes will correspond to types, that is, they will consist of the same modes as those comprising types, but other complexes will cut across the types. The structural relationships discussed above provide one example. The "traditions" and "horizon styles" of Peruvian archaeology are another (Willey 1945).

An archaeologist who studies the distributions of individual modes, then, will be in a position to reconstruct the histories of those modes and also the histories of types and of nontypological complexes of modes. On the other hand, the archaeologist who studies only the distributions of types will be unable to get at the histories of the other kinds of units. Southwestern archaeology, where it is customary to concentrate on the distribution of types (Colton and Hargrave 1937, Fig. 1), is a case in point. Several authors (Rouse 1954: 223) have commented on the lack of horizon styles in the Southwest. This may well be a peculiarity of the culture history of the Southwestern area, but there is also a possibility that it reflects failure on the part of Southwestern archaeologists, in their preoccupation with types, to trace the distribution of enough individual modes.

Studies of cultural change. If one is interested in the problem of how one complex (whether typological or not) or one culture has changed into another, modes are again the proper unit to use. As Barnett (1953: 185) has put it,

> in order to understand the innovative process, we must be prepared to analyze ideas in any fashion and without limit . . . so that we may follow the ramifications of recombination as they actually occur. We cannot deal with the gross stereotyped wholes [i.e., types] only. . . . We must treat conventional ideas, such as those of tables and men, merely as more or less stable organizations of experience that can be torn down and reassembled in the wink of an eye.
>
> In all the sciences we have come to expect very detailed analyses of data for purposes of classification. This lead, however, has not been followed by students of [culture change]. . . . In trying to understand invention it is common practice to deal with such gross units as automobiles and buggies or [pottery types] and spinning wheels. The attempt to understand one of these complex wholes in terms of the whole of another will give us no insight into their true relationships. We must view the inception of each one in terms of an analysis of its component parts.
>
> The linguists long ago recognized this necessity, and students of linguistic change do not hesitate to break down sentences, words, parts of words, and parts of these parts. . . . There can be no question that linguists are far ahead of the rest of us in their understanding of the mechanics of cultural change.

Barnett might have added that archaeologists are also accustomed to do analysis and to study culture change in terms of the resultant modes. Gladwin's (1957: 282–4) final report on Southwestern archaeology may be cited as an example. Linguists cannot claim sole credit for this kind of approach, nor to have produced the only significant results from it.

CONCLUSIONS

In the foregoing section I have attempted to indicate some of the situations in which it is better to use modes, resulting from analytic classification, or types, resulting from taxonomic classification. I do not pretend to have fully covered the subject; rather I have intended to call attention to it as a problem which deserves the consideration of archaeologists. Too many of us, in my experience, fail to discriminate between modes and types, treating them as equivalent units and substituting one for the other whenever it is convenient to do so (Webb and Snow 1945: 16–28). We need to think more about when the various kinds of modes, types,

or combinations thereof will be the most effective units to use.

This paper has likewise been intended to call attention to the way in which analysis and taxonomy complement each other as methods of classification. I think we should beware the tendency of some archaeologists to become preoccupied with one to the neglect of the other.

As already indicated, taxonomic classification has received particular emphasis in the American Southwest. We appear at the moment to be witnessing the diffusion of certain Southwestern taxonomic developments to the Southeast (Phillips 1958) and Mesoamerica (Smith, Willey, and Gifford 1960). I do not criticize this diffusion; indeed, I would recommend that it be expanded to include other Southwestern taxonomic devices, such as the key and the type artifact.

On the other hand, I share with Sears (1960) the belief that the analytic approach likewise needs to be strengthened and applied more widely. We need more studies of individual modes and of their non-typological combinations, such as the recent work of Wasley (1959) in the Southwest.

The fact is that both analytic and taxonomic classification must be done in order to make a full study of any collection. Neither, by itself, will supply a complete picture of the culture of the collection, nor will either be able to furnish all the data needed to formulate cultures or to reconstruct culture history.

Acknowledgements. This paper has been read in earlier drafts by J. A. Bennyhoff, E. M. Bruner, John Buettner-Janusch, J. M. Campbell, Patrick Gallagher, J. C. Gifford, D. H. Hymes, F. G. Lounsbury, W. J. Mayer-Oakes, Marshall McKusick, L. J. Pospisil, W. H. Sears, A. C. Spaulding, G. R. Willey, E. R. Wolf, and Stephen Williams, to all of whom I am grateful for their comments and criticisms. I have also incorporated suggestions made by J. M. Goggin, W. C. Sturtevant, and R. H. Thompson. In addition, I am indebted to the authors of the accompanying papers in this issue (Gifford 1960; Smith, Willey and Gifford 1960; and Sears 1960) for the opportunity to read these papers in manuscript form and to incorporate ideas expressed therein.

AMSDEN, C. A.

    1936 The Structural Analysis of Pottery Design. In his "An Analysis of Hohokam Pottery Design," *Medallion Papers*, No. 23, pp. 1–17. Gila Pueblo, Globe.

BARNETT, H. G.

    1953 *Innovation: the Basis of Cultural Change.* McGraw-Hill, New York.

BLACK, G. A. AND P. WEER
1936 A Proposed Terminology for Shape Classification of Artifacts. *American Antiquity*, Vol. 1, No. 4, pp. 280–94. Menasha.

BREW, J. O.
1946 The Use and Abuse of Taxonomy. In his "Archaeology of Alkali Ridge, Southeastern Utah," *Papers of the Peabody Museum, Harvard University*, Vol. 21, pp. 44–66. Cambridge.

COLE, FAY-COOPER AND THORNE DEUEL
1937 *Rediscovering Illinois: Archaeological Explorations in and around Fulton County*. University of Chicago Press, Chicago.

COLTON, H. S.
1952 Pottery Types of the Arizona Strip and Adjacent Areas in Utah and Nevada. *Museum of Northern Arizona, Ceramic Series*, No. 1. Flagstaff.
1955 Check List of Southwestern Pottery Types. *Museum of Northern Arizona, Ceramic Series*, No. 2. Flagstaff.

COLTON, H. S. AND L. L. HARGRAVE
1937 Handbook of Northern Arizona Pottery Wares. *Museum of Northern Arizona, Bulletin*, No. 11. Flagstaff.

CRUXENT, J. M. AND IRVING ROUSE
1959 An Archeological Chronology of Venezuela. *Pan American Union, Social Science Monographs*, No. 6. Washington.

FAIRBANKS, C. H.
1942 The Taxonomic Position of Stalling's Island, Georgia. *American Antiquity*, Vol. 7, No. 3, pp. 223–31. Menasha.

FORD, C. S.
1937 A Sample Comparative Analysis of Material Culture. In *Studies in the Science of Society*, edited by G. P. Murdock. 225–46. Yale University Press, New Haven.

FORD, J. A.
1952 Measurements of Some Prehistoric Design Developments in the Southeastern United States. *Anthropological Papers of the American Museum of Natural History*, Vol. 44, Pt. 3. New York.

FORD, J. A. AND G. R. WILLEY
1949 Surface Survey of the Virú Valley, Peru. *Anthropological Papers of the American Museum of Natural History*, Vol. 43, Pt. 1. New York.

GIFFORD, J. C.
1960 The Type-Variety Method of Ceramic Classification as an Indicator of Cultural Phenomena. *American Antiquity*, Vol. 25, No. 3. pp. 341–7. Salt Lake City.

GLADWIN, H. S.
1957 *A History of the Ancient Southwest*. Bond, Wheelwright, Portland (Maine).

GLADWIN, WINIFRED AND H. S. GLADWIN
1930 Some Southwestern Pottery Types. Series I. *Medallion Papers*, No. 5. Gila Pueblo, Globe.
1931 Some Southwestern Pottery Types, Series II. *Medallion Papers*, No. 10. Gila Pueblo, Globe.
1933 Some Southwestern Pottery Types. Series III. *Medallion Papers*, No. 13. Gila Pueblo, Globe.

HAURY, E. W.
1936 Some Southwestern Pottery Types, Series IV. *Medallion Papers*, No. 19. Gila Pueblo, Globe.

HEIZER, R. F. (EDITOR)
1958 *A Guide to Archaeological Field Methods*. Third revised edition. National Press, Palo Alto.

KRIEGER, A. D.
1944 The Typological Concept. *American Antiquity*, Vol. 9, No. 3, pp. 271–88. Menasha.

LINTON, RALPH
1936 *The Study of Man*. Appleton, Century, New York.

MATSON, F. R.
1952 The Contribution of Technical Ceramic Studies to American Archaeology. *Prehistoric Pottery of the Eastern United States*, No. 2, pp. 1–7. Ann Arbor.

NEILSON, W. A., T. A. KNOTT, AND P. W. EARHART (EDITORS)
1940 *Webster's New International Dictionary of the English Language*. Second edition. G. and C. Merriam Co., Springfield.

OSGOOD, CORNELIUS
1942 The Ciboney Culture of Cayo Redondo, Cuba. *Yale University Publications in Anthropology*, No. 25. New Haven.

PHILLIPS, PHILIP
1958 Application of the Wheat–Gifford–Wasley Taxonomy to Eastern Ceramics. *American Antiquity*, Vol. 24, No. 2, pp. 117–30. Salt Lake City.

PHILLIPS, PHILIP, J. A. FORD, AND J. B. GRIFFIN
1951 Archaeological Survey in the Lower Mississippi Alluvial Valley, 1940–1947. *Papers of the Peabody Museum, Harvard University*, Vol. 25. Cambridge.

PROPP, V.
1958 Morphology of the Folktale. *Publications of the Indiana University Research Center in Anthropology, Folklore, and Linguistics*, No. 10. Bloomington.

RITCHIE, W. A. AND R. S. MACNEISH
1949 The Pre-Iroquoian Pottery of New York State. *American Antiquity*, Vol. 15, No. 2, pp. 97–124. Menasha.

ROUSE, IRVING
1939 Prehistory in Haiti: A Study in Method. *Yale University Publications in Anthropology*, No. 21. New Haven.

The Classification of Artifacts in Archaeology

457

1941 Culture of the Ft. Liberté Region, Haiti. *Yale University Publications in Anthropology*, No. 24. New Haven.

1952 Porto Rican Prehistory. *The New York Academy of Sciences, Scientific Survey of Porto Rico and the Virgin Islands*, Vol. 18, Nos. 3–4, pp. 307–578. New York.

1954 On the Use of the Concept of Area Co-Tradition. *American Antiquity*, Vol. 19, No. 3, pp. 221–5. Salt Lake City.

SAYLES, E. B.

1936 Some Southwestern Pottery Types, Series V. *Medallion Papers*, No. 21. Gila Pueblo, Globe.

SEARS, W. H.

1960 Taxonomic Systems and Eastern Archaeology. *American Antiquity*, Vol. 25, No. 3, pp. 324–9. Salt Lake City.

SHEPARD, A. O.

1956 Ceramics for the Archaeologist. *Carnegie Institution of Washington, Publication*, No. 609. Washington.

SMITH, R. E., G. R. WILLEY, AND J. C. GIFFORD

1960 The Type-Variety Concept as a Basis for the Analysis of Maya Pottery. *American Antiquity*, Vol. 25, No. 3, pp. 330–40. Salt Lake City.

TAYLOR, W. W.

1948 A Study of Archeology. *Memoirs of the American Anthropological Association*, No. 69. Menasha.

TAX, SOL, L. C. EISELEY, IRVING ROUSE, AND C. F. VOEGELIN (EDITORS)

1953 An Appraisal of Anthropology Today. University of Chicago Press, Chicago.

THOMPSON, R. H.

1958 Modern Yucatecan Maya Pottery Making. *Memoirs of the Society for American Archaeology*, No. 15. Salt Lake City.

WARING, A. J., JR. AND PRESTON HOLDER

1945 A Prehistoric Ceremonial Complex in the Southeastern United States. *American Anthropologist*, Vol. 47, No. 1, pp. 1–34. Menasha.

WASLEY, W. W.

1959 Cultural Implications of Style Trends in Southwestern Pottery: Basketmaker III to Pueblo II in West Central New Mexico. MS, doctoral dissertation, University of Arizona, Tucson.

WEBB, W. S. AND C. E. SNOW

1945 The Adena People. *The University of Kentucky Reports in Anthropology and Archaeology*, Vol. 6. Lexington.

WENDORF, FRED

1953 Archaeological Studies in the Petrified Forest National Monument. *Museum of Northern Arizona, Bulletin*, No. 27. Flagstaff.

WHEAT, J. B., J. C. GIFFORD, AND W. W. WASLEY

1958 Ceramic Variety, Type Cluster, and Ceramic System in Southwestern Pottery Analysis. *American Antiquity*, Vol. 24, No. 1, pp. 34–47. Salt Lake City.

WHITEFORD, A. H.

1947 Description for Artifact Analysis. *American Antiquity*, Vol. 12, No. 4, pp. 226–37. Menasha.

WILLEY, G. R.

1945 Horizon Styles and Pottery Traditions in Peruvian Archaeology. *American Antiquity*, Vol. 11, No. 1, pp. 49–56. Menasha.

YALE UNIVERSITY
New Haven, Conn.
June, 1959

THE USE OF TYPOLOGY IN
ANTHROPOLOGICAL THEORY

Clyde Kluckhohn

Whitehead was right when he said that classification is only a half-way house in science. On the other hand, I think L. J. Henderson was equally correct in saying that in science any classification is better than no classification. A classification is useful to the degree that it sheds light on the relation between one set of facts and another. By a "typology" I mean precisely a classification that is explicitly theoretical in intent as opposed to one intended purely as a descriptive categorization.

Anthropology has had both typologies and empirical groupings for convenience. There have been the asserted evolutionary stages, posited with varying degrees of refinement. There have been categorizations based on selected criteria that were immediately observable: phenotypic "races"; culture areas; agglutinative, polysynthetic, and isolating languages. Categories based on a single feature whether technological, social, or psychological, have also been used. Thus we have spoken of plough or matrilineal or Dionysian cultures. Quite recently, certain typologies have been presented that exhibit some scientific precision or logical rigor or fairly adequate microscopic attention to the complexity of the data. I cannot give an exhaustive listing, but will limit myself to examples from publications in English. One may instance the classifications by Boyd[1] and others of genetically similar populations; Greenberg[2] and Voegelin[3] of linguistic typology; Steward[4] and his associates on types of multilinear evolution; Linton's[5] typology of nativistic movements. Redfield's work for many years has had a focus on an essentially typological problem: that of the folk society or little community. His theses have provoked much controversy[6] but are gradually illuminating many issues of the theory of types. It would be generally agreed that the British social anthropologists and certain Americans, such as Murdock and Eggan, have significantly advanced the typology of kinship and allied aspects of social structure. Lévy-Strauss[7] has proposed a typology of orders (kinship, social organization, and social stratification) and of types of connection between spatial arrangements of residence and kinds of social organization. He has likewise boldly suggested that social anthropology, linguistics, and economics can all be grouped into the single master field of communication.

Such concepts as "antagonistic acculturation" constitute a beginning for one typology of process. Vogt[8] has sketched a performance typology. Wallace[9] has sketched some types of events. Last year two typologies[10] of South American social structure were published. We have had at these meetings a typology of Indian cultures of California and are to hear a paper on the typology of the Japanese family. One could give many more examples, of course.

Steward's theory seems to be the most general and thoroughgoing to date within cultural anthropology. That of Trager and Hall[11] is also extremely interesting and more along the lines of the present paper. Steward distinguishes between culture types and classifications based on areas or value systems. He

elaborates concepts for determining cross-cultural types.[12] His own central concept is based upon two frames of reference: cultural features derived from synchronic, functional, and ecological factors; features represented by a particular diachronic or developmental level.[13] He asserts[14] that cross-culturally valid categories will apply only to similar cultural types—i.e., types that recur in a multi-evolutionary scheme will be distinguished by unique categories.

The publications of the past decade make it evident that anthropology is moving toward more ramified and more sophisticated typologies. But much remains to be done. Most classifications are still either crudely empirical or grossly impressionistic. We are relatively rich in content categories but poor in conceptual or relational categories. Steward[15] agrees that we shall "have to distinguish innumerable culture types, many of which have not yet been recognized." Anthropologists of all branches need to study the elegant work of their linguistic colleagues and also the related fields of mathematical logic such as set theory. In spite of Gödel's Proof, Russell's Theory of Logical Types[16] deserves the close attention of anthropologists, for perhaps the most frequent and serious error in anthropological theory continues to be that of confusion of levels of abstraction. Many anthropological typologies are not firmly based upon the postulate that there must be a discontinuity between a class and its members. In general, anthropologists dealing with the theory of typology could well study the careful work of contemporary philosophers upon this subject. Ryle,[17] for example, says of the determination of types:

> It has long been known that what a proposition implies, it implies in virtue of its form. The same is true of what it is compatible and incompatible with. Let us give the name "liasons" to all the logical relations of a proposition, namely what it implies, what it is implied by, what it is compatible with, and what it is incompatible with. Now, any respect in which two propositions differ in form will be reflected in differences in their liasons. So two propositions which are formally similar in all respects save that one factor in one is different from a partially corresponding factor in the other, will have liasons which are correspondingly dissimilar. . . . The operation of extracting the type of a factor cannot exclude the operation of revealing the liasons of a proposition embodying it.

There are two principal kinds of problems where typology is relevant to anthropological theory. The first is less abstract. This is that of assigning a biological or cultural specimen (or a piece of behavior) to the group to which it belongs. This is pre-eminently the task of biological anthropologists, of archaeologists, of museum ethnologists. Is a tooth ape or human? Does a pot most nearly approach "the ideal type" of Wingate Black-on-White or a similar but different pottery category? Here statistical procedures are often appropriate. The discriminant function[18] should determine whether a tooth is ape or human, *assuming it belongs to one of these groups.* The S-function is used to test whether the set of measurements is such as to make it likely that it is a member of a particular category. Since one cannot—or should not—measure everything, one is still faced with discovering what measurements are crucial or most economical to obtain such sortings. Moreover, while it is often essential to obtain the critical matrix of dimensions, measurement in and of itself may be either insufficient or actually misleading in localizing an object or event in a time or space or time-space category. Bronowski and Long say: ". . . even when no single dimension shows a significant variation from its group mean, the total configuration may still be wrong."[19]

The second class of typological problems is that of establishing groups or orders rather than that of assigning an individual entity to such a category. So far as typologies based on content are concerned, the principles involved are relatively simple, however difficult the detailed execution may become. One makes certain that the criteria chosen are actually relevant to the purpose or purposes at hand, and one investigates the inter-correlation or inter-association of these criteria so that one is not merely compounding the effects of one or two criteria. One makes one's *fundamenta divisionis* completely explicit, and one follows them consistently. One keeps one's levels of abstraction straight.

Typologies of relations are more complicated and less explored, save, to an increasing degree, in the areas of linguistics and social structure. Although I am profoundly convinced that linguistics supplies invaluable models, I shall for the rest of this paper limit myself to cultural anthropology in the narrow sense and indicate some directions that I believe might profitably be followed. These center on ways of developing typologies of cultural structure. This implies "models" rather than empirical generalizations. The "models" must embrace as much empirical fact as is convenient to the conception proposed or the hypothesis to be tested and must not be contradicted by any *pertinent* datum. But "models," by definition, represent relationships regularly prevailing between strictly selected assemblages of fact; they do not and cannot encompass a total cultural inventory.

A typology of cultures, it seems to me, should be directed toward such questions as the following:

What is apparently incompatible with what else? For example, are patrilocal bands never found among sedentary peoples who depend primarily upon agriculture for subsistence?

What is extremely likely to be found with what else? For instance, is culturally approved aggression against distributive minorities found mainly in an "atomistic social order,"[20] whereas a channeling toward segmental minorities is characteristic of more centralized social organizations? Are, as Murdock[21] suggests, the features ascribed to folk societies particularly associated with peoples practicing local endogamy?

Are some concatenations of cultural features or elements indifferent as far as minimal necessary coherence of the system is concerned and hence found associated or not associated merely as a result of the accidents of the historical process?

Enough information is now available to make possible the construction of a first approximation to an analogue of the chemical table of atomic elements.[22] Which combinations of cultural elements are, apparently, "impossible"; which are very rare and probably due to exceptional circumstances; which are so frequent as to be statistically predictable; on which is no guess justified one way or the other?

Such enquiry, exposing the principles of cultural structure, would take us some distance toward ranging cultures in an orderly way as to their respective similarities and differences. It would also help us to isolate wherein rests the distinctiveness of each particular culture at a given time level—the "without-which-not" of that culture. We require, of course, to deal with flow as well as fixity, typologies of process as well as of form. Seen through time, another dimension would be opened up. When a cultural structure assumes a radical

alteration in form, what changes first? Is Murdock's thesis that shift in the rules of residence most often initiates other major shifts in social structure an invariant property of human social organization generally or only an important statistical generalization which will turn out to be less valid for some types of cultures than for others? In short, systematic work on the typology of cultures should reveal what Kroeber[23] has called: "... the larger configurations inherent in the multitudinous data: configurations or classes that carried hidden in themselves their derivations, their historical relations."

This refers first and foremost to the implicit culture. And, if I am correct in thinking that the key to selectivity in the implicit culture is the value system, it means the devising of standard operations for exposing the value system with its hierarchy. My assumption is that every such system could be parsimoniously described in terms of not less than about ten nor more than about twenty key values and their relations of interdependence and especially superordination-subordination. Perhaps by a kind of scaling technique the number of "essential" or "distinctive" values could be reduced to a few, but, even if plausible on logical grounds, this requires empirical demonstration. Although the methods should, I think, be quite different, the objective resembles that of factor analysis. One wants to find out what value "loadings" give recognizably distinct character to each cultural structure. One avenue to this end is the cross-cultural comparison of what values are found in complementary, coincident, incorporating, and overlapping distribution.[24]

We continue to be plagued, of course, by the twin dilemmas of what constitutes "a culture" and what units within such cultures can properly be compared. On the first point, I would slightly paraphrase Lévy-Strauss[25] and say:

> A culture is a set of patterns of and for behavior prevalent among a group of human beings which, from the point of view of the research at hand and of the scale on which it is being carried out, presents, in relation to other such sets, significant discontinuities.

As to the second point, it remains unfortunately a fact that the conceptual apparatus of cultural anthropology still does not supply culture-free elemental units comparable to the phoneme and the morpheme. I do believe that some workers in social structure and folklore[26] (Goodenough and Sebeok, for example) have almost formulated the procedures for isolating such units. I suspect it is significant that Sebeok is a linguist and that Goodenough has been much influenced by linguistics. Much in the history of science in this century (physics, neurology, information theory—to name only a few fields) suggests that the dichotomous oppositions or principle of complementarity applied by the linguists with such signal success deserve sustained trial in the realm of culture in general. Niels Bohr[27] says:

> ... the viewpoint of "complementarity" forms indeed a consistent generalization of the ideal of causality ... the trend of modern psychology can be characterized as a reaction against the attempt at analyzing psychical experience into elements which can be associated in the same way as are the results of measurements in classical physics. In introspection, it is clearly impossible to distinguish sharply between the phenomena themselves and their conscious perception, and although we may often speak of lending our attention to some particular aspect of a psychical experience, it will appear

on closer examination that we really have to do, in such cases, with mutually exclusive situations. . . . The main obstacle to an unprejudiced attitude towards the relation between various human cultures is . . . the deep-rooted differences of the traditional backgrounds on which the cultural harmony in different human societies is based and which exclude any simple comparison between such cultures. It is above all in this connexion that the viewpoint of complementarity offers itself as a means of coping with the situation. In fact, when studying human cultures different from our own, we have to deal with a particular problem of observation which on closer consideration shows many features in common with atomic or psychological problems . . .

In my opinion, proper units for comparison will be arrived at along linguistic lines by determining contrastive categories rather than by any amount of measurement. As Lévy-Strauss[28] remarks, ". . . there is no necessary connection between *measure* and *structure*." Meyer Schapiro[29] has reminded us that the history of art shows that one can sometimes actually get greater precision by dealing with qualities. Anthropologists should avoid the mistake made by many American social psychologists and sociologists of putting a naive faith in numbers and especially in statistics.

The investigations by the botanist, Edgar Anderson,[30] constitute a dramatic paradigm of warning: graphic representation of a few features enabled biologists and many non-biologists to differentiate correctly two species, even when they were not told the number of species involved. In contrast, analysis of variance and regression techniques yielded inconclusive or much less efficient results. Anderson comments:

> If one sets out to analyze the difference between two species, the actual data are individual plants or animals, each individual a multiple-sense-impression of size, shape, color, texture, etc. . . . To analyze the nature of these differences we need to make a *selection* among the thousands of sense-impressions which come to us from each specimen . . . the two species may be completely separated by the resultant of seven variables even though any single variable would not suffice when used singly. . . . An impressive proportion of the best discriminators refer to *pattern* . . . In problems involving multiple sense impression, such as differences between species or varieties, where from each individual a seemingly infinite number of numerical facts could be derived . . . the customary methods of biometry are still inappropriate and ineffective. . . . Pointer readings are *not* more exact than any other kind of precise record . . . species are differentiated by combinations of characters more certainly than by single characters . . . (Emphases mine.)

I submit that there is a suggestive analogue here for the anthropologist trying to discriminate cultural "species" and sub-cultural varieties. The issue is that of discovering means for selecting the significant—and perhaps representing these features along the lines of the very interesting graphical techniques proposed by Anderson. If operations are firmly specified, "qualitative" judgments can be as systematic and as rigorous as quantitative ones. In another paper,[31] Anderson reminds us:

> Biology has advanced most rapidly when appropriate qualitative measures have been developed and used with precision. In Genetics, for example, the fundamental data are qualitative. Once obtained they are treated with such

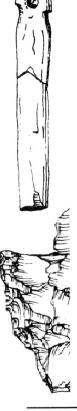

precision that most geneticists probably think of their work as purely quantitative. But the fundamental categories, "vestigial" vs. "non-vestigial," "scute" vs. "non-scute," "forked" vs. "non-forked," etc. are quite as qualitative as the fundamental categories of taxonomy. . . . If the methods of Drosophila genetics were purely quantitative, the flies would not be classified in qualitative categories but their wing lengths, eye diameters, etc. would be laboriously measured. Imagine the difficulties of conducting a Drosophila experiment in which the only available data were the lengths and breadths of the wings! Genetics has been able to advance because it was willing to take the Mendelian recessive (a qualitative unit about whose ultimate significance relatively little was known) and to use that unknown but recognizable entity as a basic unit.

For typological models of structure and of process we need to abstract from immediately visible "reality," disengaging the accidental by including in the models only those aspects of the observable that are relevant to the model being constructed. This means, among other things, as Goodenough[32] has shown in a brilliant example of the kind of analysis I am advocating, carefully distinguishing those phenomena which do tend to be associated with a particular category from those which are essential criteria for membership in that class. Only thus can we trace the intersection of systems with formally independent structure. Only in this way can we isolate the organizing principles that determine both the character of sectors of a culture and the patterning of the whole. We must, as the linguists have done, identify the significant structure points and classify accordingly, isolating the units at each succeeding level of complexity.

Eventually we can, I believe, describe the compositional pattern of each culture and construct a comparative grammar and a comparative syntax of cultures. All grammars limit freedoms and control choices. A comparative grammar of culture would delimit the necessities in cultural development: what features must precede or be associated with what others? Only the intensive and systematic study of variation, and variation through time, revealing the latent structures and latent concepts and incomplete paradigms, can make a grammar of cultures possible.

Harvard University,
Cambridge, Massachusetts.

Notes

1. See, for example, his chapter in *Anthropology Today*.

2. "A Quantitative Approach to the Morphological Typology of Language," pp. 192–211, in: Robert Spencer (Ed.) *Method and Perspective in Anthropology*, Minneapolis, University of Minnesota Press, 1954. See also: Paul Menzerath, "Typology of Languages," *Journal of the Acoustical Society of America*, 22 : 698–701, 1950.

3. "On Developing New Typologies and Revising Old Ones," *Southwestern Journal of Anthropology*, 11: 355–361, 1955.

4. *Theory of Culture Change*, Urbana, University of Illinois Press, 1955.

5. "Nativistic Movements," *American Anthropologist*, 45 : 230–239, 1943.

6. For a thoughtful discussion, see F. G. Friedmann in *The Peasant*, A Symposium Concerning the Peasant Way and View of Life, Number 7 (May, 1956). Mimeographed; Department of Philosophy, University of Arkansas.

7. His chapter, "Social Structure," in *Anthropology Today*.

8. "The Southwestern Fiesta System," *American Anthropologist*, 57 : 820–839, 1955.

9. "A Science of Human Behaviour," *Explorations*, 3 : 127–137, 1954.

10. Kalervo Oberg, "Types of Social Structure among the Lowland Tribes of South and Central America," *American Anthropologist*, 57 (1955), pp. 472–487. E. R. Wolf, "Types of Latin-American Peasantry," *American Anthropologist*, 57 : 452–471, 1955.

11. "Culture and Communication," *Explorations*, 3 : 137–249, 1954.

12. *Op. cit.*, Chapters 1 through 5.

13. *Ibid.*, Chapter 5.

14. *Ibid.*, p. 81.

15. *Ibid.*, p. 24.

16. This is not itself a "typology" but has far-reaching implications for the construction of typologies.

17. "Categories," in: *Logic and Language* (second series), Oxford (England), Basil Blackwell, 1953, pp. 79–80.

18. Cf. J. Bronowski and W. M. Long, "Statistics of Discrimination in Anthropology," *American Journal of Physical Anthropology* (1952), 10 : 385–395, 1952.

19. *Ibid.*, p. 389.

20. Cf. John Honigmann, "The Testing of Hypotheses in Anthropology," *American Anthropologist*, 54 : 429–432, 1952.

21. "Changing Emphases in Social Structure," *Southwestern Journal of Anthropology*, 11 : 361–371, p. 365, 1955.

22. C. Lévi-Strauss, "Language and the Analysis of Social Laws," *American Anthropologist*, 53 : 155–164, 1951.

23. *Method and Perspective in Anthropology*, (*op. cit.*), p. 275.

24. Cf. C. Kluckhohn, "Toward a Comparison of Value-Emphases in Different Cultures," in: Leonard White (Ed.), *The State of The Social Sciences*, Chicago, University of Chicago Press, 1956.

25. *Anthropology Today*, p. 536.

26. Stith Thompson's much earlier work on the classification of motifs was an important precursor of the search for elemental units in folklore that are relatively culture-free.

27. "Natural Philosophy and Human Cultures," *Nature*, 143 : 268–272, 1939.

28. *Anthropology Today*, p. 528.

29. *Ibid.*, p. 290.

30. "Efficient and Inefficient Methods of Measuring Species Differences," in: *Statistics and Mathematics in Biology*, (O. Kempthorne *et al.*, Eds.), Ames, Iowa, Iowa State College Press, 1954.

31. "Hybridization in American Tradescantias," *Annals of the Missouri Botanical Garden*, 23 : 511–525, 1936.

32. "Componential Analysis and the Study of Meaning," *Language*, 32 : 195–217, 1956.

The Use of Typology in Anthropological Theory   **465**

STRATIGRAPHY AND SERIATION

John Howland Rowe

ABSTRACT

Stratigraphic interpretation rests on two principles: the principle of superposition and the principle that deposition units can be identified by cultural content. The sequence of deposition units derived from a case of superposition may not give a true cultural sequence if mixing, filling, or collecting has affected the cultural contents of the units. There are two kinds of seriation: evolutionary seriation, done on the basis of an assumed general law of cultural development, and similiary seriation, done on the basis of similarities and differences in objects or deposition units compared. Similiary seriation assumes only that cultural change is normally gradual. Of the two kinds of seriation, only similiary seriation can give credible results. Some evidence of archaeological associations is necessary to control the possibility of non-gradual change resulting from sudden outside influence or archaism. If the conditions for success can be met, either stratigraphy or seriation can provide a credible sequence. Each method provides a check on the other; the most credible results are achieved by combining the two.

A FRIEND whom I regard as an archaeologist of great ability recently remarked that "a properly conducted stratigraphic analysis carries a higher degree of credibility than the best of seriations." I have heard similar statements often enough before so that it seems to me probable that the view expressed has some currency in the archaeological profession.

The statement quoted has the merit of recognizing that there are more and less credible stratigraphic studies and more and less credible seriations. Beyond this point, however, the argument is questionable. I should like to maintain that, within the conditions under which each of the methods is applicable, the right kind of seriation, properly done, carries the same degree of conviction as a good stratigraphic study. Both stratigraphy and seriation have their limitations which must be understood in evaluating results achieved by either method. The general difference, perhaps, is that it is easier to do a bad seriation than a bad stratigraphic analysis.

The principles of stratigraphy were first worked out in geology in the 18th century, and the method was adopted by archaeologists when it was already fully developed. Hence, some of the insights into stratigraphic theory provided by the development of the idea have escaped the attention of many archaeological users of it. Stratigraphic interpretation depends on two

principles ("laws"), as pointed out by Stamp (1934: 2–3) and Neaverson (1955: 1):

1. *The Law of Superposition* (Lehmann's principle, 1756). In any pile of deposition units in which the top and bottom of the pile can be identified, the order of succession from bottom to top gives the order of deposition. This principle indicates to the observer the order of particular units in a particular outcrop or site. Its geological application is explained by Dunbar and Rodgers (1957: 110–1, 289). In archaeological work the units observed may be lenses of refuse, buildings, burials, pits and hearths as well as more or less horizontal layers. The first archaeological use of this principle appears to have been made by Thomas Jefferson in 1782 (Jefferson 1787: 156–62; Fraser 1935).

2. *The Law of Strata Identified by Fossils* (Smith's principle, 1796; Fenton and Fenton 1952: 70–83; Adams 1954: 268–76). In a given outcrop or site, the deposition units can be distinguished from one another by contrasts in the features of the fossils or artifacts which they contain and by the frequency with which such features occur. Two deposition units in different sites which contain the same features in the same proportions are assumed to be contemporary. This principle makes it possible to interpret a sequence of deposition units as a sequence of biological or cultural units. The first archaeological use of Smith's principle appears to have been made by Georg Christian Friedrich Lisch in a book review (Lisch 1847).

Superposition alone is not stratigraphy, and the observation of superposition has virtually no archaeological significance unless the cultural contents of the deposition units are contrasted. Jefferson understood superposition, but he had no notion of stratigraphy.

The Law of Superposition has no exceptions, and it is this fact which gives stratigraphy its high reputation for credibility in present day archaeology. There are, however, certain conditions in which the order of deposition of the units at a particular site may not reflect accurately the order of cultural succession.

1. *Mixing of units.* Mixing of units may occur as a result of erosion, plowing, burrowing, or any digging operation which turns over the earth leaving it still in place, such as an earlier

excavation in search of antiquities or building stones. It may also occur as a result of the use of sloppy excavation techniques by the archaeologist. Some mixing of adjacent units inevitably takes place when a site with complex layering is excavated by arbitrary blocks.

There is nothing in the principles of stratigraphy which enables the archaeologist to distinguish mixed units from unmixed ones. The distinction is usually made in one or both of two ways. The first is mechanical. If two fragments of the same object are found at greatly different depths, mixing is strongly indicated. This situation occurred, for example, in some of Wendell C. Bennett's pits at Huari (Bennett 1953: 90). The second method of detecting mixed units is comparative. If certain features which occur together in a deposition unit at one site, or one part of a site, are found to occur separately at other sites or other parts of the same site, mixing in the first case is indicated. It may be impossible to identify mixing in the first excavation in an unknown area.

How seriously mixing affects the stratigraphic interpretation depends on whether the analysis is done in terms of presence and absence of features or in terms of frequencies of taxonomic types. I have contrasted these two approaches in an earlier paper (Rowe 1959). If the analysis is done in terms of presence and absence, the existence of mixed deposition units will prevent the investigator from distinguishing as many successive phases of culture as he would have been able to distinguish with unmixed units. The order of the units that can be distinguished is not affected, however. If the analysis is done in terms of type frequencies mixing may even produce a situation which can be interpreted as giving an order the reverse of the true one.

The best example of a reversal of order attributable to mixing is found in Bennett's excavations at Huari, already cited. Bennett dug 15 pits at Huari, in all of which he found pottery which he classified in four "style groups" of a taxonomic nature: Wari, Ayacucho, Acuchimay, and Huarpa. He only found one of these "style groups" in isolation; that was Huarpa, which occurred by itself in the bottom of his Pit 4 isolated from the rest of the deposit by 50 cm. of "washed stone and gravel" (Bennett 1953: 33). Above this sterile layer all four style groups were found together, and this mixture, in different proportions, was found in all

the other pits. In spite of the fact that there was mechanical evidence of mixture in the other pits, as we have noted, Bennett chose to seek indications of sequence in them by calculating the frequencies of the style groups in his arbitrary levels. He also treated the surface collection from the area of each pit as if it were a unit of superposition. All four style groups occurred from top to bottom of the pits, except, of course, in Pit 4, and there was no clear pattern in their fluctuations. However, Huarpa sherds were more frequent in all the surface units than in the levels below, and under the influence of this evidence Bennett decided that Huarpa was the latest of the style groups. This decision forced him to explain the situation in Pit 4 as a case of reversed stratigraphy. Subsequent work in the Huari area by Dorothy Menzel and me in 1958 suggests that the correct order was that given by Pit 4 which Bennett rejected. The associations of styles at other sites indicate that Huarpa must have been earlier than Wari, Ayacucho and Acuchimay rather than later. The situation at Huari which confused Bennett can be explained on the basis of certain peculiarities of Huarpa pottery. This style includes very large bowls with heavily thickened rims, usually having some simple painted decoration around them. Sherds deriving from these rims are almost indestructible and remain on the surface even when plowing and trampling have reduced most other sherds to virtually unrecognizable fragments. It was differential wear, not lateness of date, which made Huarpa sherds so abundant in Bennett's surface collections.

2. *Filling.* A fill is a deposition unit laid down for the purpose of altering the ground level. If the material for the fill is taken from an earlier midden, the result may be a "reverse stratigraphy" in which the cultural order does not correspond to the deposition order (for examples, see Heizer 1959: 328–43). Filling is common wherever monumental architecture is found but may occur even without it. Sometimes the fill differs in texture and structure from undisturbed midden, but fill does not necessarily have any formal distinguishing characteristics. The cultural material in a unit of fill may correspond to a single cultural unit; if it does, the rules for detecting mixing will not necessarily detect filling. Only other evidence of sequence will solve the problem.

3. *Collecting.* We usually make the assumption, in interpreting archaeological associations, that the date of use of an object is, for all practical purposes, the same as its date of manufacture. This assumption may not always be warranted. There are numerous ethnographic examples of the systematic collection and re-use of ancient objects (grinding stones, pottery vessels, jewelry, amulets), and some archaeological examples have been recorded (Lathrap 1956: 24). As archaeological chronologies become more refined we can expect cases of collecting to be identified with greater frequency. It may take work at many sites and very careful attention to stylistic contrasts in order to make a certain identification in such cases.

Mixing, filling, and collecting are situations which set limitations to the effectiveness of stratigraphic analysis as a way of establishing cultural sequences. A single stratigraphic excavation will not provide certainty as to the order of cultural succession unless all three of the limiting possibilities can be definitely eliminated. There are certain sites at which these possibilities can be eliminated, but the degree of certainty attainable depends as much on the situation in the ground as it does on how carefully the stratigraphic analysis is conducted. Stratified sites are rare everywhere, and ones that will yield an absolutely certain cultural sequence are even rarer.

It cannot be emphasized too strongly that the principle of superposition offers absolute certainty only of the sequence of deposition units at a particular site. The cultural sequence for the area may or may not be the same as the sequence of deposition units at the site studied; it will usually take more evidence than can be secured from one stratigraphic excavation to determine the cultural sequence with certainty.

Let us turn now to a consideration of seriation. Seriation is the arrangement of archaeological materials in a presumed chronological order on the basis of some logical principle other than superposition. The units seriated may be individual specimens of a particular kind (pottery vessels, stone axes) or units of archaeological association, such as grave lots or single deposition units of refuse, such as might be found in a "one period" site. The logical order on which the seriation is based is found in the combinations of features of style or inventory which characterize the units, rather than in the external relationships of the units

themselves. Hence, seriation involves a detailed study of style and inventory, with attention to the associations of features on individual specimens and in the units of archaeological association.

There are two types of seriation, distinguished by the principles of ordering on which they depend. We can call these types *evolutionary seriation* and *similiary seriation*, the latter term meaning "seriation by resemblance." Evolutionary seriation is done by assuming a universal rule of cultural or stylistic development, such as, for example, that development is always from simple to complex, or that artistic style always develops from realism to conventionalization. The rule which is assumed defines the relevance of the features to be studied and gives both the direction and the order of the development. No points of reference already fixed in time are needed. The credibility of the results depends, of course, entirely on the credibility of the universal rule by which the seriation is accomplished. Unfortunately, none of the rules which have been used so far for evolutionary seriation has any valid claim to universality. If approximately correct results have been achieved now and then by evolutionary seriation, it is no more than a coincidence. Until a rule of development is discovered which really does have universal applicability, evolutionary seriation is nothing but a waste of time.

Similiary seriation is quite a different matter. It is based on the assumption that, within a given cultural tradition, change in culture in general and change in style in particular are both usually gradual processes. On this assumption, objects or cultural units which are close to one another in time can be expected to resemble each other more, at least in certain features, than objects or cultural units which are further apart in time; as General Pitt-Rivers said, "like fits on to like" (Fox-Pitt-Rivers 1875: 308). No assumptions are made about the nature or direction of the changes taking place. This type of seriation was first done by John Evans in 1849 (Evans 1850).

The statement that change in a cultural tradition is usually gradual is one of the most general statements that can be made about human behavior. It appears to be valid within certain limitations which must be understood. There are two types of situations which may lead to sudden and substantial changes in a cultural or artistic tradition: strong outside influence suddenly felt, and archaism, the deliberate imitation of earlier style or custom. Both of these situations result in change which is not gradual in the sense of the general statement. Since similiary seriation depends on the assumption of gradual change, the credibility of its results depends on our ability to recognize the types of situations which do not fit the assumption, and to do so before or during the process of seriation. We shall come back to this problem after discussing some other conditions for successful seriation.

In order to obtain a sequence by similiary seriation, at least one extreme of the sequence must be known at the start of the project, since no assumption is being made about the order in which changes take place. In the New World the known extreme is often the style or cultural unit which was contemporary with European contact. If we can assume that all phases of the cultural tradition which are later than the time of contact will show some indication of European influence, we can consider that all cultural units which show no signs of such influence are earlier than the phase which we know to be contemporary with contact. The culture of the time of contact then becomes a known extreme from which the cultural units which are assumed to be earlier can be seriated back into the past by arranging them in an order of decreasing similarity to the known extreme. This type of argument enabled Francisco L. Cornely to make a highly credible seriation of five pre-contact cultural units in the Elqui Valley in northern Chile (Cornely 1950, 1956: 79–93).

Under the conditions generally prevailing in the New World, it is usually a safe assumption that cultural units later than the time of contact will show some evidence of European influence. It is not safe to assume, however, that each individual object made after the time of contact will show such influence; not uncommonly relatively few post-contact objects of native manufacture show any European influence at all. Cornely's assumption would therefore not justify an attempt to seriate unassociated objects using European contact as the later extreme of the sequence and identifying the contact by stylistic criteria. When both extremes are known and the materials to be seriated are of such a nature that it is possible to assume that they belong somewhere in the

gap we have optimum conditions for a successful and credible seriation.

Another factor which affects the credibility of the results of seriation is the way the ordering is done. Two different methods of seriational ordering are in current use: ordering by type frequency and ordering by continuity of features and variation in themes.

The method of ordering by type frequency is applicable only to refuse deposits and to objects which occur abundantly in refuse; potsherds are usually used. Standard samples are taken from the refuse, usually by collecting all sherds found in blocks of refuse of arbitrary dimensions. The sherds are then classified in formal types, and the frequency of each type is calculated for each refuse sample. Each refuse sample can be considered to be characterized by the presence of certain particular types in certain particular percentages. Ordering is done by arranging the refuse samples in such an order that the frequency of each pottery type shows a pattern of gradual increase to a maximum popularity and then gradual decrease to disappearance. This method should give the correct chronological order of the refuse samples if the following conditions are met:

1. The sherd samples are large enough so that the type frequencies reflect popularity rather than chance occurrence. It may be doubted that a sample of any type consisting of less than ten sherds gives a fair indication of the popularity of the type.

2. The span of time represented by each refuse sample is relatively short.

3. The patterns of frequency in the samples are such that they can be arranged in an order in which there are few sudden jumps. If there are long spans of time not represented in the samples this condition may not be met.

Up to this point I have been assuming that the units being seriated are excavated refuse units, perhaps from a number of different small sites no one of which shows stratigraphic differences. J. A. Ford maintains, however, that surface samples from unexcavated sites can be seriated in the same way as excavated units, and even that a single seriation can be made using both surface and excavated samples (Phillips, Ford, and Griffin 1951: 219–33; Ford 1949). The use of surface samples for type frequency seriation introduces two further assumptions which are not involved in the seriation of excavated refuse units. The first assumption is that the frequencies of types in surface collections are not affected by differences in the nature of the site; for example, that the surface of a refuse deposit with looted burials in it will give the same type frequencies as a contemporary refuse deposit without burials. The second assumption is that surface sherds are subject to the same kind and degree of "natural selection" on all the sites compared, so that frequencies would not be altered by differences of weathering, plowing, trampling, pothunting, or prior collecting. Ford apparently feels that these assumptions are justified by the fact that his seriation of surface samples from lower Mississippi Valley sites gave nearly the same sequence which Phillips arrived at by stratigraphic analysis. I am not sufficiently familiar with the archaeology of the lower Mississippi Valley to compare field conditions there with those in Peru, where I have worked, but I would certainly be very reluctant to make these two assumptions about Peruvian surface collections in the light of the surface conditions which I have observed at Peruvian sites. The results of Bennett's excavations at Huari, which we have already reviewed, reveal the danger of including both surface and excavated samples in a single seriation.

The second method of seriational ordering now in use is the method of ordering by continuity of features and variation in themes. Because this method is based on observations of presence and absence rather than frequency, it involves fewer sampling problems than the method of ordering by type frequency, and hence it can be applied to a wider range of materials, including rare and unassociated specimens as well as materials found in some kind of archaeological association. The units of discussion are features and themes, defined by contrast in the particular materials to be studied. It is unnecessary, and even undesirable, to use types as the units of this kind of seriation. Continuity of features and variation in themes are two complementary principles of ordering which provide checks on one another and should be used together, although it would be theoretically possible to use either one separately.

Ordering by continuity of features rests on the assumption that the occurrence of features of style in time is not random, but that most features have a continuous span of existence. A feature is introduced, used for a while, and then dropped. Naturally, not all features can be expected to show this ideal pattern of distribution; a feature which has been used earlier

in a sequence may reappear because it is reinvented, because it is reborrowed from another tradition, or because its use is deliberately revived. Furthermore, the investigator rarely controls a sample of material sufficiently large to document the complete span of existence of every significant feature. Nevertheless, the assumption that most features will show this pattern of distribution is defensible. In seriating on this assumption the objects or associated lots to be ordered are arranged in that sequence which provides continuous spans of existence for the largest number of features. Since there are always some features which do not show the assumed pattern of distribution, it is important to study enough features so that the exceptions will fall in a minority. Some very inaccurate seriations have been made by archaeologists who were in too much of a hurry and relied on three or four features which turned out to be among those which did not have continuous spans of existence. The larger the sample and the more features studied, the greater will be the reliability of a seriation by continuity of features.

The precision with which an individual specimen can be dated by observing the features associated on it will depend on the number of features the observer is able to distinguish on it and the length of their spans of existence. Generally speaking, the more elaborately a specimen is decorated, the more precisely it can be dated.

In ordering by variation in themes, the investigator selects some complex feature or theme which is found in several variations in the material he is studying, and he makes an arrangement of the variations in order of similarity with reference to the known extremes. In seriating pottery, for example, the profiles of food bowls might be taken as a theme, and the variations in bowl profiles used to establish a tentative ordering. Variations in the proportions of bottle spouts might provide another basis for ordering. If representational or geometric designs are present, variations in some unit of design can be seriated. In Nasca pottery designs, for example, a common figure is a man with an elaborate costume wearing a mouth mask and a forehead ornament. The variations in the way the forehead ornament and the hair are shown have proved to be sensitive chronological indicators for this style.

The important point is that the variations contrasted must be variations on the same theme, alternate ways of meeting the same technical or artistic problem. It makes no sense to treat one theme as a variation on another; for example, to treat bowls as a variation on the same theme as bottles and ask whether bowls were earlier than bottles or vice versa. The shapes were made for different purposes, and presumably people used both bowls and bottles of some kind at any given time.

A seriation of variations on one theme will give only a tentative order for those specimens or association units in which the particular theme occurs. The variations in other themes must then be studied to see if the tentative order also gives a series of gradual changes for these. Errors in the tentative order are revealed by discrepancies in the seriation of other themes, and the tentative order can be modified accordingly. The more different themes have been studied, the greater the confidence the seriational order merits.

If the seriation is done with specimens which were collected under such conditions that their archaeological context is known, the data of the archaeological associations can be used to relate the sequences of different themes to one another. When a bowl with a certain profile is found repeatedly in grave lot association with a jar with a certain curve in the neck the two varieties must be at least in part contemporaneous, even though they are decorated in very different ways. If the seriation has to be done with unassociated pieces, there will always be some pieces which cannot be seriated, because they do not share enough themes with the pieces on which the seriation is based.

In practice it is usually easier to make the original ordering by studying variations in themes and then to check it by charting the spans of existence of a substantial number of features. A minimum of 100 is recommended. The reverse procedure is also possible, however.

Now we can come back to the problem of the degree to which sudden outside influence and archaism, the situations which do not fit the assumption of gradual change, can be recognized and allowed for in a seriational study. In both cases the problem is different depending on whether the ordering is done by type frequencies or by studying continuity of features and variations in themes.

In ordering by type frequencies, sudden outside influence should be reflected in the sudden popularity of certain new types, probably correlated with an equally sudden decline in the proportion of old types. The same effect would be produced by a gap in the record, however, and there is nothing in the theory of seriation which would guide the investigator to the correct interpretation. Archaism, if it were common enough to show up at all in the sherd counts, would produce a curve showing two peaks of popularity for some of the types. If no allowance were made for the possibility of archaism the investigator would be likely to force certain samples into the wrong place in the sequence.

In ordering by continuity of features and variations in themes, specimens showing sudden outside influence could probably not be seriated in the same sequence with earlier pieces. If the earlier tradition survived at all, however, there would be certain themes discoverable in which gradual change did take place, and these themes could be used as the basis of the ordering. The problem could probably not be handled without some evidence, in the form of archaeological associations, of what kinds of pieces were contemporary with one another.

Archaistic specimens in which the archaism affects only a few features can be identified without much difficulty in ordering by continuity of features if enough features are studied. Such specimens can also be distinguished in some cases by the presence of anomalies in the combinations of theme variations they show. Really good imitations of earlier pieces cannot be identified by seriational methods alone, but they can be detected readily enough if archaeological associations of contemporaneity are available.

We can conclude that both methods of ordering are vulnerable to errors resulting from sudden outside influence and archaism, but that the difficulties can be avoided in the method of seriation by continuity of features and theme variation by checking the seriational order against archaeological associations of contemporaneity, such as grave lots or deposition units of refuse.

To sum up the comparison of stratigraphy and seriation, it appears that there are several different ways of doing both, and that the chances of attaining credible results depend on the nature of the archaeological evidence available, the alternative method chosen, and the degree to which the theoretical limitations of the method are kept in mind in the course of the work. There is one type of seriation, namely similiary seriation in which the ordering is done by continuity of features and theme variation, which can give results fully as credible as the best stratigraphic analysis, provided that associations of contemporaneity are used as well as unassociated specimens.

If the investigator has the time and the choice, he can profitably combine the methods by excavating a stratified site, making a stratigraphic analysis of the materials found, and then doing a parallel seriational analysis of the same materials. Since the limitations of the two methods are different, each provides a check on the other. If the results agree, the maximum credibility has been attained.

The common belief that stratigraphic analysis always gives more credible results than seriation rests in part on misunderstanding of the limitations of the two methods, in part on the professional bias of most archaeologists in favor of settling all problems by excavation, and in part on the fact that examples of deficient seriational studies come readily to mind. Our review does not confirm this common belief, but it does suggest that there may be more different ways to be wrong in seriation than there are in stratigraphic analysis.

Acknowledgments. This paper is a by-product of research on Peruvian archaeology being carried out on a grant from the National Science Foundation, and the Foundation's support is gratefully acknowledged. Many of the ideas presented are the product of discussions with Dorothy Menzel, Edward P. Lanning, Lawrence E. Dawson, Dwight T. Wallace, Eugene A. Hammel, and Donald W. Lathrap, and I have been influenced by their research experience as well as my own. A shorter version of this paper was read at the 4th Annual Meeting of the Kroeber Anthropological Society, Berkeley, May 21, 1960.

ADAMS, F. D.
    1954 *The Birth and Development of the Geological Sciences.* Dover Publications, New York.

BENNETT, W. C.
    1953 Excavations at Wari, Ayacucho, Peru. *Yale University Publications in Anthropology,* No. 49. New Haven.

CORNELY, F. L.
    1950 Prehistoria del territorio Diaguita chileno (provincias de Coquimbo y Atacama). *Publicaciones de la Sociedad Arqueológica de La Serena,* Boletin, No. 5, pp. 3–18. La Serena.
    1956 *Cultura Diaguita chilena y cultura de El Molle.* Editorial del Pacífico, Santiago.

DUNBAR, C. O., AND JOHN RODGERS
    1957 *Principles of Stratigraphy.* John Wiley and Sons, New York; Chapman and Hall, London.

EVANS, JOHN
    1850 On the Date of British Coins. *The Numismatic Chronicle and Journal of the Numismatic Society,* Vol. 12, No. 4, pp. 127–37. London.

FENTON, C. L., AND M. A. FENTON
    1952 *Giants of Geology.* Doubleday, Garden City.

FORD, J. A.
    1949 Cultural Dating of Prehistoric Sites in Virú Valley, Peru. *Anthropological Papers of the American Museum of Natural History,* Vol. 43, Part 1, pp. 29–89. New York.

FOX-PITT-RIVERS, A. H. L.
    1875 On the Principles of Classification Adopted in the Arrangement of his Anthropological Collection, now Exhibited in the Bethnal Green Museum. *The Journal of the Anthropological Institute of Great Britain and Ireland,* Vol. 4, pp. 293–308. London.

FRASER, A. D.
    1935 Thomas Jefferson as Field Archaeologist. *The Four Arts,* Vol. 2, No. 3, pp. 3–4, 15. Richmond.

HEIZER, R. F. (EDITOR)
    1959 *The Archaeologist at Work; A Source Book in Archaeological Method and Interpretation.* Harper and Brothers, New York.

JEFFERSON, THOMAS
    1787 *Notes on the State of Virginia,* second English edition. John Stockdale, London.

LATHRAP, D. W. (EDITOR)
    1956 An Archaeological Classification of Culture Contact Situations. In "Seminars in Archaeology: 1955," edited by Robert Wauchope, pp. 1–30. *Memoirs of the Society for American Archaeology,* No. 11. Salt Lake City.

LEHMANN, J. G.
    1756 *Versuch einer Geschichte von Flötz-Gebürgen, betreffend deren Entstehung, Lage, darinne befindliche Metallen, Mineralien und Fossilien. . . .* Klütersche Buchhandlung, Berlin.

LISCH, G. C. F.
    1847 Der Verein für Lübeckische Geschichte. *Allgemeine Zeitschrift für Geschichte,* Band 7, pp. 377–81. Berlin.

NEAVERSON, ERNEST
    1955 *Stratigraphical Palaeontology; A Study of Ancient Life Provinces,* second edition. Clarendon Press, Oxford.

PHILLIPS, PHILIP, J. A. FORD, AND J. B. GRIFFIN
    1951 Archaeological Survey in the Lower Mississippi Alluvial Valley, 1940–1947. *Papers of the Peabody Museum, Harvard University,* Vol. 25. Cambridge.

ROWE, J. H.
    1959 Archaeological Dating and Cultural Process. *Southwestern Journal of Anthropology,* Vol. 15, No. 4, pp. 317–24. Albuquerque.

STAMP, L. D.
    1934 *An Introduction to Stratigraphy (British Isles),* second edition. Thomas Murby & Co., London.

UNIVERSITY OF CALIFORNIA
Berkeley, Calif.
April, 1960

THE DOPPLER EFFECT AND ARCHAEOLOGY:
A CONSIDERATION OF THE SPATIAL
ASPECTS OF SERIATION[1]

JAMES DEETZ AND EDWIN DETHLEFSEN

IN THEIR WELL REASONED and lucid description of seriation methods employed in the lower Mississippi Valley, Phillips, Ford and Griffin (1951:219-223) state the basic assumptions which form the foundation for their analytical procedure. These assumptions can be briefly summarized as follows:

1. Population was stable in the survey area.
2. The majority of sites were of short duration of occupation.
3. Cultural change in the area in question was gradual, and migration had not occurred.
4. Pottery types used in seriation would show a single peak popularity curve when measured through time.
5. Pottery type frequency curves would differ somewhat in each part of the area at any point in time.

It is the purpose of this paper to make explicit two additional assumptions and to suggest that their inclusion with those already stated might lend some small measure of sophistication to the seriation method. The suggestions here offered should not be taken as an adverse critique of seriation methods in general; the writers subscribe to the validity of this approach to chronological ordering. Our intent rather is to attempt a modest degree of methodological refinement.

The first of our additional assumptions is that any type used in seriation originated at a single locus and subsequently spread outward from that point. An artifact type used in seriation, in order to have utility, must occur at two or more sites. This occurrence at more than one locus can either be interpreted as evidence of the movement of the mental template which was responsible for its production, either through migration or through less dramatic, secondary diffusion processes, or as evidence of the independent formulation of this template at each site of its occurrence. The latter is extremely unlikely, and Phillips,

1 This is a revised version of a paper read at the November 1964 annual meeting of the American Anthropological Association, Detroit, Michigan. The authors acknowledge the valuable suggestions of William Mayer-Oakes, who was the first to perceive the analogy between the Doppler effect and gravestone style diffusion phenomena.

196

Ford and Griffin (1951:229), aware of the role of diffusion in cultural process, select the former alternative as the only reasonable interpretation:

> The groups of ideas to whose products have been tagged such names as Mazique Incised did not spring up simultaneously all over the area. They moved from one part to another, and that took time. For example, the idea of red slipping on clay-tempered vessels (Larto Red Filmed) apparently was moving from south to north through the region, while cord-marking on clay tempered pots (Mulberry Creek Cord-Marked) was moving from northeast to south. Naturally, the former is earlier to the south, and the latter to the north.

The second assumption, anticipated in the above quotation, is that sites further removed from the locus of origin of any type will show the occurrence of that type, at a given frequency, later in time. A corollary to this proposition is that a type might still be present at some distance from its point of inception after it had disappeared from that point.

These two assumptions can be made more explicit through the use of a model in which rate of change and dimensions of spatial and temporal units are held constant (Fig. 1). The model demonstrates the spread of a single type outward in two directions from a center, indicated as locus M on the horizontal space axis. Loci N-P and N′-P′ are progressively more distant from locus M, and distances between all adjacent loci on the space axis are equal. The vertical axis of the model represents time, with each number unit, 1 through 10, representing a time segment of equal duration. As in all conventional seriation charts, the earliest time level is at the bottom. The occurrence of the type through time is indicated by percentage bars at each locus, with a constant rate of change of twenty-five percent for each time unit indicated by the width of the bar. Thus, at each locus, identical patterns of increase and decrease of the type occur. However, since the type originates at M, and spreads from M to P in one direction, and to P′ in the other, its appearance at a given frequency is later at each locus further removed from the center. For example, at M the frequency is 50 percent during time period two and reaches the same percentage at the next locus in each direction in time period three, for it is diffusing one space unit in each unit of time. Since the type originates at locus M, spreads to loci N-P and N′-P′ moving one space unit per time unit, and goes through an identical increase and decrease of popularity at each locus, its maximum occurrence is later in direct proportion to its distance from the locus of origin. Thus, during time unit 8, although it has already disappeared at locus M, the type is still relatively popular at loci P and P′, and progressively less popular at loci closer to M. This graphic presentation of the spread of a type through time and space should serve to make

James Deetz and Edwin Dethlefsen

the two additional assumptions clear. While a constant set of circumstances such as this model represents would probably never occur in reality, the variables of space, time and type frequency change are correctly shown as they relate to one another, and a clear presentation of certain phenomena is made possible.

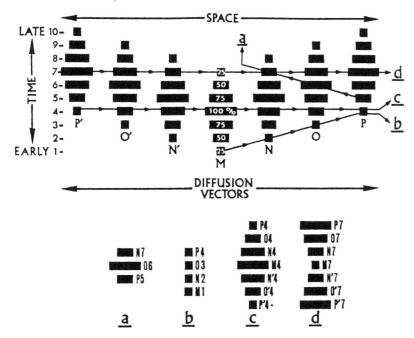

FIG. 1. Model illustrating the spread of a single type from a point (M) outward in two directions.

The non-simultaneity of inception, increase, decrease and disappearance of any type in a given area permits the construction of a number of different developmental formulations from the same set of data. Depending on whether samples are taken from short term occupation sites which become successively later in a direction running counter to the direction of diffusion (in the model P to M, P′ to M) or from sites which are located such that they become later in an alignment running with the direction of diffusion (M to P, M to P′), quite different apparent rates of change are indicated for the type. In the former case, a rate of change greater than the true rate is indicated (Fig. 1, graph a); in the latter, a rate of change is obtained which is less than the true rate (Fig. 1, graph b). This difference between the apparent and true rates and between the types

of change of frequency has a close parallel in the Doppler effect, a familiar phenomenon of the physical world. Anyone who has ridden on a train has noticed that the clanging of a station bell rises in pitch as one is approaching the source of the sound and drops sharply in pitch as one moves away from the bell. This perceived shift in frequency is due to the fact that as one is approaching a fixed source of sound, more waves are encountered per unit of time than are actually being emitted, and an apparent increase in frequency (pitch) results. Conversely, as one moves away from such a source, the perceived number of wave maxima is lower than the true number emitted in any given time interval, resulting in an apparent decrease in frequency. The variable factor in this case is the observer; his motion combined with the outward dispersal of sound waves is additive as he approaches and subtractive as he departs from the source. The more rapid his motion, the greater the discrepancy between observed and true frequencies.

The model showing the spread of a single type through space, with constant spatial and temporal units, can be used to demonstrate that a Doppler-like process should be considered in seriation procedure. As shown above, if one should sample short term occupancy sites at loci M through P, moving away from M, and if these sites are progressively later in time as one moves away from M, no change in the percentage of occurrence of the type from site to site will be indicated if one space unit is traversed for each time unit (Fig. 1, graph b). A constant percentage of occurrence results because the archaeologist, the observer in this instance, is in effect moving through space at the same rate as the type is diffusing, one space unit per time unit. In this case, although the true rate of change is twenty-five percent per unit of time, the observed rate is zero percent. Should the observer slow down, moving only one space unit for every two units of time, the apparent rate is the same as the true rate, since the observer is effectively waiting at each locus for one time unit to pass, bringing the frequency at the new location to the same level as it was in the prior one during the previous time unit.

A sampling of sites which become later in time as one approaches point M (P′ to M, P to M) produces a graph which indicates an apparent rate of change which is twice the true rate if one space unit is traversed in one time unit (Fig. 1, graph a). Increases of fifty percent per unit of time are indicated, while the true rate remains a constant twenty-five percent per time unit. In this case the increase results from the motion of the observer toward the source of diffusion. Increasing the rate of motion will make an even higher rate apparent, with two space units traversed in one time unit producing an apparent rate of change three times the true rate, or seventy-five per cent per time unit. The close analogy

James Deetz and Edwin Dethlefsen

between this phenomenon and the Doppler effect is obvious; and in a controlled model, such as the one here employed, the Doppler formula can be slightly modified and shown to be applicable. The Doppler formula, as it applies to sound waves from a fixed source, is:

$$f' = \left\{ \frac{v \pm v_0}{v} \right\} f$$

where f' is the frequency heard by the observer, v the velocity of sound in the transmitting medium, v_0 the velocity of the observer and f the true frequency. In the numerator, the plus sign is used if the observer is approaching the source, the minus sign if he is moving away from the source. The analogous formula, applicable to diffusion as demonstrated by the model, is:

$$r' = \left\{ \frac{d \pm v_0}{d} \right\} r$$

where r' is observed rate of change (percent per unit time), d the diffusion rate (space units per time unit), v_0 the observer's rate of motion (space units per time unit) and r the true rate of change (percent per time unit).

By passing through the model in various directions, a number of different formulations of rate and direction of change can be graphed from identical data. The differences are a function of differences in sampling direction in time and space. Crossing the model in the same time unit at a time when the type has reached its maximum occurrence at locus M produces a perfect "battleship-shaped" diagram, even though the spatial units are all in the same time unit (Fig. 1, graph c). A sampling of contemporary sites at a time when the type has nearly vanished at the center but remains as a popular type at more distant loci results in a wasp-waisted diagram, which if it were to result in the routine course of seriation would be considered as good evidence of improper chronological ordering of the sites in question (Fig. 1, graph d). The degree to which this effect is manifested is largely a function of the rate of diffusion of a particular style. The slower the rate, the less likely there is to be a pronounced skew resulting from direction of sampling. Furthermore, the cases demonstrated with the model

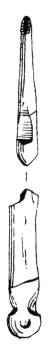

assume a selection of sites in an order which would be somewhat improbable in practice. Nonetheless, there seems to be considerable heuristic value in demonstrating this phenomenon, if for no other reason than to suggest that imperfect alignments, which almost always result in the seriation of a large number of types, might result at least in part from this cause. An awareness of this phenomenon might also lead to a more reasonable interpretation of certain evidence.

To move from a neat model, in which all variables are controlled and other quantities held constant, to the real world, where such control is rarely possible, is a constant problem in the application of theoretical constructs. Like most of the current body of archaeological method, seriation has been devised and applied using data in which a rigorous measure of control has been impossible. Recent studies in the spread of gravestone design types in eighteenth century New England have directed attention to a controlled laboratory situation in which to check a number of the basic assumptions of archaeological method (Dethlefsen and Deetz MS). These stones and their designs are admirably suited to such a study; they were the products of non-specialists who resided in small towns and provided stones for the immediate area, they are precisely dated and fixed in space, and their designs are integrally tied to the culture which produced them. The present paper stems from an awareness of some of the more detailed aspects of the spread of style which the authors gained through working with gravestone designs in southern New England.

Between 1700 and 1800, colonial gravestones in eastern Massachusetts were decorated in three universally occurring design types: death's heads, cherubs and urns shaded by willow trees. The death's head design is earliest, and is replaced by the cherub motif during the latter half of the eighteenth century, to be replaced by the urn and willow design at the close of that century. The pattern exhibited by each of these styles as it increases and decreases through time is striking support to one of Phillips, Ford and Griffin's assumptions, that the rise and decline in the popularity of a style or type will be in the form of a long single peaked curve (1951:220). Figure 2 shows the distribution of the three universal styles and two local designs between 1700 and 1829 in the cemetery at Concord, Mass. The full single peaked curve is seen to best advantage in the cherub and Roman motifs; the urn and willow design declines in popularity after 1829, a change manifested in other cemeteries but not represented at Concord. The death's head design is the earliest for which an adequately large sample can be obtained for proper quantification, and it is represented in the figure only during the later period of its existence. In addition to the three design types which are universally distributed throughout the eastern Massachusetts area, a number of

James Deetz and Edwin Dethlefsen

local styles exist and, like the universal styles, exhibit single peak curves as they are plotted for temporal change in relative frequency of occurrence. Because gravestone designs follow the predicted developmental form and can be precisely plotted in time and space, they provide a tightly controlled set of data in which to attempt a demonstration that the effect shown in the model has a close counterpart in reality.

Concord

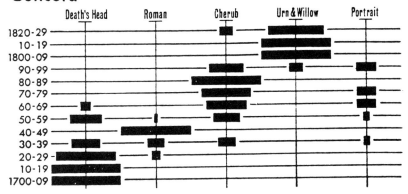

FIG. 2. Stylistic change and succession in an eastern Massachusetts cemetery.

The style selected for this demonstration is a distinctive local design, the so-called "Roman" motif. This design occurs in the Concord and Sudbury River drainages west of Boston, with the earliest occurrence falling in the third decade of the eighteenth century and the latest in the seventh decade. All stones of this type in the Harvard-Groton-Lexington-Sudbury area are known to have been carved by Jonathon Worcester, a stone cutter who resided in Harvard, Massachusetts (Forbes 1927:77). Worcester seems to have copied this design from stone cutters in Essex County, Massachusetts, fifty miles northeast of Harvard. Here, designs very similar to Worcester's occur in a number of cemeteries during the first half of the eighteenth century, including some which date to the first decade, having been cut during the years just after Worcester's birth in 1707. Worcester's rendering of this design is very conservative, showing little variation between his earliest and latest stones. He died in 1754, and apparently left a large number of cut stones to his wife, since they continue to appear until the late 1760's. At least one entry in the probate records shows that stones of this type were being purchased from his widow, this being the case of the executor of Josiah Burge of Westford, who purchased an unspecified number of stones from the "widow

Worcester" in 1756. Burge's stone bearing Worcester's unmistakable design can be seen today in the cemetery at Westford.

To demonstrate the Doppler analogue as it operates in gravestone design distributions, five cemeteries were investigated, and the percentage of the Roman motif calculated for each sequent ten year period in each cemetery beginning in 1720 and ending in 1769. The study cemeteries are located at Harvard, Groton, Concord, Sudbury and Lexington, Massachusetts. The five graphs for the design in each of the five cemeteries were then arranged in order according to their distance from Worcester's residence in Harvard. By positioning the cemeteries in this fashion, one is constructing a graph which is identical in its basic arrangement to the Doppler model (Fig. 3A). The style can then be sampled in succeed-

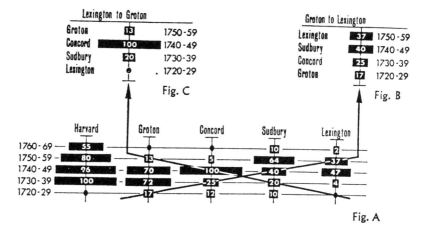

FIG. 3. Frequency of Roman design, by decades, in study cemeteries.

ing decades, moving first toward Harvard, then away from Harvard, in each case beginning in the 1720's and ending in the 1760's. If the effect observed in the model is manifested in this second construct, then relatively little change in popularity of the Roman style should be observed as one moves away from Harvard while moving through time (Fig. 3B). By sampling the same set of cemeteries in identical time ranking but moving from Lexington, the most distant, toward the Harvard center, an apparent rate of change in popularity which exceeds the true rate should result (Fig. 3C). Inspection of the graphs derived from this procedure shows such to be the case, with a high degree of agreement with the predicted results.

James Deetz and Edwin Dethlefsen

The cemetery at Harvard could not be utilized in the formulation because it is saturated with Worcester stones for three decades, a weighting of the data which results from Worcester's residence in Harvard. Frequency of the Roman design at Harvard is eighty percent or more during three decades from 1730 until 1759, a much greater popularity than observed in the other study cemeteries. The graphs are constructed, therefore, to have decade samples begin and end at Groton, the nearest of the four other cemeteries to the Harvard center. This produces a four decade series through four cemeteries. The mean rate of change in these four cemeteries is 39 percent per decade and ranges from 61 percent at Concord to 38 percent at Groton and 29 percent at both Sudbury and Lexington. The mean rate of change along the Harvard to Lexington axis (Fig. 3B) is 9 percent per decade, while the mean rate along the Lexington to Harvard axis (Fig. 3C) is 62 percent per decade. While four decade samples are obtainable moving with the direction of diffusion, only three decades, showing a rapid increase and decrease, can be graphed while moving against the direction of diffusion (Fig. 3C). At no cemetery is there only a three decade span of the Roman type.

It must be emphasized that the entity which is diffusing in this case is a preference for a certain style, since all of the stones were carved at Harvard and sent to more distant points for erection. At the two cemeteries further removed from Harvard, a significant percentage of stones was purchased and erected after this preference had disappeared in the two nearer cemeteries. At the most distant cemetery, Lexington, no Roman stones were erected during the 1720's, a time when they were being utilized in numbers at locations nearer the source of supply. The graph showing frequency of occurrence of the Roman type in the Harvard cemetery is of significance in this connection. Although the two nearer cemeteries have no Roman stones on graves of the 1760's there was apparently an adequate supply, since they are present at Harvard during this decade in 55 percent of all cases. The pattern here seems to be one of people purchasing stones from Worcester's widow for use at Lexington and Sudbury after their use had ceased at Concord and Groton. Further insight regarding the more rapid disappearance of Roman stones after 1759 in Concord and Groton is provided by the historical record, which shows that in 1756, a new carver, William Park of Groton, had filled the vacancy in the Harvard area created by the death of Jonathon Worcester. Park's stones rapidly became popular and occur in great numbers in Groton, Harvard and Concord, although they are less prominent in Sudbury and Lexington.

The progressive reduction in rate of change per decade of the Roman style

recorded in cemeteries further removed from Harvard might be a manifestation of a more generally distributed effect, that of the damping action on the vigor of a style by distance. The great popularity of the Roman style at Harvard results from Worcester's residence in that town. As one observes its popularity at greater distances, there is an expectable reduction, which probably results from the inclusion of other styles radiating from other centers at these locations. The mean frequency of occurrence of the style between 1720 and 1760 at Harvard is 83 percent, at Groton 43 percent, at Concord 35 percent, at Sudbury 28 percent and at Lexington 21 percent. Such a diminution in popularity is expectable, and it is accompanied by a reduction in rate of change, from 38 and 61 percent at Groton and Concord respectively, both equal to or greater than the mean rate, to a mean rate of only 29 percent per decade at Lexington and Sudbury, well below the mean for all four localities.

It has been shown that a simple formula can be used to state the relationship between diffusion rate, observer rate, and true and observed rates of frequency change in the model used to demonstrate the effects of spatial location on seriation ordering. While the application of the model to the distribution of a gravestone style has shown the relationships indicated by the formula to hold in a general way, the inevitable irregularities in the gravestone data which result from sampling problems, differences in distance between cemeteries and other imponderable factors might make any application of the formula to this corpus of data merely approximate. In spite of these problems, the formula was found to fit with remarkable precision. Computing the difference between true and apparent rates of change with an approaching observer, and solving for quantity r' produced a figure of 72 percent per decade as compared to a known apparent rate of 62 percent.[2] Similar results were obtained when r' was obtained for a receding observer, with an r' of 6.5 percent produced by calculation with the known apparent rate being 9 percent. Both solutions are certainly order-of-magnitude indicators at the very least.

It has been shown that a striking analogy can be drawn between the Doppler effect and certain aspects of the spread of a style or type through space and over time. An awareness of the existence of this factor in seriation ordering might aid in clarifying the relationships between different types at different locations, and in explaining discrepancies which might emerge in different seriational arrangements from the same area. This effect might conceivably produce an impression of sudden intrusion of a type, when in fact such a disruption did not occur. On

2 The following quantities were used: $d = 6$ miles per decade, $v_0 = 5$ miles per decade (mean distance between cemeteries), $r = 39\%$ (mean rate of change in four cemeteries).

James Deetz and Edwin Dethlefsen

the other hand, more gradual change within certain types might not indicate cultural conservatism but merely sampling direction. In both the theoretical model and its application, only one type was considered. Seriation, which proceeds normally using a quantity of types, can still achieve its stated purpose without introducing a spatial axis to formulations, but interpretation of results might be sharpened by taking this effect into consideration. Further refinement along the lines suggested in this paper might also eventually enable the prehistorian intentionally to sample his sites along a line known to represent a diffusion vector, thereby permitting the postulation of site interaction, rates of spread, and the existence of factors which either impede or accelerate the movement of a cultural idea. Factors of this type might include exogamy, endogamy, political boundaries, trade networks, linguistic areas or any other cultural pattern which is known to affect social interaction. As such, consideration of this as yet unnamed but seemingly important effect in cultural reconstruction has at least potential importance.

BIBLIOGRAPHY

DETHLEFSEN, EDWIN, AND JAMES DEETZ
    MS Death's Heads, Cherubs and Willow Trees. *American Antiquity* (in press).
FORBES, HARRIET
    1927 *Gravestones of Early New England.* Boston: Houghton Mifflin Co.
PHILLIPS, PHILLIP, JAMES A. FORD, AND JAMES B. GRIFFIN
    1951 *Archaeological Survey in the Lower Mississippi Alluvial Valley, 1940-1947.* Papers of the Peabody Museum, Harvard University, vol. XXV.

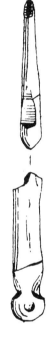

UNIVERSITY OF CALIFORNIA
   SANTA BARBARA, CALIFORNIA
HARVARD UNIVERSITY
   CAMBRIDGE, MASSACHUSETTS

The Doppler Effect and Archaeology

THE IMPORTANCE OF BOTH ANALYTIC AND TAXONOMIC CLASSIFICATION IN THE TYPE-VARIETY SYSTEM

Jeremy A. Sabloff and Robert E. Smith

ABSTRACT

The type-variety system of ceramic analysis, as currently used at many sites in southern Mesoamerica, differs in certain respects, especially in emphasis, from the system outlined by Smith, Willey, and Gifford in 1960. The reports on the pottery from the lowland Maya sites of Mayapán, Yucatán, Mexico and Seibal, Petén, Guatemala, in both their overall formats and the specific formats of their descriptive sections, have combined certain aspects of both taxonomic (typological) and analytic (modal) classification. It is argued that the type-variety system, as employed at these two sites, overcomes many of the objections to typological analyses recently raised by J. V. Wright (1967) and provides an adequate basis for both tight intersite comparisons in southern Mesoamerica and reanalyses of the ceramic data by other archaeologists in future studies.

THE PROBLEM of classifying artifacts, and specifically pottery, has been of much importance in archaeology, and, through the years, discussions of various points of view have often appeared in archaeological journals. In the New World, discussions of the methodology of ceramic analyses have tended to polarize into two positions. One position emphasizes modes while the other emphasizes types. In a recent paper, J. V. Wright (1967) has offered a perceptive criticism of the typological position and has praised the merits of attribute analysis. He advocates the use of the latter method in the Iroquois area, while eschewing use of the former. It is our feeling, however, that the type-variety system of ceramic analysis (Smith, Willey, and Gifford 1960; Gifford 1960), which essentially offers a typological approach to the study of pottery, provides an effective combination of some of the merits of attribute analysis, which Wright has delineated, in addition to nullifying some of his criticisms of typological analysis. We further feel that it is the most useful means of ceramic analysis available today in southern Mesoamerica and possibly in other areas as well. Since the manner in which the type-variety system is used at the present differs not only among various students but also differs somewhat from the strictures described in 1960, and since much of the detailed data which have resulted from the use of this kind of typological analysis is unavailable in print, we feel that a discussion of the type-variety system as used at the lowland Maya

sites of Mayapán, Yucatán, Mexico and Seibal, Petén, Guatemala may be of some value.

BRIEF SUMMARY OF THE SYSTEM

The type-variety system, like any other system of ceramic analysis, is dependent on the recognition and use of all attributes of a ceramic collection. What differentiates various systems is the manner in which these attributes are employed.

In the type-variety system, the attributes are separated into several categories: ware, type, variety, and group.

Ware. The ware attributes are those associated with paste composition and surface finish. Paste composition may be identified through paste texture, kind of temper, paste hardness (rarely used), porosity, and color. Surface finish is recognized by means of slip or the lack of slip, by smoothness or roughness, by luster acquired through burnishing, by gloss or by matte finish, and by color. A defined ware is a ceramic assemblage in which all attributes of paste composition (with the possible exception of temper) and of surface finish remain constant. A ware is not as limited in time as are types and varieties.

Type. The type attributes as used in the Maya area are basically of two kinds: those dealing with decorative techniques, and those which are concerned with vessel form. We define type as representing an aggregate of visually distinct ceramic attributes already objectified within one or (generally) several varieties which, when taken as a whole, are indicative of a particular class of pottery produced during a specific time interval within a specific region.

Variety. Theoretically, the ceramic variety (Smith, Willey, and Gifford 1960) has been viewed as the basic unit of analysis which, in due course, consequent upon an increased depth of total ceramic knowledge, either becomes the type (as the established variety) or one of a number of varieties within the type. Recent experience, however, has shown that the type provides a more practical basis for ceramic analysis. Minor, but significant, variations within the type, either intrasite or intersite, may be analyzed on a variety level. These variations may be related to the type-diagnostic attributes of

278

decorative technique and vessel form, or they may be concerned with a change in design style or the use of a different temper.

Group. This is a collection of closely related types that demonstrate a consistency in range of variation in form and color. The types of any group are (roughly) contemporaneous (that is, elements of the same ceramic complex or complexes) and are also always components of the same ware. Group is a concept which is most useful for lumping like material belonging to the same ware and sometimes not amenable to separation into types (too small or too weathered), or for material belonging to a ware (Fine Orange, Plumbate, Slate, etc.) which is associated with several phases.

Through the combined use of the ware, type, variety, and group categories, the establishment of ceramic complexes and a ceramic sequence is made possible, and the chronological development of pottery in time and space is brought to light. This is taxonomic classification by means of type-variety analysis.

Another system is that of mode analysis. The mode is considered to be a selected attribute or cluster of attributes which display significance in their own right. Modes can help in design-style analysis, in establishing a mode tradition, which is a cultural trait distribution through time, and in establishing a horizon style or cultural trait distribution through space. This is analytic classification by means of mode analysis (see also Rouse 1939).

Both the type-variety concept and the modal system form part of any ceramic picture. Although they differ in emphasis, the two kinds of study need not be kept apart. As Smith, Willey, and Gifford (1960: 331) point out, "the type-variety study should be integrated with the mode study and neither should be conducted or set forth in a mutually exclusive manner." Yet in almost all the published papers which use the type-variety system, the study of individual modes is either forgotten, limited to form modes, or relegated to a fairly minor role. As Culbert (1967: 85) has noted, this neglect can cause a serious loss of information and can damage the utility of the type-variety system.

RECENT USE OF THE SYSTEM

Three recently published ceramic studies (Culbert 1965: Wallrath 1967; Parsons 1967) make use, in varying degrees, of the type-variety concept. The Culbert report on "The Ceramic

History of the Central Highlands of Chiapas, Mexico" uses a combined seriation and stratigraphic procedure which is very well suited to the material. His types are established on a paste and temper basis, although many of them bear color or surface treatment designations such as Mercedes Red, Teopica White, Xakiltik Unslipped, and San Sebastian Fine Red. Furthermore, most of these types include various techniques of decoration which are buried in the type descriptions. Thus, the descriptions become so all inclusive that they lose the value of separation enjoyed by using *ware* to incorporate attributes of paste composition and surface finish, *type* to combine decorative techniques and vessel form, *variety* to differentiate within a type because of a new design style or a different temper or whatever, and *group* to absorb those sherds that have a number of common attributes but cannot certainly be placed in a particular type. Forms are listed under each type and then again as a mode at the end of each phase. This practice is quite commendable since, in most Mesoamerican ceramic collections, form modes are of much significance and may help determine to which group or complex a sherd belongs, when other modes are lacking. Nevertheless, there are many more modes than just those of form which deserve similar treatment.

In the Wallrath (1967) study of the Isthmus of Tehuantepec pottery, an attempt is made to follow the type-variety system. However, too often the type is actually the ware (Lieza Self-Slipped, Radani Gray, Esquipulas Burnished, Loteca Thick, Guibixo Thick, Nichi Fine-Grained, Huayabal Leathery, Mitiac Domestic, etc.). Decorative techniques which are found abundantly in these so-called types are hidden away in the descriptions instead of standing out in the names of the established types. In other words, although the descriptions under the type designation are ample and excellent, too much is lodged under "type." Wallrath also has a section on significant traits which takes care of the mode analysis.

Parsons (1967) was able to use stratigraphy to determine the sequence of ceramic complexes at Bilbao, Guatemala. He has also employed the type-variety system much as it was envisioned by Smith, Willey, and Gifford (1960) with wares, groups, types, and varieties each placed in their proper perspective, with the group as the principal unit under which other units, including form, are listed. Group is prominently positioned because of the poor condition (weathered and small in size) of much of the ceramic material at Bilbao. Some important trade and special wares are noted, but a modal study as such is not presented.

The System as Practiced at Mayapán and Seibal

In making use of the type-variety system or, in fact, of any system, more than one manner of presentation in a final report is possible. Nevertheless, one of the major aims of the method of presentation should be to provide the readers with sufficient data, without undue repetition, for any approaches, be they ones of intersite comparison or total reanalysis of the ceramic data, that they may care to take in future studies.

In the Mayapán report (Smith 1968), now in the process of being edited and to be published in 1970, one method of presentation has been used, and in the Seibal report, now in preparation by Gordon R. Willey and Jeremy A. Sabloff, another is being used.

In the discussion below, we provide a detailed description of the general, overall method of presentation of the Mayapan report and the specific presentation format for the ceramic descriptions of the Seibal report, in order to show how versatile, accommodating, and potentially useful the type-variety system can be. It should be noted that the two reports offer somewhat different approaches to the presentation of type and mode data. The Mayapán report is actually a combination of the taxonomic and analytical approaches and offers descriptions and total counts for all types *and* modes. The Seibal report, on the other hand, has added some modal features to what is essentially a typological approach. It offers data on modes and their associations, but it does not give counts for each modal feature.

It is our feeling that, ideally, a ceramic report which employs the type-variety system of ceramic analysis should combine the overall plan of the Mayapán report, with its emphasis on definitions and its extensive typological and modal analyses (complete with tables of associations and counts), and the Seibal report's emphasis on the identification of types and the criteria used in establishing them and differentiating them from other types and varieties. This ideal report would accomplish two important purposes in addition to those of establishing a ceramic sequence, investigating the historical significance of the sequence, and studying the functional significance of the ceramic associations. First of all, it would offer sufficient data for various possible kinds of reanalysis or reuse of the ceramic data which future archaeologists might wish to undertake. Secondly, it would provide tightly defined and easily recognizable typological units which workers at other sites could use to make meaningful intersite comparisons.

In actual practice, however, the type of excavation undertaken, time available for studying the pottery, and laboratory circumstances all have a bearing on the approach used; and all these factors would obviously affect the nature of a final report and may work against the achievement of the ideal. In fact, it is probably only practical to have one report in an area or subarea which approaches the ideal just noted and fully described below since it is becoming more and more difficult today to do a total excavation of a large Maya Lowland site. Moreover, it might even be argued that it is only worthwhile to do a complete dual taxonomic and analytical ceramic study, as has been done at Mayapán, if a whole site is excavated and if there is strong control on the totality of possible contexts at the site. If the archaeologist has a large and complete sample of contexts, then it becomes important and useful to have full counts of all ceramic modes and their associations, as well as detailed type descriptions. At a site which has only been partially tested, total mode *counts* may be of little relative value since there may not be complete control, let alone complete sampling, of all contexts. That is to say, when excavations at a site generally consist of stratigraphic pits and trenches and not of complete architectural investigations, total contextual control will probably be lacking. At Seibal, for example, most of the excavations in the ceremonial center proper, with several important exceptions, were of the pit and trench kind. On the other hand, in the outlying small structure ("house mound") investigations, careful attention has been paid to sampling and to context. In this case, complete analysis and counts of the ceramic modes might have great use, especially in relation to a variety of functional questions.

All in all, we would argue that, given the circumstances of an excavation as a limiting factor, it is essential that the archaeologist present as much well-described taxonomic and analytical data as possible because the two approaches are complementary, not contradictory, and they must be combined in order to bring about useful ceramic reports. The type-variety system, as will now be shown, is adaptable and compatible with analytical analysis, and at Mayapán and Seibal it has been combined with varying degrees of modal analysis to achieve what we feel are useful ceramic descriptions.

Method of Presentation in the Mayapán Report. In Part One, the matter of procedures is discussed. These procedures are described under such headings as ceramic planning and study, method of classification, and excavation and stratigraphy.

In Part Two, ceramic descriptions involving wares, types, varieties, and groups are presented. Wares are listed and described alphabetically. These descriptions emphasize the ware attributes and then mention the ware associations. These latter include groups, types, varieties, forms, quantity, provenience, and ceramic complexes.

Following wares, methods of decoration are examined under two principal headings: processes involving alteration of the surface and processes involving additions to the surface. Within this framework, each technique is discussed, and the associated types are listed with their respective ceramic wares and complexes. The techniques are listed alphabetically, from carving through texturing under techniques of penetration and from appliqué through slipping under techniques of plasticity and color.

In the next section, kinds of design are considered and listed alphabetically. Sometimes a special design serves to designate a variety, but more often certain designs are used as modes to delimit an area of occurrence, to mark a specific period in time, or to emphasize a design style. Designs are separated into abstract, naturalistic, conventional, and glyphic, and they are listed alphabetically under each of these categories.

At this point in the report, modes are studied and defined. Since a mode is considered to be an attribute or cluster of attributes which display significance in their own right, the modal list in this section of the report is a selective one. Furthermore, for clearer understanding, the list is separated into the basic ceramic categories of paste composition, surface finish, form, decorative techniques, and specific designs. For each mode there is a description, mention of ceramic complex and provenience, and a complete recording of the illustrations plus a few pertinent remarks.

In Part Three, ceramic distribution at Mayapán is considered. This section is based largely on the distributions of the categories of utilitarian and ceremonial pottery and bowls and jars. An analysis of the pottery associated with the three principal civic divisions (dwelling lots, ceremonial lots, and *cenote* lots) is made, as are studies of the pottery associated with residential, civic, and religious structures, the pottery linked with *cenotes*, middens, and stratigraphic cuts, and the pottery found in both burials and caches. These studies are followed by a summary of the intrasite distributions and associations of the pottery of Mayapán.

In Part Four, an analysis is made by ceramic complex, beginning wtih the earliest. A number of wares are associated with each complex. These wares are studied, with the aid of vessel form, which in turn is related to a number of types and varieties. Each ware analysis and each complex study is followed by a summary or review.

Part Five deals with conclusions and reflections on the ceramics of a declining culture. This is accomplished by showing the influence of earlier ceramic complexes on the late complexes of Mayapán, by reviewing the intersite distributions, connections, and interpretations, and by examining the typological and modal distributions.

Numerous illustrations are used to clarify descriptions. To further elucidate what might otherwise remain complicated, 43 tables and 3 charts are supplied. These latter have to do with (1) phase correlations of Yucatán and the central and southern Maya areas; (2) and (3) ceramic complexes, wares, groups, types, and varieties at Mayapán. The tables deal with total sherd counts in all ceramic complexes; a summary of various pit findings; certain percentage studies; Mayapán urban divisions by basic ceramic association; unslipped ware rim count by basic ceramic function and major lot designation; structure types and their associated pottery; ceramic analysis of *cenote* material; midden types and their associated pottery; Chichén Unslipped ware compared with Mayapán Unslipped ware; ware percentages and rim-body ratios; stratigraphic cuts by lots and phases; decorative techniques listed and summarized individually in alphabetical order; and temper tables involving pottery samples from Uxmal, Kabah, and Chichen Itza.

Analytic and Taxonomic Classification in the Type-Variety System   **487**

The presentation format just described makes it possible to use the ceramic material from Mayapán to develop any sort of investigation because it employs all attributes and has complete numerical counts and separations of counts into numerous fundamental categories. Thus, additional research is possible in both taxonomic classification and the analytical (or modal) classification.

Method of Presentation in the Seibal Report. The report begins with a discussion of the objectives of the study and the procedures used. Excavations, stratigraphy, and the formation of the Seibal ceramic sequence, as well as the method of classification and presentation, are all reviewed. The next section offers definitions and illustrations of forms, decorative techniques, and wares. This is followed by numerous cross-referenced indices and tables of types and varieties and of "principal identifying modes" and their associations (see below).

The main chapter offers detailed type descriptions which are all presented within a standard format. Other chapters discuss the intrasite and intersite distributions of ceramic complexes, types, and modes, and the ceramic contribution to an understanding of the general site history.

Of principal interest here is the format which is used to present the type descriptions of the Seibal pottery. The format owes a great debt to others which have preceded it, and its possible utility in tightening intersite comparisons can best be seen in light of earlier reports. Essentially, the Seibal format is a compromise between the kind of description a pure typological analysis would entail and a description which uses individual ceramic modes as a basis of analysis and presentation. Speed of analysis and conciseness of presentation were two of the major factors of decision in the compromise.

The format consists of 15 parts:

1. Type
2. Variety
3. Established as a Type and/or Variety
4. Ceramic Group
5. Ware
6. Ceramic Complex
7. Ceramic Sphere Affiliation
8–11. Description:
　　　Principal Identifying Modes;
　　　Paste, Temper, Firing, etc.;
　　　Surface Finish and Decoration;
　　　Form.

12. Intrasite Locations and Contexts
13. Intersite Locations and Contexts
14. Cultural Significance
15. Illustrations

Parts 1, 2, 4, 5, 6, and 7 systematically give all the hierarchial information which is required within the type-variety system. Part 3 states where the type or variety was first defined and is the place for the settling of name discrepancies (if any). It also notes the size of the sample upon which a particular type description is based. The ceramic description, Parts 8–11, is really the heart of the presentation. In this section, the main addition to the traditional type of ceramic description in the Maya area is the listing of principal identifying modes for the types. A similar descriptive device has been used for some time by Phillips and Williams (Phillips 1968) in describing pottery from the Southeast of the United States.

The listing of principal identifying modes can have many advantages. Among others, it can immediately give the reader an idea of the criteria which the archaeologist has used to identify a type. It can also form the basis of an attribute list to be used in a computer analysis of modal associations or of a punch card listing of modes from a large area such as the Maya Lowlands or Southern Mesoamerica. In addition, all the principal identifying modes are tied into a series of cross-referenced indices and tables which list all the modes and types and their associations. These indices should greatly facilitate the task of an archaeologist who is analyzing the pottery of a new site and who wants to make close comparisons with the pottery of Seibal. If, for example, he has a sherd lot with unsure chronological position, but with certain outstanding modes, he can quickly find out which types at Seibal have this combination of modes and see if the descriptions fit in with his sherd material. Or, he may find that there is no type at Seibal with all the proper modes, but several of them with two or three of the modes in association. He can then find the page references for these types and look at the descriptions to see if his grouping forms a new variety of a type found at Seibal or if it is not found at Seibal at all. This example illustrates just one of several possible uses to which the principal identifying modes and the indices can be put.

In the surface finish and decoration and the form sections (Parts 10 and 11) the discussions are as extensive and detailed as possible. In these two sections, slip, plastic decoration, design, vessel form, height, diameter, and wall thickness are among the areas discussed.

Part 13 of the format is the traditional comparative section. The main difference between this section and comparative sections in past ceramic reports in the Maya area is the insistence on both modal and type comparisons, and the formal recognition of both kinds of comparisons. The comparative sections of ceramic reports are often vague and may switch back and forth, inconsistently, between modal and type comparisons. It may be noted in report X, for instance, that a pot illustrated in report Y is not really the same, but the incised design and the shape are generally reminiscent of the type being described in report X. It would certainly be better and more systematic to say that the pot in report Y shares the principal identifying modes of fine-line incision and bowl with outflared sides with the type in report X, but that it differs in slip, size, and temper. To conclude, the *formal* distinction between modal and type comparisons in the format would appear to be an important step towards more useful intersite comparisons.

The cultural significance of types (Part 14) is often discussed in ceramic reports but almost never extensively and often only in a general manner in brief summary sections at the end of the reports. A short discussion of the possible cultural significance of individual types, especially the majority ones, would seem to have much to recommend it. This section includes statements on function, or on trade, or even on the importance of certain designs.

Finally, since photographs and, to a greater extent, drawings have much value in the identification of types (see Vol. II of R. E. Smith 1955; the illustrations in Brainerd 1958; or the form charts in Adams 1963, among others), as many pictures, drawings, and profiles as possible of each individual type and variety are included in the report.

SUPPOSED WEAKNESSES OF TYPOLOGICAL ANALYSES

It is our belief that the type-variety system of ceramic analysis is the best classificatory method available today in southern Mesoamerica and perhaps in other areas as well. Although any system which is essentially typological in nature has certain inherent weaknesses (such as the

five-fold weaknesses pointed out by Wright 1967), the type-variety system, at least to some extent, has overcome these deficiencies. Turning specifically to Wright's five points, it should be noted first of all that the type-variety system does not tend to "pigeon-hole" those "individual attributes whose trends extend beyond the type" (Wright 1967: 99). By combining type and mode analysis and by placing an emphasis on the ceramic group, the archaeologist who uses the type-variety system does not really lose sight of the continuities of individual attributes. Secondly, attribute variation is handled by the variety concept which takes cognizance of differences in individual attributes that are not large enough to cause the formation of a new type. Thirdly, by emphasizing decorative modes as the diagnostic criteria in the formation of a new type, the type-variety system eliminates the possibility that various workers will give greater diagnostic weight to different modes. In addition, the concept of the ceramic group enables the archaeologist to classify sherds in their proper group even when they are in fragmentary or eroded condition and therefore are lacking in one or two diagnostic modes (as was the case in Parsons 1967). Moreover, *by clearly stating what his sorting criteria are in each type description*, the archaeologist makes it much easier for others to recognize his types. Fourthly, established types are not closed systems since new varieties can be added to a type or new types to a group. Fifthly, it remains to be seen whether or not "attempts to incorporate new data into the established typology . . . (will disrupt) . . . communication by creating a host of new types, revised types, and additions or deletions of certain attributes under an earlier type name or new designation" (Wright 1967: 100). Certainly, the expandability of the system will mitigate against possible disruption as will the regular listing of new types and varieties and their sources in *Estudios de Ceramica Maya*, edited by James C. Gifford. In addition, as noted above, the tables of modes or the principal identifying modes in the type-variety descriptions are amenable to data processing.

AN IMPORTANT STRENGTH OF THE SYSTEM: INTERSITE COMPARISON

Further note should be taken of one of the type-variety system's main strengths; namely, its utility in the realm of intersite comparison. In recent years, there has been a growing realization in American archaeology that the carefully planned regional study can be of much importance (see, for example, Binford 1964). Some of the most successful and sophisticated projects with regional scope have been accomplished in Mesoamerica (MacNeish 1958, 1964; Sanders 1965; Willey and others 1965; Flannery and others 1967; and so on). In the Maya area, one can point to several projects including those reported by Ruppert and Dennison (1943), Smith and Kidder (1943), A. L. Smith (1955), and Sanders (1960), among others. But it is only in the past few years that the sophisticated problem-oriented study (which, of course, has relied in part on the historically oriented studies preceding it) has come to the fore. The Belize Valley project cited above is a good example of this kind of work as is the greater Palenque project of Rands (1967). In these studies, as in other recent projects of importance such as the Tikal settlement pattern and sustaining area studies (Puleston and Callender 1967) or the Cotzal project (Adams 1967), it is necessary to make quick and easy comparisons of pottery from a number of sites. It is precisely in this area that the type-variety system has a very useful role to play.

Since a tight ceramic chronology and knowledge of the degree of ceramic similarity among sites are simply means of reaching goals of wider scope, it should not be necessary to spend the bulk of a project's time and effort on the analysis and description of the pottery from every site. By drawing on descriptions from previously studied sites, the archaeologist can easily ascertain whether or not various types are present, especially if attention has been paid in the published reports to the delineation of principal identifying modes. Thus, through use of the type-variety system, distinctive ceramic attribute clusters (types and varieties), which have a wide areal spread and relatively limited chronological range, can be recognized without undue trouble and can greatly facilitate, as well as quicken, the establishment of ceramic sequences at neighboring sites or in neighboring regions. A case in point would be the analysis at Seibal, which was aided by the type-variety descriptions made by R. E. W. Adams (1963) at the site of Altar de Sacrificios, approximately 75 mi. downriver from Seibal.

Finally, with the growing use of the type-variety system in the Maya Lowlands, it has been possible to form ceramic spheres (Willey,

Culbert, and Adams 1967; Culbert 1967) which are based on the spread of established types and varieties and which can serve a useful purpose on a regional level of study.

CONCLUSION

We feel that the type-variety system of ceramic analysis as practiced at Mayapán and Seibal does not fall under the blanket of criticism which Wright (1967) has leveled at typological analysis. Although the type-variety system is basically typological in nature, it has absorbed some of the merits of modal analysis and has discarded some of the weaknesses of typological or taxonomic analysis. Admittedly, the system is far from perfect, and the real test of its usefulness for comparative studies has yet to come. Nevertheless, it is only a means to the end of understanding culture history and culture change ("process"), and we feel that it provides a solid and efficient foundation for the archaeological roads which lead to this end.

Acknowledgments. We wish to thank Gordon R. Willey for his helpful comments. In addition, Sabloff held a National Science Foundation Graduate Fellowship at the time that this paper was written.

ADAMS, R. E. W.
    1963 The Ceramic Sequence at Altar de Sacrificios, Guatemala. MS, doctoral dissertation, Harvard University, Cambridge.
    1967 The Cotzal Valley Project; Second Preliminary Report. Department of Anthropology, University of Minnesota, Minneapolis. (mimeographed)

BINFORD, L. R.
    1964 A Consideration of Archaeological Research Design. *American Antiquity*, Vol. 29, No. 4, pp. 425–41. Salt Lake City.

BRAINERD, G. W.
    1958 The Archaeological Ceramics of Yucatán. *Anthropological Records*, Vol. 19. Berkeley and Los Angeles.

CULBERT, T. P.
    1965 The Ceramic History of the Central Highlands of Chiapas, Mexico. *Papers of the New World Archaeological Foundation, Publication* 14, No. 19. Provo.
    1967 Preliminary Report of the Conference on the Prehistoric Ceramics of the Maya Lowlands (1965). *Estudios de Cultura Maya*, Vol. 6, pp. 81–109. Mexico.

FLANNERY, K. V. AND OTHERS
    1967 Farming Systems and Political Growth in Ancient Oaxaca. *Science*, Vol. 158, No. 3800, pp. 445–54. Washington.

GIFFORD, J. C.
    1960 The Type-Variety Method of Ceramic Classification as an Indicator of Cultural Phenomena. *American Antiquity*, Vol. 25, No. 3, pp. 341–7 Salt Lake City.

Jeremy A. Sabloff and Robert E. Smith

MacNEISH, R. S.

1958 Preliminary Archaeological Investigations in the Sierra de Tamaulipas, Mexico. *Transactions of the American Philosophical Society*, Vol. 48, Pt. 6. Philadelphia.

1965 Ancient Mesoamerican Civilization. *Science*, Vol. 143, No. 3606, pp. 531–7. Washington.

PARSONS, L. A.

1967 Bilbao, Guatemala; An Archaeological Study of the Pacific Coast Cotzumalhuapa Region. *Milwaukee Public Museum, Publications in Anthropology* 11, Vol. 1. Milwaukee.

PHILLIPS, P.

1968 Archaeological Survey of the Lower Mississippi Valley, II. *Papers of the Peabody Museum of American Archaeology and Ethnology, Harvard University*, Vol. 60. Cambridge. (in press)

PULESTON, D. E. AND D. W. CALLENDER, JR.

1967 Defensive Earthworks at Tikal. *Expedition*, Vol. 9, No. 3, pp. 40–8. Philadelphia.

RANDS, R. L.

1967 Cerámica de la región de Palenque, México *Estudios de Cultura Maya*, Vol. 6, pp. 111–48 Mexico.

ROUSE, I.

1939 Prehistory in Haiti: A Study in Method. *Yale University Publications in Anthropology*, No. 21 New Haven.

RUPPERT, K. AND J. H. DENNISON, JR.

1943 Archaeological Reconnaissance in Campeche, Quintana Roo, and Peten. *Carnegie Institution of Washington, Publication* 543. Washington.

SANDERS, W. T.

1960 Prehistoric Ceramics and Settlement Patterns in Quintana Roo, Mexico. *Carnegie Institution of Washington, Publication* 606, Contribution 60. pp. 155–264. Washington.

1965 The Cultural Ecology of the Teotihuacán Valley: A Preliminary Report of the Results of the Teotihuacán Valley Project. Department of Sociology and Anthropology, Pennsylvania State University, University Park. (mimeographed)

SMITH, A. L.

1955 Archaeological Reconnaissance in Central Guatemala. *Carnegie Institution of Washington, Publication* 608. Washington.

SMITH, A. L. AND A. V. KIDDER

1943 Explorations in the Motagua Valley, Guatemala. *Carnegie Institution of Washington, Publication* 546, Contribution 41, pp. 101–82. Washington.

SMITH, R. E.

1955 Ceramic Sequence at Uaxactún, Guatemala. *Middle American Research Institute, Publication* 20, Vol. 2. New Orleans.

1968 The Pottery of Mayapán: Including Studies of Ceramic Material from Uxmal, Kabah, and Chichén Itzá. MS, to be published by the Peabody Museum, Cambridge.

SMITH, R. E., G. R. WILLEY, AND J. C. GIFFORD

1960 The Type-Variety Concept as a Basis for the Analysis of Maya Pottery. *American Antiquity*, Vol. 25, No. 3, pp. 330–40. Salt Lake City.

WALLRATH, M.

1967 Excavations in the Tehuantepec Region, Mexico, *Transactions of the American Philosophical Society*, Vol. 57, Pt. 2. Philadelphia.

WILLEY, G. R., T. P. CULBERT, AND R. E. W. ADAMS

1967 Maya Lowland Ceramics: A Report from the 1965 Guatemala City Conference. *American Antiquity*, Vol. 32, No. 3, pp. 289–315. Salt Lake City.

WILLEY, G. R. AND OTHERS

1965 Prehistoric Maya Settlements in the Belize Valley. *Papers of the Peabody Museum of American Archaeology and Ethnology, Harvard University*, Vol. 54. Cambridge.

WRIGHT, J. V.

1967 Type and Attribute Analysis: Their Application to Iroquois Culture History. In *Iroquois Culture, History, and Prehistory; Proceedings of the 1965 Conference on Iroquois Research*, edited by E. Tooker, pp. 99–100. New York State Museum and Science Service, Albany.

PEABODY MUSEUM
Cambridge, Massachusetts
May, 1968

Analytic and Taxonomic Classification in the Type–Variety System　　　　**491**

COMMENT

SABLOFF AND SMITH'S "THE IMPORTANCE OF BOTH ANALYTIC AND TAXONOMIC CLASSIFICATION IN THE TYPE-VARIETY SYSTEM"

ROBERT C. DUNNELL

ABSTRACT

The article recently published by Sabloff and Smith (AMER. ANT. 34:278-286, 1969) adds little beyond elaboration to archaeological classification and further tends to perpetuate some common and basic errors. Some of these flaws are noted along with their manifestation in the type-variety system as propounded by Sabloff and Smith, and a direction to solution is indicated.

Department of Anthropology
University of Washington
November, 1969

The article recently published by Sabloff and Smith entitled "The Importance of Both Analytic and Taxonomic Classification in the Type-Variety System" (AMER. ANT. 34:278-286, 1969) attempts to update, at least in terms of practice and emphasis, the type-variety system proposed by Wheat, Gifford, and Wasley (AMER. ANT. 24:34-47, 1958); Smith, Willey, and Gifford (AMER. ANT. 25:330-340, 1960); and Gifford (AMER. ANT. 25:341-347, 1960) and to answer the criticisms of Wright (Tooker, ed., *Iroquois culture history and prehistory*, 1967:99-100) leveled at typology or "taxonomic classification" (Rouse, AMER. ANT. 25:313-323, 1960). It succeeds, however, in perpetuating some serious problems in classification in archaeology—problems which are of fundamental importance to the discipline as a whole if, but only if, the discipline is to be conceived of as a science. While more elaborate by virtue of being more specific, and more orderly, Sabloff and Smith do not progress beyond Krieger's "The Typological Concept" (AMER. ANT. 9:271-288, 1944), itself a milestone, but a milestone long past.

First, that Sabloff and Smith can do what they propose is unquestioned, and further, the resulting units are undoubtedly in some manner or manners "useful" and do "work," even though it may not be possible to say why such

is the case. Be that as it may, however, the "system" they propose, or rather reiterate, amounts to little more than a means of naming piles of potsherds, piles which were segregated or created according to principles and assumptions not overtly presented in the type-variety scheme or in the presentations of actual cases. Basically the flaws are these: (1) the authors, following their predecessors, do not distinguish between groups of real objects and conceptual classes to which objects are assigned; (2) they further treat modes apart from types in different but complementary systems, while failing to differentiate attributes (qualities of individual artifacts) from modes (intuitive classes of artificial attributes), a distinction which is quite explicit in the original definition of modes (Rouse, Yale Univ. Pub. Anth., Vol. 21, 1939); (3) they do not present any specific problems for which the classification proposed is intended to serve, and thus lack an objective means of evaluating the utility of the scheme (inter-site comparison, commonly voiced as it may be, is more a traditional excuse than a problem, for any class represented in two or more locations in time and space will serve to make such comparisons possible, though not necessarily meaningful); and (4) they further assume, or at least imply, lacking any specific problem, that the scheme is *the one* for all problems in the area concerned, forcing them into the untenable position of stating that they consider *all* attributes of their collections. While not directly pertinent to the form or content of the scheme as presented, but certainly affecting its use, the general nature and capabilities of classification are completely misconstrued or misunderstood by Sabloff and Smith by expecting with Wright that a device which breaks up continuous phenomena into bounded definable units or classes will embody continuity. Classification permits one only to say whether a given object is the same or different from another and in what manner. Its sole function is to break up continuity, to create discontinuities, so that units can be formulated. Classes can be and should be used to measure continuity and change as is done, for example, in seriation. They do so, however, not by embodying continuity, but by providing a fixed and defined framework of discontinuous units against which continuity and change can be measured, not entirely unlike the manner in which the calibrations on a yardstick provide a fixed system of discontinuities against which length, including that of the yardstick itself, can be plotted.

A comment of this size does not provide an opportunity to consider classification, its logic and limitations, in depth; such a detailed consideration will be published in the near future (Dunnell In press). However, it is useful to examine some of the consequences and manifestations of the flaws noted above for the type-variety system as explicated by Sabloff and Smith, and to suggest a different sort of answer.

In a volume cited by the authors (Rouse 1939), the distinction between groups of objects and classes for objects is clearly drawn when Rouse points out that "artifacts are concrete objects; types and modes are conceptual patterns" (1939:19), and further: "artifacts have little historical significance; types and modes have much. Artifacts are inert objects which exist only where they are kept. Types and modes. . .do not have the limitation of objective existence" (1939:20). An object occupies a point in space at any given time, that is to say, it has a location. As a consequence, objects cannot be shared or recur through space and time. Classes on the other hand, be they types, modes, wares, or varieties, are ideas that exist independent of time and space and when provided with explicit, intensional definitions stating the necessary and sufficient conditions for membership can be used to order real objects. Objects assigned to a class are usually termed the *denotata* of the class, the necessary and sufficient conditions or definition the *significatum* (Lounsbury; Lunt, ed., PROC. NINTH INT. CONG. LING., 1964:1073-1093). Assigning objects to the same class because they display the set of qualities required is simply a statement that these objects are identical in terms of the definitive criteria for a given purpose. The *denotata* of a class thus has (or is) a distribution in both time and space. Class *denotata* may occur in several places simultaneously. If the term "group" is taken to mean an aggregate of phenomena, either attributes or objects, then obviously the *denotata* of

a class constitute a group, a special group whose membership is governed by an explicit set of distinctive features embodied in a class as its *significatum*. Identifying the members of a class is not the only way to create groups; the term "group" is thus best reserved here for those aggregates which lack explicit rules in the form of distinctive features that govern membership.

Types, varieties, modes, and wares are all classes; potsherds and their attributes are not. Clearly, the type-variety scheme has both components of groups and classes: classes when distributions are present, when units recur from site to site, and groups when the various units in the system are treated as synonymous with a pile of sherds, when any quantification or description is involved. Quite obviously a class cannot be described or features counted. A class consists solely of its definition or *significatum*, and there is nothing to be described. Thus, one must assume that when types are "described" a description of the *denotata* of a type at a given place or set of places has been offered. Sabloff and Smith in not differentiating groups from classes confuse definition and description, as has traditionally been done in the Southeast United States they cite. It is not possible for Sabloff and Smith to convey the features which the objects must display from features which the objects may display or that the particular set of *denotata* before them happen to display; their classes lack *significata*. They come close to providing a definition in talking about the ware unit in which surface finish and paste composition would be used. It fails, however, when the "possible exception of temper" is introduced. None of the other units presented approaches a definition. The reader is deprived of the rules by which he could identify potsherds as the authors reduce the procedure to something of a mystical art. Obviously too, potential ambiguity exists in that a feature which may be constant in one set of *denotata* by chance is mistaken for a distinctive or definitive feature (e.g., in a sample of mothers all may have brown hair, a feature not part of the definition of mother as female-parent).

Anticipated in the foregoing is the second point. Sabloff and Smith's "attributes," features as termed above, have the characteristics of classes themselves, that is, they are shared or held in common by several objects.

They differ from other classes in the system in that they are classes of parts of artifacts. Further, they are intuitive; they are defined, if at all, incidentally to the classification. They are classes of attributes or more properly modes. Types, varieties, and wares must be combinations of modes, not something apart from modes. This does not mean that one cannot create defined classes for parts of artifacts such as face lugs or paste, but that this is a matter of the scale or level at which the data are conceived and not two different things. The circumstances under which one or another scale of data is appropriate have been considered frequently if not clearly in the literature (e.g., Rouse 1960; Rands, AMER. ANT. 26:331-340, 1961). That Sabloff and Smith choose to talk about the modes used in "describing" their units' contents as attributes does not change their nature as modes.

Points three and four are best considered together since they are closely intertwined. All classes, including modes, are 'created by the investigator. Taking for granted that they are defined so that they can be identified in the phenomenological world by someone other than the original investigator, there are still important difficulties—namely the choices made in creating the modes, some of which are ultimately selected as distinctive features in the definition of a type or ware. To say that *all* "attributes" are used is just as profitless as it is nonsensical. Sabloff and Smith did not consider the temperatures or the atomic structures of their sherds—they emphatically did not use all attributes, even if it were possible to define all. If one stops to consider the matter, choices are made in creating or defining modes, then further choices are made when some are selected as criteria for classes. The question then becomes: Upon what basis are the choices made? Insofar as the initial discrimination of modes is concerned, the scale at which defined classes are to be formed is the crucial factor. The modes must be at a scale beneath that of the defined classes. In the case of potsherds, the modes must be intuitive classes of sherd characteristics. Secondly, since archaeology is concerned with artifacts, not rocks, the possible modes are limited to those present by virtue of human activity, either mechanical or chemical modifications of the material or location representing selections on the part of the

makers. These choices are justifiable within the field as matters of discipline-wide interest (artifacts) and logical requirements of classification (features must be smaller than the things they are features of). The real difficulty inheres in the choice of some of these modes as distinctive features in class definitions while treating others separately or as variable features of a set of *denotata*. Why, for example, is temper not a distinctive feature of a paste, but apparently a variable? I do not doubt that Sabloff and Smith have good reasons for making this decision; however, their basis for the decision is inexplicit and unjustified.

If classifications of any kind are to be devices useful in constructing explanations, if they are done for something other than amusement, they must be capable of evaluation, susceptible to change. In short, they must be hypotheses about the ordering of data for a specific problem. Only if a specific problem is stated can the choice of definitive criteria be tested in ordinary scientific fashion as an hypothesis. If, for example, one wishes to make inferences about the use to which artifacts have been put, edge impairment (wear) is a dimension of modes which is going to be chosen, among others, for this choice can be justified in terms of the problem for which the classification is intended to order phenomena. This choice, once the *denotata* of the resulting class are identified, can be tested in many ways, for example, by examining the breakage patterns of the tools inferred to be hoes on the basis of wear. To expect that the same set of classes defined by criteria relevant to use will prove the most useful for chronology is foolish. Such would only be the case by accident, unless one is prepared to demonstrate a direct and universal correlation between the two kinds of criteria. What people do usually changes more slowly than how they do it. Sabloff and Smith, in failing to provide any specific goal for which the type-variety system is an organizational tool, do not permit their units to be evaluated. Perhaps another classification will work better, perhaps not. This cannot be assessed from the presentation.

While it may be satisfying to call a particular piece of pottery Sebonac Incised or Monongahela Plain, a sherd is not the same thing for all purposes. Brew's admonitions for more classifications, not fewer, is today just as true as

Robert C. Dunnell

when it was written (Brew, Paps. PMAE, Harvard 24:44-66, 1946). Only with specifically defined problems is it possible to evaluate the utility, parsimony, elegance, and sufficiency of a given classification. Classifications need not be taken for granted. They must suit their problem or they are useless.

In conclusion, I want to point out that the Sabloff and Smith article is not so much the offending member as an example of what is generally a very sloppy matter in archaeology. My arguments make no pretense to completeness. Such is not possible in a reasonable amount of space. I mean merely to point out some basic difficulties in "typology" which are exemplified in the article considered. Other points might well have been touched on, such as the inherent limitations of the quasi-taxonomic form employed in the type-variety system and the consequent circular definitions of units which inevitably result (e.g., the definition of type by Sabloff and Smith). Given the purpose, however, such additional criticism seems unnecessary. It is obvious too, that the Sabloff and Smith treatment is simplified for the purposes at hand. Nonetheless, it is hoped that some basic difficulties have been indicated. The direction in which solution is to be sought lies not in Ptolemaic epicycles of further elaboration and specification but in problem-oriented, thus testable, classifications explicitly defined and differentiated from the potsherds and projectile points they are intended to order. Classifications are logical constructs whose justification lies in their utility. They are not inherent, nor do they explain. They are imposed constructs that function to order data so that explanation is possible. And most importantly, they need not be taken for granted; they can be evaluated objectively.

Index

Abbott, Charles C., 19, 22
Age–area concept, 6
American Museum of Natural History, 2–4, 34, 45, 47, 57, 123
Amsden, Charles Avery, 455
Analogous similarity, 6, 9, 11, 407–409
Arbitrary levels, 3, 93
Aspect (Midwestern Taxonomic Method), 140–141, 224, 225, 245
Assemblage, 3
Association, 304
Atzcapotzalco, Mexico, 35

Base (Midwestern Taxonomic Method), 224, 227
Basic culture, 140, 218
Bennett, Wendell C., 415, 467
Binford, Lewis R., 11
Boas, Franz, 4, 35–38, 127, 208, 212
Braided stream (*see also* culture change as a flowing stream), 7, 8, 144, 268, 294
Brainerd, George W., 8, 356
Branches (see Gladwin, Harold S.), 140–141
Brew, J. O., 7, 303, 369, 409, 453, 455

Ceramic stratigraphy, 3
Class, 237
Classification, 4, 7, 10, 29–34, 94–95, 154–162, 168, 187,

219, 221, 265, 269, 273, 293, 296–297, 314–316, 348, 448, 459
Cole, Fay-Cooper, 218, 227
Colton, Harold S., 6, 268, 270–272, 279, 397, 409, 434
Component, 8–9, 140–141, 225, 227, 386–387, 397, 401–402, 455
Culture area, 6, 39–44, 219–220
Cultures, 4–5, 6, 9, 37, 40–41, 46, 140, 166, 202, 220, 222, 233, 267, 293, 371, 384, 411, 455, 461
Cultural change as a flowing stream (*see also* braided stream), 5, 7, 141, 294–295, 353
Cultural development, 2, 6, 11
Cultural evolution (*see also* cultural development), 2, 6–8, 21, 39, 117, 123
Cultural trait (or element; *see also* trait), 2, 6, 40, 116–120, 121–138, 184–185, 209, 222–224, 248, 265, 292, 372, 431
Cultural type, 36

Dall, William Healey, 22
Darwin, Charles, 269
Dendrochronology, 3
Denotata, 493
Deuel, Thorne, 146, 218, 227, 250

Diffusion, 7, 9, 10, 137, 147, 202, 206, 213, 429, 473–483
Direct historical approach, 3, 219, 405 (see also 55, 163–164)
Dixon, Roland B., 2, 130–132
Douglass, A. E., 186, 191
Doppler effect, 353–354
Driver, Harold E., 232, 242, 244, 307
Dunnell, Robert C., 10

Emic type, 6, 10, 294–295, 316–317, 319, 356–368, 489
Ethnic group (or human group), 81–86
Etic type, 6, 295, 316–317, 319, 369–381
Evans, Clifford, 297–298
Evans, John, 3, 468
Evolutionary seriation, 468

Fewkes, J. Walter, 45, 66, 85–86, 110, 188
Focus (Midwestern Taxonomic Method), 140–141, 224, 386
Ford, James A., 6–8, 201, 272, 473
Ford–Spaulding debate, 8, 365–368
Fowke, Gerard, 5
Frequency seriation, 3, 7, 8, 54–57, 468–471